A War of Patrols

Studies in Canadian Military History

The Canadian War Museum, Canada's national museum of military history, has a threefold mandate: to remember, to preserve, and to educate. It does so through an interlocking and mutually supporting combination of exhibitions, public programs, and electronic outreach. Military history, military historical scholarship, and the ways in which Canadians see and understand themselves have always been closely intertwined. Studies in Canadian Military History builds on a record of success in forging those links by regular and innovative contributions based on the best modern scholarship. Published by UBC Press in association with the Museum, the series especially encourages the work of new generations of scholars and the investigation of important gaps in the existing historiography, pursuits not always well served by traditional sources of academic support. The results produced feed immediately into future exhibitions, programs, and outreach efforts by the Canadian War Museum. It is a modest goal that they feed into a deeper understanding of our nation's common past as well.

1 John Griffith Armstrong, *The Halifax Explosion and the Royal Canadian Navy: Inquiry and Intrigue*
2 Andrew Richter, *Avoiding Armageddon: Canadian Military Strategy and Nuclear Weapons, 1950-63*
3 William Johnston, *A War of Patrols: Canadian Army Operations in Korea*

A War of Patrols

Canadian Army Operations in Korea

WILLIAM JOHNSTON

UBCPress · Vancouver · Toronto

09 08 07 06 05 04 03   5 4 3 2 1

Printed in Canada on acid-free paper. ∞

National Library of Canada Cataloguing in Publication Data

Johnston, William Cameron, 1956-
A war of patrols : Canadian Army operations in Korea / William Johnston.

(Studies in Canadian military history 1499-6251)
"Published in association with the Canadian War Museum."
Includes bibliographical references and index.
ISBN 0-7748-1008-4

1. Korean War, 1950-1953 – Participation, Canadian. 2. Canada. Canadian Army – History – Korean War, 1950-1953. I. Canadian War Museum. II. Title. III. Series.
DS919.2.J63 2003   951.904'24'0971   C2003-910028-6

Canada

UBC Press gratefully acknowledges the financial support for our publishing program of the Government of Canada through the Book Publishing Industry Development Program (BPIDP), and of the Canada Council for the Arts, and the British Columbia Arts Council.

Publication of this book has been financially supported by the Canadian War Museum.

This book has been published with the help of a grant from the Humanities and Social Sciences Federation of Canada, using funds provided by the Social Sciences and Humanities Research Council of Canada.

UBC Press
The University of British Columbia
2029 West Mall
Vancouver, BC V6T 1Z2
604-822-5959 / Fax: 604-822-6083
www.ubcpress.ca

To Emma

CONTENTS

MAPS AND ILLUSTRATIONS

Maps

Illustrations

PREFACE

I wish to thank Dr. Serge Bernier, Director of History and Heritage, National Defence Headquarters, and Dr. Roger Sarty and Dr. Steve Harris, respectively the former Senior and current Chief Historians at the Directorate of History and Heritage, for their encouragement and understanding while I wrote this book. Dr. Sarty, who has since moved on to the Canadian War Museum, was instrumental in getting the manuscript published as part of the museum's Studies in Canadian Military History series. Dr. Harris generously allowed me to complete the project and provided valuable advice for improving the manuscript.

I must also thank Maj. Mike McNorgan for his comments on the manuscript, especially in regard to proper unit and formation designations, despite his complaints about the lack of armour content. Maj. (retired) Bob Caldwell provided his expertise on army organization and the merits of various small arms as well as numerous personal insights into the post-Korean War Canadian Army. Brig. (retired) E.A.C. Amy kindly answered my questions about the Canadian brigade and Commonwealth Division headquarters. Col. (retired) Robert S. Peacock generously provided a number of photographs of the Canadian brigade's positions in Korea from his personal collection. Anne Wimmi translated Harry Pope's articles from *La Citadelle* into English. I would also like to thank my professor at the University of Waterloo, Dr. John Stubbs, for his guidance and encouragement as I made the study of history my vocation.

My deepest thanks, however, must go to Dr. Norman Hillmer and Brereton Greenhous. Dr. Hillmer first brought me to Ottawa in 1982 and gave me a job as an historian. His leadership and example as Senior Historian made the former Directorate of History the enjoyable, friendly workplace it remains to this day. It was under Mr. Greenhous's wing (or was it under his thumb?) that I received an education in writing critical military history. Not only did Ben first suggest that I write a book about the Canadian brigade in Korea, but he provided encouragement throughout, generously read the entire manuscript twice, and offered numerous editing suggestions.

I am also indebted to the staff at UBC Press, particularly Emily Andrew and Camilla Jenkins, for their very hard work in producing this book and to Eric Leinberger for adapting the maps. Sarah Wight did a marvellous job copyediting the manuscript. I must also thank the three anonymous outside readers for their (mostly) useful comments.

I also wish to thank my parents, Ruth and Lawrence Johnston, for providing such a wonderful family in which to grow up. Finally, for their tremendous love, support, and encouragement, I thank my wife, Sandra, and son, Tom. It is the two of you who make everything worthwhile.

A Note on the Text

The Korean War was fought by all Commonwealth and US forces using the imperial system of measure, and it is the imperial system that is used throughout the text. The military contour maps used during the conflict, however, were metric for both contour lines and the superimposed 1,000-metre grid used for all map references. As a result, the height of specific features was always expressed on the military maps in terms of metres above sea level. The summit of Hill 355, for example, was 355 metres above sea level. The soldiers on the ground, however, would have referred to Hill 355 but described it as 1,000 feet high. Odd as it may seem, this mixed measurement did not cause any problems for the soldiers involved.

Korean geographical names are often followed by a descriptive, hyphenated suffix: 'bong,' 'pong,' or 'san' denotes a mountain; 'ch'on,' 'gang,' or 'kang' a river; and 'dong,' 'gol,' 'kol,' 'li,' 'ni,' or 'ri' a settlement.

Map 1 is adapted from C.P. Stacey's *Official History of the Canadian Army in the Second World War,* vol. 3, *The Victory Campaign: The Operations in Northwest Europe, 1944-1945* (Ottawa: Queen's Printer, 1960) and appears courtesy of the Canadian Forces. Maps 3 through 17 have been adapted from Herbert Fairlie Wood, *Strange Battleground: The Operations in Korea and Their Effects on the Defence Policy of Canada* (Ottawa: Queen's Printer, 1966) and appear courtesy of the Department of National Defence. Several quotations from the same source also appear courtesy of the Department. Excerpts from Robert O'Neill, *Australia in the Korean War, 1950-53,* 2 vols. (Canberra: Australian Government Publishing Service, 1981) appear courtesy of the Australian War Memorial. Quotations from Anthony Farrar-Hockley, *The British Part in the Korean War* (London: Her Majesty's Stationery Office, 1995) are Crown copyright material reproduced with the permission of the Controller of Her Majesty's Stationery Office.

ABBREVIATIONS

ADS	advanced dressing station
AG	adjutant general
AHQ	army headquarters
AP	armour piercing
AWL	absent without leave
bde	brigade
BM	brigade major
bn	battalion
CASF	Canadian Army Special Force
CCF	Chinese communist forces
CGS	chief of the general staff
CIB	Canadian Infantry Brigade
CO	commanding officer
coy	company
CP	command post
CRE	commander, Royal Engineers
DF	defensive fire
EUSAK	Eighth US Army in Korea
FDLs	forward defended localities
FOO	forward observation officer
FUP	forming up place
GOC	general officer commanding
GSO(1)	general staff officer, grade 1
HE	high-explosive shell
HMG	heavy machine-gun
I&R	intelligence and reconnaissance
IO	intelligence officer
KIA	killed in action
KMAG	Korean Military Advisory Group
KOSB	King's Own Scottish Borderers
KSLI	King's Shropshire Light Infantry
LdSH	Lord Strathcona's Horse
LMG	light machine-gun
MMG	medium machine-gun
MO	medical officer

MSF	Mobile Striking Force
NCO	noncommissioned officer
NKPA	North Korea People's Army
OC	officer commanding
OP	observation post
pl	platoon
PPCLI	Princess Patricia's Canadian Light Infantry
PW	prisoner of war
R22eR	Royal 22e Régiment
RAP	regimental aid post
RAR	Royal Australian Regiment
RCHA	Royal Canadian Horse Artillery
RCR	Royal Canadian Regiment
RHLI	Royal Hamilton Light Infantry
RNR	Royal Norfolk Regiment
ROK	Republic of Korea
SP	self-propelled [gun]
sqn	squadron
TOO	tank observation officer
UNC	United Nations Command
WIA	wounded in action

INTRODUCTION

The Korean War has often been characterized as Canada's forgotten war.[1] Fought on a remote peninsula in the Far East by a brigade-sized force composed primarily of professional soldiers, the conflict failed to capture the nation's attention in the same way that the mass mobilization of the two world wars had done. Indeed, had the United States not decided to intervene in the conflict, the successful invasion of South Korea by the country's communist North in June 1950 might well have become a footnote in the history of the Cold War. As it was, Washington's willingness to rescue the Seoul regime caught the Canadian government off-guard, while the Americans' ability to internationalize the conflict made it difficult for Canada to remain on the sidelines. Aided by a temporary Soviet boycott of United Nations proceedings, the United States enlisted the support of that international body in organizing resistance to the North Koreans' aggression. The creation of an American-controlled United Nations Command with military contingents from eighteen countries (four of which sent only medical units), in addition to the forces of the United States and the Republic of Korea, made the conflict the UN's first peace-making operation.

Despite the leading role Canada had played in the formation of the United Nations, Ottawa was initially hesitant in responding to the UN's call for military force. By early August, however, the public's demand for a significant contribution to the UN Command could no longer be ignored. Because the regular army included only three infantry and two armoured units, the government decided to recruit a new three-battalion brigade group, the 25th Brigade, by drawing on the large pool of Second World War veterans who had returned to civilian life in 1945-6. A flood of volunteers quickly filled the Canadian Army Special Force, and by December 1950 the first of the new units, the 2nd Battalion, Princess Patricia's Canadian Light Infantry (2 PPCLI; the Special Force infantry units were designated 2nd battalions of the three regular infantry regiments), had been dispatched to the Far East. The Patricias arrived just as the UN forces – which had seemed on the verge of total victory in November – were being driven out of North Korea by the intervention of the communist Chinese. Over the next six months, offensive and counteroffensive would shift the front line up and down the peninsula, with 2 PPCLI's stand on a hill north of the village of Kap'yong in April 1951 becoming the best-known Canadian action of the war. The rest of the 25th Brigade arrived a month after that to take part in the UN's final advance to a defensive line just north of the thirty-eighth parallel. In July 1951, the Canadian brigade joined with British, Australian, and New Zealand troops to form the 1st Commonwealth Division, the formation in which they would spend the remainder of the war.

The opening of truce talks that same month suggested that both sides were finally willing to accept the division of the two Koreas along the line of contact, but the optimism that greeted the armistice talks eventually turned to exasperation as the negotiations bogged down over the issue of repatriating prisoners of war against their will. While the tense first year of rapidly changing fortunes may have captured the Canadian public's imagination, the protracted stalemate – both on the ground and at the conference table – meant that the war gradually faded from the headlines. Soldiers continued to fight and die on the peninsula for another two years, but it was already obvious that there would be no clear-cut victory. With no major offensives planned and operations restricted to small unit engagements, by December 1951 the Korean conflict had become a war of patrols.

As Canada's ground force commitment dragged on into a second year, Ottawa decided to replace the Special Force units with those of the regular army. The professional soldiers of the 1st battalions arrived in the spring of 1952 to take their place in the Commonwealth Division's static positions and continued to hold the front line for the next year, mounting the occasional raid against the Chinese while having their own entrenchments raided in turn. The regular units were then replaced by the 3rd battalions for the final months of fighting until an armistice agreement was signed on 27 July 1953.

Although the Canadian formation carried the same designation throughout the war, this annual rotation of units and personnel meant that, in essence, three separate brigades served in Korea during the war: the Special Force units under John M. Rockingham; the regular army's 1st battalions under Mortimer Patrick Bogert; and the original training units, the 3rd battalions, under Jean V. Allard. The yearly changeover in personnel meant that arriving units had little detailed knowledge of the brigade's previous operations and were unaware of the shifts that had occurred in the Canadians' defensive methods and tactics. This lack of continuity led to the false assumption – made by soldiers at the time and historians afterward – that the brigade's defence of its static positions must have been conducted in much the same manner by whichever battalions were holding the front. Once the shooting war had ended, few, if any, Canadians were interested in what had actually happened during the twenty months of stalemate.

Before the war could pass completely from the public's consciousness, the army's historical section published *Canada's Army in Korea* in 1956.[2] This short official account is a collection of articles by Capt. Frank McGuire, the 25th Brigade's historical officer during the last year of the war, that originally appeared in the *Canadian Army Journal.* Ten years later, the historical section produced the Army's official history, *Strange Battleground,* by another Korea veteran, Lt.-Col. Herbert Fairlie Wood, a former commanding officer of 3 PPCLI.[3] Despite the first-hand experience of the authors, these accounts were primarily descriptions of events, with Wood's history providing only the occasional suggestion that the brigade might have run into some tactical problems. *Strange Battleground* did, however, convey the professional army's disdain for the Special Force volunteers of the 2nd battalions. Placing the blame on an overhasty recruiting process, Wood gave an official endorsement to the public's perception that the Special Force had been a collection of misfit soldiers of fortune, men who were later replaced at the front by the spit-and-polish professionals of the regular 1st battalions. Even the publication of an official history did little to stimulate Canadian interest in the Korean War. Only a handful of popular histories were written in subsequent decades, with the first of these, published in 1983, appropriately subtitled *Canada's Forgotten War.*[4] Memoirs and first-person accounts have also been slow to appear – most have been published only in the 1990s – but are generally more useful, with the best being Robert Peacock's memoir, *Kim-chi, Asahi and Rum,* and John Gardam's collection of interviews, *Korea Volunteer.*[5]

Academic studies of Canada's involvement in the conflict are even fewer. Canadian diplomacy during the war was the subject of a 1974 book by Denis Stairs, *The Diplomacy of Constraint: Canada, the Korean War and the United States,* but its concentration on the US-Canada relationship meant that only passing reference was made to the situation on the battlefield. Nearly twenty years later two other historians, J.L. Granatstein and D.J. Bercuson, included three chapters surveying Korean operations in their *War and Peacekeeping: From South Africa to the Gulf – Canada's Limited Wars.* Published in 1991, the book provided only a basic narrative of events, with less analysis than the Canadian official history had contained twenty-five years before.[6]

Nor was the war of particularly great historical interest beyond Canada's borders. A year before *War and Peacekeeping* appeared, the British finally published the first instalment of their two-volume official history of the war.[7] Also written by a Korea veteran, the British history provided useful context for the Canadian experience, particularly in its use of Chinese sources, but like the earlier American army and marine official histories[8] had little new to say about the Canadian contingent other than what was already to be found in *Strange Battleground.* Aside from recognizing 2 PPCLI's stand at Kap'yong, other British and American historians have also made little reference to the Canadian brigade.[9]

The second volume of the Australian official history, published in 1985, on the other hand, contained several paragraphs that criticized the 25th Brigade's operations, particularly the Canadians' failure to patrol in sufficient strength to keep the enemy away from their entrenchments.[10] These criticisms were expanded upon by another Australian historian, Jeffrey Grey, in his 1988 study, *The Commonwealth Armies and the Korean War.*[11] The Australian perceptions of Canadian battlefield performance appear to confirm the reminiscences of Maj. Harry Pope, a company commander in Korea with both the 1st and 3rd battalions, published in the Royal 22nd Regiment periodical, *La Citadelle.*[12] Pope's articles shed further light on the views he had first expressed in two 1953 memoranda critical of the brigade's defensive methods.[13] Although the Canadian official history had acknowledged Pope's criticisms, it largely dismissed them as 'generalizations ... based, in the main on his experience as a regimental officer. The application to other units of all his statements would probably not be valid without more evidence than is available.'[14] As we shall see, the evidence already existed. What was required was more research and analysis.

Pope's memoranda and the Australian comments led me to include a description of 25th Brigade shortcomings in a chapter on the Korean War that I wrote for a history of the Canadian Army, *We Stand on Guard,* in 1992.[15] The material uncovered in preparing that chapter suggested that the operations of the Canadian brigade merited a book-length academic study, one that could provide the sort of analysis lacking in *Strange Battleground.* As this manuscript was nearing completion in 1999, however, David Bercuson's *Blood on the Hills* appeared, the first academic treatment of the Canadian Army in Korea since Wood's history had been published over thirty years earlier. Bercuson's book picked up on the shortcomings outlined in *We Stand on Guard* (there had been no mention of Pope or the Australian histories in *War and Peacekeeping*) but failed to appreciate their significance. Like the Australians' blanket assessment of Canadian difficulties, *Blood on the Hills* made little distinction among the operations of the brigade under each of its three wartime commanders. Indeed, Bercuson took the patrolling criticisms Pope had made from his observations of the 1st battalions in 1952-3 and applied them primarily to the 1951-2 operations of the Special Force battalions, units that the R22eR major had never seen in action. In almost every respect, *Blood on the Hills* accepted the official history's distinction between the regulars and the volunteers of 1950. Bercuson, however, expanded on Wood's original distinctions to conclude, inaccurately, that the professionals must have outperformed the men of the Special Force on the battlefield. He characterizes the 2nd battalions as hurriedly 'slapped together' and rushed off to Korea after a 'badly conceived' training program, while describing the professional soldiers in the 1st battalions as being 'far better prepared to fight' when they arrived in the theatre. Indeed, Bercuson goes on to state that the 1st battalions 'were probably the best-trained ground force that Canada has ever put directly onto a field of battle. They were professional soldiers in every respect. When called on to use the skills they had acquired, they did so with determination and courage.'[16] *Blood on the Hills* failed to follow that analysis with a discussion of the tactical differences between the Special Force and regular army units. Failure to recognize the operational differences of the various infantry battalions also weakens Brent Byron Watson's *Far Eastern Tour,* published in 2002. Problems, according to these historians, resulted primarily from inadequate weaponry and poor training.[17]

This book offers a new, comprehensive account of the entire Canadian campaign while placing 25th Brigade operations in their proper context within the

Korean War as a whole. It provides a detailed study and critical analysis of the training, leadership, operations, and tactics of the main Canadian Army units employed during the war and, in so doing, challenges many of the earlier assumptions about the Canadians' battlefield performance. In assessing the formation's strengths and weaknesses, this book examines, for the first time, the brigade's operational methods under each of its three wartime commanders: those that distinguished the Special Force 2nd battalions of 1951-2 from the regular army's 1st battalions that replaced them, and the reforms instituted by Allard when he took command of the brigade in April 1953. As the arm in closest contact with the enemy, the infantry battalions' abilities largely determined the brigade's success, and the infantry units are the primary focus of this study.

In contrast to *Strange Battleground* and *Blood on the Hills*, I will argue here that the officers of the Special Force units exhibited greater professionalism in their approach to operations than the regulars of the 1st battalions, a difference encapsulated in the 'active defence' of the former and the 'inactive defence' of the latter. Although up to half of the Special Force enlistees had seen army service during the Second World War, it was the combat experience and leadership of the 2nd battalions' officers and NCOs – men who demonstrated a clear understanding of the profession of arms – that gave these units their operational superiority. The Special Force was also fortunate in being led by one of the most dynamic brigade commanders the Canadian Army has ever produced. Not only was Rockingham able to hone the Second World War battle experience of his men before departing North America, his forward style of combat leadership also ensured that his officers kept on top of the tactical situations confronting them once they arrived in theatre. Far from being 'slapped together' and rushed off to war, the 25th Brigade was, in fact, the best-prepared and most combat-ready force Canada has ever fielded at the outset of a conflict. Coming only five years after the country had mobilized a mass citizen army to fight the Second World War, the Korean War's timing made the conflict unique in Canadian military history. With the nation's wars usually spaced some twenty years apart, certainly no other formation Canada has sent overseas has been able to draw on as much recent operational experience in preparing itself for battle.

A tactical study of the differences in the 25th Brigade's operations under each of its three commanders also provides a valuable insight into the nature of successful battlefield command, with the Canadian experience in Korea demonstrating both how and how not to conduct military operations. The problems the brigade encountered in 1952-3 under Bogert's command resulted primarily from poor leadership, at both the formation and unit level, rather than inadequate weaponry. While most soldiers agreed there were no new lessons to be learned in Korea, it is clear from their lethargic performance that the 1st battalions' officers either did not clearly understand the old ones or, more likely, lacked the drive and initiative that is so necessary to success in combat. The Second World War veterans who officered the Special Force battalions volunteered specifically to fight in Korea and understood the demands of combat when they joined. Slightly better armed than they had been in defeating the German army in northwest Europe five years earlier, the Special Force units proved to be skilled soldiers who believed in their superior military abilities and were not afraid to dominate the enemy. The regular officers of the 1st battalions, on the other hand, while also veterans of the 1939-45 conflict, had volunteered for a peacetime Canadian Army and were posted to the war zone simply as part of their job. At that stage of their military careers, some of them may not have been as highly motivated for combat as they should have been. As this book will demonstrate, this showed in their battlefield performance.

A War of Patrols

PROLOGUE: VERRIÈRES RIDGE, NORMANDY, JULY 1944

The commanding officer of the Royal Hamilton Light Infantry was worried. In its first major assignment since landing in Normandy with the 2nd Canadian Infantry Division in early July, his battalion had been handed the task of capturing the village of Verrières at the eastern end of a low ridge lying some five miles south of Caen (see Map 1). According to the plan laid down by II Canadian Corps, the proposed jumping-off point for the assault, an east-west road running through a farm 1,000 yards north of the village, would be captured by another battalion, Les Fusiliers Mont-Royal, only a few hours before the scheduled RHLI attack. Although 'promised that it would be cleared before dark on the night of 24 July,' the RHLI CO was concerned that the timing was 'a bit risky and late. I asked to be given the task of securing the start line myself, but was not allowed to do this and was assured that it would be secured.'[1]

On being informed on 23 July that his battalion would be taking part in the attack on Verrières Ridge, Lt.-Col. John Rockingham had sent reconnaissance patrols out to ascertain the enemy's strength and dispositions in the area of Troteval Farm and the village beyond. Not satisfied with these reports, the six-foot-two officer squeezed into a small plane the next day to reconnoitre the ground over which his battalion would be making its attack. In carefully noting the nature of the ground and possible enemy strongpoints, Rockingham was the only battalion commander taking part in the attack to undertake a personal reconnaissance of the battlefield.[2] Despite his qualms about leaving the important task of capturing Troteval Farm to Les Fusiliers, the RHLI CO had little choice once his request to have his own men secure their start line was turned down by brigade headquarters.

Since landing in Normandy on 6 June, the Anglo-Canadian army had been making slow progress against the skilled German defenders. Caen, an original D-Day objective, had not been captured until 9 July, and the industrial areas immediately south of the city had remained in enemy hands until the 2nd and 3rd Canadian Infantry Divisions attacked them nine days later as part of Second British Army's Operation Goodwood. The planned breakthrough by British armour in the Goodwood offensive, however, had been halted by the strong German antitank defences on Bourguébus ridge. Now, one week later, II Canadian Corps was being asked to mount another attack on the western end of the Bourguébus line to capture the high ground astride the main Caen-Falaise highway. The attack was to coincide with a much larger American breakout attempt, Operation Cobra, on the western flank of the Normandy beachhead.

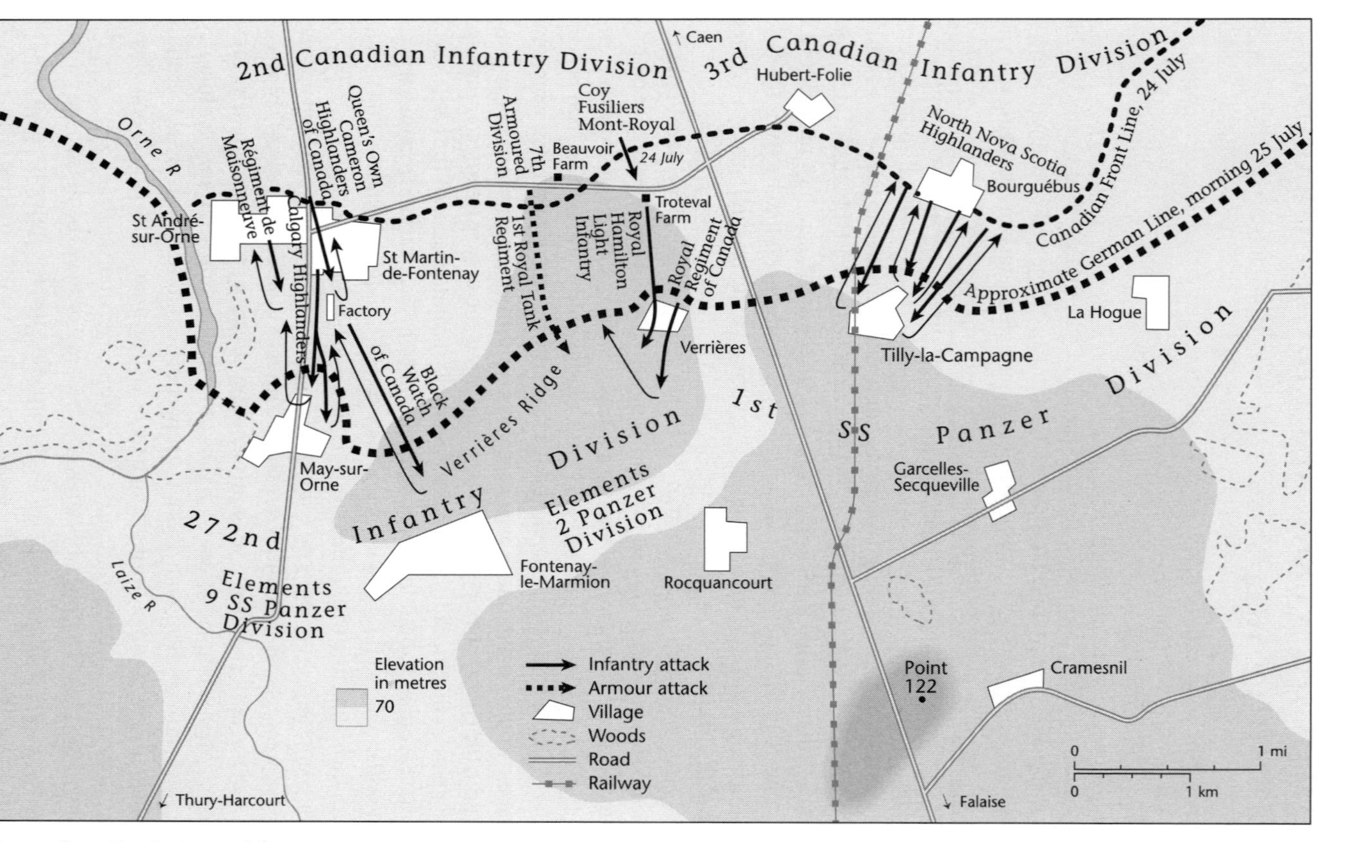

Map 1 *Operation Spring, 25 July 1944*

In keeping with the tactical views of the Canadian corps commander, Lt.-Gen. Guy Simonds, the attack on Verrières Ridge would be mounted so as to maximize the heavy supporting artillery fire.[3] Operation Spring, despite involving both the 2nd and 3rd Canadian Divisions, would be launched only on a three-battalion front, with separate battalions to clear each of the start lines, capture the intermediate objectives of Tilly-la-Campagne, Verrières, and May-sur-Orne, and make the final assaults on the villages of Garcelles-Secqueville, Rocquancourt, and Fontenay-le-Marmion beyond the ridge. Once the RHLI had secured Verrières in the centre of the II Corps' attack, the Royal Regiment of Canada was to pass through the position to attack Rocquancourt.

The RHLI commander's careful preparations were entirely in keeping with his thorough approach to all military operations. Since being posted to the Rileys as their second-in-command in September 1942 – part of the battalion's rebuilding following its heavy losses in the Dieppe disaster – John Rockingham had 'brought a new sense of urgency to the training program. The War Diary noted, with some awe, that Rockingham often went about his business on a motorcycle – "something new for an RHLI 2 i/c."'[4] He had continued to train his men hard after taking over command of the battalion in April 1943. Although their training was intensified as the invasion of France neared, Rockingham complained to brigade headquarters that realistic training was impossible in the lush countryside of southeastern England.[5] Having then been sent to a Staff College course, however, the Riley's CO did not accompany the battalion to Normandy when they were dispatched with the rest of the 2nd Canadian Infantry Division in early July. In fact, he did not rejoin them until 18 July, the same day the unit saw its first action since Dieppe. Despite the presence of a few survivors of that infamous raid in the RHLI ranks, Rockingham could not ignore his battalion's lack of combat experience as he planned the attack on Verrières.

At the orders group held on the evening of 24 July, Rockingham did not mince words with his officers: 'The intention of the RHLI was to destroy the enemy in the village of Verrières and to capture and hold the position.'[6] The battalion would be attacking on a three-company front with the fourth rifle company being held in reserve. The carrier platoon would cover the assaulting companies' flanks with light machine-gun fire while the entire operation would be supported by artillery concentrations lifting on a timed program. Shortly after 2030 hours that night, the Rileys were informed that the Fusilier attack had captured Troteval Farm and secured the start line – the understrength battalion had been forced to form a composite company under the command of Maj. Jacques Dextraze to carry out the operation. A 'still dubious' Rockingham could only wait as the scout platoon moved forward to begin taping the start line and axis of attack for each of the companies. Indeed, the RHLI scouts soon found that German infantry and three tanks had moved back into the area immediately west of the farm and were dominating the assigned start line with direct fire. The taping party was frequently interrupted in its task by bursts of automatic fire and were often forced to 'crawl about twenty yards, stop and listen, and carefully unroll the tape' in the waist-high grain. After completing as much of the start line as they could, the scout commander informed battalion headquarters at 0114 hours that the Germans had prevented him from finishing its western section.[7]

With his worst fears confirmed, the RHLI CO immediately asked brigade headquarters to allow him to use his reserve company to secure the start line. After receiving permission, Rockingham made the bold decision to send C Company forward to attack the enemy tanks even though the operation would delay the planned 0330 start of the assault on Verrières by some forty minutes. When his request to have the artillery concentration for the main attack delayed until 0400 hours was turned down by II Corps headquarters, it meant that his men would lose the benefit of the prearranged bombardment. Nonetheless, Rockingham judged that adequately securing the ground from which the attack would be launched outweighed the advantages of an artillery barrage.[8]

By 0400 hours the reserve company had driven off the enemy tanks as well as some snipers who had been holding out in the farm buildings themselves. Ten minutes later the three assaulting companies were able to cross the start line unopposed and head through the ripening wheat for their objective, 1,300 yards to the south. After an orchard immediately south of Troteval Farm, the next 600 yards was entirely open until a series of hedgerows some 300 yards short of Verrières. As the three companies crossed the open ground, they were subjected to machine-gun and mortar fire from both flanks and the hedgerow in front. Because they were without supporting artillery fire, the RHLI's two flanking companies, A and D, undoubtedly took heavier casualties in reaching the hedges, and both were pinned down by automatic weapons fire short of the objective. Only A Company on the right was able to get one of its platoons into the first German-held hedge.

In the centre, however, B Company was able to make the long advance up the slope to Verrières with fewer casualties. Entering the first hedgerow, the company commander led his men in hand-to-hand combat until he was wounded. With the capture of the first hedge, his company then 'charged across the adjoining field with the hope that perhaps the next hedge would be only a hedge! But it never was. Four successive hedges and then the headlong plunge past dung heaps and cow byres to close with the enemy. There was fighting from one stone cottage with its weathered roof to another, the painful decision of crossing a lane. Then the fruit trees to right and left, the dusty road, and finally the southern slope that was all part of Verrières.'[9]

Not until the predawn light began to strengthen was it revealed that the automatic fire holding up D Company on the left flank was coming from German tanks. A 17-pounder antitank troop supporting the Riley attack was ordered into action on the secure ground immediately south of Troteval Farm and quickly accounted for four of the tanks. After an artillery concentration called down on the right flank reduced the enemy's fire in that sector, both A and D Companies were able to rush forward and join B Company in clearing the village. In the words of the regimental history, 'Dawn was just breaking and village buildings [were] looming grey and ghostly' as they broke through the last hedgerow 'whooping like Indians, throwing grenades and firing at everything in sight with Sten, rifle and Bren. Then there was a race to the barns where the only resistance came from a few Germans who had drifted back from the hedges. Most of these surrendered.'[10]

With the rifle companies in the village, the battalion's antitank guns, mortars, and Bren carriers were brought forward, priority being given to the last in order to evacuate the most seriously wounded. The 6-pounder antitank guns were no sooner in position when the Germans counterattacked with nine tanks. Four of the RHLI guns were quickly destroyed by direct hits and the German armour had to be driven off by infantry using PIAT (Projector, Infantry, Anti-Tank) grenades and smoke. As soon as the counterattack had been repulsed, Rockingham brought up his reserve company and carrier platoon to consolidate the position and reported to 4th Brigade headquarters that the village was secured at 0750 hours. Shortly thereafter, the Royal Regiment of Canada, which had come forward in the wake of the RHLI capture of Verrières, continued the attack toward Rocquancourt, one mile to the south at the foot of the ridge. Once the Royal Regiment crossed the crest of the ridge, some 400 yards south of the village, however, they were met by heavy fire from German tanks, 88 mm antitank guns, mortars, and machine-guns that were dug in on the reverse slope. The regiment's C Company was almost annihilated when it tried to press on down the forward slope, losing all but eighteen of its men. By noon, the corps commander had to accept that the weight of enemy fire made a farther advance by the Royal Regiment impossible, and the battalion was allowed to dig in to the east between the RHLI-held village of Verrières and the main Caen-Falaise highway.[11]

Unfortunately, the RHLI success was not matched by any of the other battalions in Operation Spring. To the east, the North Nova Scotia Highlander attack on Tilly-la-Campagne, despite receiving the full support of the artillery barrage, barely managed to get a toehold in the village before it was bloodily repulsed. In the villages west of Verrières, the 5th Brigade's battalions engaged in equally futile attacks. Unlike Rockingham, the CO of the Calgary Highlanders decided to launch his attack at H-hour despite the fact that the Queen's Own Cameron Highlanders of Canada had failed to clear the start line. The Calgary Highlanders 'had trouble from the beginning'[12] with only elements of the battalion managing to fight their way to the outskirts of May-sur-Orne before falling back to St. André.

The day's greatest disaster was reserved for the Black Watch of Canada battalion attacking Fontenay-le-Marmion. Like the Calgary Highlanders, the Black Watch found its forward assembly area still in enemy hands and had to spend time clearing it, during which its CO was killed. With command devolving to one of the company commanders, Maj. F.P. Griffin, the battalion was ordered forward to capture Fontenay in support of the Royal Regiment's attack on Rocquancourt, despite the fact that its planned start line in May-sur-Orne had not been captured. Jumping off from the factory area south of St. Martin-de-Fontenay instead, the already depleted Black Watch companies set off at 0930 hours 'across the open field and the west end of the ridge directly against Fontenay.' Once they had disappeared over the crest the Canadians were pinned down by 'intense close-range fire' from the waiting Germans. 'Griffin ordered his men to make their way back individually as best they could; but very few succeeded in doing so. Officers of the battalion estimate that the four rifle companies committed to this attack numbered perhaps 300 officers and men, and that not more than fifteen of them got back to our lines. The last survivors were probably overwhelmed early in the afternoon. When we later re-occupied the position, Major Griffin's body was found lying among those of his men.'[13]

With the repulse of the remaining attacks, the Germans were able to turn their attention to the only penetration the Canadians had made. For the remainder of 25 July, the RHLI in Verrières were subjected to repeated counterattacks by German tanks and infantry. Rockingham, meanwhile, was well forward, directing the defence. During the initial assault on the village one of his company commanders had been shot dead while pointing out an enemy strongpoint to the CO. Later in the afternoon, Rockingham 'was sharing a slit trench with some of B Company's men' when 'a German tank loomed up almost on top of them ... A PIAT was prepared and fired almost directly upward, setting the tank on fire. The crew bailed out into Canadian hands.'[14] When one of the artillery's red smoke rounds, intended to mark enemy tanks, fell short and landed on Rockingham's headquarters, it was immediately attacked by three RAF Typhoon fighter-bombers. They smothered it with rocket fire but happily did not inflict any casualties.

Although supported by the arrival of a troop of British tanks in the afternoon, Rockingham took pride in reporting that his battalion's 'mortar, Bren, rifle, and even Sten, grenade and PIAT fire was just as responsible for repelling the enemy as were the tanks and Typhoons.'[15] The enemy's efforts – which included the first use of miniature robot tanks against Canadians – did not succeed in driving the Rileys out of Verrières. As one critical historian of the Canadian campaign in Normandy has pointed out, the RHLI action 'remains notable in that it was attained by so-called inexperienced, but well led and handled, Canadian troops.'[16]

The 1,500 casualties incurred on 25 July 1944 represented the Canadian Army's second most costly day of operations in the Second World War, after the Dieppe raid. Indeed, the 450 Canadians killed in the battle would prove to be 150 more fatalities than the army would suffer during the entire two and a half years of the Korean War. Although Rockingham rightly attributed the RHLI's success to the 'remarkable courage, determination and skill'[17] his men displayed in capturing and holding the position, the attack on Verrières also demonstrated the high quality of his own battlefield leadership. From his willingness to make a personal reconnaissance of the ground to his bold decision to delay his battalion's attack in order to secure the start line properly, Rockingham had demonstrated a forward style of combat leadership that was all too rare in the Canadian Army during the Second World War. Not surprisingly, his actions on Verrières Ridge marked him for further promotion. In the nine months of fighting that remained in the European campaign, John Rockingham would go on to prove himself one of Canada's best operational commanders. His record would not be forgotten five years later when the Canadian Army was called upon to fight yet another conflict, this time on an obscure peninsula in the Far East.

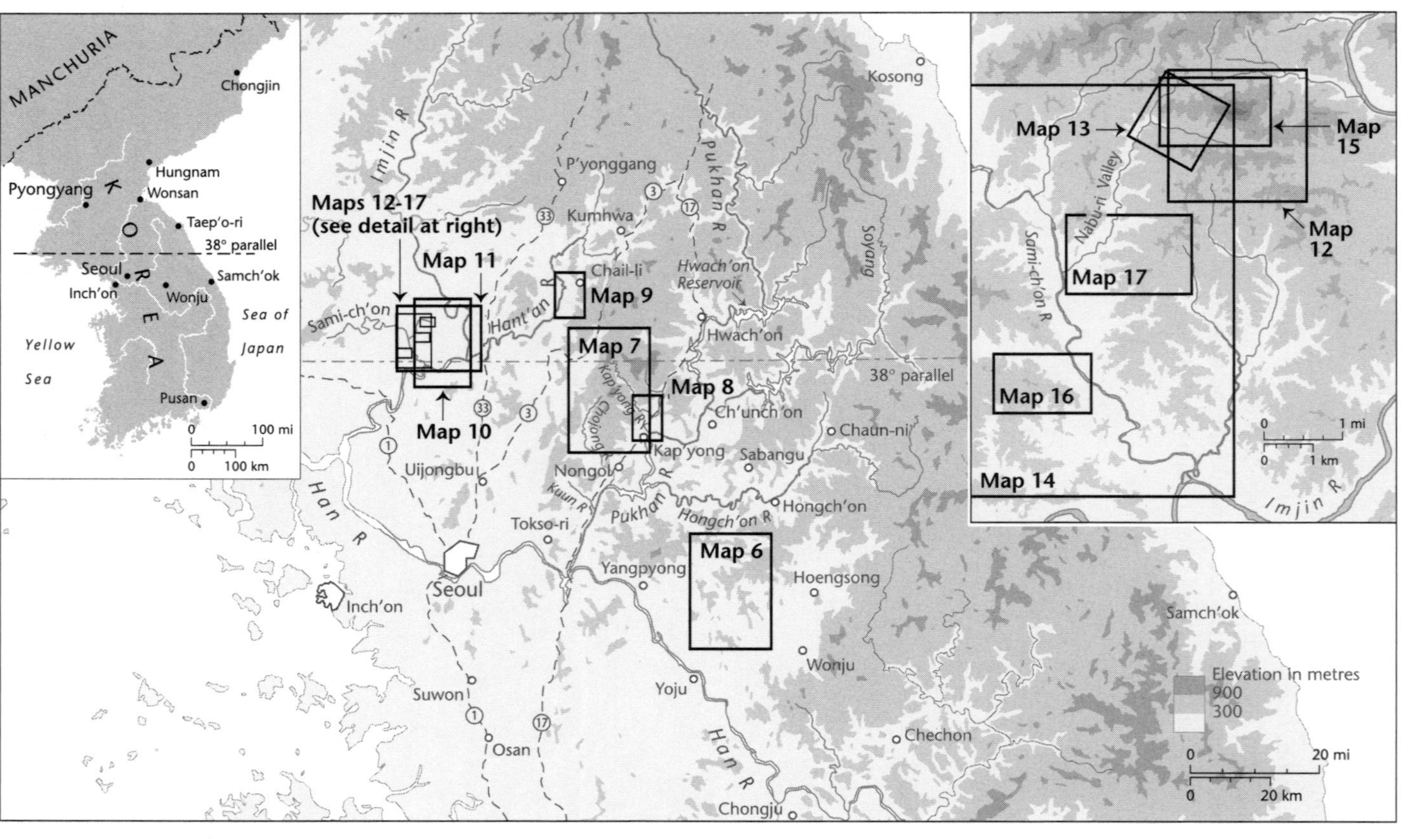

Map 2 *Korea, 1950-3*

1 WAR AND RECRUITMENT, JUNE-AUGUST 1950

The very magnitude of the Allied victory in 1945 allowed Canada to enter the postwar era with a strong sense of confidence in the world's security. Not only had much of Germany and Japan been reduced to satisfying rubble, but the former enemies were now under Allied military administration. Optimism in the peace was further bolstered by the formation of the United Nations and the apparent determination of its members to see that such conflict was never repeated. The new organization also appeared to have remedied the worst shortcomings of the failed League of Nations. For one, the United States had taken a leading role in the United Nations, giving the organization the backing of the most powerful nation to emerge from the Second World War. The UN's charter also had provisions for multinational military forces, to give teeth to the League of Nations' empty rhetoric of collective security.

With the international situation appearing to promise an extended peace, it seemed that there would be only a minimal need for national armed forces. In Prime Minister Mackenzie King's view, the security of the postwar world would allow Canada 'to get back to the old Liberal principles of economy, reduction of taxation, anti-militarism, etc.'[1] The division-sized Canadian Army Occupational Force that had been stationed in Germany at the end of the war was largely repatriated to Canada by the summer of 1946. From a total strength of 478,690 men and women in June 1945, the Canadian Army was reduced to a mere 15,852 two years later. The vast army of citizen soldiers that Canada had assembled to fight its European campaigns had returned to civilian life.[2]

If not necessarily reducing taxes, the government of Mackenzie King was at least willing to stand by 'the old Liberal principle' of antimilitarism. At war's end the three service chiefs had proposed a military budget of $290 million to maintain a navy of 20,000 men, an air force of 30,000, and a regular army of 55,000, the last to be kept up to strength by compulsory universal service. Not surprisingly the King government insisted on more modest costs. At the end of 1945, cabinet approved a defence budget of $172 million to support a naval strength of 10,000 and an air force of 16,000. Compulsory universal service for the army – the very phrase was certain to send shivers down the prime minister's spine – was rejected out of hand, as was the targeted strength of 55,000 regulars.[3] Cabinet quickly decided to reduce the army from a force that had enlisted over 700,000 men during the Second World War to only 25,000 full-time soldiers. Even so, the three services could take heart that the approved establishments were greatly in excess of the $30 million budget and 6,500 permanent personnel with which they had been asked to defend Canada by an earlier King administration in the mid-1930s.[4]

Redesignated 'The Canadian Army' in place of its prewar title 'The Militia of Canada,' the postwar army continued to be composed of both regular and reserve units. Although greatly expanded from its 1930s establishment, the 25,000-strong regular force component, now dubbed the 'Active Force' instead of the earlier 'Permanent Active Militia,' maintained its primary function of assisting 'in the training and administration of the Reserve Force and to supply the necessary staffs, services and scientific research and development personnel, augmented by a small formation of essential field units. This field formation would be maintained as a trained field force, fully equipped and organized on war establishments, ready to meet whatever commitments might arise.' The Reserve Force – the former 'Non-Permanent Active Militia' – would continue to represent 'the military potential of the country' with a paper strength of 180,000 part-time soldiers.[5]

In neither instance, however, were the establishment figures reached. With the government seeking further economies, a single minister of national defence was appointed in December 1946 to replace the three wartime service ministers, and the duplication implicit in having three service bureaucracies was eliminated. The new minister, Brooke Claxton, quickly moved to limit the size of the Active Force by restricting enlistments to three-quarters of establishment. As a result, the strength of the regular army was less than 16,000 all ranks in March 1948 and rose to just under 19,000 a year later following a recruiting drive launched by the minister. The situation in the Reserve Force was proportionally even worse. Despite the several hundred thousand army veterans in Canada, reserve units could find relatively few men who were sufficiently interested in part-time soldiering to fill their ranks. By 1947 the strength of Canada's reserve units had fallen to a mere 30,000 and rose only slowly thereafter, standing at slightly over 36,000 two years later.[6]

The field units of the Active Force consisted of three infantry battalions trained for parachute operations, two armoured regiments, and a regiment of field artillery. These units were based at army camps across Canada, often in war-built temporary barracks. The 1st Regiment, Royal Canadian Horse Artillery, was located at Camp Shilo in Manitoba and armed with the standard field gun of the Second World War, the 25-pounder. The two armoured regiments, the Royal Canadian Dragoons and Lord Strathcona's Horse (Royal Canadians), were equipped with Sherman tanks and trained with restricted establishments at Camp Petawawa in Ontario and Currie Barracks at Calgary, Alberta. Of the three infantry battalions, The Royal Canadian Regiment was at Petawawa, Princess Patricia's Canadian Light Infantry at Currie Barracks, and the Royal 22e Régiment at Camp Valcartier in Quebec. The 'sharp end' of Canada's army totalled fewer than 7,000 all ranks. The bulk of the remaining Active Force personnel were posted to the various corps schools of instruction, to static service units, and to the headquarters of the five regional commands where they assisted in the training of the reserves. In discussing Canadian defence policy in the House of Commons in June 1948, Claxton admitted the obvious: 'By themselves our forces could never deter the Russians, nor in a general conflict could they deliver a knock-out blow.'[7]

Concerns over Soviet intentions in Europe had already led to talks between Britain, the United States, and Canada about the formation of a western alliance to deter further aggression. Preliminary discussions on a possible pact were inconclusive until the Soviet seizure of Czechoslovakia on 25 February 1948. According to Escott Reid, one of Canada's leading contemporary diplomats, this event 'resulted in the opening of negotiations on the Brussels [western alliance] treaty on 7 March. Then on 8 March came the catalytic message from the Norwegian government to the British and American governments that Norway might soon face Soviet demands for a pact which would reduce it to the level of a Soviet satellite. Two days later came news of the murder or suicide of Jan Masaryk, the pro-western foreign minister of Czechoslovakia. The next day, [British prime minister Clement] Attlee proposed to the United States and Canada that officials of the three countries meet in Washington without delay.'[8] Their negotiations took on an added urgency a few months later when the USSR blockaded all land traffic into West Berlin, prompting the West to undertake a massive airlift to keep the divided city supplied and out of Soviet hands. Despite qualms in some American political circles about committing the United States to a peacetime alliance in Europe, a North Atlantic alliance treaty was signed in April 1949.

Although aimed at curbing any further Soviet expansion into Western Europe, the signatories of the North Atlantic treaty clearly did not expect the new alliance to involve them in any significant increase in defence expenditures. It was hoped that by pooling resources the pact would reduce the total expenditures which each signatory would otherwise have found necessary. According to Reid, the US State Department 'believed that the mere commitment of the United States to the alliance would be enough to deter the Soviet Union from committing aggression. The United States administration hoped that there would be "some increase" in the defence expenditures of the Western European allies but it also believed that "economic recovery must not be sacrificed to rearmament."'[9] Certainly, the Canadian government did not feel much need to launch a rearmament program because of the treaty. The entire defence budget for 1949-50 amounted to only $360 million. By the end of March 1950, the strength of the Active Force stood at just over 20,600 and the adjutant general was instructed to end an army recruiting campaign and enlist only sufficient men to replace wastage. The Reserve Force had seen its strength grow to 43,000 all ranks that year, an increase of over 6,000. Even with slightly increased numbers, however, the Active Force was far from prepared to undertake operations. A July 1950 appreciation of the field force's operational readiness concluded that if its units were brought up to strength and given intensive training, they would be reasonably efficient within six months.[10]

Canada's role in encouraging the United States to join in the North Atlantic alliance was a demonstration of the shift that had occurred in Canada's international orientation at the conclusion of the Second World War. The undersecretary of state for external affairs at the time, Lester Pearson, has explained that with the end of the war the nation's foreign policies were more heavily influenced by its neighbour to the south than from across the Atlantic. In the post-1945 world, 'The country whose policies would now concern us most would be not Great Britain but the United States. That country was now the super-power. Washington, not London, would determine, with Moscow, whether peace, progress, and even survival were possible. American policies, therefore, must be watched closely. From their consequences Canada could not escape, no more than we could from those of Downing Street from 1920 to 1939.'[11]

For the Canadian Army, the new orientation meant developing ties with the US Army. Virtually nonexistent prior to 1939, military cooperation with the United States became a recognized aim of Canadian defence policy with the Permanent Joint Board on Defence, established during the war, serving as the main instrument for its implementation. Another wartime organization, the Canadian Joint Staff in Washington, was also retained. Both governments subsequently approved a November 1946 Joint Board recommendation calling for an interchange of service personnel, the standardization of arms and equipment 'as far as practicable,' a coordinated program of military mapping, and cooperation in developing tests and exercises. This was followed by a joint statement approving the continuation of limited military cooperation, although it was emphasized that 'all cooperative arrangements will be without impairment of the control of either country over all activities in its territory.'[12] A large-scale joint Canada-US military exercise, Sweetbriar, was even held in February 1950 along the Alaska Highway.

Despite such efforts, however, the scale of North American military cooperation remained limited. The vast majority of Canadian Army officers were more comfortable with the familiar British system of command and control, and little progress was made in standardizing the weaponry of the two countries. With the formation of the North Atlantic alliance, talks between Britain, the United States, and Canada on standardization were shifted to the new organization. Canada continued to make some purchases of American military equipment, but it was not until October 1949 that Washington passed the Mutual Defence Assistance Act to allow Canadian manufacturers to sell arms to the United States.

The truth of Pearson's observation about Washington's influence on Canadian foreign policy was borne out far sooner than almost anyone could have contemplated in 1945. Although the signatories had Soviet aggression in Europe in mind when they signed the North Atlantic alliance in April 1949, in just over a year Canada found itself following an American lead in embarking upon a war half a world away from the expected flashpoint, in a country that few Canadians had ever heard of.

The country to which the world's eyes unexpectedly turned in June 1950 is a mountainous peninsula some 600 miles long and 100 to 200 miles wide, lying between the Sea of Japan on the east and the Yellow Sea to the west (see Map 2). The Yalu and Tumen Rivers separate its northern border from the land mass of Asia, the source of the country's extremes in weather. Despite being surrounded by water, in climate Korea is not dissimilar to southern Canada, with hot, humid summers and cold, crisp winters. The highest mountain range in the country, the Taebaek, runs down the eastern side of the peninsula and determines the drainage pattern of Korea's southern half, with most rivers flowing south and west to the heavily indented coastline on the Yellow Sea. Although only some 20 percent of the mountainous countryside is arable, in 1950 the 'Land of the Morning Calm' was a predominantly agricultural society that had terraced, irrigated, and cultivated its numerous hillsides to grow the national staples of rice, barley, and soybeans. The ancient Korean practice of fertilizing the fields with human waste also gave the country a distinctive odour that was immediately noticed – and frequently commented on – by almost all Western visitors.

The location of the Korean peninsula at the junction of the three major Asian powers of Japan, China, and Russia has had a decided effect on its history. A Chinese invasion around AD 100 established a strong Chinese influence on Korean society that has persisted into modern times. It was not until the Sino-Japanese War of 1894-5 that Chinese political influence over Korea was finally replaced by that of Japan. Ten years later, Japan's victory in the Russo-Japanese War firmly established its dominance over the peninsula. Despite the hostility of the Korean people, Japan annexed the peninsula as a colony in 1910 and continued to exercise an often brutal administration over the inhabitants for the next thirty-five years, until its defeat in the Second World War. Even then, the Korean people could not escape the influence of their powerful neighbours. Despite having declared war against Japan only three weeks before Tokyo's capitulation, the Soviet Union had made certain it was well positioned to move Red Army forces into Japanese-occupied areas along the Soviet border. In order to facilitate the surrender of Japanese forces in Korea the victorious Allies arbitrarily divided the peninsula at the thirty-eighth parallel into Soviet and American zones in August 1945.[13]

The Soviets had never lost sight of the peninsula's importance to their interests in the region. Since the mid-1930s, Moscow had actively supported the communist bands that had fought against the Japanese occupiers. By the time they actually declared war in 1945, the Soviets had a well-established toehold in Korea, having recruited and trained a potential communist administration among the more successful of the guerrilla leaders. Moscow's choice to head a communist regime on the peninsula, however, was not among the leaders of the Korean resistance. The Soviet-trained Kim Il Sung had fought with the Red Army during the Second World War but returned to Korea only in 1945 as a major in the Soviet occupation force.[14]

The United States, despite having defeated the Japanese, did not have the same degree of interest in, or knowledge of, Korean affairs as the Soviets. Nonetheless, when the first US troops entered the country to accept the Japanese surrender in September 1945, the Koreans enthusiastically welcomed them as the liberators they were. That goodwill was quickly squandered when the Americans, who could not speak Korean, initially turned to the former Japanese administrators to help them run the southern half of the country. The skepticism of the Korean people was not lessened when the United Nations imposed a trusteeship on the country in December 1945, overseen by a Joint Commission of the United States and the Soviet Union, to attempt to establish an all-Korean government. The trusteeship was viewed by Koreans of all political stripes as a mere continuation of their previous colonial status.[15]

While the Soviets were able to obscure their role in the northern half of the country behind the rhetoric of Kim Il Sung, the United States had to rely on the nationalist leaders of Korea's provisional government, most notably Syngman Rhee, in the South. Rhee, seventy years old in 1945, had spent much of his life in exile in the United States, but his name and reputation still garnered him sufficient political support in the American-controlled South to gain the upper hand on his rivals in the radical nationalist political movement. The Korean nationalists were no less revolutionary in their goals than were the communists, but their leadership looked to the American and French revolutions for inspiration and hoped to emulate the economic and scientific development of the West. Although many Westerners mistook their rhetoric for a commitment to liberal democracy, the Korean radical nationalists, Syngman Rhee included, viewed politics as belonging to an educated élite. American diplomats in Korea found it difficult to understand politicians like Rhee 'who could discuss the "Rights of Man" with feeling and then go off to plot the assassination of a rival or the organisation of a riot to disrupt a competing party. Like other post-colonial independence movements, leadership gravitated to the boldest, most charismatic and least compromising leaders.'[16]

Over the course of 1946-7 the US-Soviet Joint Commission was unable to reach an agreement about which Korean faction should be recognized as the legitimate government of the entire peninsula, a job made more difficult for the Americans by Rhee's decision to block the commission's work. Rhee insisted that Korea was ready to govern itself, a position that had wide popular support in the South, and he refused to accept the principle of trusteeship. His stance placed the United States in the difficult position of either repudiating Rhee in favour of Kim Il Sung or accepting his position while being unable to control him. The Soviets, meanwhile, added to the Americans' embarrassment by refusing to deal with any Korean who rejected international trusteeship.[17]

Both radical nationalists and communists were ruthlessly intolerant of opposition, and more moderate Korean politicians were attacked or even assassinated. Exasperated with the chaos of Korean politics, the United States turned to the United

Nations for the appointment of a Temporary Commission on Korea to oversee national elections and ensure that the new National Assembly was 'duly elected by the Korean people and not mere appointees by military authorities.'[18] Beginning its work in January the commission, of which Canada was one of nine members, was denied entry into the communist North to oversee the election process there, but the election in the southern half of the country, where 20 million of 29 million Koreans lived, proceeded on 10 May 1948. Roughly three-quarters of those eligible to cast ballots did so. Syngman Rhee, whose party captured the largest number of seats in the National Assembly, 55 of the 198, was elected chairman of the assembly and, on 15 August, inaugurated as president of the new Republic of Korea (ROK) in its capital of Seoul. The communist North followed on 3 September 1948 by proclaiming the Democratic People's Republic of Korea under the premiership of Kim Il Sung with its capital in Pyongyang.[19] Divided by the arbitrarily selected thirty-eighth parallel, the Korean people now had two mutually hostile administrations on the peninsula, each claiming to be the legitimate government of the whole.

On 12 December 1948 the United Nations General Assembly recommended that the two occupying powers withdraw their forces from the peninsula. The Soviet Union announced within two weeks that all its forces had been repatriated, although the lack of UN access to North Korea prevented verification of the claim; the last US Army unit departed at the end of June the following year. Neither power, in fact, completely removed its military presence. In South Korea, the US Korean Military Advisory Group (KMAG), consisting of 500 US Army personnel, remained behind to assist in the organization of the fledging southern republic's armed forces. Over the next twelve months, the American advisors helped to oversee the buildup of the ROK Army into a force of eight understrength divisions totalling some 98,000 men. Only four of these eight divisions were stationed along the thirty-eighth parallel, the remainder being employed in the interior of the country on antiguerrilla activities against the numerous communist-inspired uprisings that occurred regularly between 1948 and 1950.

Somewhat surprisingly – in view of subsequent US assistance to anticommunist forces around the world – the South Koreans created their army with little material assistance from Washington. The American government was still smarting at the defeat of the US-supported Chinese Nationalists, nor did it see Korea as a potential site of conflict with the Soviet Union. Although both the ROK Army and KMAG continued to insist that they needed more artillery, tanks, and mines, the Pentagon provided only token assistance. American apologists would later claim that Washington had taken seriously Rhee's boasts of marching north and conquering the communists, but such statements were simply meant to deflect responsibility for lightly arming the ROK forces onto the Seoul regime.[20]

Closer to the scene, the supreme commander allied powers in Tokyo, Gen. Douglas MacArthur, transferred excess war materiel from his occupation forces in Japan, but his repeated calls to arm the ROK Army to fight the North Koreans went unheeded in Washington.[21] A South Korean request in October 1949 for 189 M26 tanks was turned down, for example, while the 700 artillery pieces eventually supplied were the shorter-range (8,200 yard) M3 version of the 105 mm howitzer. The ROK Army was not given any heavy artillery. South Korean infantry battalions did receive valuable 81 mm and 60 mm mortars, some 140 antitank guns, and 1,900 2.36-inch bazookas but, as the Americans themselves were soon to discover, the 2.36-inch bazooka was useless against the armour of the North Koreans' T-34 tanks. The Americans also provided the Republic of Korea with a dozen liaison-type aircraft and ten Harvard trainers to form a fledgling air force. (Although ten P-51 Mustang fighters were also turned over to the South the day after the communist invasion, no South Korean pilots were qualified to fly them in combat.) While this lack of equipment concerned the American advisors in Korea, many KMAG officers were contemptuous of the North Koreans' military capabilities and remained confident that even a poorly equipped ROK Army was capable of repelling any invasion attempt. MacArthur's intelligence staff, moreover, believed that Kim Il Sung would attempt to unite the two Koreas by political subversion and guerrilla activity in the South rather than direct military action.[22]

Above the thirty-eighth parallel, meanwhile, the North Korea People's Army was officially activated on 8 February 1948 – seven months before the Democratic People's Republic of Korea was itself proclaimed. With strong Soviet and Chinese assistance, particularly during the first six months of 1950, the NKPA numbered some 135,000 troops on the eve of its invasion of South Korea. These were organized into eight full-strength infantry divisions, two additional (but recently formed) infantry divisions at half-strength, an armoured brigade equipped with Soviet T-34 tanks, an independent infantry regiment of three battalions, and a motorcycle reconnaissance regiment. The Soviets also provided the North Koreans with some 180 Second World War aircraft (including 110 YAK fighters and ground-attack bombers) with which to build a small air force. Particularly large shipments of equipment arrived in the spring of 1950. In addition to the excellent T-34 tanks, the NKPA also received Soviet-made 122 mm and 76 mm howitzers and guns, 76 mm self-propelled guns, 45 mm antitank guns, and numerous mortars, rifles, and machine-guns. Equipment and numbers, however, do not indicate the qualitative difference in the two forces. While many of its senior officers had been trained in the Soviet Union and the units themselves were organized under the guidance of their Soviet advisors, the NKPA also had the advantage of a large number of veterans of the Chinese civil war, about 28,000 of whom had been repatriated by April 1950: 'The Korean veterans of the Chinese Communist Forces made up about one third of the North Korean People's Army in June 1950 and gave it a combat-hardened quality and efficiency that it would not otherwise have had. Five of the eight divisions in the North Korean People's Army ... had in their ranks substantial numbers of them. Also, many of the NKPA units that did not have rank and file soldiers from the CCF did have officers and non-commissioned officers from it' (see Map 3).[23]

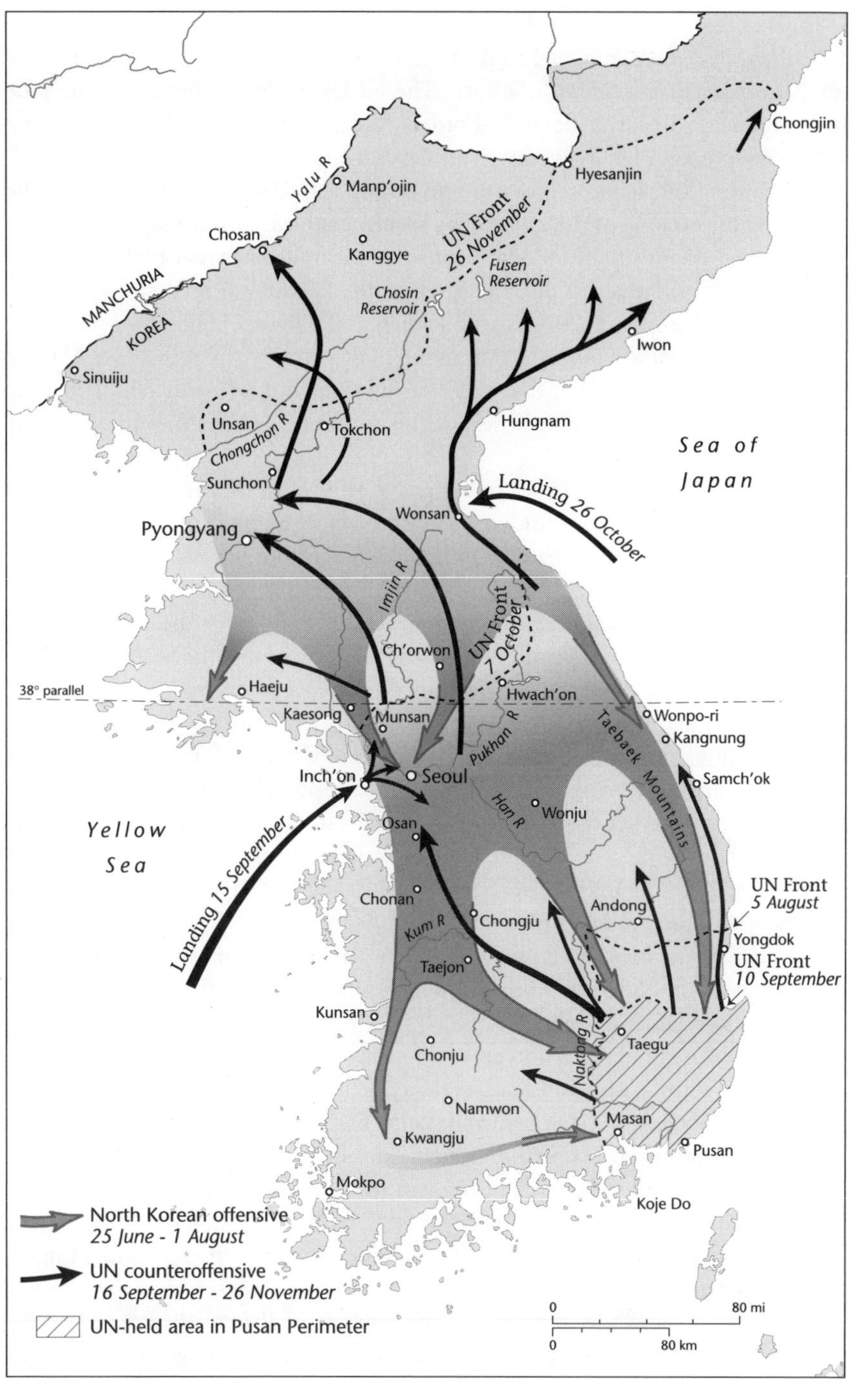

Map 3 *Invasion and counterstroke, 25 June-26 November 1950*

That combat experience, together with its large materiel advantage, proved decisive when the NKPA launched its invasion across the thirty-eighth parallel in the early-morning drizzle of 25 June 1950. The NKPA easily brushed aside the four ROK regiments deployed along the border – the remainder of each division being kept in reserve some ten to twenty-five miles to the south – and swept toward Seoul. Although the ROK forces regrouped and put up a stubborn defence north of the capital, by the evening of the 27th Rhee's government was forced to evacuate to the south. The difficult situation turned into a catastrophe later that night when the main highway bridge across the Han River south of Seoul was prematurely demolished while still crowded with escaping soldiers and refugees, killing over 500 South Koreans and trapping a large portion of the ROK Army north of the river. Having lost 44,000 men during the first week of fighting, and left with only two fully equipped divisions, the South Korean forces would take over a month to recover from the disaster.[24]

Word of the communist invasion reached Washington, DC, at 2130 hours on 24 June and the United States quickly asked for a meeting of the United Nations Security Council on the following day. In the absence of the Soviet delegation – the USSR was boycotting all UN organs on which Nationalist China was represented – the Security Council was able to pass a resolution calling for the withdrawal of North Korean forces. Freed of the Soviet veto, it appeared that the Security Council would finally be able to undertake the armed resistance to aggression that its western members had originally envisaged for it. Moving quickly, President Harry Truman announced on 27 June that he had 'ordered United States air and sea forces to give the Korean government troops cover and support.' Later that day, the Americans were able to secure the passage of another Security Council resolution recommending 'that the members of the United Nations furnish such assistance to the Republic of Korea as may be necessary to repel the armed attack and to restore international peace and security in the area.' As the NKPA crossed the Han River and continued its drive south on 29 June, Truman authorized General MacArthur to dispatch ground forces to Korea from the four divisions of the US Eighth Army on occupation duties in Japan.[25]

The commitment of American ground forces to Korea quickly led to a reorganization of the Allied command structure, the Security Council recommending on 7 July that all operations on the peninsula come under US leadership. The following day Truman appointed MacArthur commander-in-chief of a new United Nations Command, a move confirmed by Syngman Rhee when he placed all ROK forces under the American general's authority a week later. As a result, the Eighth Army commander, Lt. Gen. Walton Walker, was handed responsibility for conducting all ground operations in Korea.[26]

In Ottawa, meanwhile, the Liberal government of Prime Minister Louis St. Laurent was caught unawares by both the invasion and Washington's reaction to it. Escott Reid recalls not being 'greatly perturbed ... It never crossed my mind that the United States might intervene with military force in support of South Korea.'[27] Lester Pearson, who had left the civil service to become the minister of external affairs, also admits being 'caught completely off-guard by the North Korean aggression and by the United States response to it. At almost the exact time ... when President Truman was deciding that the United States would be giving air and sea support to the South Koreans, I was talking to some press people in Ottawa and telling them, off the record, that I did not expect a US military response to the invasion.'[28] The fact that Canadian diplomats, more closely attuned to US thinking than communist leaders in Moscow or Beijing, could so misjudge the American reaction may also explain Stalin's miscalculation in sanctioning the North Korean invasion.[29]

After expressing its concern about Korean events in the House of Commons, the Canadian government's first concrete action came on 29 June when Pearson announced that Canada was sending two military observers, Lt.-Col. Frank E. White and Wing Cmdr. H. Malkin, to serve on the UN Commission on Korea. The following day, during the final sitting of the House of Commons before Parliament was prorogued for the summer, the prime minister informed the House that 'any participation by Canada in carrying out the UN resolution [to aid South Korea] ... would be our part in collective police action under the control and authority of the United Nations for the purpose of restoring peace.' St. Laurent also stated that if such a police action under a UN commander was called for, Canada would consider making a contribution. He then announced that three Royal Canadian Navy destroyers were being dispatched to the Far East to cooperate with other UN naval forces should the need arise. HMC Ships *Cayuga, Athabaskan,* and *Sioux* sailed from Esquimalt on 5 July. Two weeks later, the government also announced that an RCAF transport squadron, No. 426, would be assigned to the UN Command to fly supplies from McCord Air Force Base in the state of Washington to Tokyo, Japan.[30]

While Canada's politicians dispersed across the country for the summer recess, the Korean situation continued to deteriorate. Immediately after the fall of Seoul, Syngman Rhee transferred his government to the city of Suwon, eighteen miles to the south, but within days was forced to move over sixty miles farther to the city of Taejon. In the meantime the leading elements of the 24th US Infantry Division had landed at the port of Pusan on the peninsula's southeast corner to join in the defence. The first American encounter with the NKPA came north of Osan on 5 July, when one of the 24th Division's infantry battalions, Task Force Smith, attempted to stop the advance of a North Korean armoured column. Understrength and ill-trained after years of occupation duties in Japan, the Americans were easily brushed aside when their 2.36-inch bazookas proved useless against the T-34's sloped armour. Further American attempts to block the path of the advance also proved futile, although two regiments of the 24th Division did manage to delay the invaders for six days north of Chonan while a defence line was established on the Kum River. When the North Koreans outflanked and breached that line on 14 July, the US and ROK units fell back on Taejon while Rhee's government fled to Taegu, a farther 125 miles to the southeast.

By 20 July Taejon was also surrounded and overwhelmed by superior numbers. As the Australian official history points out, in addition to inadequate antitank weapons, continuing poor morale and exhaustion further hampered the American efforts to halt the NKPA's advance. During these first engagements, moreover, 'The Americans were handicapped not only by poor training and lack of readiness but also by over-confidence. Many believed that the North Korean Army was a contemptible force which would stop and flee when it saw the uniforms and equipment of the United States Army in its path. Their sufferings in July 1950 were all the more severe until they shed these illusions and took their new enemy seriously. The stresses of defeat and withdrawal lowered the morale of the forward American units, and men withdrew as best they could, often abandoning their dead, their weapons and their equipment as they struggled back to the south.'[31]

With the fall of Taejon, the NKPA had driven halfway to Pusan. The American buildup in Korea continued throughout July and by month's end there were three US infantry divisions and two regimental combat teams holding the line in Korea. Two other American divisions, the 1st Marine and 2nd Infantry, were on their way from the United States. The British government, meanwhile, had announced that it would be sending the 29th Brigade, then training in England, to Korea. The UN's ground forces were also strengthened by the air superiority the US Air Force held over the entire peninsula, even though the retreat to Pusan had forced the Fifth Air Force to pull back to bases in Japan, where it joined the Far East Air Force's bomber units. Together with the close air support missions being flown by naval aircraft from Task Force 77, Lt. Gen. Walker was able to call on an average of 175 sorties a day to help make up for deficiencies in his artillery.[32]

By early August the Eighth Army had withdrawn behind the Naktong River to form the 140-mile-long defensive Pusan Perimeter about the southeastern city. For the next month the North Korean forces, by now numbering some 200,000 men in fifteen divisions, hurled themselves against the ROK-US lines in an attempt to drive through and capture the port city. Fighting with fanatic zeal, the communists were able to make small penetrations in the Pusan Perimeter but could not achieve a breach. As the situation worsened throughout the August battles, American appeals for further reinforcements were partially answered when London agreed to the additional commitment of the two-battalion 27th Brigade, stationed in Hong Kong. The British formation was brought up to strength when the Australian government decided to have its occupation battalion in Japan, the 3rd Battalion, Royal Australian Regiment, join with an artillery regiment committed by New Zealand to form a Commonwealth brigade.[33] By the time of the Australian announcement in late August, Ottawa, too, had finally taken action to provide a ground force of its own.

July's grim news from the Far East had added to the growing unease among the Canadian public that their country was not pulling its weight in the international crisis. While the Americans and South Koreans were being driven back on Pusan, there was an increasingly insistent tone in the Canadian press that the country had to provide more than mere rhetoric to support the United Nations.[34] On 14 July, the UN Secretary General, Trygve Lie, asked Canada to consider providing ground forces.[35] When the chiefs of staff met in the office of the minister of national defence three days later to discuss the Korean situation, the chief of the general staff (CGS), Gen. Charles Foulkes, was less than enthusiastic about offering Canadian troops:

> [General Foulkes] suggested that before further steps were taken it might be well to see what was being done by the United Kingdom, Australia and New Zealand in response to the United Nations request. Possibly some arrangement could be made whereby Canada might offer to participate with these countries to provide, say, a Commonwealth division. General Foulkes then outlined four alternative forms of army participation. These were:
>
> (a) one independent brigade group consisting of three battalions which would be capable of operating as an independent unit; this force to be administered by the UK forces in Hong Kong;
> (b) one brigade to operate within a Commonwealth division;
> (c) regimental combat team consisting of three battalions which would operate on US lines with a US formation;
> (d) one regimental combat team group to operate independently and to form a brigade within a Commonwealth division.
>
> General Foulkes said that, although none of these courses was recommended, he would prefer alternative (b) if the government decided that it was necessary to send ground forces to Korea. Under this system, the Canadian forces were more likely to retain their identity. Commanders would be familiar with UK methods of control, command and organization. All present army training had been done on UK lines, with British-pattern equipment.
>
> Any of these proposals would require considerable time to implement, even under ideal conditions. Moreover, each alternative would necessitate using almost every trained soldier in the regular force. In the circumstances, it was suggested that it might be well to consider the possibility of recruiting a special 'Korean Force.' Based upon experience at the beginning of the last war, it was estimated that manpower requirements for such a force could be met without difficulty. This scheme would have a further advantage in that it would leave the present Mobile Striking Force intact for the defence of Canada. In all probability, the United States would request that the Mobile Striking Force remain in Canada as part of the Canada-US arrangements for the defence of North America. In any event, the recruiting and training of a special Korean force would not alter substantially the date on which ground force assistance could be provided to the United Nations commander.[36]

Claxton was skeptical of Foulkes' assertion that recruiting the men to fill a brigade would not prove difficult, 'particularly in view of the present high employment in Canada as compared to 1939,' and suggested the possibility of offering to provide a US-equipped battalion instead. Foulkes' only caveat was to restate his strong preference that any Canadian unit should 'operate with a British formation, where its identity would be less likely to be lost and where Canadian commanders would be familiar with the system of command and organization.'[37] In the meantime, the government lifted the manpower ceilings on army recruitment in an effort to bring the Active Force units up to full strength. Unfortunately, recruiting efforts were particularly disappointing and by the end of July Canadian Army strength had actually fallen by 350 as more soldiers chose not to reenlist than could be found to fill the ranks. The Active Force alone now required some 4,000 additional soldiers to bring its field units up to strength.[38]

On 27 July, the United States government asked Ottawa to provide a brigade group for the UN force. Meeting the following day, the Chiefs of Staff Committee revisited the issue of a Canadian ground commitment. The CGS still assumed that the government was thinking in terms of a battalion-sized contribution and assured the minister that the army could supply such a unit 'and have it ready in time to operate as an organic unit of a larger British or Commonwealth formation. There were various combinations of units ranging in numbers from around 1,000 up to 2,000 personnel which could reasonably be contemplated, built around existing units of the Canadian Active Service Forces.' Foulkes did not share Claxton's belief that recruiting soldiers for overseas service would prove difficult and once again raised the possibility of contributing a larger formation. The CGS 'felt that it would be possible to recruit in Canada today, the personnel for at least a brigade from volunteer "soldiers of fortune" if at enlistment there were a firm understanding given that they would be despatched for active service overseas. In case such a scheme were put into effect he would recommend engagement for some such term as eighteen months, inasmuch as the army would not wish to retain the "soldier of fortune" type of personnel on a long term basis.'[39] As one Canadian officer has noted, Foulkes' assertion 'that people who wanted to fight a war were not what we wanted in the regular army' suggests that the CGS 'felt that what we really needed were the good, steady administrative problems' of a long-service peacetime force.[40]

Foulkes' instincts about recruiting a brigade-sized force would prove accurate in one respect and quite off-base in another. As the CGS suspected, there was little problem finding sufficient volunteers to fill the ranks of the new brigade. In fact once recruitment began the response overwhelmed recruiting offices that were used to only a trickle of applicants. On the other hand, the army quickly came to regret having labelled the new recruits soldiers of fortune, an inaccurate label that continues to stick to this day. Completely contrary to the CGS's assertion, the general staff soon became anxious to reenlist as many of the new men in the Active Force as possible. Ironically, it would prove to be the new recruits who shunned peacetime army service, rather than the army being unwilling to accept them.

According to Lester Pearson, the Canadian cabinet did not finally get 'down to the business of Korea' until the end of July, when they were all heading back to Ottawa by train from the Toronto funeral of former prime minister Mackenzie King. Pearson 'was anxious that Canada should assume a full responsibility by sending an expeditionary force. There were, however, members of the cabinet, as there were throughout my time as secretary of state for external affairs, who did not support a forward foreign policy. They asked: "What would Mr. King do?" and replied, "He wouldn't be getting involved." It was during that train ride that Mr. St. Laurent [who had hitherto been decidedly hesitant to make a ground commitment] first expressed his support for an active Canadian involvement in Korea. At a series of cabinet meetings following our return to Ottawa, the final decision to send a force was taken.'[41] Primarily at Pearson's urging, the cabinet agreed to the Foulkes proposal of recruiting a brigade specifically for service in Korea. On 7 August, Louis St. Laurent announced to the Canadian people the decision to recruit the Canadian Army Special Force to be 'specially trained and equipped to be available for use in carrying out Canada's obligations under the United Nations charter or the North Atlantic pact.'[42]

The final details of the terms of enlistment upon which a recruiting campaign could be based were not approved by Brooke Claxton until the same day as St. Laurent's announcement. In keeping with Foulkes' belief that the new recruits were not the sort of soldiers the regular army would want, the Special Force men were enlisted for only an eighteen-month period, a term that could be increased if 'required in consequence of any action undertaken by Canada pursuant to an international agreement or where the term of service expires during an emergency or within one year of the expiration thereof.'[43] As it turned out, only those Special Force soldiers in the first battalion posted to Korea in December 1950 spent the minimum eighteen months in the army; most of the rest served for nearly two years. The last of the Special Force recruits were not sent to the Far East until shortly before their initial enlistments were due to expire and had to spend two and a half years in the army, the last twelve months in combat, before being discharged.

The government's sudden acceptance of the Special Force idea caught the army's administrators off-guard right across the country. Those army recruiters who had not heard the government's announcement about the Special Force the night before arrived at work on Tuesday morning, 8 August, astounded to find several hundred young men lined up in front of their depots. Since it normally took several days to process an applicant – with some twenty forms to be filled out for documentation, medicals, and attestations – the number of enlistments officially reported to Ottawa on 9 August did not match the newspaper headlines describing the flood of volunteers. Perhaps because he had been so convinced that the army would have difficulty recruiting sufficient men for Korean service to fill even a battalion, the minister of national defence became concerned at the slow pace of the army's administrative procedures. Flying to Toronto on 10 August in the back seat of a CF-100 jet fighter, Claxton apparently wanted to straighten out the paper bottleneck before any of the volunteers changed their minds and went home. The minister arrived at No. 6 Personnel Depot determined to speed up the process:

> The MND [minister of national defence] was much agitated, and asked 'why' [of the recruiters] in a manner that could not be answered in the thirty seconds before another question was put. [Claxton] galloped about the depot where by now scores of men were in different stages of processing. Medical officers were examining men in batches, standing stripped naked and the MND spoke to several of these. The MND's party was about ten-strong, including the HQ Central Command staff officers, OC [officer commanding] 6 PD, and others. While MOs 'thumped and listened' and naked men coughed and stretched, the bizarre ministerial party stood amongst them while the MND, in a highly agitated state, talked to individuals asking if they were being fed properly, congratulated them on enlisting, etc., etc. The party rushed from room to room, looking over clerks' shoulders while MND asked why this documentation and that was necessary, etc. Press photographers were present and the MND posed shaking the hand of a would-be recruit – the 'first to be enlisted' in the press story ...
>
> The MND asked one would-be recruit if he had any problems. The would-be recruit stated that he was under twenty-one and married, but ineligible for marriage allowance [restricted to those twenty-three and older]. The MND said this was not so, that marriage allowance was to be paid. The command paymaster said 'no' and cited the regulations. Everybody was confused. The MND ruled marriage allowance!
>
> ... While the complaining would-be recruits milled around, taking cracks at the red-tape, and depot personnel were much hindered in their work by the cortege of questioners headed by the MND, the MND hit on a solution to allow him to publicly state the enlistment figures he wanted. The answer was 'attest' first and 'process' second. Therefore, the procedure was to line up the would-be recruits, swear them in *en bloc* in groups of twenty or so, give them a slip of paper ... saying they had enlisted and giving a date for their return to the depot for medical examination, documentation, etc. In addition, the MND verbally ruled out on the spot certain documents as being unnecessary and the staff were told to 'streamline' in the case of other documentation ...
>
> The MND was certainly most unhappy when he arrived. His early questions suggested that the depot was completely inefficient. He had no apparent idea of the processing system and simply could not understand why the men had not been 'enlisted.' He did get the picture, of course, and his 'attest first, process later' scheme was the solution to the bottleneck which caused official enlistment figures to be almost NIL [on 9 August], while press reports had 'hundreds joining up to fight.'[44]

Despite his agitation, Claxton had been impressed by the calibre of the recruits he had seen. Returning to Ottawa, he informed Foulkes that 'they are young, generally between eighteen and twenty-five, exceptionally fit, (out of 253 medically examined only three were rejected), generally with good background and fair intelligence. About 50 per cent were veterans.'[45] Although it had greatly overburdened the army's personnel depots, the enthusiastic response to the call to arms quickly filled the authorized strength of the Special Force. Only ten days after recruiting commenced, the CGS reported to the government that the 7,000 men authorized for the new brigade had already been enlisted. His suggestion that the authorized establishment be increased to some 10,000, in order to provide sufficient reinforcements for twelve months, was immediately approved by cabinet. Even at this early stage the general staff was already having second thoughts about the wisdom of offering the Special Force terms of service and on 23 August, after only two weeks of recruiting, enlistment under Special Force terms of service was limited to certain quotas. In Quebec Command, for instance, where recruiting French-speaking soldiers was always problematic, the enticing Special Force terms were kept in effect until 31 March 1951. Although the army continued to recruit young Canadians throughout the Korean War, from the third week of August 1950 on, virtually all new recruits were enlisted directly into the Active Force. The overwhelming response of Canadians to St. Laurent's announcement can be gauged by the fact that some 10,208 men were eventually enlisted under the Special Force terms of service, the vast majority of these during those hectic first two weeks.[46]

The larger-than-expected numbers of volunteers allowed army headquarters to expand the supporting arms and units being allocated to the brigade group. The original plan had called for a brigade of 5,000 men organized into three infantry battalions, one regiment of artillery, a field ambulance, an infantry workshop, a transport company, and two light field repair detachments. The brigade had soon been expanded to include an ordnance company and engineer, armoured, and signals squadrons. By November, the brigade's establishment had grown to 7,500 all ranks including some 1,500 men in several new administrative units. The three new infantry battalions were designated as 2nd battalions of the three Active Force units – i.e., The Royal Canadian Regiment (2 RCR), Princess Patricia's Canadian Light Infantry (2 PPCLI), and Royal 22e Régiment (2 R22eR) – and the artillery regiment became the 2nd Field Regiment, Royal Canadian Horse Artillery (2 RCHA). With the Active Force engineer field squadron being the 23rd, the Special Force squadron was designated the 57th while the armoured squadron, a composite subunit with troopers from both the Royal Canadian Dragoons and Lord Strathcona's Horse, became A Squadron, 1st/2nd Canadian Armoured Regiment.[47]

In choosing an officer to command the Special Force brigade, Brooke Claxton believed it was preferable to select someone who was not already in the regular army. The minister wanted the commander to be an experienced veteran of the Second World War who, like many of the men he would be leading in Korea, had chosen to return to civilian life after the war. General Foulkes recommended the former commanding officer of the Royal Hamilton Light Infantry, John M. Rockingham. His record in the Second World War certainly made him a logical choice for the Special Force brigade. First Canadian Army's need for good battlefield commanders had been such that Rockingham was handed command of the 9th Canadian Infantry Brigade just ten days after leading the RHLI to the only Canadian success in the otherwise disastrous Operation Spring. His appointment on 8 August 1944 coincided with the opening of Operation Totalize, II Canadian Corps' major offensive aimed at reaching the town of Falaise and cutting off the retreating German armies in Normandy. During the subsequent breakout across France, the thirty-three-year-old Rockingham continued to demonstrate his willingness to lead from the front. While closely following his forward patrols into Rouen on 30 August, for instance, his armoured car was the first to enter the main square and exchanged shots with the retreating Germans.

As the 9th Brigade's commander until war's end, Rockingham had been involved in the capture of Boulogne, in clearing the approaches to Antwerp during the Battle of the Scheldt in October 1944, and in the Rhineland battles of February 1945. In March, the 9th Brigade was selected to be the first Canadian formation to make the assault crossing of the Rhine River while attached to the British 51st Highland Division. Having gained a reputation as one of First Canadian Army's most effective brigade commanders, 'Rocky' was then selected to command one of the brigades in the division Canada was organizing to fight in the Pacific, a force that was never needed after two atom bombs were dropped on Japanese cities.[48]

Following the Japanese surrender the prewar militia officer had returned to British Columbia and become an executive with several utility companies. He had not, however, completely severed his ties with the army, and served as the commander of the 15th Canadian Infantry Brigade in the Reserve Force after 1948. On 7 August 1950, the thirty-eight-year-old superintendent of the Pacific Stage Lines bus company (he turned thirty-nine two weeks later) was in the midst of labour negotiations with the Amalgamated Transit Union over the question of lunch-hour breaks for drivers when Foulkes telephoned his office to see if he was interested in the Special Force appointment. Rockingham asked for twenty-four hours to discuss the proposal with his wife, but it seems unlikely he did not already know his answer before he hung up the telephone. Fittingly, he accepted the appointment to command the 25th Canadian Infantry Brigade on 8 August 1950, six years to the day after being promoted to his first brigade command on the eve of Operation Totalize. While the task of organizing and training an operational formation was daunting indeed, over the course of the next twenty-one months Rockingham would demonstrate that he had been a wise choice.

2 ROCKY'S ARMY, SEPTEMBER 1950-APRIL 1951

The newly appointed commander of the Special Force arrived in Ottawa only two days after receiving Foulkes' telephone invitation to begin the difficult task of building a combat-ready formation from scratch. Rockingham's immediate requirement was to select his brigade's staff and commanding officers from the numerous applications already received at army headquarters (AHQ). As he later recalled, the army directed him

> to man the brigade with as many volunteers, both ex-soldiers and civilians, as possible. I was not to ask for regulars in any particular job unless I was not able to fill it to my satisfaction in any other way. Nor were regulars allowed to volunteer. They would be detailed if required.
>
> Almost immediately, two men who were among the best infantry battalion commanders of the Canadian Army in the Second World War volunteered. Jim Stone of the famed Loyal Edmonton Regiment ... and Jacques Dextraze of the Fusiliers Montreal ... were these men. I was also told that I could take Tony Bailey as the regimental commander of the artillery with Bob Keane to command the other infantry battalion (both regulars). Thus I had the four major units commanded by men who were among the best in the country.
>
> My staff was selected mostly from regulars, headed by Herb Wood as brigade major (the senior operations staff officer in the brigade) and Goose Gosselin as deputy assistant quartermaster general (the senior administrative staff officer in the brigade) – both excellent fellows. The whole senior officer slate was filled in short order, mostly with volunteers but also with some regulars.[1]

Although the army may have preferred that most of the brigade's officers were men recruited into the Special Force, it realized that much of the expertise required for more specialized positions would be unavailable in the recruitment pool. As a result, officers in the brigade's technical corps units were largely regulars, as were most (twenty-one of twenty-eight) of the staff officers at brigade headquarters. On the other hand, a sufficient number of experienced and qualified ex-officers was available to fill most of the positions in the three infantry battalions. Indeed, some veterans who had previously held army commissions ended up serving in the ranks.[2] In the three units that would handle the bulk of the fighting, Special Force volunteers were appointed to 83 of the 113 officer positions.[3] Despite AHQ's decree that regular officers could not volunteer for a combat posting to Special Force units, it is unlikely that any of the thirty Active Force officers assigned to the 2nd battalions – eighteen of whom went to 2 PPCLI – were posted to the few infantry slots available against their wishes.

The commanding officers of the three infantry units were all combat-experienced battalion commanders from the Second World War, men who had few illusions about the nature of the task they had taken on. Jacques Dextraze, the 2 R22eR commander, had had a remarkable Second World War career, enlisting in the ranks of Les Fusiliers Mont-Royal in July 1940 and rising to company command during the Battle of Normandy where, it will be recalled, he commanded the composite company that had cleared the start line for Rockingham's attack on Verrières. Appointed CO of Les Fusiliers Mont-Royal shortly thereafter at the age of twenty-five, Dextraze led his battalion in clearing the approaches to the Scheldt in the fall of 1944 and through the 1945 battles closing up to the Rhine and on into Germany. After the war Dextraze left the army to take up a position with the Singer Manufacturing Company in Montreal but returned to the colours upon hearing the announcement that the Special Force was being organized.[4]

The wartime career of the 2 PPCLI CO, James R. Stone, had followed a similar path. Joining the Loyal Edmonton Regiment as a private soldier in September 1939, Stone rose through its ranks to become the battalion's CO in October 1944. Commanding a company when the battalion landed in Sicily in July 1943, Stone repeatedly demonstrated the ability to lead men under fire, qualities that won him a Military Cross during the heavy street fighting in Ortona, Italy, in December 1943 and two subsequent Distinguished Service Orders. As the citation for his second DSO stated, 'There were many instances throughout the actions in Italy and Holland where Lieutenant-Colonel Stone's personal leadership was the contributing factor in the success of battle. His initiative and courage are unsurpassed. He was highly regarded throughout the whole of the 1st Canadian Division as a keen, capable and courageous commander.'[5] After the war Stone had also returned to civilian life, although remaining active in the Reserve Army as CO of the Rocky Mountain Rangers during 1948 and 1949.

The third of Rockingham's battalion commanders was a regular army officer who had originally joined the militia's Lake Superior Regiment in 1935. Robert Keane served with the regiment from the outbreak of the Second World War until 1942 when he departed for several staff appointments at various headquarters. In August 1944 Keane returned to the Lake Superior Regiment, which was then the motorized infantry battalion attached to the 4th Armoured Division's armoured brigade, as the commanding officer. He led his unit throughout the remainder of the northwest Europe campaign, seeing much hard fighting during the battle for the Hochwald and earning a DSO for his battalion's success in the Wesel pocket in the spring of 1945. Unlike Stone and Dextraze, whose entire Second World War careers had been as infantry officers, the staff-trained Keane had joined the regular army after the war and was serving in the Directorate of Military Operations and Plans at army headquarters when selected to command 2 RCR.[6]

There was also a high proportion of Second World War veterans to be found among the brigade's lower-ranking officers. For example, the nominal roll of 2 RCR for March 1951 shows that the battalion second-in-command and all of the company commanders had held commissions as majors and captains during the last war, while six of its eleven captains had also been commissioned in the earlier conflict, the remainder having served in the ranks. While none of the battalion's twenty-one lieutenants had been commissioned in 1945, they were evenly divided between men who had seen war service in the ranks and men in their early twenties who had been too young to serve in 1945.[7] This common Second World War experience meant that all of Rockingham's officers above the rank of lieutenant were, in a practical sense, trained professional soldiers, whether they came to the 25th Brigade from the Active Force, a militia unit, or directly from the civilian occupations they had taken up after being demobilized in 1945-6. Eleven months of combat in northwest Europe in 1944-5 (and even longer for those who saw action in Italy as well) would, after all, have taught any officer far more about the conduct of military operations than he could have learned in twenty years of peacetime service in the regular army. By any measure, therefore, Rockingham began the task of preparing his brigade for combat with an enormous advantage over the situation that had faced the first Canadian contingents of 1914 and 1939. Army headquarters also believed that the high proportion of recruits with Second World War experience would enable the brigade to be trained in a shorter period, an assumption that had an immediate impact on the equipment question. Although the CGS had been working to replace the Canadian Army's large store of British-pattern wartime equipment with more recent American weaponry, Foulkes believed that outfitting the Special Force with US Army equipment would necessitate sufficient changes in the brigade's tactical doctrine to nullify much of the reenlisted veterans' combat experience. To avoid lengthy training, the CGS announced on 16 August that the Special Force would be equipped from Canadian stocks and immediately approached London to suggest that the 25th Brigade be maintained in the theatre from the British supply chain. Numerous items, however, would still have to be obtained from the American supply system, including 60 mm and 81 mm mortars, some wireless equipment, rocket launchers, most of the brigade's vehicles, antitank and anti-personnel mines, engineer stores, and all of the brigade's food, gasoline, and lubricants.[8]

In an attempt to speed the training of the new brigade further, army headquarters decided that the other ranks would undergo their basic training with the parent Active Force unit, thereby leaving the commanding officers of the Special Force units free to train their own officers. It was not expected that the Special Force officers would take over command of their units from the regulars until the men had completed their training to section level in mid-November. The first 252 recruits arrived at Petawawa to begin their basic training under 1 RCR's supervision on 12 August. Six days later their numbers had increased to 1,432, well in excess of an infantry battalion's establishment of 39 officers and 920 other ranks.[9] The Patricia battalion, concentrating at Currie Barracks in Calgary, received 1,162 recruits by 25

August and reached a total of 1,443 men under training in mid-September.[10] The French Canadian battalion, 2 R22eR, was only slightly slower in receiving recruits at Valcartier, Quebec, and had 1,100 men on strength by the end of August. One month later, the Van Doos had 29 officers and 1,570 other ranks on strength.[11]

As instructed by army headquarters, the regular battalions were allowed to take some shortcuts in training the Special Force recruits. The Active Force units were given details on 14 August:

> Since most personnel will be veterans, training will be of an 'in job' refresher character.
>
> A realistic approach must be taken to the problem of raising and training this Force in the shortest possible time but it must be ensured that every man is properly trained and equipped so that he has confidence in himself, in his weapons and in those who lead him. The soldier will be taught what is required to enable him to do his job but only what is necessary, not what is desirable.
>
> Programmes will emphasize training to condition men psychologically for combat. Firing courses and exercises with covering fire which accustom men to the noise and confusion of the battlefield will be included from the advanced training stage on. Troops will be prepared for operations in mountainous, wooded terrain and against guerrilla and infiltration tactics.[12]

The basic training of the Special Force recruits produced quicker-than-expected results because of the high percentage of Second World War veterans in the ranks. At Petawawa, for instance, 2 RCR recorded that 'the volunteers ... are approximately 65 per cent veterans of World War II and are above average in physique and education.'[13] The artillery unit, training at Camp Shilo in Manitoba, also had a high proportion of veterans in its ranks. Of the 1,017 men on strength on 4 October, 30 percent had been in the artillery during the Second World War while another 33 percent were veterans of other corps and branches. Thus only 37 percent of the men were new to the army. When 2 RCHA was required to provide four men for a provost course at Camp Borden in mid-September, the four soldiers selected 'had previous provost experience during the last war.'[14]

Of the men training for the armoured squadron at the Royal Canadian Armoured Corps School at Camp Borden, 90 were armoured corps veterans and 112 were 'non-veterans' who were new to the armoured branch, if not the army. After all the other ranks had been put through four weeks of basic military training, veterans were separated from non-veterans, with the former receiving 'greatly accelerated courses in the trade for which they were previously qualified. Veterans in this sense are not true veterans in the strict definition of the word but are former [armoured corps] tradesmen who, it is felt, can be easily requalified on short courses amounting to little more than a refresher. Should they prove at all slow in absorbing instruction, they will be dropped to the non-veteran classification at once.'[15] It also appears that in selecting men for the operational units of the brigade, as opposed to the reinforcement stream, priority was given to veterans of the Second World War. One-half to two-thirds of the men in the formed units were veterans, which was a higher percentage than in the Special Force manpower pool as a whole. According to a report prepared by the adjutant general, 45 percent of the volunteers had seen Second World War service of which 20 percent had served as NCOs.[16] After visiting the various training sites and observing the progress that had been made in a mere month, Rockingham announced on 20 September 'that training has proceeded so well that all units may concentrate for brigade training sooner than expected.'[17]

If the training of the troops was ahead of schedule, however, the administrative tasks associated with organizing the new force presented a much greater hurdle. Part of the problem was clearly the haste with which the recruits had been enlisted in August; the procedures instituted by Claxton left the regular army with a mountain of paperwork to sort out. Neither the army nor the individual volunteers had had time to organize their affairs properly before the recruits were hustled off to one of the training sites. Many of the units believed that the 'administration problems could have [been] made much easier by more adequate screening of personnel by the personnel selection officer at the originating personnel depot.'[18] The artillery regiment found that 'one of the more pressing problems of documentation is due to the lack of information given to the men by their personnel depots. There has been an extensive amount of trouble with marriage allowance and separated family allowance. In order to receive either of the preceding, proof of marriage, in the form of a certificate of marriage, must be attached to the entitlement forms. Very few of these men were informed of this at the time of enlistment.'[19]

Shortages of uniforms, kit and accommodation were inevitable with any sudden intake of volunteers, let alone one organized in only a few days. At Camp Shilo, for instance, the lack of mess facilities meant that the 120 men taking the driver operators course had to march two and a half miles, four times a day, from the training facilities to their mess. While that meant a loss of two hours' training time per day, it also made the truck drivers the best conditioned men in 2 RCHA.[20] As the new brigade headquarters, itself trying to train a staff to run the new formation, explained, the army's organization simply was not ready to create such a force so quickly: 'Brigade headquarters was to remain free of any command responsibilities so that it too could prepare itself to assume command in the minimum length of time. It was found, however, that units understandably approached staff officers and the commander in an effort to speed up the arrival of various needed items. At the same time, the DAA&QMG [deputy assistant adjutant and quartermaster general] found himself drawn into the planning being done at AHQ. AHQ is not geared to the task of mobilizing such a small Special Force and no co-ordinating agency existed there, as a result brigade headquarters found itself doing this co-ordinating task.'[21]

Separate training of officers and men also had its drawbacks. Lt.-Col. Dextraze of 2 R22eR was particularly dissatisfied and, after most of his men had completed their basic training, he decided 'to take direct command of [the] battalion with his own officers on October 9th. The wheel system [is] found most inefficient as far as administration is concerned. [It] results in loss of direct control of the men.' The wheel system instituted by 1 R22eR did not assign each man to a particular officer, with the result that many of their administrative concerns over family matters were left to fester. After taking over control, Dextraze immediately instructed his officers 'to attend to administration in the morning and training in the afternoon.'[22] Although training went more smoothly at Petawawa, Lt.-Col. Keane soon followed suit and the 2 RCR officers assumed command of their battalion on 15 October, one month ahead of schedule.[23] The other units in the brigade stuck to the original timetable, however, and did not become fully functioning units until the following month. Nevertheless, the high percentage of veterans in the ranks allowed the units to progress quickly. At Camp Shilo, for instance, 2 RCHA was sufficiently advanced in its training to begin artillery shoots by early November.[24]

Developments in Korea, meanwhile, were already calling into question the brigade's ultimate employment. After repeatedly attacking the Pusan Perimeter throughout August, the North Koreans launched a final offensive on the night of 31 August-1 September in an attempt to drive the Eighth Army from the peninsula. The NKPA made several dangerous penetrations into the southern and central sectors of the UN line but were held in check after a week of desperate fighting in which General Walker committed all of his reserves. Indicative of the thin margin by which the Eighth Army held the perimeter was the ten-mile front assigned to the newly arrived 27th British Brigade – the Australian and New Zealand units had yet to join it – despite that formation's strength of fewer than 2,000 men. As the momentum of the communist attacks petered out during the second week of September, however, it became clear that the North Korean forces were too depleted to renew their offensive for at least several weeks. The Canadian Army's observer in Korea, Lt.-Col. Frank White of the UN Commission, wrote to his superiors at army headquarters on the 13th with his impressions of the desperate fighting. 'I sincerely hope that our chaps don't arrive in time to participate in this shambles,' White explained, 'as it is without doubt the most ... unfriendly little unpleasantness imaginable. None of the rules apply and the poor old Yanks have had a few rude surprises.' To lessen the surprises facing a Canadian contingent in Korea, White offered some shrewd advice for those training at home:

> Everyone accepted for this theatre *must* be in the best of condition and I think should be reasonably young. Most of the important battles are decided by who holds the high ground and the hills here are really rugged. Probably the best way of describing it is by example and with the 25th [US] Division in the Masan area (south coast) where the hills are only average, it takes the CO of the 1st Battalion at least two and a half hours to

> get from his battalion CP [command post] to one company CP. If he is in very good shape, he can probably get around his battalion in a day. Food, ammunition, and water has to be man packed to the position under ordinary conditions and with the NK's [North Koreans'] unpleasant habit of infiltrating, [the NKPA was routinely sending patrols through the UN lines at this time in the guise of civilian refugees, thousands of whom still clogged the roads south] it has been fairly normal to supply companies by air drop. The example described is a bad case but by no means the worst nor is it an abnormal one. Good physical condition is a must and I suggest that training in mountain warfare is essential ...
>
> Every unit and every *individual* who comes here must be capable of his own defence. This includes padres and medical personnel. I do not want to give the impression that every NK is a murderer but certainly enough of them have never heard of the Geneva Convention to make this a most important feature of the war. These people are the descendants of Genghis Khan (or so I am led to believe) and as you know, he was one tough hombre. It might be a good idea to put out a booklet on that gentleman to refresh everyone's memory.[25]

Despite the terrible punishment the Eighth Army had received to date – and White's somewhat jaded view of its performance – its ability to hold to the Pusan defences encouraged the Canadian in his assessment of the UN's chances of reversing the situation: 'I am of the opinion that unless we make a bad mistake, it will be all over by November. However, I have always been an optimist and as I am definitely in a minority with that opinion, perhaps it is wishful thinking.'[26]

In fact, although White could not have known, the strategic situation was about to dramatically alter in the UN's favour. Against the near-unanimous advice of his immediate subordinates, General MacArthur had decided to launch a daring amphibious assault, Operation Chromite, against the port of Inch'on, twenty miles west of Seoul. Neither the continuing NKPA pressure against the Eighth Army's defensive perimeter nor the natural obstacles at Inch'on itself – a narrow approach channel and thirty-foot tides that exposed wide mud banks and high seawalls, which would greatly impede both the initial attack and subsequent unloading of equipment – could deter MacArthur from organizing a new US X Corps, consisting of the 1st Marine and 7th Infantry Divisions, to make the attack. The 70,000 men of the X Corps departed Japan on 13 September. Spearheaded by the 1st Marine Division, they landed at Inch'on two days later, overcoming the tides and seawalls to surprise the 2,000 North Korean defenders and easily overrun the entire port area. Marine casualties in capturing Inch'on amounted to only 20 killed, 174 wounded, and 1 missing. Pressing on toward the east, the Marines captured the important Kimpo airfield by the fourth day. With enemy resistance stiffening the closer the Americans got to the capital, the 7th US Infantry Division was given the job of guarding the advance's southern flank while the Marines fought their way along the main highway. By the time Seoul was recaptured on 28 September, X Corps battle casualties had risen to just under 3,000, of whom 523 were killed. Some 7,000 NKPA troops had been captured, while the Americans estimated that they had killed a further 14,000. Only ninety days after capturing the city themselves, the North Korean forces had been forced to fall back on Uijongbu to the north.[27]

As part of the Inch'on plan to cut off the bulk of the NKPA forces in the south, the Eighth Army – which had been divided into two new corps, the I and IX – was to delay for one day before launching its own breakout from the Pusan Perimeter to link up with the X Corps 150 miles to the north. NKPA strength facing the Eighth Army had by now been reduced to a mere 70,000 men, with only a third of those being veterans who had crossed the thirty-eighth parallel in late June. The UN strength in the perimeter, meanwhile, had grown to 140,000, although many of the 72,000 ROK troops were recent recruits with little training and negligible combat value. Despite overwhelming manpower and materiel advantages, it took General Walker's forces a week of tough fighting to break through the North Korean cordon and begin the pursuit. The retreat of the defeated NKPA forces quickly turned into a rout as they struggled to make their way north as best they could before the X Corps around Seoul cut them off from the thirty-eighth parallel. By 26 September, the rapidly advancing Eighth Army linked up with American forces south of Seoul and the remaining North Korean forces were reduced to small, disorganized groups that had taken to the mountains to evade capture. During the pursuit, the UN forces captured over 9,000 NKPA soldiers, and only some 25,000 to 30,000 North Koreans eventually made it back across the thirty-eighth parallel from the Pusan Perimeter.[28]

With the shattered NKPA army having left most of its weapons and equipment in the south, UN forces concentrated along the thirty-eighth parallel in anticipation of further action. On 27 September the US joint chiefs of staff gave MacArthur the green light to cross the parallel and unite the whole of Korea under Syngman Rhee but cautioned him to be vigilant against any signs of Chinese or Soviet intervention. If there was no imminent danger of either power intervening, the UN supreme commander was authorized to advance up to Korea's northern border. In case the presence of US troops might precipitate the military reaction that Washington was so anxious to avoid, MacArthur was instructed that only ROK units were to enter those provinces immediately bordering China or the Soviet Union.[29]

Fatally overconfident after the brilliant success of his audacious Inch'on landing, MacArthur chose to keep the X Corps under his own command rather than assign it to the Eighth Army, thereby preventing General Walker from planning a co-ordinated advance north of the parallel. Walker, who had gained a solid reputation during the Second World War leading a corps in Gen. George Patton's Third Army, had wanted to use the X Corps, already in position north of Seoul, to launch an immediate drive on the northern capital of Pyongyang and catch the NKPA before it could recover. Instead, MacArthur withdrew X Corps from along the parallel so that it could make another amphibious landing at Wonsan on the peninsula's northeast coast. In doing so, the UN supreme commander gave the battered NKPA forces a two-week respite to rebuild their formations while Eighth Army units moved up to the border. The decision also tied up the port facilities at Inch'on embarking X Corps rather than unloading needed supplies for the logistically strapped Eighth Army.[30]

The ROK Army crossed the parallel on 2 October to begin its own conquest of the north – Syngman Rhee was not particularly interested in whether the US joint chiefs approved or not – one week before the Eighth Army was able to launch its drive across the border. The success of the advance seemed to indicate that the campaign would soon be over. In fact, the ROK Army's drive up the peninsula's east coast allowed it to capture Wonsan ahead of the X Corps' amphibious assault on the port on 26 October. The US I Corps, fighting its way north from Kaesong, was in its own race against the ROK divisions for the honour of capturing Pyongyang. On 19 October the capital fell to the 1st US Cavalry Division coming up from the south and the 1st and 7th ROK Divisions advancing from the east. In a meeting with President Truman at Wake Island on the 15th, a confident MacArthur assured his commander-in-chief that there could be little chance of Soviet or Chinese intervention so late in the war.[31]

Neither man was aware that the Chinese had already decided to intervene in the conflict. Indeed, the same day he advised Kim Il Sung on 13 October to evacuate his remaining forces to Manchuria and the Soviet Far East, Stalin was informed of Mao Zedong's decision to move troops into North Korea. The relieved Soviet leader quickly telegraphed Kim to hold out with his battered forces until the Chinese reinforcements arrived. On the 19th, the Chinese People's Volunteers, four armies and three artillery divisions strong, began crossing the Yalu River. By 1 November, over 180,000 Chinese soldiers had entered North Korea, and more than 300,000 were on the peninsula by the 15th.[32]

MacArthur's faulty assessment of the strategic situation had an immediate impact on the Special Force. In a mid-October meeting with the head of the Canadian Military Mission, Far East, Brig. Frank J. Fleury, the American commander indicated that dispatching the entire Canadian brigade to the Far East would have no strategic impact: 'He suggests Canada might prefer to send immediately [a] small token force to show [the] flag.'[33] After further negotiations with the Americans in Washington, a planned move of the Canadian brigade to Okinawa, Japan, to train over the winter before heading to Korea was cancelled and the Canadian contribution to the UN forces on the peninsula was reduced to one battalion for occupation duties. Until its fate was decided, the remainder of the 25th Brigade would move to Washington State to spend the winter training in the rainy mountains of the large US facility at Fort Lewis.

For the men of the Special Force, who had enlisted with the specific intention of fighting in Korea, word that they would not be trained in time to take part in the war came as a major disappointment. According to the brigade war diarist, it was on 30 October that 'the blow fell. Throughout October conflicting newspaper reports had caused considerable speculation over the destination of the Special Force. At 2300 hours on the 30th, the brigade commander was phoned by the CGS [who was] in Washington [for meetings] to inform him that the main portion of the Special Force would spend the winter at Fort Lewis in Washington State. The PPCLI would, however, go to Korea as part of the United Nations occupation forces.'[34] Keane had to explain to the disappointed men of 2 RCR that 'the choice of 2 PPCLI ... was not based on training level of the battalions, but rather as an expediency'[35] because Currie Barracks was closest to the west coast. A week later, Rockingham also sat down with the RCR officers 'to dispel their feelings of unhappiness at not being selected for Korea.'[36] In fact, 2 PPCLI's officers did not take over command of their battalion until 10 November, a month after the other two infantry battalions had done so and only fifteen days before the unit boarded the troopship for the Far East on the 25th.[37]

With 'the Korean affair show[ing] signs of folding up without our help,' Rockingham was aware that uncertainty about the brigade's future employment might lower morale. It was hoped that by 'carry[ing] out advanced individual training in October at the same fast pace as September' there would 'be no slackening that might create morale problems.' As the men's individual training was concluded by mid-November, however, the Special Force's training schedule was interrupted by its move to Fort Lewis. The only untoward incident of significance came on 21 November when one of the trains carrying 2 RCHA was involved in a collision with another train near Canoe River, British Columbia. Sixteen gunners were killed and another thirty-three seriously injured in the mishap.[38]

Despite the dreariness of the rain-swept landscape that greeted them, the Canadians' reception at Fort Lewis was marked by 'the superb co-operation which has been afforded 25 CIB by the American military authorities. They have spared no effort in making American facilities and equipment available to us.'[39] While the transfer to the United States allowed the brigade to escape the bitter cold of a Canadian winter, they found that they 'had arrived in a nice, wet, soggy climate. To many it must have reminded them of England during the late war.'[40] Concentration of the Canadian brigade at Fort Lewis, however, meant that it could finally begin functioning as a cohesive formation, and Rockingham addressed his officers collectively for the first time on 22 November.[41]

For the Special Force men who had to remain behind in the American camp, watching the departure of 2 PPCLI for the Far East on 25 November only emphasized that they were missing out on the great adventure for which they had enlisted. Having eagerly joined the army to fight in a Korean war that suddenly seemed about to conclude, they now seemed likely to be stuck serving out their eighteen-month enlistments in a peacetime force, training for operations they were never to perform. In view of the situation, Lt.-Col. Keane of 2 RCR reemphasized the importance of maintaining discipline to stem the air of depression on the day after his unit arrived at the American base. 'Training is being held on an individual basis,' the battalion war diarist recorded on the 21st, 'that is each company commander is keeping his men busy mostly by drill in order to iron out the kinks formed during

Lt.-Col. J.R. Stone (left) and Brig. J.M. Rockingham watch as members of the 2nd Battalion, Princess Patricia's Canadian Light Infantry, the first Canadian Army unit to be dispatched to Korea, board the American transport USNS Private Joe P. Martinez *at Seattle, Washington, on 25 November 1950.* DND Z6252-1

our trip west. The American troops' deportment is very slack and there is already a noticeable effect upon our men. The 2 R22eR has already caused a little trouble and are now being bivouacked out in their training area ... The CO has stressed the need of rigid control over the troops at this time. He has emphasized his intention to make the price of poor soldiering on our troops' part very high. He insists on good discipline on the part of all.'[42] Despite Keane's good intentions, however, discipline was not notable when some of the Canadians were given evening passes to visit Tacoma: 'Today the 2 PPCLI left us and are now on their way to Korea. Our men are feeling none too happy about not being able to go, and as a result the morale is rather low. Tonight, a number of 2 RCR personnel made complete fools of themselves in Tacoma. Some of them were staggering around the streets improperly dressed and making general nuisances of themselves. In some cases junior NCOs were seen in the same condition, making no effort to straighten either themselves or the troops.'[43]

Although Rockingham expressed his concerns 'over the number of cases of drunkenness in the brief time since units arrived in the area,' he does not appear to have been unduly worried. Rather than deny his men access to the town, he simply ordered his COs to 'take control of the situation' and limit the number of late passes to 25 percent of unit strength.[44] The infantry battalions, where the problems were most evident, responded quickly, and within days 2 RCR reported that the 'conduct of troops in the town has generally improved. Vigilant patrolling and immediate removal of personnel unfit to be seen in public resulted in improved conditions.'[45]

Nonetheless, these problems seemed merely to confirm – at least among the national press and the army's regular soldiers – the Special Force's reputation as a collection of misfit soldiers of fortune who had difficulty adapting to the regular army's routine and discipline. According to one study by the army's historical section (prepared by a regular officer), 'men who should not have been serving and men whose morale was being undermined by the catch-as-catch-can nature of the induction procedure were suddenly confronted with the regular army. The bulk of Special Force personnel were veterans and the army that they had known was far different from the army that was to be responsible for training them.'[46] Commenting on the Special Force recruiting methods in January 1951, Brig. Geoffrey Walsh, a future chief of the general staff, stated, 'It is recognized that some chaff must be taken in with the grain. However in this particular instance this draft seemed to be mostly chaff, and it is considered steps should be taken to guard against this sort of thing happening in the future. It is again reiterated that probably the basic underlying cause of this is improper screening on enlistment, due to haste in raising the SF [Special Force].'[47]

Many regular officers pointed to the higher-than-average incidence of absence without leave among the Special Force, especially before the men moved to Fort Lewis, as the prime indicator of their unsuitability to soldiering. The historical section's report acknowledges, however, that

> absence did not become a major problem until October 1950 when, with the end of the basic training period, all ranks were granted a ninety-six hour pass. It appears that many members of the Special Force decided to either wait until they ran out of money or until they felt so inclined before they returned to their units. The situation became bad enough that the press was soon aware of it and both the minister and Brigadier Rockingham made statements trying to minimize the problem.
>
> On 1 November there was a total of 565 soldiers absent from the CASF [Canadian Army Special Force]. This figure is rather startling when one considers that it means that almost one out of every twenty soldiers was absent.
>
> The highest figures were in the infantry where it appears that the Second World War veterans took least kindly to the many strange manifestations of regular army discipline.[48]

Much of the report's analysis, particularly its condescending view that Second World War veterans were unable to adapt to 'regular army discipline,' was simple arrogance. While implicitly passing blame onto the minister for the hasty recruiting process, the report ignored the fact that these men – in contrast to the regular army's soldiers – were actually preparing for combat operations and had just completed a strenuous two-month basic training program. It also did not take into account the rather poor administration given the Special Force by the 1st battalions during basic training, a shortcoming that had often necessitated an unauthorized trip home to sort out family responsibilities. Indeed, in early October, the general officer commanding of Central Command, Maj.-Gen. Chris Vokes, had stated his belief that the number of AWL soldiers was mainly 'a symptom of our time' and 'that the sooner the 2nd Battalion officers assume command of their [own] troops the better.'[49]

The main reason for the higher AWL rate, however, was undoubtedly that the October leave coincided with the general drop in morale of the Special Force that resulted, ironically, from the good news coming from Korea. While absenteeism had been lower during 1939-45, the war news during the early years of that conflict was usually grim, with the British Empire clearly having its collective back to the wall. A soldier's motivation was far different in 1950 when the world was essentially at peace and the immediate enemy was far-away communist North Korea. Following the success of the Inch'on landings and MacArthur's invasion of the North, soldiers who had enlisted to fight were faced with the apparent ending of the Korean War before they could arrive to take part. This could only have undercut the sense of urgency that the Special Force had felt during its August-September training, when the UN forces were being hard pressed along the Pusan Perimeter.

Rockingham undoubtedly shared his men's feelings but realized that it was better to lead men who were disappointed at not going into action than men who might be reluctant to do so. And, despite the admittedly rushed enlistment procedures that had allowed a number of medically or temperamentally unfit men to enter the force – men who later had to be weeded out – the brigade commander knew that most of the Special Force volunteers would make able combat soldiers. Responding to a reporter's question about his men's unruly behaviour in Tacoma, Rockingham explained simply, 'They're fighting men. That's what they're trained to be.'[50] Years later, he recalled the basic unfairness of the early press criticism in his memoirs:

> At about this time, some of the press commenced a criticism of the Korean volunteers. I did not understand the reasons for this criticism which seemed most unjustified to me. Some of the papers printed material which said that the volunteers were useless men who could not shoulder their responsibilities in either business or domestic affairs, and that they had escaped this situation by volunteering for Korea. Naturally I rose to their defence and was soon involved in an acrimonious argument with some of the Canadian news media. Of course, there were some very rough characters among the 9,000 men who made up the force, its reinforcements and its administrative support, but the majority were a fine group of men of which Canada was to become very proud.[51]

Following the move to Fort Lewis, the brigade's AWL rate continued to decline, particularly after the end of November. The drop-off was primarily due to a renewed sense of urgency among the Canadian volunteers after hearing the latest war news from Korea. While the Special Force was concluding its basic training at the end of October 1950, General MacArthur's forces had been advancing into North Korea across a wide front against only scant NKPA resistance. General Walker's Eighth Army was on the western side of the peninsula having moved north from the capital of Pyongyang to cross the Chongchon River in an arc some 100 miles wide. On the eastern side of the peninsula, the independent X Corps was advancing north from Hungnam against only remnants of the NKPA, with two ROK divisions on its right flank moving quickly toward the Yalu River and the 1st Marine and 7th Infantry Divisions on the left moving toward the Chosin Reservoir. Between the Eighth Army and X Corps, however, lay a mountainous gap of enemy-controlled territory some fifty miles wide. By moving their soldiers rapidly at night and halting two to three hours before daybreak to allow the men to camouflage themselves and their equipment, the Chinese skilfully assembled a force of over 300,000 troops in the gap's rugged terrain up to sixty miles inside North Korea. The areas north and east of the Eighth Army concealed Gen. Lin Piao's Fourth Field Army – the victors over the Nationalist forces in 1949 – consisting of the 38th, 40th, 42nd, 50th, and 66th Chinese Armies, each of three divisions of 10,000 men. During the first half of November, Gen. Chen Yi's Third Field Army, made up of the 20th, 26th, and 27th Armies, with four divisions each, concentrated along the eastern side of the gap to strike the X Corps near the Chosin and Fusen Reservoirs. In addition to some 80,000 NKPA soldiers and guerrillas, reorganized following the September defeats, nearly 400,000 communist troops were waiting to ambush the 150,000 UN troops advancing confidently toward them (see Map 4).[52]

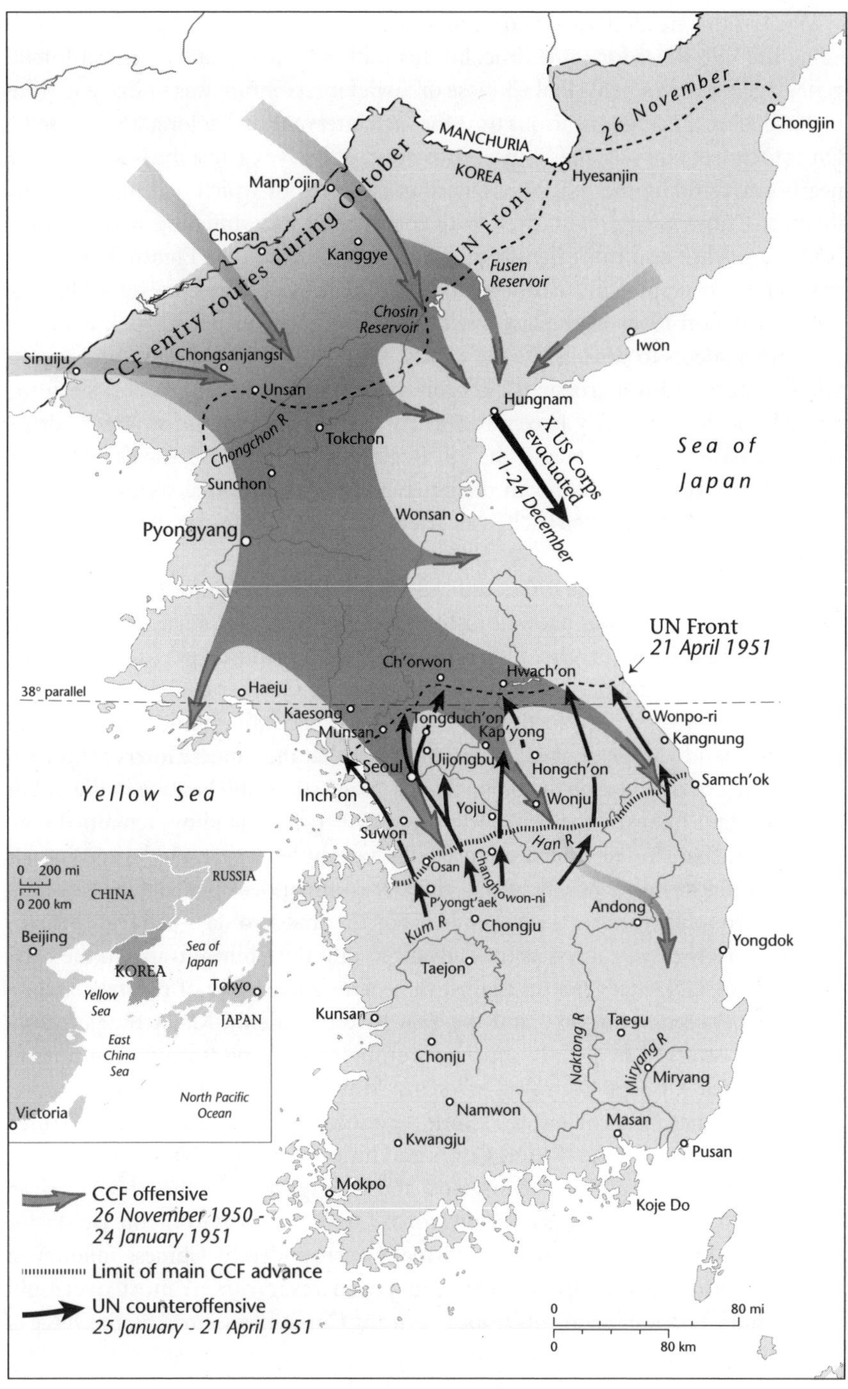

Map 4 *Chinese intervention, 26 November 1950-21 April 1951*

MacArthur's headquarters had been aware of a Chinese buildup in Manchuria along the Yalu River for some time, but his staff, relying on faulty Central Intelligence Agency assessments that Chinese or Soviet intervention was unlikely, continued to believe that 'the auspicious time for such intervention has long since passed.'[53] On 25 October, however, the Chinese opened an offensive against the II ROK Corps, nearly surrounding the 6th ROK Division, elements of which had made a rapid thrust to Chosan on the Yalu River. With enemy resistance stiffening, not only from NKPA units but also from significant Chinese formations, the Eighth Army commander was becoming more concerned. After the II ROK Corps was forced back to the Chongchon River in the last week of October, Walker pulled back his more forward elements to consolidate the Eighth Army positions in front of the important Chongchon River crossings, fifty miles north of Pyongyang. Walker's caution proved insightful in early November when a series of communist attacks drove back the 1st ROK Division and the 8th Regiment of the 1st US Cavalry Division from Unsan, twenty miles north of the river. After their initial series of attacks, however, the Chinese pulled back in an attempt to lure the UN forces into a massive ambush farther north.[54]

The presence of Chinese forces did little to weaken MacArthur's confidence. In the east, the X Corps was allowed to continue its northward advance around the Chosin and Fusen Reservoirs, fifty miles north of its landing port of Hungnam. When ten Chinese soldiers were captured in the late October clashes, with reports that they had crossed into North Korea in large formed units in midmonth, the Far East Command's assessment of the situation was that the Chinese intervention was on the order of only 30,000 to 40,000 troops. MacArthur, still basking in the public adulation that followed the brilliantly successful Inch'on landing, remained convinced that the Chinese intervention would have little impact. Declaring that his troops would be home by Christmas, the UN commander opened a major offensive all across his front on 24 November. For the first two days the Eighth Army made relatively easy progress as they advanced into the Chinese trap. On the 26th, however, the UN forces ran up against the enemy's main line of resistance about half way between Pyongyang and the Yalu River. Suddenly, MacArthur's formations were attacked by greatly superior numbers emerging from the mountains that separated X Corps from Walker's army. Moving along ridgelines to surround UN units in the valleys below, the Chinese counteroffensive struck Eighth Army's right flank to overrun the II ROK Corps and hit the 25th US Division, decimating the Turkish brigade under its command and prompting fears that the American division had ceased to exist as a fighting force. On the X Corps front, the 1st Marine and 7th US Infantry Divisions were virtually surrounded by Chinese infantry in the mountains around the Chosin and Fusen reservoirs. Almost overnight MacArthur's boast of having his troops home by Christmas seemed on the verge of ironic fulfillment as retreat turned into rout.[55]

For the dispirited Canadians at Fort Lewis, the bleak news from the battlefront came as the perfect tonic. 'The growing seriousness of the Korean situation is reflected in the demeanor of both officers and men,' the 2 RCR war diarist recorded the day after the Chinese counterattacked. 'The general feeling is an eagerness to join the "Pats" in Korea.' On 28 November he continued, 'Today the war news is very grim. The UN Army is in a general retreat before the onslaught of some 200,000 Reds. Speculation among several officers and men is to the effect that we might be on our way to Korea within thirty days.'[56] With its determination buttressed by the growing disaster in North Korea, the brigade began to 'shake itself out rapidly after the move from Canada and launch[ed] on a serious programme of sub-unit training' with the result that 'the transformation of individual soldiers from bewildered civilians to disciplined troops was well on its way to completion.'[57]

There were also morale advantages to be gained in being the only Canadian formation serving on an American base. On the last day of November, 2 RCHA noted 'a good amount of regimental pride is becoming evident ... especially during the close combat and infiltration indoctrination course when it was audibly apparent that the gunners were going to show the Americans some real RCHA gunners.'[58] The engineers of the 57th Field Squadron also trained with the Americans, commencing a five-week course in mid-November under the supervision of the 115th US Engineer Group. The 100 sappers in each of the squadron's three troops rotated through instruction on water supply, bridging, mines, and demolitions.[59] The men of the armoured squadron had 'started unwrapping' their M10 tank destroyers – a 17-pounder antitank gun mounted in an open turret on a Sherman chassis – soon after arriving at Fort Lewis and immediately commenced a busy training schedule. By early January, the squadron was able to report that 'the fighting troops are reaching a peak in training, having all been going strong on lectures and on field training. Also, they have all been to the Yakima Ranges for firing. As a result, they are gradually moulding into a fine fighting unit. The reinforcements have been unable to take advantage of this training and, as a result, will be at a disadvantage when called for duty with the fighting troops.'[60]

The two infantry battalions, meanwhile, began field exercises in the rainy mountains of Washington State, training at the platoon and company level in preparation for the upcoming battalion schemes. 'The morale of the companies is still very high,' the 2 RCR war diary recorded in early December. 'They are beginning to enjoy their experiences in the field immensely. The platoon commanders are gaining more confidence and control daily.'[61] The improved morale was in spite of the inadequacies of some of the equipment in the extremely wet weather and the continuing administrative snafus.[62]

The Canadians' morale was further bolstered in early January when the CGS telephoned to say 'that the possibility of the whole brigade going to Korea could not be ruled out' and that if they were not to be sent to the Far East then they 'would probably be sent to Europe about 1 April 1951.'[63] With the brigade entering its final three months of training, the RCR diarist noted that 'morale in the unit is on the upswing' immediately after receiving the news. 'This is probably caused by the increased tempo of training along with the possibility of a move to unknown parts.'[64] Having sorted out his battalion's administrative problems from earlier in the fall, Lieutenant-Colonel Dextraze made good progress with 2 R22eR's platoon and company training. On 4 January, he took his battalion into the mountain training area of Weir Prairie, north of Ranier, Washington, to begin a month of 'intensive field training' with emphasis 'on platoon and company tactics in the attack and defence.' Even though it was the only infantry battalion commanded by a regular officer, the training situation in 2 RCR was far from satisfactory. Following the Christmas leave period, Keane was forced to put his battalion through 'two weeks of recapitulation of basic training. It was realized that the training of this unit had been too rapid and that a series of elementary subjects would be necessary before the unit training phase was entered.'[65] Perhaps the parent regiment, which prided itself on spit and polish, had spent too much time drilling the Special Force recruits on the parade square and too little time instructing them on the more practical aspects of soldiering in the field.

The RCR's troubles were all the more embarrassing when compared with the magnificent progress the newly organized 3 PPCLI had made. Although the 2nd Battalion's replacement unit in the brigade had been authorized on 30 November, it did not receive its first draft of soldiers until 20 December and was unable to begin training 'in earnest' until 3 January.[66] The battalion was fortunate in having another experienced battalion commander appointed as its CO. Lt.-Col. Gordon C. Corbould, a native of New Westminster, British Columbia, had joined the militia's Westminster Regiment prior to the Second World War. Mobilized with his unit in September 1939, Corbould went overseas with the battalion, where it was motorized and assigned as the infantry component of the 5th Armoured Brigade in the 5th Canadian Armoured Division. (It will be recalled that Robert Keane, the 2 RCR commander, had, by coincidence, been CO of the 4th Armoured Division's motorized infantry battalion.) By late 1943, Corbould had risen to command of the Westminster Regiment, the unit he would lead through the remaining fourteen and a half months of combat in Italy and northwest Europe. The militiaman returned to civilian life after the war but reenlisted upon the formation of the Special Force. He was initially appointed to command the 25th Canadian Reinforcement Group after being bypassed in favour of Keane for command of 2 RCR, but was an obvious selection to serve as 3 PPCLI's first CO. As Corbould explained to the brigade's historical officer in July 1951, the newest battalion made remarkable progress in its training:

> The nucleus of 3 PPCLI was made up of 400 troops, some of which the 2nd Battalion considered inexperienced or unsuitable and had posted from the unit. However, they

> were all young men who had no bad habits to unlearn, and once they felt they were again part of a unit instead of merely being reinforcements, were extremely keen and eager to learn. Moreover, the senior officers and most of the senior NCOs had seen action during the last war, and their experience, coupled with the enthusiasm of the troops, made a very desirable combination.
>
> The first troops which came to the battalion were supposedly basically trained but it was soon discovered that certain phases had been neglected and required review. This posed a problem as it lessened the time that could be devoted to the advanced training and such things as bayonet sticks, rifle rests, and aiming disks could not be obtained and had to be improvised.
>
> To train the battalion to a fighting standard within the target date set by the brigade commander called for an all-out effort by every member of the unit and I had to impress on them a great sense of urgency to get the job done. Each company commander was given a readiness date to meet for each phase of training by which time it was expected that their section, platoon, and company training would be completed. Emphasis was placed on section training as this was considered the most important. When the battalion moved for three weeks under canvas at Weir Prairie during February, each company was separated and made to live and operate as individual units, as they would do in actual operations. The company commanders knew what they had to do and I carefully checked their progress without supervising too closely or appearing to be continually looking over their shoulders. During the brigade exercises of Ignes Bellum I, II, and III, I watched and checked the company commanders and not the troops and in this way they were given a sense of trustworthiness and responsibility.
>
> As time was so limited, certain subjects and phases of training such as battle first aid and common to all arms instruction for specialists, had to be deleted from the training programme. This was not too serious as they were subjects which could easily and quickly be picked up at a later date.
>
> During this period, intensive officer training was carried out and six out of seven evenings each week were spent in lectures on orders, messages, organization and appreciations. In order to become completely familiar with the proper way to give orders, each officer was made to carry a pro forma giving the sequence and information required at an orders group. This proved to be of great help during the brigade exercises.
>
> Finally, my own experience as a battalion commander for fourteen and one-half months in action stood me in good stead. I knew exactly what I wanted and how to get it which made the task immeasurably easier.[67]

In early February, the brigade began Exercise Ignes Bellum I, in which each infantry company demonstrated an advance supported by various weapons from the support company and a battery of artillery. Two platoon attacks were followed by a company attack to complete the exercise.[68] When 3 PPCLI ran through the required components on the 11th and 12th, they 'amazed everyone by the very good performance' and proved 'that they were ready to fight on the platoon and company level.'[69]

A week later, the brigade war diarist noted that Ignes Bellum II, a full battalion attack supported by all three 2 RCHA batteries, a troop of M10 tank destroyers acting as tanks, a troop of engineers, and a section from the signal squadron, 'was carried out successfully by 3 PPCLI. It was generally remarked that even though the battalion had only been in existence as a unit a little over a month, it had proven itself battleworthy.'[70] Two days after the exercise, Rockingham declared 'that 3 PPCLI was fit and ready to go into action.' As the brigade historical officer remarked at the time, 'This was a remarkable feat of organization and training and one which reflects credit upon the battalion commander.'[71]

It also demonstrated just how quickly 'extremely keen and eager' raw recruits could be moulded into an effective battalion when guided by battle-experienced officers and NCOs; in Corbould's words, the two were 'a very desirable combination.' (Indeed, many Canadian veterans could attest to its effectiveness in the case of the teenaged soldiers of the 12th SS Division in Normandy during the Second World War.) With almost all of the Special Force's veteran privates assigned to the initial strengths of the 2nd battalions, the rank and file that followed them to the Far East over the course of the next three years were largely the same sort of keen young recruits who initially filled 3 PPCLI's ranks. Given the same material with which to work, it was, as we shall see, the experience and enthusiasm of the officers and NCOs that determined the success or failure of an infantry battalion in Korea.

For his part, Rockingham also insisted on a higher, faster learning curve than the peacetime army was used to. From the outset, he did not hesitate in dispensing with anyone who failed to measure up to the required standard. In this he was greatly aided by the success of the Special Force recruiting, which gave him a large manpower pool to draw on. Infantry battalions with a wartime establishment of 950 had begun training with some 1,400 to 1,500 troops each, with several thousand more in the replacement group. An early example of the brigade commander's attitude was provided in October 1950 when the infantry battalions were commencing their platoon training. Touring the 2 RCR company training areas at Petawawa with Keane, Rockingham was not overly pleased by the younger officers' performance: 'While visiting C Company, an exercise "Platoon in the Attack" was being conducted by the platoons under new platoon commanders. The resultant "exhibition" was very poor. The platoon commanders showed an almost utter lack of knowledge re: employment of the platoon in an attack. Lieutenant-Colonel Keane has directed that a report be made on each junior officer and stated that all undertrained or poor officers [are] to be replaced by war experienced officers from 25 Canadian Reinforcement Group. The company commanders have been asked to train their junior officers as best they can.'[72]

Rockingham's emphasis on combat experience – as opposed to Active Force service time – was also evident two months later when he argued against the peacetime regulations governing the appointment of officers. At a COs' conference in early December, the brigadier stated 'that promotion would be based on ability and experience' and that a candidate's seniority on the officers list would only 'be taken into consideration on the basis of both Active Force and Reserve Force service.'[73] In midmonth he inquired of army headquarters 'if anything is being done to grant commissions to CASF other ranks who previously held commissions in the Canadian Army (Active) and, therefore, are as well qualified as many officers already in the CASF. [Army headquarters] stated that existing policy did not permit such commissioning but if commander 25 CIB felt strongly on the question he could put up special cases.'[74] Nor did Rockingham necessarily trust the training or selection process of AHQ in posting officers from Canada directly to his operational battalions. At the end of December the brigade commander 'requested authority' from Ottawa 'to fill officers vacancies in 2 RCR, 2 R22eR and 3 PPCLI from 3 RCR and 3 R22eR, when they arrive [the two battalions had been authorized but were not formed until early January 1951], rather than have these vacancies filled by reinforcement officers from Canada.' Rockingham believed that '3 RCR and 3 R22eR should be regarded as training battalions and officers [sent directly] from Canada should spend a period of time with them before being posted to the operational battalions.'[75] It took more than mere Active Force credentials to impress the hard-driving Canadian commander.

Rockingham's unwillingness to spend time on soldiers who showed signs of being either temperamentally or physically unsuited for combat did not sit well with the adjutant general in Ottawa, however. Maj.-Gen. W.H.S. Macklin was responsible for finding sufficient soldiers to meet the army's burgeoning manpower needs, which were about to be expanded to include a brigade group for NATO. Their differing priorities made a clash inevitable. In mid-February, Macklin asked Rockingham to review the criteria his officers were using to assess the usefulness of those soldiers deemed inefficient:

> In spite of a steady increase in the rate of intake into the Active Force [because recruiting into the Special Force had been drastically curtailed after August 1950, new recruits were being enlisted under Active Force terms of service], the overall gain has been cancelled to an alarming extent by the increasing rate of discharges. I had hoped that this rate would fall off when the inefficient and unfit soldiers who were accepted during the over-hasty mobilization in August had been detected and disposed of. The rate, however, has not declined; instead it has actually increased and during the month of January no less than 422 men were discharged from the Canadian Army. Since mobilization began in August, we have discharged 1764 ...
>
> In spite of the fact that we have now had roughly six months to clean house in the Special Force, the discharge rates in that Force are substantially greater than they are in the rest of the army.
>
> I do not advocate the retention of the unfit and the useless as these men are a drag on the machine ...
>
> [paragraph 5] I do feel, however, that the decision that the man is totally useless may sometimes be premature and I would therefore ask commanders to check once more within their commands to make sure that every man who has any potential ability to

> be useful to the army is, in fact, made to soldier. This can only be done with the full and whole-hearted support of the junior officers, warrant officers and NCOs. I have a suspicion that there is sometimes an unwillingness at these levels to make the real effort that is necessary to salvage some men ...
>
> I recently formulated a policy under which men of the Special Force who are re-boarded below battle profile can be absorbed into the static units of the Active Force. This should help as up till now such men have been discharged.[76]

Of course, Rockingham was trying to prepare his brigade group for active operations and was interested only in those men who had demonstrated they would make good combat soldiers. He was not in the business of salvaging soldiers for 'static' units – that was the adjutant general's job – and had no interest in men who merely had 'any potential ability' to be useful in noncombat roles in Canada. In passing on Macklin's plea to his COs, the Canadian commander simply requested 'that the contents of para 5 be made known to all officers under your command.'[77]

Although the official history takes the Special Force discharge rates as an indication of the degree to which unsuitable men were recruited by Claxton's hasty enlistment process, Macklin's belief that many of those discharged could have served quite capably in noncombat formations suggests that the totals were primarily due to Rockingham's natural emphasis on combat readiness. *Strange Battleground* makes the point that in the Special Force, 'the figure for discharges and unapprehended deserters which is more than 25 percent of the total numbers enlisted [2,731 of 10,208 to 31 March 1951], compares with 7 percent for the first seven months of the First World War and 12 percent for the same period in the Second World War.'[78] This ignores the fact that the Special Force was recruited to serve as a fighting formation and therefore had higher physical and psychological requirements than the Canadian Army as a whole. In 1945, for instance, only 44 percent of Canada's overseas soldiers were serving in its fighting formations.[79] Contrary to popular perception – and the view expressed in *Strange Battleground* – the fact that Special Force discharges were double the 1939-40 rate reflects its considerably higher proportion of combat soldiers rather than any great discrepancy in the quality of its recruits. The 25th Brigade's higher 'tooth-to-tail' ratio was a consideration that also clearly escaped the adjutant general.[80]

By March 1951, the regular army had also changed its mind about the desirability of retaining the so-called soldiers of fortune of the Special Force in its ranks. On 7 March, during a discussion at army headquarters of the likelihood that the Canadian Army would send a brigade group to Europe as part of NATO's Integrated Force, Lt.-Gen. G.G. Simonds (the new CGS, following the appointment of Foulkes to the newly created position of chairman, chiefs of staff) stressed that 'the principle of there being "one Army" had been accepted for the formation of future elements.'[81] The army's increased manpower requirements meant that the Special Force could no longer be viewed merely as a temporary addition, made solely for the purpose of fighting in Korea.[82]

Although almost all new recruits had been enlisted under Active Force terms of service since the end of August 1950, the eighteen-month engagements of the original Korea volunteers now presented a serious retention problem. Army headquarters hoped to solve it by having the Special Force men reengage in the regular army. In so doing, however, it was asking them to surrender the benefits they had received under their original terms of service. On 13 March, a team of officers from the adjutant general's office arrived at Fort Lewis to address the brigade's officers on 'the terms under which Canadian Army Special Force troops may join the Canadian Army Active Force.' Rockingham immediately set the example by applying for the Active Force, and a large majority of his officers followed suit.[83] The idea of serving in the peacetime army held far less attraction for most of his men, however, and less than a third of the rank and file did so. Over a year later, only 2,711 of the Special Force volunteers had opted to remain in the army following their tour in Korea.[84]

The training of the brigade at Fort Lewis, meanwhile, was pressing ahead on schedule. Having spent several weeks being drilled in basic infantry skills to remedy its training shortcomings, in late January 2 RCR participated in Exercise Kiwi, 'designed to demonstrate the battalion in defence. 2 RCR was dug in south of McCord Field and the syndicated officers were shown each position by the company commander concerned. The battalion put on a very good show. The infantry positions were generally well sited and the camouflage of slit trenches [was] excellent. However, the position of the supporting weapons left much to be desired and this was brought out very strongly by the syndicate leaders during the critique held afterwards.' On 2 February, 2 R22eR 'climaxed its return from four weeks of field training by a battalion attack on the radar station at the east end of the North Fort. Although the troops were tired and wet after two days and nights of movement, they were in the highest spirits.'[85]

The next week, all three infantry battalions embarked on Exercise Ignes Bellum I, 'the introduction to the most important phase of the brigade training. It consisted of progressive platoon and company controlled field firing, and with the exception of armour, included the normal complement of supporting arms.'[86] Keane's 2 RCR 'distinguished itself by the individual weapon handling and accuracy of fire' during Ignes Bellum I while the 'vigour, enthusiasm and keenness' of the Van Doo companies 'was the subject of very favourable comments from the [exercise] controllers.'[87] When Dextraze's battalion was put through its paces in Ignes Bellum II, however, it was clear that the Canadians were still not sufficiently prepared for the battlefield. The brigade's intelligence officer sent out four 'enemy' to 'test the alertness of the troops': 'As was to be expected on this, the first real battalion scale exercise in which 2 R22eR had participated, there were many weaknesses, and it would have been possible for an enemy patrol to steal at least three Bren guns, among other things ... It is felt the unit has learned its lesson.'[88] The schemes also afforded the supporting arms an excellent opportunity to train with the infantry battalions: 'Another day of valuable training in co-operation with the 2 Battalion RCR,' the armoured squadron's war diarist recorded on 2 February. Training had progressed to the point that the unit's CO, Maj. James W. Quinn, believed that the tankers 'had a good knowledge of infantry-tank co-operation' but still had 'to intensify instruction on the subject and in this way bring the squadron to the standard he desires.'[89]

It was while the armoured squadron was returning to camp after completing Ignes Bellum II on 21 February that Quinn 'halted the squadron, assembled all troops in a clearing in the bush, and informed one and all that they were at that moment warned for draft to Korea. Everyone appeared jubilant at the prospects of "getting at it."'[90] At 1000 hours that morning, Rockingham had 'received a telephone call from Lieutenant-General Foulkes to say that 25 Brigade would be going to Korea, any time after two weeks.'[91] This was exactly the information his men had been waiting to hear since the dispatch of 2 PPCLI to the Far East three months earlier. 'Colonel Keane announced the Big News that the battalion was going to Korea with the 25th Canadian Infantry Brigade,' the RCR war diarist noted gleefully. 'The announcement was greeted with cheers by the battalion which were echoed on other parade squares as other units received the news. This news should have a good effect on morale as it finally settles a good deal of speculation and rumours ... [There was] an almost immediate reaction in numerous requests from the companies [for] information about Korea and things Korean.'[92] Three days later, the same diarist reported that 'since the battalion now have some definite knowledge of where they are going, there has been a sharp increase in morale and a corresponding decrease in AWL.'[93]

Word that the brigade could expect to embark for the Far East 'any time after two weeks' also prompted the temporary cancellation of the brigade scheme Ignes Bellum III. After a quick trip to Ottawa to clear matters up, however, Rockingham telephoned his headquarters to say that they were unlikely to leave until April and reinstating the cancelled exercise. Ignes Bellum III, a final opportunity to hold a full brigade exercise with all three infantry battalions supported by the armoured squadron and 2 RCHA, took place on 7 March.[94] On the 23rd, Rockingham flew to Far East to visit 2 PPCLI in the field and get a first-hand look at Korean conditions. Before leaving, he instructed his COs 'that training in mountain warfare must be carried out and that officers and NCOs should devote time to semaphore practice. Other aspects to be concentrated upon were hip firing, night patrols and night movement, US conventional signs and symbols, air support in defence, and US artillery procedure.' Following Rockingham's departure, 'the units began hill climbing, forced marches, and general conditioning for the rugged terrain of Korea.'[95] The senior officers, meanwhile, engaged in several sand table exercises and were lectured by Maj. G. Brooks, the former second-in-command of 2 RCHA, who would later take command of the regiment in Korea and had recently returned from the Far East, where he had been serving in a staff appointment in support of 2 PPCLI. Brooks, like the men in his audience a veteran of the Second World War, 'gave a very interesting and informative lecture on the battle conditions in Korea and stressed the difference in operations between the Second World War and this present conflict.'[96] Rockingham had his own points to emphasize about the Korean fighting when he returned from the front on 3 April:

> In his opinion we were taking far too much non-essential equipment and stores. The topography and poor roads limited transport to such an extent that much of a unit's equipment had to be carried by the troops or by porters.
>
> The scale of issue, based on the experience of Northwest Europe, was entirely unsuitable for the Korean theatre.
>
> It is essential that troops be in first class condition. A unit cannot operate in Korea without this prerequisite.
>
> The country is so incredibly filthy that the most careful sanitary and personal cleanliness precautions have to be taken. Native beverages, dwellings, and women must be avoided.
>
> 17-pounder anti-tank guns have not been used to any extent in Korea, e.g. the British brigades keep theirs in Pusan. M8 scout cars and motorcycles are not popular and there is a great diversity of opinion as to the practicability of the Universal carrier.
>
> 2 PPCLI use both rubber-soled and hob-nailed boots and even within the unit no two companies agree on the most useful of the two.
>
> Parkas and windproof trousers are a necessity in cold weather.
>
> The Patricias looked very fit and battle-hardened and have established an excellent reputation as a fighting unit within the theatre.[97]

On the following two days, Rockingham also addressed the men in each unit about the living conditions they could expect to encounter during their tour in the Far East.[98] Much of the Canadians' last week prior to embarkation at Seattle was taken up in preparation for a march-past by the entire brigade in honour of a visit by the governor general, Field Marshal Viscount Alexander of Tunis, and the minister of national defence, Brooke Claxton. The 6,000 troops who took part, including the men of the replacement group, 'put on a magnificent show and, according to the brigadier, His Excellency was very impressed by the bearing, fitness, and spirit of the brigade.'[99]

Rockingham had every reason to be satisfied with the progress his men had made in the eight months since they had been recruited. Despite losing an entire infantry battalion with the early dispatch of 2 PPCLI to the Far East, the brigade was still able to field three battalions commanded by battle-tested COs. Their Second World War experience meant that unit commanders, in Corbould's words, 'knew exactly what [they] wanted and how to get it' in training their men, a situation 'which made the task immeasurably easier.' Having undergone basic training prior to the move to Fort Lewis, the Canadian brigade had been able to complete three and a half months of intense unit and formation training under Rockingham's discerning eye, a schedule that conformed with the brigade commander's original estimate of the time it would take to prepare his men for action. Added to the considerable recent combat experience of most of Rockingham's officers and men, there can be little doubt that the Special Force brigade was far better prepared for war than were the contingents that Canada had fielded in 1914 and 1939.

As well as 3 PPCLI had performed in the Ignes Bellum series of exercises, the brigade required only three infantry battalions in the field. On 2 February, Rockingham informed Corbould that his battalion would be supplying thirty-five other ranks as reinforcements to 2 PPCLI in Korea, in spite of 'the general feeling that reinforcements for the 2 PPCLI should be supplied from Canada and not the battalion.'[100] Following the conclusion of the Ignes Bellum III brigade exercise in early March, a further five officers and ninety other ranks were warned for overseas duty with 2 PPCLI. On the 14th, Corbould was posted to resume command of the reconstituted 25th Canadian Reinforcement Group at Kure, Japan, the holding and training unit for the brigade's reinforcements. (The reinforcement group was relocated to Kure in May 1951.) By 15 March further postings to the reinforcement group had reduced the battalion's strength from 900 all ranks two weeks earlier to a mere 125: 'This is the remaining nucleus of the battalion after the 25 CRG personnel have been posted. The battalion still contains a nucleus of specialists and trained personnel and, when brought up to strength, will be able to be trained and ready for service in a short time.'[101] As disappointed as the men undoubtedly were at the breaking up of their unit, the 25th Brigade had a full battalion's worth of well-trained infantry replacements at its immediate disposal. The remnants of the three 3rd battalions, brigaded in a new training formation, 25th Canadian Infantry Brigade Replacement Group, remained at Fort Lewis until early May, when they were relocated to Camp Wainwright, Alberta.[102]

The brigade's operational units left Fort Lewis for their embarkation port of Seattle only four days after Field Marshal Alexander's review. On 19, 20, and 21 April, 260 officers and 5,056 other ranks boarded three US Navy transports and set sail across the Pacific. They had been preceded by the 200-man advance water party and the six ships that had carried the bulk of the brigade's equipment, stores, and vehicles. (The port authorities claimed that the Canadians 'departed overseas with more stores and equipment than the US 2nd Division and 24th Division combined.'[103]) On the evening of 24 April, Brigadier Rockingham, accompanied by his brigade major and historical officer, followed by air from Vancouver. The rest of the Canadian brigade would finally be joining 2 PPCLI on the Korean battlefield.

3 INTO BATTLE, DECEMBER 1950-MARCH 1951

When the 927 soldiers of the 2nd Battalion, Princess Patricia's Canadian Light Infantry embarked aboard the transport USS *Private Joe P. Martinez* on 25 November 1950, they fully anticipated that they were being sent to the Far East merely to carry out occupation duties in a liberated Korea. Under those circumstances, the fact that most of the other ranks had barely completed their individual basic training – indeed, some of the men had yet to fire their weapons – should not have represented a severe handicap. The emphasis on drill and military etiquette provided by the regulars of the 1st Battalion on the parade square at Currie Barracks would prove useful to a unit that was simply 'showing the flag' as part of a UN occupation force. Since 2 PPCLI's officers had not assumed control of their men until the unit was leaving for Seattle, there had been no opportunity for any type of collective training. As we have seen, the Patricias were selected over the other 2nd battalions not because they were more ready but because of the proximity of Calgary to the west coast. The battalion, in other words, was hardly prepared to enter a front-line battle zone. This scenario appeared likely, however, by the time they arrived at Yokohama, Japan, on 13 December, following the massive Chinese intervention and headlong retreat of the UN command. The enemy had launched their offensive on the same day the Patricias departed Seattle; for the remainder of the voyage, 'speculation on the future employment of the battalion' was 'the major occupation of officers and men' as news from the battle front filtered through the deck spaces.[1]

Just as the men of 2 PPCLI were beginning to get their sea legs for the long voyage across the Pacific, General MacArthur was summoning Lt. Gen. Walker and Maj. Gen. Edward Almond of X Corps to a conference in Tokyo on 28 November to discuss the unfolding military disaster in northern Korea. It was immediately evident that the unexpected Chinese offensive had shattered the confidence of the supreme commander. Although the joint chiefs of staff in Washington were urging him to form a line of defence across central North Korea to halt the enemy, MacArthur ordered Walker to withdraw at least as far back as the communist capital of Pyongyang and instructed Almond to extricate X Corps from its encircled positions around the Chosin Reservoir and pull back to Hungnam – a difficult retreat that would eventually cost the two American divisions nearly 9,000 battle and 3,000 frostbite casualties as they fought for survival against both the Chinese and the miserable winter weather.[2] MacArthur's sense of impending doom was evident in a telegram he sent to Washington on 3 December explaining his unwillingness to halt the Chinese advance north of the thirty-eighth parallel:

> If the entire United States force of seven divisions at my disposal were placed along this defensive line, it would mean that a division would be forced to protect a front of approximately twenty miles against greatly superior numbers of an enemy whose greatest strength is a potential for night infiltration through rugged terrain. Such a line with no depth, would have little strength, and as a defensive concept would invite penetration with resultant envelopment and piecemeal destruction ...
>
> This small command, actually under present conditions, is facing the entire Chinese nation in an undeclared war, and, unless some positive and immediate action is taken, hope for success cannot be justified and steady attrition leading to final destruction can reasonably be contemplated.[3]

Defeatism quickly afflicted the Eighth Army commander as well. In addition to the heavy losses suffered by the ROK units in II Corps, IX Corps had been roughly handled in its retreat from the Chongchon River to the temporary defence line the Eighth Army was trying to establish some thirty miles north of Pyongyang. Using their great superiority in infantry and moving along the numerous ridgelines, the Chinese had swarmed past UN blocking forces in the valleys below, making retreat difficult for organized units while completely routing demoralized ones. During the retreat, the Anglo-Australian 27th British Commonwealth Brigade, which did not succumb to the widespread panic and was used as one of the Eighth Army's more reliable rearguards, believed that frequent American reports of 'large Chinese forces ... bearing down' on them were often 'fabrications produced by frightened forward units in order to gain permission for premature and quite unjustifiable withdrawals.'[4]

As skeptical as many of the Commonwealth soldiers were about the need for such a precipitous retreat, several American formations had, in fact, been hard hit by the initial onslaught of Chinese infantry. By the time it broke contact with the enemy on 1 December, for instance, the US 2nd Division had practically ceased to operate as an effective formation, having lost some 4,500 men and a large quantity of its heavy weapons and vehicles during the first five days of the communist offensive.[5] Disheartened by such losses and the panic that was gripping his retreating troops, Walker now thought that his force should fall all the way back to Pusan, from where it could be safely evacuated from the peninsula. Only if the Eighth Army was reinforced by X Corps did Walker believe that he would be able to hold out in the old Pusan Perimeter. While Washington may have been concerned at the Eighth Army's headlong retreat, it was always mindful of the Soviet threat in Europe and realized that the United States lacked additional forces with which to reinforce the Far East. In December MacArthur called for 74,000 troops to replace his heavy combat losses to the Chinese but was told that there were only 23,000 replacements available.[6] For the next several months both the Pentagon and MacArthur were convinced that the Eighth Army had to conserve its strength as best it could, even if this strategy meant withdrawal to Pusan and eventual evacuation.

In contrast the Australians believed that the precipitous retreat cost the UN Command 'an opportunity to slow the Chinese and perhaps gain the time necessary to form a firm defensive line north of the 38th parallel. In effect the Chinese bluffed MacArthur out of North Korea. There is little doubt in the minds of the Australians who participated in the withdrawal that a firm line could have been held across the peninsula from Pyongyang to Hungnam.'[7]

Although there had been little contact with the enemy along the defence line Eighth Army had established thirty miles north of Pyongyang, Walker ordered a farther withdrawal to the south of the city on 2 December. The degree to which 'bug-out fever' had gripped the American army and its commander was evident in the unnecessary speed with which the communist capital was abandoned to the enemy. Over the preceding weeks, 10,000 tons of supplies and equipment had been stockpiled in the North Korean capital, and 2,000 tons of ammunition and stores had already been left behind in dumps along the Chongchon River. Although the Eighth Army's supply staff believed they could have removed most of the stores within forty-eight to seventy-two hours, Walker allowed only twenty-four hours for the pullout even though Chinese advance elements had yet to make contact with his units north of the city.[8]

The defeatist attitude of the US forces had an immediate impact on the Patricias heading for the peninsula. As early as 3 December, the head of the Canadian Military Mission, Far East, Brigadier Fleury, had been warned that the American command wanted 2 PPCLI committed to the front line almost immediately upon its arrival in Korea. Although the possibility that the Canadian battalion might be thrown into battle before it had completed its training was disturbing to Ottawa, army headquarters' only reply was 'On understanding that content of command instructions to commanding officer PPCLI dated 13 November 1950 has been conveyed to all concerned, Canadian government had ruled that no further communications will be made to USA authorities concerning the disposition of 2 PPCLI in Korea.'[9] As it was later explained to Fleury, 'The Cabinet decided ... that having placed the 2nd Battalion under the unified command and notified that body that the commanding officer had been instructed not to engage in operations except in self-defence until training had been completed, it would be improper for the Canadian government to make further representations regarding areas of training and deployment in Korea.'[10] It would be left to Lieutenant-Colonel Stone, therefore, to ensure that his battalion was not committed to battle prematurely should Eighth Army headquarters ignore or overlook his command instructions not to engage in operations until his men were adequately trained.

Landing on the afternoon of 18 December 1950, the Canadians were greeted by military bands from both the ROK and US Armies before heading off to their temporary camp on Yong-do, an island in the harbour. The quantity of equipment issued to them on the island was 'tremendous, although certain items are not the best available' particularly 'with respect to the sleeping bags, tentage, and cooking equipment.'[11] They also found the American rations to be both plentiful and good, even though Yong-do had only 'primitive and limited' accommodation, with the men forced to live and eat under canvas in the December chill.[12] The battalion's first priority was the 'speedy uncrating of unit equipment' and 'properly equipping the men.' The war diarist noted: 'What training was carried out was confined to preliminary muscle hardening in the form of hill climbing on the island and route marches around Pusan. Twenty-three days on shipboard had left most of the men in poor physical condition, and the first few days of hill climbing produced a remarkable number of minor ailments.'[13]

Perhaps the biggest adjustment the Canadians had to face was the foreign nature of the country they were to fight in. As Lieutenant-Colonel Stone stated in his initial report from Pusan:

> Korea is a land of filth and poverty. Social amenities of a desirable type are lacking and nothing but hard work will alleviate the boredom that will soon set in. Lack of buildings will preclude the showing of movies, particularly during the winter. Beer is in fair supply, but the alcoholics in the battalion are already drinking the very poor liquor brewed in local bathtubs. Diseases, except venereal ones, probably will not be a problem during the winter, but as all fertilizing of fields is done with human excreta there is no doubt that there will be a health problem in the spring and summer. The dust at present is germ laden and is causing some respiratory trouble, but the sick bay has only a few patients, most of them suffering from common colds ...
>
> The brothel areas of Pusan, not being 'Off Limits,' have been doing a roaring business since the battalion arrived. According to the medical officer, no serious venereal disease problem exists. The troops appear to take preventative measures after contact. An attempt is being made to appeal to the men on both moral and disease grounds, but in all possibility [sic] neither will have any effect.[14]

Of most immediate concern was the fact that Eighth Army headquarters, as had been intimated to Ottawa earlier in December, wanted to commit the untrained Canadian battalion immediately. As the Patricia CO quickly discovered, convincing the Americans that his men needed further training before being committed to action was easier said than done. 'On arrival at Pusan,' Stone subsequently informed Rockingham, 'I contacted G3 operations [the operations section of a divisional or higher headquarters] research (Lieutenant Colonel Lancaster, US Army) who had instructions to ship us to Suwon as soon as we were married up with our equipment. I queried the advisability of moving within 50 miles of an unstable front with green troops, particularly as the general idea was for us to patrol against guerilla forces in the area.'[15] Recalling the incident years later, Stone remembered,

> The G3 said that he had his orders and he had given me mine, and to get going. I asked where the commander of the 8th Army was located and he told me Seoul. I asked for an

> aeroplane, which he made available, and I flew to Seoul to see General Walker. I put my position to him and his senior staff, and although he was most pleasant, he said that my troops were trained as well as the US reinforcements, and the situation was desperate. Fortunately, I had been given a piece of paper prior to leaving Canada which gave me the authority for decision on committing my battalion. I waved the piece of paper. General Walker wanted no political repercussions and agreed with my demand for eight weeks' training time.[16]

As he explained to Rockingham at the time, 'It was apparent that the result of my interview with Lieutenant-Colonel Lancaster had been communicated to General Walker, for his attitude was quite different to the one I had been advised to expect. General Walker was very gracious and discussed points of training for the remainder of the interview.'[17] Nonetheless, the Patricias' war diary, in an entry made only three days after the CO's interview with Walker, did not hide the fact that 'Lieutenant-Colonel Stone is having considerable pressure brought to bear on him to commit the battalion at an early date and training must begin as soon as possible.' For example, 2 PPCLI was given only half a day off on Christmas Day as it prepared to move to Miryang, a training area some thirty miles north of Pusan that offered better conditions than Yong-do Island.[18] The change of base consumed several more valuable days and it was not until the last day of 1950 that the Patricias were finally able to begin preparing for battle.

The battalion had barely settled into a training routine at Miryang than the Eighth Army staff indicated that the question of the Canadians' scheduled deployment had yet to be settled. 'Lieutenant-Colonel Stone is going to EUSAK [Eighth US Army in Korea] Main [headquarters] in Taegu to be told that he must commit the battalion immediately,' the Patricia war diary recorded on 5 January 1951. 'Lieutenant-Colonel Stone is under considerable pressure from both EUSAK and [British] Brigadier Brodie, Commander 29th Brigade in the Seoul area. Everyone is aware of the pressure on the CO and the troops are apparently determined to do their best.'[19] Stone was undoubtedly forced to produce his command instructions yet again to convince the Americans that the decision as to when the Canadian battalion would be committed to battle rested with himself, as national commander, and not with Eighth Army headquarters in Taegu. Despite the calls 'to commit the battalion early,' he returned to Miryang with an assurance that his men would be allowed five more weeks in which to train.[20] The Patricia CO's ability to convince the Americans that his men needed more training had other beneficial effects. As the battalion noted two days after the latest confrontation, 'EUSAK is making certain [that] officers [are] available for training lectures on Korean conditions and fighting. Eighth Army HQ is extremely co-operative in anything that will hasten the battalion's arrival at the front.'[21]

In fairness to Eighth Army headquarters, its interest in the earliest possible deployment of 2 PPCLI was prompted by both a change in army commanders and a new Chinese offensive that had opened on 31 December. On 23 December, only three days after his interview with Stone, Walker was killed when his jeep collided with an ROK army truck. His replacement, Lt. Gen. Matthew Ridgway, had arrived in Tokyo to confer with MacArthur by Christmas Day. The supreme commander was clearly discouraged by the turn of events since late November and complained about the 'mission vacuum' coming from the joint chiefs in Washington. According to Ridgway's memoirs, MacArthur had informed Washington that his current plans provided for a 'withdrawal in successive positions to the Pusan area.' The supreme commander instructed Ridgway to establish Eighth Army 'in the most advanced positions in which you can maintain yourself.' Seoul was to be held 'largely for psychological and political reasons, as long as possible but not if it became a citadel position.' The maximum that MacArthur thought might be accomplished was to inflict 'a broadening defeat making possible the retention and security of South Korea.' Assuring the Eighth Army commander of his 'complete confidence,' MacArthur also agreed with Ridgway's suggestion 'that, if we made any further material rearward movement, we should strongly reassure the South Koreans that we meant to stand by them. My final question was simply this: "If I find the situation to my liking, would you have any objections to my attacking?" And his answer encouraged and gratified me deeply: "The Eighth Army is yours, Matt. Do what you think best."'[22]

Taking over the Eighth Army on 26 December, Ridgway quickly assured President Rhee that he was 'glad to be here and I aim to stay.'[23] When he met with his corps commanders and headquarters staff to discuss the possibilities of resuming the offensive, however, he found a dispirited, defeated group that had lost its desire for aggressive action. 'I could sense it the moment I came into the command post,' he later recalled. 'I could read it in the faces of ... leaders, from sergeants right on up to the top. They were unresponsive, reluctant to talk. I had to drag information out of them. There was a complete absence of that alertness, that aggressiveness, that you find in troops whose spirit is high.'[24] Ridgway was dismayed that his front line units had failed to maintain proper contact with the enemy or sufficiently reconnoitre the terrain to their front. The failure of his formations to meet these two basic combat requirements prompted the new Eighth Army commander to order all forward units to patrol vigorously to locate the communist positions and ascertain the enemy's strength.[25]

Ridgway's hopes for aggressive action were temporarily shelved by the Chinese Third Phase Offensive that opened on 31 December. Aiming at the 1st and 6th ROK Divisions at the junction of the I and IX Corps, the Chinese quickly forced the South Koreans back along Route 33 toward Seoul. Despite only sketchy information from his forward units, it became clear to Ridgway that a broad communist offensive was under way, one that his dispirited command would have difficulty resisting north of Seoul. On New Year's Day, therefore, the new Eighth Army commander issued withdrawal orders for his forces to pull back to a new defence line running along the Han River south of Seoul to the city of Wonpo-ri on the peninsula's east coast. In doing so, the commanding general nevertheless insisted that I and IX Corps conduct strong delaying actions, with withdrawals being made during daylight in order to take advantage of the UN's strong air support. It was undoubtedly galling for the American general to issue such orders only six days after assuming command, but the condition of his defeated army did not yet allow him any opportunity to attack – or even to hold the line.

After a brief stand north of Seoul on 2-3 January, the Eighth Army evacuated the South Korean capital on the 4th and withdrew south of the Han River. Although Ridgway was encouraged by the fact that he was facing 'an enemy whose only advantage is sheer numbers, whose armament is far inferior quantitatively and qualitatively, who has no air support whatever, meagre telecommunications and negligible armor,' the unwillingness of his subordinate commanders to make a determined stand prompted him to withdraw the Eighth Army a farther thirty miles south to a new defensive Line D. Ridgway could find 'only one or two cases where a division has shown any appreciable resourcefulness in adapting its fighting tactics to the terrain, to the enemy, and to conditions in this theater' but remained confident that if he could only 'achieve the spiritual awakening of the latent capabilities of this command' the Eighth Army could still 'inflict a bloody defeat on the Chinese.'[26] His optimism was not shared by MacArthur's headquarters in Tokyo, however. Throughout January the supreme commander's staff made detailed preparations to evacuate the peninsula, and MacArthur still expected the Eighth Army to pull back to the old Pusan Perimeter before withdrawing to Japan.[27]

While I and IX Corps had broken contact with the Chinese during the retreat to Line D, on the eastern flank North Korean forces – rebuilt after the heavy losses of September and October – drove well south of the Han River during the first week of January. Ridgway, meanwhile, pulled his ROK corps back to allow them to form a new line and stem the breach in their defences. By 18 January NKPA units had advanced to within a few miles of Andong on the Naktong River, some seventy-five miles north of 2 PPCLI's training area. Despite a questionable performance by the US 2nd Division around Wonju, the steady attrition inflicted by the American and South Korean defenders eventually reduced the North Korean formations' strength and effectiveness. When the Americans managed to cut off one NKPA division near Andong, the formation scattered into the hills to engage in guerrilla operations.[28] Having just commenced their training at Miryang, the Canadians were well aware that 'pressure is heavy all along the front, with a gradual [communist] build-up becoming apparent in the East. Their apparent intention is to drive down the eastern mountains in an effort to cut off Taegu.' Taking the initiative, the Patricia's support company commander made a 'recce over the roads to the south and east of Taegu' on 5 January 'in order that, should a breakthrough occur in the eastern section, we could move quickly into the danger area east of Taegu on the defensive perimeter.'[29]

It was indeed fortunate for 2 PPCLI that the Americans and South Koreans divisions were able to turn back the NKPA drive without insisting on the Canadian battalion's premature assistance. The move from Pusan to the pleasant hills of the Miryang River valley, an area far from the noisome fertilizer of the rice paddies, had had a beneficial effect on the Patricias' morale. Nevertheless, when the battalion began company training on 2 January, the experienced officers got an indication of the magnitude of the task ahead of them. A rifle range built on 3 January, for instance, allowed weapons training to begin, but 'for many men this was the first time they had fired their weapons. Questions were raised by platoon and company officers regarding the method and speed with which this battalion [was] raised, particularly when a battalion is sent overseas with some men who have never fired their weapons.'[30] That, of course, was wisdom after the fact. As all the officers of 2 PPCLI knew, the battalion had been dispatched to the Far East in the belief that it would be employed on occupation duties only. Given the meagre training the rank and file had received before leaving Canada, the Patricias were fortunate indeed that they had a commanding officer who was willing to resist the American demands for an early commitment.

At the outset of company training, Stone called a meeting of his officers to provide firm guidance as to what was required: 'Proficiency in the use of all weapons was stressed and Lieutenant-Colonel Stone placed great emphasis on the need for rapid use of supporting arms, particularly 60mm and 81mm mortars, both weapons that are entirely new to Canadian troops [the army had used the inferior British 3-inch mortar during the Second World War]. The necessity for physical fitness presupposed by the difficulties of mountain warfare meant that the first phase of training must concentrate on the rapid development of the men's strength and endurance.' As a result, the commanders designed company training programs that emphasized 'hill climbing and section and platoon tactics in mountains. Every effort was made to show the men the necessity for meeting the enemy on his ground, i.e., the high ridges dominating the valleys, in order that our more highly mechanized army may have freedom of movement in the valleys and along the roads.'[31]

The Second World War experience of Stone and his company commanders proved invaluable in assessing the best tactics and equipment to adopt for Korean conditions. The companies' 60 mm mortars, for instance, were considered impracticably heavy, with each tube requiring nine men to carry both the weapon and ammunition. This was 'felt to take too many men from company fighting strength. Most companies plan to carry two mortars in [a] platoon truck in the attack and only man-pack one. The extra men to be used to carry extra ammunition. In a defensive position, all three would of course be employed.'[32] The officers also understood the importance of not overloading their men in the attack, particularly given the immense exertion required to climb and move along the steep Korean hillsides. It was quickly decided to follow the British practice of having each man carry only his blanket and poncho during an advance, with packs and bedding brought up after the company had formed up on a new position. The officers realized that 'carrying their packs up the mountains would leave them too tired to carry out an attack properly without a long rest. Rapid execution and exploitation of an attack is essential if the short length of the Korean winter day is to be used to the best advantage.'[33]

The bulky winter parka issued to the troops presented a more difficult problem, since 'it will not fit in the small pack, it is too absorbent to be worn or hung outside and it is far too warm and heavy for troops climbing hills. Normally, all we wear is the outer, but in action the whole of it will have to be carried and its bulk is going to present severe problems.'[34] Tactically, the Patricia officers also foresaw that battalion defensive positions would have to be organized as 'isolated company islands of defence, as the necessity for holding dominating terrain features precludes, in most instances, a very tight battalion position.'[35] The American practice of 'laying wire and positions in a straight line, irrespective of terrain,' on the other hand, was rejected.[36]

For the first two and a half weeks of January, training emphasized physical conditioning with longer and longer marches over broken country. The clear, cold weather proved ideal, although the war diarist reported that the mountains still seemed as high as ever. On the 11th, A Company embarked in full kit on a seven-mile cross-country hike, a route that included moving along a ridgeline 2,000 feet high. 'Training for the battalion continues unabated,' the unit recorded two days later, 'and though the weather continues cold the morale and physical condition of the men is steadily improving. There are still quite a few medically unfit men in this battalion, but the strenuous training is rapidly bringing them out.'[37] In fact, during the six weeks of intensive preparation at Miryang, some sixty Patricias proved to be medically or psychologically unfit for the strain of operations and were evacuated as nonbattle casualties.[38] The uncertain news from the battle front also forced the program's tempo. By 18 January, greater emphasis was being placed on company schemes, with each company 'maintaining its own pace and sequences, but the coverage of necessary training is good, despite the great need and extra time spent on physical training.'[39]

An unexpected opportunity was presented when communist guerrillas began operating on the road between Miryang and Pusan, apparently in conjunction with the NKPA drive south of the Han River. Although the Patricias were warned earlier of an increased guerrilla presence in rear areas, it was not until 14 January that the activity 'assumed serious proportions ... when two men belonging to the 16th New Zealand Field Regiment, RNZA, were ambushed and brutally treated before being killed by NK guerrillas. The 16th NZ Field Regiment, RNZA, [which had recently arrived in Korea to join the 27th British Commonwealth Brigade] is moving into a temporary training area beside ours and it was during this movement of the regiment from Pusan that the men were ambushed ... Training was partially disrupted today by the incident and the preparations for possible anti-guerrilla activity.'[40]

After making a verbal report of the incident to Eighth Army headquarters in Taegu and requesting 'permission to take counter-measures,'[41] Stone assigned B Company, under the command of Maj. C.V. Lilley, to the task. On the 16th, the company began to clear the irregulars from a 2,700-foot-high feature named T'ogok-san. Over the three days of the operation, the Patricias fired on small bands of the enemy flushed from the fields and abandoned villages, killing two and wounding several others. As Lilley remarked in his report on the guerrilla hunt, the entire operation proved to be an excellent exercise: 'Men learnt to live, keep warm and alive in the open. I consider hunting guerrillas the best company exercise ... it brings out all the tactical and administrative lessons that have to be learnt. If this area is left alone for three or four days and then a company is put in I feel certain that more enemy can be killed.'[42] The battalion diarist also noted that 'the morale and temper of the men has improved since B Company left to attack the guerrillas.' The next day he continued: 'Interest in the battalion is centered on the activities of B Company and everyone in the battalion is determined to get into the action. All the companies are envious of B Company and are eagerly waiting for what they hope will be their turn.'[43]

Despite 'considerable pressure from EUSAK to divert the battalion from training to full time guerrilla chasing,'[44] Stone realized that his inexperienced men had to press on with their company and battalion exercises. Weaknesses were revealed during the company schemes undertaken in the third week of January:

> A Company has been out all day and night and the sniper section acted as enemy endeavouring to get into A Company defensive position ... The exercise taught some valuable lessons, one being that any movement (noise) and coughing immediately revealed defensive positions. Another lesson taught the company was that even on a bright moonlight night a noiseless approach enabled Lieutenant MacKenzie and Private Butler to get close enough to leave a note under the barrel of a Bren gun. Inexperience of the company gave all advantage to the 'enemy,' but both sides learned a great deal about the tricks that night and moonlight can play on vision and hearing.[45]

> C Company returned to camp today after an all-day scheme, starting at 1900 hours last night and lasting until 1700 hours this afternoon. The exercise was designed to demonstrate methods and difficulties of night movement and occupying positions in the dark. It also gave the men a chance to experience a day in the field under trying conditions. The terrain traversed was mountainous and rough, digging was difficult and movement hazardous in the extreme, especially at night.[46]

> A Company is spending the day doing company advance to contact. Their movements appeared quite good but when actual exercise takes place and they come in for battle noise and sniping, things may be different.[47]

As the exercises continued the battalion began 'to acquire an air of competence. Section and platoon drills are becoming more connected and smooth and the men are beginning to see the necessity for the constant training and physical hardening.' On 26 January Stone was again summoned to Eighth Army headquarters in Taegu and told to accelerate his training program to allow for 'an early commitment of the battalion, probably with the 29th [British] Brigade.'[48] With the prospect of action not far off, the Patricia diarist reported that 'the spirit of competition and the men's morale has remained high. The opportunity to carry over this rivalry into the five-day [battalion] exercise seems to please the men.' The scheme devised by Stone was intended to 'serve as a gauge of the battalion's hardihood' and its readiness for operations.[49] The main focus of the exercise was to give the men some experience in setting up and defending a battalion-sized defensive position under field conditions. Each company was to send out patrols to cover its front and report any 'enemy' movement observed. As the Patricia's war diary makes clear, however, the men's vigilance still left something to be desired:

> All companies warned to look out for 'enemy' patrols after last light. Comparison of the 'enemy' commander, Lieutenant Constant's, report of his activities and the reports of the companies show little relation between them. Lieutenant Constant's patrols passed right through company areas without detection with the exception of A Company ... Reports of enemy action were so delayed as to make the CO unable to help the companies.[50]

> At 2254 hours, F Echelon was attacked by a twenty-man ['enemy'] fighting patrol which surprised the sentries and passed right through the position and the vehicle park area and continuing on down the valley where B Echelon was successfully raided, wire cut and a complete infiltration of area accomplished without difficulty.[51]

This was, no doubt, a rather inauspicious conclusion to the battalion's abbreviated period of preparation. It had been a mere five and a half weeks since the Patricias had begun serious training at Miryang, but the sustained pressure from Eighth Army headquarters for an early commitment prevented the organization of any further exercises. In his critique of the battalion exercise Stone 'stressed the necessity of accurate reporting of enemy activity in order that the CO could form an accurate and rapid appreciation of the situation. The need for good camouflage, good movement discipline, and garbage disposal was also pointed out.'[52]

Until the men developed their military skills in action, the Patricias would have to rely heavily on the combat experience of their senior officers and NCOs if they were to be successful. In addition to Stone, six of the battalion's seven majors had held commissions in the Canadian Army during the Second World War. Only three of the Patricia's captains had held commissions in 1945 – all of them Special Force volunteers – but most of the remainder had served in the Canadian Army's ranks during the earlier conflict. The battalion also had a higher proportion of officers transferred to it from the 1st Battalion than did the other Special Force infantry units, presumably because 2 PPCLI had been sent to the Far East without the benefit of collective training, and army headquarters wanted to ensure a higher level of experience in key positions. Since the unit had been expected to 'show the flag' as part of a UN occupation force, moreover, army headquarters probably believed that permanent force officers and NCOs would help instill some regular army discipline in the Special Force ranks. As a result, while Stone and his second-in-command, Maj. H.D.P. Tighe, were both Special Force volunteers, five of the remaining six majors were regular officers who had managed to get themselves posted to the 2nd Battalion. Among the other officers, seven of the fifteen captains were Special Force as were twelve of the seventeen lieutenants. The percentage of regulars among the warrant officers and company quartermaster sergeants was also higher than in the other 2nd battalions, with nine of fourteen being from 1 PPCLI. The remaining members of the battalion, however, were almost entirely Special Force recruits, with only seven of forty-two sergeants and four of seventy-nine corporals being from the permanent force. All of the battalion's lance-corporals and privates were Special Force.[53]

Although Stone would contend many years after the war that the initial strength of 2 PPCLI contained 'many deadbeats ... and other useless types,'[54] this statement is not borne out by the facts. While it is true that the 60 Patricias sent back to Canada from Miryang were eventually joined by an additional 86 nonbattle casualties culled from the ranks after the battalion's initial weeks of operations, the total of 148 unfit soldiers is not as excessive as Stone has suggested. The very high standard of physical fitness required to move and fight along the Korean mountain ridges meant that even men with relatively minor physical problems were unable to keep up. In fact, among the evacuees was one of the company commanders posted to the battalion from the Active Force. Maj. W.H.J. Stutt (a well-known Patricia regular officer who is reputed to have served as the model for the character of Major Blood – 'large and red, with a desert-army moustache, crowns on his shoulder, and a permanent glare,' an officer who 'was reasonably terrifying at any time' – in Herbert Wood's novel *The Private War of Jacket Coates*) was evacuated on 25 February with jaundice soon after the battalion began active operations.[55] Moreover, it should be noted that when the Active Force's 1 PPCLI was warned for duty in Korea the following August, the battalion placed some 200 of its regular soldiers on its X list of noneffectives, men who had supposedly been carefully screened at the time of enlistment (see Chapter 7). This represented nearly 25 percent of the unit's strength even before it was exposed to anything that resembled rigorous training, a decidedly higher proportion than the 148 unfit men of the operationally active 2 PPCLI. In his later recollections, Stone was also quick to point out that 'by the time we had weeded out the "scruff," we had a first class, high-spirited group of soldiers.'[56]

Within days of completing their lone battalion exercise, the Patricias received word that they would not be joining the 29th British Brigade, as had long been rumoured, but would instead serve with the British, Australian, and New Zealand regiments in the 27th British Commonwealth Brigade. Their deployment to the front was scheduled for midmonth. 'Interior economy and more interior economy,' the battalion recorded on 11 February, 'plus unending speculation on the conditions at the front, what battle is really like and so on, seem to be the main preoccupation of the men. Morale is good now that we are nearly ready.' When the Patricias did move to the front, they were to serve 'as a brigade reserve in the present fairly static portions of the IX Corps front.'[57] Fortunately for the Canadians, the improving situation all along the Eighth Army's front would allow them a little extra time to gain some needed experience while pursuing a retreating enemy (see Map 5).

General Ridgway had launched Operation Thunderbolt on 25 January as a probing advance by I and IX Corps to locate the enemy's main line. When the two corps met only moderate resistance in the west, X Corps was ordered to begin its own advance on 5 February. By the 10th the entire UN battle line had been advanced to the banks of the Han River, some twenty to thirty-five miles north, at only slight cost. In addition to regaining large tracts of territory, the advance dispelled the pessimism that had hung over the Eighth Army since the Chinese intervention had driven them from North Korea.[58] Their new confidence was immediately put in jeopardy, however, when the communists opened their Fourth Phase Offensive on the afternoon of 11 February, aimed at the ROK-held Hoengsong sector in central Korea.[59]

To prevent a communist breakthrough south of Hoengsong, the 27th British Commonwealth Brigade – the formation that 2 PPCLI was about to join – had been assigned to a blocking position north of the Han River near Yoju some ten miles south of Chip'yong-ni (Map 5). The brigade, which had been sending patrols north to make contact with the 23rd US Regimental Combat Team holding the village, was now ordered to fight its way toward the beleaguered Americans defending Chip'yong-ni. To its immediate west, the 5th US Cavalry Regiment was given a similar assignment. By the night of 14-15 February, the 23rd Regimental Combat Team had inflicted heavy casualties on the waves of assaulting Chinese but were running desperately short of ammunition. Fortunately, the enemy failed to put in a final attack against the weary defenders on the morning of the 15th and by afternoon had begun to withdraw their depleted divisions. At a cost of 350 casualties, the defenders had managed to inflict an estimated 5,000 on the enemy. It was the first time since the Chinese intervention that the UN Command had been able to administer such crushing losses on a major Chinese offensive.

The Chinese pullback coincided with the arrival of a 5th Cavalry armour/infantry relief column, Task Force Crombez, made up of 165 infantrymen mounted on the hulls of twenty-three tanks. The task force made a gallant, six-mile dash up a heavily defended road to break through to Chip'yong-ni at the same time that the

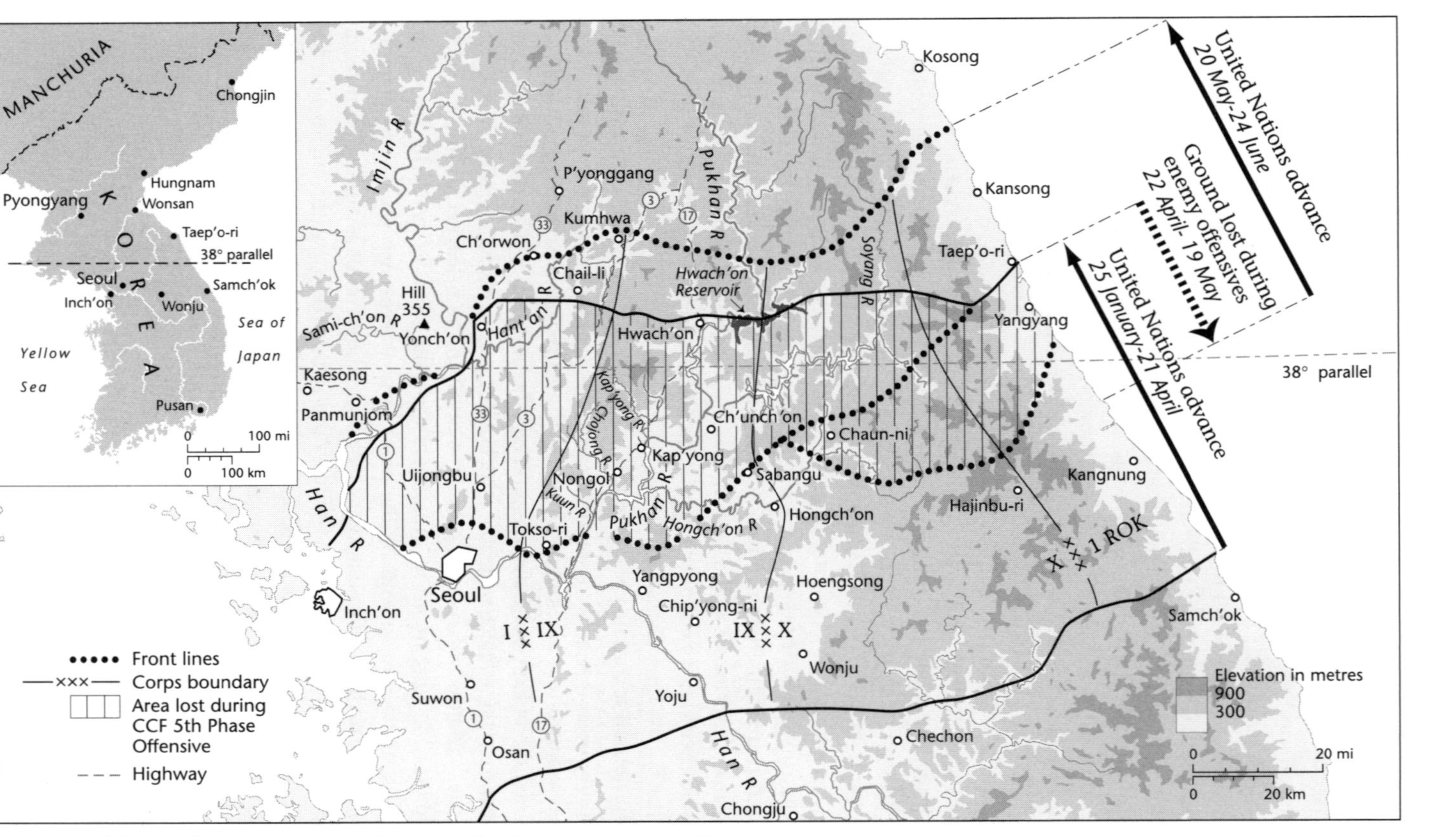

Map 5 *Eighth Army fronts, 25 January-24 June 1951, showing corps areas on 24 June*

27th Brigade was fighting its way toward Ch'uam-ni, five miles to the southeast. While far from decisive, both efforts had distracted a portion of the Chinese forces that might otherwise have been used directly against the crossroads.[60] According to the American official history,

> General Ridgway felt that the Eighth Army had reached a turning point, that it had substantially regained the confidence lost during the distressing withdrawals of December and early January. In his judgment, the successful defense of Chip'yong-ni by an isolated combat team without grievous losses against a force far superior in strength symbolized the revitalization. Task Force Crombez, in its relief role, epitomized the offensive spirit. Although being forced to place infantry aboard the tanks had proved costly, Ridgway judged Colonel Crombez' decision to advance with armor when his infantry moved too slowly to be one of the best local decisions of the war. With renewed spirit, as evidenced at Chip'yong-ni, Ridgway considered his forces quite capable of further offensive operations, which he immediately proceeded to design.[61]

The plan Ridgway implemented, Operation Killer, would be 2 PPCLI's introduction to combat.

In anticipation of his battalion's commitment, Lieutenant-Colonel Stone had visited 27th Brigade headquarters on 9 February to discuss its employment. On the 17th, as the Chinese were withdrawing from in front of the brigade's positions southeast of Chip'yong-ni, the leading elements of the Canadian battalion began arriving in the Commonwealth brigade's area. With a blizzard sweeping across their front on 18 February, the Patricias prepared for an attack against Hill 404 at 1100 hours the following day, reporting that 'everything is as ready as possible for [the] battalion's first action.' The Canadians replaced the 3rd Battalion, Royal Australian Regiment, as the brigade's left forward unit and set off the next morning for their objective. With B Company leading the advance against Hill 404, the Patricias found that the Chinese had withdrawn from around Chip'yong-ni and there were no longer any enemy on any of the brigade's objectives. The advance did provide the Canadians with 'a grim lesson on the dangers of sleeping on guard [when they found] ... the bodies of sixty-five coloured troops of the 2nd Reconnaissance Company lying dead beside the road up which the battalion advanced. These men were surprised by the Chinese at night and very few escaped with their lives.'[62] The sight made a lasting impression on the Patricias, who thereafter used only their blankets in the front line rather than risk being caught in a sleeping bag by a surprise attack.

As part of Killer's western thrust, the 27th Brigade operated in the middle of the IX Corps attack with the 1st Cavalry Division on its left flank and the 6th ROK Division on its right. To the east of the South Koreans, the 1st Marine Division would make the direct drive north along Route 29 to Hoengsong itself. The

Commonwealth brigade was to set off from the hills east of Chip'yong-ni and drive toward the operation's objective line, Albany, fourteen miles to the northeast. Although the plan called for Albany to be reached in three days, the brigade commander, Brig. Basil A. Coad, told his battalion COs that the timing seemed unduly optimistic given the onset of the spring thaw. The British general warned of the difficulties to be expected on muddy roads that could be blocked by landslides at any time.[63] In view of the difficult terrain, each of the brigade's battalions was assigned 250 Korean porters to carry supplies and ammunition forward, a feature of the Korean campaign that would become very familiar to the Canadians over the next two and a half years.

Coad's forecast of the operation's difficulties proved exactly right. Killer 'became at once a plodding affair, not so much an advance with two main thrusts as a more uniform clearing operation in which assault forces fought hardest to overcome the effects of weather. Ahead of the advance, the Chinese and North Koreans concentrated on evacuating the salient, leaving behind only scattered forces to fight occasional but strong delaying actions.'[64] In fact, one such determined rearguard was to hold up the Commonwealth brigade's progress for several days as they struggled through the melting snow and ice of successive Korean ridgelines (Map 6).

The 27th Brigade's advance was led off on 21 February by the Patricias on the left and the Argyll and Sutherland Highlanders on the right. Neither battalion encountered any serious enemy resistance as they moved north along the ridges flanking the Sokkong valley, some 4,000 yards east of Hill 404 and five miles east of Chip'yong-ni. The greatest handicap was the rain and snow that quickly turned the dirt roads and tracks into rivers of mud and made for icy climbing along the steep hills. On the first day of the advance, two Patricia officers had to be evacuated with serious injuries after falling in the treacherous conditions. The Canadians had to dig in for the night through several feet of snow along the 1,200-foot-high hills. 'Despite the miserable state and the prospect of a very cold, wet and hungry night,' the battalion diarist recorded, 'the morale of the men was very high.'[65] Continuing their forward progress the next day, C Company suffered the Patricias' first battle casualties, four killed and one wounded, in a two-platoon attack on Hill 444 at the head of the valley. The Canadians swept aside the Chinese opposition on Hill 444 and pressed on in the afternoon to approach their next objective, Hill 419, 'a very difficult feature to approach from either left or right flank.'[66] After driving off two enemy outposts, the battalion dug in at the base of the hill and began preparations to attack it the next day.

The assault on Hill 419 on the morning of the 23rd lost the benefit of an intended napalm strike when the US Air Force mistakenly hit Hill 444 in the Patricias' rear instead. The attacking companies, C and D, came under increasingly heavy machine-gun and small-arms fire as they tried to negotiate the precipitous ridges leading to the objective. By afternoon it was increasingly obvious that the strong enemy rearguard was not yet prepared to relinquish the position. Moreover, the Patricias'

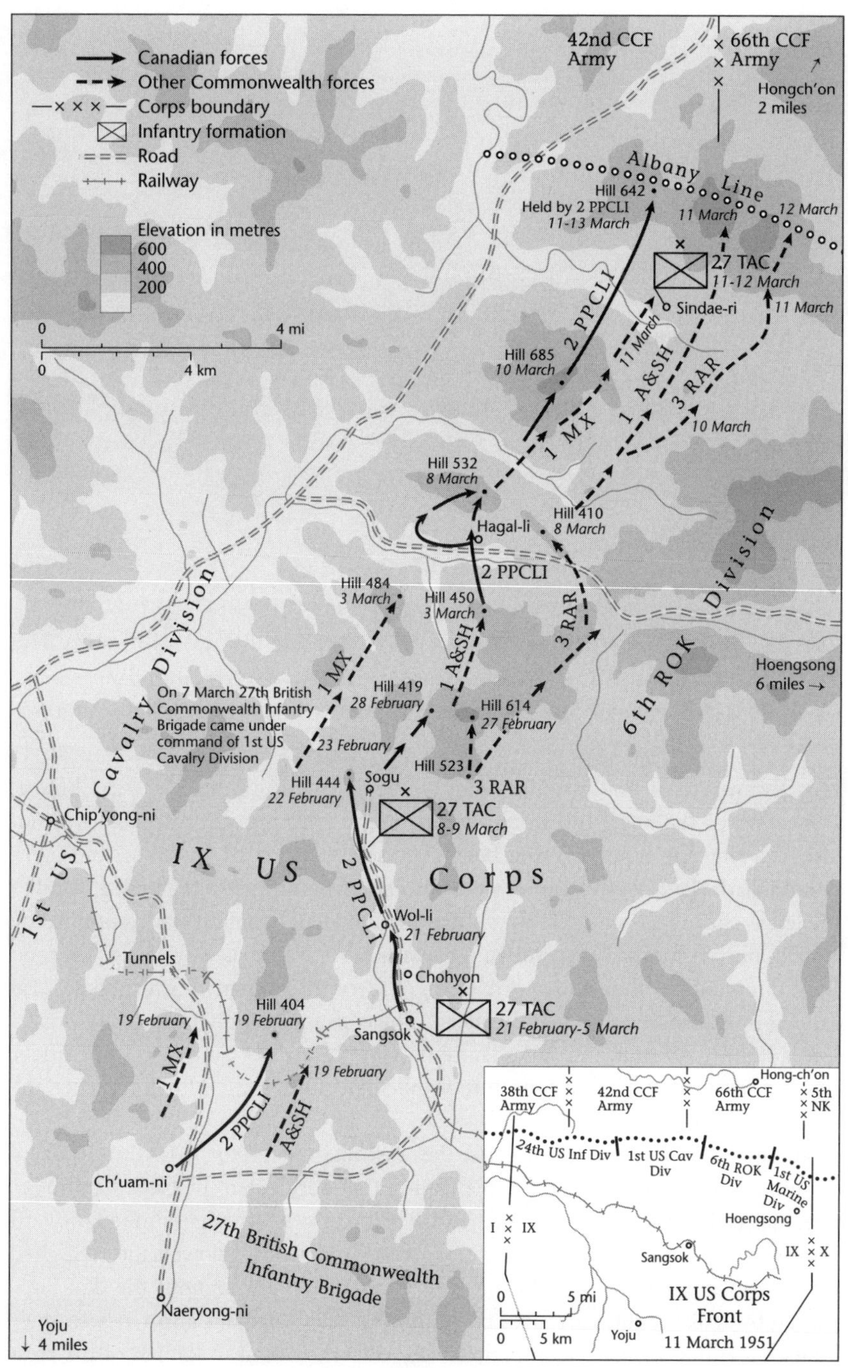

Map 6 *27th British Commonwealth Infantry Brigade operations, 19 February-11 March 1951*

Soldiers of 2 PPCLI move forward to renew the attack on Hill 419 on 24 February 1951. After two months living under canvas, the Patricias already have the look of veteran troops. NAC PA155531

objective was itself dominated by Hill 614 to the right, still held by the Chinese. Possession of the lower hill would, in any event, have proven untenable without also securing the other. Having been repulsed at a cost of six killed and eight wounded, the Patricia companies were 'forced to firm up' below the high ground to the left of the hill at last light. That night the Canadian battalion was resupplied by Korean porters for the first time. In the words of the Patricias' war diarist, the men were 'supplied by [the] native carriers ... of George Company (G for Gook) also known by the codename "Rice-burners." The company supply trains were organized and moved out in the dark. Those moving towards D Company came under fire and stampeded the first time, but supplies and ammunition finally reached the company at 2330 hours.'[67]

The next day, Brig. Coad directed the Australian battalion, 3 RAR, to make a simultaneous assault on Hill 614, the feature that dominated the Canadian objective. Just as the Patricias had found the day before, the steep ridges limited forward movement to single, eight-man sections at a time, which allowed the well-sited Chinese machine-guns to hold the Australians at bay throughout the day. Supported by artillery and air strikes on both hills, the Canadians also renewed their attack on Hill 419 with C Company trying to work around to the left of the crest while D Company made a direct assault:

> D Company moved to the high ground ... without incident and moved in to their final attack at 1000 hours and immediately came under HMG [heavy machine-gun] fire from their objective. By noon, D Company had pushed forward into the forward edge of their objective but came under increasingly heavy fire and ... were under fire from three sides.
>
> The failure of the Australians to advance onto Hill 614 on the right and of C Company to get above Hill 419 on the left enabled the Chinese to bring supporting fire to bear on D Company's attack. The line of hills which is the joint objective of ourselves and the Australians is held by two regiments [i.e., brigades] of enemy. At 1400 hours, D Company made another attempt to get on their objective but without success ... and at 1630 hours CO instructed them to firm up ... for the night.
>
> The night was passed in comparative quiet. The enemy confined themselves to light patrolling that did enter our battalion area. Brigadier Coad spent the night chasing imaginary Chinese around the battalion area in 8,000 metre bounds, four rounds gunfire from the 16th NZ Field Regiment, with the result that few of us got much sleep that night. Casualties were light today, but the battalion has been continuously engaged for two days with little sleep at night. Our battalion and the 3 RAR are in an extremely extended position so the CO has decided to confine our activities to fighting patrols for the next day ... The elements of 1 Cavalry Division have failed to come up with the result that a 5,000-8,000 yard gap exists on our left.[68]

For the next two days, the Australians and Canadians patrolled in the direction of the two objectives. A fighting patrol on the morning of 25 February encountered the enemy halfway up the slopes of Hill 419 but returned without casualties some four and a half hours later, after recovering the bodies of two Patricias from C Company who had been killed three days earlier. On 26 February a Chinese deserter reported that the two hills were being held by three battalions of the 124th and 125th Divisions. The Chinese defenders were to delay the Commonwealth brigade's advance while the remaining units of the two divisions built new defensive positions on the next ridgeline to the north. Although the Chinese had been able to hold off the earlier attacks with relative ease, the fact that a 3 RAR patrol on the 26th almost reached the summit of Hill 614 prompted the Australians to launch a platoon-sized attack on the feature the next day. Having completed the more northerly line of entrenchments, the Chinese did not mount a sustained defence and withdrew in mid-afternoon after the Australians had overrun several of their outposts. With the higher hill in friendly hands, 2 PPCLI was able to occupy Hill 419 'without a hitch. The enemy moved off to the north as the battalion advanced and by 1600 hours the battalion was firm on its objective. The four bodies of those killed in C Company's attack on the 22 February 1951 were found in the Chinese positions stripped of their clothing but otherwise unharmed.'[69]

With the seizure of the hills at the head of the Sangsok valley, the Commonwealth brigade had several days' rest to allow the 1st Cavalry Division to put in an appearance on its left flank and the 6th ROK Division to straighten out its line to the right. The difficult terrain and stiff rearguard actions aside, the caution with which the Killer advance was conducted was, in part, attributable to the scant intelligence about enemy strength and dispositions that handicapped Ridgway's planning. To negate the UN's complete air superiority, the Chinese were very adept at moving men and equipment by night and keeping them well camouflaged during the day, making it difficult for American intelligence staffs to make accurate assessments of enemy numbers. More reliable information could be gained by vigorous patrolling up to the main enemy positions, but this, too, could prove difficult during more fluid operations. Nevertheless, the Eighth Army's intelligence staff believed that seven new Chinese armies had entered Korea in recent weeks (in fact, these later proved to be three North Korean corps, totalling nine divisions, that had been withdrawn to Manchuria the previous autumn to reorganize), but were unable to tell if any of these reserves had been moved near the battle front.

While the Commonwealth brigade waited for its flanking units to join them before continuing the advance, each company was able to send back its men, one section at a time, to wash, change their clothes, and get a solid 'eight hours sleep for the first time in nearly two weeks.' The Canadians also attempted to repair their American-supplied windproof pants, which were not standing up well to the wear and tear of the campaign. The fact that the battalion had had only one case of frozen feet seemed to vindicate Stone's decision to equip his men with leather rather than rubber boots. Overall, the men were reported to be 'in very good spirits' despite the 'extremely hard conditions under which the battalion has been in action.'[70] Once the flanking divisions had reestablished contact on 3 March, the Commonwealth brigade resumed its northern advance, led by the Middlesex Regiment and the Argyll and Sutherland Highlanders. The two British battalions made a largely unopposed, three-mile hike to the edge of an east-west valley that fronted the latest rearguard defences set up by the Chinese 124th and 125th Divisions on Hills 532 and 410. There the brigade paused for several days as Ridgway prepared to launch his next advance, Operation Ripper, on 7 March.

Like the earlier operation, Ripper's primary objective was to destroy communist forces and equipment south of the thirty-eighth parallel. With the main thrust being made by IX Corps in central Korea, a secondary aim was to outflank Seoul to the east and force its abandonment by the communists, thereby avoiding the need to make a direct assault across the Han River. Ridgway had planned to commence the operation about 1 March but was forced to delay to allow the UN forces to stockpile a five-day level of supplies in the forward areas, a task made more difficult by the muddy state of Korea's inadequate road network.[71]

Unfortunately for the Commonwealth brigade, its advance to the Albany Line, some six miles north of the positions it had reached on 3 March, would first have to overcome the strongly held defences of Hills 532 and 410. With his two British battalions due for replacement at any time and their morale somewhat questionable,[72]

Coad once again selected 2 PPCLI and 3 RAR to make the assault up the steep slopes of the two hills, with the Canadians assigned the task of capturing the higher of the two on the left. Both features were heavily bombarded by artillery and air strikes on 6 March, and the two battalions moved into the valley early the next morning to make their assaults. Both units came under fire soon after they crossed the start line, with one of 3 RAR's companies pinned down barely one-third of the way up Hill 410. A second Australian company commenced climbing a parallel spur while the first company 'spent a very difficult time on slopes so nearly precipitous as to severely hamper movement.' The well-prepared Chinese defences also meant that 'supporting artillery and mortar observers were unable to locate the positions from which the enemy machine-gun and rifle fire was coming.'[73] The two assaulting Patricia companies had an equally difficult time making progress against the well-sited defences:

> At 0745 hours D Company came under heavy machine-gun fire, was pinned down and called for artillery and mortar support ... [while] A Company advanced slowly against light resistance along their ridge ... At 0920 hours D Company had suffered three casualties from AW [automatic weapons] fire and was forming for another attack. A preparation was fired by artillery and mortars to assist ... As D Company moved off, enemy HMGs that had not fired before opened up from bunkers on Hill 532 proper ... The enemy positions were too strong and their supporting arms too heavy and accurate for D Company to move successfully against the ridge immediately ahead of them without further artillery and mortar preparation. By 1410 hours A Company was encountering stiffening enemy resistance on their line of approach and were temporarily held up by a series of pimples each one held in some strength. Considerable long range, but accurate, AW fire was being brought to bear on them from Hill 443 and 532.
>
> At 1400 hours D Company began its final attack for the day and this time managed to get up on the first ridge held by the Chinese, but this ridge was in turn dominated by an even more strongly-held position about 100 yards further on. By this time D Company had become somewhat disorganized due to the intense fire which it was receiving from three sides and had had heavy casualties in the last assault. Their position was untenable and at 1600 hours the CO ordered D Company to pull back carefully. The company pulled back under heavy small arms fire and the Chinese reoccupied their last position making it impossible to recover the bodies of the men killed in the last attack.
>
> A Company firmed up ... after encountering considerable enemy resistance as they approached the ridge line connecting Hill 443 and Hill 532 ... By 1830 hours B Company had moved up to the ridge just west of the main Chinese position and firmed up ... right under a strongly-occupied Chinese position ...
>
> On the left, the Greek battalion failed to get on their objective and withdrew ... It is estimated that nearly a full CCF Division (125th Division) has been holding the high ground under attack today by 7th RCT [Regimental Combat Team], 1 Cavalry Division

> and 27th Brigade. Enemy strength on Hill 532 was at least a battalion and one-half with a position which D Company attacked held by one company at least and well-supported by enemy battalion's heavy weapons.
>
> On the right, the 3 RAR failed to get on their objective in the face of stiff resistance offered by the 3rd Battalion, 375th Regiment and elements of the 2nd Battalion, 375th Regiment which was also opposing us. Once again, the 27th Brigade is occupying a salient with long, exposed flanks. The 6th ROK Division failed to advance today with the result that the right flank of the brigade is exposed for nearly 6,000 yards.[74]

When both the Australians and Canadians dug in for the night short of their objectives' crest-line, the day's fighting had cost the two Patricia companies seven killed and thirty-seven wounded, with the majority of the casualties falling on the more heavily engaged D Company. The Australians, meanwhile, had had twelve men killed and twenty-four wounded in their assault, a fight that they considered to be the toughest since the action to defend the Chongchon River bridgehead the previous November.[75] Elsewhere on the Eighth Army front, Operation Ripper's first day had seen much easier advances against only pockets of stiff resistance. Perhaps after preparing such stout defences, the Chinese battalions facing the Commonwealth brigade had been reluctant to abandon them without first inflicting casualties on their pursuers. In any event, 'after spending an uncomfortable night during which the Chinese threw nearly 100 grenades' into their positions from above, the Patricias renewed their attack at 0500 hours the next morning to find that the enemy had withdrawn. The Canadians and Australians found large amounts of ammunition in the well-constructed enemy bunkers, and eighty-two dead Chinese.[76]

With the enemy having broken contact and retreated north in the face of the Eighth Army's general advance, the 27th Brigade had little further difficulty in making its way across two succeeding valleys to reach the Albany Line on 13 March. There the brigade was squeezed out of the front line by the advance of the 1st US Cavalry and 6th ROK Divisions and placed in corps reserve for the next two weeks. The Ripper advance continued to make substantial gains in the next few days – including the reoccupation of Seoul by the 1st ROK Division on 15 March – as the communist forces broke contact to set up another defensive line several miles north of the capital. Its important territorial gains aside, however, Operation Ripper had been disappointing in terms of its main purpose – destroying the enemy's forces. From 1 to 15 March, the known enemy dead totalled only 7,151, a figure that would not increase substantially by month's end as the communists accelerated their retreat.[77]

The move into corps reserve allowed the Canadians an opportunity to rest and refit after three strenuous weeks of mountain operations. Their clashes with the enemy, most notably the tough fights for Hills 419 and 532, had cost the battalion fourteen killed and forty-three wounded. In addition, eighty-eight men were sent home as nonbattle casualties during the Patricias' time in reserve, having proven physically or emotionally incapable of contributing to the battalion's fighting

Patricias climb past an abandoned Chinese bunker during the March 1951 advance. Climbing the rugged Korean hillsides could prove as exhausting as fighting the enemy. The lead soldier has spare Bren magazines in his pouches for the section's light machine-gun, being carried on the shoulder of the man behind. NAC PA171230

strength. In his report to army headquarters, Lieutenant-Colonel Stone indicated his satisfaction with the overall quality and performance of his, by now, battle-tested men:

> Own troops show lack of basic training, particularly in caring for weapons and equipment. Old [medical] categories very apparent on eve of battle [e.g., the sudden appearance of bad backs and knees among malingerers]. Much 'scruff' that was hastily recruited has now been returned to Canada. Troops here are fit, morale high, show lots of guts in close contact. Lack of comfort which is general in this theatre is being compensated with troops' own ingenuity covering weapon slits, etc. Officers are generally good but junior ranks show need of a company commander's school. Practical experience will help but certain basic principles of military thinking are lacking. Troops are very well led and the aggressiveness they display in attack under difficult circumstances is a great credit to the officers.
>
> Transport is being well looked after and is causing little trouble except the odd spring.
>
> Signal platoon is excellent and that is mostly due to the hard work of our signal officer.

> Battalions are given huge fronts, our own in the last show being 3,000 yards on the map, 6,000 on the ground counting the up and down. The attack itself, as is usual in the mountains, is on a narrow front with companies leapfrogging one another to the highest ground. Some softening up by artillery, 4.2 [inch] mortars (US) and 81mm (battalion) and air precedes the attack itself but on these huge hills its effectiveness is limited. Troops pile heavy gear in assembly area and attack with bren, rifle, bayonet and grenades, usually from very close range. The climbs to the assault lines are most fatiguing and it is a great credit to the troops that they show such determination in going in. Smoke plays its part in screening the assault from supporting defended localities but it is a company commander's battle at each minor objective. Once the main height is cleared, patrols can usually deal with uncleared ridges and ravines.
>
> In our last battle, at a cost to ourselves of seven dead and thirty-seven wounded (many minor), we counted forty-three enemy dead and found bloody trails going over the hill where the wounded dragged themselves away. The men themselves are a credit to Canada and to their battalion ...
>
> This theatre is a very severe test for men and equipment and it can be fairly said that both the men and equipment are standing up to the conditions very well.
>
> I would suggest that future army recruits be given at least sixteen weeks basic training and be hardened both mentally and physically before being sent into combat. Canada is the place to discover weaknesses in the individual not a battle theatre.[78]

Stone, of course, was still rueing the altered circumstances of the war that had suddenly changed his battalion's role from occupation to combat. Even so, his comments make it clear that he was pleased with the way his veteran officers – particularly the company commanders, most of whom had come to the unit from the regular army – had been able to take a raw battalion and whip it into shape in so short a period of time. Combined with Stone's own firm guidance, the battalion's performance demonstrated, just as 3 PPCLI had shown at Fort Lewis, the tremendous effect that motivated, combat-experienced senior officers and NCOs could have on an otherwise green unit.

On the equipment side, the Patricias were finding that their 'clothes wear out very readily and socks are always in demand.'[79] One of the more contentious pieces of kit in the harsh Korean conditions was boots. Since Miryang, the Patricias had debated 'the merits of our steel-shod, leather-sole boots as compared to the American issue rubber-soled boot. It has been found that the Canadian boot minus cleats in the soles wear[s] out very rapidly, especially on the sides, which are in contact with the rock and slate most frequently in hill climbing. Lieutenant-Colonel Stone has decided to try the American boot in an effort to arrive at the best equipment possible for the battalion.'[80] After three weeks of operational experience, Stone was able to report definitely that Canadian boots 'did not stand up to mountain climbing mostly because soles were not clumped and hobnailed. GI boots (US) are fairly satisfactory although some are cracking in the uppers.'[81]

Stone was also largely satisfied with the battalion's weapons, most of which he was familiar with from the Second World War. The Bren light machine-gun continued to be 'very satisfactory' while the No. 36 grenade, with its heavier explosive charge, was 'still the best in the world.' The lighter American grenades lacked the power of the No. 36 while the even lighter explosive charge in Chinese grenades generally caused only minor shrapnel wounds and few fatalities. The American 81 mm mortars that were employed at the battalion level gave 'accurate and long range support and are more satisfactory than the [British-made] 3-inch' mortar that had been used by the Canadian army during the Second World War. The smaller 60 mm mortar also provided 'heavy but accurate ... support immediately in the company commander's hands.'[82]

The relative value of the .303 Enfield rifle, the standard British and Canadian infantry weapon since the Boer War, would be debated among the troops throughout the war, but at this stage at least Stone continued to believe in its merits. 'Mud and frost shows the advantages of having a hand operated rifle,' the CO informed Ottawa, 'and I do not think a change to an automatic is desirable. Men who had acquired US Garand rifles [only four of whom had done so] have since discarded them in favour of the Enfield No. 4.' The only really unsatisfactory weapon was the Canadian-made Sten sub-machine-gun which was widely condemned as 'a poor weapon ... The magazines have all to be adjusted to fit the magazine opening and the spring is so weak that even though the mags are periodically emptied the platform will not come up with the load. Putting two springs in one mag works for a time but something should be done to strengthen the original.'[83]

Although Stone could certainly be well satisfied with his men's performance to date, he was careful not to waste the valuable training time available in the two weeks his battalion was in reserve. In addition to rekitting the men with new boots and uniforms, the Patricias opened an NCOs school under the supervision of Major Lilley while each of the companies carried 'out strenuous attacks on features in the training area with the idea of hardening the reinforcements that are now arriving in considerable numbers.'[84] The extra training would prove useful as the Eighth Army prepared to cross the thirty-eighth parallel into North Korea for a second time. The enemy's successful delaying actions on Hills 419 and 532 were a foretaste of the engagement that 2 PPCLI and 3 RAR would soon fight on dominating hills to the north of a village named Kap'yong. This time, however, the roles of attacker and defender would be reversed as the Canadians and Australians attempted to stem the tide of yet another communist offensive.

4 KAP'YONG, APRIL 1951

The 27th Brigade received word on 24 March that it was to join the 24th US Division to take part in Operation Courageous, the Eighth Army's latest attempt to move the battle line to the thirty-eighth parallel. As 2 PPCLI prepared to resume the advance it did so under new commanders. On 23 March Brigadier Coad had departed for Hong Kong on compassionate leave, and the deputy commander of the 29th British Brigade, Col. Brian A. Burke, was appointed as his replacement in the Commonwealth brigade. The next day Lieutenant-Colonel Stone had to be evacuated with a mild case of smallpox, and the battalion's second-in-command, Major Tighe, assumed the role of acting CO. The Canadian battalion was transported by truck to the village of Porunggol, twelve miles south of the parallel, on 27 March. The journey was made through a driving rain in which the 'new issue British poncho[s] which the battalion received on 24 March proved their worth.'[1] After relieving the American 19th Regimental Combat Team on the surrounding hills, the Commonwealth brigade began its advance up the Chojong River valley the next day.

The Patricias were handed the task of covering the brigade's right flank by moving along the highest ridgeline to the east of the river. From the outset of the advance, it was clear that the difficult terrain and late-winter weather would be more daunting than any resistance they might encounter from the retreating enemy. 'It began to snow at 1930 hours,' the battalion recorded on 28 March as the Canadians moved into their jumping-off positions, 'and despite extra clothing carried by the men in their large packs, a very cold night ensued. At this altitude, 4,000 feet, the ground is still frozen and the north slopes still have four to five feet of snow on them. Movement is difficult along the narrow ridges, especially so for the heavily burdened men. Steep rock faces and awkward packs made movement slow today and will continue to do so throughout this operation.'[2] Supply was particularly difficult on the high ridges and 2 PPCLI had to rely on the stamina of its Korean porters for food and ammunition. Under the circumstances, it was fortunate that the Patricias encountered only occasional long-range small-arms fire from the withdrawing Chinese.

It was on the second day of the advance that Brigadier Rockingham finally caught up with the battalion as part of his tour of the Far East. The Canadian commander arrived just as the Patricias were preparing for 'another miserable night,' in which 'freezing conditions added to wet clothing, after a day of sliding about in mud and slush, made for bad sleeping conditions.'[3] The visit provided Rockingham with a graphic demonstration of the physical demands imposed by Korean terrain and weather. Mistakenly led by his guide to the positions occupied by the Argyll battalion, he had to descend one ridge before making the 3,000-foot climb to 2 PPCLI's location. 'The approach to the company was through fairly thick cover of low trees and brush,' he later recalled, 'then up a hill which was almost vertical. It was a far cry from the country I had fought over in Europe, which had often been plains criss-crossed with excellent roads and railroads. Suddenly I was looking down the barrel of one of our Bren guns and being challenged.'[4]

After struggling north for nine miles along the difficult ridges, 2 PPCLI halted on the northern spur of Hill 1250 on 1 April. The entire Commonwealth brigade had now reached Line Benton, its objective for Operation Courageous, which lay some two to three miles south of the thirty-eighth parallel. With the Eighth Army's approach to the border, allied leaders were already questioning the wisdom of crossing the parallel for a second time. MacArthur was still operating under the joint chiefs of staff directive of 27 September 1950 that granted him the authority to move UN forces deep into North Korean territory, but there were indications that Washington, too, was now prepared to accept a stalemate on the ground while it negotiated an end to the conflict. In early March MacArthur had reasserted his own conviction that victory in the Far East would require that the war expand to include attacks on mainland China: 'Assuming no diminution of the enemy's flow of ground forces and materiel to the Korean battle area, a continuation of the existing limitation upon our freedom of counter-offensive action, and no major additions to our organizational strength, the battle lines cannot fail in time to reach a point of theoretical stalemate.'[5] Coming at the outset of Ridgway's offensive, MacArthur's statement – characterized by some as 'Die for Tie' – did little for the morale of the troops. It was left to the Eighth Army commander to point out that regaining the thirty-eighth parallel and halting communist expansion would, in itself, be a 'tremendous victory' for the United Nations while the Chinese inability to drive the UN from the peninsula would mean that communism had 'failed monumentally.'[6]

Ridgway's attitude was certainly more in keeping with the prevailing mood of both the State Department in Washington and America's non-Korean allies. US secretary of state Dean Acheson had recently come to support the possibility of a negotiated settlement based on the status quo. While not objecting to small UN advances north of the parallel for tactical purposes, Acheson hoped that a line could be established near the border that would be acceptable to the enemy. On 20 March the joint chiefs had informed MacArthur that President Truman would shortly be issuing a carefully worded appeal to the communists calling for negotiations. Four days later, however, the American general made his own public statement, tersely advising the Chinese that he was ready to confer with the enemy commander-in-chief. In doing so he belittled Chinese military power and seemed to threaten China with direct attack if hostilities continued.

Not surprisingly, the general's statement led to a quick communist rejection of the possibility of opening ceasefire negotiations. MacArthur's words also led America's allies to question whether there had been a shift in US policy. An outraged Truman believed that they so contradicted his own planned announcement that he decided not to issue it. In the president's view, MacArthur's statement was 'not just a public disagreement over policy, but deliberate, premeditated sabotage of US and UN policy' and 'open defiance of my orders as president and commander-in-chief.'[7] Truman ordered the joint chiefs to send MacArthur an immediate reminder of his command instructions while privately deciding that the wayward general would have to be relieved. The president became even firmer in his resolve on 5 April when a congressman read out in the House of Representatives a letter from MacArthur setting out his views on widening the Korean War by allowing nationalist Chinese forces from Taiwan to mount attacks on the mainland. Despite the political costs of firing a popular hero, Truman announced MacArthur's recall from Tokyo on 11 April.[8]

By relieving MacArthur and replacing him with Ridgway, the American president demonstrated his determination to fight a limited war in Korea. Soon after assuming supreme command in mid-April, Ridgway issued letters of instruction to each of his three service commanders outlining the limits under which they were to operate. The instructions to Ridgway's replacement at Eighth Army headquarters, Lt. Gen. James Van Fleet, did not represent a major shift from the guidelines in place during Ridgway's tenure. Within the overall mandate to repel aggression against South Korea, Van Fleet was authorized to advance his forces up to fifteen miles north of the thirty-eight parallel. Any greater penetration of enemy territory required Ridgway's approval. Van Fleet was also directed to inflict maximum losses on the enemy, in both personnel and materiel, while avoiding high casualties to his own forces. In drawing up his plans he was not to expect any substantial reinforcement and might be required to hold a defensive line indefinitely. In an accompanying memorandum Ridgway also insisted that Van Fleet avoid any action that might widen the conflict, a marked departure from MacArthur's views on the conduct of the war.[9]

The communist rejection of MacArthur's heavy-handed proposal, however, meant that the Eighth Army would have to continue to fight with sufficient intensity to convince the Chinese that they had no hope of a military victory in Korea. Prior to MacArthur's dismissal, Ridgway had already gained approval for his next operation, an advance to seize a strong defensive position along a new objective, Line Kansas, that ran just north of the parallel. The operation was to be quickly followed by a farther advance in the I and IX Corps' sectors to occupy the southern portion of an important road and rail junction that ran across a triangular-shaped plain – dubbed the Iron Triangle – in the mountains of central Korea. The towns of P'yonggang in the north (not to be confused with the North Korean capital of Pyongyang, 100 miles to the northwest) and Ch'orwon and Kumhwa in the south defined the triangular-shaped transportation complex, with the latter two lying some fifteen miles north of the thirty-eighth parallel. While making his plans for the advance north of the border, Ridgway was also receiving intelligence reports of a further Chinese buildup, troops that were available, at least in part, because of the Eighth Army's failure to destroy a substantial portion of the enemy forces south of the thirty-eighth parallel. Anticipating that the communists were probably about to launch another offensive, his staff also prepared plans for a fighting withdrawal through a series of phase-lines to absorb the momentum of the attacks. As a further safety measure, Ridgway planned to pull three divisions back from the front once the Kansas Line was reached in order to have them available for a counterattack role (Map 7).[10]

The 27th Brigade began its advance on 3 April after shifting from the Chojong to the Kap'yong valley several miles to the east. The two valleys were separated by the high ridgeline up which 2 PPCLI had been advancing, and the terrain forced the brigade to detour south in order to reach the eastern valley. The brigade was also transferred from the 24th US Division in I Corps, which continued to operate on its left, to become the left flanking formation of IX Corps, with the 6th ROK Division to its right. Brigadier Burke initially placed the Patricias, who had had to climb the highest hills during the previous operation, in brigade reserve for a few days' rest while the other three battalions moved up the Kap'yong valley against only limited opposition. 'Hot meals were served for the first time in weeks,' the Patricia diarist noted on 4 April, representing 'a welcome change after a steady diet of C rations.'[11] After the entire brigade paused on 6 April to allow the 6th ROK Division to come up on its right – a formation that in the Canadians' view repeatedly demonstrated 'little interest in moving forward, to judge from its present lack of activity' – the Patricias returned to the advance the following day with the assignment of clearing a ridgeline adjacent to one already secured by 3 RAR. The ruggedness of the Kap'yong valley's hills, rising some 2,500 to 3,000 feet above the river, had convinced the Chinese that fewer forces were required to delay the UN forces in that sector than in the wider valleys to its east and west. For the most part, the Commonwealth brigade was opposed by small groups of infantry skilfully dug in on the commanding hilltops (Map 7).[12]

The Canadian battalion crossed the thirty-eighth parallel on 8 April after A Company attacked and drove off a Chinese platoon from the nearest hilltop objective. Over the next three days the brigade continued to make its way north along the mountain ridges north of the Kap'yong valley – the river itself begins near the thirty-eighth parallel – to reach Line Kansas against only light opposition. The ease with which most units had reached their objectives prompted Ridgway to open the advance to the Iron Triangle in the I and IX Corps sectors on 9 April. Given the increasing concerns about a possible communist offensive, however, the two corps were to seize an intermediate position, designated Line Utah, rather than moving directly to Line Wyoming along the base of the Iron Triangle complex. In the

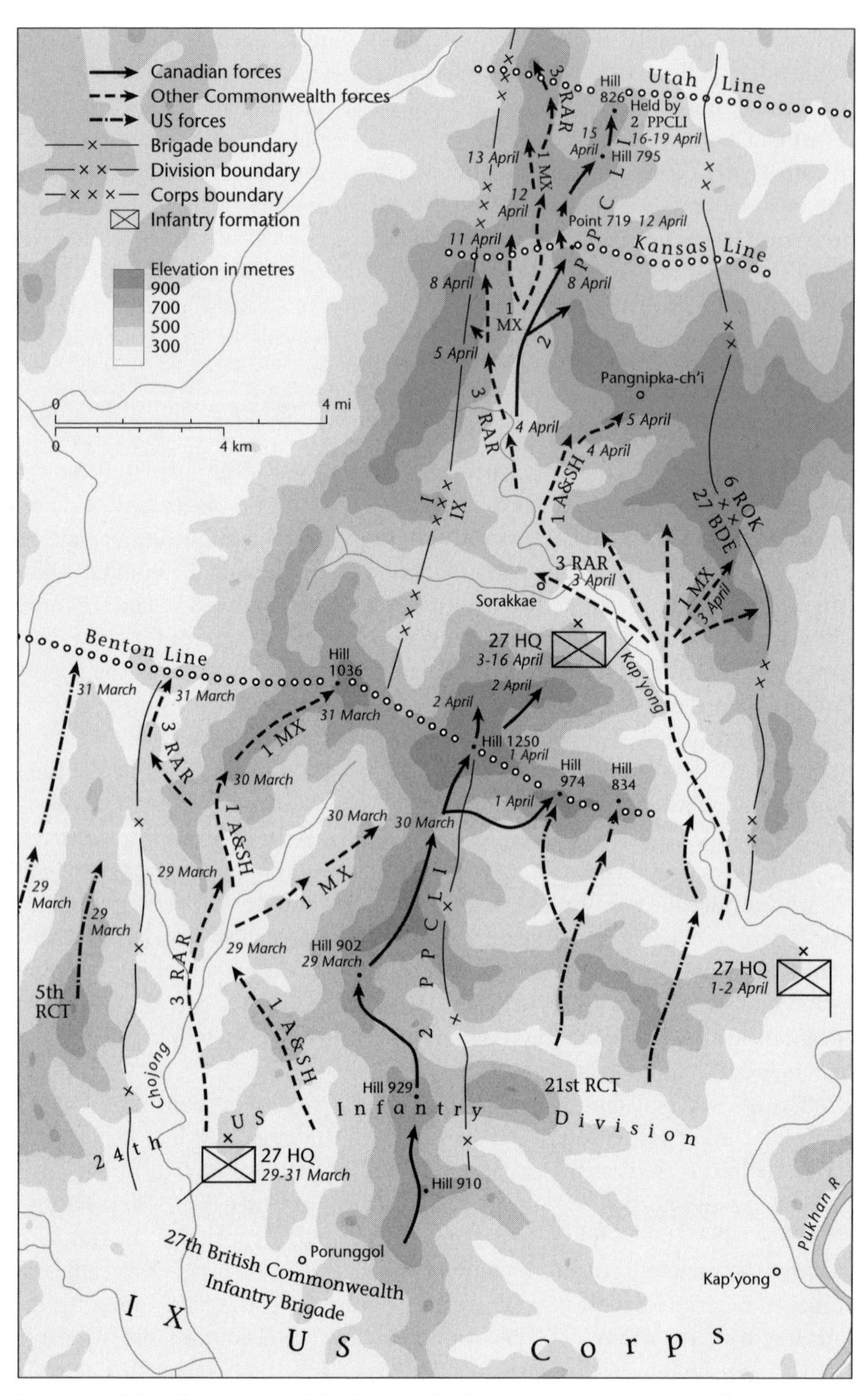

Map 7 *27th British Commonwealth Infantry Brigade operations, 29 March-16 April 1951*

Commonwealth brigade's sector on the eastern flank of the advance, the Utah objectives lay only some three miles to the north of its present Kansas positions, but the formation quickly discovered that any farther advance would have to contend with increased Chinese resistance. On the brigade's left, the Middlesex Regiment was the first to encounter the stiffening defences in clearing its assigned ridgeline on 13 April, and, following its failure to take its final two hilltop objectives the next day, it was left to 3 RAR to capture them. The Australians suffered eight wounded on the 15th in a close-quarter assault on the first objective, mostly minor injuries from grenade fragments, while counting ten enemy dead. The final hill was seized the next day against only minimal opposition.[13]

To the east, 2 PPCLI also ran into stiff resistance when D Company tried to capture the battalion's final two ridgeline objectives, Hills 795 and 826, on 14 April: 'At 1655 hours the company attack went in with artillery support on [Hill 826] and MMG [medium machine-gun] and 81mm mortar fire on [Hill 795]. This attack was successful in reaching [Hill 795] but the position was untenable due to the proximity of the dominating hill on the same ridgeline and the vulnerable position of the company on a ridge having easy flank approaches. Lieutenant M.G. Levy led the attack with great spirit and succeeded in reaching the well-held Chinese bunker on [Hill 795] with his platoon. However the company withdrew on the CO's orders.'[14] D Company suffered five wounded in the assault. A second attempt to take the more northerly Hill 826 on the 15th managed to reach the feature's lower slopes before darkness ended the attack. It was not until the next morning, after the Chinese rearguard had withdrawn in front of both the Australians and the Canadians, that the final objective was secured.

Firming up on the strong hill positions it had been assigned, the brigade waited for the 6th ROK Division, which was to take over its Utah positions, to complete the advance to its east. The Commonwealth brigade, less the 16th New Zealand Field Regiment (which remained in place to support the South Korean division), was relieved on 18 April and placed in IX Corps reserve, moving back down the Kap'yong valley to a rest area immediately north of the village of the same name.[15] Even then, there were qualms among the Canadians about the lack of professionalism exhibited by the soldiers relieving them in the front line. One day prior to the relief, 'a small group of officers from the 17th Regiment, 6th ROK Division arrived at battalion tactical headquarters at about 1100 hours. The battalion IO [intelligence officer] took the reconnaissance party forward to the positions of Baker and Charlie Company ... The reconnaissance party of the 17th ROK Regiment declined to go forward to the Dog Company positions ... For this reason the ROK knowledge of the area forward of 2 PPCLI was negligible.'[16]

With the seizure of Lines Kansas and Utah, the entire Eighth Army front, save the western section of the line running along the Imjin River north of Seoul, was now above the thirty-eighth parallel. The stiffening Chinese resistance during the 27th Brigade's approach to Utah, however, was a further indication that the communists were building up their forces for an offensive. In late February fresh Chinese reinforcements had entered Korea from Manchuria in the form of the XIX Army Group, consisting of the 63rd, 64th, and 65th Armies. At the same time, the IX Army Group, which had suffered heavily in forcing X US Corps' withdrawal from the Changjin Reservoir the previous December, had restored its three armies to fighting trim. Both army groups were reported to be in reserve positions north of the thirty-eighth parallel in the I Corps' sector. To their east, the XIII Army Group had had its three depleted armies reinforced by fresh formations in mid-March. It was against these troops that the Commonwealth brigade had been making its most recent advances in the Kap'yong valley.

Gen. P'eng Teh-huai, who had replaced Lin Piao as commander of the Chinese forces in Korea earlier in the year, planned to use these fresh forces to open a new Fifth Phase Offensive. P'eng's immediate objective was the recapture of Seoul – a prize he reputedly promised to Mao Zedong as a May Day gift – and the main thrust of the attack was to be made along the approaches to the capital by the III, IX, and XIX Army Groups, which comprised some 270,000 men. The XIX Army Group's three armies were to attack across the Imjin River on a twelve-mile front and advance on Seoul between highway Routes 1 and 33. In the centre of the main thrust, the III Army Group was to attack to the east of Route 33, between the large bend in the Imjin, where it alters course 90 degrees from south to west, and the city of Ch'orwon at the western base of the Iron Triangle. From the city of Kumhwa at the eastern end of the triangle, the IX Army Group would form the left flank of the drive on Seoul in advancing along Route 3.

General P'eng also planned to make several secondary attacks in support of the main effort against Seoul. On the western flank of the Fifth Phase Offensive, the North Korean I Corps was to cross the Imjin River and cover the XIX Army Group's flank by moving south toward Seoul between Route 1 and the Han River. In the eastern sector, two other North Korean corps were to attack down the Soyang River valley along the boundary of X US and III ROK Corps. In the area to the immediate east of the Hwach'on Reservoir, the somewhat depleted armies of the XIII Army Group were to launch holding attacks against the 1st US Marine and 6th ROK Divisions, the latter formation occupying the Line Utah positions at the head of the Kap'yong valley, directly north of where the 27th Brigade was resting in IX Corps reserve.[17] The formations committed to P'eng's secondary thrusts thus comprised a total of 149,000 troops. Together with the 214,000 supporting troops, therefore, he had over 630,000 troops available for operations. Although the failure of both the Third and Fourth Phase Offensives to oust the UN forces from Korea had disappointed the authorities in Beijing, they realized that it was not due to a lack of 'revolutionary spirit' in their soldiers so much as it was to the depleted condition of the units themselves. With the influx of reinforcements and Second World War Soviet equipment – although used, the Soviet assault rifles and machine carbines allowed many units to turn in the old Japanese rifles with which they had been equipped – P'eng believed he would be able to damage the UN forces in his path severely and make a major advance into South Korea.[18]

In proposing a Fifth Phase advance of 100 miles, roughly to the line of Taejon-Andong, the Chinese commander believed that inadequate transportation and a lack of resupply would constitute the greatest threat to success and urged his unit commanders to assign drivers and prisoners of war to salvage captured motor vehicles.[19] P'eng had initially planned to launch his offensive in early May but fears that the advancing Eighth Army would break into the relatively open country of the Iron Triangle, where its armour would be more difficult to stop, and that the UN Command would make another amphibious landing in his rear, prompted the Chinese commander to set the opening of the offensive for 22 April. In a signal to each of his armies four days before its launch, P'eng laid out his goals:

> For our Spring Offensive, we have decided to make our objective the wiping out of three divisions (less one regiment) of the American Army, three brigades of British and Turkish troops, and two divisions of the Puppet [i.e., ROK] Army to the west of the northern Han River. First of all, we will mass our forces to wipe out the 6th Division of the Puppet Army, the British 27th Brigade, the American 3rd Division (less one regiment), the Turkish Brigade, the British 29th Brigade and the 1st Division of the Puppet Army, and after this we can wipe out the American 24th Division and 25th Division.[20]

Opposing the 630,000 communist soldiers were 418,000 United Nations Command personnel (including administrative rear elements), composed of some 245,000 Americans, 152,000 South Koreans, 11,500 Commonwealth troops, and 10,000 troops from other United Nations countries.[21] Despite the disparity in numbers, Ridgway believed that the UN Command could defeat the expected communist offensive. Although he expected NKPA divisions could only have success when attacking their ROK counterparts, he was confident that US formations could stem the onslaught of the Chinese armies. Eighth Army intelligence could not pin down the timing of the anticipated offensive, but was not fooled by the apparent absence of enemy activity. Van Fleet was reminded that the Chinese had proven very adept at concealing their offensive preparations in the past and moved into forward assembly areas only immediately before the actual attack.

Rather than wait for the communists to make the first move, Van Fleet, with Ridgway's approval, decided to preempt them by resuming the advance to the base of the Iron Triangle on 21 April. The IX Corps divisions made easy progress on the first day of the operation, but by the 22nd, resistance was stiffening against the two I Corps divisions, the 24th and 25th US Infantry, on the left. Patrols sent across the Imjin River by other I Corps formations, including the 29th British Brigade holding a section of the river's southern bank directly north of Seoul, also ran into strong Chinese forces that had not been present the day before. The new positions appeared to indicate that the XIX Army Group was setting up a covering force for its assault divisions, a move confirmed by aerial reconnaissance reports of the forward movement of enemy formations opposite both the I and IX Corps. With all signs pointing to the imminent opening of the enemy's offensive, Van Fleet ordered his advancing divisions to halt in the late afternoon of the 22nd and the entire Eighth Army braced itself for an attack.[22]

The Fifth Phase Offensive opened at 2000 hours on 22 April with an attack on the 6th ROK Division in the mountains north of the Kap'yong valley. A few hours later and to the west, the Chinese launched their main thrust toward Seoul across the Imjin River. Standing directly in the path of the enemy's main drive on the capital was the 29th British Brigade, which held a seven-mile length of front on a series of hills to the south of the river. Its commander, Brig. Thomas Brodie, placed two battalions forward, the 1st Battalion, the Gloucester Regiment on the left and the 1st Battalion, the Royal Northumberland Fusiliers, on the right. There was, however, a mile-and-a-half-wide gap between the forward battalions, a space that led directly to the dominating Kamak-san feature in their rear. The brigade's third battalion, the 1st Battalion, the Royal Ulster Rifles, was in reserve southeast of the 2,000-foot Kamak-san while an attached Belgian battalion was positioned on the brigade's right flank, on high ground north of the confluence of the Imjin and Hant'an Rivers. The position of the Belgians covered the left flank of the 3rd US Division, under whose command the British were operating. The American division's line lay north of the Hant'an River covering Route 33, the main north-south road from Ch'orwon through Uijongbu to Seoul.

Although the British had held their positions since 5 April, their entrenchments were lightly constructed and were not covered by either barbed wire entanglements or mines. 'We were not really in a defensive frame of mind,' one of the brigade's officers later recalled. 'We had been crawling forward, probing forward for months. We didn't even really know exactly where on our front the Imjin was fordable.'[23] The absence of enemy activity on their immediate front in the days leading up to the Chinese offensive seemed to have convinced many in the brigade that the attack on Eighth Army would fall elsewhere. Over the next three days, the 29th Brigade provided a graphic example of the perils that could befall a force facing massed waves of attacking Chinese infantry and the sort of unnecessary losses that could occur when a national commander failed to exercise his own discretion in preserving his force.

By the afternoon of 22 April large bodies of enemy troops were reported north of the Imjin River and the commanding officer of the Gloucester Regiment spent part of the day directing mortar fire onto those who ventured too near the river bank. If the Chinese followed their usual pattern of attack, as the British expected, the men of the 63rd Army, XIX Army Group would have closed up to the Imjin during the night of 22-3 April and launched probing attacks across the river at dawn. Instead of pausing, however, the Chinese infantry forded the river before midnight on the 22nd and immediately launched their main attack. By 2230 hours, large groups of

Chinese infantry were already across the Imjin and infiltrating between the Gloucester and Northumberland positions. Following a night of sustained attack against all three forward battalions, dawn revealed that the Chinese had occupied the high ground in the centre of the brigade position.

After holding off the enemy throughout the 23rd, Brigadier Brodie became increasingly concerned by the large numbers of Chinese that were penetrating around the flanks of his battalions. He had been ordered to hold his Kansas Line positions until the 3rd US Division had pulled back from northwest of the Imjin River. The division commander's order reflected Van Fleet's own view that the Eighth Army's vast superiority in firepower – both artillery and air support – would allow the UN formations to hold their positions. As the British official history (whose author was the adjutant of the Gloucester battalion during the Imjin battle) points out,

> these were the principles on which General Ridgway had operated as army commander, but the emphasis [under Van Fleet] was different; divisions were not going to roll with the punches but to accept body blows before they drew back. This change was no doubt due to the nature of General Van Fleet's character, but he was also influenced by the apprehension that a series of premature withdrawals would draw down the confidence General Ridgway had fostered since January. He seems to have overlooked, or at any rate been unwilling to recognise, that his predecessor had drawn up a limited withdrawal plan in the face of an enemy spring offensive precisely to preserve his army's confidence.[24]

Unfortunately, Van Fleet's tactics would have worked only if the Eighth Army had been strong enough to prevent large penetrations along its line. By the end of 23 April, however, P'eng's massed infantry units were already sweeping around the UN formations' flanks and cutting lines of possible retreat. Opposite the British brigade, the Chinese 63rd Army had all three of its divisions, some 30,000 men, across the Imjin by the night of 23-4 April, virtually surrounding the isolated British battalions on the hills south of the river. Throughout the 24th, the entire brigade was again subjected to repeated attacks by masses of Chinese infantry. To the west of the Northumberland and Ulster positions on Route 11, the isolated Gloucester battalion was in dire straits. Although Lieutenant-Colonel Carne had been granted permission to withdraw at 0900 hours on 24 April, promises that a relief column would attempt to break in to their position on Hill 235 convinced him to wait rather than leave his wounded behind. The first British/Filipino armour/infantry force that tried to break through along the difficult track to the battalion's position on 'Gloster Hill' were easily turned back by the Chinese infantry. When the 3rd Division's commander asked about the state of the Gloucesters at 1500 hours, Brodie, with typical British understatement, merely informed him that the situation was 'pretty sticky.' Misinterpreting Brodie's words as indicating the battalion could hold out, the American general delayed sending a second relief column. Soon afterward,

Carne informed brigade headquarters that his battalion was 'no longer an effective fighting force.'[25]

With the entire front under heavy assault, I Corps ordered a withdrawal to a new Line Delta early on 25 April. The 3rd Division's commander, meanwhile, was fearful that the infiltrating Chinese would cut off his formation's retreat down Route 33 to Uijongbu and reassigned the regimental combat team that was planning an attack to relieve the Gloucesters. Even at that late date, however, the British brigadier does not appear to have kept 3rd Division headquarters accurately informed of the Gloucesters' true condition, having told the Americans that the isolated battalion had 'asked for some artillery [fire] but OK.'[26] Finally, at 0610 hours on 25 April, Brodie gave Carne permission to attempt a breakout back to brigade lines but the battered battalion, completely surrounded by attacking Chinese, stood little chance of doing so. Only one group of forty Gloucesters eventually managed to make its way back to the UN lines, and the bulk of the battalion was forced to surrender.

To the east, the rest of the beleaguered British brigade still had to fight its way south down Route 11 to effect an escape. Although supported by the Centurion tanks of the British 8th Hussars, the retreating infantry came under heavy fire from the swarms of enemy lining the route. The Ulsters' regimental history captures something of their ordeal: 'The road for a mile and a half south of [the pass through which they were escaping] was seething with Chinese; every bank, ditch and house was filled with them and though many were actually crushed under the tracks of the Centurions, the unprotected infantry riding on the outside came under a continuous hail of small arms fire, grenades and mortar bombs. Many were killed on the tanks and many wounded lost their grip on the wildly pitching hulls and fell to the ground. Two tanks were knocked out by pole charges but the remainder, with their loads of dead and living, broke through to the comparative safety of the brigade headquarters valley.'[27]

The 29th Brigade's stubborn defence of Line Kansas cost them 1,091 casualties. The Gloucester battalion lost 622 of the 699 men it took into the battle: 92 were killed and 530 were captured, 153 of the latter being wounded men.[28] The virtual annihilation of an entire battalion – and an allied one at that – led to understandable recriminations among the American commanders as to who was responsible for the disaster. Two weeks after the battle General Ridgway informed Van Fleet that he felt 'a certain disquiet that down through the channel of command, the full responsibility for realising the danger to which this unit was exposed, then for extricating it when that danger became grave, was not recognised nor implemented.' Certainly the loss was taken to heart by Van Fleet, who quickly warned his corps commanders to 'give when you are pressed hard. I don't want units cut off and I want you to handle UN [i.e., allied] units very carefully to avoid their being cut off. I don't want a repetition of the Gloucester loss.'[29] The Americans tried to emphasize that, in holding up the Chinese advance, the battalion's sacrifice had not been in vain, but also pointed out that Brodie and Carne had failed to keep higher headquarters informed of their truly desperate situation.

For his part, Brigadier Brodie was willing to accept only 50 percent of the responsibility for the failure in communication, possibly believing that the 3rd Division commander should have investigated the situation himself.[30] Nonetheless, as the national commander on the spot, it was Brodie's clear duty to see that his men were not discarded so needlessly. A.H. Farrar-Hockley, one of the captured Gloucesters, believed that 'the root of the matter' lay in the failure to properly heed 'the many reminders by General Ridgway that positions should be held as long as was feasible. Directives of this kind are entirely justified but implementation requires a nice judgement ... If the Glosters had been kept in position deliberately because they were destroying and delaying a substantial portion of the Chinese 63rd Army, their loss might have been justified. Actually, they were lost by oversight.'[31]

While the British brigade was being attacked on the banks of the Imjin River north of Seoul, the Chinese thrust that had struck the 6th ROK Division at 2000 hours on 22 April was quickly driving the South Koreans from their hilltop positions north of the Kap'yong valley. The Chinese infantry attacked with little supporting fire, but the 60th Division, 20th Army easily infiltrated the individual ROK units through the numerous gaps and open flanks in the South Koreans' badly organized positions. The two forward ROK regiments quickly collapsed, their troops abandoning weapons, vehicles, and equipment as they streamed south out of the mountains to reach the head of the Kap'yong valley. Three hours after being attacked, the South Korean commander was forced to admit that he had lost all communication with his units. With the 1st US Marine Division holding firm to the east, the Chinese had all night to envelop its exposed flank but, whether unaware of the opportunity or unable to alter their axis of attack quickly enough, they failed to do so.

Although the Chinese were initially slow to exploit the ROK collapse, by 0400 hours on the 23rd the sound of small-arms fire was audible in the positions of the 16th New Zealand Field Regiment operating in support of the South Koreans. In view of the collapse, Brigadier Burke instructed the New Zealand gunners to fall back to rejoin the 27th Brigade north of Kap'yong village but had to order them north again at 1000 hours on the 23rd when the ROK division's commander was able to rally some 2,500 of his men in a blocking position at the head of the valley near the thirty-eighth parallel. As a precaution, Burke directed the Middlesex battalion to accompany the gunners north 'just to make sure we can get you back if there is an emergency.'[32]

With the forward positions in both the I and IX Corps' sectors increasingly untenable as the Chinese offensive exploited gaps between formations throughout the night, Van Fleet ordered his commanders to pull their forces back to Line Kansas in midmorning. The IX Corps commander, Maj. Gen. William Hoge, ordered the 1st Marine Division to pull back to form a new defensive line along the Pukhan River

The view looking north from the village of Kap'yong toward Hill 677 (middle-left background), the feature defended by 2 PPCLI on 24-5 April 1951, as photographed by a Canadian Army historical officer in September 1953. DHH 681.009 D2

between the Hwach'on Reservoir and the new position the 6th ROK Division had been directed to take up along Line Kansas.[33] Hoge's plan was predicated on the South Koreans being able to re-form and offer some resistance. Unfortunately, the 2,500-man rearguard the ROK division's commander had pieced together was several miles south of the Kansas Line and in no condition to take up their assigned position that afternoon. Consequently, Hoge directed the 27th Brigade to take up a blocking position in the valley to the south of the ROK division so as to prevent the Chinese from breaking through to the Route 17 crossroads at the village of Kap'yong.[34] The timing of the Chinese offensive, however, had caught the 27th Brigade in the midst of a reorganization. While the brigade was in reserve, Brigadier Burke's headquarters, which had been sent to Korea during the initial emergency from Hong Kong, was to be replaced by that of the 28th Brigade under the command of another British officer, Brig. George Taylor. In addition, the 27th Brigade's two British battalions, the Argyll and Sutherland Highlanders and the Middlesex Regiment, were to be relieved by the King's Own Scottish Borderers and the King's Shropshire Light Infantry. On 23 April, neither battalion had yet arrived in the brigade's rest area, although the Argylls had already departed.[35]

The defensive line the brigade was to establish lay some four miles north of Kap'yong village at the confluence of the river and a smaller stream where the valley curved around from the northwest to the southwest toward its junction with the Pukhan River (see Map 8). To the south of the confluence a range of hills extended on either side of the Kap'yong River with Hill 504 to the east and Hill 677 to the west. To the north of 677 was an even higher feature, Sudok-san (Hill 794). Together, the three hill masses formed a naturally strong defensive position, and Burke initially intended to place a battalion on each of the three features. However, the detachment of the Middlesex Regiment to support the New Zealand gunners and the departure of the Argylls for Hong Kong left him with only two battalions to hold the five-mile length of the intended line. As a result, Burke assigned 2 PPCLI to defend Hill 677 to the west of the river and 3 RAR to hold Hill 504 to its east while leaving Sudok-san unoccupied.

The two scrub-covered hills the British general selected faced a mile-wide valley formed by a bend in the Kap'yong River at the confluence of a tributary. The valley floor was dotted with small hamlets and cultivated fields while the north side was dominated by a series of steep, 2,000-foot hills. The battalion areas were two miles apart and separated by the river, and brigade headquarters was located some three miles south of the Canadians in the Kap'yong valley. The major weaknesses of the brigade's position, aside from the length of front to be covered by two battalions, were the lack of adjacent formations to cover its flanks, and the absence of both the New Zealand gunners and the Middlesex battalion, still supporting the ROK rearguard nine miles to the north, to occupy a blocking position along the valley in the rear of the two occupied hills. Given the size of the features to be defended, each battalion had to arrange its companies in individual strongpoints, each some 200 to 400 yards across and capable of self-defence in any direction. With companies spread some 300 to 500 yards apart, it was not possible to organize mutually supporting positions in the rugged terrain. The brigade was reinforced by the addition of two companies of the 2nd US Chemical Heavy Mortar Battalion and a company of tanks from the 72nd US Tank Battalion.[36]

When informed midmorning of 23 April of the position the Canadians were to defend, Lieutenant-Colonel Stone immediately organized a reconnaissance group to decide on the best disposition of his companies. As he later recalled,

> I took forward a large reconnaissance party of company commanders, gunner rep[resentative], mortar rep, and the battalion MMG and mortar platoon commanders. We were able to look at the feature from the enemy side, which gave us a good idea of probable attack approaches. Therefore, I was able to select the vital ground which had to be defended to deny the approaches to the enemy.
>
> Hill 677 is about a mile and a half across, gullied, wooded and impossible to defend in the classic manner of deploying companies to support each other. Each company had to develop its own individual defended locality, the platoons being mutually

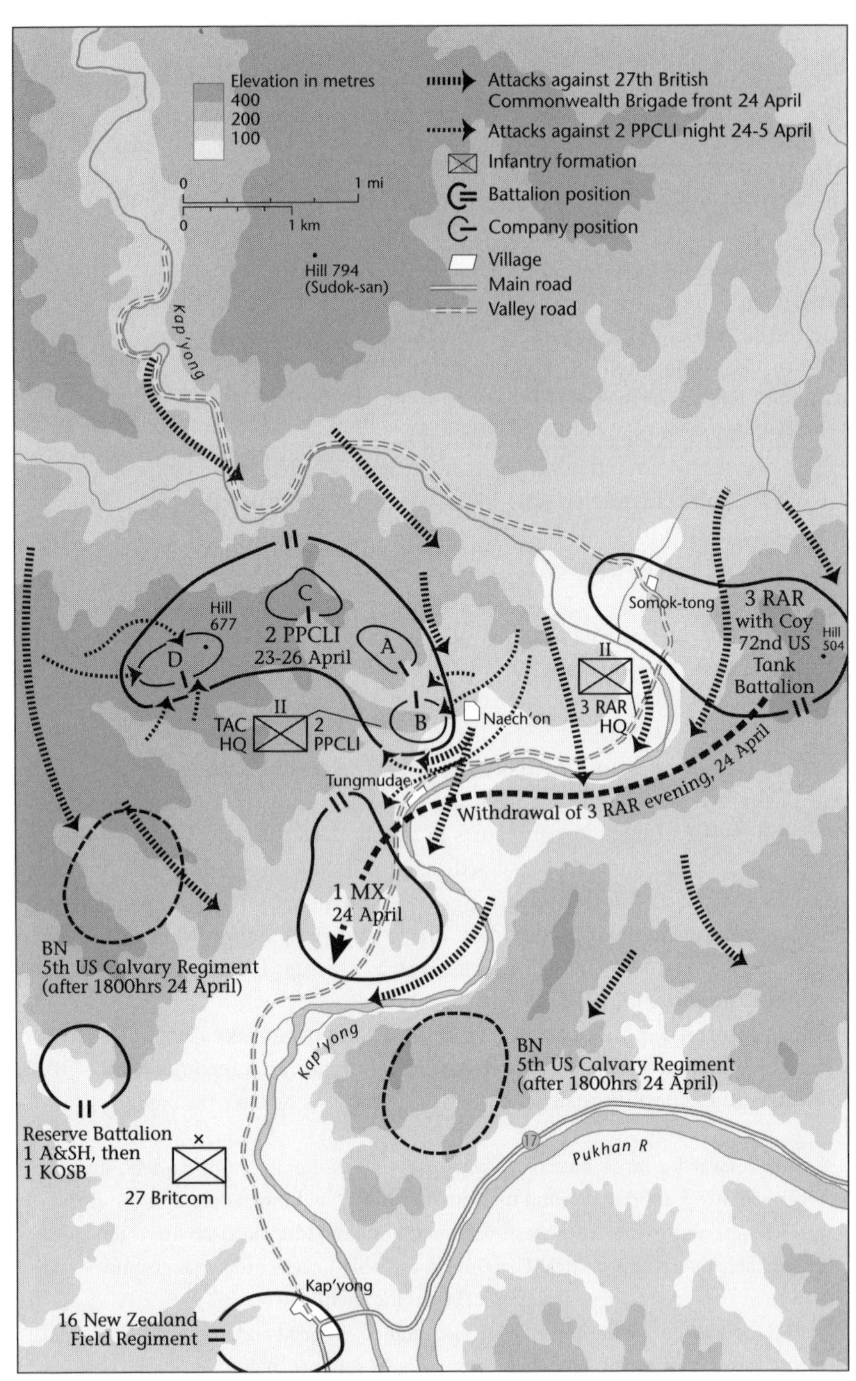

Map 8 *The action at Kap'yong, 24-5 April 1951*

> supporting. The gaps between the companies would have to be covered, to some extent, by defensive fire tasks of the MMGs, the battalion 81mm mortars, the US mortar company and the New Zealand 25-pounder regiment [which returned to the brigade on the night of the 23rd with the routed South Koreans].
>
> I issued orders in the late afternoon of April 23 and we commenced moving into position that afternoon. The defensive plan followed the lines of my appreciation in that companies were in individual defended localities, deployed so that the platoons were mutually supporting. Our six Vickers MMGs were deployed by sections, giving depth to the defence and covering the gaps between the companies. The battalion mortars supported the defensive fire tasks. A company of US 120mm mortars were supporting the total brigade effort, but when the battle got hot on the Australian front, the FOO [forward observation officer] from the US mortars on my front walked out and never a 'pop' did we get from his company.[37]

Across the river, the Australians were taking up their positions on Hill 504. The 3 RAR commander, Lt.-Col. I.B. Ferguson, arranged his companies across the western slopes of the feature nearest the river. As with the Canadians, the distances between the Australian companies prevented them from supporting each other, so each company position was laid out to permit all-round defence. An additional handicap was placed on the 3 RAR defences when Burke, responding to IX Corps directions, ordered Ferguson to place his battalion headquarters on the main valley

The view looking west-southwest across the Kap'yong valley toward Hill 677 (centre background) as seen from near the village of Somok-tong at the foot of the Australian-held Hill 504 (out of sight to the photographer's left). The Patricia A and B Company positions were located behind the first row of hills on the left. DHH 681.009 D2

road southwest of Hill 504 and across the river, to act as a check on the retreating South Koreans. The Australian battalion did have the support of the fifteen Sherman tanks of the 72nd US Tank Battalion, with two platoons deployed along the northwestern base of Hill 504 and two on the valley road near 3 RAR headquarters.[38]

Moving onto the feature during the afternoon of the 23rd, the Australians had little time to prepare their defences. The rearguard position the 6th ROK Division had set up to the north was attacked and routed just after dark by the 60th Division, 20th Army and the 118th Division, 40th Army. While the 20th Army veered off to the west to take part in the enemy's main drive on Seoul, the 118th Division continued its secondary attack down the Kap'yong valley toward the Route 17 crossroads. A flood of ROK troops began streaming through the brigade's lines from around 2000 hours. Mixed in with the routed South Koreans were the New Zealand artillery, the Middlesex battalion, and a 105 mm battery from the 213th US Field Artillery Battalion, all of whom had barely been able to deploy in support of the 6th Division when it broke for the rear. Although the New Zealand and American gunners were able to redeploy north of Kap'yong during the night, the fact that they had not surveyed their positions to determine their exact location in relation to the Australian infantry companies on Hill 504 severely limited the amount of close fire support they could provide before dawn.[39]

The advance elements of the Chinese 118th Division, intent on pursuing the fleeing South Koreans, may not initially have been aware of the Australian presence on Hill 504 and certainly did not know the locations of the RAR companies. The first enemy attack, at 2130 hours, was easily repulsed by the American tanks. A heavier assault an hour later, however, killed two of the tank commanders and prompted the first Sherman platoon to withdraw. For the remainder of the night two battalions of the 354th Regiment launched repeated attacks against the two forward Australian companies on the northwestern spur of Hill 504. B Company, supported by the second tank platoon, drove off each assault, inflicting heavy casualties on the attackers while escaping virtually unscathed themselves.[40]

Farther up the ridge, A Company had a more difficult fight on its hands. Although some of the Chinese attacks were supported by mortar fire, many were simply launched by waves of infantry. The defenders replied with heavy automatic fire from their Bren light machine-guns and Australian-made Owen sub-machine-guns as well as with rifle fire and grenades. With apparently overwhelming numerical superiority, the Chinese rushed forward over heaps of their dead and wounded to close with the A Company positions. Their assaults were preceded by a shower of hand grenades and were repeated with such frequency that it seemed at times to be one continuous onrush of enemy.[41] The beleaguered company suffered fifty casualties during the night in holding the Chinese at bay. To its rear, C and D Companies received little of the enemy's attention and were able to drive off any Chinese that approached their positions with artillery and mortar fire or small skirmishing parties.

It was a rather different situation at battalion headquarters on the valley road a mile to the southwest of the four rifle companies, however, where a second, separate battle soon developed. The 354th Regiment's third battalion had crossed the river near its confluence with the tributary, bypassed 3 RAR headquarters and its supporting US tanks, and established a block on the valley road between the Australian/Americans and the Middlesex and New Zealand positions farther south. For most of the night 3 RAR headquarters was heavily attacked by Chinese infantry from the south and machine-gun fire from the north. The sound of the battle was sufficient to stampede one of the US mortar companies located 500 yards east of the Australian headquarters. The jittery Americans abandoned their vehicles and equipment without firing a shot and fled ten miles to the east soon after the shooting started. By dawn the situation of his defending force had become so untenable that Lieutenant-Colonel Ferguson ordered a withdrawal to the Middlesex perimeter a mile and a half to the south. His four rifle companies on Hill 504, meanwhile, were given a respite from attack until midmorning when a fresh Chinese regiment renewed the assault on their positions. According to the brigade diarist, the Chinese attacks 'continued during daylight and many enemy groups were broken up by artillery fire. 3 RAR were holding their positions against enemy infiltrating parties and the situation around their battalion headquarters had cleared up and was under control.'[42]

Despite holding the enemy at bay throughout the morning and afternoon of the 24th, the problems of resupply and removing the wounded made it 'clear that 3 RAR would not be able to hold their positions for another night.'[43] Their situation prompted Brigadier Burke – in contrast to Brodie's dithering with the Gloucester battalion farther west – to order the Australians to withdraw at 1730 hours rather than risk being cut off and overwhelmed after dark. With the American tanks moving forward to cover their retreat and the New Zealand gunners providing heavy and accurate supporting fire, the four Australian companies moved off Hill 504. Only D Company, which had been holding the summit against fierce opposition, was heavily engaged and pursued as it withdrew last. The twenty-four hours they had spent fending off the enemy's sustained attack had cost 3 RAR thirty-two killed, fifty-nine wounded, and three captured, with most of the casualties falling on A Company and battalion headquarters. The Australians' stout defence and the supporting fire of the New Zealanders, however, had inflicted much heavier casualties on the Chinese attackers and halted their advance against the brigade's right flank by the time the enemy turned their attention to the imposing Canadian-occupied hill mass across the river.[44]

Sitting in their newly dug entrenchments on Hill 677, the Canadians had spent the night of 23-4 April listening to the Australian battle some two miles across the valley. It was not until morning that the Patricias reported increased enemy movement on their front. With the situation deteriorating on his right flank, Stone pulled B Company back from its forward position north of the feature's summit and redeployed it to the east of battalion headquarters on the heights overlooking the valley road. When the move was completed by 1100 hours on 24 April, the battalion's four rifle companies were deployed in a northward arc curving from the summit of Hill 677 in the west to the high ground nearest the Kap'yong River. D Company held the summit of the feature on the battalion's left flank while C Company occupied the forward slope in the centre, with A and B Companies positioned across the right flank. The feature's terrain and vegetation, while making it difficult to provide mutually supporting positions, also limited the enemy's approach routes and gave them little cover for their assaults. According to the Patricias' intelligence officer, Capt. A.P.P. Mackenzie, Hill 677 'was sparsely covered by vegetation':

> The Dog Company position on Hill 677 and the ridgeline leading to the west was covered by high grass nearly a foot to a foot-and-a-half in height and very thick. The summits of all the small ring contours along the ridgeline were topped by isolated trees. Only in the bottoms of the valleys and in steep re-entrants was tree cover heavy ... In the Able Company area the tops of the ridges were again covered by deep grass whereas the lower slopes of the hills on the north and east sides were covered by fairly dense growth of scrub pine standing from six to fourteen feet in height. In the Charlie Company area, northeast from battalion tactical headquarters, the slopes were more heavily wooded. Stand of pine twenty to thirty feet in height covered most of the area. The bottoms of the valley extending to the southeast and south of the main PPCLI position [toward the Middlesex position] were for the most part open pasture ...
>
> Most of the ridges were knife edged and it was very difficult to properly deploy an infantry platoon or company upon them. The steepness of the slopes, while it prevented approaches from all directions, made it extremely difficult to arrange platoons in mutually supporting positions. The extreme steepness of the slopes made movement between the ridges and company positions extremely difficult and tiring. Trails through the area followed the ridgelines almost exclusively and movement off the trails was rendered very difficult by the steepness of the slopes and the heavy type of grass which grew upon them. Visibility was good because of the lack of tree cover on the upper slopes of the ridges. Generally speaking the slope of the land ran from the west to the east. Spurs and ridgelines extended to the southeast from this main ridgeline. The approaches to the PPCLI positions, Dog Company and Able Company in particular, were severe. The only logical line of approach was from the west or from the east [the main directions from which the Chinese, in fact, made their attacks]. A direct north-south movement was hard for the enemy because of the steepness of the slopes and the type of cover found on the lower slopes. The steepness of the slopes made the registration of artillery and mortars very difficult. For the most part artillery and mortar DF [defensive fire] fires were concentrated on the ridgeline approaches to the positions. Invariably because of the steepness of the slope, LMGs and MMGs [light and medium machine-guns] were [also] sited to fire along ridgelines. The steeper approaches to the company and platoon positions were covered by rifle fire and hand grenades.[45]

The daylight hours of 24 April passed with little enemy activity on the Canadian front as the Chinese continued to concentrate their attacks on the Australians across the river. As recorded by the battalion war diarist, the Patricias used the time to continue digging in 'as rapidly as possible in preparation for heavy attacks that were expected that night. Throughout the day, reports continued to come in from the forward companies of an enemy build-up all along the battalion front.'[46] The Canadians also selected and registered the defensive fire tasks of their machine-guns and 60 mm and 81 mm mortars. The three 60 mm mortars assigned to each company were grouped at company headquarters and assigned fire tasks along the ridgelines out to their maximum range of 2,000 yards. According to Captain Mackenzie, the company mortars' range and accuracy 'made it possible for them to take over the role of the 81mm mortar ... Because of their stability, 60mm mortars could be fired at a high rate for some time without getting too far off their target. Their ability to hit the narrow ridgelines consistently was of great assistance at Kap'yong.' The Canadians also made use of the afternoon to bring forward supplies and ammunition to the company positions. To conceal their movements from enemy observation, they used phosphorus mortar bombs to set fire to the grass slopes. Only when the resulting smoke lifted were the Chinese able to fire accurate bursts of harassing machine-gun fire on the PPCLI positions.[47]

Although the Australian rifle companies had to be withdrawn from Hill 504 at nightfall on the 24th, the brigade's defence of the valley was reinforced during the afternoon by the arrival of the 5th US Cavalry Regiment, dispatched earlier in the day by the IX Corps commander to ensure that Kap'yong would be held. One of the American battalions was deployed to the southwest of the Patricia's D Company position on the summit of Hill 677 to cover the rear left flank while a second battalion occupied high ground across the river and southeast of the Middlesex positions. Although one of the 3 RAR rifle companies and the headquarters group had been hard hit in the battle around Hill 504, its remaining three rifle companies had emerged largely unscathed, while the 1st Battalion, King's Own Scottish Borderers had arrived during the 24th and had taken up positions with the Australians on the hills around brigade headquarters.[48] With six battalions now positioned along the valley within four miles of Kap'yong, it would have proven extremely difficult for the depleted 118th Division to have reached the important Route 17 crossroads south of the village, the road between Seoul and Ch'unch'on.

After their success in clearing the Australians from Hill 504, however, the Chinese were not about to abandon their attempt to destroy the Commonwealth brigade and, in all likelihood, were unaware of the American reinforcements that had arrived to add greater depth to the 27th Brigade's defence of the valley. Although the capture of Hill 504 had opened up a number of foot tracks through the hills to the east by which infantry groups could have reached Route 17, the valley road remained blocked to the passage of the artillery and supply vehicles the enemy would need for a farther drive to the south. In order for the 118th Division to continue its

Looking northwest toward Hill 677 from the valley road. The Chinese infiltrated down the valley to attack the Patricia's B Company, which was holding the high ground directly above the valley floor in the left-centre of the photograph. The village of Naech'on can be seen to the right. DHH 681.009 D2

advance, therefore, it still had to dislodge the Patricias from the dominating heights of Hill 677. The enemy having spotted the move of B Company earlier in the day, the men nearest the valley road were the first to be attacked by an estimated force of 200 infantry shortly after 2200 hours. The initial assault was easily beaten back by the company's own automatic fire and the battalion mortars, but a second assault an hour later managed to overrun the right forward platoon position. The men were able to withdraw in small groups back to the main company positions where the attack was defeated. The next morning fifty-one dead Chinese were counted in front of the B Company entrenchments.[49]

While B Company was driving off its attackers, its commander, Major Lilley, warned battalion headquarters that a force of some 100 Chinese had entered a reentrant to the south and were heading for its position. Having positioned six of the mortar platoon's twelve half-tracks at his headquarters, each of which was equipped with a .50 and .30 calibre Browning machine-gun, Stone was well prepared to handle the incursion. According to the CO, 'We held fire until the Chinamen broke through the trees about 200 yards away, and then twelve machine-guns cut loose together. What with the rattle of the guns and the mortars firing at their

shortest range, the enemy never had a chance.'[50] Lilley believed that the power of the defence was greatly aided by the rudimentary command and control arrangements of the attackers. From his position,

> it was a heartening sight to see the battalion 81mm mortars firing at their shortest range (200 yards) together with their .50 calibre machine-guns which literally blew the Chinese back down the ravine.
>
> The Chinese telegraphed the direction and timing of their attacks by using MMG tracer ammunition for direction, sounding bugles as signals to form up on their start line and for their assault. This gave company and platoon commanders time to bring down accurate artillery, mortar and machine-gun fire on them.
>
> Before attacking in strength the Chinese did not accurately locate our defensive positions by patrolling nor did they give accurate artillery and mortar supporting fire to their troops.
>
> The steep gradients to our positions forced the Chinese to use a monkey-run attitude in their final assault; although rifle fire in the darkness was not too effective at such small targets, grenades trundled down the hills had a devastating effect.

Rocket launchers were used in an anti-personnel role and proved deadly.

The Chinese appeared to be well-trained and disciplined but lacked initiative. Only on orders would their squads fire their weapons or throw grenades.

Their consistent attacks en masse on obvious approaches in an attempt to overwhelm our positions by sheer weight of numbers presented ideal targets for our artillery, mortars and machine-guns.[51]

In its haste to follow up the collapse of the 6th ROK Division, the 118th Division had left its artillery and supplies well to the north. What mortar ammunition the Chinese had had largely been expended against the Australians the previous day and only a few mortar bombs were fired on the Canadian positions. Moreover, the uncoordinated attacks against the various PPCLI positions allowed the entire strength of the New Zealand artillery regiment to fire in support of each company and break up many of the attacks before they closed with the Canadians. Shortly after the second attack on B Company was repelled, for instance, the Patricias spotted a large body of enemy infantry fording the river and called down a heavy concentration of artillery. In the bright moonlight, the Canadians could see the enemy break and run for cover; they counted seventy-one dead Chinese along the riverbanks next morning. The supporting artillery fire also proved crucial when the enemy turned their attention to D Company, holding the feature's summit. The Chinese launched their assaults on the battalion's left flanking company from both the northern slopes of Hill 677 and the ridgeline running off to the west toward Hill 865. According to the company commander's subsequent report on the action, his men had remained largely undisturbed as they listened to the

amazingly large volume of small arms fire from the direction of Tac HQ and B positions. This fire finally subsided until we could hear only the occasional burst. At approximately 0110 hours we received word, via the wireless, from Lieutenant Levy, 10 Platoon commander [holding the westernmost position], that Corporal Clouthier had reported the enemy were assembled in the saddle [that led off toward Hill 865] known [by the artillery fire task code-word] as FOX III. Immediately we received this word, we heard a Bren gun from 10 Platoon open fire. I called for fire task FOX III. Levy asked the MMG in 12 Platoon positions to open fire on the enemy.

The machine gunners immediately fired on the enemy with such deadly accuracy that the enemy stopped his main attack on 10 Platoon. The enemy then directed his main assault against the MMG thus relieving the pressure on 10 Platoon. The enemy in their attack against the 10 Platoon feature used machine-guns and mortars to cover their assault. The enemy attacked across the small saddle overrunning one section of 12 Platoon and the MMG. This was accomplished by sheer weight of numbers. The machine-gun continued firing until the crew was completely overrun. Four men from the 12 Platoon section which were protecting the MMG post were able to disengage and make their way over to 10 Platoon positions where they carried on the fire fight.

> They reported that the two machine gunners had been killed at their post. Also two Koreans, who comprised part of the MMG section, were able to make their way to 10 Platoon positions. The enemy having gained possession of our MMG endeavoured to use it but 10 Platoon covered the gun and the position with LMG fire by Private Baxter and rendered the MMG useless. Sergeant Holligan reported that the enemy were building up in the area known as fire task ABLE I. We asked for fire on FOX III and ABLE I, as this seemed to be the main line of approach.[52]

In engaging the prearranged target areas, the New Zealand gunners were ordered to fire at the 'slow' rate of two rounds per gun per minute so that twenty-four rounds landed every thirty seconds in a target area some 200 yards wide. The rate of fire was subsequently halved to 'very slow' to conserve ammunition, but the weight of the assaults quickly prompted the Canadians to request that it be increased to the 'slow' rate.[53] With swarms of enemy infiltrating between his platoon positions and mounting attacks on company headquarters on the hill's summit, D Company commander, Capt. J.G.W. Mills, called for the artillery to shift its fire directly onto his position. The tactic succeeded in clearing the exposed Chinese off the feature's summit while causing no casualties to the dug-in Canadians. Although the discouraged enemy persisted in launching small attacks against D Company for the remainder of the night, each was successfully driven off by the supporting artillery and the men's own small-arms fire. At first light the company was still holding firm in its position and was able to recover the abandoned Vickers machine-guns. On the opposite flank, B Company was also able to reoccupy the platoon position it had been forced to evacuate early in the fight. Stone informed brigade headquarters 'that the enemy were still pressing their attacks but the situation was under control.'[54]

The Patricias' greatest immediate concern at daybreak was the fact that the Chinese had established blocking positions on the roads south of the battalion, temporarily cutting off the Canadians from resupply. Anticipating that his men would have to continue the battle that night, Stone requested that needed ammunition, food, and water be air-dropped onto the Hill 677 position. Although the aircraft and supplies had to come all the way from Japan, at 1030 hours four American C-119 transports 'dropped, by parachute, everything requested, including 81mm mortar ammunition. When it comes to supply, you cannot beat the US forces,' he later recalled.[55] As the C rations and ammunition were distributed among the men, 'the companies continued to improve their positions in case of a delay of the battalion's relief and in anticipation of continued Chinese attack.' The Middlesex battalion had sent out patrols that morning to clear the enemy that had infiltrated behind Hill 677 during the night but it was not until 1400 hours that patrols from 2 PPCLI's B Company 'reported the road at the base of the battalion position clear of the enemy and Lieutenant-Colonel Stone requested that further supplies and reinforcements be brought up by vehicle as rapidly as possible.'[56]

For the most part, the daylight hours of 25 April were relatively quiet although the Chinese continued to direct harassing fire on the PPCLI positions. D Company in particular received heavy machine-gun fire on its forward platoons from Hill 865 to the west. The enemy made no attempt to attack; enemy activity was confined to light patrolling all across the Patricias' front, and none of the patrols was able to penetrate the battalion perimeter. The Canadians were assisted by American tanks ordered forward to help clear the remaining Chinese from Hill 677's northern slopes. Any concentration of enemy infantry the Patricias spotted was immediately hit by 'frequent artillery shoots' and an air strike that 'was put in with good effect.'[57] After the Middlesex Regiment relieved the American battalion positioned to the south-west of 2 PPCLI, the 5th US Cavalry Regiment put in an attack to recover Hill 504 from the Chinese in mid-afternoon. The American assault was resisted until 1600 hours when the 118th Division suddenly withdrew. Having left their supplies of food and ammunition far behind in their rush down the Kap'yong valley two days earlier, the Chinese now had to pull back to regroup and replenish their formations. Subsequent US patrols to the north of the feature were not engaged by the enemy, and a 5th Cavalry tank/infantry force was also able to patrol east along Route 17 toward Ch'unch'on without making contact. 'By last light the situation on the brigade front was quiet and reports of enemy had ceased,' the brigade's war diarist noted with considerable satisfaction. 'It appears that the enemy has failed completely to dislodge the [27th] Brigade and 5th Cavalry Regiment from these positions guarding Kap'yong and so has failed to cut the important Seoul/Ch'unch'on road in the Kap'yong area.'[58]

The entire brigade, and particularly the Australians and Canadians, had ample reason to be proud of their achievement. At a cost to the two battalions of forty-two killed, eighty-two wounded, and three missing – of whom ten dead and twenty-three wounded were Patricias – the brigade had held off repeated attacks by two Chinese regiments totalling some 6,000 soldiers. The Patricias estimated that they (with the New Zealand artillery) had killed some 300 of the enemy during their night action.[59] Combined with the casualties inflicted by the Australians, the two battalions likely reduced the attacking force by a quarter to a third of its original strength. As the American official history points out, 'that two battalions and a tank company had withstood attacks no weaker, and perhaps stronger, than those that twice had routed the ROK 6th Division underscored how completely control had broken down in the [South Korean] division. The huge tally of equipment lost as a result of the division's successive debacles emphasized the breakdown further.'[60] The Commonwealth units' steadiness under fire was further underscored by the manner in which Company B of the 2nd US Chemical Mortar Battalion, in position behind Hill 504 on the night of 23-4 April, abruptly abandoned their weapons and equipment and took to their heels without ever being fired upon. The fear of being overrun by hordes of advancing Chinese that still gripped some American and South Korean units was noticeably absent from the ranks of the Canadians and Australians.

Their determined stand above Kap'yong certainly did not go unnoticed by the American high command. For their efforts, 2 PPCLI, 3 RAR, and Company A, 72nd US Tank Battalion were each subsequently recognized with a US Presidential Unit Citation, the only occasion a Canadian Army unit has received such an award. Despite the honour, however, Lieutenant-Colonel Stone was still able to place the action in perspective:

> Kap'yong was not a great battle, as battles go. It was a good battle, well-planned and well-fought. Personally, I believe that Kap'yong was the limit of the planned offensive of the Chinese at that time. Had that limit been five miles further south we should have been annihilated, as were the Glosters. The numbers that the Chinese were prepared to sacrifice against a position meant that eventually any unsupported battalion in defence must be over-run. The Chinese soldier is tough and brave. All that he lacked at the time of Kap'yong were communications and supply. Perhaps death was preferable to the life he was compelled to lead, for he certainly was not afraid to die. Therefore, I say that we were lucky that he did not persist with his attacks.[61]

Of course, the situations facing 2 PPCLI and 1 Gloucesters in their respective battles were not the same. The 29th Brigade had to contend with the three fresh divisions of the Chinese 63rd Army, formations that were making their initial assaults in a drive that was supposed to take them to Seoul and, as a consequence, had supporting mortar and artillery fire available to them. The troops of the 118th Division attacking the Canadians and Australians, on the other hand, had already routed a South Korean division before moving rapidly down the Kap'yong valley in an attempt to exploit their breakthrough and reach Route 17 in the subsequent confusion. In their twenty-mile rush south, the Chinese infantry had left their supplies and supporting weapons well behind them. What mortar bombs the 118th Division's leading regiments had carried were largely used in their attacks on the Australians. In terms of support, at the Imjin battle, the 63rd Army had infiltrated large masses of infantry around the British battalions, isolating them and cutting off their retreat. Although the Ulster and Northumberland battalions managed to cut their way out with the aid of British armour, the I Corps commander, inadequately informed by Brigadier Brodie of the dire situation the British were facing, did not provide sufficient reinforcements to extricate the surrounded Gloucester battalion. In contrast, the IX Corps commander reinforced the 27th Brigade with an entire regimental combat team even though they were not as hard pressed. While the 5th Cavalry did not take an active role in the fighting until they recaptured Hill 504 on the afternoon of 25 April, they were in position behind the Canadians and available to assist them by the evening of the 24th.

Stone's contention that 2 PPCLI would have met the same fate as the Gloucesters if the Chinese had intended to drive farther south than Kap'yong is, therefore, somewhat misleading. Although groups of the enemy were able to infiltrate south of Hill

677 during the night, thus necessitating an air drop to provide immediate resupply, 2 PPCLI was far from being cut off. The Canadian unit had not suffered heavily in fending off the Chinese attacks, was completely intact for a breakout attempt if that had been necessary, and was less than a mile from the defensive perimeters of its supporting battalions. As it was, the Chinese troops that were blocking the roads south of the Patricias on the morning of the 25th were relatively few in number and withdrew when pressed by the Middlesex and Patricia patrols. The heavily depleted Gloucesters, who made their futile attempt at a breakout that same morning, had to fight their way for over four miles against a large portion of the Chinese 198th Division to reach safety. Only a handful managed to do so. It also should not be forgotten that it was primarily the bungling of higher commanders, both British and American, that lost the British battalion, rather than some unexpected action on the part of the Chinese. The Patricias were never in that position.

Nonetheless, there can be little doubt that 2 PPCLI performed well in a very difficult situation. Although the extent of the ground to be covered meant that the company positions were too spread out to support each other, Stone's battle experience had allowed him to position them on 'the ground that was vital to the defence of the area.'[62] His timely shift of B Company to cover the battalion's right flank in anticipation of an Australian withdrawal from Hill 504 also prevented the Chinese from turning the position at the outset of the contest. The steep approaches to the two company positions in the centre, meanwhile, kept them from being heavily attacked. Once companies were placed in the most advantageous positions possible, however, it was the men in the slit trenches and weapons pits – and their immediate leaders – who determined the battle's outcome. With its strong leavening of officers and NCOs with Second World War battle experience to guide and steady the men under fire, 2 PPCLI was a better prepared unit than its two months of operations in Korea might otherwise suggest. It was certainly the CO's opinion that 'the success of Kap'yong was due mainly to high morale and to good company, platoon and section commanders. In their isolated defence areas they kept their heads down, the morale of their troops up, and their weapons firing. Whatever support I could give, I gave, but the battle was theirs.' The Patricias had also 'trained and fought together for some eight months; we believed in one another, and the morale of the battalion was high. No one panicked, even when we knew we were surrounded and that there was some infiltration of the position by the enemy ... We could have run, panicked in some way, or surrendered. We stayed, fought and withdrew on orders in a soldierly fashion. This, in itself, was unique in Korea where "bug-outs" were the normal manner of withdrawing. In the circumstances, I say that the award [of the Presidential Citation] was well earned and the battalion deserved public recognition of its actions of April 24/25, 1951.'[63]

The Patricias continued to hold their positions on Hill 677 until the evening of 26 April when they were relieved by a battalion of the 5th US Cavalry Regiment. That same day Brigadier Burke passed command of the units to Brig. G. Taylor and the 28th British Commonwealth Brigade, as the 27th Brigade headquarters left the theatre to return to Hong Kong. As the reconstituted Commonwealth formation was pulled back into IX Corps reserve to the southwest of Kap'yong near the junction of the Pukhan and Chojong Rivers, the momentum of the Chinese drive on Seoul had clearly been halted. General Van Fleet could take considerable satisfaction that, although the Chinese had penetrated his line at several points, they had been unable to breach it. Nonetheless, the presence of Chinese infiltrators behind several of his forward divisions, and growing intelligence indicating a renewal of the communist attacks, persuaded the Eighth Army commander to give his forces some breathing space by pulling them back some twenty to thirty miles to a new, unnamed defence line – quickly dubbed the 'No Name Line' – running across the peninsula from just north of Seoul and curving northeast, ten miles south of Ch'unch'on, to reach Wonpo-ri on the east coast. In pulling back to the new line, IX Corps evacuated the hills above Kap'yong to take up new positions along the Han River some twenty miles to the south.

The abandonment of the Kap'yong position undoubtedly irked the Commonwealth troops who had fought so stubbornly to defend it. It was the Patricia CO's opinion that 'the withdrawal had been unnecessary. After breaking contact and falling back twenty miles, it was found there were no Chinese within eighteen miles. The withdrawal had been ordered when the Chinese had forced a retreat on the 24th Division by a flank attack.'[64] Stone's view, of course, was less a comment on the overall wisdom of Van Fleet's strategic withdrawal and more a reflection of the frustration of surrendering hard-won territory without a fight. Whatever the feelings of the Canadians, by 1 May 2 PPCLI had taken up its new defensive positions at the junction of the Han and Pukhan Rivers and, with the other units of the 28th Brigade, begun constructing strong entrenchments covered by barbed-wire entanglements and minefields. Even as they did so, the Patricias' days with the British Commonwealth formation were drawing to a close. They were about to be joined on the peninsula by the rest of the Canadian brigade.

5 THE BRIGADE ARRIVES, MAY-JULY 1951

By the time the US transports carrying the remainder of the 25th Canadian Infantry Brigade docked in Pusan harbour on 4 May 1951, the Chinese Fifth Phase Offensive had clearly lost its momentum. Prisoners captured during the last day of April had been carrying scant, if any, rations and reported that resupply from the north was now virtually nonexistent as a result of the Far East Air Force's interdiction of the communist lines of communication. Heavy casualties, particularly among the political officers responsible for maintaining motivation and discipline within the Chinese Army's ranks, were also hurting unit cohesion and coordination. It was reported that commanders had issued only vague orders for units to 'go to Seoul' or to 'go as far south as possible.' During its first week, the spring offensive had cost the communists 13,349 known dead, and Eighth Army headquarters estimated that a total of 24,000 enemy had been killed. With US Army losses at only 314 killed and 1,600 wounded – Commonwealth, ROK, and other UN contingent losses brought the totals to 547 killed, 2,024 wounded, and 2,170 captured – the disparity between the two sides' casualties reflected the devastating effect of the UN's enormous firepower when directed against massed infantry. UN Command headquarters in Tokyo estimated that the enemy lost between 75,000 and 80,000 in killed and wounded in the offensive.[1] While American casualty estimates were notorious for being inflated, there is little doubt that the communists had suffered severely. A Chinese history of the war describes the situation facing the 64th and 65th Armies north of Seoul in the wake of the fierce resistance offered by the 29th British Brigade as follows:

> The result was that five divisions, totalling about 50,000 men or more, were squeezed into a confined space of about twenty square kilometres on the south bank of the Imjin River for as long as two days, during which time they were subjected to concentrated enemy air and artillery bombardment and suffered severe losses ... After this, although the troops managed to continue their advance, the main strength of the enemy forces to the north of Seoul had already made a complete withdrawal. By 29 April ... the food and ammunition which the men of the Volunteer Army had been carrying for themselves had basically been used up, and since the situation for attacking a strongly defended city was clearly unfavourable, P'eng Teh-huai resolutely decided to halt the attack, and the troops were switched to rest and reorganization.[2]

Despite their losses, the communists still had nearly 750,000 soldiers in Korea of which 300,000 were believed to be in position to launch further attacks, primarily in the eastern half of the peninsula. General P'eng was, in fact, already planning to renew his offensive in this sector, against the X and ROK Corps. On 1 May, General Van Fleet cautioned the Eighth Army against reading too much into the present lull in the Chinese offensive, warning that the communists retained sufficient strength to continue the attack 'as hard as before or harder.'[3] To defend against a renewed offensive, Van Fleet deployed seven American and nine Korean divisions along the No Name Line that ran northeast from just north of Seoul on the west coast to Wonpo-ri on the east coast (see Map 5, p. 68). On the western side of the peninsula, covering the approaches to Seoul, was the I US Corps with the 1st ROK, 1st US Cavalry, and 25th US Divisions in the line and the 3rd US Division and 29th British Brigade – recovering from its mauling on the Imjin River – in reserve. To their right was the IX US Corps with the 7th US, 24th US, 2nd ROK, and 6th ROK Divisions in the line and the 187th Airborne Regimental Combat Team in reserve.

Throughout the first half of May, the 28th British Commonwealth Brigade was under the command of the 24th Division while it held positions along the Han River. The peninsula's central sector, from the Ch'unch'on-Hongch'on corridor to the Taebaek mountains, was held by the X US Corps with the US 1st Marine and 2nd Divisions on the left and the ROK 5th and 7th Divisions on the right. The remaining four ROK divisions, divided between the ROK I and III Corps, extended the UN line from the Taebaek mountains to the Sea of Japan.[4] It was along the X Corps' central front that the communists had placed most of their fresh troops and it was there that Van Fleet anticipated a renewed enemy offensive.

The fighting front remained relatively quiet as the 25th Brigade was disembarking in Pusan. During the first days of May, the Eighth Army patrolled intensively up to five miles north of the No Name Line in an attempt to locate and identify enemy formations, but no significant contact could be made, and it was apparent that the enemy had fallen back toward the thirty-eighth parallel to regroup.[5] In addition to allowing the Eighth Army to reorganize and rebuild supply stockpiles, the respite gave the Canadians two weeks to unload their stores and vehicles. Not least among their preparations was the need for the newly arrived soldiers to adjust to the decidedly foreign sights and smells of Pusan. As Ridgway commented in his memoirs, there was 'one feature of Korea that every fighting man will remember – the smell. The use of human excrement – night soil – to fertilize the fields, the husbanding of that commodity in pails and barrels, and in leaky wagons, give to the atmosphere of the country a fragrance so overpowering that the soul at first rebels.'[6]

Having been forewarned, virtually every member of the brigade 'was on deck and awaited for the "terrible smell" that was described by the members of the first Advanced Party' as their ship dropped anchor. For the many Second World War veterans among them who remembered war-ravaged Europe, initial impressions were tempered by earlier experience. The 2 RCR war diarist, for instance, observed, 'Though the harbour, both outer and inner, was full of ships, the odour was no worse than that found in many parts of the world.'[7] But once the Canadians had debarked the next day and were moving through the narrow, dusty streets to their new base at an abandoned prisoner-of-war camp, the stark conditions of overcrowded Pusan led them to conclude otherwise. As Brigadier Rockingham later recalled, 'The lack of sanitation when a normal population is present is bad enough, but when a place like Pusan has had its population increased from 600,000 to 2,000,000 by refugees, you can imagine the result. The stench was so bad that it seemed to slow the motors of our vehicles as we drove through a particularly heavy concentration.'[8] With most of its refugees living in temporary corrugated-iron shelters, the Korean city looked depressing to the men from North America: 'The portion of Pusan that we saw presented a pitiful aspect. The people are poorly clothed and live in foul smelling hovels. Every block has "home brew" and saki stills. "OFF LIMITS" signs are posted everywhere for obvious reasons. Congenital syphilis, active syphilis and gonnhorea [sic] are prevalent. On reaching the rural areas the scene was more palatable. The country has a peculiar beauty, with the sides of the mountains and hills terraced for growing (every inch of arable land is tilled). The vegetation is a bright green. The people appear quite picturesque, although they smell.'[9]

Fighting in a primitive countryside that had changed little in a thousand years, a soldier's revulsion toward his physical surroundings often led to disdain for the Korean people themselves. As one newly arrived Canadian recalled, 'We were on deck waiting to disembark and we could see American MPs literally beating kids with 45s and rifle butts. We were booing them and we thought that this was so terrible. They told us to mind our own business because sooner or later we would be doing the same thing ourselves. I never saw a Canadian hit a child but you did become very callous.'[10] Fraternization between the relatively wealthy young Canadians and the poverty-stricken local populace was certainly discouraged, with at least one CO warning his men not to 'associate with natives male or female. They are all disease laden and many are thieves.'[11]

The Koreans also appeared to maintain a casual disregard for human life, an attitude Rockingham noted soon after his arrival in the Far East: 'One day in Pusan, I noticed a truck driven by an ROK soldier run over and kill a Korean child of about seven. The driver got out of his cab and dragged the child by its foot to the side of the road and then headed back to his truck. The ROK truck was being followed by several Canadians who would not let the Korean just drive away. I intervened in the incident and made a report to the Korean army. They didn't actually say "so what" but managed to convey that impression.'[12]

With the Chinese offensive expected to resume at any time, the Canadians had little time to take in the exotic locale. After two and a half weeks aboard a cramped ship, one of the first priorities for the Canadian brigade was resuming physical training. Rockingham immediately ordered daily hill climbs to condition the men.[13] On 11 May, the brigade embarked on Exercise Charley Horse, with D Company, 2 RCR, as 'the first victims. Considering that the men have had very little practice in hill climbing they performed excellently. In addition to personal weapons and large packs, a section of 81 mm mortars and all platoon 3.5 [inch] rocket launchers were toted up the 2,000 foot peak.'[14] During the week and a half the brigade spent conditioning and preparing its weapons in the hills outside Pusan, Rockingham also exchanged some of its original equipment for weaponry more suited to Korean conditions. In view of the scarcity of enemy armour at the front, the infantry's cumbersome 17-pounder antitank guns were replaced by American 75 mm recoilless rifles. Their flat trajectory made them valuable for attacking enemy bunkers dug into the steep Korean hillsides, which were otherwise immune to artillery fire. The Americans had found that 'when the CCF [Chinese communist forces] have as many as four to ten days in which to organize a ridgeline position, they customarily hinge it upon machine-gun bunkers built close to the skyline.' These bunkers were so stoutly built that 'except for a direct hit, light artillery fire cannot neutralize it.' 'At ranges between 1,000 and 1,200 yards, the 75 recoilless is the only piece which can take them under direct fire, with a relatively good chance of hitting dead on and destroying the object in one round ... In this type of usage, they have justified themselves time and again,' explained S.L.A. Marshall in a contemporary report.[15]

The other equipment change involved the brigade's armoured squadron, which had been redesignated C Squadron, Lord Strathcona's Horse (Royal Canadians) on 31 March in place of the somewhat despised A Squadron, 1st/2nd Canadian Armoured Regiment (the tankers having grown weary of being referred to as the 'Half-Armoured Regiment'). Soon after arriving in Pusan, Rockingham arranged to replace the squadron's M10 tank destroyers with regular Sherman tanks. Once again, the absence of enemy armour made an antitank squadron unnecessary while tank support for infantry operations was an important element in the fluid Korean fighting. 'Since this M-10 equipment had an open turret,' Rockingham later explained, 'it was evident that they would be an easy target for enemy mortar and artillery fire and [the open turret] would form a convenient basket into which enemy ambush parties positioned on high ridges near the road could throw grenades. Permission was obtained from AHQ [in Ottawa] to purchase either Centurions, Pattons or Shermans. After much discussion with both British and American officers, and the squadron commander, it was decided to purchase Shermans. The change was made on the second day after landing and the squadron went into action with these tanks.'[16]

Although Ottawa had granted permission to buy Centurions, the British tanks had War Office restrictions placed on their employment (they were not to be captured) and the nearest repair depot was in Japan. The Patton tank, meanwhile, 'was not immediately available, showed itself to have too many novel features and certain mechanical "bugs" to be suitable.'[17] The readily available M4A3 Sherman, on the other hand, came highly recommended by the 1st Marine Division, who were already using them in Korea, and aside from having a gasoline rather than diesel engine, was the same model used by armoured units in Canada. Its reliable engine, moreover, gave the vehicle plenty of power to handle steep gradients, whereas the Centurion repeatedly exhibited shortcomings in the rugged Korean terrain. With the brigade heading to the front within days, the choice was relatively easy. On 17 and 18 May, C Squadron picked up twenty Sherman tanks from the American ordnance depot in Pusan and quickly loaded them on flat cars for the brigade's move north.[18]

With its acclimatization exercises at Pusan completed by mid-May, the 25th Brigade was ordered north to a concentration area just east of Suwon in I Corps reserve. Eighth Army headquarters insisted that the Canadian troops be transported by train while their vehicles and most of their equipment made their way north over the primitive Korean road network. Rockingham 'objected to this very strongly because I did not want them separated from their vehicles, but to no avail ... The troops moving by train were without mortars, machine guns, radio, or other essentials for fighting. The situation at the front was pretty fluid and my only victory by persuasion was that I was able to make the meeting place for the troops and vehicles much further from the front than Eighth Army wanted it. Short of refusing the order, there seemed no way out.'[19] Peering out the windows of their dilapidated rail cars as they chugged north, the Canadians were greeted by a ravaged landscape: 'The signs of war became more evident as we moved across the peninsula. Bullet holes in buildings, shell holes and finally complete havoc in Taejon. The road was littered with shattered tanks and American half-tracks. Bridges and tunnels were blown up and the tops of some of the hills had been burnt by Napalm bombs.'[20]

Even as the Canadians were en route, the renewal of the communist offensive altered the plan to move them into I Corps reserve. For the second instalment of his Fifth Phase Offensive, P'eng Teh-huai decided to shift the main axis of attack to the Taebaek mountains in the eastern sector, where most of the line was held by South Korean formations and the more rugged terrain would reduce the Eighth Army's advantages in transport, artillery, and air support. In doing so, P'eng had to overcome his continuing concern that the United Nations would mount yet another amphibious landing in the communists' rear. It was not until Beijing pointed out that the Eighth Army's withdrawal to the No Name Line indicated that they were unlikely to make an amphibious landing in the near future that P'eng reconsidered resuming the attack.[21] The stout defence of the western sector put up by the I and IX Corps – led by the actions of the 29th and 27th Brigades on the Imjin and above Kap'yong – had convinced the Chinese commander to exploit the inexperience of the South Korean army instead. Concentrating five Chinese armies and three North Korean corps east of the Hwach'on Reservoir, P'eng planned to drive a wedge down the Hongch'on River valley to isolate the six ROK divisions on the eastern flank from Eighth Army support and destroy them.

At dusk on 16 May, the Chinese 27th Army thrust its 81st Division between the ROK 5th and 7th Divisions and, like the 6th Division above Kap'yong, both formations were easily routed. To their right, the ROK III Corps also disintegrated, caught between the 81st Division and the assaults of the North Korean V Corps. By the early morning hours of 17 May 'reports revealed a familiar story of infantry units scattered by enemy attacks while they were attempting to disengage, broken communications, loss of control, a search for missing troops, and the reorganization of those that could be found.'[22] The South Korean collapse left the right flank of General Almond's X Corps wide open, and its eastern-most formation, the 2nd Division, came under attack by the Chinese 12th Army and elements of the 15th. To meet the threat Van Fleet extended the IX Corps' boundary to the east, thereby reducing X Corps' sector, and reinforced the latter formation with the 3rd US Division (less two regimental combat teams) from I Corps and the 8th ROK Division brought forward from its antiguerrilla duties in the south.[23]

While the Canadian brigade's units were strung out along the Korean road and rail network on the way to Suwon, Rockingham was summoned to an Eighth Army conference at an airstrip near the Han River on the 17th. There he was informed that a large enemy attack was being mounted on the central sector held by the X Corps, and that the 3rd Division was to move from its current positions along the Han River into X Corps reserve. Van Fleet proposed using the Canadians to man the vacated Han River defences left by the 3rd Division's 65th Regiment and asked Rockingham 'when the brigade would be ready. The brigadier replied that 2 RCHA was already in action with 28th British [Commonwealth] Brigade and needed only to be moved a few miles to support us, but that 2 RCR and 2 R22eR were still on the move up from Pusan. However, the brigadier pointed out he could have them deployed by last light on Sunday, 20 May 1951. General Van Fleet agreed to the timing.'[24] Rockingham and Van Fleet then toured the positions to be taken up by the Canadians in the 65th Regiment's sector.

Although the timing of the move agreed by Van Fleet and Rockingham had been for last light on the 20th, on the night of 18-19 May the staffs at army and corps headquarters unilaterally decided to move the Canadians' scheduled deployment ahead by some thirty-six hours. The situation the Canadian brigadier found himself in was identical to the position Lieutenant-Colonel Stone had faced the previous January when Eight Army headquarters had also ordered the Patricias to make a premature deployment. 'Ordered to commit 2 RCR by 0900 hours [on] 19 May,' the army's historical section later recorded, 'Brigadier Rockingham refused, as the brigade was in [the] process of moving up and 2 RCR would not arrive until 0200 hours that morning. They had only fifty rounds of ammunition each, and no signals communication or other equipment. Throughout the night [of 18-19 May the] chiefs of staff at corps and army [headquarters] continued to repeat the order, which the brigade commander continued to refuse, suggesting at one stage that he was prepared to be relieved of his command rather than commit his troops before they were ready.'[25]

Writing to the Canadian historical section in July 1953 to clarify the details of the incident, Rockingham stated that he 'would prefer that you said protest instead of "refuse"' and reiterated that 'the infantry, travelling in trains, had only their rifles and fifty rounds of ammunition, while the rest of their equipment was on the road which meant that they were without such essential things as wireless sets, mortars, aircraft recognition panels, spare ammunition, etc. It was the lack of these items and the uncertainty of the time of arrival of these two elements which made me reluctant to agree to put the troops in the line by 0900 hours on 19 May. Since this matter is likely to be a controversial one, I would appreciate it if you could go into more detail.'[26] In his unpublished memoir Rockingham later recalled that he had 'felt thoroughly miserable refusing my first task. However, I was determined that my troops would not be put into action when they were missing so much of their essential equipment. I felt that it was my duty to give them a fair chance on this, their first encounter with a skilful and numerous enemy. In the back of my mind was the experience of our Hong Kong troops who were not properly equipped when they had to fight their first battle. The results of that were disastrous. Anyway, I steadfastly refused to commit my troops without their proper equipment and cursed the day that I had let them separate from it.'[27] In view of Rockingham's protest and the imminent launching of a UN counteroffensive, Operation Detonate, the Americans closed the matter by cancelling the brigade's planned relief of the 65th Regiment. Instead, Eighth Army headquarters ordered the Canadians to a concentration area near Haech'on, southeast of Seoul. The incident was the closest Rockingham would come to invoking his direct channel to Ottawa when issued orders he believed would involve unnecessarily heavy casualties.[28]

Unfortunately, in a recently published monograph on the war and, based largely on that book's contention, in a subsequent article in an Australian work, it has been suggested that Rockingham's refusal to deploy the brigade thirty-six hours ahead of the agreed-to schedule was entirely a figment of his imagination.[29] Claiming that the Canadian commander's version of the events 'is at variance with the known facts,' the first account maintains that the official historian, H.F. Wood, 'uncritically accept[ed] the events as related in Rockingham's memoir ... out of respect for Rockingham.'[30] While there are indeed several areas for which *Strange Battleground* can be criticized, this is not one of them. Since the official history was published in 1966, while Rockingham did not write his memoir until 1975, the former obviously could not have been based on the latter. In fact, Wood's account of the incident was based on an interview Rockingham gave to the historical staff in November 1952 – only seventeen months after the event – and the written comments he made in July 1953 on a historical section report on the Korean War. Although the brigade war diary makes no mention of the attempts by corps and army headquarters to advance the deployment by thirty-six hours on the night of 18-19 May, the records otherwise agree entirely with the version of events given by Rockingham in his November 1952 interview and his July 1953 comments. It is possible that Canadian headquarters felt some embarrassment at having been forced to refuse its first UN order and chose not to refer to the incident in its war diary, although the 2 PPCLI diarist had shown no similar compunction in very similar circumstances. In any event, the November 1952 interviewer, G.W.L. Nicholson, noted that 'Rockingham is prepared to record this in writing for us' and that his brigade major and intelligence officer at the time could supply further information.[31]

Although Rockingham's later account, written from memory twenty-four years later, does compress the timings of these events, it would not have been at all out of character for Eighth Army headquarters to have ordered an agreed deployment moved ahead as had happened to Stone and 2 PPCLI at Miryang in January. Nor should it be surprising that the Canadian commander, given the unprepared state of the 25th Brigade on the night of 18-19 May, would have protested against such an order just as Stone had done. Not only is there no factual basis upon which to impugn Rockingham's honesty – as the recent accounts have done by suggesting that he might have fabricated the entire incident simply to please his political masters – but doing so entirely fails to understand the character of the Canadian brigade commander.

Following Rockingham's refusal to deploy his men ahead of the original schedule, the brigade concentrated at Haech'on on 19 May and was placed under the operational control of I Corps to await developments. Even with the collapse of the South Korean formations on the eastern flank, the Chinese offensive began to lose momentum within forty-eight hours of being launched. The transfer of the 3rd US and 8th ROK Divisions, the heavy expenditure of artillery rounds at 'Van Fleet Day of Fire' rates (300 rounds per 105 mm howitzer; 250 rounds per 155 mm howitzer; 200 rounds per 155 mm gun and 8-inch howitzer; and 250 rounds per 175 mm howitzer), together with the numerous ground attack sorties flown by Fifth Air Force, Marine Corps, and Far East Air Force aircraft, reduced the pressure along X Corps' front by the evening of 18 May and allowed the withdrawal of the shattered III ROK Corps. According to Ridgway, 'It was Van Fleet's aim to expend fire and steel rather than flesh and blood.'[32]

Along the coast, the two-division I ROK Corps, under the command of one of the South Koreans' more capable officers, the youthful Gen. Paik Sun-yup, had held together despite the continuing advance of Chinese and North Korean forces around and through its western flank. On 18 May, the theatre commander intervened to suggest a two-division attack in the western sector toward Ch'orwon in order to relieve the pressure on X Corps. After a personal reconnaissance of the front the following day, Ridgway judged the communists to be badly overextended and ordered Van Fleet to attack across his entire front in an attempt to cut off the penetration and trap as many of the enemy as possible. Before Eighth Army could begin its advance on the 21st, however, P'eng had accepted the futility of his offensive and ordered his badly mauled forces to withdraw. Chinese casualties were estimated by Eighth Army headquarters to be 17,000 dead and 36,000 wounded, over 20 percent of the communist forces engaged. P'eng explained his latest retreat to Beijing in a more aggressive tone:

> In order to assemble our main force for rest and reorganization, sum up our operational experience, and create favourable battle opportunities in the future, so that we shall be able to wipe out the enemy in even greater numbers, we have decided to move the main strength of the various army groups to the north of the line Haech'ang-ni – Yonch'on – Sach'ang-ni – Yangqu – Wont'ong-ni [just north of the thirty-eighth parallel]. Each army group will leave a force of between one division and an army which, starting from its present position, will adopt measures of mobile defence and repeated blocking actions to inflict casualties on the enemy and wear them down, and to gain time.[33]

With the enemy pulling back to the thirty-eighth parallel, the I and IX Corps attacks opened on 20 May in an attempt to seize those road junctions vital to the retreating enemy. Setting off from its positions five to ten miles north of Seoul, I Corps gained ground rapidly against minimal opposition. The 1st ROK Division entered Munsan on the Imjin River early on the 21st while the 1st Cavalry and 25th Infantry Divisions easily reached Line Topeka, ten miles north of Uijongbu, by the afternoon of the 23rd. As the US Army official history describes it, the attack 'amounted to a futile chase as the North Korean I Corps and [Chinese] 63rd Army backed away far faster than the I Corps advanced. Tank and tank-infantry forces probing well to the front of the main body consistently failed to make solid contact.'[34] The IX Corps' advance in the centre, despite an overly cautious pursuit that consistently left divisions short of their stated objectives, managed to capture several thousand Chinese, including most of the 180th Division, as it closed in on the western end of the Hwach'on Reservoir. The slow pace of X Corps' advance, particularly on the part of the 1st Marine Division in the rugged Taebaek mountains, drove the corps commander 'to frenzied activity' and exposed his 'predisposition for centralized command in critical circumstances.' From the British perspective, this trait proved all too common among many senior US officers.[35]

Anxiously waiting for their first taste of action after moving into the front line seven miles east of Seoul on 20 May, the Canadians had to be satisfied with watching air strikes north of the Han River from their positions on the south bank. On 21 May, Rockingham visited his units and gave them all 'an "Eve of Battle" talk ... telling them to take pride in themselves and their unit, display mental and physical fortitude. He was sure that we would do a good job ... Judging from the numbers of sing-songs held throughout the company lines in the evening, morale is excellent indeed.'[36] When the Canadians finally joined in the I Corps advance on the 22nd, they made little contact with the enemy; only 2 R22eR came under long-range small-arms fire on the right flank. The Royals did, however, capture four Chinese who 'had been left behind as part of a rear guard when their regiment had withdrawn a few days before. Their only weapons were a few grenades and they were only too anxious to surrender, very ragged in appearance and hungry.'[37]

Maj.-Gen. A.J.H. Cassels, general officer commanding-designate of the 1st Commonwealth Division, second from right, chats with Maj. R.D. Medland, A Company commander with the 2nd Battalion, Royal Canadian Regiment. The picture was taken on 22 May 1951, the day 25th Brigade joined the I Corps advance north of the Han River. To the right of Cassels is Brig. John Rockingham, while the commanding officer of 2 RCR, Lt.-Col. Robert Keane, stands to the left of the British general. NAC PA183422

By 25 May, it was clear that the enemy's rapid withdrawal had pulled the main communist forces out of reach of the counterattack. Assigned to the 25th Division northeast of Uijongbu, the Canadian brigade had the Philippine 10th Infantry Battalion Combat Team attached in place of the absent Patricias. The American division also provided a tank-infantry task force – named 'Dolvin' after its commander – consisting of three tank companies (or squadrons), an infantry battalion, an engineer company, a tactical air control party, and a signals detachment. The Canadians were instructed to 'employ armour in vigorous thrusts to keep [the] enemy off balance'[38] as they led the division's drive north to the thirty-eighth parallel. Setting off in midmorning, the 25th Brigade followed the Americans up the valley of the P'och'on River with 2 RCR moving along the high ground on the left flank and

2 R22eR traversing the heights on the right. Underscoring the completeness of the enemy withdrawal, the Canadians were fired upon only by isolated pockets of Chinese during the three days it took them to reach Line Kansas near the thirty-eighth parallel. On 28 May the brigade took over from Task Force Dolvin on high ground along the parallel, having completed an advance of some thirty miles.[39]

Although the enemy had suffered heavily in the Fifth Phase Offensive, it was clear to Van Fleet that Eighth Army had also failed in its bid to capture or destroy large portions of the retreating communist forces before they recrossed the thirty-eighth parallel. Nonetheless, the enemy's battered state convinced him to press the advance north of the parallel to recover the territory lost during the April offensive. Eighth Army quickly issued orders for a return to the Wyoming Line across the base of the Iron Triangle, the reoccupation of which would secure the roads running southeast of Kumhwa to the important Hwach'on Reservoir that supplied Seoul with water and hydroelectric power. As a preliminary to opening Operation Piledriver on 3 June, Van Fleet directed forces from both I and IX Corps to probe north of the parallel to gauge the enemy's strength and intentions. One of the first units to do so was 2 RCR, who continued the brigade's progress up the valley of the Hant'an River on 30 May. As the leading formation in the I Corps advance, the Canadians were the first to discover that a fresh enemy rearguard had been deployed immediately south of the Triangle to give the retreating Chinese time to regroup north of the open plain.[40]

In entering the Hant'an valley, the 25th Brigade had made considerably more progress than either formation on its flanks and by the evening of 29 May held a salient some 4,500 yards north of the rest of the 25th Division. At first light on the 30th, Rockingham was reluctant to continue the advance until the two US regiments on the left and right were in position to cover his brigade's flanks. After receiving assurances from 25th Division headquarters, however, Rockingham agreed to press ahead and gave orders for 2 RCR to pass through the 2 R22eR positions and take the right flank while the attached Philippine battalion moved up on the left.[41]

The Canadian thrust proved an inviting target for a Chinese rearguard anxious to delay the UN offensive before it reached the important Ch'orwon plain. The valley immediately in front of the brigade's positions was dominated by the two peaks of Hill 467, or Kakhul-bong (see Map 9). Running along the valley floor in a slight crescent about the foot of the mountain were a series of small villages linked by a dirt track that meandered past rice paddies on its left and Kakhul-bong on its right. Any progress up the valley, therefore, was contingent on the hill being captured. Unaware of the presence of fresh Chinese troops, the plan devised by 2 RCR's commanding officer, Lieutenant-Colonel Keane, was to mount one company in half-tracks and, supported by a troop of Sherman tanks, have them drive rapidly up the valley to occupy the village of Chail-li, a mile and a half directly north of Hill 467 and three miles north of the start line. Once the village had been secured, a second company was to follow and seize a smaller feature, Hill 269, that lay one

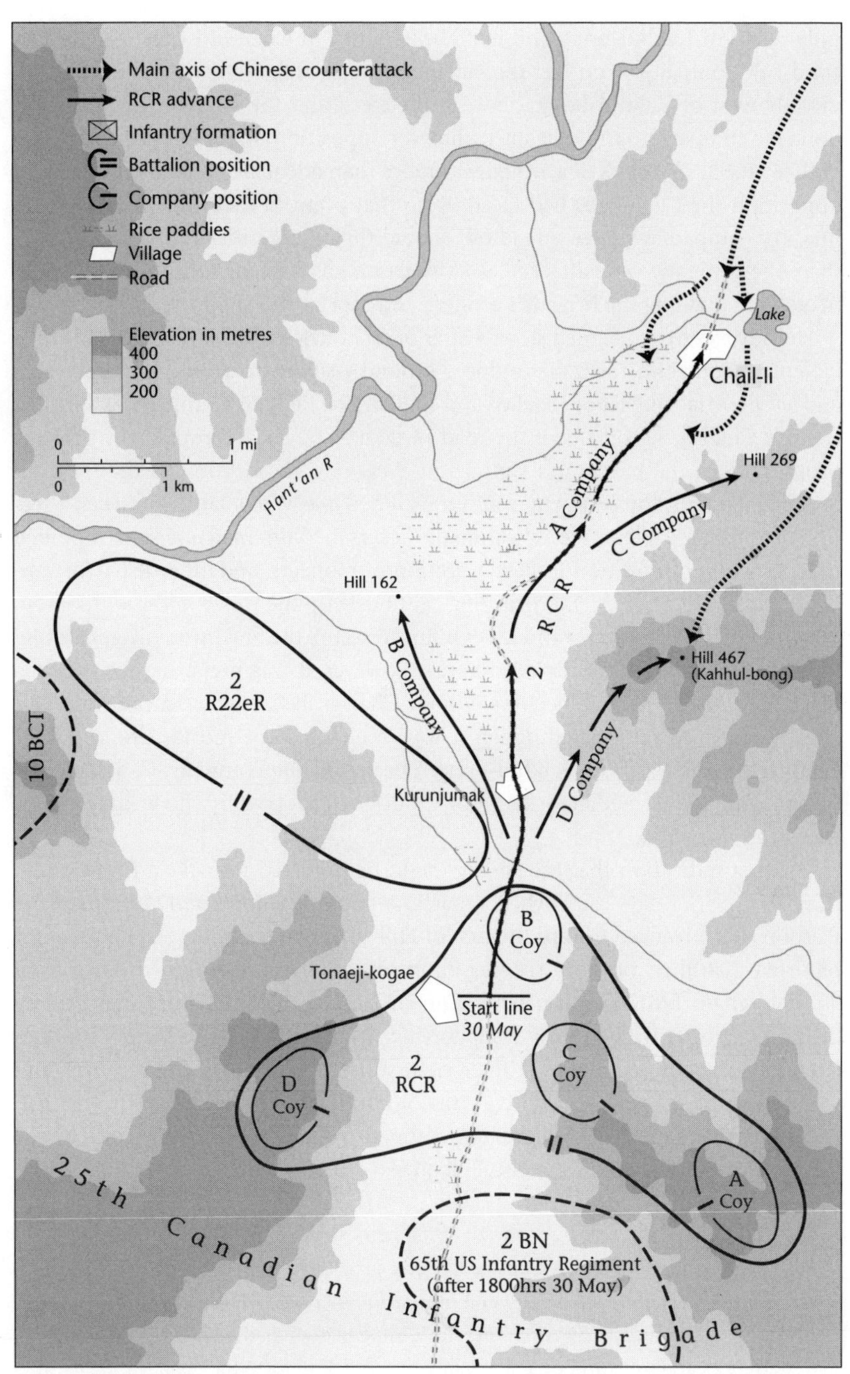

Map 9 *The action at Chail-li, 30 May 1951*

mile north of Kakhul-bong and half a mile south of Chail-li. Keane assigned his third rifle company to protect the battalion's western flank by occupying Hill 162 directly west of Kakhul-bong, between the track and the Hant'an River, leaving only one company to move against whatever opposition might be encountered on Hill 467 itself.[42] While Keane's plan was more than adequate to deal with the light opposition the Canadians had faced up to that point in their advance, it left his infantry companies rather spread out should they meet stiffer resistance. If more than one company were attacked at a time, moreover, Keane's dispositions would necessitate dividing the brigade's artillery and mortar fire support.

The advance was resumed shortly after 0600 hours on 30 May in the midst of a violently windy rainstorm that reduced ground visibility to several hundred yards and left the attacking troops soaked and chilled. The RCR's A Company, assigned to capture Chail-li, set off down the road in its half-tracks accompanied by a large proportion of the battalion's supporting weapons. In addition to the troop of Strathcona tanks, the company column included two Wasp flame throwers, a section of 75 mm recoilless rifles, a section of Vickers medium machine-guns mounted in jeeps with ammunition trailers, a section of pioneers, and an artillery forward observation officer (FOO). Proceeding cautiously up the valley in the wind-swept rain, the company took two and a half hours to secure the first three villages around the base of Kakhul-bong. By 0830 hours, however, it was preparing for the final one-mile advance to its objectives around Chail-li. B Company, meanwhile, had already occupied Hill 162, although it was receiving some mortar fire, as was D Company in its climb up Kakhul-bong. The remaining company, C, assigned to occupy Hill 269 immediately south of Chail-li, was following the leading troops down the valley road.[43]

The first indication that the enemy might be prepared to make a firmer stand than on previous days came when a machine-gun opened fire on D Company's 12 Platoon as it advanced toward the first of Hill 467's two peaks. At 0840 hours they reported that 'their position seemed impossible as they were pinned down from above by many LMGs [light machine-guns].' Despite the dire report, they pressed on up the slopes with extensive supporting fire from 2 RCHA. Twenty minutes later, D Company radioed 'that their right sub-unit was at the highest peak and were attempting to get enemy LMG at that point.' By 1030 hours, however, 'they had encountered yet another LMG nest near [the] top of their objective.'[44] The Chinese forces were securely established on Hill 467:

> The Chinese cleverly took every advantage of their extensive trench system skirting the main ridges and running back up the hill, and used their expertly camouflaged bunkers with great skill. Machine gun and mortar fire increased with every yard, but the advance was pressed on. By 1130 hours the leading platoon had scaled and cleared the western peak and were dropping down into the draw leading to the main feature itself, some 300 yards distant. From the very top of this pinnacle a well placed enemy machine

> gun completely dominated the approaches. Artillery and mortar fire was brought down, and the Platoon Commander of No 11 Platoon ordered his 3.5 rocket launcher to fire against the lone machine gun, but [the] stubborn Chinamen could not be dislodged. The leading section worked itself to within twenty feet of the crest, but found it impossible to dislodge the machine gun.[45]

As one section tried to skirt their way around to the east of the peak, they came across a group of well-equipped Chinese having lunch behind a crest. In a marked contrast to the dispirited communist soldiers they had met previously, these enemy were reported to be 'in high spirits and full of confidence.'[46] The Canadians opened fire at close range before beating a hasty retreat back to their platoon's position.

While D Company was working its way up Kakhul-bong in the face of continuous machine-gun fire, the other companies were occupying their objectives with relative ease. By 1030 hours, A Company had entered Chail-li and was consolidating its position using its tanks and Vickers machine-guns, and C Company reported itself in position on Hill 269 a half-hour later. The Chinese did not wait long before launching a strong counterattack against the penetration, however. The Canadians in the village 'began to receive increasingly heavy small arms, mortar, artillery, and high velocity, low-trajectory fire' as groups of enemy soldiers, 'estimated at company strength,' were seen dispersing into the paddy fields on either flank. Covered partially by the mist and rain, these soldiers were soon able to open fire on A Company from a range of only twenty-five yards:

> Despite the intense fire of battalion supporting weapons and 2 RCHA, the enemy pressure continued to increase. At 1300 hours, the Chinese began to infiltrate on the right flank, and with superb fieldcraft worked themselves towards the spur bordering the road on the southern outskirts of the village. At first, due to the poor visibility, this movement on the flank of the company was ignored. According to the company commander, the troops he saw were wearing ponchos and looked very much like Canadian troops. He mistakenly took them to be some men of C Company and, as he could not raise C Company on the wireless, he could not determine otherwise. It was not until this flank erupted in a hail of small arms, mortar and machine gun fire, that he realized the Chinese were circling to his rear.[47]

Half a mile to the southeast on Hill 269, the men of C Company were reduced to looking on in frustration as Chinese troops passed both of their flanks, either to surround the Canadians in Chail-li or to reinforce the resistance on Kakhul-bong. They did engage the Chinese with long-range Bren and rifle fire but without any apparent effect. At brigade headquarters, it was becoming increasingly clear that the failure of the 24th and 35th US Infantry Regiments to keep pace with the RCR's advance – by noon an 8,000-yard gap existed between 2 RCR and the nearest American troops on either flank – was allowing the enemy rearguard to infiltrate and cut off the Canadian penetration. With A Company under heavy pressure in Chail-li and C Company on Hill 269 unable to provide it with adequate support, Keane gave the order for a withdrawal from the village. The company was to 'inflict as many casualties as possible' in pulling back between B Company on Hill 162 west of the valley road and D Company on Kakhul-bong. Behind a screen of artillery barrages laid down by 2 RCHA, A Company began its withdrawal from Chail-li at 1430 hours.[48] The infantry used the hulls of the tanks to protect their wounded in the retreat down the road as 'the Chinese pressed their advantage, and harassed the returning troops at every opportunity. It was only through the excellent work done by the mortar officer and artillery FOO, and the very effective covering fire which they brought down, that the withdrawal was made with the minimum of casualties.'[49]

Even so, Keane was not yet prepared to abandon the attack on Hill 467 and ordered C Company to withdraw to the south to aid D Company. By the time the order was received, however, the situation on the upper slopes of Kakhul-bong had deteriorated as further Chinese reinforcements arrived to bolster the defence. The company commander, Major Boates, was 'seriously wounded and the company badly mortared and shelled. They requested permission to withdraw. At 1456 hours D Company reported ... the situation seemed impossible to escape from, hemmed in as they were.' Accepting the inevitable, Keane gave the company permission to withdraw 'to the bottom of the slope and consolidate. At 1509 hours D Company reported that they were slowly withdrawing down hill' despite being attacked 'by hundreds of enemy':

> Major Duncan, OC B Company, started talking D Company down the hill, at 1510 hours by RT [radio telephone], and informed D Company that his company was all set to help. D Company reported, at 1517 hours, to B Company that they were trying to consolidate until their rearguard got down ... Major Duncan's instructions were to stick to high ground and avoid the valley, and to cover troops coming down in the rear. Lieutenant Cowan, acting OC of D Company, reported that they were getting down fairly well. At 1535 hours C Company [withdrawing down the valley road] reported a large enemy group moving in on their right flank. D Company reported to B Company that all troops were now at the bottom of the hill and concentrated.[50]

Despite continuing pressure on its flanks by numerous enemy, the last company was able to recross the start line by 1900 hours. The Canadians were forced to abandon three tanks – all later recovered – as well as two Jeeps and trailers from the medium machine-gun section with C Company on Hill 269. Not surprisingly, D Company on Kakhul-bong suffered the heaviest casualties, three killed and six wounded, while B Company, who had come to their assistance, had two killed and six wounded. The two companies that achieved the deepest penetrations, A and C, escaped virtually unscathed, having no fatalities and a mere five wounded in A Company. The remaining casualties were incurred by the support company and battalion headquarters. Altogether, the day's fighting cost the battalion six men killed and two officers and twenty-three other ranks wounded, a rather small total given the scale of the enemy's resistance.[51]

Nonetheless, the engagement reinforced some important tactical lessons for the 25th Brigade. Unlike the Canadian Army's experience in northwest Europe during the Second World War, where operations usually centred on the seizure of road networks and built-up areas, in Korea occupying a valley floor was unlikely to force the enemy to withdraw if they still remained in control of the surrounding hillsides. In assessing the Chail-li operation, Keane was quick to accept the weakness of his plan: 'The by-passed enemy who were established on hills along the axis held out in spite of the penetration and made the axis insecure and was [sic] a factor in the withdrawing of the forward companies from their objectives.'[52] The C Company commander, whose men had been the least engaged while holding Hill 269, also complained,

> Some of the tactics we had been told were being employed in Korea are not necessarily the proper ones. For example, it has apparently been the custom to advance on very narrow lines, along the crests, using only one platoon up, or one company. Experience would seem to point to a much broader front, with troops advancing along both slopes and the crest, since the enemy's positions seem always to be on the slopes, often on the lower levels, and following all watersheds up to their source. These positions are mutually supporting, and any attack along a narrow front will face fire from the flanks that are unopposed. It would seem logical to attack on a broad front, on more than one slope, in order to outflank mutually supporting positions.[53]

That common-sense suggestion received Keane's endorsement along with the recommendation that 'more time should be allowed for planning at unit and subunit level,'[54] so that commanders could make a reconnaissance of the ground in daylight prior to an attack. These comments, however, suggest that the Canadian brigade may have been somewhat lulled by the ease with which they had made the first week's advance and had not taken sufficient advantage of the experience 2 PPCLI had already gained in the theatre. Within days of the Chail-li engagement, Lieutenant-Colonel Stone, who had temporarily returned to Canada to attend to a family matter, was explaining his Korea tactics to officers in Ottawa, concepts that echoed the conclusions of the RCR officers. 'In attacking ridges,' the Patricia CO explained in a talk at army headquarters, 'the tendency had been for the men to converge into single file along the path where the climbing was easiest. This had the bad result of the leading man being alone with his weapon when contact was made. Colonel Stone therefore developed the practice of attacking on three or four ridges at once, in order to cover as wide a front as possible.'[55]

It should be kept in mind, however, that 2 PPCLI had been stymied in its attempts to take Hills 419 and 532 during the northern advance three months earlier when, in similar circumstances, they had encountered a determined rearguard in well-sited entrenchments. In those instances, the features were captured only after the enemy had already withdrawn and not as a result of a direct assault. More recently, the Patricias' defence of Hill 677 above Kap'yong provided a graphic demonstration of the defensive strength of a single battalion when it had time to lay out and prepare its positions properly. In view of these experiences and the numerical strength of the Chinese defenders on Kakhul-bong, it seems unlikely that a different plan, one that committed the entire battalion to an attack on the feature, would have produced a different result. In fact, given that almost all of the RCR's casualties were incurred by the two companies that were engaged on the slopes of Hill 467, an attack that had concentrated on that hill alone might simply have produced a longer casualty list, like 2 PPCLI's carefully planned, but equally futile, attack on Hill 532 on 8 March when that battalion lost six killed and twenty-eight wounded. As it was, the 25th Brigade managed to escape its first major battle with only a small bruising.

In retrospect, the disappointing outcome resulted as much from the Canadians being at the forefront of the advance as from a poor plan. After advancing against demoralized and retreating troops for a week, the brigade had little reason to suspect that the advance on 30 May would prove much different. The leading units in such an advance may have been bound to suffer a bloodied nose as soon as the enemy introduced fresh, determined troops into their path. The inability of the flanking American formations to close the gap between themselves and the 25th Brigade allowed the Chinese to concentrate their reinforcements against the Canadians, so a battalion attack that concentrated on Kakhul-bong alone would probably not have changed the final result. As the earlier rearguard actions had demonstrated, such well-defended features were usually taken only after the defenders had been widely outflanked and withdrew to prevent being isolated behind an advancing front. Even then, a determined rearguard could delay forward movement for days at a time. When Eighth Army attempted to renew its advance to the Iron Triangle on 1 June, the stubborn Chinese defenders, fighting effectively from dug-in regimental positions arranged in depth and aided by a week of foul weather that hampered air strikes, managed to hold forward movement to a crawl all along the front. Not until 8 June, after their retreating forces had reached the safety of the hills north of the Triangle, did the Chinese finally relinquish their grip on the southern approaches to the Ch'orwon plain.

Despite the setback at Chail-li, there were still a number of positive signs in the Canadians' performance. All of the company commanders, for instance, had been impressed by the soldierly qualities of their men under fire. Maj. R.D. Medland, who led A Company into (and out of) Chail-li, reported that 'the discipline of all ranks in action has been exemplary. There is never a question or a hesitation in carrying out orders.' Morale remained 'extremely high,' while 'co-operation between platoon and sections had developed beyond my fondest hopes.'[56] Keane was similarly impressed with the men's behaviour in combat, qualities that augured well for the brigade's future: 'The troops showed a steadiness under fire which was exemplary ... they were anxious to close with the enemy, and maintained a very high morale in spite of casualties and adverse weather conditions. They were quick to take advantage of what they had been taught in training and applied the lessons without hesitation and automatically. The sub-unit commanders exhibited fine control and leadership with a good sense of judgement.'[57]

The cooperation between tanks and infantry also received praise, in particular the willingness of the tankers 'to go anywhere or to do everything to assist. It is doubtful if the successful evacuation of the forward objective could have been accomplished without their support; in fact it is doubtful if the objective could have been taken without their assistance.' The performance of the other supporting arms had proven satisfactory, although there was a requirement for additional forward observation officers. During the action, 'There were times when FOOs had to be changed from company to company during a unit action and this worked hardship on the FOO, precluded proper planning and in one case a forward company did not have fire support when required.'[58] The battle experience of the brigade's Second World War veterans was also an invaluable asset. Lieutenant Hugh Hutton, a brigade liaison officer attached to 2 RCR during the Chail-li action, later recalled 'sitting at the edge of a rice paddy' with Keane and Major Quinn, the armoured squadron CO, as 'the Chinese shells were getting closer and closer. Jim Quinn said, "Just like the big war, isn't it?" With people like that – cool in battle – we could do no wrong.'[59]

After maintaining its positions south of Kakhul-bong for twenty-four hours, the Canadian brigade – less 2 R22eR and 2 RCHA, which remained in position to support the relieving 65th US Infantry Regiment – moved back into reserve on 1 June. All across the front, however, Operation Piledriver continued to be held up by the Chinese rearguard and it was not until 11 June that the assaulting divisions were finally able to occupy their Line Wyoming objectives across the base of the Iron Triangle. Two days later, I Corps patrols advanced north to investigate P'yonggang at its apex, encountering no opposition until they discovered Chinese forces dug in on commanding ground north of the city. With I and IX Corps occupying the base of the triangle and the communists holding their positions some miles to the north, the area between the two lines was to remain a vast no man's land for the rest of the war; its flat terrain discouraged both sides from attempting to hold it.[60]

To the east, 2 PPCLI and the 28th British Commonwealth Brigade had assumed a secondary role in the Piledriver advance as part of the 24th US Division. The Patricias, perhaps because they were scheduled to rejoin the Canadian formation shortly, were given only a minor part in these operations, and the entire Commonwealth brigade was soon left behind in a reserve position. On 27 May, the Canadian battalion was sent south to the junction of the Hant'an and Imjin Rivers, where the three Commonwealth brigades were being concentrated in anticipation of the formation of the 1st Commonwealth Division,[61] to rest and refit after three months of arduous campaigning. The Patricias 'received new weapons – six 75mm recoilless rifles to replace our 17 pounders and three Wasp flame-throwers ... and a general issue of summer kit.' The battalion war diary noted on 1 June: 'Due partly to their new equipment and clothing and partly to the prospect of action again, the morale of the men is high.'[62] Visiting the unit the next day as it officially reverted to his command, Rockingham heard 'many expressions of pleasure by officers and men ... that they were at last back in the fold.'[63] The Canadian commander returned the following week 'to inspect each company of the battalion in order to acquaint himself with the troops who have hitherto seen little of him.'[64] Time in reserve also allowed the men to work on the battalion's vehicles, maintenance of which was 'one of the biggest single problems in this theatre ... The vehicles, most of which had been in storage for many years in the United States, almost immediately required shock absorbers, springs, radiators, tires and tubes, and new engines and transmissions, in that order. Many vehicles began to fail shortly after the battalion moved to Miryang in January. And since that time a very high percentage of the battalion's transport has been laid up due to a lack of replacement parts.'[65]

With the securing of its objectives east and west of the Hwach'on Reservoir, the Eighth Army had reached the limits of the northern advance laid down by the US joint chiefs of staff in their 1 May instructions to Ridgway. The defeat of the enemy's Fifth Phase Offensive, meanwhile, suggested that both sides might now be ready to admit that a decisive military victory was unattainable. On 17 May President Truman approved an official National Security Council statement that the United States would seek to conclude the fighting on the peninsula if suitable armistice arrangements could be negotiated. Two weeks later, the joint chiefs sent Ridgway instructions for the further prosecution of the war, namely, to

> inflict maximum personnel and materiel losses on the forces of North Korea and Communist China operating within the geographic boundaries of Korea and adjacent waters, in order to create conditions favourable to a settlement of the Korean conflict which would as a minimum:
>
> a. Terminate hostilities under appropriate armistice arrangements.
> b. Establish authority of the ROK over all Korea south of a northern boundary so located as to facilitate, to the maximum extent possible, both administration and military defense, and in no case south of the 38th Parallel.
> c. Provide for withdrawal by stages of non-Korean armed forces from Korea.
> d. Permit the building of sufficient ROK military power to deter or repel a renewed North Korean aggression.[66]

On the same day that these instructions were being sent to the Far East, the US secretary of state, Dean Acheson, informed the Senate hearings investigating MacArthur's relief that a ceasefire along the thirty-eighth parallel would 'accomplish the military purposes in Korea.'[67] During a United Nations radio broadcast on 26 May, Canada's external affairs minister, Lester Pearson, also stated that the UN's objective was 'the defeat of aggression against the Republic of Korea' rather than the 'complete capitulation of the enemy,' a point reiterated by the UN secretary general, Trygve Lie, in a speech in Ottawa the following week. A ceasefire along the thirty-eighth parallel, Lie said, would fulfill 'the main purpose of the Security Council resolutions of June 25 and 27 and July 7, 1950.'[68]

There were also indications through diplomatic channels that the Soviets would not be averse to a negotiated settlement, while the heavy losses suffered during General P'eng's latest offensive were forcing the Chinese leaders to a similar conclusion. According to the acting chief of staff of the People's Liberation Army, who was present at a late May meeting of the Central Committee of the Communist Party, 'the majority of those attending maintained that our troops should stop in the area of the 38th Parallel, fighting while negotiating, aiming then to settle the Korean issue through negotiations. I was one of this point of view. My opinion was, our political objective of driving the enemy away from the northern part of Korea had been achieved; to halt around the 38th Parallel consolidated the original frontier, a situation likely to be accepted by all sides. If the war continued, that would not dismay us, and we would grow stronger in combat. However, there were difficulties. Guided by Comrade Mao Tse-tung, the meeting finally adopted this course.'[69] Even so, it took another month of diplomatic sparring before General Ridgway was allowed to broadcast an appeal to the 'Commander in Chief, Communist Forces in Korea' for a meeting 'to discuss an armistice providing for the cessation of hostilities and all acts of armed force in Korea, with adequate guarantees for the maintenance of such armistice.'[70] As two five-man delegations sat down on 10 July 1951 to open armistice talks in a war-damaged mansion at Kaesong, near the thirty-eighth parallel on the peninsula's west coast, neither side could have expected another two years of difficult negotiations before an armistice would actually be concluded.

The Eighth Army still had to organize the new defensive line it had occupied following the Piledriver advance. With the communist positions often located several miles north of the Wyoming Line, Van Fleet sought to dominate the intervening no man's land by conducting deep patrols up to the enemy's outposts. One such unoccupied area lay within the large bend of the Imjin River at its junction with the Hant'an, where the river alters course from south to west on its path to the Yellow Sea. This was the same ground from which the Chinese 63rd Army had launched its attacks against the 29th Brigade in late April. On 2 June, the Patricias were ordered to establish a patrol base west of the river from which other UN units would investigate the territory within the salient. The move across the river was not without risk during the rainy season, because the Imjin 'has been known to rise as much as twenty feet in ten hours making any move across it very dependent on the weather. The problem of supplying any large unit on the west [bank] of the river

A Chinese shell explodes in the Imjin River on 10 June 1951, not far from the 2 PPCLI positions in the Hwangji-ri area. The Patricias maintained a bridgehead across the Imjin from 2 June until they were relieved by 2 R22eR on the 11th. Chinese activity in this sector convinced the British commander of the 28th Brigade, under whose command the Patricias were temporarily serving, that the enemy was about to launch a major attack. NAC PA171319

should disastrous floods occur almost renders the idea impractical at this time of the year.'[71]

In fact, wet weather prevented the Canadians from establishing a firm base on the opposite bank until 6 June. Temporarily reverting to 28th Brigade command, the Patricias were 'to provide a screen forward of the bridgehead area ... each morning to enable 28 Brigade patrols to cross the river and form up without interference.' Veterans of one Chinese offensive already, the Patricias were well aware of their exposed location, particularly with rumours that 'the CCF 6th Phase offensive is expected daily.' Nor were their concerns eased by a visit from the 28th Brigade's commander on 9 June. With the earlier Imjin battle clearly in mind, Brigadier Taylor expressed his belief 'that an all-out Chinese attack is due sometime between the 12th and 15th June on the I Corps front with the probability that the 28th Brigade occupying the hinge position would be called upon to bear the brunt of the attack.' In a tone that bordered on disdain for the British general's fears of another Gloucester-type catastrophe, the Canadian unit's war diary simply recorded that 'another quiet night was passed despite Brigadier Taylor's forecast of imminent attack by overwhelming numbers.'[72]

Nonetheless, the physical demands of maintaining the Imjin bridgehead proved to be a considerable strain for the men: 'The heat and the heavy work of preparing defences has made the troops very tired, particularly as this is the third time in thirty days that the battalion has moved into and proceeded to wire and mine a new battalion perimeter. The hills, though comparatively low, are very steep in this area and the temperatures have been in the middle nineties since the river crossing. A great deal of manual labour has been expended in an attempt to render a very precarious position at all tenable.'[73]

The battle-worn Patricias were replaced in the bridgehead by the relatively fresh 2 R22eR on 11 June. The Chinese were still recovering from their Fifth Phase mauling and could do little more than offer token resistance. Despite patrolling up to five miles into no man's land, the Van Doos usually could 'not seem to find enough enemy to make the day an interesting one.'[74] The Canadians were also somewhat surprised by the wide variety of foreign weapons that the retreating Chinese had discarded in the area, among them 'a Bren gun of Canadian manufacture bearing the Chinese markings "assembled at Hong Kong."'[75] Whether or not the Bren was deliberately left behind for the Canadians to find, it served as a poignant reminder

Soldiers of 2 R22eR patrol past a Korean farm in the Imjin salient on 14 June 1951. With the Chinese outposts normally situated some 2,000 to 3,000 yards beyond the river, the Van Doos had some ground to cover before making contact with the enemy. NAC PA183804

of an earlier Canadian military venture to the Far East. The Van Doos remained in their screening position across the Imjin until the 19th, when the entire Canadian brigade boarded their vehicles and made their way northeast along the main supply route to the city of Ch'orwon at the base of the Iron Triangle.

In taking up new defensive positions, the 25th Brigade was attached to the 1st US Cavalry Division and assigned to hold a section of the UN front that ran southwest of the city in order to conduct patrols into the wide no man's land of the Triangle.[76] Since the line had only recently been occupied by UN forces, the Canadians' initial task was to organize their positions by tying in company-defended localities, siting weapons, digging slit trenches, and carefully 'wiring in' their entrenchments.[77] With his usual attention to detail, Rockingham placed 'great emphasis ... on this phase of the operation' even though Line Wyoming was considered to be only an outpost line for the main defences on Line Kansas. Each battalion was to hold the line with three companies forward and one in reserve, with the reserve company providing the bulk of the patrols before rotating to replace one of the forward companies after a week.[78] Once again demonstrating his hands-on approach to command, Rockingham personally went over 'the whole front in detail in order to take best advantage of the ground in the disposition of the components of the brigade. The nature of the ground in Korea is such that the brigade commander must examine each battalion position in detail in order to arrive at the best possible overall disposition rather than leave it to the battalion commanders or work off a map, as was generally possible in Europe.'[79] Even by Korean War standards, each of the three battalions had to cover a very wide area: 'The battalion front is over 3,500 yards long and is very badly cut up by gullies and draws, most of them reaching from front to rear of the company positions and greatly complicating the company commander's problem of securing all round defence. Each platoon, and even some of the sections, are 100 yards apart. Due to this thinness on the ground, great emphasis has been placed on the wiring and mining of the numerous gaps that exist in the battalion front.'[80]

With temperatures frequently reaching into the low thirties Celsius, work on the defences had to be curtailed during the heat of the day. The heat and Korean insects combined to make the men's lives uncomfortable. 'Heat rashes are becoming a problem,' the 2 PPCLI war diarist noted a week after reaching Ch'orwon, and 'there is also some small insect that is bothering the men. The bites become infected and then seem to spread over the body. Very small red ants are also troublesome in this area. There is a form of poison-oak growing in the area which has added to the men's discomfort. Another ailment which owes its origins to the hot weather is the masceration [sic] of the men's feet caused by overheated feet made tender by the cold weather and wet conditions of the first part of the year. Nothing but a complete rest and treatment of the feet for four or five days seems to cure the trouble.'[81]

Having already served six months in Korea, the Patricias were also affected by continuing 'rumours concerning the time and date of rotation of personnel.' With

The layout of 25th Brigade's main headquarters on 20 June 1951, following the Canadian formation's move to the Ch'orwon area in the Iron Triangle. The effect of the US Air Force's complete air supremacy can be seen in the casual disregard for concealment from air observation. NAC PA177319

the battalion well aware of the American policy of rotating troops after six months' service, the Canadian 'government's method of handling the matter has come in for much adverse comment among the men and unless the situation is soon clarified there may be a serious deterioration in the morale of the battalion.'[82] In the meantime, the Patricias found that the 'nightly ration of beer, one bottle per man, and a chance to go for a swim in the reservoir near Tac HQ somewhat compensates for the heat.'[83] As a partial offset to the rotation grumbling, the battalion did receive confirmation that it was to be awarded a Presidential Citation for its stand at Kap'yong two months earlier: 'There was considerable speculation amongst the men as to whether or not we would be permitted to wear the citation as are the surviving members of the 1st Gloster Regiment. The feeling of the battalion is that it should be worn, or at least incorporated into the regimental flash.'[84]

Although the Canadians held a brigade frontage of some four and a half miles, the exhausted Chinese forces were content to remain well to the north and west of the UN lines. 'The distance to our FDLs [forward defended localities] may be too far for him to come during the [hours of] darkness,' the Patricia diarist noted, 'and certainly the enemy cannot operate in the valley during the day because of our air cover and superior artillery.'[85] For the most part, enemy resistance to the deep patrols, which often advanced 10,000 yards forward of the brigade's defended localities, was light, and most casualties resulted from the enemy's mortar fire. The job of the patrols was complicated by the fact that 'most movement was climbing through dry and dusty bracken, in some places four feet high. The growth in this area is very dense and movement except along the paths is very difficult. The cover afforded the enemy is very good and Chinese tactics are adapted to the terrain and cover, giving them a decided advantage in a patrol action.'[86] Specifically, the Canadians found,

> the Chinese practice of permitting us to closely approach their positions before opening fire has a twofold result. First, the proximity of our troops to the enemy when the fight begins nullifies to a certain extent our fire power superiority and forces us to attack without all our support or makes us draw back in order to engage the enemy position. This allows him to do either of two things: one, withdraw after inflicting maximum casualties in the first contact, or two, reinforce his position having determined the point of our attack. The second result is, of course, that we have little if any idea of his exact location, enabling the enemy to hold a great deal of ground with a small force and protecting his positions from bombardment by us.[87]

The wide no man's land that separated UN and Chinese lines also presented a problem regarding the local inhabitants of the forward areas. The Canadians could not forget that north of the thirty-eighth parallel they were now operating in enemy territory:

> With a military vacuum of some 8,000 to 10,000 yards between ourselves and the enemy, civilians have not been forced from their homes and villages by battle action. Consequently, when a patrol pushes forward of the FDLs to probe for enemy positions, it finds hundreds of civilians puttering around the fields and villages and showing great interest in the activities of the troops and in their equipment. There is reason to believe that when the Chinese descend from the hills to the villages after dark, there are ready informants among the villages to give them all the information they require about our own patrols.[88]

On 24 June alone, the brigade's Field Security Section rounded up and evacuated 3,400 Korean civilians from the no man's land in front of its positions for delivery to the 1st Cavalry Division's civilian collecting point some twenty-five miles south of Ch'orwon.[89] In spite of these measures, a disconcerting number of civilians remained, many of whom the wary Canadians believed were 'decidedly antagonistic, making them ideal informants for the Chinese forces.'[90] When a three-man 2 RCR patrol was ambushed and killed on the morning of 2 July, for instance, North Korean civilians were generally suspected. Rockingham promptly 'laid on vigorous security patrols for [the] following day to clear all civilians from the area.'[91] Interrogation of the civilians near the scene of the ambush subsequently 'revealed that the soldiers who ambushed the patrol were dressed in white civilian clothes. This is another aspect of the problem and makes the evacuation all the more necessary.'[92]

Even so, the tone of the war diaries reveals that the Canadians did not exactly relish the sad task of removing civilians from their homes. Their willingness to risk their lives to save Koreans had been demonstrated a month earlier when 'a party of Korean civilians had entered a minefield in the vicinity through a barbed wire fence, exploding some anti-personnel mines' and the Patricias' Sgt. F.H.W. Taylor was sent to provide medical assistance: 'Arriving at the scene, Sergeant Taylor observed that there were six Korean civilians lying in various parts of the minefield and all badly injured. He also found Private M. Kawanami, a Japanese-Canadian of the Intelligence Section, already making his way into the minefield to render assistance. These two soldiers, without thought for their personal safety, made six trips into the minefield in order to carry out all the injured. They then applied first aid and evacuated them to the Field Ambulance. These two soldiers were recommended for, and later received, "Mention in Despatches" for their bravery.'[93]

In a new position several months later, the Canadians tried to ease the hardship of the displaced population by allowing them at least to harvest their standing crops.

A battery command post in action. The 2 RCHA guns are firing in support of A and B Companies, 2 RCR, as they patrol west of Ch'orwon on 21 June 1952. NAC PA128280

As explained by a visitor to the Canadian brigade, 'The valleys looked as though they had been settled for centuries. Rice paddies filled the floor of each valley while in terraces along the sides, beans, cotton, corn and kaoliang (sorghum) were planted. In many areas the rice, beans and cotton were ready to harvest ... The civilian population had been entirely evacuated from the forward areas because of the danger of infiltration of spies. I learned, however, that arrangements were being made to let selected parties of Korean farmers come in to take off the harvest under supervision. Actually, the supervision of the programme of this kind cost more than the actual value of the crops removed but it was felt ... that such a programme would have symbolic significance in the eyes of the Korean population.'[94]

Whatever the individual soldiers' attitudes toward the Korean population may have been, they could not forget that their patrols were operating in what had, until recently, been North Korean territory. Normally consisting of an infantry company supported by troops of tanks, artillery, and field engineers, these large patrol formations had to be well organized and required great physical stamina on the part of the troops. Brigade headquarters realized that the conditions on the Ch'orwon front were unique and that 'this type of very aggressive patrolling cannot be considered standard for Korea, nor can the form of these patrols be regarded as standard tactics in this country.' The patrols did, however, demonstrate 'the versatility and the ability of the men and officers to adapt themselves to rapidly changing circumstances.'[95] Even so, they were not without risk:

> The lack of equally vigorous patrolling by the [brigade's] flanking units has made unprotected flanks 10-20,000 yards long quite commonplace. To cover these flanks the individual battalions have been forced to expend a considerable force, drawn from their patrol strength, to picket their flanks in order to prevent surprise and encirclement of their patrols. The net result of this drain upon the already limited strength of the patrols has been the substitution of fire power, in the form of the battalion's 81mm mortars and the MMG platoon, for men on the ground ...
>
> The maximum strength of the patrols put out by the battalions is determined by the necessity of keeping at least two companies in the FDLs. The inclusion of the mortars and MMGs in the patrol is necessitated by the need for close fire support if the exposed flanks are to be protected and the relatively small patrolling force is to achieve its objective and extricate itself in the event that it encounters determined enemy resistance ... For the most part the weather has been very hot and the danger of heat exhaustion in the hills is very great. The length of the patrols and the height of the hills climbed, an average of 450 metres, makes this patrolling more tiring than is normal with the result that the troops quickly become exhausted and at least one day of rest is essential before going on another patrol.[96]

The brigade's task was made easier by the fact that the boundary line between the 26th Chinese Army on the right and the 47th Chinese Army on the left fell in the middle of the Canadian front. The division of enemy responsibility made 'co-ordination of the Chinese counter measures difficult ... Enemy resistance to our patrols is strong locally but concerted action, especially on our very exposed flanks, has been totally lacking.'[97] After confining themselves 'largely to observation from a safe distance' during the latter part of June and the first week of July, by midmonth the Chinese were beginning to come 'further forward to meet our penetrations with gradually increasing strength.' The overgrown terrain restricted the means of access to the line of hills held by the enemy and meant that each patrol had to follow much the same route going out as coming in. The tactic the Canadians used to prevent a successful counterpatrol by the enemy against their extended flanks was to alternate the strength of the various patrols sent out. A strong patrol on the right supported by a smaller patrol on the left one day would often be reversed the next. From the enemy's inability to engage either patrol successfully, it was apparent to brigade headquarters that the enemy did not as yet hold their ridge line in sufficient strength to take effective action.[98]

Foreseeing the day when the enemy would be strong enough to take more aggressive measures to contest the penetrations, Rockingham repeatedly reminded his battalion commanders to remain alert against this possibility as the month wore on. In addition to daytime company patrols, the brigade commander required each battalion to send out six- to seven-man reconnaissance patrols at night to prevent surprise.[99] In keeping with his style of command, Rockingham also liked to move well forward of the FDLs to observe the progress of the patrols, often taking up a hilltop position in the wake of the advancing units. Typical of the brigade's operations at this time – and the increasing enemy resistance – were the patrols conducted on 11 July:

> 2 RCR sent out a patrol consisting of D Company, one troop of [Lord Strathcona's Horse] tanks and an engineer party from 57th Field Squadron, RCE, to patrol to the vicinity of the village of Sinchon ... The patrol left at 0730 hours and returned at 1840 hours without casualties. The 2 PPCLI patrol, consisting of one platoon of B Company and an engineer party left at 0900 hours and at 1210 hours after moving forward without contact up to this point had reached the village of Kodan-ni ...
>
> The 2 PPCLI patrol reported considerable enemy movement ... and engaged the enemy with artillery ... The leading elements of the platoon came under intense fire from at least four enemy LMGs located on the high ground on either side of the valley and to the left rear of the patrol. By 1230 hours the platoon was pinned down by LMGs firing [from the high ground]. Artillery was placed on these positions often not more than 100 yards from the troops. Smoke was used to conceal the platoon's movement and at 1315 hours the platoon began its withdrawal and all elements of the patrol [were clear] by 1340 hours. Casualties were two KIA and four WIA. Due to the nature of the engagement, no attempt was made to recover the bodies of the dead soldiers.[100]

Weary Canadian soldiers returning from patrol in the Ch'orwon hills on 22 June 1951. Company-sized patrols were often accompanied by a platoon of Sherman tanks from C Squadron, Lord Strathcona's Horse. NAC PA143367

The bodies of the dead Canadians were eventually recovered by a strong, two-company patrol that returned to the same area two days later without encountering any resistance.

The Ch'orwon patrols proved to be an invaluable training experience for the Canadian brigade as they continued to adjust to Korean conditions. During the first period when all three infantry battalions operated together, the patrols allowed Rockingham to meld them into a cohesive formation while learning the strengths and weaknesses of the various units. Facing a relatively passive enemy, moreover, the men had an opportunity to hone their military skills and develop an aggressive attitude while incurring only minimal casualties. The long distances covered under tough conditions further hardened the Special Force men, preparing them both physically and mentally to meet Rockingham's demands for routine patrolling on other fronts. Significantly, the 1st and 3rd battalions that later replaced them in the theatre did not have to endure the same hardening process before they took over well-established entrenchments at the front. The Ch'orwon experience would stand the Canadians in good stead when they returned to the important sector of the UN front along the Imjin River, where the proposed 1st Commonwealth Division was about to become operational.

6 THE COMMONWEALTH DIVISION, JULY-OCTOBER 1951

While the Canadians were patrolling along their section of the Wyoming Line near Ch'orwon, the proposed grouping of the three Commonwealth brigades under a single divisional headquarters had been going ahead as planned. Almost as soon as the Special Force was announced in August 1950, the Canadian government had been approached by the British about the possibility of forming a division in Korea by combining the United Kingdom, Australian, New Zealand, and Canadian contingents. Canada's soldiers were agreeable to renewing a relationship with which they were already comfortable. As early as 21 August 1950, General Foulkes had informed the US Army's chief of staff that he had 'already approached the UK to suggest that they should maintain us in the theatre as far as equipment and ammunition replacements are concerned. It is my hope that they will organize a division composed of the various nations armed with the UK type equipment as this would certainly ease our [supply] problem.'[1]

The politicians in Ottawa, on the other hand, were initially averse to having the nation's contribution submerged in a Commonwealth formation. The Cabinet preferred to emphasize the United Nations aspect of the Korean operation and was leery of any policy that might lead to other commitments that were of greater interest to the United Kingdom than to Canada. From the formation of the Special Force, the government had agreed that the decision as to the disposition of the Canadian force in Korea would be left to the UN unified command in the theatre, but on 8 December 1950 Ottawa gave in to pressure from Britain and agreed that, 'if it should be considered desirable by [the] unified command,' Canada would allow 'the participation of Canadian forces, for the purposes of operations, with other Commonwealth troops in a formation to be known as the 1st (Commonwealth) Division, United Nations Forces.'[2] Since the brigade group already included divisional troop elements, the government was careful to stipulate that such an arrangement not lead to an increase in Canadian personnel beyond those already assigned to the 25th Brigade.

There the matter rested until mid-February 1951, when the Canadian government's decision to send the rest of the 25th Brigade to Korea prompted London to revive the proposal. Because the two British brigades already in Korea were an insufficient force with which to form a complete division, the British government immediately asked Ottawa to allow talks between the War Office and the Canadian Military Mission in London to work out the details for including the Canadian brigade in the arrangement. Upon completion of the War Office negotiations in

March, the Cabinet Defence Committee approved the inclusion of the 25th Brigade in the scheme and the formation of a Commonwealth Division was officially announced on 23 April 1951.

Rumours that such a formation was in the works circulated among the Canadian troops during their April voyage to the Far East.[3] The United Kingdom had been anxious 'to form the division as soon as possible after the arrival in the Korean theatre of the balance of the Canadian 25th Brigade,' but the British officer designated to command the division, Maj.-Gen. A.J.H. (Jim) Cassels, did not arrive at Kure, Japan, to organize his headquarters until 11 June. Such was the British desire for Canadian participation that London 'offered eight officer and fourteen other rank vacancies on the divisional headquarters [staff], the offer including a choice of the appointments which it would wish to fill.'[4] The arrangement, as Brooke Claxton pointed out in his submission of the scheme to the Cabinet Defence Committee in April, 'would mean that we would be training staff officers and signals [personnel] in an operational formation instead of by other less realistic methods, which would be greatly to our advantage.'[5] As a result, Cassels' staff initially included seven Canadian officers – a number that soon grew – of whom Lt.-Col. E.D. Danby, serving as the division's principal staff officer, or general staff officer grade 1, was the most senior. After exercising his headquarters staff and touring the various component brigades to introduce himself, Cassels brought the Commonwealth Division into active operation on 28 July 1951.[6]

The creation of the division reduced both the size of Brigadier Rockingham's immediate command and some of his responsibilities. While the infantry battalions and armoured squadron remained under the Canadian commander's operational control, the supporting arms and services of the former brigade group – artillery, engineers, signals, transport, ordnance, medical, electrical and mechanical engineers, and provost – were integrated into the divisional organization. Even then, they generally continued to be employed in support of the Canadian brigade, which remained administratively responsible for their discipline or promotion. The amalgamation was made with little apparent friction, although some confusion was inevitable. On one occasion, Rockingham ordered the Canadian engineer unit, the 57th Field Squadron, to construct a tactical road to one of the battalion positions, while the British commander of the 28th Field Engineer Regiment ordered the unit to level an air strip at divisional headquarters. Priority was eventually assigned to the tactical road.[7]

There were decided advantages to operating as part of a division rather than as an independent brigade group temporarily attached to various American formations. The permanence of the Commonwealth Division's artillery organization allowed a better coordination of fire tasks. While the commanding officer of the 2nd Field Regiment, RCHA, Lt.-Col. Anthony J.B. Bailey, continued to coordinate fire at the brigade level, all seventy-two of the division's 25-pounder guns could be switched rapidly to fire en masse on the orders of the British Commander, Royal

Artillery. The divisional fire control centre ensured that the field regiments were located so as to cover the entire divisional front and also enabled the artillery to shift its fire to assist US or ROK divisions on its flanks. In return, the Commonwealth Division was able to call for support from the guns of neighbouring divisions as well as American corps and army artillery assets.[8]

There were advantages for the other supporting arms as well. The 57th Field Squadron joined the 12th and 55th Field Squadrons, Royal Engineers, to form the 28th Field Engineer Regiment under the command of Lt.-Col. P.N.M. Moore, RE. There was also a divisional commander, Royal Engineers, Col. E.W.C. Myers, to handle planning and arrange for engineer stores and labour from the Korean Service Corps. The Canadian squadron's park troop was integrated with those of the other engineer squadrons to form the 64th Field Park Squadron. The Canadian contingent of the field park squadron proved extremely valuable to the British because of their knowledge and experience in the operation and repair of heavy equipment more commonly used in North America than in Britain, particularly the regiment's dump trucks. The Canadians also provided a useful link between the British engineers and the Americans with whom they had to deal, acting in some instances as interpreters between the two. Administratively, the Canadians in the field park squadron remained on strength with the 57th Field Squadron, although rationed with the British elements.

With an army that was still modelled on the British example, and having served as part of 21 Army Group in northwest Europe only six years earlier, Canadian officers were fully conversant with British military practice and staff procedures. Cassels was 'an old friend' of Rockingham's 'who had commanded one of the brigades [the 152nd] in the [51st] Highland Division in the Second World War, to which I was attached for the Rhine Crossing. We had crossed the river with our brigades side by side' in 1945.[9] Perhaps the best example of their friendly personal relationship is an incident that occurred on Boxing Day 1951, as recounted by Rockingham in his memoirs:

> The Australian Minister for War came to see us as he wished to visit Commonwealth troops other than the Australians. It was snowing hard and I had arranged to take him up to our brigade OP [observation post]. At the base of the hill on which the OP stood, I had assembled a few of my soldiers from as many of my units as possible. He was inspecting them and talking to them when suddenly I was hit on the side of the head with a snowball. Although the movement had ceased by the time I swung around, I thought I saw General Cassels' arm returning to his side. In any case, there was no one else there who would have dared to do it. Because I was talking to the Minister from Australia at the time, there was no opportunity to retaliate. Also, I did not relish the idea of facing a charge of striking my superior officer. That night with the aid of my whole staff and the legal officer of the brigade, I framed a charge against my General. This caused much merriment among my officers and kept me busy most of the night.[10]

Although Rockingham believed that 'the relations within the Commonwealth Division were, on the whole, tremendous,' there was still 'a tendency for both Americans and British to treat Canadians as small-fry,' with the British initially demonstrating a propensity 'to treat my staff as mere colonials. The General never treated me like that but my staff got it from their staff. This was soon cleared up by me, as we had in fact a fully equipped brigade group which was fully manned and doing about three times the work of any other equivalent formation.'[11] Canadian sensitivity to such treatment may, in part, have led to the perception among non-Canadians that the 25th Brigade 'tended to keep to itself, and officers of other nationalities on the divisional headquarters soon came to leave liaison with the brigade to the Canadians among them.'[12]

As the second-largest national contingent in the division, the Canadian element at division headquarters – which by June 1952 had grown to thirteen officers and fourteen men – always included the senior general staff officer. The division's first GSO(1), Lieutenant-Colonel Danby, 'was a very experienced staff officer with World War II staff experience'[13] who was responsible for integrating officers from throughout the Commonwealth into the new division's operations staff. His successor at division headquarters in May 1952, Lt.-Col. Norman G. Wilson-Smith, the CO of 1 PPCLI during its first six months in Korea, reported that 'whether due to careful selection of personnel or by good fortune, no misunderstandings or clashes have occurred among the various nationalities at Div HQ. This headquarters, in fact, is the happiest he has ever served on. Differences in thought and custom, national prejudice, etc., are resolved in good-natured banter.'[14] Wilson-Smith's replacement as GSO(1) the following August, Lt.-Col. E.A.C. (Ned) Amy, believed that 'each national group attempted to accentuate the positive' within the division,[15] but also cautioned that 'professional competence is not sufficient qualification for the selection of an officer for an integrated HQ. Of at least equal weight is the man's ability to get along with others. He must show a great tolerance for such things as the food, meal hours and the manners of speech, dress and behaviour of other nationalities. Unless an officer has the right personality and a great deal of tolerance he should not be placed on the staff of an integrated headquarters no matter how well qualified he may be in military matters.'[16]

Perhaps the greatest advantage for the 25th Brigade in serving as part of a Commonwealth formation, however, was the fact that the divisional organization helped to shield the Canadians from some of the less militarily sound orders that occasionally emanated from higher American headquarters. In his initial periodic report on the Commonwealth Division's activities, Major-General Cassels explained:

> My main trouble during this period was to convince I Corps that, though we were more than ready to do anything that was required, we did like to know the reason behind it. On many occasions I was ordered, without any warning, to do things which I considered militarily unsound and for which there was no apparent reason. Eventually

> I asked the Corps Commander for an interview where I put all my cards on the table. I pointed out that we worked quite differently to them, and it was impossible to expect that we could suddenly change our ways to conform with American procedure. I then asked that, in the future, we should be given our task, the reasons for that task and that we should then be left alone to do it our way without interference from the Corps staff. The Corps Commander could not have been more helpful and, since then, things have been much better and both sides are happier. Nevertheless I regret that I cannot state that everything is now completely right. There is no doubt that they look at military problems in a very different light to us and I never know for certain what the future plan is likely to be. There have been at least five occasions when I considered invoking my directive [to refuse an order which, as a national commander, he believed to be unsound].[17]

Certainly Rockingham felt more comfortable taking his orders from a commander schooled in the British Army staff system. He later recalled:

> It was a great relief to be serving with the Commonwealth Division, where at least the language was more familiar. In the British and Canadian armies, the teaching was that the orders for military operations had to be most precise, while it seemed that this was not so important in the US Army. For example, on one occasion I received orders from a US Command to 'without delay initiate offensive action in the zone marked "P" on overlay "Q2" attached.' The zone was 8,000 yards inside enemy territory when the front was, and had been, fairly static for some considerable time. What does 'without delay' or 'initiate offensive action' mean? A Commonwealth order for the same operation would have said, 'Capture the enemy on the objective' or 'kill all enemy encountered' or 'capture the hill' or some other precise action on reaching the objective.
>
> On another occasion in defence, when an enemy attack was imminent, I was ordered by a US Command 'to inflict maximum damage.' The Commonwealth order would have said, 'Capture as many prisoners as possible' or 'Prevent the enemy penetrating beyond the river' or 'Kill as many of the enemy as you can.' In both cases the orders would have been precise had they come from a Commonwealth command. The precision seems more than ever necessary in a politically oriented war such as the one in Korea where it was most important for the soldier to know exactly what was expected. The US, and particularly its army, have had troubles before and since by not being precise.
>
> Another practice which I found hard to get used to in the US Army was that the General who was issuing the order was seldom seen at the time the order was given out. More often the operations were planned and ordered by his staff, with the General making it official by signing on a line preceded by the word 'Approved.' Under our system the commander usually gave the orders personally, giving him the opportunity to impress his personality and his belief in the success of the operation on his subordinates. At the same time, the subordinates were encouraged to voice their ideas and

> suggestions before they went away to carry out their orders. It struck me that under the US Army system the subordinate was afraid to air his views at all. One wondered where the responsibility would lie if things went wrong.[18]

Upon returning from Ch'orwon on 18 July to prepare for the formation of the Commonwealth Division, the Canadians took up much the same positions they had vacated in mid-June, on the east bank of the sweeping curve formed by the Imjin River's junction with the Hant'an. Rockingham was particularly aware of 'the vital importance of the positions of the brigade, sitting astride, as they do, the juncture of the Kansas and Wyoming Lines and on the natural axis of any Chinese attack aimed at cutting the important MSR [main supply route, which led north to] the 25th Infantry Division and the 3rd Infantry Division in the Ch'orwon apex.'[19] Although the other two brigades that were to form the Commonwealth Division were located in the same general area, Cassels' headquarters was not yet operational and the 25th Brigade was temporarily placed under the command of the 25th Division on its right. As before, the Canadians were to provide a battalion screen for a patrol base north and west of the unpredictable Imjin.

The battalion Rockingham selected for this duty, Dextraze's 2 R22eR, had seen very little action to date, either in the advance to the thirty-eighth parallel or during its patrols at Ch'orwon. Maintaining communications with a battalion on the far side of a major river at the height of the Korean rainy season, however, was enough to make any commander nervous, especially when Chinese patrols were probing the Canadian defensive positions before the infantrymen were well dug in. 'Because of the enemy patrol last night, and the extended and as yet incomplete 2 R22eR positions,' the brigade diarist recorded on 19 July, 'the brigade commander spent as much time as possible with the battalion in order to assure himself that everything possible was being done to withstand an attack.'[20] At 2315 hours that night a small enemy force engaged the battalion's A Company 'about twenty feet away from their position':

> For nearly three hours fierce fighting was carried out by A Company and the scouts platoon against an estimated 110 enemy ... Artillery was called and for what seemed like an hour shelled the forward slope of our position for 15 minutes. A few shells fell in the center of our TAC [HQ] but fortunately no one was injured, for all had dug their holes as previously instructed by the CO ... It was the first fierce battle that the unit had encountered to date. The final count was two dead, one injured for the unit while the enemy suffered two counted dead and an estimated seven wounded.[21]

Considering that it was the Van Doos' 'first fierce battle' after nearly three months in Korea, it was a rather small affair, but the battalion's position became more serious when heavy rains continued to fall on the 20th. With the rapidly rising Imjin making it difficult to maintain the ferry service to the far bank, brigade headquarters viewed the situation as 'quite critical': 'The possibility of an early enemy attack was very real and every advantage lay with the enemy should communications and the ferries fail completely. Intelligence indicated that the enemy was reacting strongly to similar patrol bases put out by the 25th Infantry Division to the northwest and the brigade commander was anticipating a strong attack on the brigade positions across the river.'[22]

In an attempt to avert a possible catastrophe, Rockingham moved the bulk of his brigade across the Imjin on the 20th to reinforce the bridgehead defences, committing all of 2 RCR, the Lord Strathcona's Horse squadron, and a company of 2 PPCLI in addition to the Van Doos. Although Rockingham's first preference would have been to withdraw his troops back to the near bank, the 25th Division's commander indicated that he would not be pleased at a withdrawal of the patrol base covering his left flank. With the Chinese continuing to threaten the bridgehead defences 'in considerable force' and the swift current forcing a suspension of ferry operations, the isolated troops on the far side of the river spent a tense night calling down artillery fire to drive off those enemy patrols that approached their positions: 'The situation was now extremely precarious. With the enemy giving every indication of probing for an attack, there were four companies of 2 R22eR, three companies of 2 RCR, one company of 2 PPCLI, the American I&R [intelligence and reconnaissance] Platoon, four tanks of C Squadron, and seventy-five vehicles completely isolated and without access by ferry, ford or footbridge to the east bank of the Imjin.'[23]

Fortunately, the front remained quiet throughout the night, but it was not until the rains finally began to let up late on the 21st and the ferry service was restored that 'the tension eased a little.'[24] Both 2 RCR and 2 R22eR sent out patrols across their front on 22 July but could find no sign of the Chinese and 'enemy activity remained at a low level' until the entire brigade moved into reserve on the 26th. Throughout the tense hours the hardest-working Canadians had been the sappers of the 57th Field Squadron. The engineers' infantry footbridge had been washed out and the anchor for the ferry cable had broken loose at 0100 hours on 21 July, prompting the Canadians to borrow an American utility boat from the 25th Division engineers to transport personnel across the still rising river. By the time river levels began to fall the following day, all three of the squadron's troops were employed at the ferry site at Hwangji-ri improving the approaches and trying to stretch a cable across the 600-foot-wide river to reestablish the ferry's operation.[25]

Although the 25th Brigade remained in the divisional area after being relieved from its positions astride the Imjin on 26 July, I US Corps headquarters assigned it the ambiguous task of acting as a reserve for the entire I Corps at the same time that it was supposed to be the reserve brigade for the Commonwealth Division. As it turned out, however, the divided responsibility had little impact. The Canadians spent much of August supporting or conducting patrols into the Imjin salient themselves and were largely unavailable to fulfill either reserve assignment.[26]

It was at this time that army headquarters in Ottawa finally got around to sorting out a rotation policy for the brigade. The Americans had a policy that required combat soldiers to serve only six months in the front line, while the British and Australians had stipulated that their soldiers would be required to serve just one winter in the theatre. A three-officer team from army headquarters (AHQ) sent to report on 25th Brigade problems in July quickly discovered that the Canadian rotation policy, or lack thereof, 'was the main topic of conversation for all ranks ... A survey of the conditions in the theatre and discussions with the brigade commander and his officers indicate that a fair policy would be to return men to Canada after six months service at and forward of division headquarters, or eight months in rear of division or twelve months in Japan. The conditions in the theatre and the lack of any announced policy are resulting in many regular soldiers, mostly tradesmen and NCO's, deciding not to re-engage. Thirty have already returned to Canada and, as an example, some twenty men have advised OC 25 Signals Squadron that they do not intend to re-engage.' Ottawa's failure to enunciate a rotation policy was seen by the men 'as "neglect" on the part of the Army and the effects of this feeling may be both long-term and far reaching.'[27]

A similar visit in mid-August by the director of infantry, Col. Roger Rowley, reached much the same conclusions. Rowley found that 'morale within the brigade group ... is generally high and troops are in good fighting trim. It is significant, however, that the major topic of conversation within the theatre appears to be rotation back to Canada. Something in the order of 3,500 to 4,000 personnel remain unwilling to join the Active Force. They talk a great deal of the government's moral obligation to release them from service at the end of eighteen months; they are not in the least interested in the "small print" which suggests that they might be retained until the emergency passes. They claim that Mr. Claxton's statements and recruiting propaganda also ignored the "small print."'[28]

A 'tentative rotation policy' for the brigade was finally announced to the men on 18 August. Ignoring Rockingham's advice that combat soldiers spend only six months at the front, AHQ decided that 'personnel will not have to spend more than one winter in Korea and rotations begin after eight months' service.'[29] The announcement was particularly important to the men of 2 PPCLI, who had already spent eight months in the theatre and whose 'originals and those eligible for rotation amount[ed] to approximately 523 all ranks.'[30] Although their Special Force status may have been perceived by many Patricias as a factor in the rotation issue, few soldiers, whether Active or Special Force, had any great desire to spend two winters in Korea or, in the case of regular soldiers, even in the army itself. The earlier AHQ report had warned that a 'substantial number' of Active Force soldiers 'are indicating that they do not intend to re-engage. It is believed that many will have a change of heart on return to Canada. However, it is an unhealthy attitude in a Regular soldier and indicates that there is a need to sell the army to the soldier as a hard and honourable profession rather than as a means of free medical treatment and security in old age.'[31] Having missed the adjutant general's reenlistment drive the previous fall at Fort Lewis, eleven of 2 PPCLI's Special Force officers, including Lieutenant-Colonel Stone and Major Tighe, transferred to the regular army on 6 August as an example – largely futile – to their men.[32]

Aside from listening to the men's grumblings about rotation, the AHQ officers also gained a valuable insight into the challenges facing the Canadian brigade, hardships that staff officers in Ottawa had not been aware of. Most importantly, the visitors were universally 'impressed with the difficulty of the terrain over which Canadian forces are required to operate.' Colonel Rowley told Ottawa: 'It is difficult to express on paper the degree of physical fitness required to fight as an infantryman in Korea.'[33] After seeing the conditions under which the Canadian brigade was operating, Lt.-Col. D.S.F. Bult-Francis of the adjutant general's office understood why more soldiers were being sent home as nonbattle casualties than his boss, Major-General Macklin, would have liked. In his report Bult-Francis emphasized that

> the terrain, the climate, the time and space factor, the filth and poverty and the complete lack of rest facilities in Korea all add up to present problems not previously met by the Canadian Army and to forbid comparison with the conditions met during the last war in Europe.
>
> The lowest position visited was that of D Company, 2 PPCLI on a height of 800 feet which involved a climb of some 40 minutes. On one occasion, this battalion had to climb a 2,700 foot hill before they could begin to clear the ridges – this climb was unopposed yet it required eight hours! Ammunition, water and supplies have to be brought up these heights.
>
> In the summer the troops are exposed to either a scorching heat and constant dirt and dust or soaking downpours and deep gumbo. The winter months bring freezing rain and sleet, or sub-zero temperatures and snow. Little if any protection against the climate is available to the infantry soldier, men of other type units are but slightly better off ...
>
> Due to the terrain and climate a high physical standard is required by all men in units of the brigade. Men with less than battle profile will not last long as drivers, signallers, mechanics etc and if so used will only reduce the efficiency of their units.[34]

Following his August visit, the director of infantry also tried to disabuse the adjutant general of his desire to see greater in-theatre employment of men with lower battle profiles, explaining 'that the hardships to which all fighting and service echelons are subjected require a high medical standard in all units.' These high physical standards meant that 'the health of all components of the force is good,' although Rowley also pointed out that the troops were 'feeding extremely well': 'The selection and variety of [ration] items available, even to forward troops in the area, is quite astonishing.' On the other hand, he was clearly dissatisfied with the welfare situation in Canadian units, describing it simply as 'poor': 'The amenities provided by the auxiliary services of the last war are noticeably missing. Such things as the provision of chocolate bars, cigarettes etc, are not well handled. The troops are very conscious of this fact. Beer, of local type, seems to be in adequate supply, however Canadian troops prefer Canadian beer, and as far as I can determine depend for their supply upon the charitable donations of certain brewery companies in Canada. Canadian cigarettes are in extremely short supply and troops, as I see it, depend entirely upon packages from home for their favourite Canadian brand.' Evidence of neglect by Army headquarters was also seen in the 'noticeable shortage of Canadian clothing both in Korea and within the reinforcement group. Many Canadians are wearing British and US uniforms and I am told that this is not by choice but by necessity.'[35]

Given the circumstances under which the Canadians were operating in the field, another of Rowley's complaints seems rather petty – a criticism that in previous wars Canadians were more likely to have heard from a British staff officer. In the director of infantry's view, 'Discipline within the force seems to be adequate, however, it was apparent to me that the hurried training of the force, although undoubtedly making these troops battle worthy and capable of meeting their commitments, had the effect of reducing the emphasis on such matters as dress, cleanliness and minor matters of deportment and appearance. Many of the junior NCOs simply have not been in the army long enough to have gained the experience and control (out of battle) that one would wish for.' At least Colonel Rowley was sufficiently shrewd to stress that the importance of physical fitness 'was the most important observation I made during my visit' rather than the dress and deportment of the troops away from the battle line. In the more important operational sphere, Rowley noted the recurring debate among Canadian soldiers in Korea about the relative merits of the Canadian-issued Lee-Enfield rifle that had been in use since the Boer War and the American M1 rifle, and the need for 'a suitable lightweight semi-automatic for close quarter fighting':

> Canadian soldiers have in many instances provided themselves with the [American M1] weapon. The questionnaire issued to all units produced the following comments – No. 4 Canadian rifle [the Lee-Enfield] is extremely dependable, the M1 is not and requires far more maintenance and attention than the troops are able to give it. The dependable factor of the M1 is markedly reduced in winter conditions ...
>
> The No. 4 rifle does not produce an adequate volume of fire. The M1 rifle, carefully maintained and 'nursed' undoubtedly produces a much more adequate volume of fire. Main complaints – the M1 is heavy and cumbersome, is more prone to stoppages than the No. 4. In defence its volume of fire is an asset. Generally, the No. 4 rifle is preferred to the M1, but there is an obvious demand for an automatic or semi-automatic weapon to deal with the mass attacks common in this theatre.[36]

Despite such warnings, however, a suitable semiautomatic rifle to replace the Enfield was not developed in time for the Korean conflict; the infantrymen – as they had during the Second World War – would continually grumble about the need for a light automatic weapon. The notorious unreliability of the Sten sub-machine-gun prompted many of the Canadians to equip themselves with the automatic American M2 carbine in trade with neighbouring US units. As is often the case with nonissue personal weapons in an army unit, however, their popularity had more to do with fashion or status than actual utility. The carbine's ready availability was in large measure a result of its almost universal rejection by American soldiers. Hypersensitive to jamming and firing a round that lacked sufficient power, a contemporary US study found that 'the clear majority of Eighth Army ... want it either eliminated or made over into a dependable weapon.' While acknowledging that 'on chance meeting engagements during patrol duty the high fire rate of the carbine may offer some advantage' the American study 'doubted that when men on patrol are armed with M1s and the BAR [Browning automatic rifle], there would be any strengthening of the fire readiness of the patrol through the substitution of the carbine for either of these weapons.'[37]

When assessing complaints about the Lee-Enfield or Sten, it should also be kept in mind that the most effective weapon in a night patrol encounter was often the hand grenade. Not only did the greater explosive power of Commonwealth grenades make them superior to those of the Chinese but in a night action grenades did not immediately betray the attacker's location like a burst of small-arms fire. Moreover, as Rockingham reminded the Canadian Army's quartermaster general in June 1951, it was easy to read too much into the brigade's complaints about certain weapons and equipment. While such griping might lead to the conclusion 'that we think all our equipment is useless ... this is not the case. Certain adjustments are necessary for this type of campaign and experience is the only way of discovering it ... Both British and Americans have had to make similar adjustments for this campaign.'[38] Whatever complaints the 2nd battalions may have expressed about some of their weapons – and they certainly would have benefited from a reliable semiautomatic rifle to replace the Lee-Enfield or a better sub-machine-gun than the Sten – Rockingham's men did not allow their qualms to inhibit their willingness to patrol no man's land aggressively. Indeed, throughout their tour the Special Force battalions maintained a strong belief in the superiority of their combat skills over the enemy's.

Of greater real tactical importance to the Canadians was the Bren light machine-gun, the weapon around which the firepower of each infantry section was organized. As during the Second World War, the 2nd battalions arrived in Korea equipped with one Bren gun per section. One of the first steps by Major-General Cassels upon taking command was to increase the section-level firepower of the division to stop Chinese human wave attacks. He issued additional Brens throughout the division to provide two light machine-guns per infantry section, which gave each rifle company a considerable volume of small-arms fire with which to defend itself.[39]

With the 25th Brigade in reserve, the newly activated Commonwealth Division was assigned to hold a six-mile length of front around the great bend in the Imjin

River that included the former Canadian positions. Throughout August the division continued to make long-range patrols from battalion bridgeheads on the far bank in order to ascertain the location of the Chinese positions within the salient. Opposing the Commonwealth formation was the 64th Chinese Army, which had lost some 40 percent of its personnel and a large number of its supporting weapons during P'eng's spring offensive. By remaining on the defensive north of the river during June and July, however, the communists had been able to rebuild the army with a substantial reinforcement of both men and material. Of its three divisions – the 190th, 191st, and 192nd – the 192nd occupied the Imjin salient, with two of its three 2,000-man regiments forward. According to Cassels, the 'enemy outposts were generally situated about 2,000 to 3,000 yards north of the River Imjin with a series of prepared defensive positions existing in depth to approximately 6,000 to 8,000 yards ... During the period from 28 July to 6 September, the enemy was strictly defensive in nature and avoided contact with our patrols as he saw fit. The enemy did very little patrolling on his own account. Enemy artillery fire was unknown to the division at this time.'[40]

Despite its reserve status during August, the 25th Brigade took an active role in the Commonwealth Division's program of long-range patrols. After supporting a combined US-British patrol into the salient in early August, the Canadians crossed the Imjin themselves on the 13th to carry out a battalion-sized patrol code-named Operation Dirk. The four infantry companies of 2 RCR were supported by a troop of Strathcona tanks, a recce party of engineers from the 57th Field Squadron, three Oxford carriers, and the divisional artillery, primarily from 2 RCHA. Their objective was to force the enemy back from the river while establishing the location of their main line of resistance and, if possible, capturing a prisoner (Map 10).[41]

With Rockingham temporarily absent in Japan and the RCR's own Lieutenant-Colonel Keane filling in as brigade commander, Maj. C.H. Lithgow led the patrol. The battalion's A Company, together with the tanks and a medium machine-gun platoon, crossed the Imjin and established a firm base one mile north of the river by 1900 hours on the 13th. Early on D-day, the three remaining rifle companies and battalion headquarters crossed to the firm base before commencing a leap-frogging advance from hill to hill. Under exhausting conditions of heat and humidity, the three companies completed their planned four-mile advance into enemy territory unopposed before making camp for the night. As Lithgow's report on the patrol makes clear, 'The physical effort required in this op [operation] was very great and although they could and would have tried, the men were too tired to fight efficiently by nightfall on D-Day. The move on D-Day was deliberately made a little longer in order to ensure a short move on D p[lus] 1, when it was expected the bn [battalion] would have to fight.'[42]

Although their movements had been observed by the Chinese throughout the 14th, the first enemy reaction did not occur until that night, when small patrols probed the area of the two forward companies. The following morning, the

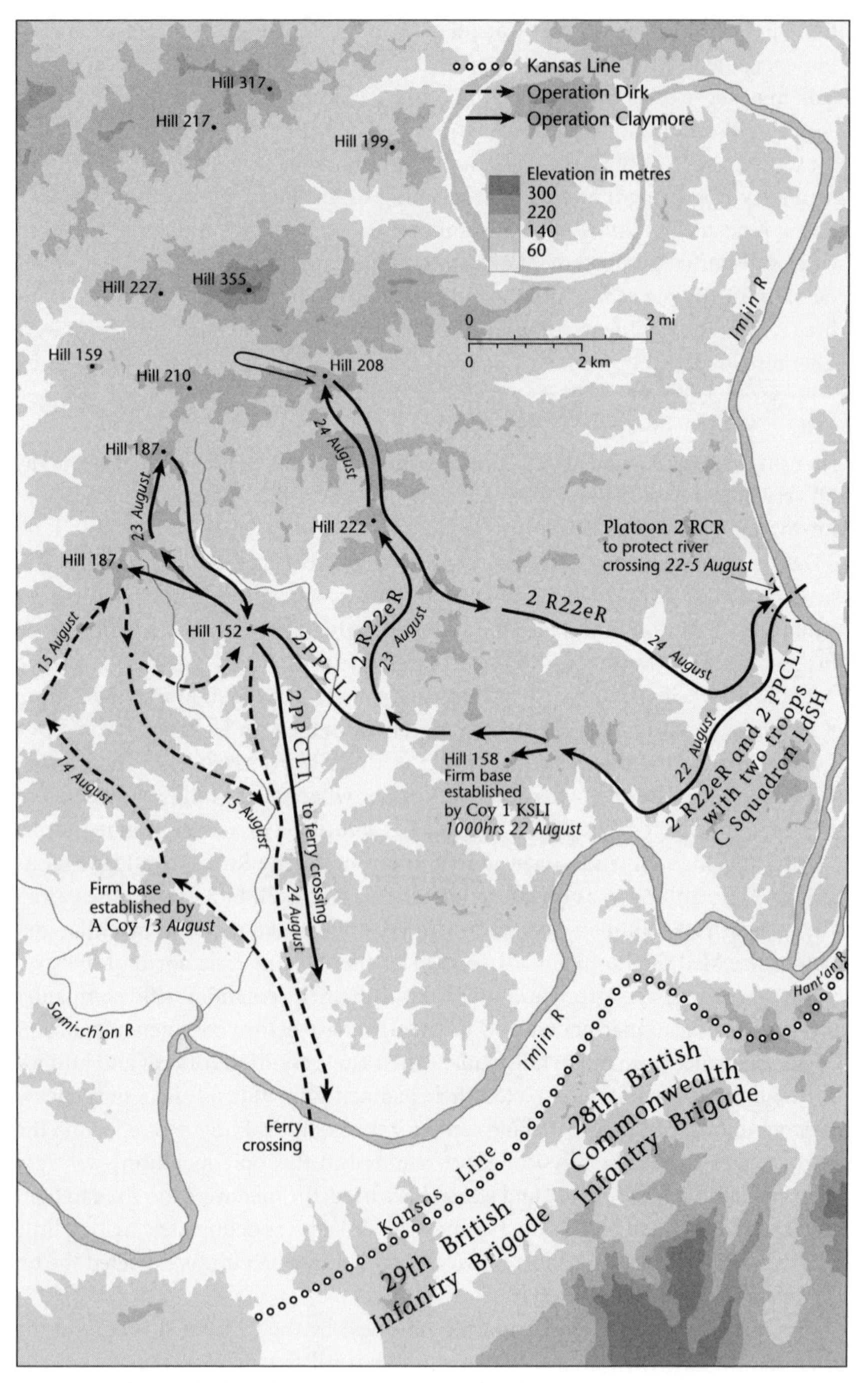

Map 10 *25th Brigade along the Imjin, Operations Dirk and Claymore, August 1951*

battalion encountered constant small-arms, artillery, and mortar fire as C Company moved toward Hill 187, its final objective one mile to the north. According to the company commander, his men were moving toward the objective when 'suddenly, along the crest of a ridge some 200 yards to our front, an enemy bunker appeared. The enemy, who were standing on top of the bunker, turned and looked at us through field glasses, apparently as surprised as we were.'[43] The Canadians were driven to ground by the enemy's machine-gun fire until a combination of artillery and the battalion's own mortar fire allowed them successfully to assault the position. Major Lithgow reported:

> The morale of the enemy opposing the advance seemed high. The position taken by C Coy had ten Chinese who refused to leave their slits [slit trenches] prior to or during [the] attack on their hill feature. In one case an enemy soldier, when ordered to surrender, came out of his bunker with a primed grenade and had to be shot.
>
> Enemy clothing, equipment and weapons found in the area were new and in good condition. North Korean money was prevalent in fairly large quantities on almost all enemy dead left behind. In addition, there was a quantity of rice found in the position taken by C Coy.
>
> The area was littered with propaganda, pamphlets, both in English and in Chinese and Korean. The 'comic-book' type of Communist propaganda was prevalent.
>
> The estimated number of enemy killed was approximately thirty-five.[44]

C Company had suffered only two wounded in capturing the platoon position, but as they continued the advance toward Hill 187, they came under accurate machine-gun fire from the objective. Lieutenant-Colonel Keane, who was circling overhead in a reconnaissance aircraft, warned the company that the Chinese were moving around its flanks and, since Hill 187 was obviously held in strength, ordered a withdrawal. B Company, meanwhile, was advancing toward its hill objective to the northeast of 187 when it, too, came under mortar and small-arms fire. As the company pressed on to the lower slopes of the objective, 'the weight of fire made it obvious that the hill was held in strength and since the object of the patrol had been to confirm this,' no attempts were made to probe any further. B Company was able to make an unhurried withdrawal to the Imjin crossings, but C was more heavily pressed and had to pass through D Company, acting as battalion reserve, before it, too, was able to break free. Altogether, Operation Dirk cost 2 RCR only four wounded.[45]

If nothing else, the operation demonstrated that the Chinese had not yet completely recovered from the heavy losses of their spring offensive. While enemy morale appeared to have been restored, they had to rely primarily on small-arms fire to fend off an attack. 'Artillery and mortar fire from the enemy was both inaccurate and inadequate,' Major Lithgow subsequently reported. 'There were few attempts at correcting fire and never did the concentration on anyone's position become intense.' Conversely, Canadian 'artillery and tank fire support was superb. Special mention must be made of the CO's rep and FOO's of 2 RCHA who, as usual, engaged targets with great enthusiasm and accuracy.' Lithgow was also well pleased with the spirit of his own men who, 'in spite of the "peace negotiations" ... are not backward about engaging the enemy and given a reasonable objective and vigorous leadership are ready to press home any attack.' Most important of all, however, the brigade's officers demonstrated an understanding that careful reconnaissance and planning were vital to success:

> Any operation of this type over such difficult and unknown terrain requires detailed planning as to routes, bounds and even estimated timings. Air photographs should be provided on the scale of NOT less than one set per company commander. Air recce by the battalion and company commanders is desirable after a tentative plan has been made.
>
> Any movement of friendly troops in the area must be ordered and planned by the comd of the op and known to everyone. The CO's orders failed to apprise coy comds [company commanders] of the detailed movement of a RCE [Royal Canadian Engineers] recce party and this party was engaged by own troops in error, fortunately without harm.[46]

The importance of thorough planning was also stressed by the CO of 2 R22eR, Lieutenant-Colonel Dextraze, in his report on a similar patrol, Operation Claymore, the following week. Unlike the earlier operation, 2 R22eR and 2 PPCLI met little opposition in their advance to Hills 208 and 187 within the Imjin salient, even when part of the advance was made at night:

> Although the 2 PPCLI's night op was successful since [it was] not opposed, I am still against such ops at night on any scale higher than pl [platoon] level. I firmly believe that it is almost impossible, at least in such a short period of time, to plan meticulously and prepare for night ops of this scope against an enemy whose strength and location are unknown over unfamiliar terrain. I fear that should contact be made at night while moving fwd with an enemy of Bn or coy strength, utter confusion and disorder would result and there would be no alternative but to withdraw along the same route with probable hy cas [heavy casualties].
>
> I would like to state, however, that I am not opposed to night infiltration on a coy, bn or Bde [brigade] level, provided that routes, terrain and possible enemy posns [positions] have previously been reconnoitred in daylight. I would venture to say that this type of country is particularly suitable for night infiltration but that it was not the object of Op 'Claymore.'[47]

Despite his qualms about the advisability of making a deep penetration at night over unfamiliar – as opposed to reconnoitred – terrain, Dextraze considered

Claymore 'to have been successful ... It has served as good battle inoculation for the batch of new recruits and unexperienced subalterns. Tps [troops] still have a tendency to bunch up, stand on the skyline and sunbathe on fwd slopes despite constant warnings. However, there is nothing wrong that a good stiff fight would not cure very rapidly.'[48] Dextraze would get his wish in the following weeks when the entire Commonwealth Division moved across the river to stay.

The decision to move the division forward to occupy a portion of the no man's land in the Imjin salient was apparently taken at the instigation of its commander prior to his receiving orders from I Corps headquarters for a more general advance all along the corps front. Cassels was concerned that patrols beyond the Imjin, even those ranging deep into the salient, rarely contacted or identified the main enemy positions. (The one exception noted by the general officer commanding was the successful patrol by 2 RCR during Operation Dirk.) As the Canadians could attest, the unpredictability of the river posed a considerable handicap to these patrols, especially during the lengthy rainy season when its current often proved too strong for ferry operations, stranding reconnaissance and fighting parties on the far bank. As a result, Cassels proposed to I Corps headquarters that he move the greater part of the Commonwealth Division north of the Imjin in order to close with the enemy's main defences and inhibit their further construction, while denying them the wide no man's land from which to launch a future assault.[49]

The resulting Operation Minden was confirmed by an order received from I Corps headquarters on 7 September 'to carry out an immediate advance and establish [a] new defence line approximately 5,000 yards north of R Imjin. New line to be an extension of I Corps' forward line Wyoming' (see Map 11).[50] The following day, the 28th British Commonwealth Brigade secured bridgeheads over the river to allow construction of two Class 50 bridges for tanks. In a series of carefully planned phases over the next several days, the division advanced to its objectives with only minimal enemy interference. The 29th British Brigade occupied the left half of the division's front while the 25th Canadian Brigade took up positions on the right, and the latter's casualties of only three killed and ten wounded attest to the light opposition of the Chinese. The stiffest fight came on 12 September when B Company, 2 R22eR, 'put in an attack on three hills across the valley to its front to clear the enemy from them so that work on the defences of the main position could be carried on without interference.' Skilfully supported with direct fire from the Strathconas' Shermans, the Canadian tanks 'literally fired the troops down the slope from Hill 172, across the valley, and on to the middle objective,' engaging enemy bunkers often no more than forty to fifty yards ahead of the advance. The attack was witnessed by the brigade commander who found it to be 'incredibly fast and executed in the very best fashion ... The soldiers of [Capt. J.P.R.] Trembley's company followed so closely behind the neutralizing fire provided by the flat trajectory weapons of the tanks that the battalion commander, Jimmy Dextraze, swore that some of the rounds shaved the heads of the R22eR company as they went over the valley and up the hill

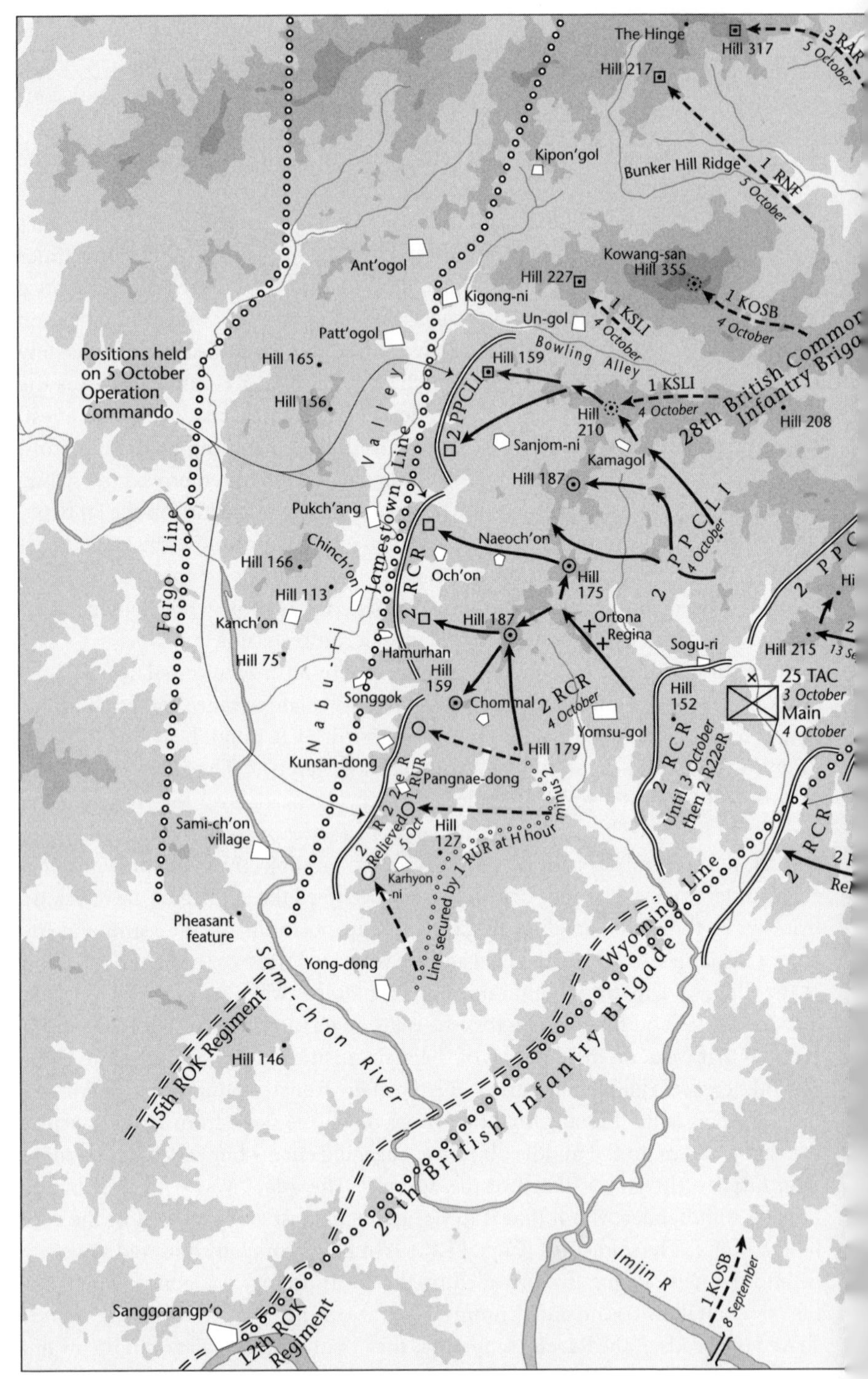

Map 11 *Operations Minden and Commando, 11 September-5 October 1951*

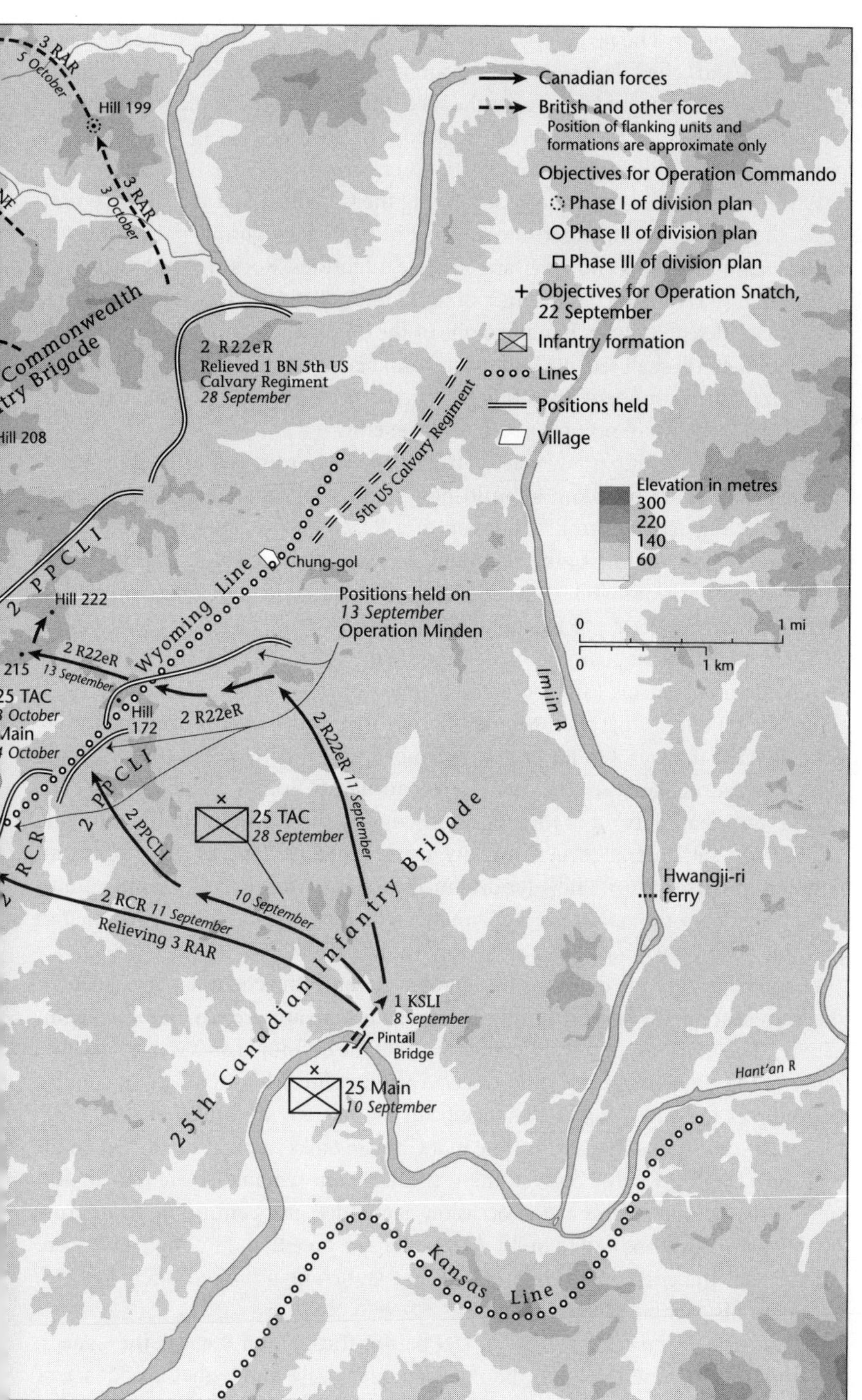

Canadian forces
British and other forces
Position of flanking units and formations are approximate only
Objectives for Operation Commando
Phase I of division plan
Phase II of division plan
Phase III of division plan
Objectives for Operation Snatch, 22 September
Infantry formation
Lines
Positions held
Village
Elevation in metres
300
220
140
60
0
1 mi
0
1 km
3 RAR
5 October
Hill 199
3 RAR
3 October
Commonwealth
ntry Brigade
Hill 208
2 R22eR
Relieved 1 BN 5th US Calvary Regiment
28 September
5th US Calvary Regiment
Chung-gol
2 PPCLI
Hill 222
Wyoming Line
Positions held on
13 September
Operation Minden
2 R22eR
13 September
215
25 TAC
Hill 172
2 R22eR
2 PPCLI
2 R22eR 11 September
Imjin R
2 PPCLI
RCR
25 TAC
28 September
2 RCR 11 September
Relieving 3 RAR
10 September
25th Canadian Infantry Brigade
Hwangji-ri ferry
1 KSLI
8 September
Pintail Bridge
25 Main
10 September
Hant'an R
Kansas Line

to rout the enemy. The next day the company shaved a strip through the middle of their heads and called themselves the "Iroquois Company."'[51] Although B Company did not remain on the objective after the successful assault, the fierceness of the Van Doo attack convinced the Chinese to abandon the position. The next day, D Company occupied the hill and counted thirty-six enemy corpses in its entrenchments.[52]

With the Imjin River no longer separating the Canadian and the Chinese positions, the brigade commander immediately instituted a vigorous patrol policy to reveal enemy locations and ascertain Chinese intentions. Rockingham's belief that maintaining a careful reconnaissance of the Chinese positions was key to a successful, vigilant defence always remained one of the dominant features of his tenure in command. As we shall see, his leadership would ensure that the Canadian brigade always remained confident operating forward of its own positions and did not surrender the initiative in no man's land to the enemy.

Following the Minden advance, patrolling was coordinated at brigade headquarters with each battalion submitting its patrol plans twenty-four hours in advance of the actual patrol.[53] The men of 2 R22eR – who, after four and a half months in Korea, still had not seen much action – maintained regular patrols in front of their positions while claiming that they 'don't mind hardship so much now that they have the chance to meet and kill the enemy.'[54] On the left of the brigade, 2 RCR manned outpost positions by day and smaller listening posts at night but also mounted larger patrols to feel out the Chinese positions. As explained in a unit report, 'Soon after [Operation Minden], occupancy patrols were edged forward to get the feel of the area. On Friday, 14 September, A Company with a troop of tanks from C Squadron, Lord Strathcona's Horse, patrolled to point 152 (codenamed Dog) [a mile and a half in front of their position], during the day but withdrew at night. On Sunday, 16 September, D Company, using point 152 Dog as a firm base, attempted to patrol to [the hill] (codenamed Regina). After hand-to-hand combat forty yards from the objective, D Company withdrew, having established the fact that this position was occupied and strongly defended.'[55]

Despite bringing the division considerably closer to the enemy's main defences, the move into the Imjin salient did not initially lead to any great increase in enemy activity. The most noticeable difference was that the divisional area was now within range of the Chinese batteries and received artillery fire. Although light in volume, the indirect fire was a marked change from the relative immunity of the Kansas Line positions. It was also at this time that Chinese tanks were first reported on the division's front. Overall, however, the 192nd Division remained 'defensive in attitude, resisting our patrols as the occasion demanded and continuing to improve his defensive positions and to build up his offensive potential. Although it was considered that the enemy had the capability of launching a limited offensive, such action on his part failed to materialise.'[56]

As was true of the vast majority of UN patrols throughout the war, the Canadians found that Chinese soldiers did not surrender easily, and higher headquarters' repeated demands for prisoners were difficult to fulfill. Given the 'stand-offish' nature of Chinese tactics and 'their genuine reluctance to become prisoners,' the Canadian brigade 'decided to go after a prisoner with a larger force by night, and if necessary to carry out a night assault in order to achieve this aim. As a result, night operation "Snatch" was conceived.'[57] As an individual operation, Snatch was not particularly noteworthy. However, since it wonderfully illustrates the professionalism that the officers and men of the Special Force routinely exhibited in their approach to military operations, it will be examined in greater detail than its size or results would otherwise merit.

Like earlier Canadian patrols, Snatch was planned only after several reconnaissances had been made of the approaches to the intended target, an enemy position located along a ridgeline running southeast to northwest some two and a half miles beyond the 2 RCR entrenchments:

> Aggressive patrolling by night continued during the early part of the week until Thursday, 20 September, when A Company was chosen to patrol at night to the area Regina. This patrol was again stopped short of the objective and withdrew. The company commander [Capt. E.K. Wildfang] sent out a recce patrol of an officer and four men just before dawn to look at the valley to the northeast of the ridge upon which lay the objective. This patrol penetrated to [the head of the valley, one mile due north of Regina] without encountering enemy.
>
> As a result of the information which had been gathered over a period of a week, it was clear that the enemy occupied the feature Regina and also [a second hill along the ridge, half a mile to the northwest] (codenamed Ortona). A route had been discovered that outflanked these positions. It appeared that the enemy were jumpy and fired on fixed line upon hearing or seeing movement. This fixed line fire was carefully charted and none came down the valley to the northeast.
>
> As a result of this information, it appeared that the capture of a prisoner was feasible. Air photographs were available for the first time and were used to confirm the information already available.
>
> B Company was selected to do the snatch and preliminary planning commenced. All officers, NCOs and men who had operated by day or night in the area were contacted and questioned by the company commander and later by platoon commanders where applicable. The air photographs were studied by all down to section leader level. In every case available information was related to the air photographs and to the maps. Time of moon rise was checked and weather reports studied.[58]

Similar care was taken in formulating the plan. The operation was to be carried out by the three platoons of B Company while company headquarters and A Company's 1 Platoon held Hill 152, code-named Dog, a mile and a half in front of 2 RCR's entrenchments. After waiting until dark at the Dog position, Nos. 4 and 5 Platoons were to make their way up the valley that lay to the north of the Ortona-Regina ridgeline and was not covered by enemy fire. Upon reaching the spur that ran up to the Ortona feature, the two platoons would make their attack from the northeast. After occupying Ortona, 'one platoon would face northwest to protect the rear and the other platoon would make for Regina and attempt the snatch.' No. 6 Platoon, meanwhile, was to form a firm base on the ridge midway between the Regina and Dog features to guard the flank of the other two platoons. A group of six scouts were to make their way another half-mile west of 6 Platoon, to the abandoned village of Yomsu-gol half a mile due south of Regina, 'to pick up any enemy who might try to escape by that route.' Once the Ortona and Regina positions had been taken, Nos. 4 and 5 Platoons 'were to attempt to clear the ridge on the way back to the firm base Dog but if this proved impossible, they were to get out by the valley through which they had advanced.' Great care was also taken in providing accurate artillery support for the patrol without tipping their hand to the enemy: 'The targets had been registered a few days before, during other operations, so that no registration was required before the operation,' which 'was to be silent until support was required.' The Royals would also receive medium machine-gun support from the Royal Ulster Regiment to their south, firing on the communist entrenchments immediately to the west of the objective. Once the snatch had been completed, B Company would reform on the Dog feature before heading back to its own lines at first light.[59]

The three platoons of B Company moved out from their entrenchments between 1600 and 1730 hours on the afternoon of 22 September and followed a covered approach to a forming-up area to the rear of Hill 152. While it was still light, Captain Wildfang – a Second World War veteran – took his platoon commanders and the scout officer to an observation post on the Dog feature from which they could see the Regina objective a little less than a mile to the northwest along the ridgeline. After getting 'a good look at the ground over which they were to move, including the recce of routes to the valley' north of the ridge, the officers returned to their men to await dark. No. 6 Platoon set off along the ridge at 2200 hours and was digging in at its blocking position halfway between Dog and Regina twenty-five minutes later. The six scouts, meanwhile, continued on to Yomsu-gol directly south of Regina.[60]

Nos. 4 and 5 Platoons set off into the valley north of the ridge just as the moon was beginning to rise at 2320 hours. For the next two hours the two platoons made their way silently up the valley to the spur leading up to the Ortona feature. During the mile and a half approach, they could hear artillery on the PPCLI front to the right, and the machine-guns of the Royal Ulsters firing on the Chinese positions west of Ortona: 'When this MMG fire started at 2300 hours, the enemy had opened up on fixed lines firing south and southeast from Regina and Point 187.' At 0150 hours, 5 Platoon led the way up the spur to clear the Ortona objective. With the enemy facing to the southeast, the position was taken in reverse and 'complete surprise was achieved.' Twelve enemy were killed, three presumed killed, and one prisoner was captured in the ensuing firefight, while the platoon commander and one other Canadian were wounded. Reorganizing on the position, 4 Platoon was able to start down the ridgeline toward the Regina objective at 0300 hours:

> They advanced approximately 200 yards when they discovered a group of Chinese who did not seem to be too alert. It is thought they had just been awakened by the skirmish on Ortona. 4 Platoon closed in on the group using grenades and small arms. Five enemy were killed and four presumed killed while one [additional] prisoner was taken. 4 Platoon suffered one [wounded].
>
> 4 Platoon proceeded southeast down the ridge until they were 75-100 yards south east of Regina. Here they came under small arms fire from Regina and mortar bombs commenced to fall on them and 5 Platoon who were 200 yards behind. The time was now 0410 hours. 4 Platoon could distinguish two or more mortar positions only 100 yards away and were waiting for 5 Platoon to close up before attacking. However, 5 Platoon had lost contact and had not closed up. At 0440 hours, 4 Platoon were ordered to return to base by the valley because daylight was due in an hour-and-a-half. Without the support of 5 Platoon they might not have had time to finish the skirmish and would have been caught behind the enemy positions in daylight. 4 Platoon arrived back at Dog at 0635 hours, withdrawing under covering fire by 2 RCHA. When the artillery fire started on Ortona, the enemy small arms fire ceased.[61]

No. 5 Platoon was also forced by mortar and small-arms fire to return to Dog by way of the valley. Out of communication, the platoon's position was unknown to Wildfang until they returned safely to the company area at 0740 hours. Despite the confusion that marked the final stages of the operation, Snatch had been a notable triumph. Two Chinese prisoners had been brought back to the RCR lines, and at least eighteen enemy had been killed, for a cost of only three Canadians wounded. The success of the operation was due to the thoroughness with which it had been planned and carried out. The narrow difference between success and failure – and the importance of careful preparation – was clearly understood by the author of the RCR's after-action report:

> It could have been an even greater success if 5 Platoon had not lost touch, [thereby] enabling 4 Platoon to attack the enemy mortar position from the rear. By the same token, an early slip might have caused heavy casualties to the company and an utter lack of success. The operation was well-planned and capably executed. Meticulous attention was given to all detail especially the briefing.
>
> No new lessons came out of this operation. It is once again established, as in general here in Korea, that there are no new lessons. The proper application of existing lessons and principles of long standing continue to ensure success.
>
> To conclude, it might be well to reiterate a few points. 'Time spent on reconnaissance is never wasted' will always be applicable. Detailed, meticulous planning is required down to section leader level. Compilation of information over a period of time is very necessary and pays dividends. Air photographs are invaluable in planning night operations. Communications are essential and must be maintained. The most important lesson re-learnt on this operation was brought out so well by the communication troubles of 5 Platoon. While they were in communication they were part of a team.

> They could be supported by an artillery regiment in addition to the battalion supporting weapons and therefore were a formidable force for the enemy to reckon with. However, once communications failed, they were merely thirty soldiers on their own behind the enemy position, not able to call upon anyone or ask for support. Also they caused confusion and prevented the last phase of the operation being entirely successful. Too much time and energy cannot be expended to ensure that communications are established and maintained.
>
> The Chinese are very nervous at night and are not the supermen that some people would have us believe. Our experience[s] by night have led us to conclude that the Canadian soldier with his adaptability, initiative and native cunning is far superior to the Chinese by night or by day.[62]

Operation Snatch had been successful because the Special Force officers understood their profession and were willing to make the thorough preparations required to give their men a reasonable opportunity of achieving the objective even when, as inevitably occurred, things did not go entirely according to plan.

Throughout the summer months, the Eighth Army had remained largely on the defensive, strengthening its Wyoming Line positions in the hope that the ceasefire negotiations at Kaesong would produce an agreement. Aside from their natural desire to go home, the soldiers' interest in the peace talks was far from academic: progress – or lack thereof – in the negotiations would determine the course and intensity of military operations for the remainder of the war. From the outset of the talks, however, it seemed to the UN delegation that the communists were more interested in scoring a propaganda victory than concluding an armistice. With the selected site for the negotiations inside the Chinese lines, the arrival of the UN delegation under a white flag of truce for the opening of talks on 10 July was represented by the communists as a UN surrender. The UN's negotiators, led by the US Navy's Vice-Admiral C. Turner Joy, also found themselves seated on lower chairs than the communist delegation, led by the North Korean Lt.-Gen. Nam Il. Moreover, the communist negotiators seemed unable to refrain from irrational outbursts of ideological rhetoric over every procedural detail and agenda discussion. Another tactic was employed on 10 August, when the communists chose to demonstrate their rejection of a UN statement by staring across the table at the UN delegates in complete silence for two hours and eleven minutes.[63]

Writing to his former boss, the president of the BC Electric company, the following March, the business manager in Rockingham emerged when he described the peace talks as 'almost exactly on the same pattern as a labour union negotiation where the labour negotiators have communist tendencies: ridiculous and unimportant points are continually dragged up to cloud the issue and delay agreement. I am not well informed enough to know what the outcome will be but it has never appeared favourable to me.'[64] His skepticism came to be shared by most of the Western public during the two-year negotiation that followed. While each side had to refer policy decisions to its superiors in Washington or Beijing, the Chinese communication system was less sophisticated and more time consuming, adding to the frustrations. While many of the communist outbursts at the negotiation table were obviously contrived, there also developed a genuine personal dislike for the members of the UN team as representatives of the hated capitalist system. Equally resentful of the evasions and abuse on the communist side, the UN delegates soon came to dislike their counterparts on a personal level as well.[65]

The Kaesong negotiations were frequently interrupted by delays and adjournments. The UN negotiating team, for instance, withdrew for two days on 4 August after spotting an armed Chinese company marching past during a lunch break. On 22 August, Nam Il broke off the talks on the pretence that the UN forces were attempting to murder his delegation by air attack, and negotiations did not resume for two months. Meanwhile, the fighting along the Korean hillsides continued unabated.

While the Commonwealth Division had been making its largely unopposed Minden advance across the Imjin River in mid-September, a much harder fight was taking place in the X Corps sector to the east. As the armistice negotiations bogged down at Kaesong, General Van Fleet became increasingly concerned that the relative inactivity of his troops was eroding their combat efficiency. 'A sitdown army is subject to collapse at the first sign of an enemy effort,' he asserted in September. 'As Commander of the Eighth Army, I couldn't allow my forces to become soft and dormant.' Although the US joint chiefs of staff had rescinded the requirement that the theatre commander secure their approval before launching major ground operations, neither Van Fleet nor General Ridgway believed that the Eighth Army had the military capability to undertake a major offensive into North Korea. They were more concerned about several sectors of the Wyoming Line that were dominated by the communist positions and believed that more limited operations would serve to correct these deficiencies.[66]

One of the most worrisome sections of line lay in the Taebaek Mountains northeast of the important Hwach'on Reservoir that supplied Seoul with hydroelectricity. Some twenty miles from the reservoir a large circular valley known as the Punchbowl was dominated by the North Koreans. From their positions on the western, northern, and eastern ridges surrounding the valley, the communists could observe the UN lines of communication and direct artillery fire onto the Kansas Line defences. Although the US 2nd Infantry Division had been able to capture the mountain of Taeu-san by late July, heavy monsoon rains delayed the opening of the main offensive until mid-August, when three ROK divisions launched an attack on one of the ridges immediately east of the Punchbowl. After nine days of attack and counterattack, the ROK I Corps was finally able to wrest control of the ridge from its defenders. Possession of the ridge not only provided protection for the UN supply route running through the Soyang valley but also allowed the ROK troops to observe and fire on enemy movements north of the Punchbowl.[67]

At the same time that the ROK I Corps was making its effort east of the valley, the US X Corps was ordered by Van Fleet to capture a second ridgeline to its west-southwest, nearer the Hwach'on Reservoir. Believing 'that the South Korean troops lacked self-confidence and needed experience to develop faith in their own abilities,' the general also ordered the corps commander to employ ROK units in the assault. The North Korean positions included thick minefields and stout bunkers and proved to be a difficult assignment. As ROK casualties mounted and their morale declined, the corps commander was forced to commit US troops to help capture what had now been dubbed by the press 'Bloody Ridge.' The experience of the US 2nd Division pointed out several shortcomings:

> The 2nd [Division] was drawn in, but then, and in following days, the tactical direction for the capture of what became known as 'Bloody Ridge,' was flawed. Successive divisional commanders applied their forces crudely and obstinately. Despite the lessons learned a year before on the Naktong, replacements for casualties were sent directly from the trucks which had brought them to companies in or entering the melee. They knew no one, could scarcely tell friend from foe. Some were young officers sent to lead a platoon they joined in darkness, among whom they fell as a stranger in the first clash of the following day.[68]

After ten days of hard fighting with little result, the corps commander widened the frontage of the attack to include a second US and three ROK divisions. By early September, X Corps's efforts finally began to pay off as the depleted communist defenders grudgingly gave ground, allowing the UN forces to capture the northern lip of the Punchbowl as well as Bloody Ridge itself. The three-week fight had cost the X Corps over 2,700 casualties. Corps headquarters estimated that it had inflicted over 15,000 casualties on the enemy.[69] The high UN casualty totals convinced Van Fleet that any major advance into North Korea would not be worth the cost in soldiers' lives, but he remained committed to the idea of more limited offensives. As the British official history has observed, 'considerable casualties among the North Koreans, and their withdrawal locally' in the Bloody Ridge fighting, 'unfortunately encouraged General Van Fleet to order the capture of the next ridge to the north. Its heights posed no disadvantage of substance to the United Nations sector but they were fought for fiercely by the North Koreans.'[70] In another difficult, month-long struggle for 'Heartbreak Ridge' to the west of the Punchbowl, the US 2nd Division incurred an additional 3,745 casualties simply to achieve a straighter-looking defence line on Eighth Army maps.[71] If nothing else, the Heartbreak Ridge fighting clearly demonstrated that a balance of military forces now existed across the Korean peninsula and it would be extremely difficult for either side to mount a major penetration of the other's line without substantial reinforcement and a willingness to accept very heavy casualties.

As the Heartbreak Ridge fighting was getting under way in mid-September, Van Fleet was still considering several plans for ambitious advances along the Eighth

Army line. One of these, Operation Cudgel, called for a nine-mile drive forward from the Wyoming Line positions to protect the Ch'orwon-Kumhwa railroad across the base of the Iron Triangle. This would be followed by a two-division amphibious assault on the east coast to cut off the North Korean forces facing the US X and ROK I Corps. After rejecting both plans as too costly, Van Fleet accepted a more modest proposal put forward by Lt. Gen. John Wilson O'Daniel, the recently appointed commander of the US I Corps. O'Daniel's plan called for a five-division, six-mile advance to a new defence line, Jamestown, a move that, like the Cudgel plan, would secure the Ch'orwon-Kumhwa railroad and reduce the I Corps' reliance on trucks to haul its supplies. There were sound tactical reasons behind O'Daniel's proposal: the ground held by the Chinese gave them direct observation of several of the Imjin crossings and long stretches of the numerous roads leading up to the I Corps' current defence line. Since the new Jamestown Line included

After occupying the Chinese positions overlooking the Nabu-ri valley during Operation Commando in early October 1951, the Canadians quickly set to work improving the entrenchments and re-siting them to face from east to west. Here men of 2 RCR make themselves at home in the former Chinese entrenchments as a supporting LdSH tank runs its engine, most likely to recharge the vehicle's batteries. NAC PA193470

portions of the enemy's main defences as well as important observation posts, however, the Chinese were expected to resist the advance with considerable force.[72]

On the Commonwealth Division's front, the Jamestown objective lay from two to four miles northwest of the Wyoming Line positions occupied during the Minden advance (see Map 11, p. 154). Some eight miles long, the new line was to run along a series of hills fronting an unnamed tributary of the Sami-ch'on River from its junction with that river north to two large mountains, Kowang-san, whose peak was 355 metres above sea level, and Maryang-san, Hill 317, two miles north of Hill 355. In devising a plan for the division's first – and only – major attack, Major-General Cassels decided to employ just two brigades. The 28th British Commonwealth Brigade would attack the two mountains, Kowang-san and Maryang-san, while the Canadian brigade attacked the line of hills fronting the Sami-ch'on tributary in the south. Each brigade was to be reinforced by a battalion from the 29th British Brigade – the 1st Battalion, Royal Ulster Rifles would advance to cover the 25th Brigade's left flank – with the bulk of the division's armour employed in support of the northern attack. The operation was to be divided into three phases, with the Commonwealth brigade assaulting Hill 355 on D-day, the Canadians capturing the line of hills south of Hill 210 on D plus 1, and the Commonwealth brigade pushing on to take Hill 317 on D plus 2, while the 25th Brigade's right two battalions completed their advance to Hill 159 and the heights above the village of Och'on. Despite the considerable frontage involved, the employment of only two brigades attacking on successive days allowed Cassels to maximize his striking power by concentrating the entire divisional artillery, plus any batteries allocated from corps or army resources, to support each brigade's attack.[73]

The Commonwealth Division's engineers, which included the Canadian 57th Field Squadron, spent the days leading up to Operation Commando building the roads and tracks needed for its support. As a preliminary to the main advance, the 25th Brigade's three infantry battalions occupied the enemy's outpost line, 2,000 yards in front of the Minden positions, on 28 September. It was subsequently learned that the 64th Army had relieved its 192nd Division with the 191st five days before the Canadian advance. Even so, the fresh formation offered only token resistance to the occupation of its outposts. On 1 October, the division's 25-pounders and 4.2-inch mortars began their preliminary bombardment without departing sufficiently from the previous program of harassing fire to arouse suspicion. As the 28th Brigade's infantry battalions moved out from the start line in the predawn twilight of 3 October, the divisional artillery was joined by heavier-calibre guns from corps and army batteries. On the Commonwealth brigade's left, the King's Shropshire Light Infantry (KSLI) had more than 10,000 yards to cover before reaching its objective, Hill 210, to the south of 355. In the centre, the King's Own Scottish Borderers (KOSB) had a similar distance to go to reach the dominant heights of Hill 355 while the right-hand battalion, 3 RAR, was to take Hill 199, two miles to its northeast, in preparation for its assault on Hill 317 on the third day of the operation.[74]

An early morning mist greatly aided the initial advances, particularly that of 3 RAR, which set out for Hill 199 at 0300 hours. Despite 'darkness, river mist, thick vegetation and rocks,' the battalion was in position to assault the summit five hours later and had cleared the feature by 1015 hours, killing or wounding most of the occupying Chinese platoon at a cost of only three Australians wounded.[75] The two British battalions also made early gains but soon found enemy resistance growing as they neared their objectives. Supported by the Centurion tanks of A Squadron, 8th Hussars, 1 KSLI had reached Hill 208, halfway to Hill 210, without resistance by 0600. By 1000 hours, however, 1 KOSB and 1 KSLI had met strong enemy opposition, and progress for the rest of the day was difficult. Facing elements of two Chinese regiments, both battalions had to contend with enemy snipers, who laid low in the dense undergrowth and opened fire only after the leading platoons had passed them by. Detailing infantrymen to clear snipers along the approach route reduced their fighting strength while the advance brought them 'within range of previously silent enemy artillery and a considerable volume of artillery fire was received during the operation. An estimated 2,500 rounds fell in one brigade area in twenty-four hours, which was unprecedented at that time.' The volume of enemy fire was dwarfed by the response of the division's supporting artillery as a total of 22,324 rounds were fired on the Commonwealth Brigade's front but, by last light, 1 KSLI was still 1,000 yards short of its objective while 1 KOSB was a similar distance from Hill 355.[76]

The failure of the two British battalions to secure their initial objectives meant that the plan for the Canadian brigade's advance had to be altered. During the evening of 3 October, Cassels decided to postpone the Canadian attack from 0600 hours the next day to 1100 hours. This would make the divisional artillery available to the 28th Brigade when it renewed its assault in the morning, after which it would have only the direct support of the 16th New Zealand Field Regiment on call.[77] Although the Australian battalion had hoped for a day of rest before launching their assault on Hill 317, it was not to be. At dawn on 4 October, one company of 3 RAR crossed the valley between Hill 199 and the shoulder of Hill 355 to occupy the long spur that ran northeast from the peak. The Australians launched their assault on the Chinese platoon holding Hill 220 at 0900 hours, quickly killing or driving off the enemy before pressing on up the spur to rout the remainder of the company. Exhibiting their usual drive and determination, the RAR company took advantage of the initiative they had gained and pushed one of their platoons on toward the peak of Hill 355 even though they had no orders to do so. By clearing the eastern slope of Kowang-san, the Australians eased the task of 1 KOSB, which was making a simultaneous assault up the western face of the mountain.[78] The Chinese defenders, for fear of being trapped between the two attacks, abandoned the peak with little further resistance, their retreat to the northwest being harried by the divisional artillery. On the Commonwealth brigade's left, 1 KSLI met only light opposition in finally securing Hill 210, three-quarters of a mile southwest of 355, by 1010

The view north from Hill 187 (east of Hamurhan village) along the line of hills occupied during the Commando advance as they appeared on 26 June 1952. The entrenchments on Hill 210 are visible directly below Hill 355. The company position on the ridge leading to Hill 159 (out of sight to the left) can be seen below the enemy-held Hill 227. The Canadian positions directly north of the photographer's location are facing west toward the Chinese-held hills across the Nabu-ri valley. DHH 410B25.014 D2

hours. It was subsequently relieved by A Company, 2 PPCLI when the Canadians opened Phase II of the Commando operation, and 1 KSLI moved on to occupy its final objective on Hill 227, west of Hill 355, by nightfall on 4 October.[79]

In view of the stout enemy resistance on their right, the men of the 25th Brigade were expecting an equally stiff fight when they crossed their start line promptly at 1100 hours. Fortunately for the Canadian battalions, however, the loss of Hills 355 and 210 had convinced the enemy regiment facing them to make 'an unexpected withdrawal from well-prepared positions.'[80] The Royals met no opposition in easily securing their Phase II objectives, Hills 159 and 175, halfway to the final Jamestown Line position. Only on the 2 PPCLI front did the enemy put up any resistance, when D Company advanced on the main battalion objective, Hill 187. At 1530 hours, D Company's 'leading platoon (10 Platoon) under command of Lieutenant C.E.S. Curmi came into close grips with the enemy right in amongst their crawl trenches and dugouts. The enemy stayed in their dugouts firing and refusing to surrender until killed.'[81] Although the assault cost the Patricias one killed and six wounded, they captured four of the enemy and counted a further twenty-eight Chinese corpses in the entrenchments. Only four other Patricias were wounded during the day.

The ease with which the brigade's Phase II objectives had been secured allowed the Canadians to press on to occupy most of their final Jamestown positions by last light. No further enemy troops were encountered during the advance. However, as 2 RCR advanced to its final objectives 'in the early evening, B Company came under heavy artillery fire and suffered thirteen casualties, three killed and ten wounded. There was great difficulty in getting the wounded out due to the jeep ambulances having much trouble in going over the bad roads.'[82] Once again, fortune smiled on 2 R22eR. Held in reserve during the advance on 4 October, the Van Doos did not move forward to relieve the 1st Battalion, Royal Ulster Regiment on the brigade's left until the next day. As recorded in their war diary, 'The troops walked about two miles and were very tired due to the hot sun and their heavy loads.'[83] The ground occupied was 'covered with Chinese equipment,' evidence of the enemy's hasty retreat and the numerous casualties inflicted by the divisional artillery. With 2 R22eR on the left, 2 RCR in the centre, and 2 PPCLI on the right, the Canadian brigade had reached the approximate position it was destined to hold for the next twenty-two months of fighting:

> The positions overlooked what was called the Nabu-ri Valley [where that stream flowed south] and formed a no man's land between the brigade positions and those of the Chinese on the other side. These [Chinese] positions were dominated by Hill 166, whose shell-scarred top dominated the forward companies of 2 RCR, and Hill 156, opposite 2 PPCLI. The Nabu-ri valley joined the broader Sami-ch'on (whose river was the divisional boundary) across [from] the left flank of 2 RCR, and formed opposite 2 R22eR a broad plain some 2,000 metres square. 2 R22eR held the best defensive positions as any attempt on their lines could be easily seen and countered on the valley floor. In contrast, 2 PPCLI held the least enviable [positions] of all, its right forward company [on Hill 159] was considerably ahead of the left forward KSLI company [on Hill 227], its right flank was the lateral road forming the inter-brigade boundary and its positions on the right, at least, were dominated by Hill 355.[84]

The success of Phase II left only the Australian assault on Hill 317, two miles north of 355, to complete the Commando advance. Although the 317 mark was its highest point, Maryang-san was a two-mile long, crescent-shaped ridgeline with numerous spurs that made it readily defensible. Faced by an enemy that was sheltered in deep bunkers across the entire feature, Cassels detailed the 1st Battalion,

Looking west-northwest from Hill 187 toward the enemy positions on the far side of the Nabu-ri valley. The combined effects of extensive Chinese digging and Commonwealth artillery fire are evident on the main enemy-held hilltops. DHH 410B25.014 D2

Royal Northumberland Fusiliers of the 29th Brigade to support the Australian effort with an attack on the ridgeline's western end centred on Hill 217. The 3 RAR, meanwhile, was to have one company 'feint from the southeast while attacking successively with two companies from the east. On this basis, the Chinese defending Maryang-san would be distracted.'[85] As it turned out, however, the capture of Hill 317 was to be the Commonwealth Division's longest and toughest fight of the operation.

After 'another very quiet night with no enemy contact,' the assaulting battalions set off in the predawn darkness of 5 October to cover the two miles between Hill 199 and their objectives. Receiving 'a generous share of the 9,000 rounds of preliminary bombardment' and air strikes with napalm, the Northumberlands managed to capture Hill 217 by 1500 hours but made little progress in driving a well-entrenched enemy from the reverse slope and were forced to withdraw. The Australians also had a difficult time attacking 'against very strong enemy opposition from well dug in defensive positions' as they made their way toward Hill 317 from the southeast. After committing all four of its infantry companies, 3 RAR eventually captured its objective at 1700 hours when C Company, which had assaulted Hill 355 the previous day, occupied the summit.[86]

The two battalions renewed their attempts to clear the ridges on the 6th 'but enemy opposition remained as strong as ever.' The Northumberlands eventually succeeded in reaching Hill 217, but in the late afternoon 'were again forced to withdraw due to heavy enemy artillery and mortar fire on to the feature.'[87] After yet another day of tough slogging, the Australians finally managed to seize the 'Hinge' feature directly above the Hill 217 objective. Fighting off three determined Chinese counterattacks during the night, 3 RAR woke up on 8 October to discover that the enemy had abandoned the defences on 217.[88] The casualties the two battalions suffered attest to the stubbornness with which the Chinese had defended Maryang-san. The Northumberlands lost 16 killed, 94 wounded, and 3 missing in the action, while 3 RAR suffered 20 killed and 104 wounded. Overall, the five days of Operation Commando cost the Commonwealth Division 58 killed and 262 wounded. The enemy's decision to withdraw from the defences facing the Canadians prior to the 25th Brigade's attack was reflected in the brigade totals of only 4 killed and 28 wounded.[89]

On the Commonwealth Division's immediate right flank, where the 1st US Cavalry Division's objectives threatened the Chinese supply base of Sangnyong-ni, the enemy's resistance to the I Corps advance was fiercest. By their reaction,

> the Chinese had shown how valuable they considered the control of the terrain in this area. For the first time they had shifted from the fluid defense system that formed part of their basic doctrine and had dug in in depth. The deep bunkers, complex system of trenches, and large stocks of food, supplies, and ammunitions stored at the front-line positions showed that they intended to stay and defend in place. When the 1st Cavalry Division tried to storm the enemy's main line of resistance, the Chinese poured in first-class reinforcements, freely expended their ammunition stocks, and fought fanatically to hold on. Only when losses in men and exhaustion of ammunition supplies forced them to withdraw, could the 1st Cavalry take possession of the Jamestown Line. Intelligence reports at I Corps headquarters pointed out that there seemed to be a definite lack of interest among the Chinese commanders in the fate of front-line regiments which had been ordered to resist to the end. According to the G-2 [intelligence staff] officers, this suggested that the Chinese might have come around to the belief that fewer troops would be lost through these tactics than in trying to retake lost territory with heavy counterattacks.[90]

Continuation of the view across the Nabu-ri valley from Hill 187 as photographed on 26 June 1952. The Canadian company entrenchments clearly visible on Hills 123 and 97 were part of the position held by C Company, 3 RCR, when they were attacked on the night of 2-3 May 1953. DHH 410B25.014 D2

The 28th Brigade had encountered such stiff fighting because the enemy's main line of resistance included Maryang-san and Kowang-san on the Commonwealth Division's front (the former lay as close to the communist supply base at Sangnyong-ni as any of the 1st Cavalry Division's objectives). Just how fortunate the men of the Commonwealth Division were that only a portion of their Jamestown objectives lay within the strongest belt of enemy fortifications was demonstrated by the experience of their flanking division. Attacking directly against a series of commanding features, the 1st Cavalry Division had to struggle for sixteen days to wrest each hilltop from the determined grasp of the Chinese 47th Army. By the time it had secured all of its Jamestown objectives on 19 October, the US division had lost more than 2,900 killed and wounded, almost three-quarters of the 4,000 casualties I Corps incurred in the entire operation. On the other hand, corps headquarters estimated that Commando had resulted in over 21,000 enemy casualties, including more than 500 prisoners. Almost 16,000 of those had been inflicted by the 1st Cavalry Division in reducing the 47th Army to half strength.[91]

The large discrepancy between UN and communist losses, despite the fact that it was the former who were on the attack, was not only due to the US Army's tendency to exaggerate enemy losses. It also demonstrated how greatly the communists relied on their manpower advantage, and how vastly superior the Eighth Army's firepower was. In the case of the 1st Cavalry Division, that superiority included bringing forward self-propelled 155 mm guns to fire directly into enemy fortifications, and scores of B-26 medium bombers dropping 1,000-pound bombs on bunkers that resisted all other fire. The completion of the Commando advance also coincided with the capture of Heartbreak Ridge, as X Corps wrapped up its Punchbowl operations on 13 October. In a final move, Van Fleet ordered IX Corps, in the centre, to occupy the enemy's outpost line in midmonth. After incurring nearly 11,000 casualties in the previous six weeks, the majority by American formations, the Eighth Army suffered few additional losses when IX Corps made its two-mile advance against only light opposition.[92]

On the Commonwealth Division's front, meanwhile, 'the enemy remained content to readjust his defence lines and to harass our FDLs [forward defended localities] with a moderate volume of mixed artillery fire' in the week following its advance. The opposing 192nd Division had lost 935 counted casualties in the operation, and another 119 of its soldiers had been taken prisoner. By 12 October, the 64th Army had withdrawn the division and replaced it in the line with the 191st Division on the left and the 190th Division on the right.[93] Having gained all of its objectives in its first attack as a unified command, his division's performance pleased Major-General Cassels. 'I never had the slightest doubt,' he explained in an order of the day, 'that this [success] would happen because I knew that I had well-trained and aggressive troops who could, and would, achieve anything that was reasonably demanded of them. The result has more than proved that my conviction was right.'[94]

Although the Canadian brigade's role in Commando had turned out to be a relatively easy one, the men continued to demonstrate the aggressiveness and determination that they had shown throughout their first five months in Korea. Even as they began digging in and wiring their new Jamestown entrenchments, each battalion was already sending out reconnaissance patrols to ascertain the enemy's new dispositions across the valley. Led by officers with invaluable Second World War combat experience who approached each operation with the professionalism it required, the Special Force volunteers were fully justified in believing, as the 2 RCR report on Operation Snatch had stated, 'that the Canadian soldier with his adaptability, initiative and native cunning is far superior to the Chinese by night or by day.'[95] This belief would have to be sustained as the war of movement came to an end and both sides settled into a long, drawn-out war of attrition along the Jamestown Line.

7 THE FIRST ROTATION, OCTOBER 1951

Even as the various national units of the Commonwealth Division were digging and wiring their new positions on the Jamestown Line, the cohesiveness and esprit de corps that the division had developed during Commando were about to be dissipated by the scheduled departure of several of its infantry battalions. In accordance with the British policy that units were required to spend only one winter in Korea, all of the major units of the 29th Brigade were due for replacement in the theatre. The Canadian brigade, meanwhile, was about to undergo a similar – if smaller – upheaval. The rotation of 2 PPCLI back to Canada not only highlighted the manpower difficulties faced by the expanding Canadian Army but also indicated that its Active Force units may not have been as prepared to meet the call to war as army headquarters anticipated.

As we have seen, it was apparent by the early summer of 1951 that the Canadian Army needed to establish a replacement policy to avoid a serious morale problem among the Special Force volunteers, most of whom would see their eighteen-month enlistment term expire in February 1952. In a memorandum to the chief of the general staff on 16 July, the adjutant general, Maj.-Gen. W.H.S. Macklin, had reminded Lt.-Gen. Guy Simonds that

> rotation policies are already in effect for US and UK forces. The US policy provides for repatriation after six months in a combat formation. The British and Australian policy is less definite but requires troops to serve only one winter in the theatre ...
>
> A year is considered the maximum period any officers and men should serve in Korea ... In view of the fact that 2 PPCLI arrived in Korea in the early winter of 1950, and have been subject to substantial periods of combat, personnel of this unit should be repatriated or rotated during this coming autumn and should be in Canada before Christmas. This must apply to Active and Special Force enrolees alike. The introduction of such a plan will undoubtedly improve the morale of the entire force.[1]

The question of a Canadian rotation policy was complicated by the fact that the Canadian Army was also now responsible for providing a brigade group, the 27th, to meet its NATO commitment to Europe, in addition to its Mobile Striking Force commitments at home, thereby putting a substantial squeeze on its resources. Since the army's efforts to have Special Force soldiers reengage under Active Force terms of service had met with only partial success – in all, 2,823 eventually agreed to join the Active Force – by the summer of 1951 some 4,500 of the 8,000 Canadian soldiers in the Far East remained subject to Special Force terms of service, making them unavailable once they were rotated back to Canada. While that requirement had little impact on the 25th Brigade, it was a much greater concern for the adjutant general given his responsibility for organizing the army's total manpower requirements. In his July memorandum, Macklin warned Simonds that the problem would be most acute in the infantry:

> Provided, however, that approximately 500 officers and men can be withdrawn from each battalion of the Mobile Striking Force to augment manpower available in the [3rd battalions of the] Wainwright Replacement Group, there is sufficient strength in sight to replace infantry personnel who will be eligible for repatriation or replacement late this year and early in 1952. This will, however, entail:
>
> (a) Reduction of first battalions to one parachute company plus a nucleus for subsequent restoration.
>
> (b) Priority of posting from first battalions to Korea rather than to 27 Brigade Group [in Europe].
>
> (c) Reduction of third battalions to the minimum required for training of recruits.
>
> Our ability to maintain the rotation policy after the initial replacement is dependent on the recruit intake. It is important, therefore, that the intake which is now going almost entirely to 27 Brigade Group and its replacement units be diverted for duty in Korea. To effect this with a minimum reduction in the recruit flow it is recommended that 25 Brigade Replacement Group be redesignated and become a "neutral" training formation processing recruits for all formations at home and abroad. A high percentage of its output will, however, be required for Korea and will thus delay the build-up of infantry units of 27 Brigade Group and their replacement companies.[2]

Macklin was clearly operating on the assumption that the 2nd battalions would remain in Korea and that only individual soldiers from the 1st battalions would be rotated rather than complete units, a course of action that followed the American and Australian examples. Even so, he recognized that a large proportion of the army's regular soldiers would be sent to Korea as replacements. The adjutant general's assertion that the 3rd battalions would continue to function solely as training units was contrary to the understanding of the men in 3 PPCLI, however. They believed they would replace 2 PPCLI as a unit, an assumption that their high turnover and lack of logistical support had done nothing to alter.

Since leaving Fort Lewis in May, the 3rd battalions had been living under canvas at Camp Wainwright, Alberta, training replacements for the 25th Brigade. While the crude living arrangements were manageable during the summer months, if detrimental to unit morale, the acute shortage of equipment and training aids was proving the greatest impediment to operational efficiency. It was not until 11 August that 3 PPCLI was able to record that 'a few items of much needed training equipment have arrived in the unit. To name a few of them: 81 mm mortars, bayonet training sticks, aiming rests, [and] photo and map reading kits.'[3] Upon visiting Wainwright in early July, the director of military training, Col. F. Clift, had 'listened to a summary of the unit's training difficulties as outlined by the CO,'[4] Lt.-Col. H.F. Wood. Among Wood's complaints was the method of instruction the 3rd battalions had been required to implement, namely the practice of mixing soldiers at all levels of training within companies:

> It has been observed that far from being encouraged to learn his trade by watching the complexities of collective training, the new soldier who participates is discouraged by the assurance displayed by his seniors and the "new boy" feeling is only partially dissipated by the appearance on the next exercise of even greener arrivals ...
>
> Were this unit suddenly presented with 1,000 men and its full complement of officers and NCOs and told to get ready for war in the shortest possible period of time, as was its problem in Fort Lewis in January 1951, some such method would be effective, and, in fact, was effective.
>
> When the problem is complicated by the reinforcement of two other battalions [primarily of 2 PPCLI] at the rate of about 100 men per month, with a corresponding intake of green men, the method must be altered. The criterion in such a case is not that a man be fitted into a team in the 3rd PPCLI and be prepared to fight as well as his training permits, but that 3 PPCLI turn out an acceptably trained soldier to take his place in one of two other battalions, where men expect that a new teammate be thoroughly versed in his trade.[5]

Training was also bound to take more time since almost all of the new recruits lacked previous military experience. In view of the number of replacements 3 PPCLI had already sent to the Far East, it is not surprising that the Special Force men in its ranks had largely disappeared by the summer of 1951 (unlike the other 3rd battalions in the replacement group, which still contained slightly more than 2,000 Special Force personnel in mid-July). A 'census' of 636 other ranks in 3 PPCLI undertaken by two of the battalion's officers at the end of June 1951 found that 'the age group is generally under twenty, Roman Catholicism predominates, few of the men had left their home province before joining the army and most were single.'[6] Although the new recruits had been enlisted under regular army terms of service – Special Force recruitment having been severely curtailed after August 1950 – it would appear that they were just as keen to see action in Korea as the initial influx of Special Force enlistees. When 3 PPCLI received 'word from brigade that no NCOs will be sent on draft to Korea by the battalion' in early June, for instance, a sudden 'lack of morale in the NCO course' was immediately noted: 'It is felt that if NCOs were brought out of the line [in Korea] and sent here to train the new troops and those who qualify on the course were to be sent overseas, morale would be much higher.'[7]

The question of which unit would proceed to Korea was finally settled in late July when Simonds ruled that the regular force veterans of 1 PPCLI would replace 2

PPCLI beginning in October.[8] In reaching his decision, the chief of the general staff stated that 'morale was the primary consideration. Units of the Mobile Striking Force were entitled to their tour of overseas duty.' The rotation 'would be by unit and sub-unit wherever there was in Canada a unit or sub-unit corresponding to units or sub-units in Korea.' For the infantry battalions, 'rotation would proceed two companies at a time. When two companies from first battalions have arrived in Korea, battalion HQ would switch. By December 1952, third battalions would be ready to relieve first battalions.' With its MSF obligations to North American defence in mind, however, AHQ also stipulated that 'at any one time there would be no less than one fully trained airborne company from each battalion operationally available in Canada.'[9] As Simonds later explained to his minister, the reduction of one of the MSF battalions to a single parachute-trained company would not have significant operational impact 'since available airlift at this time is only sufficient to sustain an operation by one company group ... The 2nd Battalions which will eventually make up the Mobile Strike Force units will have as a nucleus the 1st Battalions' parachute companies [one per battalion] remaining in Canada. It is intended that the remainder of the 2nd Battalions will be trained in their airborne and northern operations role as soon as possible.'[10]

By the time the details of the rotation plan were finally telegraphed to Western Command Headquarters in Edmonton on 16 August, however, AHQ had increased the number of parachute-trained soldiers that 1 PPCLI was to leave behind in Canada. In addition to the five officers and 125 men of the parachute rifle company, Ottawa instructed the 1st Battalion to designate a further 150 parachute personnel to 'be retained in Canada until sufficient personnel can be trained to replace them.' The replacements would come from 2 PPCLI by calling 'immediately for 200 volunteers' to return 'to Canada by air' to commence parachute training. In the meantime, a rifle company from 3 PPCLI would replace the 1st Battalion parachute company being left behind. In addition, the 3rd Battalion was warned that 'replacements now with 3rd Battalion ... may be required for posting to 1st Battalion to make up deficiencies resulting from the retention of 150 parachute personnel per battalion over and above the formed parachute company.' In the interest of maintaining operational efficiency at the front, only two infantry companies were to rotate with their 2nd Battalion equivalents at any one time. As a result, the rotation plan called for a staggered departure of 1 PPCLI's subunits with 'two rifle companies, 1 PPCLI, to embark not before 21 September 1951, one rifle company, battalion headquarters, and headquarters company 1 PPCLI to embark not before 3 October 1951, [and] support company 1 PPCLI and rifle company to be formed from 3 PPCLI to embark not before 15 October 1951.'[11]

The Patricias' regimental history claims that when the regular soldiers of 1 PPCLI were informed by their commanding officer, Lt.-Col. N.G. Wilson-Smith, that the battalion would be proceeding to Korea, the announcement was met by 'a spontaneous whoop of joy.'[12] Although that description is in keeping with the spirit in which regimental histories are generally written, the facts suggest that the regulars' enthusiasm may have been considerably more subdued. Required to leave 280 parachute-trained officers and men behind in Calgary, the battalion's call for volunteers for the parachute company received an overwhelming response from the veteran Patricias. Within a week of Wilson-Smith's announcement that the battalion would be proceeding to Korea, 1 PPCLI had posted 301 of its other ranks to fill the vacancies in the parachute company. By the time the first two Patricia companies, A and C, departed for Korea on 20 September, 53 more soldiers had managed to wangle a posting to the already oversubscribed parachute company, bringing its total strength to more than 360 all ranks. With so many more volunteers than needed, it seems unlikely that any paratrooper who actually wanted to go to Korea would have been kept in Calgary against his will. The fact that parachute sections were led by sergeants, while infantry sections required only corporals, also meant that the battalion had about forty extra sergeants. Seven section commanders were willing to revert to the rank of corporal in order to sail for the Far East with their battalion – a good indication that at least a portion of the 1st Battalion were enthusiastic about the prospect – but the remainder were simply posted to administrative and training duties or left with the parachute pool.

Those 1st Patricias who were not keen to see action in Korea but had been unable to obtain a posting to the parachute pool still had the option of being transferred to the battalion's X list of noneffectives. Normally numbering between twenty and thirty men, the announcement that 1 PPCLI would be proceeding to Korea quickly brought out an abundance of the 'old categories' of trick knees, bad backs (perhaps strained in whooping for joy?), and deaf ears. Within a week, the unit's noneffective list had swelled by an additional 176 soldiers, of whom 38 had gone absent without leave since the announcement and another 11 had been placed in custody for various offences.[13] Given that the strength of the battalion on 31 March had been 34 officers and 873 other ranks,[14] the decision to leave over 550 reluctant regulars of the 1st Battalion behind in Canada placed an enormous – and unexpected – strain on 3 PPCLI to supply the required combat soldiers within a very short time frame. The fact that so few 1 PPCLI soldiers were actually being sent to Korea seems to have caused little concern for higher headquarters judging by the absence of written comment in the files. Since it was AHQ that decided to leave 280 paratroopers behind in the first place, even though the army still had two other parachute battalions available and the RCAF had the capacity to airlift only one parachute company at a time, perhaps the lack of comment is not surprising.

News of the rotation decision, on the other hand, was a genuine disappointment for the soldiers training at Wainwright. Lieutenant-Colonel Wood returned from Western Command Headquarters on 20 August to make the discouraging announcement that '2 PPCLI will be replaced by 1 PPCLI less one parachute company plus one company from 3 PPCLI. D Company under Maj. J. George [the officer commanding the NCOs course, who had only recently returned from Korea himself] will be the company to go from 3 PPCLI. In addition 3 PPCLI will be called upon to fill all vacancies in the 1st Battalion. Our D Company is due to leave for Korea in October.' Speaking to the assembled battalion that morning, Wood wanted 'to stop the wild rumours that have been circulating, also he wanted to put the unit in the picture first hand. He explained that he was most sorry that the 1st Battalion was going instead of the 3rd.'[15] The keenness of the troops for overseas service was amply demonstrated by the fact that D Company's ranks were quickly filled: 'The officers chose their section commanders and the section commanders chose the men that they wished to [have] serve under them ... The morale is high and the company office is besieged with requests to join its ranks.'[16]

In accordance with the instructions Wood received from Western Command, 3 PPCLI dispatched a draft of 274 all ranks to Currie Barracks in Calgary on 26 August to replace the 280 parachutists the rotation order designated to be left in Canada. This draft included all of Major George's D Company, which was expected to remain intact to fill the gap left by the parachute company in 1 PPCLI's order of battle, as well as a large portion of the 3rd Battalion's C Company to fill vacancies in the other three rifle companies of 1 PPCLI. With such a large draft draining 3 PPCLI of most of its trained soldiers, the 3rd Battalion's B Company had gathered 'all the untrained men in the battalion. Their strength now is 280 all ranks of whom sixty are trained soldiers ready for draft.'[17]

If Lieutenant-Colonel Wood was under the impression that this draft would be the extent of 3 PPCLI's contribution to the 1st Battalion, the truth must have come as a rude surprise. Only a day after the 274 men left for Currie Barracks, Wood was told that a further draft of 100 men would be required for 30 August. The already heavily depleted C Company had 'only eleven men available for the one hundred-man draft' while B Company managed to make 'up a nominal roll of seventy-two trained personnel to be posted to C Company for the draft,' despite having had only sixty trained men available on 23 August.[18] The standard required to be considered a trained soldier, ready for draft, was clearly being lowered to meet 1 PPCLI's sudden demand for combat soldiers. On 28 August, B Company was 'preparing to post seventy-eight men to C Company [an addition of six trained personnel overnight] ... for the 100-man draft this Thursday, [30 August] ... C Company has only twenty-one men available for draft [an increase of ten 'trained' soldiers from the day before] but men from other companies will completely fill the requirement with ten to twelve men as spares.' That same day 3 PPCLI was informed that it would have to furnish a third 'draft of 106 men for the 1st Battalion for Monday, 3 September.'[19] Having already run out of trained soldiers, a concerned Lieutenant-Colonel Wood hurriedly left for Calgary later on the 28th 'to establish the requirements for replacements in the 1st Battalion which will be supplied by 3 PPCLI.'[20]

Although undoubtedly wondering what had so drastically reduced 1 PPCLI's 900-man strength that they required over 500 immediate reinforcements, Wood had little option but to meet the demand as best he could. With 3 PPCLI's reserve of trained men exhausted in filling the second draft, the need for yet another hundred-plus soldiers placed the CO in a quandary. With no one else available, Wood 'decided that forty men presently on advanced training would be available for the [106-man] draft [of 3 September] but would remain here [in Camp Wainwright] to continue training for a further three weeks. Also included in the draft were forty-one men now on leave ... leaving thirteen men to be found.'[21] Unfortunately, allowing soldiers time to complete their basic training had now become a secondary consideration to filling the 1st Battalion's ranks before the unit embarked for the Far East. Wood's request that the departure of the latest draft of 3 PPCLI soldiers be delayed to allow them a few more weeks of badly needed training was not approved. As a result, on the originally scheduled date of 3 September a 'draft of sixty-nine trained men left for Calgary to reinforce 1st Battalion. The balance of the 100 men required for this draft are to be sent as they return from leave.'[22]

However, the 3rd Battalion men in the last draft appear to have been far from the 'trained' soldiers the war diary claims. According to Ted McNamara, one of the young 3 PPCLI soldiers sent to Calgary to join the 1st Battalion, he and many of his comrades had just completed their first six weeks of basic training at Wainwright when they were paraded and asked to volunteer for an immediate posting to the Far East. McNamara, who had joined the army with the intention of fighting in Korea, had heard the rumour being widely circulated through Wainwright that the reason untrained men were being asked to volunteer for combat was because three-quarters of the regular soldiers in 1 PPCLI had deserted rather than serve in a war zone. While untrue – the regulars had simply volunteered to remain in Canada – rumours of a mass desertion may well have resulted from the reports of friends in the first draft already at Currie Barracks that a large proportion of the 1st Battalion's soldiers did not want to go to Korea. With the regular unit apparently desperate for men who were willing to fight, McNamara and his other untrained buddies felt it was their duty to fill the breach left by the veteran Patricias and stepped forward to volunteer.[23]

Knowing the large number of administrative tasks required of a unit proceeding overseas – documentation, inoculations, embarkation leave, cross-postings, etc. – Wood was undoubtedly aware that the untrained men he was forced to send to Calgary would have little chance for further training before they were shipped off to Korea. Moreover, the better-trained men who had made up the bulk of the first draft of 274 that arrived at Currie Barracks on 26 August – including what was to have been the intact D Company from 3 PPCLI – appear to have been redistributed to reinforce A and C Companies of 1 PPCLI before they departed Calgary on 20 September. Writing fifteen years after the event, Lieutenant-Colonel Wood, by then the official historian for the Canadian Army in Korea, only hinted at the actual story, stating that 'the paratroopers who had to be left behind were replaced by the best troops available in the 3rd Battalion, but A and C Companies left for the Far East with few experienced private soldiers, although the officers and NCOs were all Regulars [from the 1st Battalion].'[24]

Wood's point about the officers is significant. Any 1st Battalion officers who, like so many of their men, might have preferred to continue their military careers in Canada rather than face the perils of combat in Korea would have had a more difficult time than the other ranks in avoiding the war zone. As Wood suggests, three-quarters of the officers who accompanied the 1st Battalion to the Far East were already serving with 1 PPCLI when the unit received word it was being sent to Korea. There were only a few officer positions in the parachute company available for those who might have preferred to continue their service in Canada, and the only officers who arrived to augment the 1st Battalion were those from 3 PPCLI's D Company. Moreover, 1 PPCLI had already supplied eighteen officers to the Special Force 2nd Battalion – presumably those officers in the regular unit who were among the most eager to see action in the Far East. As we shall see, any reluctance on the part of combat officers could have a decidedly negative impact on a battalion's front-line performance.

Although three-fifths of 1 PPCLI's other ranks were from the 3rd Battalion drafts, the Wainwright infantrymen formed an even larger proportion of the four rifle companies. The more experienced regulars, meanwhile, had the training required to fill the ranks in the specialist support and headquarters company. Most of the last two drafts of largely untrained 3 PPCLI soldiers – the 'best troops available' to use Wood's phrase – were used to form the 1st Patricias' B and D Companies, particularly the latter company, which continued to be commanded by Major George. Despite receiving the final hundred-man draft from Wainwright on 3 September, it was not until 4 October that 'B Company held its first parade as a company since it commenced reforming for the overseas move. Inoculations, embarkation leave and cross-postings are nearing completion and the platoons are now able to commence training in earnest.'[25] Just how complete that training could be in the week left before the company headed off for Korea is left to the reader's imagination.

The situation in the least experienced of the subunits, the reconstituted D Company, was little better: 'Today [3 October] D Company did a tactical move to the Sarcee Ranges, rifles were zeroed and every man in the company threw at least one 36 and one 77 grenade. This was the first company training the company has conducted although previously the platoon commanders have been conducting their own platoon training including 60 mm mortars and signals. Major George has given the entire company lectures on advance to contact in mountainous country and company defence, based on his experience with the 2nd Battalion in Korea.'[26] Theoretical lectures and zeroing rifles was about all the training D Company could manage before it joined the headquarters company and battalion HQ in embarking for the Far East four days later. With little training under his belt when he left Canada, Ted McNamara remembers feeling very green and unready when D Company filed into the entrenchments of the Jamestown Line a few weeks later.[27]

The 3rd Battalion's own war diary entry for the end of August 1951 conveys a little of the bitterness which the events resulting from AHQ's decision to send 1 PPCLI on rotation – and then fill the bulk of its ranks with men from 3 PPCLI – inevitably fostered: 'All ranks were looking forward to the [battalion's] collective training phase planned for September. Those who couldn't stand the pace had gone AWL, and the balance conducted themselves admirably both on duty and on leave. The decision to send 1 PPCLI to Korea, reinforced from this battalion was thus doubly disappointing. Ten officers and over five hundred ORs [other ranks] were to be sent to Currie Barracks, which completely stripped the unit of its trained soldiers and many of its specialists.'[28] Even those 3rd Battalion Patricias who had gone absent without leave seem to have thought they were simply granting themselves some unauthorized preembarkation leave before they left to fight in Korea. As the battalion's war diary admits, by the first week of September the majority of the AWL men had returned to their unit 'evidently expecting to be posted to 1st Battalion for Korea. However, the CO is standing by his policy of not sending men with long periods of absence until they have proved themselves good soldiers.'[29]

In retrospect, the circumstances surrounding 1 PPCLI's rotation to the Far East contradict the commonly held view that the administrative problems resulting from the hurried recruitment of the Special Force led to an inordinate number of misfits entering its ranks. Certainly many of the army's regular officers, who generally viewed the Special Force volunteers with considerable disdain, believed that a better calibre of soldier would have been produced if the army had been allowed a more leisurely approach to screening recruits. The army's official history subscribes to this view and points out that the 25 percent rate of discharges from the Special Force was twice that experienced during the Second World War. In overlooking the fact that a far higher proportion of Special Force men were assigned combat roles than had been the case with 1939-45 recruits, it also ignores the observations of Colonels Bult-Francis and Rowley that the fitness level required for combat soldiers in Korea was much greater than it had been in northwest Europe.

Nor does *Strange Battleground* mention that 1 PPCLI categorized a quarter of its strength as noneffective upon being warned for service in Korea, men who had presumably been through the careful screening process that the Special Force lacked. Considering the 1st Battalion's willingness to overfill the ranks of the parachute company, it would seem that far more than 25 percent of the army's regular soldiers were either unfit, or unwilling, to go to war. Regardless of the traditional view of the Special Force as 'soldiers of fortune,' it should not be forgotten, as Lieutenant-Colonel Stone has pointed out, that the strength of a combat unit lies in 'those who joined the army because there was a war to fight and they wanted to be there.'[30] Whatever criticisms might be made of the hasty recruiting procedures of the Special Force, it did produce a far higher proportion of keen, physically fit soldiers than the regular force was able to muster when it finally received the call to arms.

The first two 1 PPCLI companies to cross the Pacific, A and C, disembarked at Pusan on 6 October 1951. Whether or not Rockingham was aware of the new arrivals' relative lack of training is unclear, but the brigade commander made the most of the one week the two companies had to accustom themselves to Korean conditions. After arriving at the 2nd Patricias' B Echelon south of the Imjin River on 7 October, the men underwent several days of acclimatization training, including courses on American weapons and a series of route marches and hill climbing exercises to condition them after their long sea voyage.[31] On 11 October Rockingham guided the officers and NCOs of the battalion over the ground where 2 R22eR had attacked during Operation Minden in preparation for a battalion exercise the following day. The two companies 'marched by road to Pintail Bridge which crosses the Imjin River and on the other side picked up a guide from the Royal 22nd Regiment who led across country along the ridges. The march was very difficult due to the terrain, the extreme heat, and the large packs that all were carrying.' The Patricias then followed the 'attack made by a company of the R22eR two weeks previously. In support were two tanks of the LdSH plus several LMGs to lend a warlike air to an otherwise dull procedure. The exercise was under the supervision of Brigadier Rockingham and Lieutenant-Colonel Wilson-Smith.' Afterwards, the companies moved through the 2 RCHA gun lines, picked up their next days' rations, and marched to the top of Hill 152, still some 4,000 yards behind the front line positions, where they spent the night. With a 50 percent stand-to enforced to accustom the men to front-line duty, the newcomers found 'there was little sleep to be had as the guns of 2 RCHA fired over our heads all night.'[32] Two days later, the two companies replaced 2 PPCLI's C and D Companies in their Jamestown Line entrenchments.

This was meagre preparation for war compared with the six months' training the Special Force had conducted at Fort Lewis the previous winter, or even the additional four-week training course that replacements received with the Reinforcement Group in Japan. Whereas Rockingham's brigade had been put through a comprehensive training schedule of progressive company, battalion, and brigade exercises at Fort Lewis, Washington, 1 PPCLI had barely managed minimal company training before it departed North America. That should have been an even greater concern for the army planners in Ottawa given that the bulk of the battalion's riflemen were drafted from Wainwright, where equipment shortages and inadequate facilities had greatly hampered individual training – for those who were fortunate enough to receive more than six weeks of basic training. Even 2 PPCLI had been able to undergo six weeks of unit training at Miryang before heading north to the battle front. Moreover, their 2nd Battalion cousins had been inserted into a fluid battle front in February 1951 where they were physically toughened by months of continual tramping up and down the steep Korean ridgelines in pursuit of the enemy. The men in 1 PPCLI, on the other hand, were destined to spend their entire tour in the Far East holding the same hilltop positions for months at a time. Vigilance and physical fitness remained just as essential in a static war, but to maintain them in the Jamestown Line positions would require strong leadership at all levels. Fortunately for the soldiers of 1 PPCLI, during their first six months in Korea they had both a brigade commander who was determined to keep his units sharp and the example of the veteran 2nd battalions to spur them on.

In the immediate aftermath of Operation Commando, the Chinese were preoccupied with constructing new entrenchments and took only limited offensive action. 'Enemy patrols were practically non-existent,' Major-General Cassels reported for the last few weeks of October, 'and contacts by our night reconnaissance and fighting patrols were generally made in the vicinity of the enemy FDL [forward defended localities]. Enemy artillery was harassing in nature and averaged approximately 200 rounds per day.'[33] However, the apparent calm that had descended across the Commonwealth front, as viewed from the perspective of division headquarters, could seem quite different to the men in the forward positions. While the remainder of the month was generally quiet, the Canadians were not entirely free from enemy attention. During the afternoon of 10 October, both 2 PPCLI and 2 RCR 'received considerable enemy shell fire,' and both battalions reported a number of enemy patrols in front of their positions early the next morning. On the night of 11-12 October, the forward company positions 'were heavily shelled and mortared. Casualties for the night were 2 RCR four dead, and 2 PPCLI one dead, four wounded, and one missing.' On the following day, Rockingham had the honour of firing 'the 100,000th round to be sent against the enemy in Korea by 2 RCHA' even as the shelling of the RCR and PPCLI positions continued. The reason for the Chinese artillery fire became apparent at 2030 hours that evening when 'the enemy began to shell 2 PPCLI very heavily. At 2230 hours, A, B and D Companies were strongly attacked by an enemy force estimated at a battalion. These attacks were repulsed and by 0100 hours the next morning the enemy had withdrawn. Casualties suffered by 2 PPCLI w[ere] one dead and ten wounded. Twenty-four Chinese bodies were counted.'[34]

The first two companies from 1 PPCLI, A and C, were placed under Stone's command and relieved the 2nd Battalion's C and D Companies in the early daylight hours of 14 October. The 1st Battalion's C Company occupied one of the Patricias' three forward company positions on Hill 210 while A Company took over the battalion's reserve position on Hill 187 (see Map 11, p. 154). For the first two weeks, at least, the new men were able to enjoy a relatively quiet introduction to combat in Korea by contributing to the Canadian brigade's patrols. On the 19th, for instance, the 1st Battalion's C Company provided 'a small patrol to recce the spur leading up to Hill 156' on the far side of no man's land. Successfully making its way across the Nabu-ri valley, the patrol 'bumped a small enemy group' on the forward slopes of the feature but continued on to scout the position before returning safely to their own lines. The patrol's leader 'showed skill and determination on his patrol and received the compliments of Lieutenant-Colonel Stone.'[35]

For the most part, however, the Commonwealth Division was content to remain on the defensive, making minor adjustments to the company positions and improving its defences by covering the reentrants between the hilltop positions with barbed wire fences and mines, both antipersonnel and antitank. The fighting power of the division was somewhat reduced during the period because the 29th British

Brigade was in the midst of replacing all three of its infantry battalions at the conclusion of their one-year rotation in Korea. Moreover, the 28th British Commonwealth Brigade had carried the brunt of the fighting – and absorbed the bulk of the casualties – during the advance to the Jamestown Line and were in need of some rest. The Canadian brigade, on the other hand, had come through Commando relatively unscathed and was in the best position to conduct offensive operations in the weeks that followed. Unsurprisingly, therefore, the 25th Brigade was most active in probing the enemy's new defence line and carried out the division's only major raid of the period.

Unlike most raids in Korea, which were passed down from corps to division, Operation Pepperpot grew from the bottom up. After the relative ease with which they had occupied the hills on the left of the divisional front, 2 R22eR had been busy conducting regular reconnaissance patrols to the far side of the valley. Despite investigating the enemy positions on the forward slopes of Hill 166, the dominant feature on the Chinese side of the Nabu-ri valley, the Van Doo patrols had few contacts with the enemy. After five and a half months in Korea, 2 R22eR, through no fault of its own, had yet to be involved in any major engagements; the unit's casualty total was 11 killed and 36 wounded compared with 2 RCR's 18 killed and 69 wounded and 2 PPCLI's 46 killed and 120 wounded.[36] The unit's relative lack of action may explain Lieutenant-Colonel Dextraze's desire for more aggressive operations once the Van Doos had settled into their Jamestown positions. On 18 October, Dextraze 'informed the BM [brigade major] that he would like to send a company in to take Hill 166 on Sunday [21 October], providing it was approved by the [brigade] commander.'[37] Not only did Rockingham approve the scheme, he immediately expanded it to involve all three of his battalions. At an orders group held at brigade headquarters on the 20th, he outlined his intentions:

> The objective of Operation Pepperpot (as the raid was code-named) was (1) to discover enemy dispositions, (2) to maintain the offensive and (3) to capture prisoners. The commander stated it was imperative to find out what the enemy was doing on the front. He explained that Pepperpot was originally the idea of Lieutenant-Colonel Dextraze, who wished to raid Hill 166 with one company. It was then decided that one company was not enough and that one company from each battalion should do the job. The GOC [Cassels] had asked 28 Brigade to help with a diversionary raid and these have now spread across the whole front. The brigade intention was to raid Hill 166, capture it, booby trap it, and then withdraw.[38]

While the Van Doos raided their objective on Hill 166, a Patricia company would seize Hill 156 to the north while an RCR company occupied two smaller features on the ridgeline running between the larger hills. Planning had been aided by the capture of a talkative Chinese medical orderly on 10 October by a 2 RCR patrol. The orderly reported there were three companies in and around Hill 166, each of which included a platoon from the heavy mortar company, and three heavy machine-guns sited on Hill 166 itself, information confirmed by a recce patrol from 2 RCR that infiltrated to Hill 166 after dark on the 17th.[39] A secondary aim of the operation 'was to create the impression that a major attack was about to be launched along the whole divisional front by putting down heavy fire concentrations and a series of feint attacks over a wide area.'[40] This impression would be enhanced by the fact that, unlike most raids, Pepperpot would be conducted in daylight, with H-hour set at 0630 on 23 October. To aid the raiders in crossing the half-mile-wide no man's land, all the divisional artillery and heavy mortars would lay down a barrage to smother the Chinese defences. A troop of Sherman tanks from C Squadron, Lord Strathcona's Horse would directly support each of the companies, firing on fixed lines at bunkers and enemy troop movement for thirty minutes before H-hour and remaining on call thereafter. A troop of British Centurion tanks was also positioned on each flank to provide additional covering fire. To assist in the destruction of the enemy fortifications, the Van Doo company would be accompanied by a section of engineers from the 57th Field Squadron and the Patricias would have a smaller demolition party in support.[41]

In keeping with the thoroughness 25 Brigade routinely displayed in preparing for its operations, on 21 October, two days before the raid was scheduled to take place, Rockingham 'ordered each battalion to send patrols this evening to recce their start lines across the valley.' The brigade commander himself made a visual reconnaissance of the objectives from an observation post near Naeoch'on that afternoon. At a conference of commanding officers held on 22 October, Rockingham reported that the patrols had found enemy in front of 2 PPCLI at the reentrant northeast of Hill 156, and in the valley in front of 2 RCR.[42] Although H-hour remained set for 0630 hours the following morning, the brigade commander was sufficiently flexible to allow the CO of 2 RCR, Lieutenant-Colonel Keane, to advance the starting time by one hour for his battalion. As Rockingham explained it, Keane 'wished to have his company across the valley by that time [0630 hours] as he believed it would have more success in gaining its objective if it began climbing the opposing slopes at first light and not have to cross the valley in daylight. He believed this would outweigh the disadvantage of risking exposure in the valley. Consequently, it was decided that H-Hour (when the companies left their respective FDLs) would be 0530 hours for 2 RCR and 0630 hours for 2 R22eR and 2 PPCLI.'[43]

The Patricia company chosen for the operation was the newly arrived A Company of the 1st Battalion, currently occupying the reserve company position on Hill 187. According to the battalion war diary, Lieutenant-Colonel Stone 'was reluctant to employ a 1 PPCLI company but felt he had to use a reserve company' rather than one of the ones holding a front-line position. Wilson-Smith 'gave a complete release and requested that A Company be employed.'[44] On 22 October Maj. E.J. Williams of A Company and his platoon commanders made a visual reconnaissance of Hill 156 from the left forward Patricia company position opposite the feature:

Artillery spotters report the fall of shot on Hill 166 during Operation Pepperpot on 23 October 1951. As the Canadian in the foreground demonstrates, soldiers will take every available opportunity to catch up on their sleep. NAC PA183974

> The ground was carefully searched with binoculars. If looks could kill, Hill 156 would have been blasted this morning.
>
> Hill 156 is a rise in the main ridge line approximately 300 yards long and is almost razor-backed. Running out from 156 are two fingers each 500 yards long and approximately 800 yards apart making the entire feature a half-moon shape. The valley in between is rice paddy and hugging the left spur are two small villages. The spurs are broken and rolling especially the right (most northerly) one. The growth is only small scrub trees not over waist high ...
>
> Enemy movement was observed only at the very top of the hill, and it is thought they occupy the spurs at night but by day only the very top of the hill. Tomorrow should tell us the story ...
>
> Late on into the evening, weapons were cleaned, tested and retested, grenades primed, checked and rechecked. A quiet calm settled on the company but it was the calm of confidence and not of apprehension.[45]

Early on the 23rd, all three companies crossed the start line promptly at their assigned H-hours 'behind a very heavy and very accurate barrage,'[46] and made rapid progress toward their objectives. The RCR company, having left their FDLs one hour ahead of the other companies, reported themselves in occupation of the middle hilltop at 0732 hours, having killed six and wounded eleven of the enemy while capturing the only Chinese prisoner taken during the operation. One hour later, the other two companies were also closing in on their objectives.[47] Seeing their first action, the Patricias in A Company were 'most impressed by the fire being put down in their support. Some ineffective long range enemy MG fire came in from the left flank but no other interference was met in the FUP [forming-up place].' The Patricias moved across the valley and captured their initial objectives on the spurs with little difficulty. The leading 2 and 3 Platoons 'had met no enemy but had been subject to both mortar and MG fire. One man had been wounded.' Major Williams then ordered 1 Platoon to take Hill 156 'and then to press on to the top' of the ridgeline just beyond:

> The ground between the positions secured by 3 Platoon and the final objective was interspersed by three distinct crest lines. Mortar fire of increasing intensity was met by 1 Platoon in the valleys in between, and the crest lines were being sprayed by enemy MG fire.
>
> 1 Platoon fought its way stubbornly forward in the face of this fire and established itself under cover of the crest of Point 156. The final objective lay less than 100 yards away and ten meters up a steep climb. The fire intensified and Captain Gunton [of 1 Platoon] requested fire support and suggested that perhaps a two platoon assault, which would divide the enemy fire, might be advisable. On hearing this on his wireless, Sergeant Stone [of 2 Platoon], who had the nearest platoon, came up on his set before Major Williams could speak and said 'Easy 1 Baker, moving now, over.' Major Williams gave his OK and 2 Platoon, covered by the fire of 1 Platoon who were engaging the ridge top, moved forward ...
>
> A quick consultation between Captain Gunton and Sergeant Stone produced the plan whereby 1 Platoon was to assault covered by the fire of 2 Platoon and as soon as 1 Platoon was well launched, 2 Platoon would follow immediately on the heels of 1 Platoon.
>
> Supporting fire was ordered and 1 Platoon surged forward as one man led resolutely by Captain Gunton. Observers at the battalion OP could see him moving calmly in the mortar fire directing his platoon by pointing with his cane. The tank fire clipped in just above the assaulting troops' heads, bursting less than twenty feet from them. 1 Platoon reached the top and then quickly reorganized as 2 Platoon swept through them clearing the ridge to the south. 2 Platoon moved along communication trenches grenading bunkers and shooting down fleeing Chinese. The advance of 2 Platoon was halted [on the ridgeline 400 yards southwest of Hill 156]. Sergeant Stone had some difficulty in restraining his men who were ready to plunge into the next valley beyond. Nine Chinese were counted dead and many more [dead] could be seen beyond the objective.[48]

Hill 156 was secured by the Patricias by 0945 hours. The assault cost A Company one corporal killed while leading his section forward and three others wounded, including another of the section commanders. As the 1 PPCLI war diary concluded, 'This Korean fighting is hard on section commanders who must lead in order to keep control while moving over the broken ground. On flat ground men can be

Two soldiers of D Company, 2 R22eR, watch the explosion of Canadian shells from the base of Hill 166 during Operation Pepperpot. Both men are carrying type 36 grenades on their web belts, while the soldier at left holds a Bren light machine gun, the offset sight of which (to compensate for the centre-mounted magazine) is clearly visible. NAC PA185023

relied on to keep section formations and the section commander can move towards the rear of his section. Here he must lead and be the pivot on which his section moves. This calls for leadership of the highest order.'[49]

The Van Doo company assaulting the main feature, Hill 166, encountered greater resistance, particularly from five of the enemy's well-entrenched machine-guns. With the other objectives in Canadian hands, the supporting Strathcona tanks were able to concentrate their fire entirely on Hill 166 and succeeded in reducing the number of active enemy machine-guns to one. Despite the concentrated fire of 2 RCHA's guns over the next two and a half hours, however, the Van Doos could get no closer than 150 yards from the top of the feature. A final assault was mounted at 1115 hours when 'after some delay, the right platoon of D Company assaulted from the shelter of [the] draw [immediately northeast of the feature] up the slopes of Hill 166. The platoon advanced under cover of artillery in perfect formation to within 150 yards of the top when it received several hand grenades thrown by the Chinese in the slit trench encircling the feature. Unfortunately, a short artillery round fell close to the advancing troops and the platoon began withdrawing rapidly to their start line.'[50]

When it was reported at 1205 hours that at least two enemy platoons remained in possession of the hill, Rockingham, 'in view of the [2 R22eR] failure and the lateness of the hour,'[51] issued instructions for the return of all three companies commencing at 1315 hours, the withdrawal to be covered by the combined fire of the brigade's mortars, tanks, and artillery. As Rockingham later recalled, 'The interesting part of this raid was the tremendous smoke screen we placed on the ridge when we were ready to withdraw, still in daylight. The enemy's reaction, as soon as the smoke screen was laid, was to fire all his defensive fire tasks, made up of artillery, mortar and machine gun fire. We anticipated this reaction and gave our troops time to get clear of the defensive fire tasks by preceding the smoke with heavy HE [high explosive] concentrations on the hills ahead of them with the intention of making them [the Chinese] believe that we were going to attack further into enemy territory. This had the desired effect and enabled our troops to disengage with little trouble.'[52]

The veterans of 2 RCR and 2 R22eR did not delay in pulling back from their objectives and making their way across no man's land. The dispatch with which they conducted their withdrawal allowed them to avoid the Chinese artillery and mortar fire in the valley. The Van Doos reported all their men back in their FDLs at 1355 hours while the RCR company made a similar report seven minutes later. The inexperienced Patricias – who up to this point had performed quite well – did not, however, seem to appreciate fully the importance of making a quick withdrawal and they were not reported as beginning to cross the valley until 1407 hours, five minutes after the last of the Royals had reentered their FDLs. The slower pace meant that the Patricias were caught in no man's land when the enemy began firing defensive fire tasks. As planned, the gunners of 2 RCHA soon switched from high explosive to smoke to help cover the withdrawal. Major Williams, the Patricia company commander, recalled that he 'had successfully got the two leading platoons away to the rear [to reenter the valley and head back toward their own lines] and was following with company headquarters when the gunners moved the smokescreen back from the top of 156. Pots of 25 pr [pounder] smoke began raining around the ears of company headquarters and I was not pleased to find that in accordance with standard gunner practice one round in four was HE. I instructed my very gallant FOO [forward observation officer], Berthiaume, to get that unprintable stuff off our necks. He sat down in the midst of the mixture of Chinese and Commonwealth artillery fire and lifted the concentration off us by wireless.'[53]

The withdrawal cost the Patricias a further ten casualties, including one killed by artillery or mortar fire and another soldier who died when he wandered into a Commonwealth minefield, misfortunes not suffered by the RCR and R22eR companies that left on time. It was not until 1440 hours, forty-five minutes after the Van Doos had returned to their lines, that the Patricias radioed brigade headquarters to say, 'Think all troops are back now – will confirm in a few minutes.'[54] The state of confusion that existed during the company's withdrawal is indicated by the fact that two of the dead Patricias were left in the valley and their bodies had to be recovered after nightfall. The veterans of 2 RCR and 2 R22eR, despite having the same distance to travel in returning to their lines, suffered only twelve of the operation's twenty-six casualties, and only two of the five fatalities.[55] Many of these points were brought out by Stone when he held a meeting with A Company the following day 'to discuss the operation. He was very frank and the company officers learned much from his remarks. He praised the fighting qualities of the company but had critical comments to make on the loss of an LMG, the failure to bring out the body of one of the dead, and the slowness with which the company withdrew.'[56] These were important lessons for the new men to absorb, because the Chinese were preparing to launch a series of counterattacks.

Having broken off the peace talks at Kaesong on 22 August 1951, the communist delegation finally proposed a resumption of the negotiations on 19 September. However, General Ridgway insisted that a more neutral site be selected. The two sides eventually agreed to hold all further meetings in Panmunjom, a small village southwest of Kaesong that lay between the communist and UN lines. US Army engineers promptly constructed a tented conference centre in the no man's land between the armies and negotiations resumed on 25 October. The talks immediately focused on the second item on the conference agenda: the establishment of a demilitarized zone. Although agreement was easily reached to establish a two-and-a-half-mile-wide zone along the line of contact, the date on which the line would be set was a matter of contention. General Ridgway feared that acceptance of the current line of contact as immovable would impose a de facto ceasefire and allow the communists to prolong the negotiations indefinitely. Moreover, a ceasefire would allow the enemy to thin defences and concentrate forces for a new offensive. UN negotiators therefore insisted that the final line would be the one actually held at the conclusion of the negotiations, thus allowing Eighth Army to continue to exert military pressure on the enemy.[57]

Even as agreement on the line of contact principle seemed imminent, however, the UN delegation was also concerned that the communists would use the period prior to a final settlement to attempt to recover some of the ground lost to the Eighth Army in early October. It did not take long for the UN negotiators' fears to be realized, as the light shelling and occasional probing attacks that had characterized the enemy's reaction in the weeks immediately following the Commando advance gave way to more aggressive thrusts.

The 25th Brigade's defence against the Chinese counteroffensive was strengthened by the continuing drive of its commander and his insistence that they remain vigilant for any signs of unusual activity in the enemy's forward defences. On 27 October, Rockingham ordered his battalions 'to send nightly recce patrols forward of their FDLs to obtain information concerning the enemy's dispositions. The first of these would commence tomorrow.'[58] By insisting that his men routinely leave the relative safety of their own entrenchments and move across the valley, he ensured that the aggressive attitude the brigade had developed in its past operations would not fade during the stalemate on the ground. A detailed knowledge of both the terrain in front of their own entrenchments and the enemy's day-to-day activities on the far side of no man's land would maintain that initiative and prevent surprise.

The commander's patrol instructions soon amounted to a standing order that was to remain in effect until Rockingham relinquished command the following April. On the first night of the aggressive policy, 28-9 October, a seven-man RCR reconnaissance patrol investigating the village of Pukch'ang on the far side of the valley encountered three Chinese soldiers, who fled when fired upon.[59] The next night 2 R22eR and 2 PPCLI sent patrols to the vicinity of Hills 166 and 156 respectively. The 2 R22eR patrol 'neither saw nor heard any enemy, although the patrol commander reported Hill 166 very thoroughly searched. In view of the heavy opposition this feature has provided in the past, this appears to be most surprising. The patrol leader said the best approach to Hill 166 and the feature [a spur running to its southwest] was from the south and that tanks could easily get across the creek' that divided no man's land. The Patricia patrol, meanwhile, reached its objective and returned without incident.[60]

The defence was also aided by the fire support provided by the armoured squadron whose tanks were dug in on the hilltops overlooking the Nabu-ri valley. During Operation Pepperpot, for instance, the squadron had fired over 2,000 rounds of 76 mm high explosive and 300 of white phosphorous smoke. Throughout the raid, 'The tank troops of the squadron were switched from target to target either by the TOOs [tank observation officers] or, [in the case of] the complete squadron, by Major [Victor] Jewkes, the squadron commander. This proved the flexibility of a tank squadron in support of infantry, in good fire positions.' Stone, for one, 'was quite sure that if it had not been for the well-aimed tank fire that his D Company would never have reached their objective.'[61] Although the Shermans were repeatedly shelled by the Chinese, they usually emerged undamaged, even by direct hits. When Trooper J.F. Smillie was wounded by a 105 mm shell fragment on 16 December, he was only the squadron's third battle casualty. Instead, the Canadian tanks routinely inflicted greater damage on the enemy, engaging bunkers and antitank guns whenever they were not directly supporting the infantry.[62] As one of the squadron's young tank drivers recalled,

> the war was nothing like I had envisioned it to be. The tank was dug in alongside the infantry trenches and bunkers and our role appeared to be that of providing direct sniper fire support for the endless infantry night patrols. The night turret/radio watches were particularly nervewracking, although one would never admit to it. The noise of patrols going out or returning through the wire, the constant thumping of Vickers and .30-calibres firing on fixed lines, the frequent lighting of the sky by some equally nervous infantryman firing off flares, the shadows created by the searchlights providing

> artificial moonlight, and every shrub exposed by the flares appearing to move – all had the tendency to make one rather anxious. These two-hour watches were the longest and loneliest times that I have ever experienced.[63]

The Commonwealth front also benefited from US air strikes that hit strongpoints and disrupted any suspected Chinese buildup. On the last day of October, for instance, the Commonwealth Division called in two air strikes to hit enemy positions west and northeast of the Maryang-san defences held by the 28th Brigade. On 1 November, three more air strikes were put in on the high ground surrounding Hill 166 'with apparent good effect.' The strikes followed a strong, twenty-one-man Van Doo patrol the night before that had been directed to investigate the spur that ran down from 166 above the abandoned village of Chinch'on. A half-mile south of the village, the patrol encountered a group of Chinese and was forced to return.[64] On the night of 1-2 November yet another 2 R22eR patrol was sent to investigate the slopes of Hill 166. Dextraze had decided to illuminate the patrol area with searchlights: 'This was the first time that they had been used for an operation since the two [searchlights] had been established on Hill 152 [4,000 yards behind the forward positions] some four days ago. The [searchlight] detachment was made up of rep[resentative]s from 2 RCR and 2 R22eR and had undergone quite intensive training by the Americans. Lieutenant-Colonel Dextraze reported the lights to be most satisfactory.'[65] The next day Dextraze held an orders group to discuss another raid planned for Hill 166, an operation that had to be cancelled after increased enemy movement was observed across the valley.

The growing enemy activity was part of the Chinese buildup in preparation for a counterattack on the Commonwealth line. At 2330 hours on 1 November, an enemy patrol 'estimated at twenty to twenty-five in strength penetrated through the minefield and tactical wire'[66] in the reentrant southwest of the PPCLI company position on Hill 159, but 'it was successfully beaten off and four dead Chinamen were found near the position. These were later identified as belonging to 3rd Bn, 570th Regt, 190th Div, 64th Army.'[67] On 2 November, artillery-spotting aircraft had reported groups of from twenty-five to fifty of the enemy in and about Chinch'on and in the valleys behind Hills 166 and 156. Perhaps not surprisingly, the report was followed by an attack that night:

> At 1800 hours A Company, 2 RCR reported enemy artillery fire on its forward positions and the PPCLI OPs [observation posts] reported considerable vehicle movement to its front. At 2100 hours the forward platoon of A Company, 2 RCR, which held the Songgok feature, was heavily shelled and mortared before being quickly attacked and surrounded by an estimated enemy company. The attacks were pressed almost continuously between 2100 hours and 0300 hours the next morning when the RCR platoon was forced to fall back to the company position, with the enemy harassing closely behind. The platoon suffered one killed and thirteen wounded, and accounted for thirty-five dead Chinese

Dead Chinese of the 1st Battalion, 568th Regiment, 190th Division, 64th Army on the morning of 3 November 1951 after that unit's night attack on A Company, 2 RCR, holding the Songgok feature in the Nabu-ri valley. The Royals are checking their wire entanglements before burying the enemy's dead. Given the nature of their wounds – the soldier on the left is missing his legs – the Chinese either tripped a mine or were hit by artillery or mortar fire. NAC PA184292

> and two wounded prisoners of war from an estimated battalion of enemy. At 0630 hours, No 3 Platoon re-occupied the position without opposition. The PWs were identified as belonging to the 1st Bn, 568th Regt, 190th Div, 64th Army.[68]

When the platoon position was reoccupied the next morning, 'they found everything almost as it had been left, bedrolls, parkas, etc., untouched along with seven dead Chinese within the platoon wiring,' indicating that the communists had only hastily occupied the position with no intention of staying. An interrogation of the

Soldiers of 2 RCR search the lower slopes of the Songgok feature for wounded Chinese on the morning of 3 November 1951. NAC PA183960

prisoners 'revealed later that the enemy attack consisted of one full battalion. One company attacked frontally, one flanking with the third in reserve. A heavy weapons company positioned on and around Hill 166 gave their support. [The] reserve company [was] utilized during the third attack.' The enemy attack cost the Royals one killed and fourteen wounded, all but two of the wounded being from A Company.[69] Given the location of the RCR company position, across the valley and southeast of Hill 166 and four miles south of Hill 355, the enemy raid was in all likelihood meant to divert attention away from the 64th Army's main offensive thrusts to the north. On 3 November, the Patricias' B Company received five rounds of direct fire on its entrenchments. The direct fire 'and the number of reports of enemy heavy vehicle movement in the last few days indicate that the Chinamen have moved tanks or SP [self-propelled] guns into their forward areas opposite the battalion position.'[70] With their own entrenchments lying immediately south of the 28th Brigade positions on Hills 227 and 355, the Patricias were more acutely aware of the gathering strength of the enemy.

With the buildup of their forces nearly completed, the Chinese were poised to attempt to recover the valuable ground lost to the 28th Brigade during the Commando advance. Beginning on 4 November, the Chinese 64th Army launched a series of determined counterattacks to recapture Hills 355 and 317, the two most dominant features within the Imjin salient, held by the 28th Brigade. On the morning of the 4th, South Korean 'agents returned to our lines with information indicating a considerable increase in enemy forces in the area north of 28 BritCom Inf Bde, previously known to be lightly held.' Reconnaissance aircraft also made repeated sightings of groups of Chinese infantry close to the division's forward positions as well as a number of enemy tanks or self-propelled guns, which were 'immediately engaged from the air.'[71] After 1300 hours, the enemy's artillery fire intensified on the 28th Brigade's positions, eventually reaching a rate of 90 to 120 rounds a minute. Finally, at 1645 hours, the enemy 'launched a very heavy attack from the north' against the 1st Battalion, King's Own Scottish Borderers, holding Hills 217 and 317, and the left company of 3 RAR on the ridgeline to their east. For the next seven hours 'heavy fighting ... took place with the main effort of the enemy [directed] against 1 KOSB, who were eventually forced back off the two dominating features Points 217 and 317 captured during Operation Commando. Effective strength of 1 KOSB [was] reduced to two companies, but [the] line remained intact ... Soon after midnight it appeared the second phase of the enemy attack would start, but it is believed this was broken up by two radar bombing attacks and intense artillery fire.' The Chinese seizure of Maryang-san (Hill 317) was supported by a second determined – but unsuccessful – assault on the 1 King's Shropshire Light Infantry company holding Hill 227 immediately north of the PPCLI positions. Nonetheless, by first light on 5 November, Hills 217 and 317 were held by a three-battalion regiment of Chinese infantry. The loss of 317 was 'a galling experience for the Australians who had fought so hard to gain it four weeks previously.'[72] The KOSB did not surrender its positions easily, however, having lost most of two companies in suffering casualties of seven killed, eighty-seven wounded and forty-four missing. Chinese losses were estimated to have exceeded 1,000.[73]

On the morning of the 5th, the Borderers were joined in their positions below Maryang-san by the recently arrived 1st Battalion, the Royal Leicestershire Regiment, temporarily transferred from the 29th Brigade. At noon, the Leicesters 'counter attacked towards Point 217 supported by diversionary probes by 3 RAR towards Point 317.' A thirty-man Australian diversion managed to overrun one platoon position on a knoll just below the main height, but the British battalion could make little headway against the hillside bunkers and heavy small-arms fire from the heights above in its assault: 'By last light, 1 R Leicesters was finally held up short of their objective, having been heavily engaged all afternoon by the enemy, supported by accurate artillery fire.'[74] The next morning, an Australian patrol 'crept forward to the wire defences around the summit of Hill 317 and observed Chinese in trenches, without being detected by them. The Chinese position was too strong, however, for the Australians to attack. Heavy rains set in and the battlefield soon became a quagmire, covered by mist and low cloud.'[75]

While the 28th Brigade was attempting to recapture Maryang-san on the 5th, 2 PPCLI was completing its official handover to the 1st Battalion. The Eighth Army commander, General Van Fleet, presented Lieutenant-Colonel Stone with the Presidential Citation in recognition of the battalion's stand at Kap'yong the previous April during a small ceremony at brigade headquarters on 5 November. The day before the handover ceremony, 1 PPCLI had placed the third of its four companies in the line when its recently arrived D Company occupied the entrenchments on Hill 159. Although led by the combat-experienced Major George, D Company, it will be recalled, had a high proportion of men with only six weeks of basic training under their belts when they were drafted to fill out 1 PPCLI's ranks.[76] As he had with the first two 1 PPCLI companies, Rockingham had put D Company through 'an intensive five day training period' – referred to by the previous Patricia companies as the 'death march' training exercise – before committing them to the line. The newest Patricias found the Korean terrain 'so completely different from anything most of the men have seen, that many just stare in awe at the steep scrub-covered hills. The men are anxious to get up the line for their first taste of action.'[77] They would not have long to wait.

On its first afternoon in the front line, D Company received 'moderate mortar, artillery and direct fire ... By 1725 hours, 160 shells and bombs had fallen, mostly on D Company.' The direct fire came from self-propelled guns that had recently been

The handover parade from 2nd Battalion to 1st Battalion, Princess Patricia's Canadian Light Infantry, on 5 November 1951. The CO of 1 PPCLI, Lt.-Col. N.G. Wilson-Smith, is to the left of Rockingham, while the CO of 2 PPCLI stands to the right of the Canadian brigade commander. NAC PA133399

placed in the Chinese entrenchments opposite the battalion, two of which were spotted and engaged by artillery: 'This is the first actual sighting which confirms our suspicions that the enemy has moved tanks or SP guns forward. The enemy tanks or SP guns rolled up to the crest line in previously prepared positions, quickly fired several rounds, retired behind the crest line then repeated the process.' That night, as the fighting was raging on Hill 317 4,000 yards to the north, 'an enemy patrol of an estimated eight men reached [the reentrant immediately southwest] at 2150 hours and commenced cutting D Company's wire fence. The patrol was beaten off with small arms and 81mm mortar fire with unknown results.' D Company's casualties had been 'amazingly light considering the heavy volume of fire' with only three Patricias 'slightly wounded' although one Korean porter was killed and two others wounded.[78]

As the battalion handover ceremony was taking place the next day, the enemy was preparing an even rougher initiation for the green Patricias. From early afternoon on the 5th, D Company's entrenchments on Hill 159 were subjected to continuous mortar fire. By 1630 hours, shells as well as mortar bombs were falling and the Chinese had shifted part of their fire to include the neighbouring company positions to the east and south. Ninety minutes later, the enemy added the flat-trajectory fire of a self-propelled gun to the mix as their infantry, estimated to be in battalion strength, began to form up across the valley for the assault.[79] 'At 1810 hours, enemy machine guns started firing on D Company from the vicinity [of] Kigong-ni and enemy were forming up in the vicinity of Pattagol.' Having been spotted, however, the Chinese infantry were decimated by the Commonwealth Division's artillery as they crossed no man's land beginning at 1815 hours: 'Many artillery and 81mm mortar tasks had been fired and repeated and disorganized the first enemy attack before it reached the assault phase. This first attack was beaten off with ease by small arms fire from the company. Searchlights were requested and came on at 1825 hours assisting the visibility of the companies.'[80]

After a ninety-minute lull to reorganize, the Chinese prepared to renew their assault on Hill 159. This time the enemy infantry was more successful in reaching D Company, in part because the division's artillery had been diverted to deal with a simultaneous attack against the 1 KSLI company holding Hill 227 to the north. Whether it was meant as a diversion or not, the attack on 227 met the same fate as the first assault on 159, being largely broken up by indirect fire before it even came under small-arms fire. In front of the Patricia positions to the south, meanwhile,

> the enemy was seen forming up in the vicinity of Pattagol for [its] second attack on D Company. The searchlights assisted the RCHA FOO with D Company, Lieutenant Dalke, in bringing down several 'Uncle' [seventy-two gun] and 'Mike' [twenty-four gun] targets on the attacking enemy in the valley in front of D Company. Our MMGs and mortars also brought down a heavy volume of defensive fire on the attacking enemy. Wireless communication was working well to all companies but line communication had been knocked out to the forward companies by enemy shellfire ...

> By 2020 hours, 10 and 12 Platoons were under heavy attacks. Supported by artillery, mortar and MG fire, the enemy came up the spur to the right of 10 Platoon, up the spur to the left of 10 Platoon, and up the spur in front of 12 Platoon. A 10 Platoon section position ran out of ammunition and withdrew to the main platoon position. Wave after wave of enemy charged at D Company's wire with bangalore torpedoes [tubes filled with explosives] and small arms fire, to be beaten off by our small arms fire and grenades. By 2200 hours this second enemy attack had been repulsed and the section of 10 Platoon was back in its position.[81]

In an attempt to break up any further attacks before they developed, divisional headquarters arranged for a radar-guided air strike on the main Chinese positions opposite the Canadians. Although the bombs did not hit the exact targets they were meant for, landing instead at the foot of the hills on the far side of the valley, the explosions proved to be 'another morale booster as troops can now depend on air support at night.'[82] (When brigade headquarters was later 'asked to query 1 PPCLI on the results of the B-29 radar-controlled bombing early on the 6th in order to ascertain if it had been "of assistance," the Patricias answered with a "definitely yes."'[83]) The enemy was still not willing to give up the assault, however, and a third attack was made on D Company at 0130 hours on 6 November, once again concentrated on Lt. J.G.C. McKinlay's 10 Platoon on Hill 159's forward spur. Like the company commander, Maj. J.H.B. George, Lieutenant McKinlay was one of the five 3 PPCLI officers who had transferred to the 1st Battalion with the original D Company draft on 26 August. The third attack was also hard fought:

> An estimated two enemy companies came down the Pattagol valley across the main valley floor in front of D Company and attacked 10 Platoon from both sides of the ridge to the north. A smaller enemy element did a right flanking [movement] and came up the ridge to the south. Again the enemy took a terrific pasting in the main valley in the vicinity of [Patt'ogol] from our artillery defensive fire. Artillery DF task[s were] fired time and again with all the guns in the regiment and the division when available. As the enemy attack approached the ridges leading up to 10 Platoon, they were hit by our 81mm mortar defensive fire ... Our mortar fire was crept up to the edge of our wire where the fire fell a scant fifty yards from our positions. This task was fired repeatedly and with devastating effect. The accuracy of the 81mm mortar astounds us; such close support would be unheard of with a 3-inch mortar. Tonight completely sells us on the 81mm. The Mortar Platoon hammered for hours and hundreds of mortar bombs fell on the enemy. Our MMGs were firing at 500 yards range on enemy on the [southern spur of Hill 159]. Still this last attack came in such strength that numbers of the enemy got through the wire only to be killed by small arms fire and grenades from 10 Platoon. The right forward section of 10 Platoon was under attack from three sides and in a somewhat precarious position but the men held firm in their slit trenches and beat off each enemy assault. Smaller bodies of enemy penetrated to 12 Platoon's wire with bangalores and were killed or beaten off but 12 Platoon was not under heavy attack

> at any time. At 0245 hours, one hour and fifteen minutes after the attack commenced, the enemy fired two red flares in D Company's area which were evidently the signal to withdraw, for D Company was left alone for the remainder of the night.[84]

In analyzing the first large-scale attack to be made on 1 PPCLI since its arrival in Korea, the Patricia war diarist identified three factors in D Company's successful defence of Hill 159:

> The enemy attack had come in three waves, at 1815 hours, 2020 hours, and 0130 hours and appeared to have been battalion in size, with a company in each of the first two waves and two companies in the last. Despite the heavy artillery and mortar fire preparation on D Company, and the fact that practically all of the enemy battalion attack fell on one platoon, 10 Platoon, the attack was a failure. Apart from enemy shortcomings, a number of factors were responsible for the enemy defeat. First, our artillery defensive fire broke up and disorganized each enemy wave in the valley in front of D company and our mortar fire kept him disorganized as he approached the base of the spurs leading to the company. The success of our defensive fire is of course due to the excellence of wireless communication both in the battalion and artillery channels. Secondly, our defensive wire, though damaged in many places by enemy shellfire, kept the enemy from making any well organized rushes at any of the section or platoon positions. Lastly, the mettle of the men of 10 Platoon in remaining in their slits to fight it out at close quarters with the enemy and the excellence of the leadership of the officers and NCOs in the company was a predominating factor.[85]

The last point applied particularly to the 10 Platoon commander, Lieutenant McKinlay, whose action in strapping a wireless set to his back and moving about the platoon entrenchments to organize the defence and call down the battalion's supporting fire earned him a Military Cross.[86] Even before first light on the 6th, the stretcher bearers commenced the arduous task of carrying the wounded back to the regimental aid post near the battalion's tactical headquarters in the valley 1,000 yards southeast of Hill 159. Like the 2nd battalions, 1 PPCLI found the evacuation of wounded from hill positions which could not be reached by Jeep ambulance to be a great problem: 'Stretcher parties become fatigued rapidly and reliefs are required if the wounded are to be evacuated quickly. The Korean Service Corps personnel are generally as loath to carry our wounded as we are to trust our wounded in their hands, and in no circumstances will they carry our dead down the hills so for the most part the "rice-burners" are useless to us as stretcher bearers.'[87] Soon after dawn, Wilson-Smith and the battalion intelligence officer proceeded to the D Company positions on Hill 159, where he 'found a haggard but smiling crew. With Major George and Lieutenant McKinlay, they went over the 10 Platoon positions attacked during the night and the CO spoke with many of the men.' While making their tour, the officers stopped to interrogate one of the wounded Chinese prisoners waiting to be evacuated:

> He had a serious arm wound but was conscious and appeared quite frightened. Major George, who understands two Chinese dialects [in addition to his previous service with 2 PPCLI, George had served with the British Military Mission to China during the Second World War], briefly interrogated him on the spot and determined that he was a member of the 2nd Battalion, 570th Regiment, 190th Division, 64th Army ... The IO [intelligence officer] managed to determine from the PW that he had been in the CCF for eight months and across from our position for twenty days. Approximately 100 attacked in his company and he estimated that 400 from other companies in his battalion were involved. He stated that our artillery fire had caused many casualties. Their task had been to capture and hold Point 159.[88]

By any measure, the neophyte soldiers of D Company had acquitted themselves admirably in their first taste of combat. When one considers that many of their number had received only a few weeks of rudimentary military training at Wainwright before being sent to 1 PPCLI and that they had been in the line for only thirty-six hours, they demonstrated outstanding determination in defending their positions. Patricia casualties during the night amounted to three killed and twelve wounded, a rather small total given the volume of enemy fire and the scale of the attack. Not surprisingly, all of the dead and eight of the wounded – five 'more seriously' and three 'less seriously' – were from D Company, the majority of casualties being caused by enemy shells and mortar bombs. Half of the D Company casualties were from 11 Platoon, who were not under direct attack themselves. The enemy's casualties were understandably much heavier. 'In all thirty-four enemy dead were counted within fifty yards of the company wire,' the Patricias' war diary recorded the next morning. 'How many more were killed or carried away from the ridges by the enemy or killed in the valleys by our artillery and mortar fire, or wounded and carried away, we do not know. However, it is unusual for the Chinamen to leave so many dead on the battlefield. He will usually go to considerable lengths and risk to carry off all his casualties.'[89]

Despite D Company's successful defence, Pte. Ted McNamara believed that their inexperience must have been all too obvious to the Chinese during their first day in the line and that they had been singled out for attack because of it.[90] Since the capture of Hill 159 would also have been tactically important for the planned Chinese assault on Hills 227 and 355 to its north, that conclusion would appear to be unwarranted. The quantity of equipment found on the enemy's dead tended to confirm the statement of the wounded Chinese prisoner that they had attacked the feature with the intention of staying: 'Each Chinaman was dressed in his khaki padded-cotton winter dress, and many had padded-cotton jackets rolled on their backs. Each had a Chinese shovel, and carried cloth pouches of loose ammunition, bandoliers and potato-masher type hand grenades. Many rifles, "burp guns" (SMGs [sub-machine-guns]) and two Russian-made Degtyarev LMGs were found near the dead.'[91] Nonetheless, McNamara's perception indicates the degree to which the men of D Company were conscious of their lack of military training.

Although the Special Force Patricias had officially handed over to 1 PPCLI on 5 November, it was not until the 11th that 2 PPCLI's A Company was finally relieved by the 1st Battalion's B Company. For the Patricia veterans, 'the last night in the line, as always, was restless.' They were sufficiently aware of the importance of constant vigilance, however, to send out two snipers in front of their position. The snipers detected a fifteen-man Chinese patrol in no man's land and directed mortar fire to drive them off. One of the last 2 PPCLI officers to leave was the battalion's battle adjutant, Major Lilley, the former commander of C Company, who had led the hunt for the communist guerrillas back at Miryang. According to the 1st Battalion's war diarist, 'He had been awaiting patiently the arrival of Major Mainprize, and when he finally heard his "relief" had arrived in the car park, he said to one of the subalterns: "Go down and guide him up. If any shells come in, fall on him."'[92]

8 NO WITHDRAWAL, NO PANIC, NOVEMBER 1951

The repulse of the Chinese attempt to seize Hill 159 from 1 PPCLI's inexperienced D Company meant that the success of the enemy's attacks on the Commonwealth Division had been limited to the recapture of Hill 317 in the 28th Brigade's sector. The extent of enemy buildup opposite the division, however, indicated that the Chinese counteroffensive to recover the dominant features lost during the Commando advance was not yet over. The next enemy effort came on the night of 8-9 November, when 3 RAR, still holding its positions immediately east of Hill 317, came under attack. After a hard, three-hour fight, the Chinese assault was repulsed with heavy casualties.[1] The enemy's position on the heights above the Australians, however, meant that they could observe and fire on any movement in the 3 RAR forward platoons. Along with irregular shelling and mortaring, the nervous strain resulted in over forty cases of shell shock and battle fatigue among the defenders. Two of the battle fatigue cases were severe enough to be evacuated to Japan, while two other Australians were disciplined for refusing to return to duty. In the understated words of the Australian official history, 'the morale of the battalion suffered considerably during November.'[2]

In view of the heavy attacks being made against the 28th Brigade, the few offensive operations undertaken by the division during November were made by the Canadians. The largest of these came on the night of 9-10 November, when 2 R22eR staged yet another company raid to probe the enemy's defences on Hill 166, the main hill mass across the valley from the Canadian positions. Having raided the same position during Operation Pepperpot the previous month, the Van Doos were well acquainted with the layout of its defences, and Dextraze had been planning a follow-up raid since early in the month. Originally scheduled for the night of 2-3 November, Operation Toughy had been postponed by Rockingham because of the obvious Chinese preparations to make an attack of their own. In the words of the 2 R22eR war diarist, 'It was with mixed feelings that those who were to have participated in the operation heard the enemy attack come in at approximately 2100 hours on the forward platoon of A Company, 2 RCR.'[3] Two days later the operation was postponed 'for an indefinite period' as it was 'felt that by curtailing our patrol activity for a while that the enemy may relax his present alertness.'[4] Whether or not Dextraze saw these raids as a means of keeping his battalion battle-ready – 2 R22eR was largely immune from enemy attention in its positions on the brigade's left flank – the Van Doo CO did urge his men to remain vigilant, stressing 'that all guard duty and watch was to be done in the slit trench proper, dugouts are for sleeping purposes only.' Exhibiting his typical common-sense approach, he also issued orders 'that all dugouts would be rebuilt so that the roofs conformed to ground level and all camouflaged carefully. It seems that during the large scale attack yesterday [4-5 November] on 28th Brigade that the apparent [i.e., easily observed] dugouts received a large percentage of the enemy fire resulting in a large number of casualties. These revisions are to be completed in forty-eight hours.'[5]

Having already planned the operation, Dextraze was undoubtedly pleased with Rockingham's decision to remount Toughy four nights after the Chinese assault on Hill 159. In preparation for the raid, 'an air strike was directed on the ridge leading to Hill 166' on the afternoon of the 9th, while '2 RCHA was kept busy firing at numerous targets' throughout the day. The patrol set out that night:

> The Scout [platoon] and C Company of 2 R22eR began the operation at 2100 hrs, and C Company reached within 75 yards of the top of Hill 166 before the brigade commander ordered the patrol to withdraw. The Scouts achieved complete surprise left [southwest] of the hill but were forced to withdraw because of superior numbers ... According to the patrol, Hill 166 is covered with very deep bunkers, and the zig-zag crawl trenches (which are visible from this side of the valley) and covered by machine guns sited on fixed lines. On the morning of the 10th, three air strikes were brought in – two on Hill 166 and the other on Hill 156.[6]

Operation Toughy cost the Van Doos four wounded and two men missing. The bodies of the missing men were discovered on the 13th, when they were found 'in an RCR minefield into which the two men had apparently wandered on their way back to Company HQ' after returning to their lines.[7]

When operations are not intended to gain ground but merely to probe the enemy's defences, it is difficult to assess their ultimate value. The Eighth Army commander, General Van Fleet, and his subordinate corps headquarters clearly placed a great deal of importance on raiding operations as a means of keeping the front-line troops combat-sharp and maintaining a tactical initiative over the enemy once the ground campaign had settled into a stalemate. The desire to keep his men sharp certainly motivated Dextraze in recommending that his battalion carry out both Pepperpot and Toughy. If nothing else, Operation Toughy confirmed that the Chinese defences on Hill 166 had not been significantly weakened by the enemy in order to make their main efforts to the north against the more dominant Maryang-san and Kowang-san. It also indicated to the Chinese that their counterattacks would not go unchallenged and that the Commonwealth Division had not reverted entirely to the defensive even if they had been forced to relinquish their hold on Hill 317.

Nevertheless, the balance to be struck between maintaining the troops' readiness and the needless wasting of soldiers' lives was always a matter of some debate. While emphasizing that his relations with his American commanders 'have remained extremely amicable and we have been given all the help and support that was possible,' Major-General Cassels believed that there were still

> some awkward moments when I have been ordered to do certain operations which I considered either unsound or pointless. I have made the point that, so long as the Peace Talks [at Panmunjom] continue, I consider it wrong to undertake any operation which is likely to involve a high proportion of casualties unless there is some very definite and worthwhile object. So far the only objects I have been given are to show the enemy that we can still be offensive and to keep our soldiers sharp. I have said that I do not think that either of these objects are necessary so far as this division is concerned and it has now been more or less agreed that we shall confine our activities to active patrolling of all kinds, occasional limited platoon-sized raids to destroy enemy defences and capture prisoners and limited raids by armour. A comprehensive harassing programme by all arms continues all the time.
>
> I have not had to invoke my charter [to refuse an operation Cassels considered too costly] but on one occasion it was a very near thing. This was when I was told to put in an armoured raid to Kuhwa-ri (about 6,000 metres behind the enemy forward defended localities) [a village in the Sami-ch'on valley, three miles west-northwest of Hill 166]. This operation involved two [infantry] battalions and an armoured regiment against considerable opposition. In my view it would have led to very heavy casualties and the loss of a number of tanks and the corresponding gains would have been very small. After some argument the operation was cancelled for the time but it has not been totally abandoned and still hangs over our heads. However, I do not think it is ever likely to be staged.[8]

Nonetheless, patrolling was to remain an important feature of the division's active defence even during the enemy's November counterattacks. In the ten-day lull following the Chinese seizure of Hill 317 on 4-5 November, the 25th Brigade continued to send out regular reconnaissance patrols to determine the enemy's dispositions and intentions. Three nights after the Toughy raid, for instance, both 1 PPCLI and 2 RCR dispatched small patrols to investigate Hills 156 and 166. The Patricia patrol did not encounter any enemy in or around Hill 156, but the RCR patrol to Hill 166 'returned at 0100 hrs the following morning to report that Chinese on Hill 166 had forced the patrol to fight a rearguard action back to the battalion lines.'[9]

On the night of 13-14 November, a five-man Patricia patrol – consisting of an officer, a signaller carrying a number 88 wireless set, two soldiers from A Company, and one from the sniper section – set out at 2100 hours from 10 Platoon's FDLs at the base of Hill 159's western spur. Although not particularly remarkable, the patrol does provide a good example of what could be accomplished when the Canadians were willing to penetrate to the far side of the valley to gain information about the enemy's defences. As we shall see, such efforts are in marked contrast to the complete lack of reconnaissance patrolling undertaken by the Canadian brigade the following year, when infantrymen seldom ventured more than a few hundred yards in front of their entrenchments.

With good visibility provided by the full moon, the five Patricias headed west across the valley floor following paths through the 'comparatively dry' rice paddies and easily waded the eighteen-inch-deep creek that generally marked the Nabu-ri valley midpoint. On reaching the spur opposite their starting point, the patrol found concealment on its pine-covered slopes as they circled north of a village in the reentrant below. The Patricias 'believed enemy were first heard talking and coughing in the houses' but they 'could not determine whether people were enemy or civilians although patrol came within twenty-five yards of one house. There were no bunkers, weapon pits, or defences observed near these houses. At the west end of the unnamed village, patrol observed three well-camouflaged cross-type slits. The camouflage consisted of small trees and scrub in a square about each slit. These positions were unoccupied.' From the village, the Patricias moved northwest across the ridge and into the next valley containing the larger village of Patt'ogol. The road through the village 'appeared to have borne heavy foot traffic and was built to carry veh[icle]s, with log[s] inset' in the road bed. Crossing the valley west of Patt'ogol to the spur that ran up to Hill 165 northwest of the village, the patrol made its way through terrain consisting 'of scrub, vines, grasses, dried leaves and, in general, noisy going low cover.' As they reached the top of the spur,

> the patrol was challenged by an unseen enemy in words sounding like 'EE – I.' A few seconds later a grenade of a small percussion type was thrown by the enemy. The patrol retired to the west end of Patt'ogol village where it observed several camouflaged bunkers, not believed to be occupied.
>
> The patrol was fired on ... from the centre of Patt'ogol, first by one LMG, and a few seconds later by three. The fire continued for several minutes and was described as aimed steady bursts of two to four rounds. The patrol leader called for arty HF [artillery harassing fire] which appeared to land [on the ridge south of the village]. The enemy fire ceased upon the arty, and the patrol returned to D Coy without further sign or contact with the enemy.[10]

The following night it was 2 RCR's turn to dispatch a six-man patrol to reconnoitre Hill 166. Three hours into the patrol, the Royals were fired on from the village of Chinch'on and 'forced to withdraw under cover of arty to its own lines.' On the night of 16-17 November, each of the three Canadian battalions again sent out reconnaissance patrols to the Chinese-occupied hills across the valley. A Van Doo patrol uneventfully investigated two groups of buildings in the wide no man's land immediately east of the Sami-ch'on while a 2 RCR patrol returned to Hill 166 where it was again fired upon and forced to withdraw under the cover of artillery fire.[11] A five-man Patricia patrol, meanwhile, was sent out to determine if there were any enemy either in the village of Kigong-ni, which lay in the valley northwest of D

Company's positions on Hill 159, or on the high ground behind the village. Once again, this patrol's activities demonstrate the willingness of the Canadians to investigate the Chinese defences and gain information about their intentions without necessarily engaging them.

The patrol set out from 10 Platoon's FDLs at 2100 hours on 16 November and headed due north toward the eastern end of Kigong-ni. The 'valley between D Company and Kigong-ni and Patt'ogol spurs consists of dry grain fields. Only water is in stream which was about one foot deep when crossed by the patrol ... All buildings in Kigong-ni appear to be burnt out except one still standing at the eastern end of the village.' After skirting the village, the Patricias continued north along a trail not shown on their maps which ran 'north up [the] valley close to west edge of spur area. This trail will apparently support t[an]k traffic as it has been reinforced in a wet spot for some forty yds with large trimmed timbers presumably taken from buildings in the village of Kigong-ni. The ground rises sharply from the trail running north close to the east edge of the Kigong-ni spur. The spur itself is covered with scrub and patches of scrub pine. The house [in a reentrant northeast of the spur] appeared to be lived in. There are tended vegetable gardens, beaten paths and stacked, cut rice adjacent to the house.'[12]

After retracing their route down the unmarked tank trail, the Patricia patrol headed north, deeper into enemy territory, along the eastern side of the Kigong-ni spur. Near the head of the spur, the patrol stopped to rest while the sniper was sent to investigate the crest. There he 'came within ten feet of enemy soldier with steel helmet apparently in slit trench. Sniper was not seen, and returned to patrol.' Despite the presence of the enemy, the Patricias pressed on up the spur to the northwest before heading west along a sunken trail. They had now penetrated more than half a mile northwest of Kigong-ni and about the same distance north of Patt'ogol. As they headed farther west along the sunken trail away from their own lines, they came across 'a large rectangular pit approximately eight feet by eight feet and seven feet deep' located 'some ten feet west of the crest of the spur':

> There is a similar pit some fifty feet further down the spur. Patrol comd [commander] believes they are mortar pits. Appeared unused for two or three days. No empty cases were seen, but a piece of paper with Chinese writing which appears to be a range card was found in one of the pits. This paper has been forwarded to 25 Cdn Inf Bde IO [intelligence officer].
>
> Between the second pit and the house [south of the pit], there are several small bunkers and weapon pits. They were unoccupied and showed no signs of recent occupancy. The house at MR13451895 [map reference] is occupied. The patrol heard snoring and coughing in it.
>
> Within fifty feet of [the] two houses at MR133189, (not shown on [the unit's] map) while proceeding west along trail previously described, the patrol heard noises which at first sounded like digging. The patrol stopped to listen, and the noise turned out to

> be a body of approximately fifty persons moving south quickly in two groups along a trail just east of the Patt'ogol spur. The people were carrying heavy loads and the noise was caused by the rattle and clang of the loads, the patrol was not able to see if the party carried arms or how they were dressed. The patrol comd is of the opinion they were a carrying party ... This party went onto the Patt'ogol spur and continued proceeding south in the direction of Patt'ogol. The patrol were not observed and disengaged, stopping at MR 136188 and 138186 [on the way back to Kigong-ni] to listen. The enemy party was heard at both patrol halts to continue moving somewhat noisily through the brush still toward Patt'ogol. Some words were spoken, presumably orders. The patrol passed a wireless message giving the position of the enemy which was passed to arty. When the patrol arrived at 10 Pl D Coy wire at [0130 hours] ... a Mike target was fired [by 2 RCHA] at Patt'ogol.[13]

For both the outgoing and incoming routes, the Patricias' machine-guns had provided directional fire north of Patt'ogol and at Kigong-ni village, which was 'a great help to the patrol leader in keeping direction.' On the basis of the information gathered by the patrol, the number of enemy in the carrying party was believed to indicate that 'a sizeable enemy position is likely at' Patt'ogol. Of more immediate interest to the battalion's intelligence officer, however, was the trail running north from Kigong-ni: 'The reinforced road running north from [the village] and the fact that the valley in front of D Company is dry point to a possible enemy tank approach. This possibility is being closely investigated by CO 1 PPCLI and destruction of the road is planned.'[14]

The vigilance of the Canadian brigade was, in large part, due to the character of its commander. As Rockingham confided in a letter to his former boss at BC Electric in March 1952, he was 'not particularly keen about soldiering when there is no fighting involved.'[15] At his best as a combat soldier, Rockingham worked hard to maintain the initiative and drive of his officers by personal example. He clearly understood the importance of thorough preparation to the success of operations and always ensured that he kept himself closely attuned to the front line. According to his deputy assistant adjutant and quartermaster general (the chief administrative officer at brigade headquarters), the very able Maj. Charlie Hamilton, 'Rockingham was a soldier's soldier. He rose early each morning and after breakfast set off for the front to visit the troops. On occasion I accompanied him and noticed that he made a point of visiting the most exposed positions. He had a good sense of the battlefield and many times correctly noted sub-units receiving enemy artillery fire. This would happen while having dinner in the mess tent.'[16]

Hamilton's observations are borne out by the various unit war diaries which contain frequent references to Rockingham's routine inspection of their front-line positions, in itself a physically demanding job even if there had been no threat from enemy shells. 'The commander left Main [Headquarters] for 2 RCR,' the brigade war diary records for 0930 hours on 9 October, 'where he discussed last night's patrol with Lieutenant-Colonel Keane. From B[attalion] HQ he visited A Company [2 RCR] then walked across to B Company 2 R22eR, A Company 2 R22eR, and D Company 2 R22eR, before returning to Main at 1736 hours. To visit four company positions in this type of terrain is an almost superhuman task, and the commander appeared to be very tired when he finally returned.'[17] A typical example of Rockingham's tenacious ubiquity is described in the 1 PPCLI war diary the following month: 'The rain continued during the night and by morning the roads were all but impassable in places. Vehicle movement in the brigade was restricted to a minimum ... Brigadier Rockingham visited the battalion this morning, arriving at 1000 hours. With the CO, battery commander and IO, he sloshed through the mud up to B Company and inspected the company position. He agreed with the CO that the left forward platoon position was too tight and that a section should be moved farther south which will be done. He appeared satisfied with the takeover and the work being done by B Company improving the defences.'[18]

As this quotation suggests, the brigade commander's frequent visits to the front were not cursory. Aware of how difficult it was to take best advantage of the broken Korean countryside in laying out a battalion's field defences, Rockingham used his experience to help correct any faults he found in the positioning of entrenchments or the siting of weapons. During a routine tour of the 2 RCR positions south of the Imjin River in late July, for instance, the brigadier had made certain that the battalion's defences were properly adjusted even though the unit's commanding officer did not necessarily agree:

> The reconnaissance of the two left flank company positions [by Rockingham and Keane] required the balance of the morning as considerable differences of opinion were expressed over the position of the left forward platoon of A Company and the forward platoon of B Company. Map reading in broken country, so typical of Korea, requires careful application and a good eye for ground ... The brigadier remained at 2 RCR HQ for lunch in order to complete his tour of the C and D Company positions in the afternoon. At 1315 hours, the brigade commander and Lieutenant-Colonel Keane left to visit D Company. The brigade commander expressed considerable concern over the poor disposition of the left forward platoon of the D Company and the CO 2 RCR agreed that they would have to be repositioned immediately. The feature occupied by the platoon was a long series of small pimples all densely wooded with pine and brush. The position of the platoon as laid out by the platoon commander illustrated the folly of 'contour chasing.' Each section was out of sight of one another and completely incapable of supporting each other in any way. Each successive knoll or pimple appeared, and in most instances was, to be dominated by the next little feature. In his efforts to secure dominating ground, the platoon commander completely removed any chance the platoon might have had for usefulness or mutual support.[19]

Rockingham also made sure that his headquarters was placed sufficiently close to the fighting to guarantee that he was seldom out of earshot of major developments along the brigade's front. Following the Commando advance, the main brigade headquarters was set up to the east of Hill 152 near the abandoned village of Sokchang-ni, some 5,000 yards behind the most forward company positions and 2,000 to 3,000 yards from the various battalion headquarters. As the head of the Canadian liaison mission in Japan, A.R. Menzies, remarked following an October visit to the 25th Brigade, 'The guns of the British 45th Field Regiment of Artillery were located a quarter-mile down the valley from brigade headquarters and fired over the top of my tent all night long, in what they called harassing fire. If they were only as successful in keeping the Chinese enemy from sleeping as they were in harassing me, they should be given full marks for their nuisance value.'[20] Being so close to the front, however, meant that brigade headquarters was subject to periodic shelling from the Chinese, which caused problems whenever headquarters had to entertain a high-ranking Canadian politician. First shelled on 17 November, Rockingham later recalled receiving

> a teletype from Ottawa that the minister of fisheries, the Honourable Robert Mayhew, was in Japan and wanted to visit the brigade. The visit was nice for me as I had known him and his family since my youth in Victoria. He had not been in action before and kept us amused by asking, 'Are those guns theirs or ours?' every time a salvo of artillery was fired. Unfortunately during his visit, I am afraid that they were mostly 'theirs,' directed, I suspect, by an observation post which they manned somewhere in the surrounding hills – because whenever he appeared, he got shelled. I was not too happy as I supposed it was all right to get the minister of defence killed when visiting the front, but I did not fancy having the minister of fisheries killed in my area. We promptly had the sides of the officer's mess tent sandbagged up to the junction of the walls and roof to help reduce the odds of the minister being hit by shell fragments.
>
> After a somewhat exciting morning, he was offered a drink at lunch; he accepted a rum. He had no sooner got the drink in his hand than in came a shell, very close. As I went to the ground, I pulled him with me. A very alert and ambitious newspaper photographer who was part of the minister's party got the picture of him on the ground, but with his drink still firmly gripped in his hand. His wife was strongly against drink, and I think he very seldom used it, but I believe she saw the picture in a Canadian newspaper titled 'Minister hits the dirt without spilling a drop of rum.' He warned me that she would not be pleased if she knew that he was having a drink with us![21]

The brigade commander's frequent presence in the forward positions was not unnoticed – or unappreciated – by his men. Reporting on their reaction to Rockingham, Menzies wrote that 'it was wonderful to see the way in which he was received in all the units and by individual soldiers we met along the road. Everyone had a smart salute and a cheery greeting for him. It was quite evident that he was not only looked up to as an able commanding officer [sic] but also much liked by officers and men.'[22] For his part, Rockingham understood the significance of the military salute: 'It was not unusual, for example, when I was driving near the gun lines flying my flag (with or without a visitor) to be saluted from a great distance. This may seem rather useless and an imposition to the uninitiated, but those who have fought with real fighting men will tell you that the distant salute is a great indicator of morale and mutual trust, particularly when it is not solicited or insisted upon.'[23]

The ten-day spell of rainy weather that followed the Chinese recapture of Hill 317 in the first week of November had given the battered Commonwealth brigade a brief respite from the enemy's counterattacks. Despite UN air attacks on their defences and gun positions whenever the weather allowed, the Chinese were not yet prepared to accept the results of the Commando advance, particularly the loss of Hill 355. With that goal in mind, the Chinese 190th Division renewed the attack against the 28th Brigade's positions north and west of Kowang-san on 17 November.[24] During the afternoon, enemy shelling increased on the Commonwealth brigade's sector as well as on the PPCLI positions immediately to its south. At 1645 hours, the Chinese 'suddenly launched a strong attack against the forward company of 1 KSLI holding the high feature Point 227,' which lay directly west of Hill 355 and across the 'Bowling Alley' valley immediately northeast of the PPCLI position on Hill 159. This was followed by a probing attack against 1 Royal Leicestershire Regiment facing Maryang-san to the north and the continued mortaring and shelling of 1 PPCLI to the south:

> After very heavy fighting, the forward company of 1 KSLI was gradually forced back off the Point 227 feature, although one platoon with a MMG section, east of the feature, held their positions and were never dislodged. At about 2100 hours a lull developed in the fighting, by which time the enemy had overrun one platoon position of 1 R Leicesters, and captured Point 227. About this time, radar bomb attacks were put in close to our own troops, on likely enemy forming up places. Possibly as a result of this bombing, together with the heavy artillery concentrations, the enemy made no further attempt to exploit the slight gains that had been made. Soon after midnight, D Company, 1 KSLI attempted to counter-attack on to Point 227 but the company soon came under heavy fire, and the attack was postponed to first light.[25]

The postponement proved to be a wise decision as the dawn attack found that the Chinese had largely withdrawn; the KSLI company reoccupied the position against only light opposition. The chief consequence of the night's action had been the eighty-odd casualties suffered by the two British battalions. By late evening on the 18th, Canadian brigade headquarters was informed 'that it was tentatively planned for 2 R22eR to move from its position on the left and relieve 1 KSLI. The latter battalion had suffered heavy casualties and the commander of 28 Brigade no longer considered it to be in condition to withstand a further attack.'[26] Nonetheless, the British battalion had to remain in position when the Chinese resumed their attack on the company holding Hill 227 at last light that night: 'Once again heavy fighting took place for several hours and the company was forced to withdraw after inflicting very heavy casualties on the enemy. However, soon after midnight, [the] enemy broke off the engagement, and by dawn had withdrawn from Point 227 allowing it to be re-occupied by 1 KSLI.'[27]

The odd pattern of these attacks was continued the following night, 19-20 November, when the Leicesters had to fend off two more Chinese assaults: 'Both attacks [were] broken up after much bitter fighting, although one company [was] forced to fall back, but [the] lost ground [was] re-occupied at first light without opposition. Enemy estimated to have suffered further heavy casualties from artillery, radar bombing and ground troops. The exact aim of the enemy [is] difficult to understand whereby the division is attacked each night in strength, but any ground gained [is] given up in the morning.'[28] The enemy's tactics appeared more curious because during the initial attack on Hill 227 on the 17th, the remnants of one KSLI platoon 'came into the lines of 1 PPCLI to report that they had been captured by the Chinese and then released.' In the early morning hours of 20 November, 1 PPCLI informed brigade headquarters 'that they had picked up a wounded British soldier outside their wire who was left there by the Chinese after being a prisoner for three days':[29]

> At 0800 hours, it was discovered that the Chinamen had performed a rather interesting stunt during the early morning in front of C Company [which had relieved D Company]. Shortly after first light, an English voice was heard shouting for help outside C Company's wire. A small patrol sent to investigate found a wounded British soldier lying on the ground beside a roughly lettered sign saying 'Come pick up your buddy' stuck in the ground. Beside the soldier was a large neatly tied bundle of propaganda. The patrol carried the soldier back to the company, and as they were leaving several bursts of burp gun fire were heard across the valley. The soldier was brought to the RAP [regimental aid post] and questioned by the IO. He turned out to be Private P. Smith of 2 Platoon, A Company, KSLI, and was suffering from a fractured hip and several flesh wounds. Smith had been captured by the enemy on the night of 17/18 November during the Chinese attack on the KSLI on our right. His slit trench was blown in by shell fire and he and four others hid in a bunker. A Chinaman with a burp gun entered the bunker, captured the five and took them to the base of the hill on the way back to enemy lines. The party was caught in our artillery and mortar DF [defensive fire], the Chinaman lost a leg and all five KSLI soldiers [were] wounded. Smith lay for over an hour, was twice again wounded by our fire, and lost touch with the other four soldiers.
>
> A Chinese stretcher party picked him up and after a three hour carry he was laid in a bunker with a wounded Chinaman. There he remained until last night. He was accorded

> good, though limited, medical treatment, as verified by the MO who states that the dressing on his wounds were well put on. He received enough to eat, was given cigarettes and visited by a number of Chinese soldiers who all seemed very friendly. He was interrogated for several hours, apparently by a Chinese officer through a Chinese interpreter. The interrogation appears to have been skillful in that it succeeded in getting Smith involved in a long political discussion and argument. Few questions of military significance were asked. It appeared to Smith that the enemy were well in the picture on our order of battle. Last night he was told that adequate medical attention was not available and asked if he would like to return to his own lines. He was told that a Corporal Jones of his unit had been released the night before. (This was later verified by the KSLI.) Early this morning he was carried by relays of stretcher bearers for several hours, deposited with the bundle of propaganda and told he was outside Canadian lines. He was to wait until first light and yell for help. The Chinamen said they would watch him and fire a burp gun signal when he was picked up.
>
> The Chinese were quite successful in creating the desired impression on this soldier and Smith talked freely of his good treatment. While we have reason to believe the Chinese do accord prisoners good treatment (in contrast with the North Koreans), it was obvious they had bent over backwards in Smith's case. Smith was duly warned of the significance of this enemy propaganda stunt and a report made to Brigade Headquarters and the CO, KSLI. The bundle of propaganda, though in great demand as souvenirs, was dispatched to intelligence at brigade.[30]

Such humane behaviour clearly had the political motive of easing a Commonwealth soldier's fear of capture. Given the continuing Chinese counterattacks, however, it was an impression that division headquarters did not want to see spread beyond the grateful Private Smith.

If the object of the repeated Chinese attacks and withdrawals against Hill 227 was to cause the KSLI company to abandon its position, they eventually achieved their purpose. North of the Bowling Alley, where the Sami-ch'on tributary flowed west before making a sharp turn south in front of the Canadian positions, the hill was somewhat disconnected from the rest of the division's line. It had been important when the division was also in possession of Maryang-san to its north, but the loss of Hill 317 in early November had rendered Hill 227 less essential to the integrity of the Jamestown Line. A properly organized defence of the western and northern slopes facing the Chinese would have required at least two companies, far more men than its tactical significance warranted, while attempting to hold the 227 summit with a single company left those men especially vulnerable to counterattack – as the KSLI's D Company had already discovered. Complicating the situation was the long stretch of front line, some 20,000 yards, that the Commonwealth Division was expected to hold. As Cassels later explained to London, the long front left the division with

The view looking west down the Bowling Alley from the ridge east of Hill 210. DHH 410B25.014 D3

> seven battalions in the front line, one battalion in a back-stop position on the left and one battalion in reserve. Obviously it would have been desirable to have more in reserve but, without leaving gaps so large that they were unacceptable, it was impossible to reduce the front line units. As it was, they were very thin on the ground and gaps existed in many places. If the enemy had launched a large scale offensive I am of the opinion that we could not have held him, and I said so at the time.
>
> On 22 November, after many representations that we were over-stretched, we were side-stepped to the left and our front was reduced to 15,000 metres [16,000 yards]. Apart from the reduction of our front, we also lost a considerable part of the area where the enemy was most active and where most of the fighting had been. We took over an extra bit on the left which was, and always had been, a comparatively quiet area. Thus we were able to have two brigades forward and one in reserve. We are now in a position to give a very good account of ourselves but the front is still a long one by any standards and again I am doubtful if we could hold a really large scale offensive, but we can cope with anything else.[31]

With the shift of the divisional boundaries to the left on 22 November, 28th British Commonwealth Brigade was relieved by the 7th Regiment, 3rd US Division, and the company position on Hill 227 was abandoned to the enemy. The two company positions located on and immediately south of the saddle of high ground that linked the feature to Hill 355 to the east were retained and left within the Commonwealth Division's boundary even though they were an integral part of Hill 355's defences. With the badly battered Commonwealth brigade moving into divisional reserve for some well-deserved rest, the boundaries of the 25th Brigade shifted to the right in order to take over the two positions from the KSLI. These were occupied by 2 R22eR, moved by Rockingham from the left to the right flank; 2 R22eR also took over the two company positions on Hill 210 and the ridge to its west from the Royal Norfolk Regiment.[32] Sandwiched between the Chinese on Hill 227 and the Americans on Hill 355, the two exposed companies were separated by the Bowling Alley from the rest of their battalion on Hill 210 and 1 PPCLI's C Company on Hill 159 farther southwest. The Royal and Patricia positions remained unchanged (Map 12).

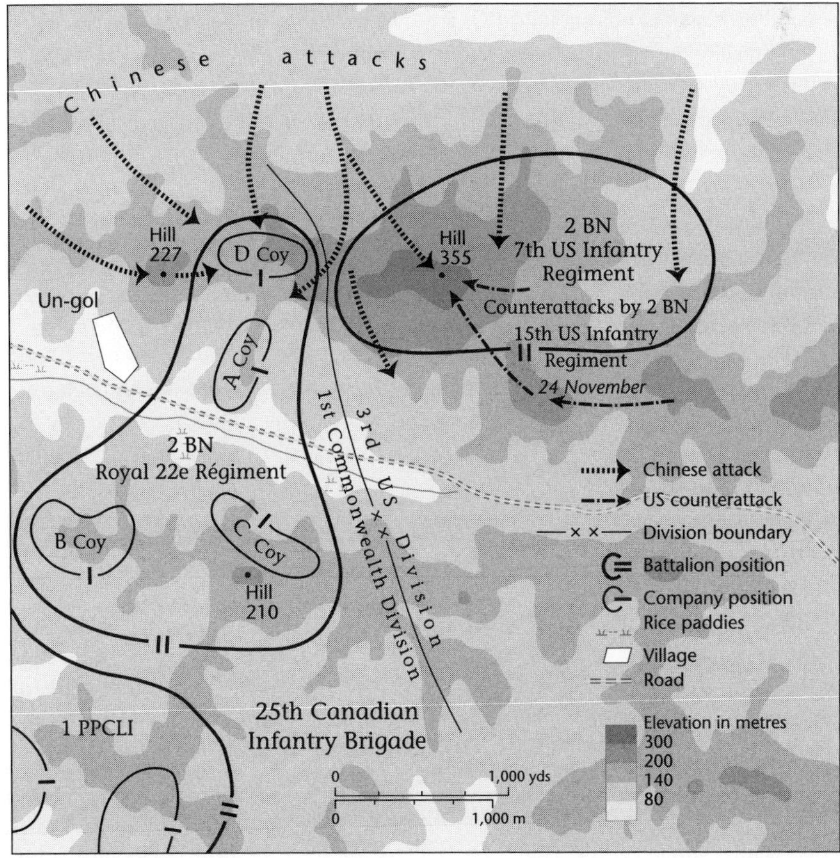

Map 12 *Defence of Hill 355, 23-5 November 1951*

When first informed on 19 November of the intended shift of his battalion, Lieutenant-Colonel Dextraze undoubtedly realized that in moving from the relative security of their positions on the brigade's left flank to a sector of the front that had been under assault since early in the month, his men were likely to come under heavy attack for the first time since their arrival in Korea. He communicated the heightened vigilance and military efficiency that would be required of the unit in its new positions at an orders group later that day. From his comments, it is apparent that Dextraze harboured some concerns that the men's inactivity had had a detrimental effect on the unit:

> For some time now, the CO stated, there had been a noticeable lowering of standards within the battalion. We seem to be adopting a 'Dugout Complex' with all the resulting ill effects. All movement in the future would be done in a military manner ... Men are to stay off forward slopes and crests, observation must be continuous and not confined to the one man in the company OP ... Saluting is poor and infrequent, must improve. [Platoon] officers and NCOs are to be instilled with drive and initiative, explain qualities of good leadership and man management. Careful attention is to be directed towards relationship between junior officers, NCOs and men so that efficiency and discipline will not be impaired. All present, the CO concluded, will give immediate attention to these matters, so that in a short time a marked improvement will be noted.[33]

In addition, Dextraze also went over the organization and control of the battalion's supporting weapons to refresh his officers on their importance in the defence. Most importantly, he emphasized 'that in the event the battalion does take over and is attacked, there will be NO withdrawal, NO platoons overrun and NO panic.'[34] Whatever his concerns, over the course of the next four days the men of 2 R22eR would amply fulfill Dextraze's underlying confidence in their abilities and determination. The stalwart defence of the saddle position between Hills 227 and 355 by the battalion's D Company stands as one of the finest feats of arms of any Canadian unit in the Korean War.

The Van Doos began moving into their new positions on the night of 21-2 November and were in place by 0630 hours the next morning (see Map 12). C Company and battalion headquarters were located on the relative safety of Hill 210, and B Company occupied the entrenchments on the ridge running west toward the Patricia company on Hill 159. The two companies in the most exposed positions were D and A, with the former taking over the more northern defences on the saddle of high ground between Hills 227 and 355 and the latter in the entrenchments to the south on a spur running down to the Bowling Alley. Typical of the sort of leadership exhibited by Rockingham and his officers, both the brigade commander and Dextraze went forward to examine D Company's exposed position on the slopes of Hill 355 after lunch on the 22nd.[35] There Dextraze took the time personally to site his men's automatic weapons, using his extensive combat experience to help ensure

Hill 210 as seen from the ridge to its east. DHH 410B25.014 D3

the best defence possible. Despite his efforts and those of his company commanders, however, D Company was defending a vulnerable position with entrenchments that were less than ideal: 'Captain (Acting Major) Réal Liboiron, commanding D Company, found that without Hill 227 the platoon positions he had inherited were much too crowded and lacked mutual support. One of his platoons were now squeezed into a position originally designed for a section. Some fire positions were of the "hotdog stand" or "sandbag castle" variety – built up instead of dug down, and thus perfect targets for high-velocity weapons. "I intended to readjust the positions at the first opportunity," Major Liboiron stated, "but as events turned out there was never the time."'[36]

Throughout the 22nd D Company received some light shelling on its position but the heaviest concentrations fell on the American company immediately to its east on the upper slopes of Kowang-san. On the following day, amid a snowfall that blanketed the ground in white, the light shelling continued while the Canadians improved their positions, most notably by building a jeep road across the Bowling Alley to the A and D Company positions. Reports of considerable enemy movement to the north and west of Hill 227, meanwhile, continued to filter in. At 1600 hours the shelling intensified into 'a terrific barrage of enemy fire directed on Hill 355 and vicinity' as the Chinese prepared to assault Kowang-san.[37] Thirty minutes later, an estimated battalion of enemy attacked the three companies of the 2nd

The 81 mm mortars of 2 R22eR fire in support of the battalion's D Company, holding out on the lower western slope of Hill 355, 23-5 November 1951. From their position behind Hill 210, the battalion's mortars fired over 4,000 rounds each night to aid D Company's stalwart defenders. NAC PA184317

Battalion, 7th US Regiment holding the western slopes of Hill 355. The Van Doos' D Company in the saddle position, meanwhile, had to contend only with pairs of Chinese soldiers advancing toward them from Hill 227. As the left forward platoon commander later reported, the enemy 'were like sitting ducks and the men shot them two at a time with the greatest of ease.'[38] To the north and east of D Company, the Chinese moving against the Americans on Hill 355 presented equally good targets for the right forward platoon.

Despite D Company's flanking fire, the Chinese pressed home their attack against the Americans, forcing two of the 2nd US Battalion's companies to contract their defences while the third, nearest the Van Doos, was overrun. 'With all means of communication destroyed and platoons fighting independently in hand-to-hand combat,' the American unit's journal recorded, 'the company could not contain the overwhelming assault and was pushed southward from the hill.'[39] At 1735 hours the Van Doos' A Company, on the spur directly south of D, reported American soldiers filtering into their position after having been driven from their own entrenchments by the Chinese attack. Fifteen minutes later the 3rd US Division informed 25th Brigade headquarters that 'Hill 355 is lost. 2/15 battalion [2nd Battalion, 15th Regiment] will counter attack. They were warned fifteen minutes ago and are on the move now. Part of the company on 355 is still intact and will join in the counter attack.'[40]

Two days later, Rockingham talked 'to the corporal who commanded the [right-hand] section [of D Company]. In reply to my question as to whether our friends had moved off their position quickly or had just trickled off, he replied, "Did they move fast? They moved so fast that their cigarettes looked like tracer bullets going down the hill!"'[41] The loss of Kowang-san had serious implications for the Van Doos' D Company, which was now under direct observation from both east and west. As Dextraze had indicated at his orders group on the 19th, however, he was not about to allow his men to abandon their exposed entrenchments. According to the battalion's war diary, at 1750 hours on 23 November 'Lieutenant-Colonel Dextraze, although extremely concerned over his now open right flank, expresses his resolution, in a net call to all sub-units, to hold the present positions. His quiet air of confidence impresses all and it is with frank anticipation the forthcoming night is awaited.'[42]

While it was the 3rd US Division's policy that all Jamestown Line positions were to be held with 'nothing less than an impregnable defense,'[43] the loss of Hill 355 had 'left a very large hole in the Corps perimeter.'[44] As the 25th Brigade diarist pointed out, Kowang-san had long been recognized as the key to holding the section of line running through the Imjin salient and its permanent occupation by the Chinese 'would mean their control of the lateral road running through the American sector and would make the 1st PPCLI and 2nd R22eR positions untenable.'[45] Despite the hopeful tone of the 3rd US Division's report of an impending counterattack, it took over six hours for its reserve battalion to move into position to begin the assault to recapture Hill 355. In the meantime, D Company had to hold its position in the face of imminent encirclement by the Chinese now holding both 227 and 355.[46]

The defence of such an exposed position was made easier, however, by the volume of firepower the company had at its disposal. In addition to the Commonwealth Division's three artillery regiments, the beleaguered Van Doos could call for supporting fire from the Strathcona tanks positioned on the Hill 159-Hill 210 ridge to the south and the 2 R22eR and 1 PPCLI mortar platoons. More distant targets, or those not visible to direct fire weapons, were engaged by the 4.2 inch mortars of the division's 120th Light Battery, Royal Artillery. Good communications were also required to coordinate the supporting fire, and D Company had both a mortar fire controller and artillery forward observation officer in its platoon positions in radio contact with company headquarters. Major Liboiron was in both radio and

Artillery illumination rounds light up Hill 355 during the Chinese attacks of 23-5 November 1951. Although the 7th US Regiment was temporarily forced off the feature, D Company, 2 R22eR, held out on the hill's lower western slope, to the left of the illuminated summit held by the Chinese. NAC PA188710

telephone communication with Lieutenant-Colonel Dextraze in the battalion command post on Hill 210, although the telephone wire had to be repaired repeatedly after being cut by shell fire.[47]

The first enemy attack on D Company's entrenchments came at 1930 hours from the direction of Hill 355. It was successfully beaten off after an hour-long fight, primarily because 2 RCHA and the battalion's own mortars maintained a curtain of fire around D Company's forward perimeter. At 2127 hours, Dextraze relayed a report to brigade of 'fifty enemy approaching D Coy from top of 227. Engaging with artillery, mortar and small arms.' Ten minutes later, the sounds of 'bugles, voices and yelling coming from west and north' of the saddle position indicated 'considerable number of enemy.' For the next three hours, all Chinese movement in front of D Company was immediately engaged by artillery and mortar fire. It was not until 0145 hours on 24 November that the Van Doos were seriously threatened, and the left forward platoon was reported as being 'practically surrounded.' Once again, a heavy bombardment from 2 RCHA and the battalion mortars, 'very close to [the platoon's] position,' succeeded in forcing the enemy to withdraw toward Hill 227.[48]

As the night wore on, the Canadians waited hopefully for the American attack on Hill 355 to relieve the pressure from that flank. At 0220 hours the Van Doos saw troops moving up the western spur of Hill 355 and asked brigade headquarters if they were American, only to be told that the 15th US Regiment's counterattack was 'having some difficulty clearing their way through our own wire and mines' and was still at the southeastern base of the hill, a mile east of D Company's position. It was not until 0540 hours that the Americans were able to report that the 'leading elements of F Company 15th Regiment are two-thirds of the way up Hill 355 and are receiving small arms fire. F Company 7th Infantry Regiment receiving mortar fire.' That was of limited consolation to the men of D Company, who were in the midst of beating off the heaviest Chinese attack of the night from the direction of Kowang-san's western spur. Reporting 'many Chinese are at [the] wire,' the company needed the combined effect of small arms, grenades, mortars, tank, and artillery fire to drive off the attacking infantry. The next morning, Dextraze reported his casualties in the night's action as being five killed, eleven wounded, and one missing.[49]

Throughout the night, the Van Doos had been assisted by C Squadron's tanks and the Patricias' mortars firing on Chinese infantry concentrations spotted around the village of Un-gol and Hill 227. At 0830 hours on the 24th, Wilson-Smith offered the support of 1 PPCLI's mortars in firing designated DF tasks against Hill 227: 'Lieutenant-Colonel Dextraze had been without sleep for some time, but was full of his usual zest and wit. The [Patricia] IO tied in with him Lieutenant-Colonel Wilson-Smith's Montreal and Quebec fire plans. Lieutenant-Colonel Dextraze made a rough sketch of the plan on a scrap of paper and said "You think I won't remember this? I may not have been to staff college, but you'll see."'[50] Later that morning, both Rockingham and Cassels visited Dextraze to discuss 'last night's clash and the GOC is high in his praise of the battalion's stand. The mortar platoon OC, Captain C. Forbes, performed nobly, firing over 5,100 rounds from the time of the initial attack 'til 0800 hours [on] the 24th November.'[51]

During the daylight hours of the 24th, the two Van Doo companies holding the saddle position were subjected to intermittent shelling, at times heavy, as indeed were the other two Canadian battalions. The most troublesome of the Chinese batteries were eventually silenced by the divisional artillery and several air strikes. The American counterattack against Hill 355, meanwhile, was finally making progress. At 0735 hours, the Canadians reported seeing 'what we believe to be Chinese digging in on northern slope of point 355' and asked for permission to engage them with mortars, only to be told that the soldiers they could see were likely to be American as the 7th and 15th Regiments had 'taken all of Pt 355 except one strong point.' Ninety minutes later, the situation on D Company's right was made clearer when the Americans reported themselves to be 'holding Point 355 and two thirds of crest line to the west. One strong point remains on the western end of the feature [nearest the Canadians] and an attack is now going in on it.'[52]

Despite that good news, further Chinese infantry attacks seemed likely against the 2 R22eR positions and in midmorning A Company dispatched a recce patrol to investigate the situation on Hill 227. At 1130 hours they were reported as being 'short of 227 – receiving grenades from top but not holding them up. Moving on, sniping at the enemy. Tks are helping.'[53] Thirty minutes later, 'assisted by the extremely accurate fire of C Squadron tanks,' they were on top of the feature with the intention of staying there to observe enemy movements until 1600 hours.[54] By early afternoon, however, it was clear that the enemy was massing his forces for another attack, based on the 'tremendous' amount of Chinese movement seen to the immediate north and northwest of Hill 227. 'Small groups of ten to fifteen each could be seen moving down from the hill and concentrating in larger groups in the valleys,' the commander of D Company's left platoon later recalled. 'These in turn would concentrate in still larger groups closer to our lines. They were in plain view and beautiful artillery concentrations must have killed and wounded a great many. I would estimate that the largest group of Chinese numbered approximately 500.'[55]

The presence of so many enemy massing for an apparent attack convinced Dextraze to withdraw the A Company patrol from the top of Hill 227 forty-five minutes earlier than originally planned. Even so, the Chinese offensive had not curbed the Canadians' willingness to patrol across the valley to investigate the enemy's intentions. To the south, the Patricias had planned to send a seven-man recce patrol 'to observe and listen for enemy activity in area of Patt'ogol' over a nine-hour period that night but it was eventually cancelled, undoubtedly as a result of the heavy Chinese attack that developed against Hill 355 some three hours before the PPCLI patrol was scheduled to depart its FDLs at 2100 hours.[56]

At 1745 hours on the 24th, the Chinese began moving in on the Van Doos' D Company position, with one section advancing down from Hill 227 on the left platoon of D Company and others coming from the western slopes of Hill 355 where the enemy was still holding out against the American counterattack. A half-hour later, the Chinese were reported as 'coming on D Coy from all directions. Left forward platoon might be overrun.'[57] Attacking in three waves – the first armed with sub-machine-guns, the second with heavy matting for getting over barbed wire, and the third simply with bayonets attached to sticks – 'they came over the wire like buffaloes over a bridge and there was no stopping them,'[58] the commander of the forward platoon recalled. As feared, the weight of the attack soon overran the platoon position, although its commander was able to gather his three sections together and lead them back to cover A Company's right flank and the two Vickers and recoilless rifle detachments located there. The company commander immediately called down mortar, tank, and artillery fire on the overrun position while making plans for its recovery. The right forward platoon was also surrounded by the swarming Chinese infantry but was able to hold its entrenchments. At 1925 hours Dextraze reported, 'one enemy company on the left platoon D Company and one enemy company on the right platoon. 30 per cent of the left platoon came into the center platoon area. Rest of the company [is] firm. Counter-attack to restore left platoon position planned for 2300 hours.' By 1930 hours, the Chinese attacking

The officers of 2 R22eR's D Company in one of their sandbagged entrenchments on the lower western slope of Hill 355. They are, from left to right, Lt. R. MacDuff, company commander Capt. Réal Liboiron, Lt. Mario Côté, and Lt. Walter Nash. NAC PA184260

D Company had largely withdrawn and the Van Doos were able to report that all was quiet.[59]

On the 3rd US Division's front, a strong enemy attack was being mounted about the time that the threat to D Company was petering out. At 2035 hours, the Americans reported, 'E and F Companies still holding. F Company has lost two squads. They are getting heavy tank fire from west and north. Getting heavy casualties ... G Company has been pushed off and is re-organizing with twenty-five men on reverse slope. They are thinking of sending one more company.' American casualties in the latest attack on Hill 355 were already reported to exceed 100, and 25th Brigade headquarters was advised that the 15th Regiment's counterattack to recover the lost positions would not be going in before 0300 hours. In the event, the American companies did not begin their advance until nearly 0500 hours, when they were able to move forward 'against no opposition apart from sporadic shell fire.' By 0850 hours on the morning of 25 November, the 3rd Division was finally able to report Hill 355 as being 'entirely secured.'[60]

The R22eR scout platoon, eighteen strong, set out at midnight on 24-5 November to recover the left forward platoon position lost earlier in the evening. Forty-five minutes later, the scouts advanced to their objective against minimal opposition: a solitary machine-gun firing from the eastern slope of Hill 227 which was quickly put out of action. Once on the ground, the scouts found that 'there was nothing left to occupy in [the] old position ... Not a bunker left.' As a result, the scout platoon had to take shelter in shell holes when 300 Chinese from Hill 227 launched an attack on them at 0130 hours. Fortunately, the battalion's mortars were being registered when the attack began and, together with the supporting fire of the Patricias' mortars, the Chinese infantry was decimated in the ensuing barrage.[61] In all over 3,000 rounds of 81 mm mortar ammunition were fired during the night, burning out one complete set of mortar barrels. Following the attack, the scout platoon left an outpost in the old platoon position and reorganized 150 yards to the east.[62]

With snow falling heavily throughout the day on 25 November, the Americans reestablished their defensive positions on Hill 355, placing a company on their left to make contact with the Van Doos in the saddle position and fill the existing gap. Although it was hoped that the enemy's efforts to seize Kowang-san might be over, they did make one final attempt to drive the stubborn Canadians from their entrenchments at 2120 hours that evening. As the Chinese infantry moved down from Hill 227 they were hit by the defensive fire tasks of the artillery, battalion mortars, and the Strathconas' tanks. Once again, the attack was broken up in less than twenty minutes as the defensive fire proved to be 'most effective – 100 per cent coverage ... Inf[antry] came in from 227 and north – they were shouting and making noises but now they are moaning but no yelling.' Based on reports from the scout platoon outpost that the Chinese were retreating by way of the valley immediately north of 227, Dextraze hit them with fire from the battalion's workhorse 81 mm mortars. At 2214 hours the 2 R22eR commander was able to inform brigade headquarters that the 'last shoot was very effective. Could only hear moaning and groaning [from the retreating Chinese]. Quiet now. Scouts will go out again in 30 minutes.'[63] As on the previous night, the 2 R22eR mortar platoon had 'done magnificently ... again firing over 4,200 rounds. The DAA&QMG [deputy assistant adjutant and quartermaster general] at brigade is literally combing the country for mortar ammunition. We have exhausted all the supplies in the Corps as trucks rushed ammo to the mortars throughout the night.'[64]

On the 26th, Dextraze ordered B Company, who had largely been bystanders in their position just west of Hill 210, to relieve the beleaguered soldiers of D Company. The men were in a state of near-exhaustion as they left the entrenchments they had stoutly defended during four days and nights of near-continuous shell fire and combat.[65] In the words of the brigade's war diarist, 'The troops of D Company 2 R22eR had reached the limits of their endurance. They had been exposed to the snow, the cold of the day, the freezing nights and had had no sleep since the evening of the 21st.'[66] The defence of the exposed saddle position cost D Company eleven men killed and thirteen wounded, while the 'lack of sleep and ... near-hits by shells further depleted the company's strength by twelve men.'[67] Overall, 2 R22eR lost

The commanding officer of 2 R22eR, Lt.-Col. J.A. Dextraze (left), briefs the CO of 1 R22eR during Lt.-Col. L.F. Trudeau's orientation visit to 25th Brigade in November 1951. NAC PA184311

sixteen men killed and forty-four wounded between 22 and 26 November, the casualties in the other companies primarily due to Chinese artillery fire. Known enemy casualties incurred on the Commonwealth Division's front from 17 to 26 November, eight days that included the capture of Hill 227 from the KSLI, amounted to 742 counted killed and seven prisoners of war. In view of the general Chinese practice of policing the battlefield and removing their dead – and eyewitness accounts of large groups of up to 500 enemy infantry being caught in the open and decimated by the divisional artillery – the actual numbers must have been considerably higher. Enemy casualties inflicted by the 3rd US Division in its defence of Hill 355 were estimated to be 1,500 killed.[68]

By any standard, D Company's four-day defence of the saddle position reflected well on the Canadian brigade's fighting abilities. It was, moreover, deeply appreciated by the Americans on its right. Commenting on the willingness of 3rd Division drivers to keep 2 R22eR supplied with US mortar ammunition from their own dumps, Dextraze observed that he had 'never seen, while in the field, such desire to help the fellow occupying a position next door to yours.'[69] By tenaciously holding on to their entrenchments even when they were virtually encircled by the enemy, the Van Doos provided a firm shoulder for the American defence of Hill 355, prevented the Chinese from flanking the Kowang-san feature by penetrating down the Bowling Alley to its rear, and made the American counterattacks to recover their positions a more straightforward proposition. Although the 7th US Regiment was twice driven off the feature by the Chinese attacks, it should be kept in mind that D Company, being the only unit of the Commonwealth Division under attack, had the entire divisional artillery of three regiments at its disposal to drop a cordon of shrapnel around its entrenchments as well as the squadron of Strathcona Shermans firing from positions on Hills 210 and 159. Nevertheless, the fact that the Canadian company was able to hold its exposed position at a key corner of the Jamestown defences must have made a good impression on its American allies.

D Company's defence of the saddle position also compares favourably with 2 PPCLI's better-known stand at Kap'yong. Whereas the Chinese attack on the Patricias was over within twenty-four hours, 2 R22eR's D Company had to remain alert and ready for action for more than ninety-six straight hours under miserable winter conditions. The actual number of assaulting infantry was undoubtedly greater at Kap'yong, but 2 PPCLI never had to contend with a large volume of enemy artillery fire. In Cassels' view, one of the most marked features of the November attacks 'was that the enemy produced a lot of artillery, including self-propelled guns, which he used very accurately in heavy concentrations. The enemy not only followed these concentrations extremely closely but on occasions actually reached the objective before their own artillery had lifted.'[70] The high proportion of men killed to men wounded (eleven to thirteen) was because the majority of D Company's casualties resulted from artillery fire, as a number of its entrenchments received direct hits. On the other hand, as mentioned above, D Company was supported by three artillery regiments in its fight while 2 PPCLI could call upon only the 16th New Zealand Regiment and one attached American battery to provide it with defensive fire. The Van Doos were at a disadvantage in comparison with the Patricias at Kap'yong, however, in that the defences they had to occupy were in a saddle between two higher features, both of which were, at various times, in the enemy's possession. As a result, D Company was usually under direct enemy observation and often received machine-gun fire from the surrounding high ground.

There were also some notable similarities between the two contests. Both 2 PPCLI and 2 R22eR received strong leadership at the battalion and company level. It will be recalled that Lieutenant-Colonel Stone made a personal reconnaissance of the northern slopes of Hill 677 prior to the attack at Kap'yong, studying the feature from the enemy's perspective to discern likely avenues of approach, before designating the specific ground that his companies were to occupy. Similarly, Rockingham and Dextraze both went forward to inspect D Company's entrenchments when they were first occupied on 22 November, in the process of which Dextraze personally sited each of the company's automatic weapons. He also kept on top of the battle by placing the battalion's 81 mm mortars under his direct control and ensuring a close cooperation with the artillery regiments in laying down a cordon of shell fire around D Company to break up Chinese attacks before they reached his men. As the official history records, 'to one officer who was with Lieutenant-Colonel Dextraze and his artillery representative, the battalion commander seemed "always about two jumps ahead of the Chinese in his thinking."'[71]

Finally, some mention must be made of the Van Doos' willingness to leave the relative security of their bunkers and scout for enemy activity. In his periodic report for the period, Cassels emphasized the importance of receiving early warning of attacks: 'We broke up a number of attacks before they reached us when we could get early warning. Without it, the attack is on you and round you before the artillery defensive fire can be used.'[72] Despite the presence of hundreds of Chinese infantry in the immediate vicinity, 2 R22eR maintained a recce patrol from A Company on top of Hill 227 throughout the early afternoon of 24 November to observe the enemy's intentions. Upon relieving the exhausted members of D Company on the 26th, B Company immediately sent a section to patrol 'towards Point 227. They got to within twenty-five yards of the top – two men then went forward – they swung around the southern edge and have been engaged [with the enemy] for the last two or three hours with grenades and small arms ... There were six enemy who were reinforced and got MG [machine-gun]. Tanks from 1 PPCLI [positions] hit bunker where Chinamen were and it is believed to have knocked them out. Now harassing with mortars and tanks.' That night 1 PPCLI also sent a nineteen-man patrol to the far side of no man's land 'to clean-up from frontal area' and make a reconnaissance of the village of Patt'ogol where previous attacks against Hill 159 had formed up.[73]

While the important Kowang-san feature had been successfully defended, Hill 227 still remained in Chinese hands, overlooking the now vulnerable Patricia company position on Hill 159 to its southwest. On the morning of 25 November, Rockingham visited the 1 PPCLI headquarters to discuss Wilson-Smith's concerns about the enemy situation on his right. The Patricia CO 'emphasized the threat that an enemy-held 227 held for us and recommended offensive action to regain it.' The brigade commander did not immediately dismiss Wilson-Smith's suggestion but pointed out 'the problem of holding it ... Unfortunately there are only four rifle companies in a battalion. It seems there is never enough infantry.'[74] The Chinese occupation of Hill 227 remained a thorn in the Commonwealth Division's northern flank for the remainder of the war.

With the successful repulse of the Chinese counterattacks against Hill 355, the fighting all along Eighth Army's front line temporarily paused as a result of the truce talks at Panmunjom. On 27 November, division headquarters informed the Canadians

> that until further notice all future patrols will be recce and not fighting, with the object of gaining information and not fighting the enemy. Artillery would fire only DF tasks and active CB [counterbattery] tasks. The object ... was to show the Chinese that the Allies were willing to honour a cease fire if one was agreed.

> This was the result of the agreement reached at the Peace Talks for a tentative demarcation line. Effective today the Allies and the Chinese had agreed that for a period of one month each side would not take offensive action while negotiations were carried out for a ceasefire. If a ceasefire was agreed within the 30 days each side would withdraw a set distance from the present line to establish a neutral zone. If an agreement was not reached, then each side was free to begin hostilities on a large scale again.
>
> There was no doubt that the Chinese attacks [in November] were prompted by the desire to establish the most favourable line for themselves and, in the sector west of the Imjin, the inclusion of Hill 355 in such a line would make it the most favourable.[75]

According to the Canadian brigade's historical officer, the November fighting had provided 'the most dangerous situations and anxious moments the brigade has experienced since its arrival in Korea.'[76] Thanks in large part to the magnificent defence of the saddle position by D Company, 2 R22eR, the Commonwealth Division continued to hold a strong defensive line across the Imjin salient for the twenty months of fighting that remained until the anticipated armistice was finally signed.

9 THE ACTIVE DEFENCE, DECEMBER 1951-APRIL 1952

For the weary soldiers on the Jamestown Line, the night following the agreement at Panmunjom provided a strange contrast to the preceding week of heavy fighting. Not a gun was fired and no enemy activity was reported anywhere along the Eighth Army front. Although General Van Fleet informed his corps commanders that they were responsible for ensuring that every soldier was aware that hostilities would continue until an armistice was actually signed, his operational instructions confirmed that a ceasefire was in effect: 'Eighth Army should clearly demonstrate a willingness to reach an agreement while preparing for offensive action if negotiations are unduly prolonged to this end. A willingness to reach an agreement will be demonstrated by: Reducing operations to the minimum essential to maintain present positions regardless of the agreed-upon military demarcation line. Counterattacks to regain key terrain lost to enemy assault will be the only offensive action taken unless otherwise directed by this headquarters. Every effort will be made to prevent unnecessary casualties.'[1]

In conjunction with the Eighth Army directive, Commonwealth Division headquarters informed the Canadian brigade that 'during the remainder of the armistice negotiations, every effort will be made to avoid casualties and to demonstrate our willingness to honour a cease fire.' For the immediate future, the Commonwealth Division was not to mount any offensive operations or raids, sending out recce patrols only, and generally to 'avoid engaging the enemy unless he threatened our positions by fire or movement.' Artillery and mortar fire was to be limited to counterbattery tasks except to fend off 'concentrations of enemy troops threatening our positions or fire in support of a counter-attack,' and the troops were to refrain from exposing themselves 'on features that would draw enemy fire.'[2] The de facto ceasefire proved to be short-lived, however. When word of Van Fleet's ceasefire order leaked to the Associated Press, American newspapers quickly proclaimed that the order had 'brought Korean ground fighting to a complete, if temporary, halt.' Embarrassed by the truth of the newspaper analysis, Gen. Matthew Ridgway quickly explained that Eighth Army headquarters had assumed 'a function entirely outside its field of responsibility,' and that the fighting would, in fact, continue. In the words of the American official history, 'The unfavourable news stories put an end to the virtual cease-fire and insured that at least lip service would be paid to the oft-repeated avowal that hostilities would continue until an armistice was signed.'[3]

On the Commonwealth Division's front, 2 R22eR received sporadic shell fire on 28 November and had to call in artillery fire on a Chinese patrol that was spotted on Hill 227 shortly after midnight. The following day, division headquarters issued fresh instructions easing the previous fire restrictions. The new directive 'stated that artillery and air activity would revert to normal, that infantry on recce patrols could direct artillery on[to] observed enemy, and that in general the brigade could attack "with everything but infantry."' The divisional artillery was allowed to resume its counterbattery tasks and engage targets of opportunity, such as groups of enemy soldiers that presented themselves.[4] For most front-line soldiers, however, the brief ceasefire meant little discernible change in the war. The Patricias recorded that 'the men in the forward companies notice little change in activity. Many are, if anything, a little more leery of the Chinaman than before. All are fully alert.'[5] On 30 November, 2 RCR reported that its B Company, on the heights above the village of Hamurhan, had received

> numerous mortar bombs with no casualties, however, considering the number of times B Company has been shelled and mortared since 2 RCR fought their way into these positions in Operation Commando, it is well worth mentioning that the low percentage of casualties they have received is chiefly due to the excellent dugouts, arrangement of weapon slits and crawl trenches. Concealment is practiced very extensively. The men are battle wise and heed all safety precautions ... Along with engaging the enemy, both when the Chinese attacked our front and on patrols, a lot of work has been completed towards making everyone warm and comfortable in the cold weather to come, improving the defensive positions by the laying of more barbed wire, mines and booby traps and generally preparing for any future offensive action on the part of the enemy. Daily transportation of men from throughout the battalion to A Echelon for showers ... and a daily laundry service being set up makes life in Korea, even in the front lines, that much more endurable. Every man has an ample supply of warm clothing and a sleeping bag plus good footwear and he faces the winter and the Chinese with determination and high spirits.[6]

For the most part, the Chinese activities during the month-long ceasefire apparently consisted of countering the Commonwealth Division's nightly patrols and deepening and strengthening their defensive works. 'In such areas of the divisional sector where the demarcation line as agreed at Panmunjom resulted in a no man's land,' Cassels explained, 'the CCF embarked upon a series of manoeuvres to close up to this line. This was skilfully achieved with a minimum of contact by successively occupying terrain features over a two month period. Enemy artillery fire was very light, due no doubt to the necessity of replenishing the large amount of ammunition used during the November offensives and the efficiency of our counter bombardment. It has been learned that the CCF move active guns from their firing positions at the first practical moment after the completion of their shoot.'[7]

Despite the partial ceasefire of 27 November, the 25th Brigade did not sit passively in its entrenchments to await developments. Within days, the Canadian battalions resumed sending out nightly reconnaissance patrols to keep abreast of enemy strengths and positions. On the night of 1 December, for instance, 2 RCR sent a seven-man patrol to scout for enemy positions on the high ground above the village of Pukch'ang, northeast of Hill 166. After laying up on the ridge above the village and listening to Chinese singing and talking on the reverse slope, the Canadians encountered an enemy section but returned without mishap after receiving some inaccurate automatic fire from them.[8] On the 4th, Cassels 'directed' his brigades 'to use fighting patrols to locate and engage enemy positions and to secure prisoners.'[9] Two nights later, the RCR carried out a fighting patrol, 'the first in quite a while.' One officer and ten men probed the defences around Hill 166 in an attempt to capture a prisoner, but 'they encountered enemy small arms fire at every attempt to snatch a POW, every ridge was occupied.' After attempting three separate approaches to the feature, the determined patrol was finally driven off by Chinese machine-gun fire. The next night, 'a game of cat and mouse was played with enemy patrols' by a four-man RCR reconnaissance party:

> D Company's recce patrol first encountered an enemy patrol of five men at [the Naburi stream northwest of Hamurhan]. Our patrol didn't fire but went to ground and later followed the enemy. Fifteen minutes later a second patrol of three enemy were encountered [across the valley near the village of Chinch'on] who fired three bursts of burp gun fire and threw one grenade. Our patrol didn't return fire. This last patrol of three went to Hill 166. Our patrol proceeded [southwest] and at [the road south of Chinch'on] heard the first enemy patrol following. Again [the] D Company men went to ground and the enemy went to Hill 166. Our patrol, after a wait of twenty minutes, went to [the ridge south of Hill 166] and climbed up along the feature and then NE. In the valley they heard nothing at all. No sight nor sound of movement at 166. Patrol was ordered back at 0100 hours so didn't proceed further. With no further enemy contact, the patrol arrived back at 0130 hours.[10]

Such efforts, however, should not be misconstrued as an attempt to satisfy a futile notion of dominating no man's land simply for the sake of it. As in the past, Canadian patrols were sent out with the primary goal of scouting the ground leading up to the enemy's positions and gaining information about their activities. Given the nature of the war and the enemy's methods, it was important to know just what the Chinese were up to so as not to be surprised. The information reported by each patrol – the best routes across the valley, concealed approaches to the Chinese positions, the presence of a light machine-gun here or a medium machine-gun there, the position of mortar pits and dugouts – could be assembled by the brigade's intelligence staff into an up-to-date picture of the far side of the valley. The cumulative intelligence could then be used to plan future operations and provide patrollers with an accurate briefing of the enemy's routine, the nature of the ground to be covered, places to avoid, and more generally, what they might expect to encounter in any given area.

The size of the reconnaissance patrols used to achieve these goals is a further indication that mere domination was not, in itself, the objective. Like the four-man RCR patrol cited above, smaller parties could easily blend into the underbrush and avoid detection by larger enemy patrols. Such reconnaissances were not meant to engage the enemy directly but merely to observe and, if circumstances were favourable, to call down artillery fire on exposed groups of Chinese. Given the much slower response times of Chinese artillery, that latter option was not available to enemy patrols despite their, by now, widespread use of wireless sets.

As we have seen, Cassels was also under pressure from the US corps commander to launch larger company and battalion-sized raids against the Chinese positions to keep the soldiers in shape and maintain an offensive posture. Although he had managed to dissuade I Corps headquarters from ordering operations that he found unnecessarily risky, he was certainly receptive to any operations proposed by his own troops that had a sound tactical basis. In addition to addressing the concerns of his unit commanders over aspects of the enemy's line, they conveniently demonstrated the type of aggressiveness that higher American commanders were seeking from all of their divisions.

One such operation was the raid on the night of 10-11 December made by 1 PPCLI against the high ground west of Hill 227, enemy occupation of which posed a problem for the company position on Hill 159. During a visit by Dextraze to the Patricias' tactical headquarters on 6 December, Wilson-Smith had again raised the issue of these Chinese positions:

> This enemy-held ground is particularly tricky. While it lies within R22eR responsibility, a large part of the ground is dead to view of the R22eR companies. On the other hand, our C Company [on 159] has full observation on all the southern slopes of the features ... Both COs agreed they would like to see the feature in the hands of friendly troops and felt the ground could be taken with relative ease. However, because of limitations of the present army policy, the COs decided on a plan of close coordination of observation and fire on the features and are bearing it in mind as a possible objective for a raid or large fighting patrol. In the immediate future both battalions will carry out recce patrols in the area.[11]

By the next day, however, the 'possible objective' had been transformed into a plan to raid the enemy entrenchments west of Hill 227. On 7 December the Canadian brigade major, Major D.H. George, issued a patrol plan covering the four nights leading up to the operation. As explained in the brigade war diary, these patrols were 'to obtain the dispositions and strength of the Chinese on the feature west of Hill 227. This was in aid of a forthcoming raid by 1 PPCLI (Operation Janus) on Hill 227 and the ridge west of it.'[12] The plan directed each of the infantry battalions to send out one fighting patrol before the 10th, with the 1 PPCLI and 2 R22eR patrols to operate in the area west of Hill 227 and 2 RCR to dispatch its fighting patrol to Hill 166. The battalions were also directed to send out recce and ambush patrols on each of the nights they were not engaged in a fighting patrol.[13] On the 1 PPCLI front, the busy patrol schedule prompted Wilson-Smith to divide up his front into specific patrol areas named for 'Greek and Roman gods: Mars, Janus, Atlas, Bacchus, etc. Patrols in these are given numbers so patrols in say area Janus will be known as Janus I, II, etc.'[14] The raid by D Company on the night of 10-11 December would be Janus III.

While the main focus of the brigade's patrols was to make a thorough reconnaissance of the enemy's positions prior to launching the company raid, a prime objective for all of the division's patrols was to capture Chinese prisoners, a recent lack of which had drawn some negative comments from the I Corps commander. Shortly after midnight on 8 December, therefore, 1 PPCLI sent a five-man recce patrol to obtain information about 'enemy dispositions and strength on feature west of Point 227.' If little enemy presence was detected, the Patricias were to send out two snipers 'approx one half hour before first light and lay up all day' to the west of the 227 hill mass, half a mile north of the company position on Hill 159. The recce patrol found footprints left by small Chinese patrols in the fresh snow that covered the valley and heard 'considerable traffic' from the direction of Kigong-ni, but encountered only one enemy soldier, who fled up a hillside upon their approach. At the same time that the Patricias were scouting the defences west of Hill 227, a four-man ambush patrol from 2 R22eR laid up south of the feature in what turned out to be an unsuccessful attempt to capture a prisoner. The four-man RCR patrol dispatched to investigate Hill 166 encountered two small groups of Chinese on their way up the far slopes of the feature but reported that many of the enemy slit trenches had 'not been used since the first snow' and that they had 'heard no movement or sound from Point 166.'[15]

The following night a four-man Patricia patrol was again sent to the high ground west of Hill 227 to 'dissuade the enemy from operating in the area' and, if possible, capture a prisoner. Upon reaching the summit of the high ground, the patrol encountered four Chinese in bunkers: 'Enemy threw approx twenty grenades at patrol, wounding three slightly. Patrol did circling move, closed on enemy and killed one, the rest escaped. Could not get a PW. While there, received red tracer fired from a rifle ... Shortly after seven rounds of mortar landed in area. Enemy body searched, but no identification obtained. A number of bunkers and a crawl trench around [the area as well as] bunkers on forward [i.e., the enemy's reverse] slope.' Despite slight wounds, the Patricias continued up the valley to the village of Kigong-ni and the high ground of Ant'ogol before returning to their lines. That same night, three miles to the southwest, a six-man RCR patrol encountered entrenched Chinese behind the village of Chinch'on on the spur leading up to Hill 166. The

Royals called in artillery fire on the position and withdrew across the valley without casualties.[16]

The brigade's aggressive patrolling culminated in the raid on the night of 10-11 December. The company Wilson-Smith selected for the operation, D Company, were the same young men who had put up such a stout defence of Hill 159 in only their second night in the line one month earlier. The company's orders group was held at 1000 hours on the morning of the 10th, when the Patricia CO 'gave verbal orders for the operation, Janus III, and issued the written [orders] ... which he had prepared and which the Intelligence Section had produced during the night in the event the operation was ordered.' Although heavy fog in the morning prevented the orders group from observing their objectives, it did allow the experienced Maj. J.H.B. George to lead his platoon commanders into no man's land to make a valuable reconnaissance of the routes they would use 'up to 800 yards beyond the start line.'[17]

Led by George, the company 'crossed the start line at 2200 hours as planned' (see Map 13). They were supported by the guns of 2 RCHA, the 81 mm mortars of 2 R22eR, a troop of British 4.2-inch mortars, and a troop of C Squadron's Sherman tanks. From their positions on Hill 159, the tanks were assigned to provide direct fire on each of the three platoon objectives: three hilltops lying to the west of 227 code-named, from west to east, Tank One, Tank Two, and Tank Three. Two other armoured fire tasks were the saddles lying to the immediate east of Tank Two and Tank Three, code-named Tank Four and Tank Five respectively.[18] Ten minutes after crossing the start line, the three rifle platoons and company mortar platoon had reached the stream midway across the Bowling Alley. With 12 and 11 Platoons leading the way to the first objectives, Tank One and Tank Three, the Patricias started up the southern slopes of the 227 high ground:

> The first enemy reaction was encountered at Ungol where 11 Platoon came under light mortar fire. Advance continued without casualties until approximately 2235 hours when enemy guns started shelling of spurs leading to Tank Two, Three, and Point 227 forcing 11 Platoon to the right (east) side of their spur. 11 Platoon suffered two or three casualties. Leading platoons began to find difficulty in establishing their exact place on the spurs, each false crest appearing to be the top of the hill. At approximately 2233 hours, 11 Platoon began to run into heavy shelling on top of the ridge on the objective. Our artillery fire on Tank Three was asked to be lifted but it was found that this shelling was enemy fire. It was in the exact place that our preparation had been put down. At this time it was deduced that the enemy had evacuated Tank Three and a message was passed asking if the advance should continue on to the objective in view of the enemy shelling and probable evacuation. The CO ordered the attack to proceed. When the shelling ceased, the advance was continued and 11 Platoon immediately came under small arms fire and grenades from positions in the area on which our preparation fire had been falling. 11 Platoon rushed these positions up a very steep open slope but were driven back by the intense weight of grenades thrown down on them.[19]

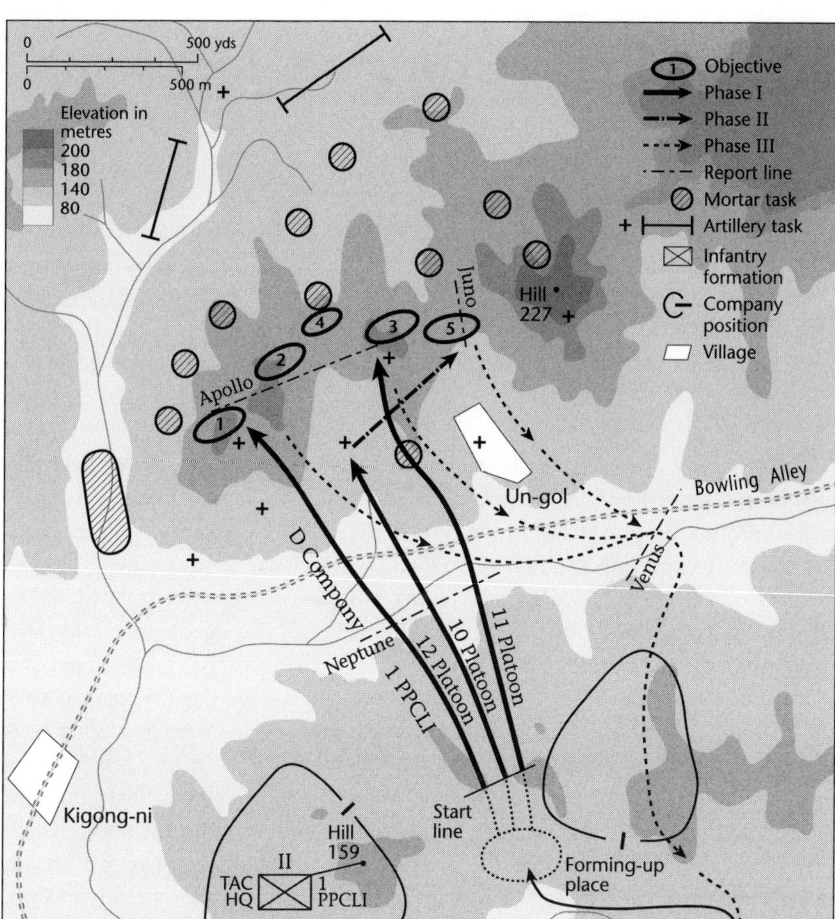

Map 13 *Operation Janus III, 10-11 December 1951*

No. 12 Platoon, meanwhile, trying to capture the Tank One objective, was also having a difficult time. They had 'come under small arms fire and grenades at very close range' on the saddle to the immediate east of its objective and twelve men had been wounded 'in the first few minutes.' Moreover, the platoon commander and most of the NCOs were among the wounded and the platoon's radio was damaged, leaving them unable to communicate. In view of the situation, the platoon commander 'used all his effective personnel to evacuate his wounded and withdraw to the report line' in the valley floor. No. 11 Platoon was also experiencing communication difficulties but, led personally by Major George, was making a determined effort to capture its objective:

> 11 Platoon and Company HQ proceeded to bring the [supporting] fire on the enemy positions. Difficulty was found in directing tank fire because a phone line was out, the 300 set was damaged, and the tanks could not be heard on our set. Fire control orders were passed by Major George to the CO at Tac HQ. The fire was placed near the enemy positions three times. These positions immediately became silent but [the Chinese] called a 60 mm DF on top of themselves. The signal for this was one red Very light and bombs arrived on the ground thirty to forty seconds after the signal. Enemy LMGs on Tank Two and in the saddle [of] Tank Four made the ridge of [the] spur leading up to Tank Three untenable. Enemy artillery shells continued to arrive sporadically on the west slope of all spurs. 11 Platoon made four unsuccessful attempts to take out the bunkers and the fifth rush by 11 Platoon, led by Major George, took this position (Tank Three).[20]

Unfortunately, as during the earlier large raids that attempted to capture a prisoner, Operations Toughy and Pepperpot, 'all enemy had got away by means of tunnels and communication trenches to the reverse slope of the ridge.' Immediately after the success in capturing Tank Three, 10 Platoon, which had been waiting in reserve near the base of the hill, was switched from its Tank Two objective and ordered to advance onto the saddle that led to the Hill 227 peak and occupy the Tank Five objective. It did so 'with no opposition except LMG fire from the reverse slope.' The platoon was led onto its objective by a corporal who had assumed command after the platoon commander had been badly wounded and his signaller killed by a Strathcona tank round that had fallen short. Following 10 Platoon's success, Wilson-Smith ordered D Company to withdraw, a task that was delayed thirty minutes while a section from 11 Platoon was sent to make contact with 12 Platoon, which had not been heard from since the beginning of the operation. No. 12 Platoon, being without functioning radios, had already withdrawn from the vicinity of Tank One to the report line. The remaining two platoons also returned to the report line without further difficulty.

Although the raid failed in its attempt to capture a prisoner, it did provide an example of the importance an officer's leadership could have in action. Despite being wounded, Major George personally led 11 Platoon's successful assault on Tank Three and then 'made certain every man was off the hill [before] he withdrew himself. He continued to refuse medical attention for his neck wound and personally conducted a count of his men ensuring that all were accounted for. The sight of the company returning to the position is best described in the words of Padre Captain Felchie, "They were magnificent, stepping out with arms swinging and chests out." Major George then reported to the CO ... and was debriefed while medical attention was forced upon him.'[21] He was later awarded a DSO for the skilful handling of his men during the operation.[22]

Nonetheless, the raid had cost the company the dead 12 Platoon radio operator and thirty others wounded, including Major George and two of his platoon commanders. Fortunately, the wounds were mostly slight ones from grenade splinters

The reverse slope dugout of 2 RCR, overlooking the Nabu-ri valley in December 1951, provides an indication of the underground existence experienced by front-line battalions. NAC PA184267

and did not require evacuation. No. 10 Platoon had been particularly hard hit by machine-gun and grenade crossfire, but overall the Patricias believed that the enemy's 'small arms fire was surprisingly ineffective. At one time a burp gun fired at 11 Platoon [from] a distance of about forty yards. No one was hurt by the fire, although ten or fifteen men were walking around or lying in open ground in bright moonlight ... Artillery fire, [both] our own and the enemy's, had no apparent effect on the enemy's positions. Tank fire anywhere near them made the enemy get out immediately.'[23]

The Patricia raid had been supported by a thirty-five man fighting patrol mounted by 2 RCR against Hill 166. The Royals exchanged fire with the enemy in their entrenchments but were also unsuccessful in capturing a prisoner. Their patrol 'suffered ten slight casualties, with only one serious enough to be evacuated.'[24] Acknowledging that neither raid succeeded in capturing a prisoner, the formation's war diarist had to admit 'that it was the general opinion that this was a very expensive night for the brigade.'[25] Given the fact that only one man had been killed and that the vast majority of the wounds were superficial, it may not have been that high a price to pay for demonstrating – both to the enemy and the American high command – that the Commonwealth Division would remain aggressive even during the developing stalemate on the ground.

As the two sides settled into the long period of static fighting, Rockingham continued to ensure that there would be no let-up in the Canadian policy of active patrolling. Until the 25th Brigade moved into divisional reserve along the Wyoming Line on 18 January, each of the Canadian battalions sent out an average of five to seven patrols a week. In the week immediately following the Janus III raid, for instance, 2 R22eR sent out two recce, four fighting, and four ambush patrols, primarily covering the ground around Hill 227 and the village of Un-gol. Over the five-week period as a whole, the three infantry battalions sent out thirty-four reconnaissance, thirteen fighting, and thirty ambush patrols across its front. These totals do not include the numerous standing patrols – two- or three-man static listening posts positioned 100 to 200 yards forward of the FDLs to spot enemy movement – that were also sent out at night but cannot be considered aggressive in nature.[26]

Nor were Rockingham's men content simply to investigate as far as the Nabu-ri stream that divided no man's land across much of their front. Most patrols centred on the enemy-held hills across the valley, and the unit war diaries for the period make routine references to destinations such as Hills 166 and 227, the more distant Ant'ogol feature, 1,500 yards west of 227, and the Kipon-gol ridge a similar distance to its north. Despite the constant patrolling, however, the resulting casualties were exceptionally light with almost no fatalities and few men wounded. What casualties the brigade did receive usually stemmed from the routine shelling of its entrenchments. Casualties were almost nonexistent among the small reconnaissance patrols that dominated the patrol schedule but gathered valuable intelligence on the enemy's positions, movements, and patrols. Typical of the stealth used in these operations was the 2 RCR recce patrol to Hill 166 on the night of 23-4 December, which observed both an enemy ambush on the Canadian side of the stream east of Chinch'on and an eight-man Chinese patrol on the ridge leading up to the feature. Although followed by the second enemy patrol, the Canadians returned to their lines without shots fired by either side.[27]

While the fighting and ambush patrols were, in part, a response to the pressure the Commonwealth Division was receiving from I Corps headquarters to capture prisoners, the level of the Canadians' activity was primarily a continuation of Rockingham's emphasis on probing the enemy's forward defences to monitor their dispositions and intentions. This was a particular concern of the brigade commander during the Christmas period. At an orders group on 19 December, Rockingham told his battalion commanders 'that he wanted a very strict vigilance kept by all troops during the Christmas season. All enemy movement would be engaged immediately and any enemy activity would be reported promptly. Every effort must be made by the COs to keep their men on their toes, for in his opinion, the Christmas period would be a most likely time for the Chinese to attack.'[28] The Special Force veterans could appreciate the importance of thorough reconnaissance and were unwilling to abandon no man's land to the Chinese. They accepted Rockingham's emphasis on patrolling as a necessary part of the brigade's job whenever it was in contact with the enemy, realizing that a proper defence of the Jamestown Line could not begin at its own wire but had to extend across the valley to the forward slopes of the enemy's positions.

The one object of the raids and patrols that remained difficult to fulfill was the capture of Chinese soldiers. From the end of the November battles to the middle of February, in fact, the Commonwealth Division succeeded in capturing only seven prisoners. Of these, two were taken by the Canadians: a wounded Chinese was picked up on the far side of the valley by a 2 RCR fighting patrol on the night of 12-13 December, and another was apprehended by 2 RCR on 29 December after he had become entangled in the battalion's barbed wire.[29] The capture on the 13th was the result of a thirty-five man fighting patrol to Hill 166. Armed with two Bren guns and a 300 radio set, 'D Company's fighting patrol, although suffering one casualty, Private Hilton who was hit in the hand by grenade fragments, achieved their objective of capturing a wounded prisoner after a fire fight ... Interrogation of the wounded prisoner at the ADS [advanced dressing station] brought forth the information that the enemy opposing 2 RCR and 1 PPCLI is the 570th Regiment, 190th Division of the 64th CCF Army.'[30]

The divisional commander attributed 'the dearth of PWs' to three factors: 'the nature of the fighting which is virtually restricted to short patrol contacts at night'; 'the effective propaganda campaign inaugurated by the CCF to counter desertion'; and the 'close supervision by officers and NCOs of rank and file to physically prevent desertion.'[31] An equally important factor that Cassels did not cite was the elaborate system of deep underground bunkers and passageways the Chinese were constructing, which allowed their soldiers to retreat to safety whenever they came under attack. Understandably, UN soldiers were loath to follow a retreating enemy into his maze of underground tunnels. Although the Eighth Army were not yet fully aware of the extent of the enemy's underground defences, they could easily see the great effort the Chinese had put into constructing their trenches. Commenting in February 1952, Cassels noted that 'the amount of digging accomplished by the enemy in the preparation of his defensive positions has reached fantastic proportions. Enemy FDLs are a maze of fire trenches, bays and bunkers and dug outs connected by deep communication trenches. These latter trenches extend down the forward slopes of some positions and of all positions rearwards for as many as three to four miles, thus providing concealment from view and protection from our artillery fire when moving to and fro. The greater part of this digging, especially in forward areas, was carried out under the cover of darkness.'[32]

With the approach of the Christmas season, the communists began to leave handmade signs and Christmas cards in no man's land in a primitive attempt to influence the men of the division. As the 2 RCR war diarist makes clear, however, the Chinese efforts served largely as light entertainment for the Canadians:

> A Company, 3 Platoon, observed another sign standing [just outside Hamurhan] at dawn also. This one, although identical in size and construction [six feet high and twelve feet long], had these words painted on it 'Come home Darling' with a crudely drawn painted sketch of a big fat woman pawing the photo of a soldier. Here again numerous greeting cards were found, all from the Chinese Peoples Volunteer Forces,

> wishing the UN soldiers a Merry Christmas and asking them to surrender and enjoy their Christmas out of the battle. It has become quite a joke and the men get a great laugh out of them, anxiously awaiting each new dawn to see if there is any more. The enemy has certainly made a mistake if he thinks his childish attempts at psychological warfare is having any effect on the morale of the men. It remains exceedingly high.[33]

In accordance with Rockingham's desire to maintain the brigade's vigilance, there was no let-up in the Canadians' patrol program over the holiday period. Nonetheless, individual companies were taken out of the line to enjoy a Christmas dinner. The Royals built a large log bunker on one of their reverse slopes to seat the men in relative comfort and safety close to the front lines. The men – according to the RCR war diary, at least – found their food to be 'prepared very tastily by the unit cooks. These men do wonders with the bulk rations and everyone is quite satisfied with the meals. Good food and lots of it.'[34] In his memoirs, Rockingham explained that 'we in the Commonwealth Division thought the provision of proper Christmas dinner, under as comfortable circumstances as possible, was most important to the morale of the troops. We all went to great extremes to provide other meals through the whole year in as much of a state of hotness and attractiveness as the circumstances would permit. Long lines of Korean porters were continually seen carrying "hay boxes" (insulated food containers) on their backs up to the ridges and hills so that our men could get a hot, decent meal in the line.'[35]

Although the Korean Service Corps labourers did invaluable work in hauling food and ammunition up to the forward positions, relations with their officers were not always smooth. 'We have been having trouble with the KSC officers,' the Patricias noted in early December. 'They seem content to sit on their fannies in the KSC village of Kamagol while their "rice-burners" roam lazily through the battalion area up to the hills with their loads. This necessitated Major Mainprize to call in their company commander this afternoon and, with the aid of our number one interpreter Lee, to lay down the law in no uncertain terms. The Korean word for courtmartial seems to bring results with them.'[36]

With the peace talks dragging on at Panmunjom and the fighting stalemated on the ground, American higher headquarters had begun taking an ever greater interest in ever smaller operations all along the UN front. Following his late-November public relations gaffe about the ceasefire, Van Fleet had told his corps commanders that they were 'to keep the Army sharp through the smell of gunpowder and the enemy' by conducting ambush patrols to capture prisoners of war. Although this directive had little apparent impact on the number of prisoners – only 247 were captured by the entire Eighth Army in December, a quarter of the previous month's total – it did prompt corps headquarters to take a detailed interest in each division's patrol activities.[37] On 23 December, for example, division headquarters wrote to the Canadian brigade major, D.H. George to explain that 'a complaint has recently been made by the Corps Commander that insufficient information has been passed to Corps in respect of patrol activity during the night.'[38]

Although the infantry battalions were responsible for conducting the patrols, a brigade's patrol schedule was coordinated by its brigade major to ensure proper coverage of the brigade front, to prevent friendly patrols from bumping into each other by mistake, and to keep the supporting arms informed of friendly troops' whereabouts in no man's land. In the British staff system, a brigade major held a status and influence that exceeded his actual rank. Normally selected from among the most intelligent and efficient of the staff-trained, combat-arms officers, a brigade major served as the formation's de facto deputy commander. As we have seen, his counterpart at division headquarters was the general staff officer grade 1, or GSO(1), a lieutenant-colonel who ran the division's operations, or G, staff. The initial appointee, Lieutenant-Colonel Danby, headed the division's operations staff until 30 April 1952. His immediate subordinate, the GSO(2), was British Army officer Maj. R.C.W. Thomas who 'co-ordinated the work of the G Staff, ran the Ops Room and co-ordinated the daily staff briefing for the GOC.'[39]

In his 23 December letter to the Canadian brigade major explaining the 'difficult matter' of the corps commander's desire to be briefed on all patrol activity by 0800 hours each morning, Major Thomas acknowledged 'the difficulties of all concerned (including Div HQ) of keeping to this timetable' but asked that each brigade report its patrol plans – including unit and strength, time in and out, and all routes – by 1800 hours each evening. The patrol reports themselves, with details of any contacts with the enemy, were to be received at division headquarters by 0700 hours although 'this info c[ould] be passed in respect of individual patrols anytime during the night as the patrol reports come in and should not be held back for one long report at 0700 hours ... It is suggested that brigades might maintain some sort of 24 hours chart showing details of all patrols and results, which could be used as a "check list" to ensure all details and results of patrols are in fact received and reported to Division HQ.'[40]

With little progress being made at the peace talks in Panmunjom, it was apparent that the American command was concerned that the Eighth Army would lose its fighting edge if the stalemate was prolonged. The American emphasis that all patrols should make contact with the enemy was the cause of some concern at Commonwealth Division headquarters, which often held a rather jaded view of Eighth Army operational directives. Writing to the three brigade majors on 21 January 1952, Major Thomas gave some indication of the pressure corps headquarters was exerting on its divisions to engage the enemy and inflict casualties:

> I Corps has issued a horrid order saying every patrol WILL make contact.
>
> At present we have NOT issued this order to brigades officially and are trying to cover up by 'adjusting' NO contact reports.
>
> Corps has now called for a daily return showing number of patrols and contacts for info of Corps Commander so we must go easy.
>
> As I see it, if in future we refer to static listening posts and static ambushes, we can get away with NO contact reports in respect of these, but in the case of patrols that

move about we MUST 'have' some contact even if it is only: Noises at ... Suspected enemy at ... Suspected enemy digging ... Enemy believed seen ...

In future we shall have to write up this sort of thing in the Ops Reports so when you see [it] you will know why.

As regards your HQ, I suggest:

(a) You better tell your Commander 'off the record' what is the official position in case Corps Commander blows in on you and talks about it.

(b) Battalion commanders [had] better be let into the picture.

(c) Everyone must help by 'having' some contacts.

Please accept this as DO [demi-official] info only as at present the GOC has NOT ordered officially every patrol to make contact, but I personally feel that pressure from I Corps might lead to this order having to be issued.[41]

Upon reflecting on the tangled web that might result if patrol contacts were simply invented, particularly given the close working relationship between the division's own intelligence staff and their counterparts at corps headquarters, the GSO(2) continued to keep the brigade majors abreast of the evolving policy at division headquarters. 'I have discussed this with GSO 1 at length,' Thomas wrote on 23 January, 'and he is fully in the picture and we have decided: (a) Truth must be told; (b) If NO contact or nothing to report then we must say so; (c) If we get a comeback, it must be accepted; (d) But really every patrol that moves around (other than the tiny recce patrol) OUGHT to make contact with enemy so close. This is all very difficult and I fear it is up to you. We must NOT invent false info obviously, but any tiny incident that happens needs to be reported so we can suggest to Corps the patrol did something. If somehow we can avoid the cold curt NTR [nothing to report] description of a patrol I think we can bat this somehow.'[42]

The American high command's obsession with patrol contacts – and their statistical calibration – could easily degenerate into the emphasis on 'body counts' that would afflict the US Army in Vietnam fifteen years later. As it was, the Americans' need to measure the success of operations in a stalemated conflict lent itself to exaggeration. In his memoirs, Rockingham related his own experience during a visit to General Ridgway's headquarters in Japan:

The night before we left for Japan, a three-man enemy patrol had come in against us and I had reported that we killed one, captured one and that one got away. Later US Army HQ said that the report did not match their statistical methods, which required them to multiply the killed by three, [and] add three times that to the captured or wounded. So the figures should be three killed, ten wounded or captured and any number got away. I said that I was sorry, but only three had come in and what I reported had indeed happened to them. The next day in Tokyo, I visited the C-in-C's HQ and found that the board had the US figure for the patrol against us. I again explained that only three had come in and what had happened to them. A rather tolerant shrug greeted my announcement as much as to say these crazy Canadians don't know the rules.[43]

In any event, the American fear that the troops would become dull during a protracted stalemate was unwarranted as far as Rockingham's units were concerned, even though the remaining two of the brigade's original three battalion commanders were posted to other duties. On 16 December, 2 R22eR's second-in-command, Lt.-Col. Joseph Vallée, took over command of the battalion when Dextraze – a future chief of the defence staff – received a posting to staff college. Vallée's previous combat experience had come as a company commander with the Van Doos during the Sicilian campaign of 1943. On 3 January 1952, the RCR's Lieutenant-Colonel Keane also returned to Canada to take a staff posting, to be replaced by Lt.-Col. Gordon C. Corbould, the former CO of 3 PPCLI at Fort Lewis and, more recently, commander of the 25th Canadian Reinforcement Group in Japan. As will be recalled, Corbould had commanded a motorized infantry battalion in action throughout the final fourteen months of the Second World War. His combat experience had proven valuable in overseeing the training organization in Japan. According to Corbould, Canadian reinforcements arrived in Korea 'in excellent condition, [with] a sound knowledge of weapons and tactics, and have gone through four

Two of the searchlights the Commonwealth Division borrowed from their American allies to provide 'artificial moonlight' over no man's land. Hill 355 lies on the northern horizon between the two lights. NAC PA184242

weeks of training designed to approximate as closely as possible battle conditions in Korea.'[44] His experience would also make for a smooth transition as Corbould settled in to the command of 2 RCR.

Despite the changeover in his immediate subordinates, Rockingham continued the brigade's vigorous patrol policy. During the first half of January 1952, each battalion continued to send one or two patrols across no man's land each night. Nor did they allow their patrol routine to become stale, introducing innovations to try to keep the enemy off-balance:

> A different type of patrol was carried out tonight. Sergeant Urquhart and two snipers went into the valley at 1900 hours to make a nuisance of themselves to the Chinaman. They moved about the valley floor [across the stream south of the village of Kigong-ni], intentionally making noise, coughing, and firing at the enemy outpost positions on the spur tips. A fire plan was laid on to be called for at the highest point of enemy reaction. The object of this patrol was to convince the Chinaman that our patrolling effort for the night was over, in the hope that he would slacken off for the rest of the night. Then our fighting patrol against the tip of Pattagol spur would hit him in the waning hours of darkness in the morning. The snipers were successful in making their presence known to the enemy and were chased around the valley by an enemy section or two.[45]

Despite careful planning, however, the Patricias' fighting patrol came up empty when it tried to capture a prisoner: 'The Chinaman is very crafty about occupying his prepared outposts on the tips of the spurs running off the ridge line that comprises his main line of resistance. The early morning fighting patrol was planned against an outpost which he is known to have occupied on several occasions in the last few weeks. The patrol went as planned and doubtless would have cleaned out the outpost were it occupied. Unfortunately, Lieutenant Jans and his two sections found no Chinamen on the objective.'[46]

Not all patrol surprises were a result of the enemy's actions, however. On the night of 8 January, the Patricias' intelligence officer, Lt. R.J. Frost, led a group of snipers to the northern base of Hill 159 to set up an ambush 'in coordination with an aggressive R22eR recce patrol around the features to the west of Point 227.' The Van Doo patrol failed to flush any enemy toward the waiting Patricias but, as 'the R22eR patrol hove into sight of our ambush, Lieutenant Frost saw his old friend Lieutenant Nick Sincennes, R22eR, for the first time in some years, though not exactly to speak to. People meet again in the funniest places.'[47] Four nights later, Frost led out 'a sundry crew of snipers, intelligence section personnel, drivers and the Signals Sergeant' to set up another ambush just across the Nabu-ri stream to the west of Hill 159. This odd assortment of Patricias was just moving into the valley off the spur north of the company position on 159 'when they bumped an enemy ambush patrol. After a small fire fight in which one enemy was hit, the patrol withdrew to A Company. At 2045 hours, a second attempt to make for the ambush position was engaged by enemy on both sides of the spur. Mortar fire was called on the enemy, and one group was seen by the FOO with A Company and chased across the valley with 25-pounder shells. Said one of the swanners [out to enjoy himself] on the patrol, "Hell, why didn't you tell me there were Chinamen in the valley. I just wanted to go out for a look."'[48]

For the next several nights, a full moon lit up the valley and limited Canadian activities to a few standing patrols out in front of their positions. Although the entire brigade was to move into divisional reserve on the 18th, each of the Canadian battalions resumed a full schedule of reconnaissance, fighting, and ambush patrols during their final three nights in the line, including yet another reconnaissance of the eastern spur of Hill 166 on the night of 16-17 January.[49] Despite having been in the front line since early September, the Canadians' high morale was reflected in the fact that 'not all battalion commanders were in favour' of the proposed move into reserve, 'owing to the good positions their units had built, maintained and held.' As much as they may have been reluctant to relinquish their entrenchments, Rockingham 'had decided that after four and a half months in the line, the troops needed the opportunity to rest and clean up and for the units to re-equip themselves.'[50] The brigade's main task in reserve would be 'to prepare the defence positions on Lines Wyoming and Kansas ... and to complete these defences as quickly as possible. Units would make use of the time to rest, re-equip and provide maximum recreation for the troops.'[51]

Before the Canadians moved out of the line on the 18th, however, 1 PPCLI suffered sixteen more casualties in the type of unfortunate accident that can easily occur in a war zone. On 15 January a Patricia on standing patrol accidentally set off a mine in one of the numerous Commonwealth minefields, wounding himself and two others. One of the stretcher parties sent to bring in the wounded men inadvertently exploded a second mine, killing two soldiers and wounding four more. That evening a Chinese patrol infiltrated behind a Patricia company position and ambushed one of the battalion's vehicles, wounding three of the occupants with a tank grenade. One of the soldiers who came to their rescue found a second, unexploded tank grenade near the vehicle and casually tossed it aside. The grenade detonated on contact with the ground and wounded four more Patricias.[52]

While having two men killed and fourteen wounded in such incidents on the same day was a rather high total, the mishaps themselves were not out of the ordinary but simply reflected the inevitable carelessness that can afflict young men when they are routinely surrounded by live ammunition and high explosives. While the enemy's daily mortar and shell fire inflicted the most casualties, wandering into friendly minefields or the accidental discharge of a weapon also took a surprising toll. One notable incident had occurred on 16 July when the Van Doos' acting second-in-command, Major Y. Dubé, was fatally wounded at A Echelon when a pistol being cleaned by a Korean went off accidentally.[53] A more typical occurrence was described in a Patricia war diary entry on 22 November 1951: 'At 1050 hours [a private] of B Company was seriously wounded when he wandered off the beaten path in the company area and ran into one of the booby traps laid by the 2nd Battalion. All ranks in the company had been warned to stay out of this area because of the booby traps. A few days previously, it was [the same private] who accidentally shot and wounded another B Company soldier.'[54] You do not have to read too much between the lines to sense the relief of his fellow soldiers as they watched the unfortunate Patricia being evacuated to hospital by jeep.

The January move into reserve also provided an example of why the US Marines had recommended the Sherman tank so highly for the rugged terrain of Korea. As C Squadron was being relieved in the front line by the Centurion tanks of the 5th Inniskilling Dragoon Guards, the Canadian Shermans had to tow the British tanks into their positions. Even then, 4 Troop on Hill 159 had to wait an extra night for the Centurions to reach them. Next morning,

> the squadron leader left the new harbour area at 0600 hours to supervise the relief of 4 Troop ... The relieving Centurion troop was by this time at the base of 4 Troop's hill (Point 159). Upon the arrival of Major Jewkes, the Centurion troop leader started his tank up the hill. Immediately he threw a track. All day the troop leader's tank endeavoured to reach the top of the hill but met with continual mishaps. The other Centurions fared little better. By 1600 hours ... two of the Centurions had succeeded in reaching the top of the hill where they had become immobile due to throwing tracks. The third Centurion was half way up the hill also with a track off. At this point the CO of 1 KSLI released 4 Troop who drove to the new harbour area without difficulty.[55]

In divisional reserve, the Canadians were not immediately affected by the Eighth Army's renewed emphasis on having all offensive patrols make contact with the enemy. Their reliance on the use of smaller reconnaissance patrols, which were best suited to gathering information on the enemy's dispositions and routine activities without having to engage them in a firefight, had already proven effective. Nonetheless, Rockingham informed his COs at a conference held in early February that Eighth Army had 'directed that patrols and outposts in the future will be more aggressive' and warned that the 25th Brigade 'would be patrolling again very shortly' even while in reserve.[56]

Although the brigade had always been active patrollers, Rockingham made sure that his battalions made good use of their time in reserve to keep the men's skills sharp. In early February the RCR's Lieutenant-Colonel Corbould ordered all of his companies to commence refresher patrol training under his personal supervision: 'Training will be done in daylight and darkness and will consist of the following: individual fieldcraft and use of ground; patrol formations; dress and weapons; movement before and after enemy contacted. Companies will demonstrate a fighting patrol which will be judged on formations, dress, weapons, movement, aggressiveness, etc. All companies will then train along the lines of the best patrol demonstrated.'[57] As the unit's war diary recorded on 20 February, 'The weather was sunny and clear and the companies continued to take full advantage of it with training. Their days are full lately, extending into darkness when night patrolling is practised.'[58]

The Patricias were also busy, setting up a patrol school that put 'a new flock of students' through their paces with each course. The school eventually provided a demonstration of patrol techniques for selected observers from within the division, following which Rockingham conducted a discussion on patrolling.[59] Brigade headquarters also distributed 'some common Chinese sayings for use when on patrol' to its battalions and also circulated a paper prepared by the 29th British Brigade 'discussing patrol activity on [the Commonwealth Division's] front. It is very interesting and will be most useful in helping us get the "feel"' for the latest developments when the Canadians returned to the line.[60]

Even in reserve, however, the Canadians were required to carry out one fighting patrol each week, with the battalion concerned receiving ninety-six hours' notice of its task and the 'unit through which [the] patrol will pass. Battalions will then conduct recces and make all further arrangements with battalion of 28th British Commonwealth Infantry Brigade or 29th British Infantry Brigade concerned. Patrols will be under [the] operational command of [the] battalion on whose front they operate.'[61] The Royals sent a fighting patrol to a ruined bridge on the Samich'on River on 10 February to investigate the enemy-held high ground to its northwest. The Royals exchanged fire with a Chinese ambush patrol at the base of the high ground but managed to return without casualties. Although the three battalions continued to send out periodic reconnaissance and fighting patrols through the 29th Brigade's positions, such contacts remained rare despite Van Fleet's urging to the contrary. The patrols did allow the Canadians an opportunity to become familiar with the terrain and conditions on the section of front they were scheduled to take over on 10 March.

In fact, throughout the brigade's time in reserve 'the enemy showed little aggressive action' and the majority of Commonwealth patrols were able to report only 'no contact.'[62] The lack of enemy contact was in part the result of Operation Snare, 'an idea cooked up by some wild-eyed dreamer at Eighth Army HQ to make the enemy curious, then careless.' For a one-week period in mid-February, all patrolling was suspended and all artillery, mortar, and tank fire forbidden. 'No one is hopeful of this plan,' the Patricias' war diarist noted at Snare's outset, 'but we are playing along.'[63] Four days later, it was clear that 'Operation Snare is producing very little. There have been no curious patrols against us and the enemy seems to be taking full advantage of his unexpected respite from shelling. He is quite boldly digging by day on the forward slopes and creeping his positions closer to our lines ... Our tanks crews are practically dying of frustration.'[64] Cassels was similarly skeptical of Snare's value, fearing

> that the operation would give the enemy exactly the opportunity he wanted to improve his defences on the forward slopes and to work his way forward with impunity. As we had spent the previous month using every possible means to force the enemy back and

> off the forward slopes and had destroyed many of his bunkers, I protested strongly against this operation. I was overruled. I regret to say that the result has been exactly as I and all my commanders anticipated. The enemy is now right down the forward slopes in very deep and strong bunkers and all our previous efforts have been completely nullified. The enemy sent out a few patrols and found we were still there and then calmly proceeded with his digging. We are now trying to force him back again but it will take a long time and considerable effort.[65]

One of the brigade's training programs that continued to run whether the Canadians were in reserve or the line was the NCO school originally established by 2 PPCLI in June 1951. 'The establishment of the school,' the Patricias proudly recorded at the time, 'came after the recommendation made by Lieutenant-Colonel Stone ... had been considered and found feasible by the brigade commander. The decision to locate the school near Uijongbu and remove it from the other establishments of the brigade is a good one as it reduces interruptions and distractions to the minimum [whenever the brigade moved]. The establishment of the 25 CIB NCO School is a continuation of the policy laid down by Lieutenant-Colonel Stone before the arrival of the brigade [and] will enable the battalions to have a reserve of qualified NCOs on hand rather than have to take untried men from the reinforcement stream.'[66] As this quotation indicates, the NCO school was strongly supported by Rockingham, who believed that it gave 'any bright and ambitious soldier the opportunity to raise his qualifications. The standards were very high and the conditions so much better than at the front that it became a real showplace. It was one of the smartest NCO schools I have ever seen and highly sought after by the troops. I tried, and was mostly able, to take each graduation parade and naturally was not averse to showing it off to all and sundry.'[67]

Such an opportunity presented itself at the school's passing-out parade on 10 February, to which Rockingham invited both General Van Fleet and the I Corps commander, Lt. Gen. John O'Daniel. Rockingham later returned to his headquarters to report 'that the performance put on by the NCOs was excellent and one of the best he had yet seen. Apparently the Army and Corps commanders were very much impressed as were the numerous American visitors from I Corps HQ and EUSAK [Eighth US Army in Korea]. One [American] officer was heard to remark that the candidates looked proud of being soldiers to which the [brigade] commander replied "Of course. Why shouldn't they?"'[68]

With the Canadians set to return to the Jamestown Line on 10 March, Rockingham ordered the entire brigade to conduct Exercise Limber. Its purpose was 'to exercise the units in battle techniques, drills, and procedures, and to test communications, in order that the brigade would "unrust itself" from the static role which the units had held for so long.'[69] Beginning at first light, the three infantry battalions, 2 RCHA, C Squadron, Lord Strathcona's Horse, and the 57th Field Squadron pulled out of their Wyoming Line positions and moved south of the Imjin from where they recrossed the river in assault boats and 'began to "counter-attack" to their original positions. These were reached by 1700 hours, when the exercise came to an end. That evening a review of the scheme was held, when the criticisms were made by the umpires (the CO 2 RCHA and the three battery commanders) and when the brigade commander gave his summary. He said that the scheme was satisfactory, although the brigade was "rusty" on many of the battle techniques.'[70] Although such training and exercises might seem routine, they are a further example of Rockingham's determination to keep his officers and men on their toes, a trademark of his entire tenure in command. With the war stalemated on the ground and just over a month to go before being rotated back to Canada, it would have been very easy for the 25th Brigade's officers to let standards slide and simply return to their dugouts on the Jamestown Line to await the end of their twelve-month terms. Rockingham did not allow that to happen, yet another sign of a very good brigade commander.

The positions the Canadians took over from the British brigade on 10 March were on the opposite end of the Commonwealth Division's line to those they had previously occupied. With the shift to the left in mid-November, the division had taken over a group of hills west of the Sami-ch'on River known as the 'Hook' position (see Map 14). With their former entrenchments now being held by 28 Brigade to their right, the Canadians' new positions lay astride the Sami-ch'on: both 2 RCR and 1 PPCLI occupied the Hook, and 2 R22eR, to the northeast, faced the river from the high ground north of the village of Yong-dong. 'The general feeling is one of excitement and in some cases apprehension,' the brigade diarist noted before the move, 'which is normal preceding a move into the line.'[71] As we have seen, the Canadians had already developed some familiarity with the area by conducting a number of fighting and reconnaissance patrols there while still in reserve. Nonetheless, the battalions were not entirely satisfied with the entrenchments they inherited from the British. 'The new positions are only fair by Canadian standards,' the Royals reported immediately on taking over on the 10th. 'The English have a tendency to construct their bunkers as small as possible. The Canuck likes lots of room and comfort. Consequently, reconstruction was seen on all sides throughout the day.'[72] As usual, Rockingham's concerns had more to do with tactics than comfort and at a COs conference several days later, he 'emphasized the importance of improving the positions as quickly as possible which everyone had agreed had been far too cramped and tight [in relation to each other]. This had been a common criticism by the Canadians of the British positions which invariably have been much closer together [on the ground] than ours.'[73]

In order to familiarize themselves with their new sector, the Canadians resumed patrolling during their first night in the line with the usual mix of reconnaissance, fighting, and ambush parties from each battalion. As they always had, patrols roamed some 1,000 to 2,000 yards forward of their positions to search out the enemy's entrenchments. The Royals also began to send snipers to a position on Hill 163, half

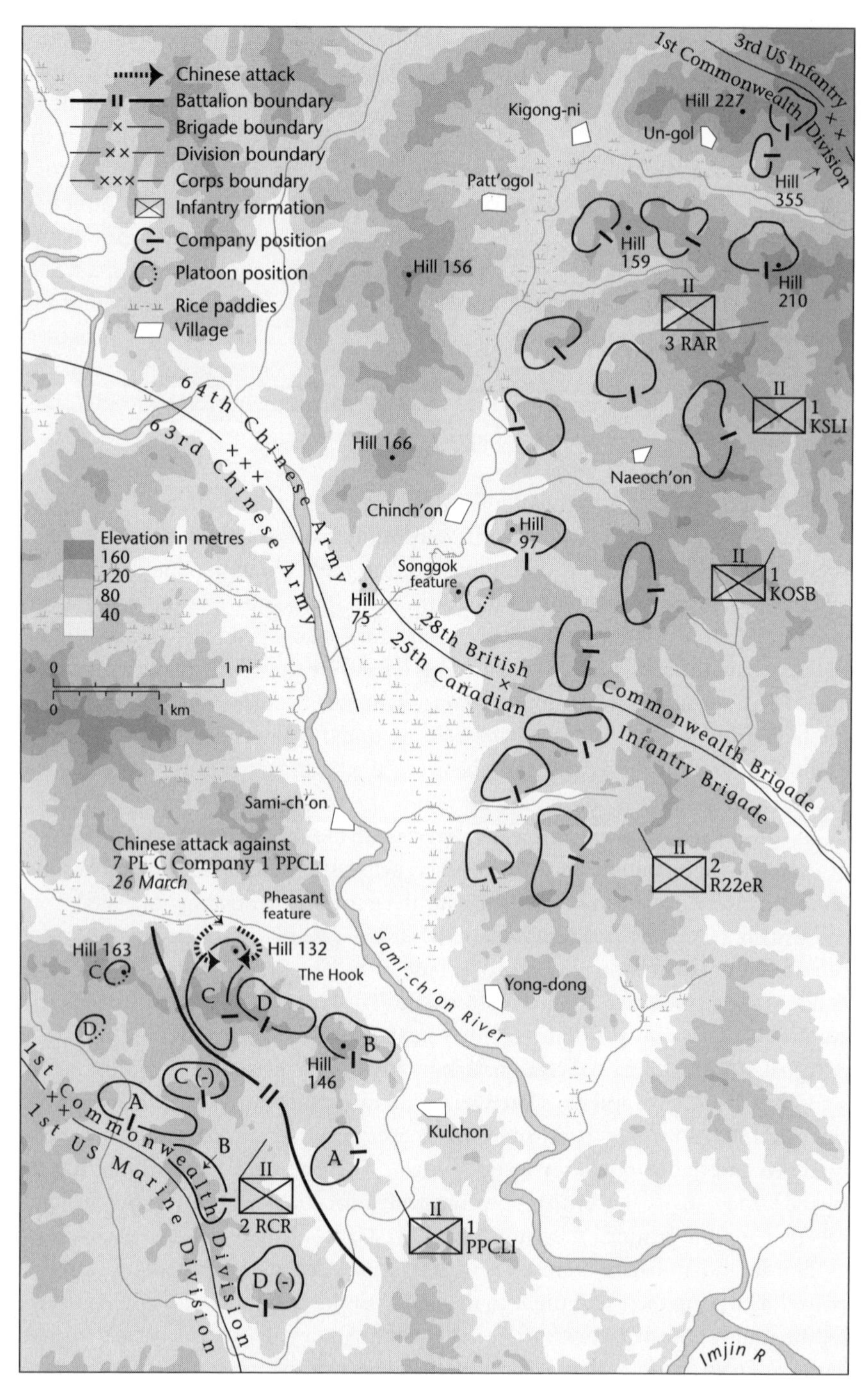

Map 14 *1st Commonwealth Division front, 31 March 1952*

a mile northwest of their lines, from which they were able to account for seven Chinese by the 17th. After a quiet initial week in the line, the Canadians began to make the sort of contacts that Eighth Army headquarters was looking for, although, as was usually the case, they entailed a more active enemy. On the night of 19-20 March, for instance, an RCR fighting patrol of a sergeant and eleven men was attacked while probing the enemy-held high ground a mile northwest of their Hook positions on Hill 163. The Canadian patrol 'was setting up its machine-guns when it was suddenly attacked by an enemy platoon. The patrol withdrew successfully but when it got across the stream in the valley it found that two men were missing ... 2 RCR sent three snipers down into the valley to try and find the missing men but they returned at 0555 hours without finding any trace of the two soldiers. However, at 1625 hours, the battalion reported that they had turned up unscathed. They had apparently been cut off when the Chinese attacked and were forced to lay low until daylight. They said the valley was "alive with Chinese" and it was impossible to move for fear of being seen.'[74]

The next night a sixteen-man Patricia fighting patrol was sweeping a prominent enemy hill across the valley north of the Hook when 'the Chinese had come running down the hill throwing grenades. The Patricia patrol threw grenades back at them and then withdrew without casualties.'[75] Although most patrols proved less eventful, with 'no enemy seen or heard' despite probing the Chinese-held hills across the valley, a Van Doo patrol moving north along the Sami-ch'on on the evening of 24-5 March 'was attacked from the rear by fifteen enemy. Four men were wounded, one seriously, but the patrol accounted for five Chinese dead.' Later that night a 1 PPCLI patrol ran into 'an estimated two platoons of well-entrenched Chinese' across the valley north of the Hook. Four men were wounded, one mortally, before the Patricias extricated themselves.[76]

Such patrol losses were the exception, however: most casualties continued to result from enemy mortar and shell fire. On 22 March, for instance, five Patricias were wounded by enemy mortar bombs falling on their entrenchments, and two days later eighty-eight artillery rounds were counted falling on the Canadian lines, primarily in the sector held by 1 PPCLI. The most intense action of the entire month occurred on the night of 25-6 March against the Patricia position that had received the greatest number of shells. The daylight hours of the 25th were noteworthy in that, 'for a change, there was no enemy artillery fire and at 2315 hours the battalions and division reported all quiet across the front.'[77] The reason for the calm became apparent shortly after midnight when the forward platoon of the Patricias' C Company on Hill 132, the northern-most tip of the Hook position, was heavily attacked by an estimated company of Chinese. Thirty minutes after midnight, a four-man outpost located in the valley at the base of 7 Platoon's hill reported that a small group of Chinese had crossed the stream in the valley that separated Hill 132 from the enemy-held high ground to the north, 'heading in the direction of our positions.' The enemy raiders followed trails of paper laid by reconnaissance parties through the minefields and closed in on the platoon position to await their supporting artillery and mortar fire. 'Suddenly at 0120 hours the Chinese opened up with a very heavy barrage of shelling on the company positions, and particularly on No 7 Platoon,' the company commander reported two days later:

> I estimate that 150 shells fell in the first initial barrage.
>
> The Chinese came up the valley on each side of the position and attacked from the rear where the platoon headquarters was located. Two platoons came up the west valley and one up the east. These approaches had been reported mined by the ROKs but as far as we could tell afterwards, no Chinese were killed by mines. They blew the wire in three places, twice on the ridge leading down to the platoon position and once on the west side of the headquarters. They were carrying stick grenades which had been made more powerful by wrapping cloth containing an explosive yellow powder of some type, around the head. The Chinese were also carrying propaganda leaflets which they dropped as they attacked and their route up the valleys and to the position is still very plainly marked by these leaflets.[78]

Having moved into position close to the 7 Platoon entrenchments prior to the opening barrage, the Chinese infantry were able to launch their assault 'almost simultaneously' with the first shells landing. 'The Chinese were upon us before we knew it,' the acting platoon commander, Sgt. F. Buxton, explained, 'and they were able to breach the wire at the rear of my headquarters in short order. One of my men who was handling a .50 Browning covering the rear was knocked out which enabled the Chinese to get in very close. I took it over but several of the enemy were by this time inside the wire. However, I managed to knock them off. They seemed to have complete disregard for their own personal safety. One of their officers, believed to be the company commander, led the attack and was killed right at the entrance to the position.'[79]

Surrounded by the initial assault, the Patricias tenaciously stuck to their positions and held the Chinese at bay with small arms fire, despite running short of ammunition. No. 7 Platoon's entrenchments were 'below and forward of the rest of the company positions,' with the result that C Company's own medium machine-guns 'were unable to give any supporting fire. The greatest help came from D Company on the right which was able to lay down a very heavy fire on the Chinese coming up the east valley.' After an hour and a half of fighting, 'the pressure on No. 7 Platoon began to slacken, and although the mortar and artillery fire stopped, there still was a lot of small arms fire. At 0400 hours the Chinese apparently had [had] enough and began to withdraw although there w[ere] still a few of them near the position.' Two sections from C Company's rear platoon were dispatched by the company commander to carry ammunition to the beleaguered platoon. They 'had literally to attack in single file' down the trench leading to Hill 132 'and shoot their way through the Chinese who were still milling about the area.' The relief party reached 7 Platoon at 0415 hours and by 0500 hours 'everything was quiet.'[80]

At the same time that the Patricias were being assaulted, a separate Chinese attack overwhelmed an RCR outpost north of Hill 163, three-quarters of a mile to the west. According to the battalion war diarist, 'The outpost was ordered to withdraw to the main platoon location on Point 163 but suffered two killed and one wounded during this intense enemy shelling on the move. Lieutenant H.R. Gardner [the first 1 RCR officer to arrive in Korea for familiarization with the 2nd Battalion] led a section out to Point 161 to bring these three in, and during his attempt, was wounded in the legs. Heavy mortar and artillery fire was falling on Point 163 continuously which caused four more casualties. The enemy swarmed over Point 161 but withdrew immediately.'[81] The outpost position was reoccupied by 0730 hours the next morning.

Both battalions had been subjected to a heavy barrage estimated at some 550 artillery and 300 mortar rounds. Patricia casualties totalled four killed and nine wounded, while the Royals lost four men killed and four wounded in the outpost action. Twenty-five Chinese corpses were counted about the 7 Platoon entrenchments although, as the divisional intelligence staff pointed out, this was 'not a true indication of the enemy's casualties as it is standard procedure with the enemy to remove his dead often at the risk of incurring additional casualties.'[82] One wounded enemy was taken prisoner three days later when he was discovered hiding near the Canadian position. The wounded soldier stated that the raid on 7 Platoon had been made by eighty men of the 1st Battalion, 562nd Regiment.[83] According to the division's intelligence staff, the Chinese soldier reported that their objective had been '"to surround a platoon of 29 Brigade and to take PW" ... It is significant that the enemy thought that 29 BRIT Infantry Brigade was in the sector even though 25 CDN Infantry Brigade had moved in on 10 March and despite the fact that many of the Canadians were wearing red berets, using Sherman tanks rather than Centurions, and were using different weapons, i.e., recoilless rifles. This is indicative of our measure of control over the forward slopes thus rendering enemy observation ineffective.' There were also indications that the Chinese had attempted to fire some counterbattery tasks 'as a portion of his artillery fire was uncomfortably close to several of our gun positions.' This was noteworthy since the enemy lacked the necessary expertise for counterbattery fire and seldom engaged in it.[84]

For the next two weeks, the Canadian battalions continued to send out from two to four patrols each night. As the 2 RCR diarist admitted at the end of March, 'Constant night patrolling and one fairly large attack on the night of the 25th, has kept everyone on their toes. Feeling is running high with rotation coming in April.'[85] Since the Canadians had returned to the line on 10 March, the enemy had been quite active all across the Commonwealth Division's front, with the defences of a forward company of the 1st King's Own Scottish Borderers receiving particular attention in early April. After some 750 rounds fell on the battalion area on the 3rd, it appeared that the Chinese were preparing to mount a similar raid to the one staged against 1 PPCLI on 26 March. Two nights later, 'an estimated two enemy companies of 1 Battalion, 568 Regiment of 190 CCF Division attacked elements of two forward platoons of 1 KOSB. The attack was supported by approximately 3,000 rounds of mixed artillery and mortar fire plus medium machine guns.' The attack was dispersed within an hour of its commencement and 'probably became completely disorganized due to our artillery, who fired over 7,000 rounds. Enemy wireless net very active during the battle and monitored the whole time, allowing our troops to get the "feel" of the attack. Exhortations heard for enemy to get on, with promises of extra rice and medals. Later these exhortations changed to threats when enemy could make no progress. Our casualties were two KIA, five WIA. Later twenty-eight enemy dead were found.' The Chinese had approached the Commonwealth positions carrying 'a number of bundles of faggots' which, it was later concluded, must have been 'used as a form of camouflage,' given the clear weather during the night, 'or possibly a secondary purpose of preparing a pathway through the low wire.'[86]

In the days that followed the attack on the KOSB, the Commonwealth front was relatively quiet despite several patrol contacts in no man's land. On the night of 8-9 April, for instance, a 2 R22eR fighting patrol 'was suddenly attacked by approximately forty Chinamen' in the Sami-ch'on valley in front of their positions. After an intense struggle that included some hand-to-hand fighting, 'three of the patrol were wounded and one seriously wounded Chinaman was brought back but later died.' The day before, 2 RCR had captured a Chinese deserter who wandered into its lines claiming he was 'tired of Communism.'[87] On 12 April a Chinese patrol threw grenades into one of the Patricia outposts north of the Hook but, on the whole, the enemy confined his offensive actions to the sporadic shelling that had become a common feature of the soldiers' everyday life in the line.

No matter how annoying the Chinese artillery might prove, however, it was no match for the much greater firepower that UN divisions could muster in response. The effectiveness of the Commonwealth artillery was demonstrated during a surprise visit of the theatre, army, and corps commanders to 25 Brigade headquarters in mid-March:

> At 1345 hours, without warning, Division notified Ops that General Matthew B. Ridgway, General James A. Van Fleet, [and] Lieutenant-General John O'Daniel would be arriving at Main [brigade headquarters] in fifteen minutes. Frantic preparations were made to have the required number of jeeps at the helicopter strip outside the gate. The GOC [Cassels] ... arrived shortly after this news and at 1415 hours the visitors arrived. The Commander [Rockingham] took them to Ops where he showed them the brigade front on the maps. He then, in the M8 [Rockingham's armoured car], took them up to a position in the PPCLI area from where they could see the Chinese positions. The Commander picked out a hill and asked if the visitors would like to see a demonstration of an 'Uncle' target. The GOC suggested it would be a better idea if one of them picked out the target. The Army Commander volunteered and made it as difficult as possible by selecting an obscure feature in the distance. The Commander and Lieutenant-Colonel Brooks [the commander of 2 RCHA] made a hurried consultation and decided on the

Rockingham shows his replacement, Brig. M.P. Bogert (right), around the brigade's front-line positions on 21 April 1952, six days before formally handing over command. NAC PA184728

> map reference. The fire order was given and in sixty seconds seventy-two rounds were falling right on the target. The GOC then said 'Sir, didn't you mean those two trees just down the slope?' Colonel Brooks made the correction and again seventy-two rounds fell right on the target. General Ridgway said it was the finest artillery shooting he has ever seen. When the Commander returned to Main he was in high spirits and promptly bought Colonel Brooks what he termed the most deserved drink in Korea.[88]

The reduced Chinese activity in mid-April came at an opportune time for both the Canadians and the Commonwealth Division. With the remaining Special Force units of the 25th Brigade about to be rotated back to Canada at month's end, the veterans were undoubtedly relieved that the enemy cooperated in making their final weeks in Korea quiet ones. The first two rifle companies of both 1 RCR and 1 R22eR had reached Pusan on the 10th and 11th respectively and, after a few days of acclimatization training, relieved four 2nd battalion companies in the line six days later.[89] The division, meanwhile, had received word on 8 March to prepare for a shift of divisional boundaries back to the right, turning over the Hook defences west of the Sami-ch'on to the 1st Marine Division while reassuming responsibility for the defence of Hill 355. As the Patricias began their move to the right on 13 April, they found that the Hook defences were 'now alive with Marines. Our men are very impressed with them but cannot understand why the Marines get so angry when you call them soldiers. They seem to hold the US Army in very low regard indeed.'[90]

By the time Operation Westminster, the shift to the right, was completed on 19 April, the Commonwealth Division had reoccupied much the same positions it had first captured during the Commando advance, with the obvious exception that it was no longer responsible for defending the Maryang-san feature around Hill 317.[91] The shift also returned the 25th Brigade to virtually the same entrenchments it had originally constructed the previous October on the line of hills facing the Nabu-ri valley. While 2 R22eR remained in position on the hills north of Yong-dong overlooking the Sami-ch'on River, it now became the division's left flank battalion. The Royals moved into the battalion entrenchments extending to the north of the Van Doos, and 1 PPCLI took up positions to their right, north and west of Naeoch'on. The 29th British Brigade, meanwhile, relieved the 28th Brigade on the division's right flank, with one battalion on Hills 159 and 210 south of the Bowling Alley and two battalions defending Hill 355 from the saddle position on the feature's western slope to a point some 2,000 yards to its east. In taking over the more easily defended positions facing the Nabu-ri valley, the Canadians were well positioned for the final relief of 2 R22eR and 2 RCR by the 1st battalions on 24 and 25 April respectively. Two days later, Rockingham officially handed over command of the brigade to Brig. Mortimer Patrick Bogert.[92]

10 THE PROFESSIONALS, MAY-JUNE 1952

The arrival of spring in the bleak Korean hills along the Jamestown Line brought with it a marked change in the character of the Canadian brigade. For the first time in the conflict, the regular soldiers of Canada's Active Force battalions would now take up the fight in place of the Canadian Army Special Force volunteers. Although several hundred 2nd battalion men whose time in Korea had not yet expired were absorbed into the newly arrived units to help fill out their ranks, the officers and NCOs of 1 RCR and 1 R22eR were almost exclusively members of the two Active Force battalions. From the outset many of these regular force officers exhibited an air of superiority toward the 'non-regulars' they were replacing in the line. The disdain for the Special Force shown by the commanding officer of 1 RCR, Lt.-Col. Peter R. Bingham, was typical: 'A regular soldier should not only fight better than the non-regular,' he announced soon after reaching the front line, 'but should at all times conduct himself as a professional. Hence also a greater emphasis on saluting in the RCR than apparently in other units.'[1] The day after arriving in the 25th Brigade's rear area on 11 April, for instance, his officers held a mess dinner in formal dress uniforms, an event in which their CO took considerable satisfaction. Even when they were in the line, the officers of 1 RCR were proud of their regular formal 'Mess Dinner in the Officer's Mess. All officers of the battalion attended wearing No. 1 Dress (Blues). Every Wednesday this will be occurring.'[2]

The future official historian of the Canadian Army in Korea, Lt.-Col. H.F. Wood, who commanded 3 PPCLI in Korea and was himself a regular, also noted a difference in attitude between the Army's regular soldiers and the Special Force veterans they replaced, commenting that 'the original 25th Brigade had a morale all its own – with the emphasis probably deriving from its name, "Special," and its commander who managed to instil a sort of "Errol Flynn" attitude (for want of a better word) towards the Korean War. The regulars in the Force who were good, got caught up in this atmosphere; the ones who did not were either sent home, or found themselves training reinforcements or doing administrative jobs at the base.' The regular battalions, on the other hand, had a morale that was 'more of the "stiff upper lip" brand. Troops shined their kit in the positions, kept themselves clean in spite of the difficulties, stressed orderliness, neatness, calmness, "form."'[3] Wood found the difference in attitude between the 1st and 2nd battalions in Korea significant enough to comment on in the Canadian official history, *Strange Battleground.* The changeover in battalions meant that 'the character of the 25th Brigade had changed ... The atmosphere of "spit and polish" the professionals brought with them to

Korea was difficult to maintain in that country but ingenuity and perseverance overcame the difficulties. The brigade took pride in immaculate lines, pressed uniforms and gleaming boots. A cartoon of the period showed the commanding officer of the 1st RCR pointing indignantly at some tarnished barbed wire defences [left by 2 RCR] and exclaiming, "I won't take over the position until it's *all* polished."'[4]

As we shall see, however, the professionalism of the Canadian regulars was more readily visible in matters of appearance than in their battlefield performance. Indeed, Wood's description of the 1st battalion professionals in the official history would have brought a wry smile to those Australian soldiers who had formed a very different impression of the Canadians' military abilities during 1952-3. During their year-long tour in the Jamestown Line, many of the officers of Canada's regular battalions did not exhibit the drive and initiative that had characterized the more thorough – and professional – operations of the Special Force units under Rockingham's command. Contrary to the image of competence suggested in *Strange Battleground,* the Canadian brigade languished in mediocrity throughout Brigadier Bogert's year in command – much to the annoyance of at least some of its allies within the Commonwealth Division.

Such problems, of course, were most evident in the infantry, the arm that was in direct contact with the enemy (as demonstrated by the fact that infantrymen incurred 93 percent of the brigade's casualties during the war).[5] Given less frequent exposure to danger, reticent officers would be less of a handicap in the armour, artillery, engineers, and signals units and, by and large, those arms were equally efficient under all the brigade commanders. They provided valuable support to the infantry battalions throughout the conflict. Indeed, the infantry's increasing reliance on the 'Chinagraph Curtain' of defensive artillery fire, whether to defeat enemy raids or to drive away aggressive patrollers from around their wire, strongly indicates the importance of the artillery. In a war of patrols, however, it was the infantry who were at the tip of the sharp end, and that arm is the continuing focus of this study.

The two regular infantry battalions that arrived in Korea in the spring of 1952 had spent most of the previous year conducting their normal peacetime training schemes with an emphasis on qualifying men as parachutists. During the first part of 1951, the 1st battalions had also provided some basic training to new recruits earmarked for the 25th Brigade's reinforcement stream. The Royals, for instance, trained several hundred recruits in a holding establishment before sending them to Camp Wainwright in June and July 1951.[6] Thereafter, transfers of personnel from the 1st battalions to the reinforcement stream were few, as the Active Force units concentrated on their regular training.

Although 1 RCR 'received the first intimation' in October 1951 that they would be sent to the Far East, the move was not officially confirmed until early January 1952. Nonetheless, the remaining two 1st battalions had more time to sort out the personnel they would be taking with them than the Patricia regulars had had the previous August. In accordance with the same rotation orders that 1 PPCLI had received, both 1 RCR and 1 R22eR were required to leave a reinforced parachute company behind in Canada around which those Special Force veterans who transferred to the regular army could re-form the 2nd battalions. Although there was not the same degree of mass posting to either the parachute company or the noneffective list as 1 PPCLI had experienced the previous August, both units did receive a large influx of new recruits from their 3rd battalions immediately after being officially warned for duty in Korea. As the 1 RCR war diarist admitted two days after the unit received its formal warning, 'The administrative problem of accepting young soldiers from 3 RCR is uppermost at present.'[7] The early January draft from 3 RCR was followed by two more drafts, totalling another 125 soldiers, at the end of the month.[8] The French Canadian battalion, meanwhile, had 182 soldiers transferred to its ranks from 3 R22eR.[9]

Unlike 1 PPCLI, which had embarked for the Far East at full strength, both 1 RCR and 1 R22eR proceeded to Korea as understrength units of only two rifle companies each, as well as battalion headquarters, support, and headquarters companies. The rifle companies were, as in the Patricias' case, largely made up of the recent transfers from the 3rd battalions. The men needed to fill each battalion's remaining two

Lt. D.G. Hanson shakes hands with Rockingham as the brigade commander welcomes 1 RCR's officers to Korea on 10 April 1952. The 1st Battalion CO, Lt.-Col. Peter Bingham, stands to Rockingham's right. The battalion moved up to the brigade's rear area for its short period of acclimatization training the next day. NAC PA140699

rifle companies would come from 2nd battalion personnel who had not yet completed their full tour in the Far East. While few of their other ranks were veterans of the Active Force, all of the officers and NCOs for each unit's four rifle companies were supplied by the 1st battalions. According to Bingham, 1 RCR 'brought over 100 per cent 1st Battalion officers, warrant officers and senior NCOs, and 75 per cent junior NCOs' while many of the men who were transferred from the 2nd Battalion 'were ex-1 RCR.'[10] The character of the 1st battalions, therefore, remained 'regular force' despite the large influx of infantrymen from the 2nd battalion units they were replacing.

The decision to send understrength battalions to Korea, while solving the problem of what to do with those 2nd battalion soldiers who were not yet eligible for rotation, reduced the amount of training the men of 1 RCR and 1 R22eR received in Canada prior to embarkation. In discussing the preparation of his battalion for the Far East, Bingham later explained that there had been 'only a short time in which to deal with administrative problems, such as securing driver-mechanics, cooks and other specialists, and providing for leave, inoculations, etc. Various personal problems arose which could not be settled before embarkation, resulting in certain people being left behind. Administrative factors inevitably complicated training problems. The training was already seriously hampered by weather conditions. Although both administrative and training requirements were met on schedule, it was only with considerable effort which should not have been necessary.' As for the training program itself, 'the training of the two rifle companies selected, B and D, consisted mainly of weapon training with emphasis on firing, drill, and platoon tactics. This despite the weather, which was generally below zero. Lecture-room subjects were reserved for the boat trip.'[11] As the 1 RCR war diary admitted, 'practical field work' was largely restricted to time spent on the rifle ranges. Company-level schemes were virtually nonexistent, with most training being carried out 'under platoon arrangements. When they're finished training they will be able to shoot straight at least.'[12] The training of the battalion's support company was also hampered by a shortage of equipment. Writing to Rockingham at the end of January, Bingham acknowledged that his support company's 'training was weak because there was no 3.5-inch rocket launcher ammunition available, no 75-mm recoilless rifles, no mines, no wire, no 60-mm mortar ammunition, and very little 81-mm mortar ammunition.'[13]

Compared with the training program that Rockingham had organized for the Special Force at Fort Lewis the previous winter, with its regular progression from platoon and company training schemes to battalion and brigade exercises, the men who accompanied the 1st battalion to Korea received only a limited preparation for their tour in the Far East. This was despite the fact that the regular battalions had the advantage of being – at least in theory – already formed and trained for combat with experienced, professional officers in place to teach the men. With the dispatch of 1 PPCLI the previous September strongly indicating that the remaining 1st battalions would follow in the spring, the regular units had had the same seven-month period to prepare themselves that the Special Force had received, even if they were not officially warned until 2 January. Nonetheless, an apparent peacetime attitude continued to prevail during the unit's last four months in Canada, and the 1 RCR war diary does not indicate any particular sense of urgency in its training program. Perhaps the number of parachute descents and field exercises the battalion had conducted in the summer and fall of 1951 – the latter intended 'to ensure proficiency in both basic and advanced fieldcraft skills, to reach a high standard in the battle techniques of the rifle section and platoon in the attack, defence, advance and withdrawal'[14] – had convinced its officers that the battalion was well prepared, an attitude that the influx of new men into its two rifle companies did little to alter.

Unfortunately, the 1st battalions had little time to address any shortcomings after their arrival in Korea in mid-April. Although Bingham later asserted that 'a newly-arrived unit should not be committed before one month's training in a rear area,'[15] the two rifle companies of both 1 RCR and 1 R22eR had only one week for orientation before taking over the front-line entrenchments from their 2nd battalion counterparts. For the most part, the 1st battalions' acclimatization program was a continuation of the section and platoon level training they had undertaken in Canada, with none of the arduous hill-climbing exercises that Rockingham had insisted upon for his own men. B and D Companies of 1 RCR arrived in the brigade's rear area on 11 April (one day after disembarking in Pusan), where they were met by Lieutenant-Colonel Bingham who 'worked with them until the 14th, on which date he was accidentally wounded' in stumbling across a booby-trapped grenade. A witness to the incident recalled that the CO 'had just given us a big lecture and ended by saying: "Now go up to the hills and dig in for the night, and watch for booby traps." The next thing we know, there was an explosion. Colonel Bingham himself had walked into a booby trap and he had to be away for some time. I imagine he was quite embarrassed about the whole thing.'[16]

That same afternoon, the two companies held a battalion exercise – the first such scheme to be conducted by the unit during its four months of preparation – before relieving two companies of 2 RCR on the 16th and 17th. Despite their lack of training, 1 RCR's B and D Companies were immediately assigned to conduct all of the battalion's patrols 'for the ensuing month ... to familiarize the unit with the methods employed and the feel of the ground. The first patrol was an ambush patrol by Lieutenant J.W. Martin to a deserted and demolished village' in one of the reentrants between the company entrenchments.[17] The 1 R22eR companies, under the command of Lt.-Col. Louis Frémont Trudeau, had reached Pusan on 11 April and they, too, had only one week to acclimatize themselves to the theatre before taking over front-line positions from 2 R22eR on the 17th.

The changed character of the 25th Brigade was evident in the service background of the incoming brigade and battalion commanders. While many of Rockingham's

Special Force officers had had a militia background prior to enlisting during the Second World War, and had then returned to civilian life in 1945, the 1st battalion officers were career soldiers, some of whom had spent a large portion of their service in staff positions. The new Canadian brigadier, Mortimer Patrick Bogert, graduated from the Royal Military College in Kingston in 1930 before receiving his commission in the Canadian Army. His Second World War experience included stints serving on the staff at Canadian Military Headquarters in London, England, as the GSO(1) with II Canadian Corps, and as the commanding officer of the West Nova Scotia Regiment. It was in the latter capacity that Bogert first experienced combat, leading his unit ashore during the invasion of Sicily in July 1943. Following the Allied invasion of southern Italy in September, he had led 'Boforce' – a task force made up of the West Novas reinforced by tanks, artillery, medium machine-guns, and engineers – in a well-executed advance inland to the city of Potenza. Subsequently wounded, Bogert returned to the staff of CMHQ in London before spending five months as GSO(1) of the 1st Canadian Infantry Division in Italy. After temporarily taking over command of the 3rd Brigade during the Battle of the Rimini Line in September 1944, he was given permanent command of the 2nd Brigade the following month and led it for the remainder of the war in Italy and Northwest Europe.[18]

After the war Bogert had attended the National Defence College in Kingston and in 1952 was serving as the director general of military training at army headquarters in Ottawa when he was informed of his appointment to succeed Rockingham as commander of the 25th Brigade in Korea. E.A.C. Amy, who served as GSO(1) of the Commonwealth Division from August 1952 to August 1953, thought that of the Canadian brigade commanders, 'perhaps Brigadier Bogert, the eldest of the three, was less charismatic than the other two [Rockingham and Allard] but nonetheless [was] a solid, unflighty and competent commander.'[19] Although Bogert was a combat-experienced officer, his qualifications would not, of themselves, ensure a successful command. In a static ground war, success would depend on his willingness to instill in his battalion officers the energy and determination needed to keep the troops from developing a lethargic attitude toward operations.

Bogert's difficult task was not made any easier by the fact that his most experienced battalion commander, 1 PPCLI's Wilson-Smith, was posted to Commonwealth Division headquarters at the end of April 1952 to replace Lieutenant-Colonel Danby as the division's GSO(1). Wilson-Smith's replacement as the Patricias' CO was Lt.-Col. John R. Cameron, a prewar regular officer who had most recently commanded the reinforcement group in Japan.[20] Cameron's previous tactical experience had been gained as a company commander with the West Nova Scotia Regiment in Sicily and Italy – where his CO was Bogert – from July 1943 until he was wounded in October 1943. Returning to the West Novas in early 1944, he served as second-in-command of the battalion for the remainder of the war. Despite his regular force credentials and battle experience, however, Cameron was passed over for command of the unit on each of the three occasions that the battalion's CO was replaced between September 1944 and April 1945.[21]

The CO of 1 R22eR, Lieutenant-Colonel Trudeau was, like the other two battalion COs, a prewar regular who had joined the Van Doos as a lieutenant in 1936 after graduating from the Séminaires de Saint-Hyacinthe et Rimouski with a bachelor of arts degree. Despite three years of regular army experience, Trudeau's Second World War career got off to a slow start and he was left to languish as a company commander in reinforcement units in the United Kingdom. It was not until April 1944 that he was finally posted to his regiment in the field, serving as a company commander until war's end. His career did not really begin to gather momentum until after 1945 when he received several staff appointments (he would eventually retire as a brigadier-general). Following a fourteen-month posting as resident staff officer at the University of Ottawa, he was selected to command 1 R22eR in January 1950. It was as CO of the 1st Battalion that he organized the poorly conceived initial training of 2 R22eR at Valcartier the following August.[22]

The commanding officer of 1 RCR, Lt.-Col. Peter Bingham, was also a prewar veteran, having joined the Royal Canadian Regiment as a private soldier in 1931. A warrant officer at the outbreak of war in September 1939, Bingham was commissioned the following year and held a variety of regimental appointments until being posted to the staff of the 1st Canadian Infantry Division in 1942. According to one Canadian officer, Bingham 'was a too typical example of those who had attended British Officer Cadet Training units in the early days of the war and had become caricatures of proper Edwardian officers, perhaps because they didn't know any better.'[23] He continued as a staff officer with the division until being appointed brigade major of the 2nd Infantry Brigade ten days after the invasion of Sicily in July 1943. After returning to Canada to take a war staff course in September, Bingham continued to serve as a staff officer for the remainder of the war, first on loan to the 5th Indian Division in 1944 and then with the headquarters of 1st Canadian Army in 1945. He was appointed to command of 1 RCR in December 1948 and in that capacity had overseen the early training of 2 RCR at Petawawa in August and September 1950. Since his previous operational experience had been exclusively as a staff officer, the 1 RCR CO would have his first taste of commanding a unit in combat while facing the Chinese on the Jamestown Line in May 1952.[24] The lack of operational command experience of Bogert's three infantry COs, therefore, stands in marked contrast to Rockingham's selections, all of whom had seen action as battalion commanders during the Second World War. While the 1st Battalion commanders were all capable, well-regarded staff officers, the fact that they had never before been tested as battalion COs in combat had serious consequences for the future efficiency of the Canadian brigade.

After taking over the entrenchments from the departing battalions, the newly arrived units were at least fortunate in being granted a two-month breathing space by the Chinese. Following the aggressive patrols and raids the enemy had launched against the Commonwealth Division in March and early April, the Chinese lapsed into several months of relative passivity, allowing the incoming Canadian units to adjust to Korean conditions without undue interference. One reason for the lack of enemy patrol activity was the relief of the 64th Chinese Army – which had been opposite the Commonwealth forces in the Imjin salient since April 1951 – by the 40th CCF Army on 19 May. The incoming army's 119th Division held the high ground facing the Nabu-ri valley from the Sami-ch'on River south of Hill 166 around to Hill 227 with two regiments forward and one in reserve. The 40th Army's 118th Division had its three regiments in line between Hill 227 and the Imjin River, holding, most prominently, the Maryang-san hill mass 2,000 to 3,000 yards north of Hill 355.[25]

As they had all winter, the communists continued to tunnel into the hillsides to create extensive underground defensive positions immune from UN artillery fire. At the same time, they were bringing forward additional artillery pieces, ammunition, and supplies for their front-line forces. This nearly impregnable belt of fortifications across the entire 155-mile width of the Korean peninsula enabled the communist negotiators to take a tough stance in the truce talks at Panmunjom and test the resolve of the Western powers, confident that their armies could not be driven from their current entrenchments without inflicting heavy casualties on the UN forces attacking them. While the Chinese were forced to spend a large portion of their digging efforts repairing the damage routinely inflicted by UN artillery and air strikes, they had so much manpower that they were still able to concentrate on the more important task of improving the 'existing positions by producing additional communication and crawl trenches, tunnels and caves.' According to Major-General Cassels' report on the spring 1952 period, 'It is now possible for the enemy to move between any defensive position and rear area by means of deep communication trenches. The effect of this on our HF [harassing artillery fire] on isolated enemy groups moving to and from the forward areas is obvious. These trenches now extend at least four to five miles back from his front-line positions. He is therefore able to supply and transfer his troops in these areas with little danger of detection as was evidenced in the relief of 64th CCF Army by 40th CCF Army,' a move that was not confirmed by the Commonwealth Division's intelligence staff until early June.[26]

With progress apparently being made in the negotiations at Panmunjom, the outgoing American theatre commander (General Ridgway was replaced by Gen. Mark Clark in May 1952) had prohibited UN forces from launching any attack larger than battalion strength without his prior approval. He instructed the Eighth Army commander that 'offensive action will be limited to such reconnaissance and counter-offensive measures as necessary to provide for the security of your forces.'[27] Ridgway's edict did not entirely suit General Van Fleet, who had been planning a series of limited objective attacks, primarily using his South Korean divisions. Blocked in that scheme, the Eighth Army commander now sought to keep his forces sharp by maintaining an aggressive patrolling and raiding policy across the entire UN front. While such a policy required, in the words of the British official history, 'a sense of proportion' to ensure that the casualties incurred did not outweigh the advantages, the American high command

> would have been in breach of their duty if they had allowed a wholly passive mood to develop among those required to defend the United Nations line. Adoption of a purely defensive attitude among the United Nations divisions would have encouraged Communist aggression and weakened the means to resist it. Soldiers occupying positions from which they never make a sortie rapidly develop an acute sense of self-preservation. If the enemy in contradistinction dominates no man's land, raids freely to take prisoners or seize local points of vantage, the image of his invincibility grows. The idea is nurtured that when a defensive position is pressed it cannot be held, so it is abandoned. And it is abandoned more readily by those who have been in position for a number of months and are thus looking forward to being sent home at the end of a set term of operations. Similarly, when there seems to be a strong chance that an armistice will be concluded shortly, even those who have recently come into the line think twice about holding a piece of ground tenaciously. Survival becomes the first aim of the soldier.[28]

In accordance with Van Fleet's raiding policy, I Corps headquarters instructed its divisions, which included the Commonwealth Division, to capture one prisoner every three days. In response to these demands, the Commonwealth troops were instructed to mount a number of raids on the Chinese entrenchments in May and June 1952, in groups ranging from section to company strength. As Cassels admitted, prisoners of war continued 'to be a scarce commodity' in spite of the division's efforts. In fact, from mid-February until the end of June, 'only eleven prisoners of war have entered the confines of the division PW cage' and of this number 'ten were deserters. There is ample evidence that CCF counter-measures against deserters mentioned in our previous report have now been improved upon to the extent that the CCF soldiers have been told of the type of welcome [Chinese] deserters may expect when they are returned to Chinese hands at any future date. Ten deserters in four months vividly demonstrates the success of this campaign.'[29]

Undergoing their baptism of fire – 1 PPCLI excepted – the Canadian regular battalions shared in the Eighth Army's general record of futility in capturing prisoners, a task that was not made easier by their facing, at least initially, a passive enemy who seldom ventured into the valley to challenge their patrols. One benefit of the Chinese decision to limit their patrol activities was that it allowed the newly arrived battalions to establish some confidence in their ability to patrol in no man's land, even if the Canadians did not take much advantage of it. During the month of May, the brigade conducted a total of 484 patrols, of which the vast majority, 419, were passive standing patrols mounted only 100 or 200 yards in front of the forward positions. Of the remainder, 43 were futile ambush patrols, usually set up no farther forward than the stream in the middle of the Nabu-ri valley, waiting for Chinese who never came. Only 22 of the Canadians' patrols were aggressive in nature, with 20 larger fighting patrols and only 2 reconnaissance patrols.[30]

This last number is particularly striking. Given that two of the three infantry battalions had just arrived in the theatre and were completely unfamiliar with the ground in front of their positions, the absence of a vigorous program of reconnaissance patrols to acquaint the forward troops with the terrain is inexplicable. The fact that the enemy was relatively inactive in no man's land should have allowed the newly arrived units to conduct nightly recces right up to the forward slopes of the Chinese positions against only limited opposition. Even the normally uncritical Canadian official history, after noting that the Canadian brigade's patrol task tables for the last half of June do 'not list a single reconnaissance patrol,' acknowledges that 'this lack of detailed information about the enemy's hour-to-hour routine (best provided by reconnaissance and "lie-up" patrols) must have made the planning of fighting or, more particularly, ambush patrols very difficult.'[31]

The absence of reconnaissance patrols from the regulars' tables stands in stark contrast to the full slate of reconnaissance patrols conducted by the Special Force. Not only did these small patrols result in few casualties, they also gave the Special Force soldiers confidence in their ability to move about in no man's land, even in the face of enemy patrols. As expressed in 2 RCR's October 1951 report on Operation Snatch, Rockingham's men believed 'that the Canadian soldier, with his adaptability, initiative and native cunning is far superior to the Chinese by night or by day.'[32] On the other hand, the preference of the regulars to send only large groups of men into no man's land eventually instilled an unnecessary awe – bordering on fear – of the enemy's patrolling skills. Just as importantly (as Wood acknowledges and the Special Force veterans repeatedly demonstrated), the success of a military operation depended on a thorough reconnaissance of the ground before a large fighting patrol or raid was undertaken. The operations of the 2nd battalions had always been preceded by a number of reconnaissance patrols to assess the enemy's routines, dispositions, and strengths. The complete absence of preliminary reconnaissance from the 1st battalions' raiding program indicates the degree to which the so-called professionals either failed to understand the keys to successful military operations or lacked the drive and determination to carry them out.

Although a number of ambush patrols were laid on near the Nabu-ri stream that divided no man's land, the Canadians made only two reconnaissances during their first two weeks in the line. Both were made on the night of 27-8 April but only the 1 PPCLI patrol – which could draw on its six months' experience under Rockingham's command – crossed the valley to investigate enemy activity on the spur leading up to Hill 156. Although the Chinese were less active in no man's land than before, their ability to move and fight on the Canadian side of the valley was starkly demonstrated to a fourteen-man 1 R22eR patrol assigned to establish an ambush along the Sami-ch'on River on the night of 6-7 May. Led by an officer, the Van Doos were just entering the valley near the abandoned village of Polmal, at the southern end of the Canadian line, when their radio failed:

> [The] patrol commander ordered the patrol to take defensive positions while [the] set was being repaired and while he went forward with Corporal LeBlanc to recce. Reached river without seeing or hearing anything. Left the corporal at the river and returned half way to patrol. Signalled to patrol to come forward. As patrol officer signalled, Burp gun and mortar fire opened, estimated one platoon. [The] lieutenant ordered patrol to withdraw and leave him to get Corporal LeBlanc at the river. Lieutenant [was] wounded [by] two rounds [in the] right arm, one left arm (fractured). Private Dubois put the lieutenant on his shoulder and began withdrawal. Burp gun opened on right (south) and Private Gendron was shot in the face. Patrol opened fire and withdrew. Wireless operator fired into set and left it. As the patrol reached [position] Joker, Private Dupuis stated that enemy were on left (north). Enemy fired Burp gun, killing Dupuis (two bullets in the heart). Friendly outpost engaged enemy to assist the patrol. Patrol states that Corporal LeBlanc almost certainly killed by fire that hit him at the river. Total casualties one killed in action, three wounded in action – two of whom [are] missing and [presumed] dead. Second patrol found no signs of missing men.[33]

The body of the unfortunate Corporal LeBlanc was not recovered until a month later, when it was stumbled upon by a Van Doo fighting patrol operating in the same vicinity.[34]

One of the first operations the regular battalions conducted on the far side of no man's land was the demolition of the abandoned village of Chinch'on at the foot of Hill 166 by 1 RCR. The village 'constituted a potential enemy patrol base' and was the reported location of enemy snipers. On this occasion the regulars demonstrated some of the thoroughness that had characterized the operations of the Special Force veterans they had replaced. To its credit, one week prior to the planned demolition 1 RCR sent a fighting patrol to scout both the village and the horseshoe-shaped Hill 113 behind it, to establish if either site was occupied by the enemy at night. On the night of 1-2 May, sixteen men from B Company's 5 Platoon were led across the valley by their platoon commander, Lt. J.B. Kelly. They had been briefed on the patrol and shown the ground from the company observation post, and then allowed a rest period prior to moving out through one of the company's outposts at 2307 hours that night: 'The night was chilly and there was no moon. Visibility ranged between ten and twenty yards. The ground was rolling, with unused paddy-fields and dykes. Hill 113 was covered with low, noisy brush.'[35] After crossing the Samich'on tributary the patrol set up a firm base 100 yards southeast of Chinch'on before proceeding through the empty village. Moving up Hill 113 behind the village, Lieutenant Kelly detached a corporal and four men to scout southwest along a series of crawl trenches halfway up the slope while continuing toward the summit with seven of his remaining men:

A Sherman tank of B Squadron, LdSH, fires its main 76 mm armament on 15 June 1952 from its entrenchment in the 1 R22eR positions, on the left of the Commonwealth Division's line overlooking the Sami-ch'on River valley. NAC PA188577

On almost reaching the summit, the forward group was greeted by a shout in Chinese. Immediately a Bren gunner opened up and fired one magazine. The enemy replied with burp guns and grenades, and the Bren gunner fell wounded in the leg and shoulder. A second soldier ... was hit in the stomach and hand.

The grenades used by the Chinese carried an additional charge, wrapped in canvas, for greater blast effect. Some of the men were thus blown off their feet, down the slope, losing their weapons.

Lieutenant Kelly then ordered his men down off the hill. When the patrol regrouped at the bottom of the slope, the wireless set was found to be damaged. The officer therefore decided on a further withdrawal. As the first stage of this, Corporal Lemoine's group was to return from the crawl trenches back down to [the firm base] ...

Instead, the NCO and his party remained in their position and from there covered the withdrawal of the remainder with fire. Again on reaching [the firm base], Lieutenant Kelly ordered Corporal Lemoine to come down. In due course the entire patrol rallied on the firm base, including the two wounded.[36]

After debriefing the returning Royals, the battalion intelligence officer reasonably concluded that the fact that the Chinese section had not been entrenched 'suggests a clash between two patrols, rather than a case of our own patrol having bumped a defended position. Furthermore, the trenches on Hill 113 had evidently fallen into disuse, being now only three feet wide and belt-high.'[37] Although the patrol had gathered important information on the absence of Chinese from Chinch'on and the state of defences on Hill 113, a smaller reconnaissance patrol might have obtained the same intelligence while avoiding contact with the enemy.

In any event, it was with at least some knowledge of the area that a twenty-one-man RCR patrol – seventeen soldiers from 8 Platoon and four from the pioneer platoon – moved into Chinch'on on the night of 8-9 May. After setting charges and spraying gasoline on the remaining buildings, the demolition party was informed by the firm base group of 'some movement on the right of the village ... The pioneer officer accordingly concentrated the covering party on this flank and prepared to detonate the charges also from the right. The fuse was then lit, and the withdrawal commenced. The patrol had leap-frogged its way back as far as [the stream crossing point] when, at 0350 hours, the charge blew. Thus the village was completely blown and burned down, flames lighting up the whole valley. Covered by our own artillery firing DF tasks, and by an ambush patrol ... of B Company, the party returned to the company area. Some fifteen minutes later (about 0420 hours) the ambush patrol also returned. Casualties were nil.'[38]

For the next two weeks, the Canadians remained passive in their patrolling assignments, mounting mainly standing and ambush patrols, none of which encountered the enemy. A steady stream of patrol returns with 'nothing to report' apparently did not satisfy the needs of higher headquarters, particularly the wishes of I Corps that its divisions should continue to act aggressively. Acting on orders, the Canadian brigade major, Major J.C. Allan (who had replaced D.H. George in the change-over), issued instructions on 17 May that 'battalions will carry out at least one strong fighting patrol each per week, with the aim of establishing contact with the enemy.' The new orders did prompt a few additional contacts: a twenty-two-man Patricia patrol skirmished with the Chinese on the night of 20-1 May and suffered one man killed and four wounded. Two nights later, a large RCR fighting patrol was engaged by the enemy and had two officers and four other ranks wounded and one man missing. On the night of the 26-7th, a forty-two-man Van Doo raid had a brief firefight with the Chinese before withdrawing behind an artillery barrage with two men wounded.[39]

One of the bolder Canadian fighting patrols of the period was a twenty-three-man raid by 1 RCR on the night of 31 May-1 June. Crossing the wide valley that separated the Chinese and Canadian positions shortly after last light, the patrol, led by Lt. A.A.S. Peterson, attacked a platoon position on Hill 113, following both an air strike and artillery bombardment of the feature. The lower trenches on the hill were found to be largely abandoned – one section briefly cornered a prisoner in a bunker opening but was forced to shoot him when he attempted to flee – but those nearer the summit were fully manned. The Chinese entrenchments erupted with small arms fire as soon as the Royal's supporting fire lifted, and Lieutenant Peterson quickly gave the order to withdraw to avoid being overwhelmed by superior numbers a mile away from reinforcement. The Royals managed to regain their lines successfully with only four men wounded in the operation. The fact that the patrol had not captured a prisoner did not deter Cassels from praising the effort as 'a specially daring raid against a strong enemy position.'[40]

However, it was increasingly evident that Canadian operations were not as well staged as they should have been – a situation made worse by the complete absence of proper reconnaissance. Despite the lack of Chinese activity during May, an uneasy Patricia war diarist admitted that 'it can truly be stated that this is a twilight war. But somehow one feels as though we are sitting on a powder keg.'[41] One of the few Canadians to provide a frank assessment of the 1st battalions' performance in Korea was Maj. W.H. Pope, who served as the commander of C Company, 1 R22eR during 1952-3. The son of Lt.-Gen. Maurice Pope, Harry Pope already had considerable combat experience by the time he was posted to Korea in the spring of 1952, having led many successful patrols as a platoon commander with the Royal 22e Régiment in Italy during the Second World War. Reflecting on the poor record of the 1st battalions in Korea while serving as the head of the belatedly established brigade patrol school in June 1953, this outspoken officer admitted that 'for the past year and more the enemy has held the tactical initiative in no man's land. He has raided our outposts and forward positions and ambushed our patrols at will. We, on the other hand, with only one or two exceptions, have not carried out any successful operations forward of our lines.'[42]

According to Pope, difficulties were usually the result of poor planning and bad leadership at the battalion level. One operation in particular stood out in his mind as an example of how not to conduct a raid. While his own company was occupying a reasonably secure position on Hill 210, Pope was selected by his battalion commander, Lieutenant-Colonel Trudeau, to oversee a forty-two-man raid on a Chinese platoon position. The raiders were divided into two equal groups, each led by a lieutenant, with one group acting as a firm base in the valley while the other group carried out the assault. Much to Pope's dismay, none of the men were drawn from his own company but were selected, several from each platoon, from the remaining companies in the battalion. As a result of Trudeau's decision, 'only three men of one group were known by the lieutenant who had to lead them to the attack, with only eight known by the other.'[43]

The Van Doo CO also did not allow time for 'training together in preparation for the attack; no rehearsal on ground similar to the enemy position; not even time for the two groups to begin to think and act as teams.' To make matters worse, Trudeau specifically prohibited Pope from making a reconnaissance 'of at least twenty-four hours duration' of the enemy position, a preparation that Pope believed was essential if the raiders were to have any hope of success. Nor did his CO allow him to accompany the men into the valley, ordering him instead to remain in his company command post on Hill 210, nearly a mile from the action, so that his only contact with the raiders would be by radio.[44] Not surprisingly, the operation failed entirely. The lack of reconnaissance precluded anything other than a frontal assault and the Canadians were immediately driven to ground by Chinese machine-gun fire as they approached the enemy position. Warned by radio intelligence that the enemy was preparing a strong patrol to encircle the raiders, Pope recommended to the patrol commander that he return immediately to the Canadian lines, a task that was accomplished without loss. 'For the raid to have been successful,' Pope later declared, 'the enemy would have to have been sleeping until our patrol was actually in their trenches (or cave – or whatever their position consisted of ... we did not know!). Since all preparatory recce patrols had been forbidden me, we had no exact idea of where the enemy was. Therefore a frontal attack was necessary. And that no longer worked as soon as the enemy machine gun opened fire. Not one of the forty-two officers and men in the valley had previously taken part in an assault.'[45]

Although few others were as vocal and clear as Pope in stating the shortcomings of the brigade's operations, it was not because the procedures of the other battalions were any better than those of 1 R22eR. Officers in the 1st battalions were routinely satisfied to conduct their reconnaissances from secure observation posts on the hills behind the forward positions, thus restricting the knowledge of the ground on which their men were to operate to what could be observed through a pair of binoculars. Typical was the patrol briefing held by the Patricia CO at the battalion observation post on 13 June: 'Lieutenant-Colonel Cameron and Lieutenant Howard made a visual reconnaissance with Major Isnor, Major Leach and Sergeant Helligier for the forthcoming ambush patrol. At this time the specific locations for the patrol were chosen and a rough briefing for the ambush patrol [was given where] the plan was present[ed] in its entirety to the patrol commander, Sergeant Helligier.'[46] As with virtually all of the brigade's ambushes that were planned without any knowledge of the enemy's routine, the one commanded by Helligier returned with 'nothing to report.'

The hesitancy of commanding officers to venture forward had an inevitable effect on their men. In assessing the performance of the 1st battalions, Pope decried the fact that Canadian troops under attack almost never manned their platoon weapons in their own defence. Instead,

> they were taking cover from the enemy artillery and mortar fire in their Chinese holes or, worse still, in their bunkers. In truth, they were following the example of their platoon commander who was in his so-called command post – a bunker on the reverse slope, nice and safe, but utterly useless to control or even to observe the battle. And the subaltern was merely following the example of his company commander who was fighting a map board and telephone war on *his* reverse slope one or two hills behind ... The

> rear platoons would not have engaged the enemy if they were under neutralizing shell fire (as they assuredly were) without their commanders exercising decisive leadership – and decisive leadership cannot be exercised by runner from inside a nice, safe bunker. It cannot be exercised by wireless or line either.[47]

Reflecting on his Korean experiences with the 1st battalions many years later, Pope maintained that the Canadians 'ended up with higher casualties because of the "sit tight" mentality.' Even more disturbing is Pope's belief that the brigade's ineffective leadership was a direct product of the fact that 'many majors and lieutenant-colonels with Second [World] War experience were most concerned not to get themselves killed in a sideshow like Korea.'[48] Unlike the officers of the Special Force who had returned to the army specifically to fight in Korea, the regular officers of the 1st battalions had remained in the military after the Second World War to serve in a peacetime army. Those regular infantry officers who were the most eager to see combat again would, moreover, have already been posted to the Far East to fill the few officer vacancies that had been open in the 2nd battalions. For the remainder, postings to Korea were the result of their general service with the 1st battalions and did not necessarily stem from any desire to see more fighting at that stage of their careers. Indeed, if Pope's assertion is accurate, many of the 1st battalion officers – upon whose energy and aggressive professionalism an operational brigade depended – were lacking those very qualities.

In commenting on his experience as the division's GSO(1) for much of this period, Lieutenant-Colonel Amy remarked that 'after a time you begin to live with your mistakes without seeing them. A tremendous amount of drive is required on the part of the company and platoon commanders to keep the division in fighting trim.'[49] Unfortunately, the necessary 'drive' appears to be have been missing in more senior 1st battalion officers as well. In his memoirs of the Korean War, Robert Peacock, a platoon commander with both 1 and 3 PPCLI, also notes that the 1st battalion's senior officers had little connection with the men in the front line. He recalls that 'battalion HQ was a remote location to which we went for patrol briefings and debriefings. There was an awful temptation to develop an insularity which could be damaging to unit morale. There was always joy and cheering when shells intended for us overshot and dropped into the battalion HQ area.' That attitude was not helped by the fact that 'command post bunkers tended to be large and solidly built with a log framework, layers of sandbags, corrugated metal, waterproofing and at least five feet of rock and dirt on top of all this to provide maximum protection from shellfire. These structures, however, used the majority of the defensive stores and engineer support that were available to the battalion. Farther down the scale of affluence in the rifle platoons, we were left to do what we could using any local resources we could lay our hands on from time to time.'[50]

Ironically, when interviewed in October 1952, Peacock's CO, Lieutenant-Colonel Cameron, stated that two of the most important 'lessons learned' in Korea were related to road building in the rear areas and bunker construction. He proudly reported that his own command post 'was recognized as the strongest in 1 Commonwealth Division.'[51] Nor were Cameron's energies necessarily concentrated on matters of operational concern. 'There has been a report received here that late one night early in the month,' the battalion's diarist recorded at the end of May, 'one of the company commanders was phoned, the voice asking "Do you hear an owl hooting?" to which the company commander replied, rather caustically, "No, the bullfrogs are making too much noise." The voice then said, "This is the Commanding Officer speaking." It is understood that this [company] officer is now paying the strictest attention to the various bird calls of Korea.'[52]

Indeed, many of the 1st battalions' senior officers and NCOs appear to have substituted an emphasis on spit and polish for effective combat leadership. Peacock, for one, believed that the 1st battalions were 'a fussy group as far as dress was concerned. We were always properly dressed for the field, cleanly shaven and boots shone. Some individuals carried the spit and polish routine to extremes as their way of occupying leisure time.'[53] Without question, one of the fussiest battalions was Lieutenant-Colonel Bingham's 1 RCR. At the end of September, while 1 RCR was occupying the exposed entrenchments on Hill 355, the battalion's war diary records that 'the brigade commander visited the Regiment in the morning and with the CO inspected E Company, A Company and C Company. While visiting E Company under the shadows of Hill 227, the brigadier was pleased to note in one of their fighting trenches, grenades with highly polished base plugs, a can of Brasso and a polishing rag. He remarked between chuckles, "It is no more than is to be expected."'[54]

For soldiers in the forward positions, the emphasis placed on spit and polish by seldom-seen superiors safely ensconced in the battalion's rear area often seemed petty. Returning to the front line after a day spent improving a reserve position, Lieutenant Peacock's work party was passing through 1 PPCLI's F Echelon when

> an imperious figure strode over, saluted, and introduced himself as the Regimental Sergeant Major. We exchanged a few pleasantries and I thought little about the encounter until we returned to the company when the company commander said my presence was required at battalion HQ, immediately, to see the adjutant. This was usually an ominous sign and I went off, by foot, over the hills to see what was in store. It turned out that the RSM had witnessed my trouser legs not being fully tucked into my boot tops and had reported me to the adjutant for unseemly dress. We had been working all day digging trenches and had become hot and dirty, and were on our way to wash and clean up when spotted by the RSM. I was a bit upset at the nature and manner in which the complaint was raised and said so to the Adjutant. The adjutant, Captain Bob Dudley, listened, then gave me the adjutant's lecture on dress standards for wayward subalterns and said I should get back to my duties. This was the only time with 1 PPCLI in Korea that I ever met or saw the RSM.[55]

Such remoteness was in sharp contrast with Rockingham's practice of continually touring the front-line positions, both to check on their layout and to keep in touch with his men. The Australian commander of the 28th British Commonwealth Brigade, Brigadier Daly, displayed his disregard of 'the dangers of the forward areas by visiting his men in their trenches and bunkers almost every day.' According to the Australian official history, his familiarity with front-line conditions was an important ingredient in 'his leadership of what many members of the Commonwealth Division, including the General Officer Commanding, regarded as its best brigade.'[56]

Sudden visits from senior officers do not appear to have been a common occurrence in Harry Pope's C Company, 1 R22eR. During Christmas 1952, for instance, his men set up a Christmas tree, complete with lights, on top of the Sherman tank entrenched near their company position. Pope realized that he 'would have been accused of revealing my position to the enemy' if his battalion CO ever ventured forward to see it but was apparently unconcerned that that was likely to happen.[57] Although Pope may not have had his own CO specifically in mind when he wrote that 'decisive leadership cannot be exercised ... by wireless or line,' Trudeau's performance suggests that he was one of the regular officers who was quite content to exercise command via the telephone.

Pope has offered two possible explanations for the lethargic leadership of 1st battalion commanders. The first, put forward in his critique of the brigade's patrols in June 1953, was that the Canadians had 'been waging war on the assumption that the peace talks at Pan Mun Jom were going to be successful from one day to the next. A humane desire of commanders to avoid risking lives in the possible last days before an armistice has led to a purely defensive patrolling policy of which more aggressive enemy commanders inevitably have taken full advantage.'[58] Writing in the Van Doo periodical *La Citadelle* thirty-five years later, however, Pope alluded to another, more serious, cause for the Canadian malaise. After relating the story of a C Company private who refused to move forward with his platoon to occupy the company position on Hill 159 – until a half-hour, rain-sodden conversation with his company commander convinced him to change his mind – Pope explains that when the company needed a storeman for A Echelon a couple of days later, he sent this man: 'Nothing would have been gained, either by the company, or by the soldier, to push him any further.' The Van Doo major emphasized, however, 'that the way to treat a private who lacks a bit of courage and the way to treat an officer who lacks it, must be handled in two totally different ways. And, by this I am not saying that we send the officer on vacation or on leave to become an instructor somewhere behind the lines. Nor am I saying that we send the cowardly officer back to Canada so that he can instruct recruits and get a promotion because of his experience on the battlefield. I am not joking: this happened regularly during the Second World War.'[59]

Although Pope was willing to treat the laggard from C Company leniently – the private would have faced ninety days' hard detention and a dishonourable discharge from the army if he had been dealt with in the usual manner – he insisted that harsh treatment was the only option for officers who similarly lacked the requisite courage: 'The officer who cannot perform his duty facing the enemy must be dismissed immediately, either by court-martialling him or, if we want to be kind, forcing him to resign from the army, to return his certification as an officer. Nothing is worse than to give such an individual a second chance: a cowardly lieutenant will be a cowardly company major or cowardly battalion major. At each level of superiority, the wrong he does becomes greater and greater.' Whether the battlefield was in Europe or Korea, it was 'the primary duty of an infantry officer ... to lead soldiers under his orders against the enemy. If he is not ready to do this at all times, he has no business in the army. A cowardly infantry officer is a threat to the army and an insult to the troops.'[60]

While Pope's assertion that an officer returned to Canada for cowardice during the Second World War might remain in the postwar army and later be posted to command combat troops in Korea might seem incredible, his experience in both Italy and the Far East meant that he was well placed to have known of such incidents. It says a great deal about AHQ's indifference toward an officer's actual ability to command units on active operations that they would not consider an officer's previous combat service record in making such appointments. Given the less intense nature of Korean operations, however, the 'inefficiency' of an officer was less likely to be starkly revealed and certainly not on a daily basis. Pope's comments about the predilection of some officers for self-preservation aside, problems of lethargic leadership were more likely to be identified simply as a lack of motivation among tired or disinterested long-service officers. In a June 1953 interview, for instance, the commanding officer of 3 RCR, Lt.-Col. Kenneth L. Campbell, pointed out that veteran officers from the Second World War, after some seven years of peacetime service, could be more of a liability than an asset in combat despite their experience:

> It was a poor policy to post ... as company commanders officers who had been company commanders during the Second World War. These officers felt they were back doing the same job they had done almost ten years ago. They felt they had not progressed and in many cases lacked drive and enthusiasm. Even where they retained these important qualities, age and/or physical condition made them unsuitable. This made it necessary to replace many of these officers before the unit proceeded overseas. Company commanders must be fighting fit. They must be able to run up and down hills with the youngest of their men. Besides, in choosing the old war horses, AHQ prevented the unit from developing the future commanders. A company commander should be young, tough and ambitious ... Lieutenant-Colonel Campbell would rather have keen young captains commanding his companies than slow old majors.[61]

Understandably, old, slow officers who lacked drive and enthusiasm were also unlikely to place themselves in harm's way in the manner that a commander must if he was to exercise effective combat leadership. Troops who saw that their own senior officers 'were most concerned not to get themselves killed in a sideshow like Korea' could hardly be expected to fill the leadership vacuum themselves and maintain an aggressive vigilance.

A clear example of the new tone of Canadian leadership set by the 1st battalion regulars was provided in early June when Brigadier Bogert decided to move brigade headquarters from its more exposed position in front of Line Wyoming to a secure location behind it. When the Canadian brigade had occupied virtually the same hilltop positions after its Commando advance in October 1951, Rockingham made a point of locating his headquarters within a few thousand yards of the forward battalions, in the valley behind Hill 152, in order to remain within earshot of the front lines even though this meant being subjected to occasional shelling. After his first month in the line, on the other hand, Bogert selected a new location some 5,000 yards southeast of Rockingham's previous headquarters and more than 10,000 yards from the farthest Canadian company position. The brigade war diarist justified the move by claiming 'that the present location is in front of the second line of defence, called Line Wyoming, and should a penetration by the enemy occur, the HQ would have to move at a time when their presence would be most required.'[62]

In its new location Bogert's headquarters was well out of sight of enemy observation, and thus immune to enemy artillery fire. The move was matched by the change in emphasis that occurred in the brigade's war diary as soon as Bogert replaced Rockingham in April. Under the Special Force commander, the brigade diary concentrated almost exclusively on descriptions of operations, with frequent observations on weapons, the position of entrenchments, and the tactics being employed. Once Bogert took command the war diary became more of a social chronicle, recording only those events that could be observed directly from headquarters itself, with detailed descriptions of mess layouts, bar bills, and high-ranking visitors, but little or no reference to the brigade's actual operations.

Major-General Cassels, who had always been opposed to the I Corps directive ordering each forward battalion to conduct one strong fighting patrol a week, finally suspended the policy in early June. Freed from the necessity of mounting a set number of fighting patrols, each of the Commonwealth Division's brigades resumed establishing its own patrol schedule. Since the British GOC tended to provide guidance to his Commonwealth units rather than rigidly asserting command – he took a more direct role with the British units in the division – each brigade had a fairly wide latitude in determining the scale of its patrol activity. For the 25th Brigade, this freedom quickly led to a strictly defensive approach. 'Until further notice,' the Canadian brigade major informed the battalions on 3 June, 'fighting patrols may be discontinued. Ambush, recce and standing patrols will continue. The object of these patrols is to destroy or capture any enemy moving in the valley in front of battalion areas.'[63]

Since reconnaissance patrols were never a part of the 1st battalions' repertoire, the new instructions effectively limited the brigade's operations to passive ambush and standing patrols. Cassels had hoped that ambushes might secure the necessary prisoners I Corps was looking for but, on the Canadian front at least, the failure to conduct any recce patrols made it exceedingly unlikely that their ambushes would achieve anything of value. By further limiting the scope of ambush locations to positions 'in the valley in front of battalion areas,' moreover, the Canadians were unnecessarily handing control of no man's land over to the Chinese – despite the fact that the enemy had made only a few forays of their own in the past month and a half.

This defensive mindset was reflected in the observations Lieutenant-Colonel Cameron appended to Major Allan's patrol instructions of 3 June. While suggesting in his notes that he felt 'very strongly re: aggression of patrols,' the main focus of Cameron's comments was the situation immediately in front of the Patricias' own wire defences rather than what might be happening on the Chinese side of the valley. 'Known enemy movement to our own FDLs,' the Patricia CO asserted in his 'Observations by Commander,' 'can be stopped or certainly limited by strongly mutual supporting ambush patrols and by searching the valley. When enemy patrols do get to the wire, we should send out patrols to outflank them and not only rely on mortars and MG fire to disperse [the] enemy.'[64] Unfortunately, Cameron did not follow up these comments with concrete action and his battalion remained as passive in the defence as ever. No man's land would eventually become a forbidding place for Canadian soldiers to enter, and mortar and machine-gun fire would become the primary method used to drive the enemy away from the brigade's entrenchments.

The inactivity of the Chinese in May and June also masked the problem that the 1st battalions' lack of reconnaissance patrolling and defensive mentality eventually created, by instilling in the Canadians a false sense that their limited patrol programs were effective. Their initial bravado was reflected in the 1 RCR diary entries for 7 and 8 June that proclaimed, 'Brigade requests that 1 RCR eases up on patrols to let the other two units get in the show ... The 1 PPCLI had the most patrols of the brigade in the month of May (all kinds). But 1 RCR had the most fighting, and the most contacts with the enemy [five of the meagre total of seven contacts]. Now we know who is doing the work.'[65] In his own patrol instructions in early June, Lieutenant-Colonel Bingham made it clear that he would take personal control of his battalion's patrol assignments: 'The CO will personally detail the initial orders for all patrols, giving timings, routes, objectives and type of patrol. A controller will be designated in the order ... Large patrols, or when several patrols are being co-ordinated, will be controlled by the CO personally. The final O Group being held at Tac HQ under the CO's direction.'[66]

One innovation the Royals were responsible for was the 'jitter' patrol. First recorded on the night of 28-9 May, a second jitter patrol was conducted on the night of 12-13 June and explained in the brigade war diary the following day:

> The use of Jitter patrols by 1 RCR are proving effective. The name 'Jitter' has been given by 1 RCR to this rather unorthodox type of patrol. What actually happens is as follows:

> a patrol of usually one officer and twelve men in strength move towards the enemy lines after last light. When they are sufficiently near to the enemy to arouse his suspicion, they get down in a firing position and open up with every weapon at their disposal. By doing this, they give the impression to the enemy that an attack or raid is pending and invariably cause the enemy to disclose his position by opening fire. Once the so-called Jitter patrol has caused the enemy to reveal his position, they withdraw some three or four hundred yards and take up an ambush position in the hope that the Chinese will follow them and be caught in their trap. The RCR are now using these patrols practically every night with considerable success. They are obviously making the enemy jittery and secondly they are gaining valuable information about the enemy strength at various enemy-held positions. The brigadier is keen for the other battalions to try this form of patrol.[67]

In the event, however, the new type of patrol did not fulfill the expectation of the hopeful brigade war diarist. The only other unit to attempt a jitter patrol was 1 R22eR, also on the night of 12-13 June, but its automatic weapons drew 'no answering fire' from the wary Chinese. The Royals themselves made only six more jitter patrols before abandoning the practice on the 22nd. Even the 'valuable information' that such patrols gathered was highly dubious given that the Chinese could choose when – and if – to return the nuisance fire. Such patrols could not replace the more accurate intelligence that could be gained by a regular series of reconnaissance patrols that routinely probed to the enemy's entrenchments. The brigade's operations log, however, records only two reconnaissance patrols for the entire month of June and both of those barely entered the valley before returning to their lines.

The lack of effective intelligence on the Chinese dispositions had a decidedly negative effect during the last half of June, when the Commonwealth Division was again ordered by I Corps to capture prisoners and passed this directive on to its brigades. On 11 June, 'The brigade [was] once again requested to take aggressive action in its patrol policy and endeavour to capture at least one prisoner every six days.'[68] Ten days later, with Cassels 'emphasizing the necessity for capture of prisoners,' each of the Canadian battalions was obliged to mount a large raid against the Chinese positions.[69] The first such raid was mounted on the night of 20-1 June by 1 PPCLI, against Hill 133 on the ridgeline that ran between Hills 166 and 156. Although the raiders were briefed for the patrol on the 18th, no attempt was made to make a reconnaissance of the ground to determine the enemy's strengths and dispositions beforehand. In fact, to that point in June – despite Cameron's rhetoric about aggressive patrolling – the entire Patricia patrol schedule had consisted only of standing patrols and five uneventful ambush patrols, none of which proceeded beyond the stream that divided no man's land. The fighting patrol on 20-1 June was the first time that the Patricias had attempted to penetrate to the enemy side of the valley since late May.[70]

The results of such an ill-prepared operation were, perhaps, inevitable. Led by Lt. A. Bull of B Company, the thirty-seven Patricias set up a firm base 'at the end of the spur forward of D Company' at 0030 hours: 'Here they stopped for a period of five minutes as an enemy patrol had been heard in the valley and had been dispersed by our mortars. The patrol moved through the firm base into the valley at 0035 hours.' After moving across the valley floor, they were 'in the assault position about thirty-five yards below the enemy crawl trenches' by 0225 hours:

> When the patrol got strung out in assault formation, the commander called for Bofors to engage two previously arranged targets ... the tracers could be seen overhead and forward hitting the specified target. It was at this time that there were three briefly intervalled crumps in the patrol area. The first one inflicted several casualties. Lieutenant Bull himself was wounded and blown back some feet down the hill. There were calls for help and men went to aid. The second crump occurred closely followed by a third. More casualties resulted. At 0226 hours a message was received from the patrol stating that there were uncounted casualties. From the debriefing no satisfactory explanation for the three crumps could be given by the patrol. The consensus of opinion is that there was nothing 'come in.' They are very sure that there was no whine of shells or swish of mortars at this time. The Bofors were making some noise, normal harassing was being carried out both to the right and left of them – considerable bedlam ... At 0230 hours Lieutenant Bull reported that he was unable to continue and was returning ... Getting the dead and seriously wounded down from the hill was a big job. Corporal Reding and Private Hughes (though Hughes was wounded and bleeding considerably), Corporal McLaughlin and Private Bertrand did most of the evacuating. They made three trips up and down the hill. The last trip was just to make sure that no was left behind.
>
> This group organized at the foot of the hill on the road south of the start line at [the stream] ... No help was sent at this time. The patrol proceeded after caching the weapons of the casualties at [the stream] (three Stens, one Bren, two or three rifles). From here to the firm [base] was tough going. About 600 yards of muddy paddy fields, a stream to cross and a hill to climb. They took turns at carrying the casualties (one per one) and supplying protection from possible enemy in the valley. The last man finally reported to the stretcher bearers at 0402 hours.[71]

The divisional intelligence staff eventually concluded that the 'three crumps' were caused by the explosion of 'a new "super-type" concussion grenade. On one occasion this weapon was seen to be hurled through the air, emitting a trail of sparks, as though the grenade was fuze ignited. This may be another of the many improvised grenades in which the CCF seem to specialize.'[72] With the Patricias venturing up the slopes of Hill 133 for the first time, the explosion of the well-timed grenades had 'resulted in 50 per cent casualties including the patrol commander and the majority of his NCOs. The battle then changed from offensive to one of evacuating the dead and wounded.' Chinese casualties, if any, could have resulted only from the Canadians' supporting fire coming from across the valley. The raiders themselves had nothing to show for their six dead and eighteen wounded – certainly no prisoners. Even the Patricias' own war diary acknowledged that they 'took a beating from the enemy.'[73]

The following night, 1 RCR staged a company-sized raid in an attempt to capture a prisoner, this one to Hill 113, part of the spur directly above the demolished village of Chinch'on that led up to Hill 166. The Royals had been only slightly more active in their patrolling than the Patricias, having actually sent a patrol to 'jitter' Hill 113 from the village of Chinch'on on the night of 12-13 June. Their patrol's fire had 'brought one LMG burst from [the] right spur of Point 113 and two grenades from [the] left spur of Point 113'[74] – not particularly significant information on which to plan their 21-2 June raid on the feature. (The battalion's other three jitter patrols that month had sprayed some ineffective small-arms fire toward Hill 75, over 1,000 yards to the south of Hill 113, in preparation for an uneventful fighting patrol against the lower feature on the night of 15-16 June.) Despite two rehearsals in the battalion's rear area for the assault on Hill 113, things did not go well for the RCR raiders either:

> When the main body reached the base of the hill [113], the firm base came forward to the track. All the fire on the objective was now lifted except one tank troop. This was done on the code word 'Charles,' which was also the signal for the assault up the draw.
>
> Two tanks were now to engage the second of three rows of communication trench around the hill; the other two were to fire on the top row. This was to be carried on for eight minutes. Then, for a further seven minutes, all four tanks were to concentrate on the top.
>
> The end of the first five minutes found Coy HQ midway between the two lower rows of trenches. Here three heavy explosions occurred, resulting in four casualties. It is believed that these explosions were anti-tank mines used in an anti-personnel role. Major Holmes [C Company commander] is positive that they were not thrown.
>
> The attached FOO, however, assuming that the friendly tanks were responsible, promptly called their fire off. (As it happened, the fire of all four tanks had been going on or over the top of the hill. Thus of the 15 minutes' tank fire planned, only five was produced; and even it was not properly on the target.)
>
> Despite the three explosions in its rear and the cessation of supporting tank fire, the Aslt Pl [assault platoon] kept going. On reaching the top of the hill, it came under enemy MG fire, burp guns and grenades. One man was killed. All three section leaders were wounded. The Platoon wireless operator and three other men also were wounded.
>
> The strength of the enemy holding the top of the hill was estimated as one platoon plus. Major Holmes appreciated that the action had reached that stage where one determined effort by either side would swing the balance. His next step would have been to push 8 Pl through No 7. But at this point someone (identity not established) shouted

'Get down' – meaning to keep low – and the warning was misinterpreted as an order to withdraw off the feature. Consequently the attack, which might well have been successful, ended in a mad scramble down the hill.

Meanwhile 9 Pl had failed to take up its proper position. The Firm Base was some 100 yards left of where it should have been. This was due to 6 Sec (8 Pl) having neglected to lay tape behind itself. One result of this was that, in looking for the right spot, the Firm Base Pl ran into our own artillery fire on the base of Pt 72; two minor casualties occurred here.

Thus the company found itself at the bottom of Pt 113 with one dead and 15 wounded, and the Firm Base out of position. The wounded included the CSM [company sergeant major], three section leaders and three signallers.[75]

By the time C Company regained the battalion's positions, the raid had cost 1 RCR one dead and twenty-four wounded, four of them seriously.[76] The FOO concerned, Captain F.W. Webb, RCHA, was convinced that the Chinese had been 'well aware of our intentions,' not least because of a lack of imagination in the plan. 'The route had been used many times before by our patrols,' the FOO claimed, while 'the fire plan was substantially a repetition of previous fire plans.' To introduce at least

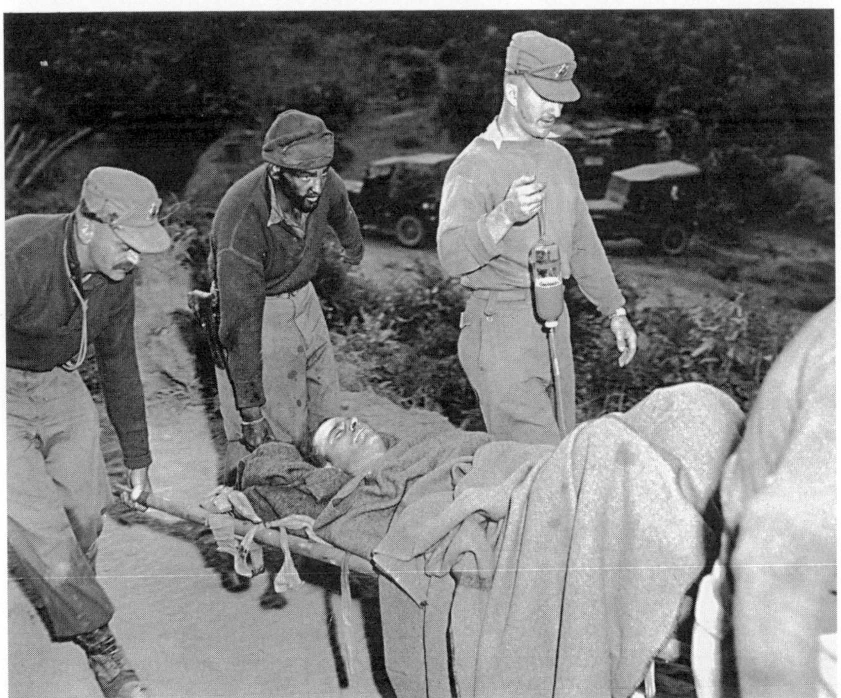

One of twenty-four Royals wounded during the 1 RCR raid on Hill 113 on the night of 21-2 June 1952 is brought into the Canadian lines. NAC PA184805

one element of surprise, Webb had asked that there be no registration in the days leading up to the raid and that only heavy mortars be used in the counter-bombardment role. Nonetheless, 'seven hours before H Hour, all types of weapon were in fact registering' and Webb's pleas to cease firing – 'this is an open invitation, we'll probably get the RSVP when we get there' – fell on deaf ears as the artillery fire controller 'considered that the registration fire would be regarded as routine.' Despite harbouring 'strong misgivings' about the raid, however, Webb chose to keep them to himself until after the operation had failed.[77]

The next night it was the turn of the 1st Battalion, The Welch Regiment, holding the saddle position on the western slope of Hill 355, to mount a raid against Hill 227. The British operation was preceded by an air strike and the raiders were able to reach their objective without serious opposition. Even so, they were unable to capture a prisoner when they were forced to withdraw under heavy Chinese mortar and shell fire. The British did manage 'to collect the effects of one enemy killed, but these proved to be of little value,' a negligible return for suffering three dead and nineteen wounded in the attempt.[78] On the night of 23-4 June 1 R22eR tried to capture a prisoner. Wearing body armour borrowed from the 1st US Marine Division on their left flank, the French Canadians attacked the Chinese positions on the hill behind the village of Sami-ch'on. Although they reported being hit by twenty-five of the 'super-heavy grenades,' the body armour reduced Van Doo casualties to only two killed and six wounded, with one of the latter, Lance-Cpl. P. Dugal, falling into the hands of the Chinese. The raid was also only the second time in the past month that a 1 R22eR patrol had ventured west of the Sami-ch'on River.[79]

A final Commonwealth raid, made by the recently arrived 1st Battalion, Royal Australian Regiment against the Chinese defences on Hill 227, managed to achieve somewhat more success than the Canadian sorties. Although 1 RAR was sent to Korea in early June to reinforce the 28th Brigade (giving that formation four infantry battalions for the remainder of the war, as opposed to the three battalions in the Canadian and British brigades), it was initially attached to the 29th Brigade and put into the line on Hills 159, 210, and the saddle position on the western slopes of Hill 355 when the British formation relieved the Canadian brigade on the 30th. Attacking at 0900 hours on 2 July, the Australians were on top of the Chinese entrenchments within thirty minutes despite coming under heavy small arms, artillery, and mortar fire. A number of Chinese were trapped in their bunkers and disposed of with explosives and flame throwers. As the enemy's artillery fire intensified, the order to withdraw was finally given at 1030 hours after four bunkers had been demolished and an unknown, but probably considerable, number of Chinese had been killed. Australian casualties were three killed and twenty-eight wounded. Although the 1 RAR raiders did not capture a prisoner – the main purpose of the operation – they did overrun the position and inflict significant damage.[80]

As the division's intelligence staff later reported, the enemy's extensive use of tunnels and reluctance to surrender continued to make the capture of a live prisoner a difficult proposition. During the Australian attack, the 'four large bunkers on the summit were found to be occupied by an unknown number of enemy who offered considerable resistance and refused to come out. Despite the use of flame the occupants preferred to perish in the bunkers rather than surrender. One bunker bore the signs of recent occupation and in the vicinity numerous dug-out slits were observed, but the entrances to these could not be located. These undoubtedly were some distance away, on the reverse slope, connected by underground tunnels and with well camouflaged entrances. Reports from intelligence sources indicate that a number of enemy did in fact remain in these dug-outs during the operation.'[81]

The Australian rationale for aggressive action resembled the Canadian brigade's own attitude during Rockingham's tenure. As the British official history points out, 'The pursuit of active operations had a sound basis. Mastering no man's land by laying ambushes, reconnoitring the enemy's positions, occasionally raiding by fighting patrols or larger forces to take prisoners or knock out particularly vexatious enemy observation posts were doubly advantageous. These limited enterprises checked enemy aggression and heightened the morale of those undertaking them. But their use required a sense of proportion. The advantages would be dissipated if they led to unwonted casualties.'[82] It was the appropriate sense of proportion that the Commonwealth soldiers felt was missing from I Corps' arbitrary fighting patrol directives.

The costly nature of the large raids – more than 120 casualties in late June and early July alone, mostly Canadian and Australian – finally prompted Cassels to order their suspension while promising his American superiors that his division would attempt to obtain prisoners by other methods.[83] Writing in early July, the GOC explained the problem to his superiors in London:

> During the last month we have been ordered to produce one prisoner every three days and have been authorised to use up to a battalion to achieve this. In fact we have put in a series of company raids which have killed many enemy but have not produced a prisoner. As these raids have had to go a long way to find the enemy, who are sitting back in their main positions, they have been comparatively costly. As a result I have ordered that they should be suspended and we are trying some other methods. Meanwhile I am being harassed and ordered by Corps to produce a prisoner every third day, apparently regardless of cost. As we know quite well what enemy divisions are in front of us I cannot see the point in this and have said so and have asked if there is any special reason behind the request. I have made it clear that I will do all in my power to get as many prisoners as possible, but that I consider a series of battalion or company raids a most unprofitable way of doing it, unless the need is considerably greater than I think it is. At present this has been agreed, but I do not know how long it will last. Personally I believe the reason behind the order was to keep the US Army divisions 'sharp' regardless of casualties, and at least one of their divisions has taken very considerable casualties –

> between 2,000 and 3,000. The Commander of 1st US Marine Division on my left visited me on 29 June, and raised this very point. He is in complete agreement with my views.[84]

Overall, Cassels recognized that the May-June period 'has generally been very static with both sides patrolling and doing the occasional raid. Latterly we have dominated no man's land to such an extent that the enemy has been very loath to enter it. In some ways this has been a considerable disadvantage as it makes it extremely difficult to get a prisoner. We are now trying to lure him forward again but, so far, he has not reacted.'[85] While Cassels was undoubtedly confusing cause and effect – the division's 'domination' was due to temporary Chinese passivity and was not the result of their being driven from no man's land by Commonwealth patrols – there was no debating the failure of Eighth Army's raiding policy. Even the American official history admits that 'from an intelligence point of view [these] patrols and raids often proved quite futile; few prisoners were taken and frequently no enemy contact was effected.'[86]

Cassels' suspension of the raids in early July 1952 coincided with the Canadian brigade's move into divisional reserve. During their initial two months in the front line, the 1st battalions had been most fortunate to have faced a passive enemy. In many ways their relatively easy first tour was similar to the time Rockingham's men had spent patrolling at Ch'orwon. Unlike the aggressive program the Special Force formation had instituted – and without the warnings Rockingham had given his men that the enemy was unlikely to remain passive forever – the regular battalions were content to remain close to their own entrenchments until ordered to raid an enemy position. Had the 'professionals' been more attuned to the military situation on their front, they could have used the valuable time to remedy the inadequacies of their patrol program – notably the complete absence of reconnaissance patrols – and familiarized their men with the terrain on the enemy side of the valley. The problems caused by the lack of detailed information about the enemy's routine and positions should have been obvious from the difficulties Bogert's men experienced whenever they ventured across the valley to attack the Chinese in their entrenchments. Unfortunately, the regulars squandered the opportunity the enemy had provided for building the confidence of the newly arrived units in operating well forward of their positions. By the time the Canadians returned to the line in mid-August, their shortcomings would be magnified by an enemy that was once again patrolling no man's land in strength.

11 THE INACTIVE DEFENCE, JULY-OCTOBER 1952

While the Canadian brigade was in divisional reserve during July and early August, the Chinese resumed patrolling aggressively, raiding Commonwealth forward positions and generally operating on the UN side of no man's land. The new commander of the Commonwealth Division was Maj.-Gen. Michael M. Alston-Roberts-West (he preferred to be called by the more American-sounding Mike West while he was in Korea), and he replaced Cassels on 7 September. West reported at the end of October that 'the [summer] period has again been a static one, with the tempo of enemy shelling and general activity rising appreciably. It cannot be said any longer that we dominate no man's land – it has become a battleground for patrols with the enemy holding at least one good card in the form of expendable manpower.'[1] The renewed enemy aggression, while never approaching the scale of the Chinese counterattacks of November 1951, nonetheless sternly tested the Commonwealth Division's drive and initiative in keeping the enemy back from its forward defences. The Canadian brigade faced a particularly severe test following the formation's return to the line in mid-August.

The increased Chinese activity had not been immediately evident to the men of the 28th Commonwealth Brigade, however, when they took over the front-line positions vacated by the Canadians at the end of June. Through the first three weeks of July the divisional front remained relatively quiet 'except for the usual enemy shelling and patrol contacts.'[2] The 3rd Battalion, Royal Australian Regiment began regular patrols in no man's land immediately on moving into the battalion position opposite Hill 166. Despite the suspension of the futile raiding policy, the Australians' vigorous patrolling culminated with the dispatch of a strong fighting patrol to capture a prisoner from an enemy outpost on Hill 115, a knoll on the lower slopes of Hill 166, on the night of 12-13 July. Unfortunately, the Chinese position was much better defended than the twenty-five man patrol had expected. Although the Australians fought up to the trenches, their assault failed and there were thirteen casualties, three of whom were killed.[3] The advantage of smaller patrols was demonstrated two nights later when 'two enemy sections on Point 133 commenced firing on each other ably refereed by a 1 RAR patrol positioned within good view of the battlefield. Whenever the battle showed signs of waning, it was pepped up by the watching patrol who called down a few rounds of artillery, both sides of course being treated with absolute impartiality.'[4]

One of the first signs that the enemy was becoming more aggressive came on the night of 13-14 July when a standing patrol of the 29th Brigade's 1st Royal Norfolk

Regiment was rushed by two enemy platoons wielding 'long stabbing knives' during hand-to-hand fighting. Although the Chinese were repulsed on that occasion, a week later another 1 RNR standing patrol 'was overrun by fifty enemy and forced to withdraw after suffering three killed in action, four wounded in action and two missing.' On 1 August another of the British brigade's battalions, 1st Black Watch Regiment, 'received a small probing attack during the night which was easily repulsed.' Two nights later, an 'outpost of 1 Welch [Regiment] was attacked strongly and forced to withdraw suffering four killed in action, five wounded in action and one missing.'[5]

A measure of revenge was extracted when 1 RNR set up a company ambush that 'fought a successful action against the enemy' that same evening. According to the division's intelligence staff, 'the enemy appears to have no objection to a wide, unoccupied no man's land but has demonstrated his aversion to our holding ground in this area and reacts strongly to any attempt to establish a firm position close to his doorstep.' This observation provided the basis for the ambush:

> This attitude was quite apparent in the case of our operations on Point 118 (a small hill feature in no man's land). Between 31 July and the night of 2/3 August, Point 118 was occupied by a section during the day. By night a company, reinforced by a platoon-sized protective patrol laid a large ambush to the east, north and south of the feature and a Royal Engineer battle simulation team prepared the ingredients of a battle on the feature itself. On the night of 2/3 August at about 2130 hours, the enemy attacked in strength. This action by 1 Royal Norfolk (Operation Harvest) was a complete success. The enemy was caught off balance by the strength of the ambush and by the fact that Point 118 was apparently occupied and in action. In this action it is known that twenty-one enemy were killed, including six prisoners of war who later died of wounds. It is, however, not known how many enemy died or were wounded under the heavy artillery fire placed west of Point 118 in the counter-attack launched by him which was completely unsuccessful, or in his encounter with the [RNR] cut-off platoon.[6]

British casualties were three killed and eighteen wounded, with most of the latter being only slightly injured.

Of more immediate concern to the forward battalions than the return of enemy patrols to no man's land, however, was the increasing volume of harassing artillery fire being directed against the Commonwealth entrenchments. Over the course of the winter, the Chinese had managed to build up the ammunition supplies they had depleted during their November counteroffensive. Since most supplies had to be carried on the backs of both man and animals all the way from the Chinese border – the primitive North Korean rail system had been hard hit by UN air power – the static front line greatly aided these stockpiling efforts. By early summer it had become apparent that 'the enemy now slightly outnumbers us in guns and has continued to improve his artillery technique. His harassing fire has been more accurate and more effectively used ... He can still put down accurate and heavy concentrations in support of an attack and he has improved his technique for placing defensive fire with both artillery and mortars.' During July, the Chinese fire 'showed a marked increase over previous months with a daily incoming average of 140 shells and ninety mortar bombs' in the divisional area. The daily average increased to 222 shells and 200 mortar bombs for the first three weeks of August, the highest sustained average the Commonwealth Division had seen. This figure fell to 137 mortar bombs per day in the last ten days of August.[7]

During the first half of September, however, the Chinese increased their harassing fire even further, sending over an average of 300 artillery rounds and 180 mortar bombs each day except for the 13th when they 'indulged in a large scale divisional artillery exercise in which he expended nearly 2,000 rounds ... Enemy shelling dropped off during the last half of the month with an average of just over 200 rounds a day. This may have been due to the greatly increased enemy artillery activity on our flanks in support of ground action.'[8] To put the volume of fire into perspective, a high average of 500 artillery and mortar rounds landing in the divisional area per day would, if fired over a ten-hour period with the majority falling on the two forward brigades, amount to an average of one incoming round every forty minutes on each forward company position – annoying but hardly enough to cause excessive damage. Of course the enemy was likely to concentrate his fire, in both time and space, so that a particular battalion or company could experience a much greater volume of fire over a shorter period.

Despite their increased artillery capability, the communists continued to lag well behind the Commonwealth Division in terms of both quantity of firepower and its accuracy. Even relatively heavy concentrations of Chinese artillery fire were answered with two to three times that number of Commonwealth shells. The superiority of UN artillery fire had led the communists to dig from three to four gun pits per gun in an effort to move their artillery quickly after each shoot and avoid the accurate counterbombardment. The enemy was also

> considerably hampered by poor communications, but given time he can conduct very accurate destructive shoots on tanks, observation posts, etc., with a minimum of wastage of ammunition. In the case of opportunity targets, he may take up to twenty minutes to get the first round on the ground. No serious counter battery fire has been received by this divisional artillery during the period, though other divisions have received casualties in equipment and personnel from very accurate counter-battery. Periodically, an unobserved 'hate' is carried out [by the Chinese] on an obvious harassing target area picked off a map. This target may be up to a few thousand yards behind the [Commonwealth Division's] main line of resistance. In one case, such an area received five hundred rounds of field calibre in one hour.[9]

The relatively long time it took for the Chinese to place their initial round on a target of opportunity was advantageous to Commonwealth patrols. Whereas the speed of their own divisional artillery (often only a minute elapsed between providing the map coordinates for a target and the landing of the first shells) allowed them to use indirect fire for sniping at enemy patrols, the delay in registering Chinese artillery meant that Commonwealth patrols had to contend only with sporadic mortar fire in the event of a clash in no man's land. When the enemy did have time to register a target, as against well-established Commonwealth entrenchments, his increasing artillery resources posed a much greater threat. The exact number of artillery pieces available to the Chinese, however, remained little more than guesswork:

> The artillery support within a CCF army continues to be the subject of much research and few conclusions. Information is obtained from shell fragments and the sound of shell bursts. PW have been of slight assistance. 64th CCF Army, on leaving the front in mid-May, was firmly believed to have twelve battalions of twelve guns, each division having thirty-six 75/76mm howitzers and the army having a regiment of twelve 122mm howitzers, a regiment of 105mm howitzers and twelve 37mm anti-aircraft guns. They were deployed in depth according to the layout of the divisions. 40th CCF Army are still an unknown quantity and their complement of guns may be anything from seventy-two to one hundred and forty-four ...
>
> No special anti-tank guns have been discovered on our front but it is known that all Russian light and medium artillery can fire AP [armour piercing] shot. Many unoccupied pits close to the front could be used for anti-tank guns deployed along the main tank avenues of advance.
>
> The number of 122mm howitzers deployed on our front has increased from one battalion to a suspected three battalions and a possible four. Some are certainly organic to the army but others are believed to belong to the 1st CCF Artillery Division, which is known to be deployed on our right flank. Recent shell fragment identifications indicated [the presence of] a possible 122mm gun and a possible 152mm gun/howitzer.[10]

Even before leaving the line at the end of June, 1 PPCLI had remarked on the shelling of its B Company by a Chinese 122 mm battery. Although the fire itself did little damage, the Patricias noted that 'the fragmentation of these shells cover[s] a tremendous area, actually neutralizing the entire company area. It appears to be harassing fire and possibly a try for the tanks. Usually a two minute interval between rounds, continuing for periods up to two hours at various times of the day. Strange, as this position had not been a target for the enemy at any other time. B Company is somewhat perturbed with this type of nonsense as they had been looking forward to a serene stay there.'[11]

The men of B Squadron, Lord Strathcona's Horse, who had relieved C Squadron in the front line on 8 June, quickly came to appreciate the sturdiness of their Sherman tanks. 'What is believed to be the first Canadian tank [of B Squadron] suffering a direct hit occurred today,' their diarist reported on 21 June (C Squadron tanks had received direct hits during the previous tour): 'Codesign 1B, commanded by 2 Troop's Corporal R.W. Graville, was hit with an HE [high explosive shell] and began to brew. Corporal Graville had the tank backed out of position so his ammo pile would not ignite and managed to subdue the flames. The tank was not damaged to any extent and was driven back into position shortly after.'[12] Three days later another of the troop's tanks 'was hit with an HE, the shell landing on the driver's hatch and pieces of the hatch and periscope wounded Trooper W.A. Kea. The crew commander, Corporal R. Peart, suffered [the] full concussion of the explosion, and though not wounded, was evacuated as a battle fatigue case.'[13]

According to the new Canadian operations staff officer at divisional headquarters, Lt.-Col. E.A.C. Amy, by the time he arrived in Korea to replace Wilson-Smith in mid-August, the Chinese had brought forward sufficient artillery to 'concentrate one hundred guns to blanket a single company position,' making them, in his opinion, 'a much more dangerous foe.' Of course the fact that the enemy could hit the Commonwealth positions with a larger number of shells should have underlined for the Canadians the need to patrol no man's land vigorously to contest its control and prevent being surprised by enemy forces moving to the attack. With the increased enemy firepower over the summer, Amy noticed that 'a certain uneasiness was apparent in the division.'[14] While Amy's boss, Major-General Mike West, shared the view that no man's land had 'become a battleground for patrols,' he also realized that the Commonwealth Division 'has had less attention from the enemy than any other formation in Eighth Army. The reason for this is difficult to assess but I think our system of defence may have a lot to do with it.' West maintained that since the enemy 'prefers isolated "outposts" as objectives,' the American tactical system of two lines of defence, an outpost line and a main line of resistance, provided more attractive targets. 'In the Commonwealth Division,' its commander explained, 'we studiously avoid the word "outpost" and refer to "standing patrols," "screens," etc.'[15] Nonetheless, it would take more than differences in terminology to keep an aggressive enemy back from the Commonwealth defences, particularly because the 25th Brigade's standing patrols returned to the same well-known positions night after night.

When the Canadians returned to the front line in the second week of August 1952, they, too, soon discovered that the Chinese infantry were becoming more active in no man's land. While in reserve, the 25th Brigade had made little effort to practise its patrolling skills, even though patrolling was now the only offensive activity in which the Commonwealth Division was engaged. The Canadians did continue to operate the junior NCOs school set up by the 2nd battalions near Uijongbu a year earlier, but it mainly provided refresher training in weapon handling, drill, map reading, and platoon and section tactics. Only eight hours of the five-week course were devoted to patrolling.[16]

Back in the line, the Canadian brigade was assigned to the division's right flank to hold the all-important Hill 355 with two battalions. The Van Doos were positioned astride the Bowling Alley, with three companies on Hills 159 and 210 and one company on the spur south of the Hill 227-Hill 355 saddle. The Bowling Alley road, being under direct enemy observation, had a reputation as 'a hot spot' since those vehicles that did make the crossing routinely received at least a few CCF shells for their trouble: 'People are not noted to linger on its route.'[17] The Royals held the more vulnerable entrenchments on the feature's crest and western slopes, facing the Chinese dugouts on Hill 227 immediately to the west, while 1 PPCLI was assigned the relatively secure positions to the east of Kowang-san. For the first two weeks after reentering the line, an effort was made to confuse the enemy by issuing the Canadians with American helmets and having them adopt US wireless procedures 'in the hope that the enemy would believe that US troops were holding the sector. During the next seven days there were several indications that the deception plan achieved its aim,' as demonstrated by the occasional 'Hello American' or 'Hello Yank' from Chinese radio operators.[18]

The ground east of Hill 355 (out of view to left of photograph), held by 1 PPCLI from mid-August to the end of October 1952, as seen from the ridge one mile east of Hill 210. The inter-divisional boundary with the 1st ROK Division lies to the right, while the Chinese-held Hill 317 can be seen in the left background, two and a half miles to the north. DHH 410B25.014 D3

Despite the increased enemy presence in no man's land, there were few actual patrol contacts on the Commonwealth front during August because Chinese reconnaissance patrols deliberately avoided engagements.[19] The most noticeable change for the Canadians was the increased scale of the enemy's harassing artillery fire since June. 'The enemy continued to shell [the] forward positions of the R22eR and the RCR comparatively heav[il]y,' the brigade war diarist commented on the 16th. 'It is interesting to note that neither the first battalion of the RCR nor the first battalion of the R22eR have previously been subjected to shelling on this scale before in Korea. They appear to be standing up to it extremely well.'[20] The Canadians could also take heart from the amount of fire the divisional artillery was able to return. For three days in midmonth, the gunners engaged in an artillery 'hate' against the Chinese positions. '1 RCHA went out of their way to make the enemy realize that our shelling capabilities were at least ten times greater than that of the enemy,' the brigade diarist noted with some satisfaction. 'The effort of 1 RCHA counter-bombardment was, to say the least, rather remarkable, as during the afternoon the enemy shelling was remarkably reduced. Under somewhat trying conditions, the infantry battalions have the height of morale and seem to be standing up to the rather aggressive enemy artillery fire extremely well. The division as a whole is proud of the brigade.'[21]

Since the Commonwealth brigade to their left was receiving the same enemy shell fire and had been in the line longer than the Canadians, the last comment may have been more firmly rooted in the 25th Brigade's view of their own stoutheartedness at surviving their first week and a half of artillery harassment rather than a true reflection of the division's attitude toward them. A favourable opinion of the Canadians' performance could not have been based on the cautious approach the 25th Brigade had adopted toward routine patrolling. Despite the fact that they were occupying a new sector of the front that was quite unfamiliar to them, the Canadians did not send out a single reconnaissance patrol in August to scout out approaches to enemy positions, old minefields, or wire entanglements in no man's land. In contrast, 1 RAR, the 28th Brigade battalion to the Canadians' immediate left, regularly covered its front with a mixture of reconnaissance, fighting, and ambush patrols.[22]

Just as in May and June, its failure to mount reconnaissance patrols prevented the 25th Brigade from establishing a picture of the enemy's routine – let alone determining the nature of the opposing positions. Until the end of August, the battalions sent out only passive standing patrols, occasionally described in the operations log as ambush or anti-infiltration patrols, 100 to 200 yards in front of their company positions. The farthest that the Canadians routinely penetrated into no man's land was a standing patrol 1 PPCLI frequently assigned to a long east-west ridge north of Hill 355, some 600 yards in front of its left forward company. Although the ridge, nicknamed Bunker Hill, lay 1,000 yards south of the main Chinese positions on Maryang-san and was unlikely to be permanently occupied, keeping it clear of enemy was 'of vital importance to this section of the front.'[23]

Having been assigned to the most secure battalion position within the Canadian brigade area, 1 PPCLI was well situated to patrol forward of its entrenchments in the wide no man's land that separated it from the enemy. Fortuitously located over 2,000 yards south of the main Chinese positions, where an inward bend of the Jamestown Line placed their right forward company 'behind and between B Company [in the centre company position] and the American battalion on our right,'[24] only two PPCLI companies actually faced the enemy. With its flanks well protected by Hill 355 to the left and the Americans to the right, the battalion had, in effect, two companies in reserve and available for patrolling. Despite this advantage, however, the unit's war diary described its August patrol policy 'as aggressive protective. Two standing or anti-infiltration patrols are established each night at the gates in the wire of [the forward] D and B Companies,'[25] in addition to the standing patrol that normally moved out to Bunker Hill at last light. The caution of these patrols meant that they were inevitably more protective than aggressive. There was little in the way of offensive action to drive the Chinese patrols back toward their own lines, even though on 11 August, two days after 1 PPCLI's return to the line, the enemy had been 'active all along the brigade front.' That night a forty-man enemy patrol had swept the Bunker Hill ridge, prompting the Patricia standing patrol located there to withdraw to its FDLs and call down artillery fire on the intruders.[26]

On 23 August, Lieutenant-Colonel Cameron held an orders group to inform his officers 'that the patrol policy for the battalion was becoming increasingly offensive. He outlined that the plan was to begin easily, close to home, with well placed ambush patrols progressing to more bold ventures in tactics and ultimately demanding the necessity of fighting patrols to probe known occupied enemy positions. A strong standing patrol of one [officer] and nine [men] will be maintained in the vicinity of Bunker Hill. This patrol will in the future act as a firm base for ambush and fighting patrols operating from it.'[27] Once again, however, Cameron's aggressive rhetoric was not matched by action. Three days later the unit's war diary recorded that the battalion's 'patrol activity was confined within our defensive wire.'[28]

By the last week of August, the continuing passivity of the Canadian brigade's patrol scheme – both 1 RCR and 1 R22eR were also mounting only standing and ambush parties close to their defensive wire – had apparently drawn the attention of Major-General Cassels. On the 27th, Cameron was summoned to brigade headquarters where the GOC's wishes were explained. On returning, the Patricia CO 'announced a change in the patrol policy. We were to go further afield until PWs are taken and we ascertain exactly the enemy dispositions on our front. It is emphasized, however, that PWs are the primary object.' The Patricias finally mounted their first ambush patrols on consecutive nights on 29-30 and 30-1 August on the western end of the Bunker Hill ridge, Cameron having explained that 'time will be spent there at first to feel our way out.'[29] The 1st Battalion officers still did not understand the importance of preliminary reconnaissance patrols to determine either the lay of the land or likely enemy patrol routes, and none were dispatched. In the absence of any detailed knowledge of the enemy's routine, it is not surprising that both ambush patrols returned with nothing to report.

Cassels had clearly been hoping for more determined action and finally ordered the Canadians to send out two fighting patrols for the night of 31 August-1 September. As the brigade diarist reported, 'The first two fighting patrols since the brigade moved into its position were provided by RCR and PPCLI' in response to the GOC's wishes.[30] Feeling their way out in the absence of previous reconnaissance, neither patrol made contact with the enemy, although the Patricia patrol 'suspected that the Italy feature [at the western end of the Bunker Hill ridge] is an enemy lay up position at times.'[31] The following night 1 PPCLI showed greater initiative by dispatching a nineteen-man ambush patrol to a spur some 500 yards north of Bunker Hill, its most northerly penetration to date, although still about 500 yards south of the Chinese positions. The ambush returned uneventfully with the standard 'nothing to report.' A second Patricia fighting patrol on the night of 4-5 September to the ridge west of Bunker Hill again returned without contacting the enemy.

The Royals also sent out fighting patrols on the nights of 2-3 and 6-7 September to probe no man's land north of Hill 227 but these, too, failed to find any Chinese. In fact, the only Canadian patrol to encounter the enemy was a Van Doo ambush party which was attacked by a large enemy patrol at 0400 hours on 6 September on the northeastern spur of Hill 159, soon after it left its own entrenchments. There was an exchange of fire as the Canadian patrol quickly withdrew back up the spur, missing one man.[32] The missing man, who proved to be the patrol leader, was found by a second Van Doo patrol sent out to look for him. Approaching the spot where the first patrol had been ambushed, they heard the missing Van Doo shout a warning that the Chinese were still in the area and immediately went to ground as the slopes erupted with small arms fire and grenade explosions. By the time the second Van Doo patrol got back to its entrenchments farther up the hill, it had lost four killed, five wounded, and one missing.[33]

The Chinese attack on the 1 R22eR ambush patrol was indicative of the increased enemy presence just beyond the 25th Brigade's wire defences. Unlike the Canadians, whose most aggressive patrols were the recent fighting patrols to the ridge north of Hill 355, the Chinese made nightly reconnaissances to investigate their opponent's positions, noting the location of Canadian standing patrols, cutting their wire entanglements, and scouting avenues of approach to their entrenchments. On 8 September the Royals reported that 'activity around the outposts was increased last night by a number of Chink patrols probing about,'[34] while the following night the Patricias noted that their own standing patrols 'reported that the enemy were throwing stones into the wire.'[35] 'This is not the first time the Chinaman has thrown stones,' brigade headquarters noted, 'presumably with the object of getting the outpost to give its positions away by firing and possibly to detract attention from wire cutting on the other side of the outpost. An "Enemy Probes" map was started in [brigade] Ops. The map will have marked on it the location and date of enemy probes into our FDLs and outposts over a period of two to four weeks. The purpose is to try to determine the general trend of enemy probes with the ultimate [goal] of foretelling where his next company or battalion sized attack will come.'[36]

Given the Canadian unwillingness to contest either the enemy's reconnaissance or fighting patrols, it is not surprising that the abilities of the Chinese patrollers soon came to be held in high regard. 'The enemy is most meticulous in his recces before a raid or an attack,' an envious Harry Pope observed in his June 1953 patrolling memorandum. 'Apparently all the [Chinese] commanders – up to regimental level – carry out lay-up recce patrols up to and behind the area to be attacked.' The Van Doo company commander's assessment of the relative effectiveness of Chinese and Canadian patrols also demonstrates one of the problems of the mass rotation of 25th Brigade units in the spring of 1952. With the departure of the 2nd battalion officers in April 1952, the Canadian brigade was left with little in-theatre experience and no idea of Rockingham's operational methods – even if the regulars had been willing to accept that the Special Force veterans might have had something to teach them. Having never seen the 2nd battalions in action himself, Pope was quite unaware that the Chinese practice he so greatly admired of making a thorough reconnaissance of the ground and defences prior to an operation had been routine Canadian procedure under Rockingham. With only his observations of 1st battalion methods to draw upon, Pope found a marked difference between Canadian and Chinese patrol standards. In his view, the professionalism of the enemy's reconnaissance carried over to his fighting and ambush patrols:

> He gets his information for aggressive action from his skilled recce patrols which NEVER make contact with us. However, when the enemy has decided on the time and place for his raid or ambush, he apparently always details at least a company for the job. Regardless of the size of the party he uses for his fighting patrol in the valley, he always has sufficient men standing by in the FDLs to bring his total force in the valley up to 100 to 150 men immediately contact is made. He never risks contact in the valley, that is he never sends out more than one to three men recce patrols, unless he has sufficient men of a well-trained reserve or patrol company standing by to ensure his retaining control of the battlefield once contact has been made ... For this purpose he does NOT use front-line troops for patrolling but instead uses specially trained patrol companies which are kept in the rear echelons until a fighting patrol is ordered. Even if he only sends a small ambush of 20 men into the valley he will keep the remainder of the patrol company standing by in the FDLs for instant action.[37]

A platoon commander recently posted to 1 PPCLI, Lieutenant Robert Peacock, shared Pope's respect of the enemy's patrolling abilities. Expressing a view that contrasts starkly with the Special Force's earlier belief in their superiority over the enemy, Peacock thought that Chinese 'movement was quiet and quick and they were expert at patrolling in small groups to find gaps between our companies. I was to learn later that they had special patrol companies at their regimental level which did the specialized reconnaissance and infiltration work but the average Chinese soldier was also a well trained and reliable soldier. When contact was made on patrol, the Chinese would all fire their weapons immediately and start a flanking movement which was obviously a drill which had been practised a number of times. Our training was weak in this area and we worked hard to develop the same immediate response to fire or ambush as the Chinese.'[38]

Conducting the second of the Patricias' two early-September fighting patrols, Peacock thought that his men were lucky to have escaped attack by the alert enemy patrollers. According to Peacock, the patrol 'was ordered by brigade HQ to capture a prisoner and dominate no man's land, a simple task until the problem was put in perspective. The enemy position where the action was to take place was some two thousand yards away [from his own company position] at the other end of a long ridge [Bunker Hill] with obstacles to lateral movement which kept any movement constrained to a predictable series of narrow trails. Another factor was that roughly the same patrol task had been done every night for almost a week with very little to show for it.' Although he was briefed by Cameron more than twenty-four hours before the patrol was to set out, allowing time for his men to test fire their weapons and get a good night's sleep, the results were predictable when Peacock led his platoon forward the following evening:

> Movement out was fast and quiet and we got to the firm base on schedule, paused briefly to do last minute orientation to the ground and moved forward. We had not gone too far when we ran into some unexpected wire obstacles which severely limited our movement. These wire obstacles had not been spotted by our OPs, or our own personal observations, nor had they been reported on by recent patrols which had been in the area. At the same time word came from the north flank of the patrol that there was a lot of enemy movement on the north flank. The enemy were heading to the area where our firm base was established. We warned the other platoon by radio and I recognized that we were no longer the hunter but had become the hunted. We called in artillery fire on the area where we judged the enemy would be and pressed forward to the objective only to find the position was empty. After a sweep of the position we made a quick withdrawal and regrouped to start our return journey. It now became obvious that we were almost cut off and would have to fight our way through a superior force if we retraced our steps as planned. At this point I ordered a change in direction and we worked our way to the south across what was supposed to be a minefield and, after some problems of identification, came into our lines through the RCR, avoiding the Chinese ambush ... To us it was another patrol from which we emerged unscathed by good luck and great teamwork.[39]

The ground north of Hill 355, as photographed from the 1 PPCLI forward positions by Lt. Robert Peacock in October 1952. The Chinese-held Hill 317 is in the centre background, nearly two miles to the north, while Hill 355 is out of view over the photographer's left shoulder. Robert S. Peacock collection

Simply escaping disaster should not, however, have been the main purpose of the patrol. Had the Patricias spent the last three weeks of August sending out preliminary recce patrols to gain confidence and familiarize themselves with various routes along the Bunker Hill ridge, Peacock's men would not have encountered 'unexpected wire obstacles which severely limited our movement.' As it was, the Canadians' fighting patrols were likely to make contact only with those enemy parties that chose to engage them and stood very little chance of ambushing the small Chinese reconnaissance parties – who undoubtedly knew exactly where all of the wire obstacles were located – ranging skilfully across no man's land. Reflecting on his experiences with 1 PPCLI forty years later, Peacock remained vaguely uneasy about the Canadian brigade's 'sit tight' attitude to defence. Although he claimed – rather dubiously – that 'what we were doing was workable for this theatre of war under these particular conditions,' he was realistic enough to caution that it 'should not be taken as gospel for use in future doctrine and training.' More to the point, he had to admit that 'the worst never happened to our company but I felt we were learning bad lessons about how a defence should be conducted.'[40]

In a surprisingly candid entry, the Patricia war diarist also explained some of their patrol problems in the wake of the failed series of fighting patrols during the first week of September:

> A word or two on the conduct of our patrols may be in order here. The majority of them have been carried out with despatch and deliberation, however, there have been a few [which], if through ignorance or contempt, broke all the rules of good patrolling. Members of a fighting patrol were seen to go out wearing trousers which due to regular scrubbing and washing, were bleached almost white. Ambush members were seen to light cigarettes and smoke them out in no man's land. Another night, members of the patrol were boisterous and jocular whilst proceeding to a position at the foot of a suspected enemy position. With no stretch of the imagination can we expect patrols conducted in this manner to succeed.
>
> To continue on this same trend, patrol leaders (on more than one occasion) took it on themselves to change their routes without first notifying the patrol master. Some patrol commanders have failed to report by wireless or telephone when they have crossed or arrived at a report line. To relate one incident, a patrol reported it was returning. Prior to this we had no report of its progress after it had left the FDLs. Neither the firm base nor the patrol master had any idea of the patrol situation until after the objective had been reached, exploited, and the patrol assembled for the return trip. It would pose somewhat of a problem if supporting fire was necessary to extricate the patrol from a superior enemy force.[41]

Given these shortcomings, it was just as well that none of the Patricia patrols came to grips with the enemy. Despite Lieutenant-Colonel Cameron's bold pronouncement that his battalion was to go 'further afield until PWs are taken,' 1 PPCLI soon retreated back to the relative safety of its own entrenchments. Although it came only a week after Cameron's announcement of a new aggressive patrol policy, Peacock's fighting patrol of 4-5 September was the last such operation mounted by the Patricias for the remainder of the month. The brigade's patrol task tables, moreover, list just ten Patricia ambush patrols during all of September, with only one moving farther afield than the Bunker Hill ridge. There were, of course, no reconnaissance patrols.[42] On 11 September, the unit's diary records that 'it was decided tonight to postpone heavy patrolling for the next few nights' without stating why the decision was taken or why a mere two fighting patrols over a one-month period – neither of which contacted the enemy – would be considered 'heavy.'[43]

One week after that decision was taken, the battalion on the Patricias' right, the 3rd Battalion, 65th US Regiment, engaged in a fight with the Chinese for control of a company outpost named Kelly. In the words of the American official history, the Chinese were 'probing for soft spots in the UNC lines' and appeared to have found one when they overran the American outpost position. After a week of heavy fighting in which the 3rd Battalion failed to demonstrate the required offensive dash needed to eject the stubborn Chinese defenders, despite suffering 350 casualties, the American divisional commander decided to call off the attempted recapture of the Kelly position.[44] Whether or not the fighting on their right flank influenced the Canadians, 1 PPCLI limited its activities to standing patrols only. Two other Patricia fighting patrols planned for month's end were cancelled 'because of expected enemy activity against the RCR,' even though the presence of the enemy on its flanks might suggest the need for more – not fewer – patrols. For most of September, therefore, 1 PPCLI was content to keep to four standing patrols immediately in front of its wire.[45]

The Patricias' relative inactivity was matched by the performance of the understrength 1 R22eR on the hills south of Kowang-san. By early September, a shortfall in French Canadian recruits had reduced the Van Doos' total strength to 687, some 250 soldiers below establishment. As a result, the battalion's A Company was disbanded and its men redistributed among the remaining three rifle companies while 1 RCR formed a composite E Company of men from its rifle companies and echelons to take over the Van Doo position on the spur running south from its own left forward company.[46] With the redistribution, 1 R22eR was left to hold the three company positions on the Hill 159-Hill 210 ridge with reasonably full-strength companies. Even so, however, Lieutenant-Colonel Trudeau was unwilling to mount any patrols into no man's land, restricting the battalion's activities to passive standing and ambush patrols on the lower slopes of the Van Doos' own hills.[47] Undoubtedly recalling his own battalion's poor performance, Major Pope believed that the 25th Brigade's lack of success was linked to the Canadians' unimaginative employment of their outposts, the three- to ten-men detachments that were sent out each night to occupy secondary features or minefield gaps and provide warning of the enemy's approach. According to Pope, the 'exact positions [of the Canadian standing patrols] became well marked not only by the telephone lines leading to them but also by the quantity of empty tins of self-heating soup and the occasional beer bottle surrounding them ... Their sole chance of carrying out their object of giving early warning of the approach of the enemy without being destroyed themselves lay in the enemy not knowing where they were. But because of their rigid employment the enemy always knew where they were.'[48]

Pope's criticism was equally valid for 1 RCR, which deployed the same nine standing patrols to the lower slopes of Hill 355 night after night throughout August and September, even naming their rigid outpost positions Calgary, Winnipeg, Vancouver, and so on (see Map 15, p. 307). The RCR standing patrols were listed in the patrol task tables as 'permanent,' including the Vancouver outpost on the saddle between Hills 227 and 355 that was normally manned by an NCO and fourteen men. Not surprisingly, the Chinese were soon well aware of the exact location of the Canadian standing patrols and could easily avoid them in approaching the RCR entrenchments. A typical contact was made on the night of 6-7 September when 'four small groups of enemy were reported moving between Calgary and Vancouver outposts. The enemy exchanged grenades with the outpost, and mortar fire was brought down – movement ceased. When Calgary outpost withdrew this morning, they discovered one dead enemy. Between 0100-0200 hours, ten to fifteen enemy surrounded [another] outpost [farther south]. Enemy apparently recce'd area and withdrew. No exchange of fire.'[49]

Much of the standing patrols' task of reporting enemy movement could have been accomplished by nightly reconnaissance patrols that moved about no man's land, just as Rockingham's men had done throughout their tour on the Jamestown Line. In the case of the 1st battalions, however, Pope found that on the rare occasions that the Canadians did attempt a reconnaissance, it was 'usually inadequate, rarely, if ever, penetrating behind or even up to the enemy position selected for attack. Little use was made of the lay-up recce [in which a patrol would spend a day or two in a concealed position observing the enemy], and those that were made were not deep enough. It was unusual for the officer selected to lead a fighting patrol to be allowed to do the preliminary recces.' Their absence 'always caused us to attack straight from the front ... Without exception all our raids have failed.'[50] But even Pope does not appear to have appreciated the extent to which reconnaissance patrols of any sort were absent from all three 1st battalion task tables.

Without a reconnaissance on which to base their plans, the 1st battalions' fighting patrols were similarly futile exercises, typically ordered 'to sweep an area in search of the enemy and then to engage him.' Canadian ambush patrols, normally consisting of a lieutenant or NCO and five to twenty men, suffered from an equally serious lack of information: 'The schedule called for ambush patrols and so they were duly sent out to places where it would be most convenient for us for the enemy to pass. Rarely was provision ever made to reinforce the ambushes should they have accomplished their object, that is, of ambushing the enemy ... The company commanders concerned were simply quite incapable of reinforcing their ambushes adequately without denuding the entire company position – an impossible risk. So on the rare occasions when our ambushes did fire first, the initiative quickly passed to the enemy who alone had the power of quick reinforcement.'[51]

All of the Canadian ambushes during August-October were sent out without the benefit of an earlier reconnaissance patrol to establish the enemy's routine and likely avenues of approach. Although many of these ambushes were sent to identical locations several nights in a row and would, as a result, gain some limited local knowledge, their chances of success were exceedingly small. As during the May-June period in the line, the location for an ambush was selected by the battalion commander based on his limited view of the ground from a hilltop observation post and his ability to read a map. Given that most of the ambushes during this period were set up near or slightly in front of the standing patrol locations, the difference between the two was usually more a matter of semantics than tactics.

During the last three weeks of September, the 25th Brigade once again limited its patrols to its routine standing and ambush patrols, despite the almost nightly presence of small groups of Chinese lurking around – and often cutting – the Canadians' wire entanglements. The stealth and thoroughness of the enemy patrollers also allowed them to clear paths through the brigade's minefields. When two mines were set off in front of 1 PPCLI's B Company on the night of 13-14 September, an examination the next morning discovered that it had not been an accident: 'Two holes in [the] minefield itself' were found with 'two paths ... leading to the holes.

No drag marks [are] visible indicating that no casualties were dragged out but rather that the trip wire was pulled from a distance.'[52]

Since the front had reached the Jamestown Line in October 1951, it had been standard UN practice to lay extensive minefields, and the Commonwealth Division was no exception. Between November 1951 and October 1952, when minelaying was finally curtailed, the division's engineers laid more than 56,000 mines covering over 100,000 yards of terrain, the vast majority in trip-wire minefields.[53] As late as September 1952 the 23rd Field Squadron had laid a 500-yard-long mine belt over rugged terrain immediately north of the 1 R22eR company position on Hill 159.[54]

By the end of 1952, the Commonwealth engineers were questioning the wisdom of having laid so many minefields across their front. In December the commander, Royal Engineers, estimated that the division's trip-wire minefields remained only 15 percent effective. The CRE felt that the engineers would have laid fewer mines if they had known how the war was going to develop. The extent of the mined terrain meant that there were some 140 miles of minefield fence that had to be regularly maintained in no man's land and a farther 100 miles of fence in the division's reserve areas. Originally intended to slow down an attack and provide time for the defensive fire tasks to defeat it, the minefields had been rendered largely ineffective by the Chinese skill in reconnaissance. Indeed, the division's limited access to the valley through the minefield gaps was a tactical liability. Their entrances and exits were well known to the Chinese patrols, who could lay down mortar fire on those gaps they suspected a returning Commonwealth patrol might use. Moreover, the minefields themselves were proving as deadly to friendly troops as they were to the enemy. To the CRE it seemed as though the Chinese could walk unscathed through almost any minefield while Commonwealth soldiers had only to step across the perimeter fence to set off a mine, an impression borne out by the statistics. Between August 1951 and October 1952, casualties to Commonwealth personnel from the division's own minefields totalled fifty-one killed and eighty-one wounded, while known enemy mine casualties amounted to only twenty killed, although the actual total must have been higher. The CRE's intelligence section estimated that at least twenty casualties would be incurred in any attempt to lift the majority of the trip-wire fields; the only other solution – pulling the division back to virgin soil – was clearly not an option.[55]

The continuing aggressiveness of the Chinese during September produced only a cautious response from the Canadians. Although the enemy probes often threw stones at their standing patrols, at times with sufficient accuracy to hit individual soldiers, the brigade relied almost exclusively on artillery and mortar fire to drive off the intruders.[56] In fact, the only battalion to undertake any offensive action during the last three weeks of September was 1 RCR, holding the western slopes of Hill 355. On the night of the 16-17th, a twenty-one man RCR fighting patrol ventured toward Hill 227 in search of a prisoner. The Canadians had little knowledge of the

Chinese dispositions, having made no earlier reconnaissance, and limited their penetration to the no man's land at the northern base of the hill, well below the Chinese entrenchments. Not surprisingly, they did not make any contact and returned with the usual 'nothing to report.'[57]

The value of prior reconnaissance was brilliantly demonstrated the following week, however, when an RCR lieutenant pulled off a well-executed prisoner snatch during a daylight raid northwest of Hill 227. It is noteworthy that the patrol's commander, Lieutenant H.R. Gardner, was the first 1 RCR officer sent to Korea, having joined 2 RCR's C Company in February 1952.[58] While attached to the 2nd Battalion, Gardner had a month and a half to observe how the Special Force veterans conducted operations. Unfortunately, Gardner had been wounded during the 26 March Chinese attack and did not rejoin his regular battalion until 26 August, when he assumed command of B Company's 6 Platoon.[59] Even so, the young lieutenant had obviously not forgotten his experience with 2 RCR. Gardner had been back with his battalion for barely two weeks when, apparently on his own initiative, he took one of his corporals with him to make a forty-eight hour lay-up reconnaissance of the Chinese positions from 9 to 11 September. The two Canadians observed the enemy from the Kipon'gol ridge some 1,300 yards northwest of Hill 227 (see Map 11, p. 154). From their concealed location, Gardner and Cpl. K.E. Fowler made notes on the enemy's activity around a field kitchen on the northern slope of the Hill 227 hill mass, some 800 yards to their south.

With first-hand intelligence of the enemy's routine to guide his planning, Gardner devised a daring scheme to capture a Chinese soldier in a dawn raid. Departing the Winnipeg outpost at 0247 hours on 24 September, the RCR lieutenant led a six-man patrol back to the kitchen area on the northwest slope of Hill 227 (see Map 15, p. 307). Positioning three of his men as a firm base along his intended line of retreat, Gardner, Corporal Fowler, and Private Moody proceeded to an enemy bunker they had noted during the earlier patrol. In Gardner's words, the three Royals 'found the bunker to be unoccupied and apparently of little importance. Before, on the layup, we had noticed people coming to and from this bunker quite frequently. We still haven't determined what use the bunker is there. It has two entrances. I covered Corporal Fowler while he went in one door and out the other.'[60]

With their hope of capturing a prisoner at the bunker dashed, the three Canadians shifted their attention to the field kitchen, where they 'could hear and occasionally see people in the kitchen area ... Meanwhile it was getting lighter and lighter. At approximately 0610 hours, I said "to hell with it." Corporal Fowler and I strolled over to the communication trench at the foot of the kitchen area, leaving Private Moody as a secondary firm base. We entered the communication trench which proved to be a dried out creek bed.' Proceeding along the creek bed, they eventually spotted a telephone line, which they broke before concealing themselves in the undergrowth to await developments. According to Gardner's report,

> within five minutes our present prisoner doubled down from [Hill] 198 going in a southerly direction along the path past us and up to the kitchen area, supposedly doing a rough check of the line. His only weapon was a pair of pliers. He went part way up the hill and cried out to friends of his in the kitchen area. He returned almost immediately, this time checking the wire carefully. In order to do so he had to come to our place of concealment. He noticed the break in the wire. As he turned to examine it I hit him on the head with my blackjack. Immediately Corporal Fowler leaped up and pinned his arms. He was crying out loudly by this time so I struck him again and again. He refused to be silenced or pass out.
>
> Corporal Fowler was still holding his arms and I stuffed a handkerchief into the Chinaman's mouth, trying to poke the gag down with the big end of the blackjack. In the struggle he succeeded in spitting the gag out and crying out again. I struck him again and again with the blackjack. Then I succeeded in getting the gag back into his mouth and tried to tie it in with a shoelace. At this point we succeeded in tying his hands. Again he spit the gag out. When I forced it back in he bit my thumb. He spit it out again so Corporal Fowler struck him on the head with his pistol and I hit him on the jaw with my gun butt, still trying to silence him. I believe this pacified him somewhat because he ceased struggling and when we threatened to shoot him he made a gesture of submission.
>
> This struggle had gone on for some time and as there were hostiles within 75 yards who could easily hear his cries we felt that it was no place for us. We succeeded in getting him to take the gag voluntarily and allow us to tie it in place. We got him to his feet just as the first two armed Chinamen were coming down from the kitchen area. We got about 25 or 30 yards on the way back when we were fired on by burp [guns] from 30 yards range. We were fairly well concealed by the deep creek bed. Private Moody, meanwhile, had started to pull back, firing as he did so, I turned and fired a couple of bursts also which slowed down the pursuit somewhat. I called to Moody to get back to the firm base. We followed the creek bed as far as was feasible, being under fire all the time from at least two burp guns, rifles with the pursuers and LMGs [light machine-guns] on the hills. Corporal Fowler was prodding the PW along with his pistol and I was watching our rear and also picking a route out.
>
> When we left the creek bed the fire was much more intense, one rifleman coming very close. By this time our firm base was delivering very good fire which stopped the pursuers but not the firing. The firm base fire killed one Chinaman for certain and possibly wounded two. We, after crossing the open paddy, found another creek about hip deep which gave us excellent cover to right in behind our firm base. We proceeded some 200 yards homeward and I called to the firm base to pull back. They acknowledged. Our route back was the same as our route out.[61]

For carrying out such a daring and well-planned patrol, Gardner and Fowler were awarded, respectively, the Military Cross and Military Medal.[62] It seems unfortunate that the young RCR lieutenant did not receive a promotion as well, since he was one of the very few 1st battalion officers who understood how such operations should be conducted.

Despite having clearly demonstrated the benefits of making a proper reconnaissance before a raid, Gardner's success had absolutely no impact on subsequent Canadian patrols. Four nights later the Royals reverted to form in dispatching yet another large fighting patrol around the northern slopes of Hill 227 to attempt the capture of a second prisoner. This time the patrol's objective was some 600 yards closer to the feature's summit and nearer the Chinese entrenchments than the more isolated kitchen area to the northwest that Gardner had selected for his successful snatch operation. Once again, the Canadians did not carry out any reconnaissance patrols to scout out avenues of approach or the actual enemy positions prior to sending the raiders stumbling off in the dark. Planning was based solely on what could be deduced from examining a map. According to the patrol commander, Lt. Dan Loomis, the objective 'was thought to be an outpost' but 'higher headquarters wanted to find out exactly what was on the top of the feature.' Moving against an alert enemy, whose own vigorous patrolling allowed it to chose when and where to engage any Canadians that dared approach them, the result of the fighting patrol was as predictable as it was futile:

> As we climbed up Hill 227, my patrol went through rows of old rusted barbed wire – at night this is not easy – and when we stopped we heard rustling in the brush behind us. The Chinese were moving in and setting an ambush on the path we had used and would be waiting for our return. This was hairy, in that other possible withdrawal routes were through old British minefields. I dropped off half my patrol of twenty-two soldiers to form a firm base on a small ridge to provide direct fire support as we advanced to the top. Some fifty paces further I heard many clicks as heavy weapons were cocked. This was no outpost.
>
> We looked up the hill and could see heads silhouetted against the moonlit sky looking down on us. A vicious firefight began with weapons firing, grenades being thrown, a lot of noise and people being hit. Everyone in my entire assault group was wounded. We were in a jam.
>
> We could not have got away but for one Strathcona tank. It had been previously laid [aimed] on one of the suspected Chinese positions near the top of the hill, which turned out to be a heavy machine-gun that had pinned us down by its fire from its pit about thirty yards off our left flank. [The tank] got the machine-gun with its first round! We took out its mate providing crossfire from the right with a well-thrown phosphorous grenade. At the time we were barely ten paces away from the central Chinese fire position, but we were below them on the steep hillside. They mostly shot over us. While we could see them, luckily they could not see us. With some of the Chinese heavy weapons destroyed under a hail of fire from our firm base, we were able to withdraw after fifteen minutes. With my assault group wounded we still faced a serious situation. We were still deep in no man's land and a long way from home.

> Major Don Holmes was patrol master that night. [He] had taken up a position to direct the patrol from a forward company observation post. He ordered us to withdraw and coordinated the covering fire. Salvoes of artillery hammered the Chinese as we went down the side of the hill through ancient British minefields. With nearly half the patrol tied up carrying two wounded and assisting others, we stole single file through rows of old barbed wire and minefields churned up by previous artillery bombardments and, amazingly, never set off a single mine. The barbed wire was a real obstacle. The teams carrying the badly wounded in ponchos kept getting caught in it. However, we surprised the Chinese by taking a different route and managed to slip away. The artillery fired on targets where I thought Chinese had established their ambush position on our inbound track. Finally we made it across the valley and back to our own trenches on Hill 355.[63]

With their own patrols roaming freely over no man's land, the Chinese had probably been aware of the approaching RCR patrol soon after it left its own lines. As was so often the case with the 25th Brigade's fighting patrols, the only soldiers in danger of being captured were the raiders themselves.

Not only did the Canadians disregard the example of Gardner's well-executed raid but they also ignored the patrol tactics of the Australian battalions to their left. Like the Canadian 1st battalions, the 1st Battalion, Royal Australian Regiment had recently arrived in Korea, having joined 3 RAR in the Commonwealth Division in March 1952. With the addition of a second Australian unit to the 28th Brigade, command of the formation, which still included two British battalions, was handed to an Australian officer, Brig. Thomas J. Daly, in June.[64] Facing the same tactical problem as the Canadians – i.e., an aggressive enemy that was now willing to contest control of no man's land – Daly opted for a more vigorous response. The Australian brigade commander 'had learned this style of warfare from Lieutenant-General [L.J.] Morshead while a brigade major in the siege of Tobruk' during the Second World War.[65] Demonstrating the wide latitude division headquarters allowed each brigade in conducting defensive operations, Daly directed the 28th Brigade to carry out a more intense patrol scheme than Canadian officers were willing to implement. As their official history explains,

> When Australian troops first occupied a new position in the line, they undertook a series of familiarisation patrols, so that they came to know the terrain, the barbed-wire obstacles and the minefields in front of their defences intimately. They then fought for domination of the approaches to their positions before attempting to force the enemy's patrols back into their own defences, thereby giving the Australians dominance over no man's land. These activities, together with the need to maintain and strengthen the defences in the line, taxed the manpower resources of all units heavily. Patrols were particularly exhausting. They did not cover great distances, usually no more than several kilometres, but the exertion of fighting and the rigours of the climate made heavy

> demands on all patrol members. All patrols could call for artillery fire support and for assistance from other patrols of their own unit or from stand-by forces within the line ... Care also had to be taken that patrols did not set a regular pattern of activity so that the enemy could predict their routes and set ambushes accordingly.[66]

Holding the battalion position immediately south of the Van Doos, 1 RAR maintained a regular program of ambush and fighting patrols throughout August. For instance, during the first three weeks of September (at which point they were relieved in the line), the Australian battalion sent out twenty-seven fighting and twenty-eight ambush patrols to cover its front along the stream in the middle of the Nabu-ri valley. The RCR totals for the entire month – six fighting patrols, including Gardner's successful 'snatch' operation, and four ambush patrols – compare poorly with the Australian effort, and 1 RCR was the most active of the Canadian battalions. The Patricias mounted only two fighting and ten ambush patrols during the month, none of them successful, while the Van Doos confined themselves to what amounted to standing patrols only (several of their nightly standing patrols were described as 'ambush' in the operations log although positioned on the lower slopes of Hill 159 only a few hundred yards forward of their FDLs).[67]

On the other hand, 1 RAR mounted ambushes, often two per night, along the Nabu-ri creek bed that divided no man's land, and much of the time these thirteen-man ambushes were supported by an eleven-man fighting patrol waiting nearby to come to their aid in the event of a clash. The fighting patrols were also used to sweep down the enemy side of the Nabu-ri stream to flush out Chinese patrollers and drive them into one of the ambush patrols. These tactics led to a successful ambush on the night of 13-14 September when one of the fighting patrols captured a prisoner, the first to be taken by 1 RAR. The more experienced 3 RAR, occupying the battalion position immediately south of 1 RAR, had also captured a prisoner during a patrol clash earlier in September. Like Gardner, the Australian battalions made use of lay-up patrols in the Chinese-occupied hills across the valley to more closely observe the enemy's activities.[68]

For most of 1952, each Australian battalion sent out from one to three fighting patrols each night to cover its front. By early 1953 their nightly totals had increased so that

> up to six fighting patrols of about sixteen men (occasionally up to thirty), and one or two ambush patrols of ten men, ranged deeply into no man's land in front of each Australian battalion to lie in wait for enemy patrols, endeavouring meanwhile not to be ambushed themselves by the many Chinese groups who were on the same mission ... Normally, two or three reconnaissance patrols of four men were each night stationed to cover the areas between the larger patrols, providing warning of any enemy attacks or movement. Usually over sixty-five men were out on patrol at night and when the weather became colder and patrols could not stay out long, many more reconnaissance

> patrols had to be sent out to ensure coverage of the approaches throughout the hours of darkness.[69]

Numbers alone, however, do not provide the only contrast between Australian and Canadian practice, as both the preparation and execution of Australian patrols also appear to have been more thorough. Australians occupying a new position were urged 'to have all members of the unit familiarise themselves with the ground in their vicinity' by patrolling to standing positions, mine gaps, and around the perimeter fences of minefields. Battalion commanders were instructed to plan their patrols one week ahead and submit their 'patrol forecast to brigade headquarters where they are checked and marked on the master patrol map to ensure that there is complete coverage of the brigade front.'[70] The patrol commanders were then briefed as to the nature, route, and timing of their patrols at least forty-eight hours in advance in order to allow them 'to warn members of [their] patrol, to arrange that they have a good night's rest on the night prior to the patrol, to prepare equipment and to study the ground, particularly in darkness, over which they will pass.' Detailed briefings using aerial photographs, sand tables, or earth landscape models were conducted on the day of the patrol, it being 'essential that at the end of [the briefing] the company commander knows exactly what the patrol commander intends to do.' Thereafter,

> the company commander, the patrol commander and his NCOs should visit observation posts and discuss the patrols in relation to the actual ground. The patrol commander must always call his men together and fully explain the object of the patrol to ensure that every man fully understands the importance of it. If this is not done the patrol becomes pointless from the soldier's point of view. Patrolling merely for the sake of patrolling is a needless sacrifice of human life. It is advisable to discuss and lay down definite plans of action to cover certain varying situations which might occur, but such plans must be kept to bare essentials as too much detail will confuse members of the patrol. It is well to remember that the soldier can often offer some very sound suggestions which may greatly assist in arriving at a workable plan ... After the reconnaissance has been carried out, and the plan is known to all, a rehearsal should be carried out on a piece of ground similar to that over which the patrol will operate ... The wireless operator must be the most thoroughly briefed man in the patrol. He must also be of higher mental calibre than most of the others. He should at all times keep his headset over his ears and should never leave the side of the patrol commander.[71]

These Australian patrol methods were eventually summarized in a 28th Brigade memorandum, 'Notes on Patrolling in Korea,' issued in April 1953. When passed to the Canadian brigade major later that month, Maj. T.M. MacDonald forwarded them to the incoming commander, Brig. Jean Allard, with the endorsement that it was 'a worthwhile resume of patrolling. Suggest we give a copy to each of your battalions.' The notes provide a sharp contrast to the inadequate patrols conducted by the Canadians during Bogert's tenure, particularly the aggressive Australian approach laid out in the memorandum's introduction:

> During the last twelve months the major activity in 1 Commonwealth Division has been patrolling. For this reason the [28th] Brigade has had ample opportunity to learn a great deal about this important part of warfare. It has learnt the importance of dominating the ground between opposing forward defended localities and how, by so doing, enemy patrols have been gradually forced back to the vicinity of his own positions. As a result, enemy forces of any size have been unable to move without our receiving ample warning.
>
> In the line, our battalions sometimes provide an average of two fighting patrols and three to four reconnaissance patrols each night over long periods. In addition, there have been up to twelve standing patrols along a battalion front throughout the hours of darkness ...
>
> A close study of past patrol actions has shown that aggressive action 'pays-off' every time. By taking such action casualties have been avoided and the enemy has been thrown off balance.[72]

Inevitably, of course, the 28th Brigade's aggressive approach did produce casualties, and its wisdom was questioned by Australian army headquarters in early 1953. Daly justified his policy 'by pointing out that far heavier casualties could have been suffered had the Chinese been allowed to get close enough to the 28th Brigade positions to mount a major attack.'[73] The Australian brigadier's contention is borne out by comparing the casualties suffered by the Canadian brigade with those of the Commonwealth Division as a whole over the period from 1 June to 12 November 1952. Despite providing 33 percent of the division's front-line strength during the period (sixteen weeks in the line and eight in reserve), the 25th Brigade suffered 43 percent of the division's killed and wounded (83 of 191 fatalities and 344 of 803 wounded) and 59 percent of the division's missing (twenty-three of thirty-nine).[74] This was in spite of the timid Canadian practice of sending only a small fraction of its patrols into no man's land forward of its outposts. In justifying his patrol casualties to Canberra, Daly pointed to a US regiment that had relieved the Australians on Hill 355, explaining that they had not patrolled aggressively and within days had had a complete company overrun in a surprise attack that resulted in some 200 casualties.[75] Although he chose not to, Daly could just as easily have used the Chinese attack on B Company, 1 RCR, on the night of 23-4 October 1952 to illustrate his point.

Despite the increased Chinese presence in no man's land and the fact that the RCR positions on Hill 355's western slope were only some 700 to 800 yards from those of the enemy on Hill 227, the Canadians reduced their patrol activity even further during October. For the first eleven nights of the month, 1 RCR did not venture into no man's land beyond sending out the usual standing patrols immediately forward of its wire. Indeed, one of only two offensive patrols conducted by anyone in the Canadian brigade during that period was an uneventful 1 R22eR fighting patrol to the village of Un-gol at the foot of Hill 227 on the night of the 9-10th. However, by early October the Chinese were clearly applying pressure on the RCR positions on the northwest slope of Hill 355, routinely maintaining a harassing fire of approximately 150 shells and mortar bombs daily on the battalion's forward companies (Map 15).

On the morning of 1 October, some 150 rounds fell on the exposed left-forward company position nearest Hill 227 – the one that B Company would occupy on 23-4 October. That same afternoon an intense bombardment of over 400 rounds destroyed the Vancouver outpost on the saddle of ground midway between the left-forward company and the enemy defences on 227. The bombardment killed six Royals and wounded six others, and the outpost was abandoned to the enemy. Throughout the day some 800 shells and mortar rounds fell in the brigade area, 'the greatest number of shells since records [were] started on 1 January 1952,' the brigade diarist reported. 'They were all on A, C and E Companies, RCR ... This appeared to be in preparation for an attack. It was expected that the Chinese would go for Hill 355 tonight.'[76] The anticipated attack never materialized, but a 'severe shelling' the following day, mostly on the left-forward company, killed three more Royals, wounded five, and caused the evacuation of three others with battle exhaustion. A 122 mm shell also struck a glancing blow on the sole remaining Sherman tank positioned on the western slope of the feature. The shell 'buckled the side of the turret and killed Trooper Waldner' and prompted the withdrawal of the damaged tank.[77] Having formed a fifth rifle company to replace one from the undermanned 1 R22eR, 1 RCR still remained well up to strength despite the shelling, with over 1,000 all ranks reported available for duty on 7 October. Following the bombardments of 1-2 October, however, the volume of enemy fire returned to normal across the entire brigade front for the next two weeks.[78]

Although the RCR's wire was 'continually being probed by small numbers of enemy' and an enemy attack was expected at any time, Lieutenant-Colonel Bingham proceeded on leave on 11 October, turning his battalion over to his second-in-command, Maj. F. Klevanic.[79] The Royals undertook their first offensive operation of the month when Klevanic sent an entire company to raid Hill 227 on the night of 12-13 October. While the brigade's war diarist described its outcome as 'a bit of bad luck,' the raid once again demonstrated the overwhelming advantage that their domination of no man's land gave the Chinese whenever the Canadians ventured out of their entrenchments. Ordered to 'attack and seize Point 227,' the B Company commander, Maj. E. Cohen, set out from the Calgary outpost northeast of the objective with his 4 Platoon leading in single file with two scouts on the point. No. 4 Platoon was followed by Company Headquarters and 5 Platoon while the remaining 6 Platoon was stationed at the Edmonton outpost in support. The raiders had

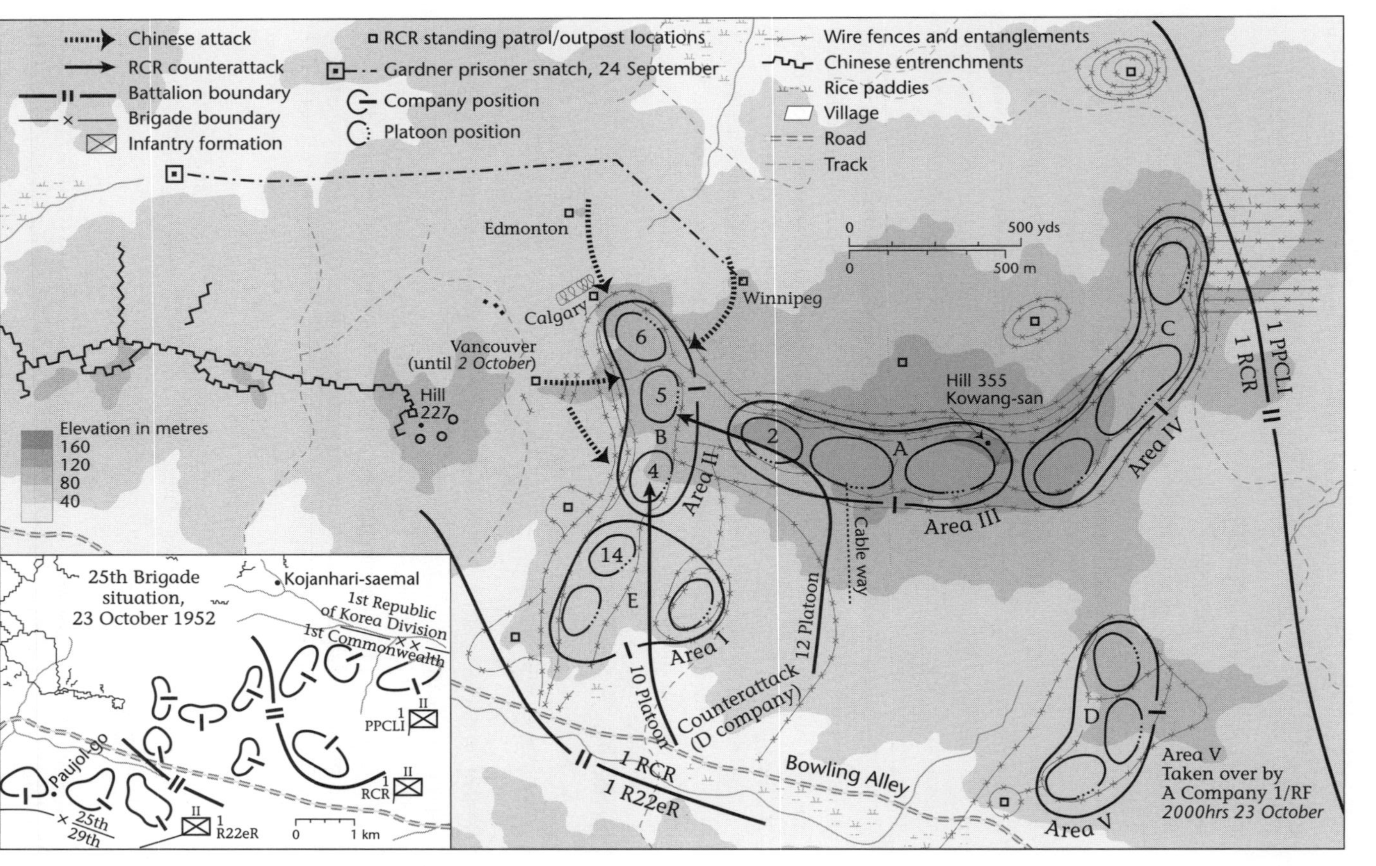

Map 15 *Attack on B Company, 1 RCR, 23 October 1952*

proceeded only 100 yards northwest of the Calgary outpost – and were over 600 yards short of their objective – when they met an ambush:

> This ambush was apparently well-planned and co-ordinated. It consisted of a reinforced enemy platoon sited on ground which was advantageous to the enemy. The ambush was in the form of a U, or three sided box, and well-armed with burp guns, at least one LMG and grenades. In addition, the enemy called a mortar DF into the centre of this U. The two scouts were immediately wounded and no more was seen of them.
>
> The platoon commander [of 4 Platoon, Lt. S. MacDonald] found he was out of wireless contact with the company commander and having sited his group to the best advantage reported to the company commander. He then returned to the leading element.
>
> The company commander immediately put out flanking Bren groups, reported to the co-ordinating group and overcame the temporary confusion. He ordered No. 5 Platoon commander and one section to attempt a right flanking movement.
>
> No 4 Platoon commander, on his return to the leading element, found the enemy to be on his immediate front, on high ground to his left and at the top of a reverse slope to the right. About this time MMGs from Point 227 [600 yards to the southwest] joined in the fire-fight. Approximately 50 per cent of his group was by now wounded.
>
> No 5 Platoon commander's attempt to outflank the ambushing force was unsuccessful owing to the darkness, confusion and lack of suitable ground for manoeuvre.
>
> The company commander had, by this time, called for DFs ... He received very satisfactory close artillery support ... He ordered Nos. 4 and 5 Platoons to withdraw [to the northeast].
>
> As No. 4 Platoon withdrew, it found itself closely followed by enemy small arms fire and grenades. Enemy mortars continued to fall in the area. This fire effectively prevented attempts to recover the two wounded scouts. This withdrawal was gradual and orderly. At this point two green flares were sent up by the enemy and the enemy gradually broke contact ...
>
> On reaching [a position 200 yards north of the Calgary outpost] the company reorganized ... No 5 Platoon commander volunteered to take a small group back to the scene of the fire-fight and recover the two missing scouts ... [They] carried out a thorough search of the area, moving well forward of the ambush area and to the right and left of the route out. A Bren gun and rifle were recovered. The missing men were not found. No further contact with the enemy was made ...
>
> The company commander ordered the withdrawal of No 5 Platoon and directed No 6 Platoon to cover the withdrawal of this group and Company Headquarters. The whole returned to our lines without further incident.[80]

This abortive raid cost the Royals the two scouts killed and ten others wounded. In addition, the Vancouver outpost had been reoccupied for the operation, and the Chinese took the opportunity to mortar the well-known position, killing another three Royals and wounding five others. What was particularly foreboding about the failed sortie was the fact that the enemy had been able to set up a well-planned ambush so close to the Canadian positions. Since the leading 4 Platoon had moved only 100 yards beyond the Calgary outpost when they were hit from three sides, the Chinese could not have had much time to prepare their ambush and must have had sufficient men close at hand near the RCR standing patrols. Brigade headquarters should also have been disturbed by the fact that an entire company could not deal with a single enemy platoon despite far greater numbers, an abundance of Bren machine-guns (two per section), and a large volume of highly accurate artillery support to call on. No. 5 Platoon's claim that it was unable to outflank the Chinese ambush 'owing to darkness, confusion and the lack of suitable ground' sounds particularly feeble given that they were operating just beyond their own outposts on a route of their own choosing. Although fighting patrols had operated in the area on several occasions in the past, no Royal had been forward of the battalion's outposts since a demolition party had destroyed several houses in the vicinity of the ambush two weeks earlier. Able to move right up to the RCR wire with little fear of interference by Canadian patrols, the Chinese reconnaissance parties must have been thoroughly familiar with the ground on which they organized their ambush.

Not surprisingly, given the apparent malaise of its senior officers, 1 RCR was satisfied to remain in its entrenchments following B Company's attempted raid and send out the usual nightly standing patrols in front of its positions. The battalion's patrols ventured beyond its outposts on only one other occasion before the Chinese attack on the 23-4th and that was for an uneventful ambush that set up several hundred yards north of the Edmonton outpost – some 500 yards north of the position where B Company had been hit. The basis for selection of this site was obviously not reconnaissance patrols, since none had gone out since 1 RCR had returned to the line in mid-August. In fact, the only aggressive action taken by the entire Canadian brigade in the ten days before the raid on Hill 355 was a forty-two man fighting patrol mounted by 1 PPCLI on the night of 15-16 October, one of two fighting patrols carried out by the battalion during the month. On the night of 4-5 October, a Patricia patrol had been sent to the base of the Chinese-held Hill 217, part of the Maryang-san hill mass, where it had engaged in 'a five minute fire fight' before withdrawing with one killed and one wounded.[81] This was the closest to Hill 317 that any 1 PPCLI patrol had ever attempted to penetrate and, as usual, the operation was undertaken without prior reconnaissance, leaving the patrollers to find their own way across no man's land in the dark with only their maps to guide them.

That pattern was repeated by the Patricia fighting patrol of 15-16 October. The second patrol was dispatched to a new position 'Tombstone,' a north-south spur some 800 yards north of the Bunker Hill ridge and an equal distance south of Maryang-san. Since Tombstone lay several hundred yards farther north than any previous patrol had ventured, and was 1,000 yards east of the objective given the earlier October fighting patrol, the twenty-five Patricias were entering unreconnoitred territory. The alert Chinese defenders received ample warning from their own patrols and the Patricias were 'assaulted by [an] estimated enemy platoon' as they approached their objective. The result was a 'firefight involving many burp guns and percussion grenades lasting ten minutes. The first section of the patrol suffered almost complete casualties including the patrol commander. Communications went out and [the] fighting section of [the] patrol [was] cut off from the firm base ... Extremely accurate and effective shelling was put down by artillery which enabled the section to withdraw wounded. The enemy continued to throw grenades and attempted to follow up but was beaten back. Artillery and mortar fire was brought in more closely and discouraged the enemy. The patrol reorganized in their location and helped its wounded as much as possible.' Since the patrol had suffered two killed and nine wounded, the Patricias had to send out carrying parties to help bring in the wounded to battalion lines.[82] Because 1 PPCLI held the most easily defended of the battalion positions on the Commonwealth Division's front, however, lack of patrolling did not have the same consequences there as at the more vulnerable 1 RCR positions to its left.

Hills 355 and 227 as seen from the turret of a B Squadron, LdSH tank on 21 November 1952. Lying across the turret in front of the binoculars is an example of the much-maligned Sten sub-machine-gun. The purpose of the rather elaborate sight on this particular Sten, a personal weapon of one of the tank's crewmen, is something of a mystery. NAC PA128836

Beginning on 17 October, the enemy's harassing fire against 1 RCR increased in intensity during the daylight hours, with the two company positions facing Hill 227 receiving particular attention (see Map 15). In twenty-four hours on 19-20 October, for example, the battalion was hit by 170 shells and 647 mortar bombs.[83] From 1200 hours on 21 October until 1200 hours on 22 October, the brigade received 451 shells and 1,034 mortar bombs mostly concentrated on the two exposed positions facing 227.[84] Throughout the 22nd, some 2,426 rounds fell on the Royals with 'no attempt [made] to distinguish between mortars and shells.' When B Company relieved D Company in the entrenchments on the northwest slope of Hill 355 that evening, they 'found that much of the ammunition [for the immediate defence of the position] had been buried or destroyed by recent shelling. Darkness and unfamiliarity with the area made an effective search impossible. Further shelling and mortaring during the night severed communications and destroyed much of the remaining earth-works. [No. 6] Platoon, which was initially the right-forward one, had all its bunkers caved in; at first light it moved into the centre position, where it became interspersed with 5 Platoon.'[85]

Having failed to control the ground in front of their positions, the men of B Company remained in their weapon pits that night and listened to the Chinese making their preparations for an attack. Lieutenant MacDonald, the 4 Platoon commander, 'heard some twenty explosions which he was sure were bangalore torpedoes. All during the night, the men heard noises in the draw in front of 4 and 5 Platoon areas. In the meantime, at about 0300 hours Private Morrison reported to MacDonald that he had killed two Chinamen in the act of charging his position. At first light, three dead Chinese were found within ten feet of Morrison's weapon pit ... The fact of so much enemy movement during the night, Lieutenant MacDonald suggested, supported a theory that the Chinese were present in strength immediately in front of B Company throughout the next day.'[86] (The bangalore torpedoes were being used to cut the Royals' wire; the soldiers killed by Morrison likely had simply wandered too far forward in the dark.)

The Chinese resumed their bombardment on the morning of the 23rd, 'working up to high pitch by about 1730 hours. At th[at] time complete silence fell until 1830 hours (last light) when an intense bombardment came down on A, B, and E Companies.'[87] During that thirty-minute bombardment, more than 3,000 shells and mortar bombs fell on the battalion, half of which landed on the B Company position and the remainder on its two flanking companies.[88] The concentration on B Company lasted for some eight to ten minutes before shifting to the company positions to the left and right, effectively sealing it off from its neighbours. Once their artillery had shifted, the Chinese infantry moved onto the position before most of the Commonwealth artillery's own defensive fire tasks could hit them. As was typical of a Chinese raid, 'the enemy bombardiers approached our trenches and threw their grenades (which our survivors were later to insist meant the Chinese attacked through their own artillery fire). The enemy machine carbine assault teams then passed through, entered the single line of trenches, and practically unopposed, went about their work of execution and securing of prisoners.'[89]

When the Chinese bombardment began, the B Company commander, Maj. E.L. Cohen, and the 5 and 6 Platoon commanders, Lieutenants Clark and Gardner respectively, were pinned down in the 5 Platoon position, where they had been discussing reorganizing the defences of the two understrength platoons. Even during the shelling, the officers could hear Chinese burp gun fire as the enemy commenced their attack. Once the artillery fire had shifted,

> preparations were made for immediate, local defence. Lieutenant Gardner went down the communication trench to the left [toward 4 Platoon], came back with the report that nothing was doing there, and then went towards the forward communication trench; this was the last that Lieutenant Clark saw of him for some time. Meanwhile Clark and Major Cohen had gone to the right [toward 6 Platoon] and collected a number of people including Corporals Smith and McNulty ...
>
> The right-hand group augmented itself with two D Company details who were passing through B Coy area on the way to Calgary and New Vancouver outposts, thus bringing its strength to about twelve. But, as a result of the shelling, some of the B Company members had no weapons and others no ammunition. Two Light Machine Guns fired from the top of the crawl trench in the direction of the sound of a burp gun. One of the D Company personnel (Private McInnis) was hit by either rifle or burp fire, and died before he could be evacuated. Those men who lacked weapons were sent down the communication trench towards A Company in search of grenades and small arms ammunition. When they returned they did so with a quantity of SAA [small arms ammunition] – some in LMG magazines, some in bandoliers – and grenades. A group of perhaps four or five, under Corporal McNulty, was organized as a grenade throwing party and sent down towards the right; no more was seen of this lot for some time.
>
> Now the remainder, consisting of five or six (including a signaller without a set), fought its way along the communication trench to the left-hand platoon of A Company. Darkness and the general confusion made an estimate of the enemy's strength impossible. On arrival at the position they found it unoccupied. Lieutenant Clark presumed (as it turned out, correctly) that the A Company platoon had been withdrawn when the enemy barrage had lifted to that area. Major Cohen now proceeded to A Company HQ, from where he could communicate with Main [Battalion Headquarters].[90]

The grenade-throwing party sent out to the right soon reversed direction, however, and returned south to the 5 Platoon position manned by Lieutenant Gardner, who, apparently alone in the position,

> decided that he had better man a slit [trench], for targets had begun to appear. But now people of both his own and 5 Platoon started coming down from the right, stating that the Chinese were into the circular communication trench. Thus he ended up with five men, of which he recognized only one – Lance Corporal Bawdin, of 5 Platoon ...

> It seemed that the others had either no weapons or no ammunition; all they were doing was indicating targets. Gardner engaged these with his TSMG [Thompson sub-machine-gun]. (During the whole engagement he killed five of the enemy.) Up to now, all the enemy were coming in from the right; but then one appeared on the left. At this, Lt Gardner decided to withdraw. He ordered the men to get out over the top of the hill and go to A Company.
>
> They were being heavily grenaded; some of the explosions could have been rifle grenades. Light mortar bombs were landing just behind them. Gardner saw someone he thought to be Lance Corporal Bawdin get an almost direct hit from a mortar. The officer himself must have received one of his wounds at this time. (He was hit by shrapnel in the right forearm and in both legs, and was superficially wounded in the right upper-arm by a bullet.) With Private Perry of 5 Platoon, who also had been wounded in the legs, he played dead.
>
> Meanwhile, the Chinese were milling about, shouting and blowing horns. It must have been about 2100 hours that the enemy disappeared, at which time Gardner and Perry made their way to A Company.[91]

The company's left-hand platoon, No. 4, abandoned its position as soon as the Chinese bombardment shifted to the flanks: 'Already the enemy were into the platoon position; two, in fact, were on top of [Lt. S.] MacDonald's bunker.' The platoon commander later remembered telling 'someone – he did not know whom – to tell the Company Sergeant Major and Company Signals to "get the hell out of here."'[92] At 1836 hours, six minutes after the shelling began, MacDonald arrived at battalion headquarters to report that his platoon had been overrun.[93] The 4 Platoon commander explained that 'the shelling had been very accurate; the attack, coming in as it did immediately on the concentration being lifted, was a complete surprise; and it was simply impossible to fight back.'[94]

It was not until 1943 hours, however, when battalion headquarters received a report from Major Cohen that no friendly troops remained in action in B Company, that the Commonwealth Division's artillery fire was shifted from its defensive fire tasks on the forward slopes to the company area itself. At 2100 hours enemy artillery and mortar fire suddenly increased on the flanking company positions. Battalion headquarters, which was bringing the reserve D Company forward in anticipation of a counterattack, interpreted the renewed shelling as the preparatory bombardment for a Chinese attack on E Company but it was almost certainly made to cover the Chinese withdrawal; Lieutenant Gardner, playing dead in the 5 Platoon position, stated that it was 'about 2100 hours that the enemy disappeared.' (It will be recalled that Rockingham had employed the same artillery ruse to cover the withdrawal of his companies during the Pepperpot raid the previous October.) By the time D Company's counterattack did go in at 0110 hours, it met minimal resistance. As the official history records, 'After a brisk fire-fight during the approach [one wonders whom they were shooting at], the left platoon [of D Company] moved into the former positions of No 4 Platoon without meeting further opposition and the right platoon occupied the No 5 Platoon area in the same manner. By 3:30 am the platoons had linked up and the situation was restored.'[95]

RCR casualties in the engagement, most of which were sustained by B Company, amounted to eighteen killed, thirty-five wounded, and fourteen captured, twice as many casualties as 2 PPCLI had suffered at Kap'yong in April 1951.[96] Only nine Chinese bodies were later found in the B Company position, although, as division headquarters recognized, 'enemy casualties must have been quite heavy. It is difficult to give an accurate estimate especially in view of his practice of removing both dead and wounded from the battlefield. Movement heard in the area on the following night indicates that the enemy was searching the area for his casualties.'[97] Since few of the Royals fired their personal weapons in their own defence, the overwhelming majority of Chinese casualties were likely inflicted by the division's artillery and mortars. A comparison of the relative volume of fire delivered by the two sides indicates the large advantage the Commonwealth Division enjoyed over its opponents. While 1 RCR was hit by 8,503 Chinese shells over the course of the week from 18 to 24 October, the division's three artillery regiments fired 11,035 rounds against the attackers during the evening of 23-4 October alone. That total does not include the 3,279 rounds fired by the heavy 4.1-inch mortars of the division's 61st Light Regiment.[98] Such a volume of shell fire must have exacted a heavy toll on the attackers.

In his veiled description of the raid, Harry Pope lamented its effect on Canadian morale: 'Since our "counter-attacks" always went in after the enemy had withdrawn with his own wounded we took no prisoners in our turn. Without doubt the enemy's ability to raid successfully our strongest platoon and even company positions adversely affected our morale ... If the men become aware that the enemy can successfully raid any forward company position along the entire divisional front, the troops will "take off," "bug out," when the enemy hits. Defeat breeds defeat.'[99] Perhaps the most concise summary of the attack was provided by the Patricia war diarist in describing how the Royals had been taken 'practically by surprise ... Evidently the enemy got into assault position the previous night and laid there all day.'[100]

The initial impression that the Chinese had laid up in no man's land prior to the attack was confirmed four days later when an RCR two-man patrol finally ventured back to the old Vancouver outpost. There they discovered six recently excavated bunkers, each capable of holding from ten to twenty soldiers, and a quantity of discarded Chinese equipment.[101] The Commonwealth Division's intelligence staff agreed with this conclusion:

> The assault force at least, moved up during the night [of] 22/23 October and spent the next day in lie-up positions in the vicinity of the objective. This is confirmed by the amount of enemy movement reported on 22 October and the fact that a number of caves and bunkers were found in the forming up area which had obviously been used

> by the attacking force. Some of these were in the vicinity of the 1 RCR outpost position [Vancouver] which had been destroyed by artillery on 1 October. In addition, the fact that the assault went in immediately after last light indicates that the force did not move a very great distance, otherwise they would have been detected by our Ground and Air Observers.
>
> Explosive charges found in bunkers on the position and information from other sources suggests that this was an enemy raid and that he did not intend to remain on the position.[102]

Because 1 RCR had failed to control the ground immediately in front of its own entrenchments, thus allowing the Chinese to dig lay-up caves around the outpost position from which to mount a close-in assault, the divisional artillery and mortars were denied an opportunity to decimate the attackers before they reached the Canadians' wire. A successful defence usually entailed spotting the Chinese assault formations as they crossed no man's land and reducing their numbers – if not breaking up the attack altogether – before they reached the Commonwealth positions (although the artillery also had to fulfill its important counterbattery role in the defence). Those attackers that did manage to escape destruction in the valley and reached, or breached, the wire entanglements, could then be dealt with by a platoon's considerable small-arms fire while the battalion's 81 mm mortars laid down fire immediately in front of the rifle pits. By permitting the Chinese to lay up so close to their positions, the Royals made it highly unlikely that they could have stopped the raiders' momentum before they overran B Company's entrenchments.

The lack of Canadian control of the approaches to their positions did not seem of any great concern to Brigadier Bogert, however. On the 31st, the brigade diarist was full of praise in reporting that 'the highlight of the month has been the failure of the attack by the Chinese on Hill 355 – called Little Gibraltar over the radio – due to the fine defence by 1 RCR and the shooting of our gunners.'[103] Just how brigade headquarters was able to conclude that 1 RCR had put up a 'fine defence' when, in fact, the Chinese raiders had successfully overrun their objective, inflicting sixty-seven casualties, including fourteen prisoners, before voluntarily withdrawing, was never explained. As long as the line was subsequently restored, Bogert was apparently willing to tolerate the temporary loss of a company position, and the heavy casualties that resulted, rather than end his brigade's inertia and contest the enemy's control of no man's land.

12 ON THE HOOK, NOVEMBER 1952-APRIL 1953

A week after the raid on 1 RCR's B Company, the Canadians turned over their battered entrenchments to Brigadier Daly's 28th Brigade and moved back into divisional reserve. The move was part of the regular rotation of brigades in and out of the line, and the battalion commanders of the Commonwealth formation had made their first inspections of the Canadian positions on 16 October, before the Chinese raid. The RCR's defences on Hill 355's western slope were taken over by the 1st Battalion, Royal Australian Regiment, under the command of Lt.-Col. Maurice Austin. During the relief, the Australian CO received a tongue-in-cheek handover certificate from Lieutenant-Colonel Bingham (who had finally returned from his leave) stating that Hill 355 'and attached real estate had been handed over complete, slightly worse for wear and tear, but otherwise defendable.'[1]

The Australians were less than amused by either the state of the Canadian defensive works or the tactical situation they had inherited. The Australian official history does not hide the dissatisfaction the incoming battalions felt toward the Canadians' defensive malaise, clearly stating:

> Austin found a difficult situation on Hill 355 ... The Canadians had not dominated no man's land by patrolling and the Chinese had relatively easy access from hides which they had dug close to the wire. Austin had to reconstruct the damaged trenches and bunkers, some of which had collapsed completely, and then had to re-establish control over no man's land. Daly ordered a heavy patrol program and hard fighting was necessary until the Chinese were forced to relinquish their grip ... The Canadians had not maintained concealment of their defences and advertised their presence by throwing empty food cans around their pits. The cans reflected the rays of the sun and enabled the Chinese to pin-point the locations of individual defences by day.[2]

With Chinese patrols operating close to the outer barbed wire each night, 'It took some ten days of aggressive Australian patrolling to regain control of the approaches, during which nearly fifty Australian casualties were suffered.' Some of the casualties resulted directly from the poorly maintained RCR defences. The sides of weapons pits and communication trenches had not been repaired by the Canadians, for instance, leaving large openings that acted 'as funnels for incoming shells and mortar bombs.' Nor had 1 RCR maintained the perimeter fences around minefields if, in fact, they were marked at all. One of the early Australian patrols 'was badly blown up when it unwittingly entered an unmarked and unrecorded minefield which the

Canadians had laid around an outpost position,' leaving one man dead and four wounded.[3] Although the Australians occupied the position until the Commonwealth Division was placed in I Corps reserve at the end of January 1953, the Chinese made only 'occasional forays' but 'no serious attack' on either of the RAR battalions. Lieutenant-Colonel Austin was subsequently awarded the Distinguished Service Order 'for the outstanding way in which he had taken charge of an unfavourable situation on Hill 355 in November 1952, restored the position's battered defences and established domination over the approaches to it by aggressive patrolling.'[4]

No less serious from an operational perspective – and equally disturbing as an indication of the lack of supervision being exercised in the forward positions by the spit-and-polish Canadian officers – was the 25th Brigade's lax attitude toward the disposal of garbage in its forward positions. Interviewed many years later, Lieutenant-Colonel Austin compared relieving the Canadian battalion in the line 'to occupying a fresh midden.' This lapse of field discipline had serious consequences for the concealment of defensive positions. Discarded ration tins in front of positions not only revealed their location but indicated their strength. In his book on the Commonwealth Division, the Australian historian Jeffrey Grey generalizes Austin's complaints about 1 RCR to assert, 'Canadian units tended to dispose of rubbish by the simple expedient of throwing it out in front of the wire ... British and Australian battalions relieving the Canadians had then to send out working parties beyond the wire for the dangerous and totally unnecessary task of cleaning up the position.'[5] While a certain amount of grumbling is inevitable whenever one military unit replaces another, there can be little doubt that the Australians were most unhappy at the situation left behind by the 25th Brigade's combined traits of timidity and sloth.

Possibly as a result of the Australian complaints, the Canadians had barely settled into their new reserve positions when Major-General West decided to alter the deployment of his three brigades. Rather than rotating entire brigades in and out of the line every couple of months, West now placed all three of his formations in the line, each with two battalions forward and one (or two) in reserve. The GOC's explanation for the move was that brigade commanders would 'now have a two-battalion frontage instead of a three-battalion one, which was proving too much for them to control properly; their own reserve battalion with which to counter-attack and with which to carry out inter-battalion reliefs at their own convenience; and a complete sector in depth instead of just a front line.'[6] If the three-battalion front was too wide for brigade commanders to control, that was the case only within the Commonwealth Division, the sole UN division to make such a change. Given the complaints about Canadian practices, Jeffrey Grey implies that the decision to redeploy the brigades was, at least in part, a response to the Australian objections. By handing each brigade responsibility for its own sector of the front, the tactical problems created by one formation's malaise would no longer be routinely inherited by another. As the leader of a multinational force, West was not in a position to order either the Canadians or Australians to change their procedures. According to his senior staff officer, E.A.C. Amy, the GOC was well aware of 'the national sensibilities and sensitivities' of his various units and felt that within the Commonwealth Division 'the chain of command is more a chain of suggestion.'[7]

As logical as it may be to infer that the November redeployment of the division's brigades was undertaken to minimize the need for continual reliefs, Grey's interpretation is questioned by Amy. The former GSO(1) does not believe that the Australian complaints were 'a motivating factor in the redeployment and I have no recollection of this being an issue at our headquarters. If it had been, I certainly would have heard of it. If the GOC was aware, he certainly would have told me and most likely would have asked me to go and see Brigadier Bogert if he himself had not already done so.'[8] According to Amy, the Canadian brigade 'had a favourable reputation within the division and within the theatre. The Australian perception of the performance of the Canadians was not apparent and neither General Cassels nor West ever suggested otherwise to me.' As a result, the senior staff officer of the division

> had no knowledge that the Australians had complained about the Canadian brigade ... In my estimation the Australian soldiers in Korea were superb and without question eager and aggressive with their patrolling. While I am disappointed and surprised to hear of their complaint [years later], I have no basis for questioning its validity. To put it in perspective, however, some level of dissatisfaction was undoubtedly expressed, at one time or another, by most if not every unit in the division after taking over a position from another regiment regardless of its nationality. This is not to condone it but soldiers will be soldiers and having been associated with them for a long time, I don't think many would disagree with this view.'[9]

Amy recalls the following rationale for the redeployment:

> General West decided, in consultation with his brigade commanders, that this arrangement of each brigade having a sector of the front would ensure a more consistent development of each of our battalion positions. I remember the excitement over the redeployment as it was viewed as a change for the better. It broke the monotony of months of the same routine and offered new challenges to brigades and their troops. The GOC's periodic report ... indicated that three battalions in the line were too much for the brigade commanders to control properly. This was the reason for the new deployment and I don't believe that 28 Brigade allegations had any bearing on his decision although perhaps the Australians may have considered that it did. It did have other benefits as well including: a greater measure of control by brigade commanders over the long term maintenance and improvement of their defenses; a more manageable arrangement for the engineer support in the forward area; and an improved capability to develop intelligence of the enemy opposing them and his defences thus enhancing the integrity of brigade patrol programmes.[10]

As the division's senior staff officer, Amy was well positioned to have been aware of any problems brought forward to division headquarters. Of course, the Australians' disapproval of Canadian practices may have been aired strictly within the 28th Brigade. As Amy admits, his 'comments were based solely on a normal relationship between division headquarters and its brigades, and without knowledge of such intimate details contained in [internal brigade memoranda]. As GSO 1, I was more aware of problems within a couple of the British battalions than within our Canadian brigade since the GOC frequently briefed me on what he was doing about them.'[11] Clearly, if West was aware of the Australian complaints about the Canadians, he did not bring them to either Amy's or Bogert's attention.

It may well be that Daly, himself the commander of a multinational brigade and therefore aware of the limitations on the division commander's powers, chose not to complain about the Canadian shortcomings to division headquarters. In any case, West's decision to redeploy his brigades served to eliminate the problem by ensuring that poor Canadian practices would be confined to the 25th Brigade's front. The redeployment did mean that in the event of a major Chinese attack – as opposed to a mere raid – the divisional commander's role would be reduced since he would have no infantry reserve under his control with which to launch a counterattack. While each brigadier would have one battalion for that task, there was no longer a brigade in reserve to plug a breach in the division's line. Given the static nature of the Korean fighting, this may have been deemed an acceptable risk by West if it precluded the need to tread on sensitive national toes.

Meanwhile, the peace talks at Panmunjom had broken down over the question of the forcible repatriation of prisoners of war. By the time of the final meeting on 8 October, the United Nations Command had reached the end of its patience with the enemy negotiators. Following yet another communist insistence on full repatriation of all prisoners, an exasperated Lt. Gen. William Harrison, speaking on behalf of the UNC delegation, made a thirty-four-minute speech reminding the communists that they had started the war and were stubbornly rejecting the UNC's various proposals to reach a settlement. Insisting that his negotiators had no intention of meeting at Panmunjom simply to listen to communist abuse and falsehoods, he announced that the UNC delegation had no further proposals to make. The American general then declared a recess in the negotiations until such time as the communist side was willing either to accept one of the UNC proposals or submit a constructive one of its own.[12] The deadlock seemed likely to last for a considerable time, since the opposing positions of the UN and the communists on the question of repatriation were not susceptible to compromise. Although lower level talks continued, the main delegations did not in fact resume their sessions until 26 April 1953.[13]

With the suspension of the negotiations, there were several bitter clashes as the communists tried to improve their defensive positions before the onset of winter. The Canadians on Hill 355 had not been singled out for attention. Indeed, American and South Korean divisions along the I Corps front were subjected to more raids and limited attacks on their positions, while even larger battles were being fought farther to the east in the IX Corps sector. Some of the heaviest of the October fighting occurred on the front of the 9th ROK Division, near Ch'orwon. The focus of the Chinese attacks was White Horse Hill, four miles northwest of the city. From 6 to 15 October, the Chinese 38th Army launched twenty-eight separate attacks to seize the feature from its very determined South Korean defenders, committing some 15,000 infantry to the various assaults. Subjected to over 55,000 rounds of enemy artillery fire during the battle, the 9th Division suffered over 3,500 casualties but provided a graphic example of the great strides the ROK Army had taken in developing its military skills and leadership.[14]

Twenty miles east of Ch'orwon, at the other end of the base of the Iron Triangle, General Van Fleet decided to launch his own attack in early October to improve the American defensive positions north of the city of Kumhwa. Although this was originally intended as a small, two-battalion attack to seize the Triangle Hill-Sniper Ridge bunker complex, the 7th US Division was able to capture its objectives only after a twelve-day battle that cost it over 2,000 casualties. After the complex was turned over to the 2nd ROK Division on 25 October, however, the Chinese mounted their own counterattack and drove the South Koreans off Triangle Hill. Chinese attacks continued against Sniper Ridge until 18 November, when the battle finally ended in a draw. Ultimately there were over 9,000 UN casualties and an estimated 19,000 Chinese casualties, but as always, the enemy had no shortage of manpower. Time and again during the past year they had shown themselves willing to incur heavy casualties in order to hold on to key terrain features.[15]

When judged against these other battles, the 23 October raid against 1 RCR had been a minor affair indeed. Perhaps with the high cost of the Iron Triangle battles in mind – or the earlier fighting for Outpost Kelly on his right flank – the Commonwealth GOC was not overly impressed with the American strategy of rigidly maintaining an outpost line. Although I Corps headquarters had stipulated that units were 'not expected to hold outpost positions at all costs,' West believed that 'this teaching ... is not always followed by some higher commanders who feel that the retention of an outpost is a matter of honour and insist that it shall be defended to the last man and the last round, regardless of its tactical significance.' The Commonwealth system of defence, with its greater reliance on patrolling rather than maintaining isolated outposts, was viewed by West as the main reason 'the division has had less attention from the enemy than any other formation in Eighth Army.'[16] West's analysis may nevertheless have been an oversimplification of the tactical situation. Since the Chinese often used their attacks to influence the ongoing truce talks at Panmunjom, their lack of attention to the Commonwealth Division was more likely due to communist recognition that the British Commonwealth exerted only a limited influence on American policy. In either case, there can be little doubt that the 25th Brigade's inclusion in the Commonwealth Division saved the Canadian formation from the sort of heavy casualties often incurred by American and ROK divisions.

It is apparent that 1 RCR's officers believed that their battalion had held its own against the attack on 23 October and that the Chinese had been successfully repulsed. There is no indication of concern that their inactive patrolling had contributed to the ease with which the Chinese had overrun B Company. Indeed, while in reserve the battalion quickly reverted to the peacetime routine with which it was most comfortable, emphasizing smart drill and neat tent lines rather than fieldcraft or operational procedures. A diary entry for early December decried the fact that their reserve 'area leaves much to be desired in the way of cleanliness. However, in true Royal tradition, everything we touch will be benefitted.'[17] Three days later the battalion borrowed a tank dozer 'to level the uneven ground and so set up all tents in a military manner.'[18]

Nor did 1 RCR set up a patrol training scheme or undertake any battalion exercises while in reserve. Instead, the Royals' 'emphasis on training stresses drill, weapon handling and range work. The object of all range training is, in this case, to obtain accuracy rather than speed. The result of the many drill periods may be seen in the smart guard that is turned out daily to protect the Pintail Bridge [over the Imjin River]. This guard would do credit to any of the Guards battalions.'[19] Unfortunately, the regular officers of 1 RCR seem to have mistaken the ability to hold mess dinners in dress uniform, polish the base plugs of its grenades, keep cans of Brasso and polishing rags in forward positions, and mount well-drilled bridge guards as the essence of a good unit. At its best in reserve, that was exactly where the battalion was destined to spend four of its remaining five months in Korea. Whether or not Brigadier Bogert had any questions about 1 RCR's operational effectiveness, it returned to the front line only during January 1953 before being rotated back to Canada in late March.

While the brigade was in reserve in November, 1 PPCLI's year-long tour in the theatre came to an end with the arrival of 3 PPCLI from Canada. It will be recalled that the 3rd Battalion had been formed at Fort Lewis at the end of November 1950 before moving to Camp Wainwright the following May to serve as a training unit preparing reinforcements for Korea. As such, the battalion had provided the bulk of the men for the rifle companies in 1 PPCLI before that unit's sudden dispatch to the Far East the previous autumn. Unfortunately, equipment shortages in Canada continued to plague the battalion's training program even as it prepared for its rotation to Korea. 'As the unit approaches the collective training stage,' its war diary recorded at the end of May 1952, 'the many shortages of training elements are beginning to be felt. There is little concertina and barbed wire, practically no ammunition for the 60mm and 81mm mortars, no stripless belt for MMG, no ammunition for the 3.5[-inch] rocket launchers, no mines of any sort, not enough vehicles, no mobile or portable flame thrower equipment, no air photographs, no recoilless rifles, and an overall restriction on the use of live ammunition. Many of these shortages have existed for nearly two years and they have placed a heavy strain on the ingenuity and imagination of the instructors.'[20]

In the Canadian official history, the battalion's CO, Lt.-Col. Herbert Fairlie Wood, recalls that it was not until 'the 1952 summer training period' that 3 PPCLI

> began to take shape for battle, gradually losing the appearance of a 'training centre.' In spite of the unit being told that 1 April would be the last date on which drafts would be called for, seventy-five men had to be sent to Korea as late as 29 May. At Wainwright, Patricia sub-units became involved in mine-laying, wiring, target grid procedure, rifle training, mortar firing, compass marches, anti-tank gun drill, wireless and all the many other skills required to make an infantry battalion operationally fit. There were a number of deficiencies in tradesmen and specialists, but an agreement was reached with the 1st PPCLI in Korea to make up these shortages on arrival in that theatre.[21]

The 3rd Battalion left its Wainwright home on 4 October and sailed for the Far East three days later aboard the USS *Marine Adder.* Like the 1st battalions, Wood's unit would have to face the enemy without the benefit of any battalion or brigade exercises. The Patricias arrived at the 25th Canadian Reinforcement Group in Hiro, Japan, on 21 October and spent the next week engaged in 'a training program [that] was designed to prepare the men for the hills of Korea, hence long route marches, hill climbing exercises and physical training were emphasized.'[22] On the 27th, the battalion made the short voyage across the Sea of Japan to Korea, with the last leg of its journey north 'via a clap-board train from Pusan to Tokchon where the troops encountered "C" rations for the first time. It was a slow, uncomfortable trip "sans" light, "sans" heat, "sans" beds.'[23]

With the Canadian brigade in divisional reserve, the battalion was able to assume 'an operational role' on 4 November without enemy interference, taking over 'the areas previously set up by 1 PPCLI. They will commence training immediately in order to fuse the elements of 1st Battalion and the new arrivals into an operationally sound unit.'[24] The 3rd Battalion had arrived in Korea understrength, prepared to absorb about 300 men from 1 PPCLI who had not yet served their twelve months in Korea.[25] The unit quickly began '"shaking down" and sorting people into their proper slots' with a general military training program that emphasized 'small arms and section co-ordination.'[26] It was soon apparent, however, that the equipment shortages in Canada meant that the new troops were less than fully trained. On 7 November, the battalion diarist recorded that 'the men need further training in all their weapons. A grenade was accidentally detonated and CSM Green was injured slightly with grenade fragments.'[27] The unit was fortunate that it was able to enjoy a month in reserve to remedy the worst of its deficiencies.

One important area that did receive attention was the battalion's patrolling skills. 'A short course on patrolling is being conducted for platoon commanders and platoon sergeants,' the Patricia diarist noted on the 12th. 'The object of the instruction is to recapitulate the normal drills for the preparation and conduct of a patrol and to discuss patrolling for the theatre. Three hours are spent in the class room and two evenings are to be spent on patrol. The objects of the exercises are a practice in the conduct of the patrol and to familiarize the leaders with cross-country travel by night.' Given the prominence of patrolling along the Jamestown Line, a two-day course could hardly have been expected to inculcate the requisite expertise needed to face a determined enemy, but it was certainly better than no instruction at all, as was the case with the two remaining 1st battalions. By the time the Patricias had concluded their last patrol course in midmonth, 'a total of thirty officers and sergeants will have had the benefit of the instruction. Though the course is of short duration, it is felt that a great deal is being learned from it and the effectiveness of our patrols will show it.'[28]

Of course the effectiveness of a battalion's patrols would be determined by the thoroughness with which they were mounted and the degree of confidence their officers could instill in their men to take offensive action. Judging by the inactive defense that Bogert's brigade had maintained during its recently completed tour, his battalion COs had yet to meet the demands of commanding front-line units. Interviewed on 27 October 1952 just before 1 PPCLI left the line to return to Canada, the battalion's CO demonstrated an amazing lack of appreciation for the tactical situation that had confronted him. In Lieutenant-Colonel Cameron's view, his unit's final six months in Korea had been a period of 'watchful waiting, coupled with intensive patrol activity.' He went on to assert that 'PPCLI patrols have retained control of no man's land; though recently there has been evidence of the enemy's outpost line being advanced somewhat, and of a general tightening of his main defences.'[29] Since the Chinese had routinely probed the Canadians' wire defences close enough to throw stones at the defenders, while only a handful of Patricias had ventured within 1,000 yards of the enemy's entrenchments, his conclusion is difficult to understand.

Nor did Cameron seem aware that the two-company front the Patricias had held, with its flanks securely anchored by more exposed neighbouring units, was virtually immune from attack. 'Yet, while on the right and left of the Patricias hostile activity has increased since August,' he stated, making an apparent link to his battalion's fictitious control of no man's land, 'the PPCLI front had been quiet.' As for tactical lessons, the Patricia commander believed that 'there actually had been very few; it was mainly a case of old lessons being re-emphasized. The 1st Patricias have, for example, gradually reverted to using only weapons of those types which are authorized on the establishment ... It was emphasized that types, not numbers of weapons, were restricted; for example, in defence, the unit carried double the normal scale of Bren Guns.'[30]

The commanding officer of the incoming 3 PPCLI, Lieutenant-Colonel Wood, had been a militia officer with the Irish Regiment of Canada at the outbreak of the Second World War. After proceeding overseas with his unit, Wood soon became a staff officer, eventually serving as GSO(3) of the 10th Canadian Infantry Brigade and then GSO(2) of the 4th Canadian Armoured Division during the campaign in northwest Europe. He transferred to the regular army in 1947 and was the chief instructor at the School of Infantry from April 1948 until appointed Rockingham's brigade major in August 1950. Assuming command of 3 PPCLI in March 1951 when

The view looking west toward the Hook positions across the Sami-ch'on River, as photographed on 26 June 1952 from the heights above the village of Yong-dong (out of sight at the foot of the hill). DHH 410B25.014 D1

the unit was still at Fort Lewis, the future author of the Canadian Army's official history of the war spent his first eighteen months as CO overseeing the training of reinforcements. Although an experienced trainer of troops, Wood may have lacked the drive sufficient to command soldiers in active operations. After observing him for two months with the Commonwealth Division, the GOC wrote to the chief of the general staff in Ottawa to express his concerns about the Patricia commander. West explained that 'Herb Wood has started well' and 'is very keen,' but questioned 'if he has the personality to drive his men if required.'[31] Certainly Wood appears to be one of those who subscribed to the Canadian Army's Second World War practice that commanding officers did not go forward to oversee operations but remained at their tactical headquarters in radio contact only – a style of command exemplified by Simonds himself in the last war. For example, in an account written a few years later, Wood recalled the night of 28 December 1952 'when Peter Bingham's Royal Canadian Regiment relieved us on the Hook':

> Into our command post, which we were occupying jointly during the relief, strode two American Army officers. They identified themselves as a general staff lieutenant-colonel and a captain of signals from First Corps headquarters. They had come down, they said, to ensure that the Corps commander's intention was being carried out. Peter raised his eyebrows and I shrugged. Such a procedure was unheard of in our army.
>
> The [American] lieutenant-colonel allowed as how he would like to see the relief taking place and asked when we were going forward to supervise it. 'Supervise it!' exclaimed Peter, 'why should we supervise it? We have given our orders, they have been understood, we would only be in the way were we to stand around behind the company commanders.' The American colonel looked slightly stunned. 'But how,' he asked, 'will you ensure that your orders are carried out?' We looked at him dumbly. Finally I broke the silence. 'If I thought for one minute that a company commander with twelve years service in the army could not carry out a simple operation like relief in the line without supervision from me, I would send him back to Canada tomorrow.'
>
> 'You would?' Our American friend had not come across this method of soldiering before. While he was puzzling this out, Peter spoke up again. 'My B Company,' he said, 'is passing here in about forty-five minutes. The company commander will be coming in to report and you could go with him when he moves up to relieve Wood's A Company. In the meantime, how about a drink?'
>
> Our two guests accompanied us to our little mess looking as if they had been caught by [the] teacher eating a candy bar during class. The relief proceeded smoothly, our guests went up to the front with B Company, RCR, and in due course returned with A Company, PPCLI. As he was leaving for his HQ, the [American] lieutenant-colonel handed me a piece of paper and said, 'Would you be kind enough to sign this?' 'Certainly,' I said, 'What's it all about?' 'Well, you see,' he said, 'if I can prove to my superiors at Corps Headquarters that I have been on duty past midnight, I get to sleep in tomorrow morning.'
>
> It was our turn to look dazed.[32]

While there can be little doubt that as the war in Korea stalemated higher American commanders injected themselves to too great a degree into small unit operations, the 'remain in the command post' attitude of Bingham and Wood – both of whom had served exclusively as staff officers during the Second World War – reproduced the style of command they were most likely to have observed during that conflict. It was, however, at odds with Rockingham's and the Australian Daly's hands-on approach. In contrast to Rockingham's frequent presence in the front line – whether to resite a machine-gun, offer suggestions for improving the layout of the defences, or simply observe his men first-hand – the absence of the 3 PPCLI commander from the forward positions was noted by at least one of his subordinates.

Lt.-Col. J.R. Cameron (left), CO of 1 PPCLI, and Lt.-Col. H.F. Wood, CO of 3 PPCLI and the future author of the Canadian Army's official history of the Korean War, pose with a map board on 25 November 1952. NAC PA185014

Lt. Robert Peacock, who was one of the soldiers transferred from 1 PPCLI in November 1952, later recalled that Wood 'was my commanding officer for a few months in Korea but I had very little personal contact with him. At that time I felt, rightly or wrongly, that he was a remote individual who stayed at battalion HQ and didn't know what was going on. I would like to have known him better because his novel [*The Private War of Jacket Coates*], shows how well he observed and understood his soldiers.'[33]

Particularly revealing was an incident that occurred shortly after Christmas 1952, a month after 3 PPCLI had entered the line, as Wood accompanied Bogert on a rare tour of his battalion's forward positions. Peacock remembers one of his soldiers asking

> who the Patricia lieutenant-colonel was and I replied that he was our commanding officer. I thought about it and realized that in almost five weeks on 'the Hook,' this was the first time any of us had seen the commanding officer around our platoon trenches. I knew that Lieutenant-Colonel Wood had visited company HQ on many occasions, but he had not toured our platoon trenches and talked to our soldiers. He was unknown

> to most of the soldiers, especially those who had been left behind [in Korea] when 1 PPCLI departed for Canada. I feel to this day that not enough was done to bring those of us from 1 PPCLI quickly into 3 PPCLI and create a new battalion identity. We did, very quickly, develop a strong company identification and loyalty which was the great strength of 3 PPCLI in its first period in action. Many years later when I had command of 2 PPCLI in Germany, I must have driven my company commanders and NCOs crazy with my impromptu visits to every nook and cranny of the unit. I was determined to be known, for good or ill, by everyone in the unit.[34]

If the newest members of 3 PPCLI did not feel that their CO had made himself sufficiently known or attempted to mould a strong unit identity, for his part Wood was disappointed by the number of his men who were turning out for 'orders and sick parades. Lately there have been quite a number present on both. It appears that the brief sojourn in Japan has disrupted both discipline and moral[e] of some members of the unit. The 1 PPCLI personnel who stayed on with 3rd Battalion also were strongly represented though mostly on the delinquent side. They probably suffered from neglect due to their leaders and buddies preparing for rotation.'[35] Nonetheless, by 17 November the battalion's rifle companies were reporting 'good progress in their training. The men are showing a keen interest as most of them realize and accept the purpose of it all.'[36] The importance of their preparation was highlighted two nights later when a company of the 29th Brigade's Black Watch came under attack on the exposed Hook position and the Patricias were called upon to take over two of the company positions to allow the British battalion to counterattack.

It will be recalled that Rockingham's brigade had previously occupied the Hook position on the high ground west of the Sami-ch'on River in March 1952, when 1 PPCLI's C Company had been heavily attacked on the 26th. Since that time, however, there had been some changes in the layout of the position's defences. With the periodic shifting of divisional boundaries, there was now only one battalion position on the Hook in the Commonwealth Division's sector, as opposed to the two battalion positions they had previously held. The defences themselves had also been contracted since the previous spring with Hill 132, the high ground held by the Patricias on 26 March 1952, now lying some 700 yards beyond the entrenchments of the left forward company and code-named Warsaw (see Map 16). Following the shift in divisional boundaries during Operation Westminster in April, the Hook position had become part of the 1st Marine Division's front. The Marines' left forward company, occupying the Hook itself, had been strongly attacked on the night of 26-7 October, with the Americans suffering heavily before finally restoring the situation. Like 1 RCR on Hill 355, the Marines did not patrol sufficiently to prevent the Chinese attackers from being able to 'lie-up in caves and bunkers in a forward position the day prior to the attack.' One day after the assault, the Hook position was handed back to the Commonwealth Division as part of yet another readjustment of divisional boundaries.[37]

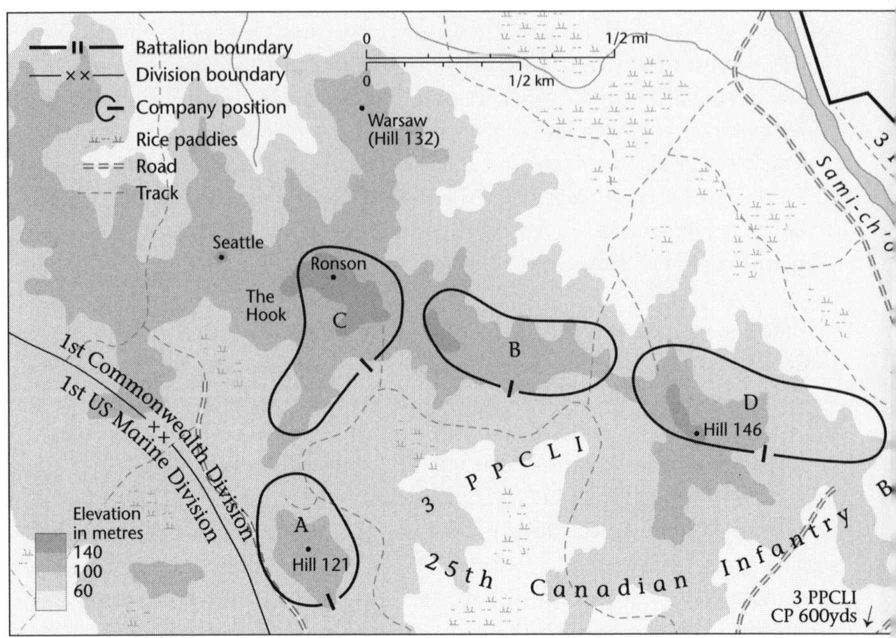

Map 16 *The Hook positions, 7 December 1952*

The changeover from American to Commonwealth control did not end the enemy's interest in the position, however. Given that the Hook was the last defensible piece of ground north of the Imjin River along that particular section of the Jamestown Line, the attention paid to it by the Chinese is not surprising. On 4 November,

> a party of forty to fifty enemy assaulted a standing patrol from 1st Black Watch in the area of Ronson [a high point 100 yards northeast of the forward company position]. The patrol came under fire from enemy small arms and grenades and immediately withdrew. The enemy attack followed the familiar pattern, no preliminary artillery or mortar preparation, a noisy rush and a large scale use of burp guns at close range. At the same time the enemy put down 180-200 rounds of mortar fire on the Hook which lasted for thirty minutes. Undoubtedly the object of this fire was to prevent the patrol being reinforced and to inflict casualties as the patrol returned to their company position. An attempt at a repeat performance was tried by fifty enemy who engaged the standing patrol on Ronson on 12 November. The patrol withdrew and artillery and mortar fire were placed.'[38]

On the 18th, the Chinese mounted their second large attack on the feature in less than a month. Despite a two-hour warning provided by an eleven-man Black Watch patrol reconnoitring some 600 yards north of the Hook, a Chinese battalion, advancing under a heavy barrage, successfully infiltrated portions of the British battalion's A Company position. The Black Watch platoon 'on the western end of the Hook, being under heavy attack, went to ground in its tunnels and brought down artillery fire with VT [variable time] fuzes on its own position.' The Black Watch's B Company, to the right, was relieved in its position by 3 PPCLI's A Company, allowing the British company to launch several counterattacks against stubborn enemy resistance: 'For the rest of the night hard fighting continued but the Black Watch remained firm in the position despite repeated attacks and enemy penetration. By about 0430 hours the battalion started slowly to mop up small parties of the enemy remaining on the position. At about 0630 hours the enemy withdrew.' Later that morning, the Patricias' C Company relieved the Black Watch's hard-pressed A Company on the Hook to allow the British to evacuate their casualties.[39]

The tenacity with which they had held their positions exacted a heavy toll on the Black Watch: twelve men killed, seventy-two wounded, and twenty-one missing – a total, in terms of wounded and missing, that far exceeded 1 RCR's casualty figures on Hill 355. Enemy casualties in the attack could only be estimated, but 'over eighty enemy dead were counted. The area of the Hook was littered by what can literally be described as shattered humanity. It is not known how many dead there were in forward areas in dead ground or in enemy forming up places. A [British] soldier from an ambush patrol who laid up all night in a bunker forward of the Hook reported that throughout the night a constant stream of enemy wounded were evacuated past his position.' The Chinese artillery preparation in the days leading up to the attack 'was nowhere near as heavy as that prior to the attack on 1 Royal Canadian Regiment' the previous month 'except immediately prior to the assault when an extremely heavy barrage was placed.' It was estimated that the Chinese fired between 4,000 and 5,000 artillery rounds in support of the Hook attack.[40]

While the remainder of 3 PPCLI continued with their training program, A and C Companies received some front-line experience while temporarily occupying the Black Watch entrenchments. On the night following the attack, 'three-man standing patrols were despatched from C Company to Warsaw [Hill 132] and Ronson. At intervals they would report enemy movement [as the Chinese recovered their dead]. They would return to our FDLs while artillery and mortar fire was laid down. They would then return to their positions. This activity continued throughout the nights of 19/20 [and] 20/21 November with obvious success. On three occasions the screams of enemy wounded were heard and each morning more enemy bodies were seen.' Nonetheless, their first exposure in the front line convinced the Patricias that they still had much to learn. 'The enemy was found to be fast and efficient in his evacuation of dead and wounded by night,' their war diarist recorded. 'He did not hesitate to risk new casualties in order to evacuate others and did so with a rapidity that failed two attempts to secure a wounded prisoner. Our patrols did not move with the speed necessary to forestall his evacuation of casualties caused by our artillery and mortar fire.'[41] Three nights later, an eleven-man fighting patrol attempted by B Company 'did not go well at all. A searchlight prevented the patrol from proceeding to its objective. While the patrol was waiting for the light to go out, enemy patrols were active in their vicinity in the valley. They were ordered back and to try and have the enemy follow them into our firm base. Instead of following, the enemy directed mortar fire on them while they were returning.' Fortunately, the Patricia patrol was able to reach its entrenchments without incurring any casualties.[42] With the Black Watch companies hastily reorganized after their ordeal, 3 PPCLI's C Company was relieved from the front line on 22 November while B Company returned to the battalion two days later.[43]

The lack of success confirmed the need for further patrol training and, to Wood's credit, the Patricias continued to run patrol courses in their B Echelon for the remainder of November. Although short, two-day affairs, the courses ensured that 'at least two members from each platoon' would have some patrol training, including 'a number of corporals and senior privates.'[44] It was also expected that the battalion would have an additional month to prepare themselves for the front. On 24 November, the unit's war diary recorded that 'the plan at present is for 3 PPCLI to be [in] the reserve position' when the division implemented the scheme to place all three of its brigades in the line.[45] As wise as it would have been to allow the newly arrived Patricias further time to acclimatize themselves to Korean conditions, however, Bogert had a change of heart at the last moment. When the 25th Brigade did move back into the line on 30 November, the Canadian commander decided to put his most inexperienced battalion on the important Hook position while assigning 1 R22eR – still some 200 other ranks below establishment despite having seen almost no action during its first eight months in Korea – to the relative security of the high ground east of the Sami-ch'on River and keeping the experienced 1 RCR, now fully up to strength after its October losses, in reserve.

Between them, the Chinese attacks in October and November had convinced division headquarters that greater attention had to be paid to improving the Commonwealth Division's field defences. Interviewed in June 1953, Lieutenant-Colonel Amy stated that 'it was the attack on the RCR last fall which supplied the clear warning. It was obvious then that the Chinaman could smash our existing defences almost any time he chose.'[46] Following the redeployment, the Canadians occupied the left of the divisional front astride the Sami-ch'on River. The entire division then commenced a comprehensive program to construct more effective field defences, with top priority being assigned to both the Hook and Hill 355 positions. Trenches were deepened to a minimum of six feet, overhead cover was provided for fire trenches and bays, and prefabricated concrete bunkers were put in place. Although the infantry battalions were responsible for the work, under the supervision of the engineers of the 23rd Field Squadron, the Korean Service Corps provided the bulk of the labour. Understandably, the existing defences in the Hook were in a poor state of repair after the heavy bombardments and infantry attacks of the previous two months. Nonetheless, British engineers had already begun construction of six tunnels, three in each of the Hook and 'Right of Hook' company positions, which ran into the hills from the forward trench fire bays and were intended to serve as shelters from enemy shelling or as refuges during Chinese attacks should the infantry decide to call for artillery fire on their own positions. Faced with difficult digging conditions the Canadian sappers worked shifts to complete the tunnels by the end of January. Aside from tunnelling, 650 yards of new trenches were also dug in the Patricia positions and a farther 1,035 yards of the original trench system was deepened to a standard six feet.[47]

In addition to improving its entrenchments, the Canadian brigade also appeared to take a greater interest in developing a better patrol scheme to cover its front. On 2 December, the brigade major, Maj. J.E. Leach, issued a long overdue memorandum on 'Patrol Policy' for the 25th Brigade. In a belated recognition of a major Canadian weakness, Leach informed the battalions that 'the practice of standing patrols going to the same location night after night is obsolete. The function of standing patrols will be carried out by two-man listening posts. A listening post will not go to the same location each night but rather to different locations within a definitely defined area. Listening posts will be defensive rather than offensive in nature; they are to give early warning of enemy approach.'[48] The simple common sense of the instruction makes the fact that it was necessary – and that it took Bogert's headquarters seven months to issue it – all the more remarkable.

The patrol instruction also allowed for 'routine recce patrols within battalion boundaries up to the Sami-ch'on River. On certain occasions recce patrols beyond the river will be carried out when specified information is required.' Even here, however, it was clear that the Canadians were not about to be overly aggressive in probing the enemy's entrenchments, the memo stating emphatically that 'no scope for recce patrols exists near the Hook feature.' Instead, the Canadian reconnaissances would be confined to the wide valley of the Sami-ch'on that lay between the Hook position and the entrenchments of 1 R22eR on the hills above the village of Yong-dong. Well over 1,000 yards from the nearest Chinese positions, such patrols were mainly organized to prevent enemy infiltrators from moving down the valley to the Imjin River. If the Canadians were to probe near the Chinese positions, they were instructed to use only fighting patrols 'to go to enemy side to see if certain features are held' or 'to gain information when it is considered necessary to fight for it.'[49] As in the past, battalions were left to work out their own patrol schemes while coordinating them through brigade headquarters by submitting a 'daily forecast of all patrols one day in advance. That is to say that patrols going out on any specific night will give information to this HQ the date before patrols are due to go out. Confirmation is required by telephone by 0900 hours of the day concerned to confirm that there are no changes, or otherwise, of the patrols for that day.'[50]

As the least experienced of the Canadian battalions, 3 PPCLI was fortunate that December 1952 was a quiet month. Wood's official history relates that 'no really serious contacts developed from any of these patrols, since the action in most cases was to withdraw on detecting the enemy in order to bring down artillery or mortar

The view north from B Company, 3 PPCLI position in the 'Right of Hook' or 'Sausage' entrenchments, December 1952. The unoccupied Pheasant feature (middleground centre) is across the valley fronting the Hook positions. Hill 355 is visible in the far background right centre. The wide Sami-ch'on valley is in the right middleground, while the hills occupied by 1 RR2eR across the river are just out of sight to the right. Robert S. Peacock collection

concentration on the spot where the Chinese had been seen.'[51] The greatest change from earlier Canadian operations were the frequent references to Patricia 'recce' patrols in the brigade's patrol task tables. Despite their name, these patrols, in strengths of from three to eleven men, were routinely assigned a single map coordinate position usually only 100 to 200 yards in front of the company entrenchments. These locations make it clear that these recce patrols were simply 3 PPCLI's version of the listening posts advocated in the brigade major's memorandum. By midmonth these patrols, still assigned to the same locations immediately in front of the battalion's defences, had been reclassified as 'standing.' Importantly, however, the Patricias' standing patrols did heed Leach's admonition about remaining in one place throughout the night and moved about within their patrol areas rather than adopting the previous tactic of occupying the same location night after night while the Chinese threw stones at them.[52]

While patrol contacts were few, it was not because the Chinese were completely inactive. The Patricia standing patrols routinely found that the 'sounds of [enemy] digging and movement ... are becoming common,' particularly around the Ronson feature, a hundred yards north of the Hook corner, and Hill 141, code-named Seattle, which lay only 200 yards west of the Hook company position. Both features had been well within the Hook defences the previous spring but had since been abandoned. Based on the sounds of enemy digging coming from Seattle, a twenty-seven-man Patricia fighting patrol assaulted it at 0250 hours on the night of 5-6 December with encouraging results: 'The enemy were taken completely by surprise and a short

fire fight ensued. The patrol suffered one casualty and claim to have inflicted seven on the enemy. On the return route the enemy directed mortar fire on the patrol and neutralized the firm base on Ronson with small arms fire. Lieutenant Campbell was wounded slightly by a mortar bomb fragment, and Private Mudd at the firm base was killed.'[53] The first real reconnaissance patrol undertaken by the Patricias came on the night of 10-11 December when thirteen men swept across the battalion front on the northern slopes of Hill 132, the Warsaw feature some 700 yards north of the Hook corner, to search for signs of recent enemy tunnelling.

Throughout the month, however, the Patricias remained timid about allowing any of their recce patrols to proceed farther afield, confining their operations to their own forward slopes and never moving out to investigate what might lie nearer the main Chinese positions. Contrary to brigade headquarters' assertion that there was 'no scope for recce patrols ... near the Hook feature,' however, on 16 December four inebriated Patricias conducted their own daylight reconnaissance of the enemy's defences across the valley to the north of their positions. According to the battalion war diary, 'At 1645 hours the FOO with B Company reported seeing two Canadian soldiers on Pheasant,' a hill on the Chinese side of the valley some 1,500 yards north of the Patricia entrenchments:

> When the full story was unfolded, it was found that four soldiers from B Company had left their platoon positions without permission. They had all been under the influence of alcohol. One fell asleep [in the valley in no man's land] and was apprehended and

> returned to his position with no trouble. One returned to his position after searching out Warsaw [Hill 132]. The other two, one a corporal, went to Pheasant, became involved in a fire fight during which they claim to have killed five enemy. They returned through B Company unharmed. They reported seeing the bodies of three US Marines near [the foot of Pheasant]. All four soldiers were sent to A Echelon under close arrest.[54]

The ease with which the drunken Patricias had penetrated across the valley to investigate the Chinese positions indicates that there was indeed scope for authorized patrols to range farther afield. The Canadian units that occupied the Hook defences (3 PPCLI and, after 28 December, 1 RCR), however, preferred sniping at the Chinese – an activity that allegedly ran up an impressive score of kills – and hitting enemy positions with mortar and artillery fire.[55]

That the Chinese did little to harass the Hook positions during the winter months was simply a reflection of the general lull in operations across the entire peninsula rather than the result of any Canadian effort to dominate no man's land. Following its lone true reconnaissance patrol on 10-11 December and an uneventful fighting patrol three nights later, 3 PPCLI was satisfied with mounting the usual standing patrols and the odd uneventful ambush for the remainder of the month.[56] The Chinese, meanwhile, largely confined their activities to reconnaissance patrolling and digging in no man's land. As they had the previous year, the communists used

Hill 132, code-named Warsaw, as photographed from the B Company, 3 PPCLI positions by Lt. Peacock in December 1952. Hill 132 was directly north of the Hook company position (out of view left) and was the feature held by C Company, 1 PPCLI, when attacked on 26 March 1952. Robert S. Peacock collection

the approach of Christmas to stage a propaganda campaign, efforts the Canadians mostly found humorous. On 22 December, for example, the Chinese made a 'gift of Christmas trees, cards and small trinkets, the whole surmounted by a huge banner over twenty feet long, which dawn disclosed on Ronson,' only 100 yards in front of the C Company positions.[57]

For 1 R22eR, on the other side of the Sami-ch'on, the Chinese entrenchments were some 2,000 yards away across the wide river valley and contacts were exceedingly few. Throughout its time in Korea, the Van Doo battalion failed to demonstrate much interest in mounting patrols forward of its standing patrol line, although the wide no man's land in front of their positions above the village of Yong-dong allowed them to 'carry out routine recce patrols within battalion boundaries up to the Sami-ch'on River.'[58] According to C Company's Harry Pope, if aggressive action was contemplated, it was better to inform the battalion commander after the fact. The Van Doo major later recalled that in December 1952 two privates proposed a patrol 'in broad daylight' to the enemy side of the Sami-ch'on River opposite the Hook 'to see what was to be seen there. I admired this aggressive spirit and the example it gave to the rest of the company.' After warning the adjoining companies and requesting the forward observation officer 'to hold himself ready to massacre with his twenty-four guns any enemy showing a disposition to annoy the patrol,' Pope had Lt. Bruce Rutherford, commanding the Lord Strathcona's tank that was dug in on the crest of C Company's hill, 'follow the patrol with his tank gun, ready at any moment to fire 100 yards in front of it. In effect I did everything except to tell the CO and that for the excellent reason that I knew he would not authorize the ... patrol.'[59]

To Pope's surprise, the enemy did not react to the Canadian intrusion even when the two Van Doo patrollers reached the far side of the Sami-ch'on and 'stamped out "Merry Christmas from C Company" (in English) in the snow' only '200 yards from the enemy position and 2,000 yards from ours.' Although the entire patrol had been conducted without the knowledge or approval of Lieutenant-Colonel Trudeau, the fact that 'the total lack of enemy reaction was useful military information' prompted Pope to report it to his battalion: 'The IO [intelligence officer] ... transmitted my report with all the other patrol reports (no doubt all authorized, these) to Colonel Trudeau on his entering the CP that evening. It didn't take long for me to learn that I was to be paraded to the brigadier.' The Van Doo major does not say what, if any, punishment he received for allowing the unauthorized daylight patrol.[60]

Despite the fact that December 1952 had been a relatively quiet month – enemy artillery and mortar fire had 'dropped off steeply' to an average of only seventy-three shells and fifty-six mortar bombs a day on the entire Commonwealth Division – the daily grind of occupying a front-line position was bound to take an emotional toll on some soldiers. Lieutenant Peacock recalls an incident when a returning Patricia patrol was attacked by Chinese mortar bombs in the approaches to his platoon's position. Having made a head count when the patrol passed through on its way out, Peacock believed that the incoming soldiers were a man short and 'questioned the sergeant [in command] as to what had happened and where the missing man could be located. He said that the patrol was complete and that they had to get back to battalion HQ as quickly as possible to report to the battle adjutant. I questioned the patrol members and they said that a couple of mortar bombs had landed by the rear of the patrol as they were returning and that the last man in the patrol was missing.' Peacock's own platoon sergeant quickly organized a search party and brought in the wounded soldier:

> Meanwhile, the sergeant still maintained that the patrol was complete. At this stage it was obvious that the patrol leader had panicked and lost control when the mortar bombs hit the rear of the patrol. I placed him under arrest and sent him back to battalion HQ, separately from the rest of the patrol, informing battalion HQ of the circumstances. The matter was eventually dropped by those in charge as the sergeant was obviously worn out from desperately trying to achieve too much. His psychological fitness to cope with the pressures of patrolling had deteriorated before his physical strength, and he had almost caused a wounded man to die of exposure or to be captured. The sergeant had had extensive combat experience in World War 2 and had a previous tour in Korea. He was regarded by all of us as a first-class fighting soldier. In both campaigns he had served with distinction but he had tried to continue when he knew he was pushing himself beyond his limits. I felt that his immediate superiors should have recognized that the man was wearing out emotionally and should have taken some action to place him where he could have rested and regained his stability. Each of us felt that 'there but for the grace of God go I' and was relieved the situation was ended.[61]

Even so, battle exhaustion cases within the Commonwealth Division remained exceedingly few, in marked contrast to the army's experience during the Second World War. For the thirteen-month period from 1 June 1952 to 30 June 1953, for example, Commonwealth medical units reported only thirty-six battle exhaustion cases but 1,863 battle casualties, for a neuropsychiatric casualty to battle casualty ratio of less than 2 percent. More intense fighting during the Second World War had produced ratios closer to 25 percent.[62]

At the end of December, 3 PPCLI was replaced on the Hook by 1 RCR. In keeping with the patrol instructions Major Leach had issued on 2 December, the incoming battalion also demonstrated a greater willingness to patrol than it had during its defence of Hill 355 the previous October. For the first time since arriving in Korea, 1 RCR even began to make reconnaissances prior to mounting its fighting patrols. On 2 January 1953, for example, Lieutenant Ferraday 'led a recce patrol towards Pheasant in preparation for a fighting patrol. The recce was uneventful though informative.'[63] The RCR's reconnaissance clearly had not extended to investigating

Part of the entrenchments in the Hook position occupied by C Company, 3 PPCLI, in December 1952. Robert S. Peacock collection

the feature itself, however, since 'to almost everyone's surprise no enemy was found'[64] when Ferraday returned with the fighting patrol later in the week. Nor was the enemy's absence a chance occurrence. When the heavily armed fighting patrol – its twenty-one men were carrying six Bren guns – easily swept over its objective on the night of 6-7 January, it found 'no evidence of any recent digging, defensive construction, bunkers or cover. Trenches all shattered and caved in ... No evidence of enemy occupation for some time.'[65] Of course this information could have been gathered by Ferraday if he had pressed on with his original reconnaissance four nights earlier to observe the objective itself. Nonetheless, the Royals were well aware that the use of reconnaissance patrols was a new feature in their operations. 'Tonight is unique in that four officers are on recce patrols,' their war diary recorded on 9 January, continuing on the 10th: 'Little by little an accurate and complete intelligence picture is being built up. Tonight the same [four] officers were to lead the same patrols out but to extend their roving deeper into enemy territory. However, enemy movements and artillery/mortar [fire] curtailed the movement of our patrols' before any contact was made.[66]

As encouraging as the sudden use of reconnaissance patrols was, they were not quite as wide ranging or informative as the war diary suggests. As a general rule, the Canadian patrollers seldom ventured beyond the abandoned entrenchments the 25th Brigade had occupied in March and April 1952, well short of the main Chinese entrenchments across the valley north of Warsaw. The only enemy encountered were on patrol themselves, often in close to the Canadian defences. As had been the case during the summer, the skillful Chinese patrollers quickly established the initiative in any clashes that did occur. On the night of 12-13 January, for instance, a fighting patrol was sent to investigate the Seattle ridge, a finger of high ground running northwest from the feature to the left of the Hook entrenchments. Moving in three groups, the RCR patrol planned to approach the objective by heading north from their FDLs before turning toward the west. Three hundred yards from their FDLs, however, the Canadians were, like so many previous 1st battalion patrols, jumped by an alert enemy patrol:

> The leading group, headed by the patrol commander, had reached a shell crater twenty yards from a horseshoe-shaped trench when one enemy was clearly seen to throw a fragmentation grenade. This wounded the patrol commander. The 2ic [second-in-command] was detailed to carry out the assault but was pinned down as he moved forward by machine gun fire which came down from either the right or left hand arm of the horseshoe-shaped trench. The patrol was ordered to withdraw. The patrol commander split the patrol into two groups. One group retraced its route [to the north-east]. The other group came in via Ronson. As the first group moved north they came under direct fire from two machine guns and burp guns. Light mortars followed the withdrawal of this group up the valley and caused further casualties. Additional [enemy] fire was brought to bear from Seattle [to the south] by two machine guns. The withdrawal of the second group was also followed by small arms and mortar fire but without effect.[67]

The twenty-three-man patrol returned to their lines with eleven wounded, including the patrol commander who had suffered a broken leg among other wounds.

Fortunately for the Royals, the enemy remained passive throughout January 1953 and such patrol clashes were rare. The reduced Chinese activity meant that most RCR patrols were able to move as much as 500 to 600 yards into no man's land without contacting the enemy. Typical entries in the unit's war diary describe patrols as 'successful but uneventful' with patrols moving 'into, through, and behind enemy tunnels without making contact but gaining useful intelligence.'[68] Given that the Canadians largely confined their activities to their own side of no man's land and did not venture across the valley north of Hill 132 to investigate the main Chinese positions, however, the RCR claim that its uneventful sweeps of the unoccupied Ronson and Warsaw features 'clearly demonstrate that this battalion is the master of the valley'[69] is a considerable overstatement. With the Canadians patrolling only directly in front of their own positions, it was left to the division's other two brigades to try to capture Chinese prisoners.

Not surprisingly, the most active patrollers during December and January – and the ones who clashed most frequently with the enemy – were the Australians, engaged in their continuing battle to keep the Chinese away from their defensive positions on Hill 355. Unlike the Canadians, fighting patrols from the RAR battalions often penetrated across the valley in search of prisoners and engaged the enemy in their own entrenchments. On the night of 10-11 December, for instance, a two-platoon raiding party from 1 RAR 'reached its objective, destroyed bunkers and an ammunition pit, killed fifteen enemy and wounded five. The raiding party occupied the position for thirty minutes. The trenches on the feature were found to be ten to twelve feet deep and the parapet between three and four feet in height.' The raiders killed an estimated ten to fifteen enemy but, as was usually the case, failed to capture the desired prisoner. The Australians themselves had two men killed, eighteen wounded, and two missing. A fighting patrol sent out the following night to search for the missing men encountered four Chinese platoons in the valley that were apparently preparing to attack one of the 1 RAR standing patrols. The enemy's company-sized raid was then broken up by small-arms and artillery fire.[70]

The British battalions of the 29th Brigade, in the division's more secure centre, held positions that were over 1,000 yards from the Chinese entrenchments, and the much wider no man's land meant fewer patrol contacts. Nonetheless, the 1st Battalion, Duke of Wellington's Regiment attempted 'two well-planned snatch patrols' in December but 'were unlucky in their attempts to capture a prisoner of war. One patrol entered an enemy bunker and found breakfast cooking, also eating utensils and jacket which they brought back. It is believed that the enemy heard the patrol coming and withdrew. The second patrol cut enemy telephone lines [in the manner of Lieutenant Gardner's successful snatch] and after waiting an hour two linesmen appeared and were engaged. However, in the hand-to-hand struggle which ensued the enemy managed to escape.' The following month a seventeen-man fighting patrol from the battalion crossed the valley to make a daring daylight raid against the Chinese entrenchments. 'After long observation and much careful and painstaking reconnaissance of the enemy position,' the operation took place on 24 January:

> The approach to the objective was made whilst the sun dazzled the enemy and under cover of supporting artillery, mortar and tank fire. The party had been given intensive training for the operation whilst a careful deception plan was also arranged. The patrol crossed the valley by the most direct route to the objective. Advantage was taken of the shadows thrown by the sun and cover of the morning mist. On reaching the objective, one enemy was seen running into a tunnel and excited talking was heard inside. One enemy in a trench was killed by a grenade. His body was recovered and taken back to our own lines. Identification indicated that he was a platoon grade political officer. All attempts to induce the enemy in the tunnel to come out failed. An unknown number of enemy within responded by firing burp guns from undetected weapon slits. The patrol finally blew up the tunnel, the roof beams going twenty feet into the air and burying the occupants. Enemy reaction to this patrol was slow and consisted mainly of mortar, defensive fire spread across the front. There is every indication that the enemy was completely confused by the operation and had no idea of what was actually happening. All adjacent enemy positions were engaged by artillery fire. The smoke and dust created was so great that the enemy were quite unable to see what was going on.[71]

If nothing else, the raid demonstrated the value of taking an unexpected approach to disorganize the enemy, in this case attacking during daylight. The Chinese confusion allowed the British raiders to withdraw back to their lines without incurring a single casualty.

The Chinese continuing ability to deploy large numbers of men in no man's land whenever they chose to do so was vividly demonstrated one night later when a 3 RAR snatch patrol northwest of Hill 355 found itself facing overwhelming numbers of the enemy. The result was, in the divisional staff's opinion, 'the fiercest fighting during the period.'[72] The platoon-sized patrol consisted of a snatch party of five Australians and two thirteen-man groups acting as firm bases along the planned withdrawal route through no man's land. Unfortunately, the snatch party was spotted soon after entering the Chinese trenches and the alarm was raised. A large enemy force then moved forward and eventually overwhelmed one of the thirteen-man firm bases after the snatch party withdrew to the second. As the division's intelligence staff later acknowledged, 'The presence of so many enemy in this area was a surprise. It is believed that the enemy employed between 150 and 200 troops in the operation. Considering the defences in this area, it would have been possible for the enemy to have deployed so many troops on such short notice only if he had reinforced these forward positions, which in fact was established later.'[73] Despite having inflicted an estimated ninety casualties on the enemy, the Australian losses totalled ten wounded and the thirteen men from the overwhelmed base missing. The Australian official history admits that 'it had been an expensive and vain attempt to capture a prisoner' but suggests that the patrol clash was also a 'fitting finale to a bitter winter of continual contest between small groups of determined men for control of no man's land.'[74]

By the time the entire Commonwealth Division moved into I Corps reserve at the end of January 1953, West was sufficiently pleased with the tactical situation to report that the division's 'great efforts in patrolling' during January had allowed it to 'just about dominate' no man's land by month's end.[75] Whether or not it was due to the division's efforts, Chinese patrolling had noticeably slackened during January with no contacts reported on fourteen separate nights during the month. According to Lieutenant-Colonel Amy, there was a continuing belief at division headquarters that 'aggressive patrolling will save lives in the long run.'[76] Nonetheless, West was concerned by a recent trend within Eighth Army to seek more prisoners of war. In particular, the divisional commander feared that 'there were indications that I Corps was going to bring out a patrol policy ordering every forward battalion to send out so many patrols per night or week.' To forestall that development, the GOC issued his own divisional patrol directive, which 'had the desired effect as we have now received a Corps instruction deprecating the practice of laying down an arbitrary number of patrols to be carried out by forward units.'[77] Beginning with the assertion that 'the overall object of patrolling is to dominate No Man's Land,' the memorandum cautioned that

> each patrol must have its own specific object.
>
> No patrols will be sent out without some such specific object. On no account will commanders send out patrols for patrolling sake, nor will they order sub-units to provide so many patrols per so many days. Any form of routine patrolling is dangerous because it invites enemy ambush, it kills initiative, it wearies the men both mentally and physically and it achieves little.
>
> Patrols must be sent out as and when the situation demands and the situation often varies between battalion sectors and sometimes even between company sectors.
>
> If the enemy is suspected of building up prior to attacking it may be necessary for a battalion to send out eight recce patrols in one night in order to cover the whole area throughout the hours of darkness.
>
> In order to divert the enemy's attention from a projected raid on Thursday, it may be desirable to send out 'noise-making' fighting patrols in another area on Monday, Tuesday, and Wednesday.
>
> If the enemy is attempting to dominate No Man's Land it may be necessary for a series of strong fighting patrols to go to selected points each night over a period of time, thereby slowly pushing the enemy back.
>
> If a company commander wants to get his company familiar with the terrain in front of it, he may institute an extensive programme of small recce patrols to various features. In other words the tactical situation demands and dictates the patrols.
>
> Every patrol must be a carefully organized and worthwhile operation, complete in itself – not 'just another patrol.'[78]

Perhaps the most striking feature of West's patrol directive is that its detailed suggestions were most apt for the 25th Brigade. Certainly the aggressive patrollers of the Commonwealth brigade had no need for such common-sense reminders. Its essential points, moreover, had been standard operating procedure in Rockingham's brigade but were the complete opposite of the patrol schemes of Bogert's sluggish battalions. As the GOC's directive went on to point out, 'There is no doubt that for purely recce missions the answer is the one and one patrol. Two men can see and appreciate as much as ten men, and moreover, if making contact with the enemy can "fade out" in a way which a section or platoon never can.'[79] This concept had been well understood by the 2nd battalions but Bogert's professionals seemed unable to grasp it. While Rockingham's units routinely sent out small reconnaissance patrols to cover their front and observe the Chinese positions across the valley, the 1st battalions ventured forward of their standing patrols only if they were in large 'fighting' groups of at least a dozen men. As a result, the 1st battalions' fighting patrols had been left to stumble blindly across no man's land until ambushed by the ever-alert Chinese.

On 27 January the 1st Commonwealth Division began preparations to hand over its positions to the 2nd US Infantry Division, prior to moving into I Corps reserve south of the Imjin River. Its artillery units were to remain in place to support the

American formation, whose own artillery was being used to support a South Korean division. One interesting feature of the relief was that the 29th Brigade's two front-line battalions had to be temporarily placed under command of the 25th and 28th Brigades in order to conform with the normal Eighth Army – and, until recently, Commonwealth – deployment of two regiments (i.e., brigades) in the line and one in reserve. By 31 January the handover had been completed, and the division was out of the line the first time since its formation in July 1951.[80]

The division's two and a half months in reserve were largely unremarkable. A prominent feature in the training program was a renewed emphasis on mobile operations. By the end of its reserve period, West believed that his division was 'capable of moving and deploying rapidly, a state of affairs almost unheard of when we were in the line.'[81] Given the static state of the war, however, rapid movement was unlikely to be called for. The rationale for the training seems to have been the concern of Gen. Mark Clark that the communists might be building up their strength for an offensive. The reduced scale of operations resulting from the onset of winter weather had allowed the enemy to increase troop strength from 970,000 at the end of October 1952 to 1,070,000 by 1 February 1953, to stockpile ammunition and rations at the front, and to replace three of the seven Chinese armies and one of the two North Korean corps in the front line with fresh, fully equipped combat units. The Eighth Army's commander, General Van Fleet, remained confident despite the buildup, certain that the UN force of eighteen divisions could defeat any enemy attempt to break its line. Due for retirement, Van Fleet handed over command to Lt. Gen. Maxwell Taylor, who had commanded the 101st Airborne Division during the Second World War, on 11 February 1953.[82]

From the Canadian perspective, any training undertaken in February and March was of marginal value to the brigade's future operations since, at the end of March, the Canadians began their second major rotation of units. While still in reserve, the 3rd Battalion, Royal Canadian Regiment replaced the 1st Battalion on 25 March. Interestingly, during 1 RCR's eleven months in Korea, they had spent only five and a half months actually in the line. Nonetheless, the battalion had incurred the highest number of casualties – 48 killed, 206 wounded, and 17 missing – of any Canadian battalion in the war, and a total that was considerably in excess of the 31 killed, 134 wounded, and none missing suffered by 2 RCR during its nine months in the front line. While in reserve the Canadian battalions also received their first quota of Korean Augmentation to Commonwealth troops, South Korean soldiers assigned in groups of 100 to infantry battalions in Eighth Army to augment their fighting strength.[83] Between the newly arrived units and the influx of inexperienced Koreans, therefore, the Canadian brigade could not have been expected to be at peak efficiency upon its return to the line in early April.

Nor was the division, as a whole, expecting an easy time once it reoccupied its former positions. During its absence, the 2nd US Infantry Division was attacked several times by the Chinese. On 1 March a company-sized attack, preceded by a heavy bombardment, struck the French battalion attached to the 2nd Division but was driven off after a brief hand-to-hand combat. Two days later, an American outpost on the Hook was overrun. The heaviest attack was launched on 17 March when a Chinese battalion attacked the 9th US Infantry Regiment's positions on Hill 355. The Chinese were able to reach the American trenches but only one platoon position was overrun, with the remaining platoons holding firm until reinforcements arrived. Although enemy casualties were estimated to be in excess of 400, the 9th Regiment's stubborn defence of Little Gibraltar cost it more than 100 men. Even that action had to be considered minor, however, compared with the four-day fight of the 1st Marine Division to recover two hilltop outposts, two to three miles southwest of the Hook, that were overrun by the Chinese on 26 March. By the time the marines had retaken the outposts and repelled the last of several battalion-sized attacks on 29 March, the Americans had suffered 1,017 casualties while inflicting over 1,300 on the Chinese.[84]

It was the increasingly tentative nature of most US patrols, however, that was the Commonwealth commander's greatest concern prior to the division's return to the front. 'With the change over in Army commanders' from Van Fleet to Taylor, West wrote on 1 April, 'there has been a noticeable increase in centralisation in the control of patrols. Strict, almost hide-bound, orders are in force regarding the briefing of patrols and any set-back, however minor, is the subject of a searching inquiry in US units – indeed the unfortunate patrol commander may even have to report to the Army Commander. As a result there is a tendency in US units for patrols to become less and less aggressive. I anticipate that we shall have to patrol and fight exceptionally hard in order to regain no man's land when we return to the line.' Of less concern was the recent Chinese tactic of 'the silent attack, so as to avoid our defensive [artillery] fire.' West was confident that the new tactic 'should be fairly simple to defeat with our infantry weapons' but added the important caveat 'providing our patrols are alert.'[85]

The Commonwealth Division's relief of the 2nd US Division was completed on 8 April 1953. In arranging his brigades, West handed the difficult task of defending Hills 159 and 355 to the always aggressive 28th British Commonwealth Brigade, in the same positions they had occupied prior to the move into reserve, and placed the 29th British Brigade astride the Sami-ch'on River in the equally exposed defences of the Hook. That left the division's least vulnerable sector, its centre, to be occupied by the 25th Brigade. In making these dispositions, West was undoubtedly influenced by the fact that 3 RCR had only recently arrived in the theatre while 1 R22eR was due to be replaced by 3 R22eR in a couple of weeks. It was probably hoped that the wide no man's land of the central sector – from 1,000 to 2,000 yards between the Chinese and Commonwealth positions – would compensate for any continued Canadian shortcomings.

As West had predicted, the Commonwealth Division 'found on our return to the line that the enemy completely dominated no man's land and we had to embark on some aggressive and costly patrolling.'[86] That was certainly the case with the Australian battalions, 2 RAR (which had replaced 1 RAR on 21 March) and 3 RAR, when they relieved the two British battalions of 28th Brigade on Hills 355 and 159 on 5 and 7 May. According to the Australian official historian, 'The Americans ... had not maintained dominance of no man's land at night and when the Australians returned they found the Chinese "leaning on our wire." In this situation it was easy for the Chinese to make raids and more serious attacks on the Jamestown Line and the two battalion commanders ... set about restoring the situation' by reestablishing 'an aggressive patrolling program.'[87]

On the Canadians' central sector, Bogert placed 3 PPCLI on the brigade's right and 1 R22eR on the left while initially keeping the novice 3 RCR in reserve. Maj. Harry Pope's C Company drew the task of defending the forward positions on Hills 97 and 123, north of the village of Hamurhan. On the night of 7-8 April while the Van Doos were moving up to relieve the Americans, the US company occupying the position had had one of its outposts overrun for a second time in less than a week, and lost all ten men in the valley. With rotation close at hand, C Company made no attempt to contest the Chinese control of the valley floor during its last week and a half in the line and 'life was pleasant and uneventful' despite averaging some 200 shells per day on the company position. Nonetheless, the pattern of the shelling convinced Pope 'that the Chinese were preparing an attack. Their destruction of the two [US held] outposts was very much in the pattern of their October 1952 attack on Hill 355. Their shelling was not harassing; it was the pin-point registration of, I believe, no less than 100 guns, each registering for its troop.'[88]

When the Chinese, speaking over a loudspeaker, offered to turn over several wounded UN soldiers if some Canadians would go into the valley to collect them, Major Pope 'asked nothing better than to go for a walk in the valley to see my positions from the enemy's point of view.' Aware that his CO was 'not fond of patrols going out from C Company in broad daylight,' he decided that it would be better to go 'into the valley without telling him.' Pope and the commander of 9 Platoon headed out at dawn carrying a stretcher. After reaching the centre of the valley midway between the Chinese and Canadian entrenchments with no sign of enemy reaction, Pope contemplated 'strolling like that along the whole front of the Commonwealth Division' until 'the man on duty at the Chinese loudspeaker woke up and threw this one at us: "What are you doing?" ... "Are you just going for a walk?"' Showing the Chinese their stretcher, the two officers decided to make a quick about-turn and quietly reenter their own positions: 'At every instant, we were expecting a burst in our backs but it seemed to me that to break into a gallop – as I had a very great desire to do – would certainly have brought enemy fire down on us. Better then to continue to stroll like a couple of idiots who had nothing better to do than to spend breakfast time between the lines with a stretcher.'[89]

The lack of an enemy response, or any sign of lay-up caves or cut wire, convinced Pope that a Chinese attack on the 1 R22eR's positions was not imminent. Having assured himself 'that the enemy was doing nothing crooked on our side of the valley,' the Van Doo major decided to phone his battalion commander to make his report. 'Colonel Trudeau was one of the rare 22nds who never swore – but if he'd ever come close [to it] with me, he certainly came close again that morning. But, in effect, without cause. In seizing the opportunity the enemy was offering me to examine my position from the point of view of the enemy's position, I was precisely carrying out my mission: defend my company position with the least loss possible. And precisely because it was abnormal to make reconnaissance patrols in broad daylight, I would have been ashamed to send anyone else to do it.'[90]

In any event, an attack would not be Pope's problem. On 20 April, 3 RCR relieved 1 R22eR in its positions as the last of the 1st battalions prepared to return to Canada. Interviewed about his battalion's experiences the following day, Trudeau, like his fellow 1st battalion COs in similar interviews, did not admit to any problems if, indeed, he was aware of them. He did acknowledge that his officers, many of whom had had operational experience during the Second World War, lacked 'first-hand knowledge of defensive warfare' but would comment only that 'they had applied standard teachings for the defence and thus had come to appreciate more fully that these were sound. In the defence, as much as in offensive warfare or even more so, the importance of weapon training, leadership and man management at all levels had come out.'[91] Given Pope's criticisms of Canadian performance in 1952-3, first-hand experience of which was gained in Trudeau's battalion, it is not clear whether 'come out' was meant in a positive or negative sense. On the same day that Trudeau was interviewed by the brigade's historical officer, 1 R22eR handed over its reserve positions to the recently arrived 3 R22eR.

With the peace talks at Panmunjom about to resume, it appeared that the war might well be moving toward its final phase. Despite the possibility that an armistice might finally be concluded in the near future, the rotation of units in the Canadian brigade continued. By 1 May, the other Canadian units in the division, the artillery field regiment, the engineer field squadron, the transport company, the Royal Canadian Electrical and Mechanical Engineers workshop, and the field ambulance unit had all been replaced as well. By the time the second rotation was completed on 24 May with A Squadron, Lord Strathcona's Horse, taking over B Squadron's Sherman tanks, the Canadians were already revamping their defences under the guidance of their new commander. After replacing Bogert on 25 April 1953, it did not take Brig. Jean V. Allard long to realize the difficult task that lay before him in correcting the worst of the brigade's deficiencies.

13 THE THIRD BATTALIONS, MAY-JULY 1953

On the day after Jean Allard assumed command of the Canadian brigade, the plenary sessions of the armistice negotiations were resumed at Panmunjom following a six-month recess. The impasse in the stalemated talks had been broken on 28 March when the communists informed the United Nations Command that they were agreeable to an exchange of sick and wounded prisoners that had been proposed by Gen. Mark Clark. At the same time, the communists expressed the hope that the prisoner exchange would 'lead to the smooth settlement of the entire question of prisoners of war, thereby achieving an armistice in Korea for which people throughout the world are longing.' The new attitude was undoubtedly influenced by recent changes in leadership in both the Soviet Union and the United States. Dwight Eisenhower had been sworn in as US president in mid-January, while the death of Joseph Stalin on 5 March appeared to inject a fresh incentive to settle the Korean question so that the new Soviet leadership could consolidate its power base at home free of a major international distraction. Operation Little Switch, in which the UNC exchanged 6,670 North Korean, Chinese, and civilian internees for 684 UN prisoners at the end of April, seemed to indicate a new willingness to pursue a negotiated settlement of the forced repatriation issue. Although the numbers exchanged may seem disproportionate, they represented a roughly equal percentage of the 132,000 communist prisoners held in the South and the 12,000 UN prisoners held in the North.[1]

While past experience with the communist negotiators dictated caution on the part of the UNC, it seemed that a final settlement of the repatriation question was now within reach. Tempering the United Nations' optimism, however, was the rising tide of opposition from the South Korean government. President Syngman Rhee remained strongly opposed to any settlement that left the two Koreas divided and had vowed that South Korea would fight on alone if a negotiated armistice failed to address Seoul's objections. As the talks reconvened at Panmunjom on 26 April, therefore, the UNC delegates not only had to conclude an agreement with the communists but also had to ensure that its terms were acceptable to the South Korean government. Trying to predict President Rhee's reaction to any one of their proposals often proved embarrassing for the UNC negotiators as they attempted to resolve the difficult repatriation issue.[2]

It was against the backdrop of renewed optimism for a final ceasefire, therefore, that Brigadier Allard assumed command of the Canadian brigade in late April. Like his two predecessors at brigade headquarters, Allard was a combat veteran of the

Brig. J.V. Allard, wearing an American helmet and a Van Doo scarf, on a night tour of 3 R22eR's entrenchments in June 1953. Behind Allard is the Van Doo CO, Lt.-Col. J.L.G. Poulin. The flashbulb could have done little for either officer's night vision. NAC PA134496

Second World War, having commanded the 2nd Division's 6th Brigade during the closing months of the campaign in northwest Europe. The native of Trois-Rivières had been given the 6th Brigade after successfully leading the R22eR through much of the Italian campaign. Consequently, he was already familiar with some of the officers he would command in Korea, particularly those in the French Canadian battalion. During the crossing of the Rhine in March 1945, moreover, Allard's brigade had followed Rockingham's 9th Brigade to the far shore and one of his battalion commanders had been Jacques Dextraze of Les Fusiliers Mont-Royal. After an appointment as Canada's military attaché to the Soviet Union immediately after the war, Allard served as commander of the Eastern Quebec area – in which capacity he had a hand in the selection of Louis Trudeau to command 1 R22eR – and on the staff at army headquarters in Ottawa. Having been sent directly to Korea from his post as vice quartermaster general at army headquarters, the new brigade commander had had little contact with the 3rd battalions in Canada.[3]

Of his three battalion commanders, Allard was most familiar with the CO of 3 R22eR, Lt.-Col. Jean Poulin. A permanent force officer since August 1939, Poulin had served with the R22eR until August 1942 when he was transferred to Les Fusiliers Mont-Royal to help reorganize that unit after its losses in the Dieppe raid.

Returning to the R22eR in May 1944, Poulin spent ten months as a company commander under Allard in Italy. Like Poulin, the other two infantry COs were also combat veterans of the Second World War. Lt.-Col. Kenneth Campbell, who had commanded 3 RCR since the battalion's formation at Fort Lewis, had seen action with both the Princess Louise Dragoon Guards and the Lanark and Renfrew Scottish Regiment in Italy and northwest Europe. The replacement for the Patricias' ailing Herbert Wood (suffering from the weak heart that would kill him a year after the publication of *Strange Battleground*) was Lt.-Col. Malcolm MacLachlan, an officer who had twice been wounded while in action with the Cape Breton Highlanders during the Second World War. He was posted to 3 PPCLI directly from Canada's recently formed NATO brigade in Germany, where he had been serving as the second-in-command of 1 Canadian Highland Battalion.[4] Although Allard's group of infantry commanders had not commanded battalions in action during the Second World War as Rockingham's COs had all done, they did have more combat experience than Bingham, Wood, or Trudeau had had on arrival in Korea.

Like the regular battalions they were replacing, neither 3 RCR nor 3 R22eR had the advantage of collective training, at either the battalion or brigade level, before arriving in Korea. Having served as training units in the two years since their formation, the two battalions had managed to conduct only a limited training program prior to embarking for the Far East. The continual infusion of new recruits to replace those men drafted to Korea meant that many of the men in the 3rd battalions had spent little time in the army prior to embarkation. In 3 RCR, for instance, the ranks of the support company were finally filled 'for the first time since it was formed' only on 22 January 1953. Although the company then underwent 'a vigorous training programme,' it had less than two weeks to learn its job before the men were sent on embarkation leave on 5 February. When the battalion's B and D Companies conducted a field firing exercise on 23 January 'supported by one section of mortar and two sections of MMG,' it 'was the first battle inoculation for many of the men of the rifle and support companies.'[5] The unit was visited by Allard for the first time on 25 February but left Petawawa for the Far East the next day. Fortunately for 3 RCR, it arrived in Korea during the Commonwealth Division's period in corps reserve and had nearly a month to become acclimatized to Korea before entering the Jamestown Line on 20 April.[6]

If Allard had not been aware of the 3rd battalions' lack of training prior to arriving in Korea, he was quick to recognize it after sizing up his brigade under frontline conditions. The new brigade commander's immediate worry was the fact that the 'deliberate defence is in many respects foreign to the average Canadian officer.'[7] According to Allard's memoirs, he had two great concerns after taking over command from Bogert: 'First of all, at night, no man's land was under enemy control ... Secondly, our defensive positions – especially our shelters – were not very solid. I also felt that the young officers were lacking in initiative: they arrived in their allotted positions and settled into them, usually making only minor adjustments. Then they waited. This was quite normal since the doctrine of training these men had received was essentially based on offensive warfare; they had received little instruction in the art of entrenchment.'[8] On 1 May, Allard issued the battalions with 'Notes on Defence,' a memorandum 'intended as a compilation of some of the most important aspects of the daily life in defence.' The instructions were primarily aimed at reminding company and platoon commanders that their leadership was just as important when holding defensive positions as it was in the attack. The new Canadian commander insisted, for instance, that the siting of all automatic weapons must be personally coordinated by the company commander: 'It must be ensured that each platoon commander and section commander know exactly the location of the weapon and its arcs of fire. The men in the platoon must be familiar with the arcs of fire and area of responsibility of each of the automatic weapons in their platoon.' Allard's greatest emphasis, however, was on the importance of officers demonstrating daily leadership while on the defensive. Allard particularly wanted his company and platoon officers to make routine visits to each forward position during the night:

> Company and platoon commanders ... should go amongst their men talking to them and instilling them with the importance of their work and assuring them of their presence. There should be no doubt at any time that company and platoon commanders are not personally commanding their sub-units. In defence this is more difficult to realize than in the offence where personal leadership becomes so necessary. Because of the very nature of defence in that so much time is devoted to watching and waiting for something to happen, all ranks should be kept extremely busy during working hours. The criteria is to work constantly developing your defensive locality and keep alert for any overt action of the enemy.[9]

Problems were readily apparent to 3 RCR when they occupied the former 1 R22eR positions on 20 April. In this instance, however, the difficulties were not entirely of Canadian creation. The RCR's commanding officer, Lieutenant-Colonel Campbell, found the entrenchments his battalion had taken over to be 'badly run down. The wiring was insufficient. The trenches were not deep enough. There were gaps in the communication trenches. The fire bays were of a poor design and had no adequate overhead cover. The bunkers were too high, too lightly timbered and had too little overhead cover. They were also too far removed from the fighting positions.' As part of the less-exposed central sector, this portion of the Commonwealth line had received the lowest priority during the division's digging program of the previous December and January, and the Americans, apparently satisfied with the field defences they inherited, had made no improvements. The 3rd battalion officers, like all of their predecessors, were initially taken aback by the problems imposed by the rugged Korean terrain in laying out defensive positions. 'The type of defensive position seen in this campaign,' Campbell explained,

> was very specialized. The terrain was made up of steep-sided hills joined by steep-sided ridges and separated by valleys varying from narrow bush-choked ravines to wide flat bottomed valleys floored with [rice] paddy ... Because of the width of front allotted to a battalion, usually twenty-five hundred to four thousand yards, the defensive position usually consisted of platoon positions on the more prominent hills loosely grouped into company localities suited to the ground pattern ... The fashion was to have a platoon position consist of a more or less circular trench around the hill with the fire trenches spaced along the front and sides of the hill and the living quarters on the back.[10]

As was being done elsewhere in the Commonwealth Division, 3 RCR willingly blamed the Chinese dominance of no man's land on the Americans, claiming that the 2nd Division had not patrolled effectively. It was a situation, Campbell claimed, which the Van Doos, 'being in the line for such a short time and being so close to rotation,' had not attempted to correct.[11] Unaware that the enemy had routinely dominated the Canadian front since the previous summer, Campbell could not have appreciated the irony of his comments. Rectifying the situation, however, would require the 3rd battalion officers to exhibit the sort of drive and determination that had been lacking in the Canadian brigade since Rockingham's departure a year earlier. It was now up to Allard to reinstill that commitment throughout the formation. As the brigadier explained in his post-armistice report, the task was not made any easier by the inexperience of his men:

> Both of the forward battalions were kept busy restoring the defences and familiarizing themselves with the front so as to wrest from the enemy the control of no man's land. While 3 PPCLI had been in action before, 3 RCR had not, and so Lt-Col Campbell set about familiarizing his patrol commanders with the terrain, and practising his men in the art of patrolling in Korea and against the Chinese. To achieve this, the battalion started with a program of recce patrols. By the end of the first week, fighting patrols were sent out. At first the enemy interfered very little with this patrolling but, as time went on, there were more and more contacts. It became quite obvious that our men were not sufficiently trained to gain control of no man's land. They barely reached the valley and returned too early.[12]

Of course a major revamping of the brigade's defences would take some time before becoming effective. Even as Allard was sizing up the difficulties he was facing, the Chinese exploited the Canadian weaknesses in yet another raid on a company position.

Major Pope's suspicions that the Chinese were preparing an attack against the company position on Hills 97 and 123 gained credibility in the days immediately following 3 RCR's takeover of the Van Doo entrenchments. In response to RCR complaints about the volume of enemy artillery fire that was falling on its C Company,

Allard sent his counterbattery officer to investigate. The officer 'found shell fragments from so many different types of artillery and mortar weapons, that he described the shelling as clear evidence of registration rather than harassing fire.'[13] Campbell, for one, was impressed by the subtlety of the registration: 'One day a whole new battery would fire and then it would quit and not be heard again. Later on another battery would come in but in such a fashion as to appear to be the same battery in a new form of harassing role.' The stealth of the registration came as a surprise to Campbell, who had been misinformed by his less-than-insightful counterpart, Lieutenant-Colonel Bingham, that the Chinese 'registered targets in a fairly obvious fashion.'[14]

Chinese patrol activity was also on the increase by the end of April, with the enemy paying particular attention to the wire defences to C Company's right front in the draw between the RCR positions and those of 3 PPCLI to their right (see Map 17). Although Campbell believed that some reports of enemy activity 'were quite obviously the product of imagination' resulting from 'the greenness of his men,' enough were verified to indicate 'that the enemy were feeling out the wire.'[15] On the night of 1 May an enemy patrol, employing the same tactic that had been used against the Canadians prior to the attack on Hill 355 in October, closed on C Company's wire and threw stones at the defenders. The Royals promptly called down their defensive fire tasks, a result that Allard believed 'had been the chief mission of the Chinese patrol' in the first place.[16] Given all of the signs, the Canadian brigadier strongly suspected that an attack was imminent: 'During this period of preparation the enemy [artillery] fire cut and kept open a gap in the tactical wire on the right flank of the right forward platoon. His patrols had drawn our DF tasks, had discovered the positions of our standing patrols and the few gaps through our wire and minefields. From these reports, I expected that the enemy would stage a raid, or possibly make some special effort on May Day. He did not. Apart from maintaining his fire on the gap created in the wire, there were no other activities during the daylight hours of 2 May to distinguish that day from the previous ones.'[17]

Allard's situation was complicated by an invitation he had received from Gen. Maxwell Taylor to dine at the Eighth Army headquarters mess in Seoul. Having been in command of his brigade for less than two weeks, Allard did not feel that he was in a position to refuse the commanding general. As he later recalled in his memoirs, however, 'I was so worried [about an attack] that I asked permission to leave again right after the meal, promising to complete my visit later. Taylor, who had seen many problem situations, pointed out that his units were constantly coming under fire that usually led to nothing more. I was not convinced and he readily let me do as I wanted. As soon as the meal was over, I climbed into my jeep which I had had specially equipped so that I could hear what information my HQ was receiving during the sixty-mile return journey.' Apparently Allard had not communicated his concerns to his headquarters staff, however, since upon returning to 25 Brigade at 2300 hours he had to close down 'a small party celebrating the departure

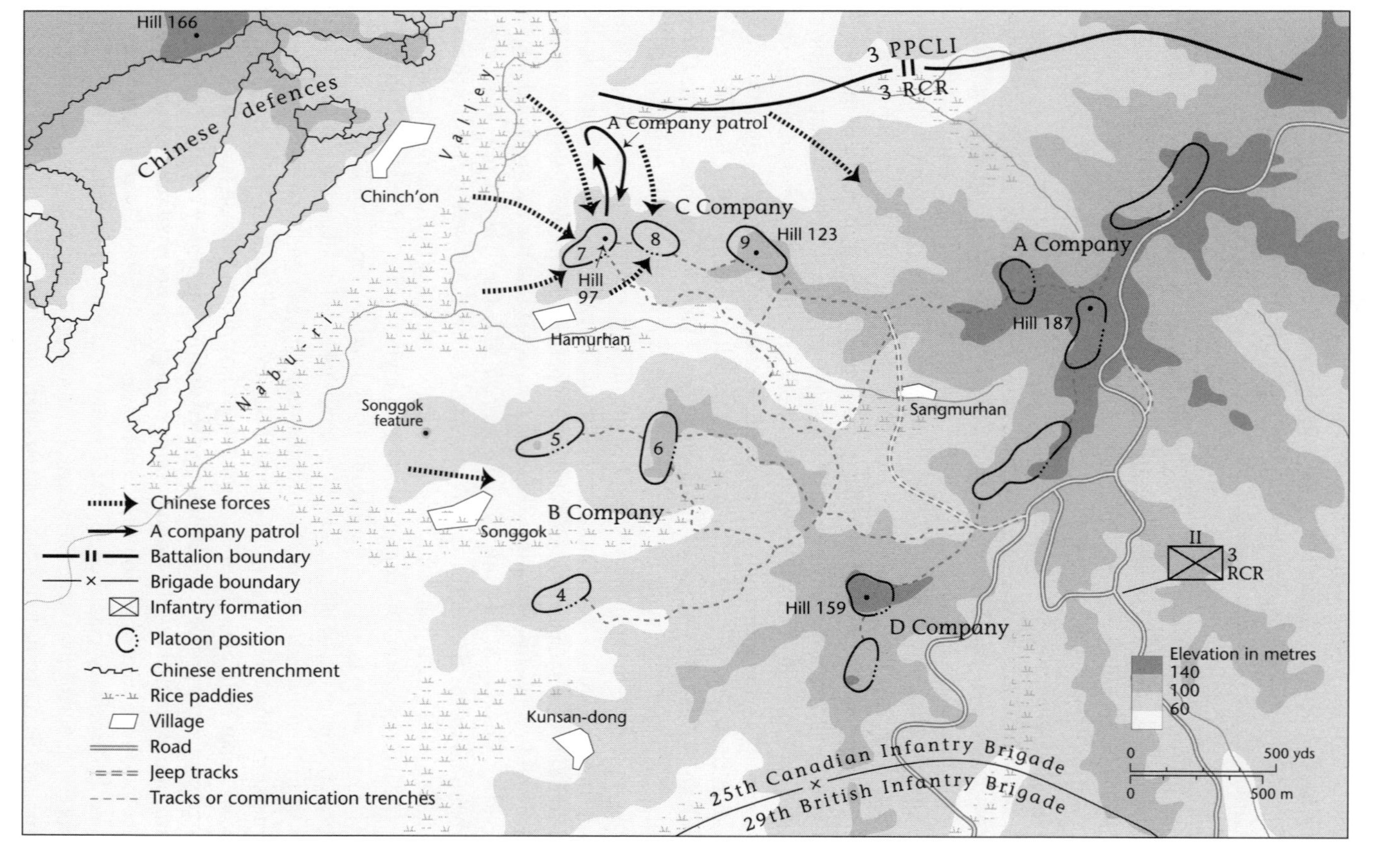

Map 17 *Attack on C Company, 3 RCR, 2-3 May 1953*

of one of our officers for Canada' in the officers' mess and order 'everyone to take up their battle position.'[18] By that time the Royals were already under attack.

At 2030 hours, as soon as it was sufficiently dark to screen movement in the valley, a sixteen-man patrol from A Company under the command of Lt. G.B. Maynell had moved out through a minefield gap to set up an ambush for the Chinese patrols that had been working on the wire covering C Company's northern flank. Once in position, however, the inexperienced Canadians found that some Chinese were already behind them. Moving to a nearby rice paddy wall, the RCR patrol requested a flare from C Company and opened fire. As one of the patrol members recalled,

> the enemy were close. I could see them. We were firing our Brens and Stens and tossing grenades and the enemy returned with burp guns and grenades. I heard Mr. Maynell shout 'You're doing good boys, keep pouring it to them.' It must have been shortly after this that he was hit.
>
> Our patrol called for artillery support but the shells landed too close so we had the support called off.

Hills 97 and 123, held by C Company, 3 RCR during the Chinese raid on 2-3 May 1953, as seen from the company position to the north on 13 July 1953. DHH 681.009 D6

> After we had been firing for about half an hour we ran short of ammunition. Cpl [J.C.] McNeil went around checking to see how much we did have ... Then McNeil told us to follow him. We moved out slowly for we had a few guys hurt. The flares that were going up made things tough for us. The Chinese caught us in the open as we were trying to come in. The man carrying Mr. Maynell was hit so he had to put the officer down but Mr. Maynell must have been dead anyway.[19]

On the way in, the survivors met the C Company standby patrol, a section of 8 Platoon under the command of Lt. D.W. Banton, that had been detailed 'to deal with enemy spotted by the recce or standing patrols but too large for the spotters to handle.'[20] Warned of the large numbers of Chinese in the valley, Banton nonetheless continued on, intending to rescue the wounded left behind by the first patrol. After travelling some 125 yards from the Canadian positions, however, Banton and his section were themselves ambushed, and the lieutenant was killed in the initial firefight. The survivors of the second patrol also scattered and made their way back to C Company as best they could.[21]

The intelligence staff at divisional headquarters, meanwhile, was able to gain a reasonably clear picture of the well-planned attack, primarily by monitoring Chinese wireless traffic. They were later able to surmise the composition of the enemy forces:

> a counter patrol force of three patrols designed to engage the battalion's patrols and draw attention to one area and if possible gain local domination of the area; selected groups to gap the wire in several places and hurl concussion grenades to simulate continuation of the mortaring programme; three bunker and trench destruction groups of approximately fifteen men each; two main assault/snatch groups each of platoon size; [and] one company group as immediate reinforcement.
>
> In front of 3rd Battalion, Royal Canadian Regiment, the enemy's patrols ventured out early and these he supported with artillery and mortar fire. However, while these patrols drew our attention, the enemy's wire gapping groups moved out on either flank, screened by a steady fire which fell on wire defences as well as on the objective. As the gapping groups closed to the wire, part of the fire was to lift to the rear of the company position.
>
> The task of the first group of the wire gapping parties was to establish where the wire had been most damaged by mortar fire, enlarge the gaps with bangalore torpedoes if necessary, and roll concussion grenades through the wire area to clear any mines. The second group was to move up on either side of the wire gap and hurl large numbers of concussion grenades towards the objective to create the impression that heavy shell and mortar fire was still falling in the area of the wire.
>
> During all this, while the gapping groups remained fairly secure near the gapping sites (shelling and mortaring of the wire had evidently made sufficient holes to provide local cover), the objective itself was subjected to very heavy shell fire. At the same time guides had been dispatched to bring forward the assault groups.

> By 2300 hours the enemy was sufficiently sure of his routes and the assault troops had begun to move forward in phases. Each phase had been paced off on the ground and as each phase was completed it was reported. Finally by 2350 hours all forward moves by the assault troops had been completed and the reserve company was in position some 1,000 metres in rear to the northeast. The wire had been gapped and special assault groups were hidden just inside the wire and the stage was set for the raid.
>
> At three minutes to midnight, the enemy announced that his main fire plan would start at midnight. At the appointed time shells and mortars rained onto the forward platoon of the right forward company [C] of 3rd Battalion Royal Canadian Regiment. For three minutes this fire continued, then it lifted onto the rear of the position. The enemy at the wire began to hurl his concussion grenades and the bunker and trench assault groups broke forward from two directions. He was soon in our forward trenches. Bunker charges were lit and tossed in and to add to the confusion, grenade throwers rushed from one side of the position to the other, thereby making the Canadians think that a much larger force was upon them.
>
> Now came the main assault/snatch groups, specially selected for the task, they threw themselves into our defences and soon had a dozen odd prisoners. As these were being hustled back [to the Chinese lines] the shelling and mortaring continued on the rear of the company position, while at the front and on the sides the enemy hurled more concussion grenades.[22]

With the 7 Platoon position on Hill 97 overrun, its commander, 2nd Lt. E.H. Hollyer, called for artillery concentrations on his own position. Lieutenant-Colonel Campbell then ordered the countermortar and close-in defensive fire tasks to be shot by the guns of the 81st Field Regiment although, with the Chinese already on the position, the DF tasks would only have made it costly for the attackers to be reinforced. At brigade headquarters, Allard used the balance of the divisional artillery and heavy guns from the supporting American Corps artillery to concentrate on isolating the fighting and preventing reinforcement.[23] Under this weight of fire the Chinese attack soon lost its cohesion. According to the intelligence staff who were monitoring Chinese radio communications, 'The enemy was very pleased at his quick success but orders by local commanders for withdrawal were countermanded on several occasions by a higher headquarters. His losses however in this period of uncertainty mounted and soon it became clear that the action would have to be broken off. For a time confusion and some panic was evident, for no sooner had the break off order been sanctioned than his rear company received another tremendous battering.'[24]

After overrunning Hill 97, the Chinese moved up to attack 8 Platoon. One of the 8 Platoon soldiers was Cpl. J.J.A. Pelletier:

> To the best of the Corporal's knowledge the enemy came upon 8 Platoon from two directions – from the north when they overflowed from the 7 Platoon positions and

> followed the communication trench back, [and] from the south-east when they temporarily cut off 8 Platoon from Company headquarters and 9 Platoon. In the close range fighting which followed, Corporal Pelletier was wounded first in the right leg by a burp gun and then in the left leg by the splinters from the wooden handle of a stick grenade. The Chinese were obviously seeking prisoners for they had ample opportunity to kill him had they so desired. Corporal Pelletier is rather surprised that they didn't for the three who took him a prisoner had just seen him shoot down one of their comrades.
>
> With two other Canadian prisoners, Corporal Pelletier was escorted off the hill and down the gap between 7 and 8 Platoon. When the party got to the base of the hill, a concentration of our own artillery made all go to ground. When the bombardment ceased, the group made its way across the floor of the valley but had to go to ground once to take cover from another of our concentrations. There were about thirty walking Chinamen and about fifteen wounded Chinamen being carried on the backs of their comrades ... Although the enemy had 'quite a few casualties,' the Corporal did not himself see more than this fifteen.[25]

Another Canadian captured that night, 2nd Lt. C.G. Owen, the battalion pioneer officer, also found the Chinese anxious to take prisoners. As Owen surrendered, 'a Chinese called out, "Hey Joe! Come out Joe! No Harmo!"' following which they 'grabbed my hand and shook it.'[26] Although the Chinese managed to enter the 8 Platoon position, a stout defence forced the attackers back toward 7 Platoon on Hill 97. By 0130 hours Lieutenant Hollyer, still in his 7 Platoon command post, had reported that the enemy was withdrawing and asked for the artillery fire to be shifted onto the forward slopes while the surviving members of his platoon withdrew to No. 8's position. Campbell was preparing a company attack to recover Hill 97 when Hollyer reached the C Company command post and reported that the position could be retaken by a fighting patrol. Twenty-one men from A Company subsequently reentered the position, both to secure it and to evacuate casualties, despite the heavy Chinese mortaring that covered the communist withdrawal.[27]

Even as the attack against 3 RCR had been developing, it was apparent to the division's intelligence staff that the engagement was, in fact, part of a larger action:

> The first suspicions were aroused at approximately 0025 hours. At that time [the enemy's] troops in action against the Canadians were told to keep up the fight because the other mission would come. A glance to the right [i.e., to the area of the Bowling Alley] served well at this time and it was soon evident that two enemy companies were on the move towards point 159 [west of Hill 210] from the north. The eyes and ears of special intelligence agencies were now turned in this direction. There was heavy movement there, no doubt of that, and two groups of medium machine guns were positioned on either side of Kigong-ni [northwest of Hill 159] firing into the Royal Fusiliers who held point 159. Moreover the enemy on the Apostles [feature] to the north east was also pouring small arms fire into this area.

> Throughout this time the command controlling the forward observation groups was urging them to press on to carry out the mission.
>
> The medium machine guns north of point 159 however were fast annoying the tenants of that area and the divisional guns were turned on to that fire. In all eight battery targets were fired; from all accounts with devastating effect. In turn the forward observation groups were also taken under fire.
>
> At 0400 hours on 3 May the enemy was still trying to extricate his hard-pressed forces, both in front of 3rd Battalion Royal Canadian Regiment and Point 159, and it must have been a gruesome task. By 0500 hours, however, his remaining elements in both areas were in full retreat, battered along their withdrawal routes by gun and mortar alike.[28]

Although the British defenders 'were engaged heavily by enemy artillery, mortar and small arms fire,' the Chinese attack on Hill 159 was broken up by Commonwealth artillery fire before it reached the lower slopes. In all, it was estimated that the enemy had fired over 2,000 rounds of mortar bombs and artillery rounds in support of their attacks while the Commonwealth divisional artillery replied with over 8,000 rounds in the defence.[29] That the attack on Hill 159 in the 28th Brigade's more exposed sector was spotted and broken up by artillery fire before an assault could be made was a clear indication that the tactical inadequacies that had plagued the Canadian brigade for nearly a year still remained. 'It came as rather a rude shock' to division headquarters, Lieutenant-Colonel Amy reported the following month, 'that the Chinese were able to move across such a wide no man's land and get in position for the attack without being spotted. 3 RCR could not have had an adequate screen of patrols out in front of their positions.'[30] Certainly Brigadier Allard had no doubt that the engagement was a Canadian defeat, even if the raiders had suffered far heavier casualties than the defenders. RCR casualties totalled thirty killed, forty-one wounded, and eleven missing, the biggest losses suffered during the war by any Canadian unit in a single engagement. Twenty-two of the eighty-two casualties were South Korean soldiers attached to the battalion. In the words of the Canadian official history, 'The Chinese achieved their objectives of inflicting casualties, taking prisoners, destroying defences and clearing their dead and wounded from the battlefield.'[31]

In contrast to the lethargy that characterized his predecessor's command (and the false victory claims made by brigade headquarters following the raid on 1 RCR the previous October), Allard not only acknowledged the 25th Brigade's tactical shortcomings but was willing to take corrective action. Among the more pronounced Canadian deficiencies was the continuing lack of effective leadership at the company and platoon level. While the problem had been ignored during Bogert's tenure – if indeed his indifferent battalion commanders, suffering from the same malaise, had the ability to recognize it – the question of leadership was quickly identified by Allard. Sharing the brigadier's desire to correct these deficiencies, his battalion COs gave frank assessments of the problems in their wartime interviews with the brigade's historical officers. As quoted in Chapter 10, Lieutenant-Colonel Campbell believed that his older, Second World War-experienced company commanders 'lack[ed] drive and enthusiasm' and expressed a preference for 'keen young captains commanding his companies [rather] than slow old majors.'[32] The commander of 3 R22eR, Lieutenant-Colonel Poulin, was more charitable, noting that all of his 'present company commanders bar one had served as company commanders or 2/ics during the Second World War' and that their 'experience, guidance and admonitions' during training in Canada 'were a tremendous help in making the subalterns good.' Nonetheless, his unit's initial performance at the front in May 1953 convinced Poulin that his battalion had 'lost our aggressive spirit. Commanders and men are dug-out minded. The fear of receiving casualties deadens our reactions and lessens our effort. We are thoroughly defensive minded and yet not thorough in our defence.'[33]

Maj. C.E.C. MacNeill, the acting CO of the Patricias until Lieutenant-Colonel MacLachlan arrived in mid-May, was also critical of 'the young soldiers in the ranks' of his battalion when he was interviewed in May 1953, noting that they 'have not a highly developed sense of duty, not even to each other.' MacNeill reported that 'three [of four] rifle company commanders have served in action during the Second World War' while 'the majority of the subalterns are young officers who graduated from OCS [officer candidate school] in the post-war period,' which was typical of the Canadian battalions. MacNeill, like Harry Pope, believed that too many officers were reluctant to leave the shelter of their command posts: 'Successful man management is fundamental to sound tactics. Too often, the platoon commanders try to run their platoons by telephone. They pick up the phone, talk to the section commanders and accept, without personally checking, the sector commander's assurance that all is well. The platoon commanders must get about from man to man. However, when the positions are being heavily bombarded it is almost impossible to move about and a certain amount of control by telephone must be accepted.'[34] Of course Pope would have added that the young platoon officers were simply following the example set by their company and battalion commanders.

The opinions of his infantry commanders were confirmed in Allard's post-armistice report. In touring the front-line positions, the brigadier was taken aback by the disturbing lack of professional knowledge exhibited by many of the brigade's career officers. Allard explained, 'Some of my impressions on first contact were of surprise, and some not too favourable. Since we were already in contact with the enemy I had no alternative other than "do what you can with what you've got."' Among the company commanders – about whom the brigadier felt obliged to state that they 'were all brave and loyal' – the 'most serious weakness ... was their apparent ignorance of infantry weapons, and particularly of their tactical handling.' As almost all of the company commanders were Second World War veterans for whom the infantry weapons in use in Korea were basically unchanged from the previous conflict, the brigadier's comments are a shocking indictment indeed. Allard was also critical of the 'lack of knowledge of the defensive battle' among his experienced regular officers: 'The co-ordination of fire was not existent. Fortunately there were some exceptions, but I would say that the majority did not know how to build a defensive fire plan and here is where the "Chinagraph Curtain" [i.e., the reliance on defensive artillery fire to stop enemy attacks] was at its worst. Too many took their last war experience of reorganization on an objective, or hasty defence, as the example for the preparation of a defensive position and defensive plan. This had to be corrected and it was. Unfortunately, a few officers had to be relieved of their commands.'[35]

The lack of understanding of infantry weapons in the defence also made it more difficult for company commanders to instruct their men properly on their specific roles during an attack or to instill a sense of confidence in their ability to defeat the enemy:

> Company after company occupied the same hills, lived in the same bunkers and fought from the same trenches, and there was a tendency for the platoon and company commanders to display little initiative. As long as he observed certain fundamental principles he felt safe. This required constant vigilance on the part of battalion commanders and myself, because the width and depth of our front necessitated co-ordination, impossible without the closest co-operation between sub-units.
>
> The true worth of a company commander was measured by the determination with which his men fought ... At the most crucial time – the period of the bombardment before the attack – the company commander could do almost nothing to reassure and to encourage his men. Only with a clear understanding of the company defence plan by all ranks was it possible to maintain the men at their posts. Leadership that comes squawking out of a telephone is hardly inspiring.[36]

Given the inadequate level of professional knowledge among the long-serving regular officers who made up the bulk of the company commanders, it is not surprising that Allard found the platoon leaders, who depended on the more senior battalion officers for their training and were too young to have served in the Second World War themselves, to be 'very deficient in professional knowledge.' Although 'the junior officers were all potentially good,' the brigade commander

> was astonished at their lack of appreciation of their problems. They all, without exception, took their ready-made defensive positions, sat down and waited to be attacked. When asked if they had a battle plan, the obvious answer came 'we are here' and pointing at some distance away, they indicated fields of fire, often beyond the maximum range of platoon weapons. The tendency was to rely on artillery fire. The knowledge of dead ground [ground shielded from direct fire] and of protective patrols, seemed a great mystery. To correct this situation, they all attended the patrol school and were asked to produce a dead ground trace of their position. To this, the reaction was very good and an improvement of the defences was immediately noticed.[37]

Also lacking Second World War experience, the infantry's NCOs were found to be deficient in 'knowledge of minor tactics and employment of weapons.' The NCO raw material, like that of the junior officers, was judged to be good – provided they were taught their trade. 'In all fairness,' Allard concluded, 'I must say that they reacted very well to battle conditions, were brave in front of the enemy and were resourceful in difficult situations.' However, the lack of professional knowledge among the officers and NCOs was bound to have a detrimental effect on the young soldiers in the ranks. 'The men were generally good and willing but their standard of knowledge in the handling of weapons was poor,' Allard reported. 'Their attitude to patrolling was one of inferiority, and it took a long time before they attained sufficient confidence in their ability to move in no man's land, to be effective. This weakness could, in many cases, be traced as far back as basic training. With a few exceptions, they had no knowledge of either the purpose or the method of patrolling.'[38]

Indicating the indifferent officership that had plagued the Canadian brigade during Bogert's tenure in command, similarly critical comments by 1st battalion COs are virtually nonexistent in their post-tour interviews. Indeed, 1 RCR's Lieutenant-Colonel Bingham seemed quite unaware of any shortcomings in either his own officers or the replacements coming from 3 RCR. Interviewed prior to departing Korea for Canada, Bingham had reported that 'the calibre of reinforcements who had come from 3 RCR had been very good. Of the newly arrived unit itself, Lieutenant-Colonel Bingham was pleased to say, "Their standard of spit and polish is just as high as ours."'[39] Typically, Peter Bingham's appreciation of a soldier's attributes was more acute in matters of appearance and drill than in those of professional knowledge or ability.

It was not until he wrote the official history that Lieutenant-Colonel Wood explained that the inadequate preparation many infantrymen had received in Canada was in part a product of the regimental training system the army adopted. According to Wood, the regimental system

> was an admirable method from many points of view but it had one disadvantage: it was inflexible. If a draft demand arrived that could not be met with fully trained soldiers, there was no other source – so those with the *most* training had to be sent. Training experts of the period felt that a newly joined recruit needed a minimum of seven months' training to equip him to perform in a field unit in action: four months' learning the basic skills of his arm, two months for such specialist training as driver or mortarman, and at least one month collective training. These timings however were seldom met, since they disregarded the amount of time consumed in 'housekeeping' duties, leave, special parades and punishment for infractions of discipline. Any sickness or absence without leave during the training period would of course further delay the process in individual cases. Since the intake of volunteers is not a predictable factor, while the demand for trained reinforcements is, there is no way of ensuring under this system that the soldier gets his ten to twelve months' training before being called forward as a reinforcement.[40]

Of course, as the long-time CO of 3 PPCLI, Lieutenant-Colonel Wood was well placed to describe the system's shortcomings – even if he chose not to mention the chronic equipment shortages that had hampered the 3rd battalions' ability to train recruits during 1951-2. As the performance of 1 PPCLI's inexperienced D Company in November 1951 demonstrates, however, the problem of inadequately trained reinforcements could be overcome if the men were led by dynamic officers. Even though Rockingham had combat-experienced battalion COs, he still kept on top of his officers with continual visits to the forward positions to ensure that operational standards were maintained. Unfortunately, the permanent force officers in the 1st battalions failed to exhibit that same drive and professionalism. Although Allard's report specifically addressed the problems of the 3rd battalions, his assessment is an accurate description of the lethargic performance of many regular officers. The problem of having 'old, slow majors' in command of rifle companies was compounded in the 1st battalions by the indifferent quality of their COs and Bogert's unwillingness or inability to recognize that a leadership problem existed. Harry Pope's observation that 'many majors and lieutenant-colonels with Second World War experience were most concerned not to get themselves killed in a sideshow like Korea' certainly suggests that a tour of combat duty in the Far East was not the posting of choice for many of the army's regular officers.[41]

To his credit, Allard not only accepted that problems existed within the Canadian brigade but moved quickly to address them. As mentioned in his report, the new brigade commander emphasized forward leadership among his officers and had to relieve several of their company commands. Only days after the attack on 3 RCR, Allard and the CO of the 81st Field Regiment, Lt.-Col. Henry Sterne, made a personal reconnaissance of no man's land in order to gain a first-hand knowledge of the approaches to the Canadian positions from the enemy's perspective – a course of action previously advocated by Harry Pope but one that his own CO had frowned upon.[42] In keeping with Major-General West's own patrolling memorandum, Allard concluded that the very wide no man's land on the Canadian front required

> numerous, two-man, wireless-equipped, combination recce patrols and outposts. These patrol-outposts must be in position on the enemy side of our DF fire zones as soon after last light as possible. It is their task to warn of the enemy approach and to remain out in no man's land even after the battle starts. Their work does not end when the enemy makes contact with our FDL's. By careful movement, our two-man patrol-outposts can supply vital information as to enemy manoeuvres, casualties and reinforcements even while the battle rages. They are just as safe in no man's land as they are back in the hill positions.[43]

Since the Canadian brigade had not mounted a program of reconnaissance patrols since Rockingham had turned over command to Bogert the year before, patrol techniques had to be retaught in order to instill a suitably aggressive spirit in Canadian patrols. To help accomplish that goal, Allard established a brigade patrol school under the 'masterly direction' of Major Pope.[44] Beginning its first course on 25 May, the patrol school provided week-long instruction to junior officers and NCOs on such subjects as camouflage and fieldcraft, recce patrols and outposts, stalking by day, night fighting patrols, and enemy formations and tactics. Since only fifteen or sixteen soldiers were enrolled in each course, however, fewer than a hundred infantrymen would have the benefit of the patrol training by the time the fifth and final course was concluded at the end of June.[45] Despite the small numbers, Allard believed that the patrol course had 'solved the majority of their weaknesses.'[46]

The brigadier also reorganized the brigade's defensive fire plan, placing primary emphasis on the infantry's own weapons instead of the Chinagraph Curtain of artillery fire: 'It is bad for the morale of the infantry if they are left with few responsibilities in the DF plan. They must be given a task which requires them to fire in the event of an assault.' Under Allard, each battalion's fire plan was now to be organized around its Bren and Browning light machine-guns, to which would be added the defensive fire tasks of the unit's medium machine-guns and mortars. Finally, the fire of supporting tanks was added to the plan. Only then were the brigade's artillery tasks assigned: 'The artillery should be left free to fire a few, very important DF-SOS targets but their main job is counter-bombardment. The fire power of a brigade without artillery is ample to stop any conceivable infantry assault. The chief danger to us is not an assault by the enemy infantry but in the mortar and artillery concentrations in support of it. Our artillery must be left free to engage enemy mortars and guns. That is their major role. That is the manner in which they can provide the most assistance to the infantry.'[47]

Allard also upgraded the brigade's field defences, primarily by strengthening the overhead cover and fields of fire of Bren positions to enable gunners to continue firing during a bombardment, and by digging more tunnels. Where that was impractical, trenches were deepened and barbed wire strung across their tops to prevent Chinese who reached the fieldworks from jumping into them. The brigadier also tried to restore a greater mobility to the battlefield by lifting some minefields and moving four tanks from the armoured squadron's reserve troop to the valley floor 'to give their support when needed. We hid them by day, and at night they patrolled the land near the former rice fields.'[48] He also had his battalions prepare plans for flanking companies to counterattack enemy raids more quickly than had been done on 2-3 May. Finally, Allard had an accurate plot made of all visible Chinese trenches and observation posts, using a powerful telescope procured in Japan, and ordered the tanks now located in the valley floor to conduct a destructive shoot each day as soon as the morning mists had lifted sufficiently to allow direct observation. According to the official history, 'All Chinese movement and any new positions which the telescope disclosed were taken on, day after day, with single rounds by all the guns, mortars and heavy machine-guns that could be spared from other tasks. This special effort, combined with vigorous and aggressive patrolling, kept the Chinese on the far side of the river. Brigadier Allard felt that he had discovered the key to successful defence in Korea.'[49]

Fortunately for the Canadians, the division's central sector remained relatively quiet for six weeks following the attack of 2-3 May, allowing time for Allard's reforms to be implemented. On the Commonwealth Division's left, however, where the 29th Brigade was holding the Hook position, the Chinese were not so passive. On 8 May a company-sized probe was made against the left forward company position held by the Black Watch but was driven off by artillery, mortar, and small-arms fire. A platoon-sized fighting patrol sent out to sweep the Ronson feature was engaged in a fierce firefight after the enemy had withdrawn but managed to capture three wounded Chinese. Unfortunately the prisoners all died before they could be interrogated.[50] During the final four months of fighting, in fact, the Commonwealth Division captured only five prisoners, all of them badly wounded, including the three taken by the Black Watch patrol. The division generally found that the Chinese soldiers fought 'fanatically when faced with the prospect of being taken a prisoner. The cause of this fanaticism may be ascribed to the constant communist political indoctrination to which all ranks of the Chinese Communist Forces are subjected by their political officers. Thus all five of the prisoners taken outright died before interrogation could take place. One of the five men even went so far as to attempt resistance to the medical personnel who were aiding him, stating that he preferred death to assistance from the United Nations.'[51]

Chinese deserters, on the other hand, of whom four were taken by the Commonwealth Division during the same period, 'talked freely under interrogation.'[52] The information provided by a Chinese who deserted on 18 May about an intended attack on the Hook on the 28th also demonstrated the thoroughness with which the Chinese forces prepared an attack. The soldier in question had taken part in a detailed reconnaissance of the Hook as part of his commanding officer's reconnaissance group. According to the Commonwealth Division's intelligence section, which monitored Chinese radio transmissions, these reconnaissance patrols

> stressed the techniques taught under Soviet Tactical Doctrine to determine the opponent's defensive fire tasks, fire lanes and patrol stations. The other information required from patrols was positions of light machine guns and medium machine guns, tanks and routes of protective patrols. The enemy spent considerable time in trying to locate our patrols and reported sightings of personnel and tank fire with the greatest care for several nights prior to the attack ...
>
> The most meticulous care was taken in placing [Chinese] observation posts and many were readjusted time and time again to take in definite areas near the objective ...
>
> Observation was of a most detailed nature and was passed back to a special station well in rear. These stations continually asked questions of the observers. The positions of our tanks and mortars were of particular interest ...
>
> Specialists, such as forward observation officers, radio operators, guides and unit leaders, were out on ground reconnaissance eight days prior to the attack. They were asked to remember landmarks and routes and in some cases to leave some marker on the spot as a guide.[53]

In the ten days before the 28 May attack, there were several enemy probes 'and much movement' around the Hook defences, 'supported on occasions by heavy enemy shelling and mortaring.' The enemy buildup opposite the Hook was parried by moving a second battalion onto the position – the 29th Brigade's third battalion was across the Sami-ch'on on the heights above Yong-dong – and transferring a fourth, 1st Royal Fusiliers, from the 28th Brigade on the division's right to act as a reserve. The British brigade also deployed extra tanks and 4.2-inch mortars while the divisional artillery engaged in a program of heavy harassing fire. The latter was in turn supported by the I Corps heavy artillery, which alone fired 5,000 rounds on one night, and by twenty-four air strikes totalling 102 sorties and 129 tons of bombs. The pattern of enemy shelling on 28 May indicated that 'the long awaited attack on the Hook was about to start and considerable damage was done to the defences in the area.' The assault was finally launched at 1953 hours after 'a tremendous weight of fire was brought down on to the forward positions ... Within a few minutes the enemy attacked, throwing grenades and satchel charges into the weapon slits as they assaulted. Gradually the defenders were forced to withdraw into the tunnels which were defended until the entrances were blown in. Three other assault waves were scattered by artillery, tank and small arms fire. A second attack against the right platoon position of the Hook company at 2045 hours made some penetration but the platoon was reinforced, the penetration stopped and the position soon restored by a counter attack.'[54]

Other assaults were made against the company positions to the right of the Hook but the attackers 'suffered very heavy casualties and were forced to withdraw without having achieved any penetration of our defences.' By 0430 hours on 29 May the entire Hook position was reported clear of the enemy. An engineer reconnaissance of the two forward platoon positions on the Hook found that the platoon bunkers were all damaged, that the eight-foot-deep trench system had in many places been levelled by the bombardment, and that tunnel and covered entrances had been blown in by the enemy's satchel charges.[55] Despite having accurately anticipated the attack and taken measures to defeat it, the Hook's defenders still suffered significant casualties. Their tenacious resistance cost the 29th Brigade 23 killed, 105 wounded, and 20 men taken prisoner. The Duke of Wellington's Regiment, holding the Hook position itself, was hardest hit, taking 126 of the 148 casualties. The added defensive measures, together with the support of both divisional and corps guns, which fired over 38,000 shells, mortars, and rockets, inflicted far heavier casualties on the Chinese attackers, however. Nearly 100 enemy corpses were counted on the position the next day and a further seventy dead were seen to be lying on enemy held ground. In all it was estimated that the Chinese force had lost some 250 killed and over 800 wounded in trying to capture the Hook.[56]

The attack had been made by a full regiment of Chinese and was viewed by Lieutenant-Colonel Amy at division headquarters as 'a serious attempt by the Chinese to seize the feature'[57] rather than the sort of raid experienced by the RCR battalions in October 1952 and May 1953. His opinion was supported by the weight of enemy artillery fire used to support the attack. In the raid on 3 RCR, the Chinese had averaged 150 to 200 shells and mortar bombs a day in the two weeks leading up to 2-3 May, followed by a barrage of 2,000 shells and mortar bombs during the assault. In the attack on the Hook four weeks later, the enemy hit the position with an average of 1,100 rounds on each of the nine days prior to the 28th and some 10,000 shells and mortar bombs during the actual assault.[58] Of course the other major difference between the two raids on the RCR positions and the attack on the British brigade was that, on both occasions, the Canadian defenders had been taken by surprise.

The attack on the Hook was part of a larger operation against the Turkish brigade holding the Nevada outpost complex in the 25th US Division's sector to the immediate left of the Commonwealth Division. With the resumption of the peace talks, the communists had launched a series of limited objective attacks of which eighteen were of battalion size or larger, timed, they hoped, to allow them to claim a military victory prior to the signing of an armistice. While hardly a general offensive, the communists concentrated on capturing dominant terrain features along the front to improve both their battlefield position and their negotiating power at Panmunjom.[59] The heaviest of these May attacks fell on the neighbouring 25th Division southwest of the Hook. The Nevada outposts were regarded as critical by I Corps headquarters, since their capture would have given the Chinese improved observation of the 25th Division's main line of resistance. After a four-day bombardment, the Turkish brigade was heavily attacked by four Chinese battalions on the same night as the 29th Brigade to its immediate northeast. While the attacks on the Hook had largely ended by the early hours of 29 May, the desperate, often hand-to-hand, battle for the Nevada complex continued on into the next day with numerous attacks and counterattacks. By mid-afternoon on the 29th, the strength of the attacks convinced the American commanders that the Chinese intended to capture the outposts whatever the cost and they ordered the defenders to withdraw from the remaining outposts. Over 150 men, mostly Turks, were dead and a further 245 wounded, while Chinese casualties were estimated to be in the range of 3,000.[60]

From the intensity of the attacks, it was apparent that the Chinese were willing to accept heavy casualties to improve their positions. After the winter lull in operations, the communists had been able to build up stockpiles of ammunition and material and bring their front-line units up to strength. There was consequently a growing belief that the Chinese would launch a final offensive on the UN line in the weeks leading up to an armistice in order to create the impression that they had won a military victory. One of the weakest parts of the Eighth Army's line, and the most vulnerable to attack, lay in the I Corps sector that included the Commonwealth Division's front. As General Taylor pointed out to General Clark on 2 June, the UNC positions north of the Imjin and Hant'an Rivers had not been chosen for their defensive strength. Even a relatively shallow penetration of the UN line, such as in the Hook-Nevada sector situated only three miles north of the Imjin, would have forced I Corps to pull back behind the river and expose the main supply route to Ch'orwon to attack. Had the Chinese made a concerted effort north of the Imjin, Taylor would have had to choose between launching costly counterattacks to regain lost territory or conceding the area to the enemy. Eighth Army made preparations to defend against such an offensive but the question of how long I Corps should hold its Jamestown positions if attacked in strength was never resolved.[61]

Just how well the inexperienced Canadian battalions would have fared had the Chinese launched a major offensive north of the Imjin River became a moot point when the communists chose to attack the ROK divisions holding the IX Corps central sector instead. Fortunately for the Canadians, their front remained quiet throughout May and June with relatively few patrol contacts. That was not due to any lack of initiative on the part of the 25th Brigade, however. Allard's insistence on a more active defence resulted in a patrol schedule that had each of the forward battalions maintaining from one to four reconnaissance or fighting patrols across its front each night in addition to the normal allotment of a dozen or so standing patrols. For the remainder of May following the raid on 3 RCR, brigade headquarters directed the two forward battalions to mount a total of fifty-six reconnaissance, thirty fighting, and eighteen ambush patrols between their FDLs and the stream in the middle of the Nabu-ri valley – totals that, for the first time in over a year, compared favourably with the Australian patrol effort. They did not, however, operate on the enemy side of the valley. The reconnaissance patrols were instructed 'not to engage in any fire fight but will withdraw by shortest possible route to our own line when task is accomplished or if spotted by enemy group. If feasible, location of enemy troops will be reported on wireless to enable [battalion] to engage them with artillery and mortar fire.'[62] During the last week of May, 3 R22eR also mounted two uneventful two-man sniper patrols that lay up at the Nabu-ri stream for forty-three hours.[63]

The lack of enemy activity on the Canadian front produced a large number of 'exceptionally quiet' days. On 9 May the Patricia war diarist recorded 'the tedium being broken by ... the brigade's [patrol] task table directing one of the normal standing patrols to a grid reference which happened to be C Company garbage dump. The patrol commander thought he must have forgotten how to read a map.'[64] The absence of Chinese patrols was fortunate, however, since the Canadians did not have much success on those few occasions when contact was made. On the night of 19-20 May, for instance, an eleven-man Van Doo fighting patrol was ambushed at the stream. Chinese small-arms fire and grenades wounded two of the soldiers, with another seven reported missing in action. Two of the bodies, including that of the patrol commander, were not recovered until 13 June.[65] At month's end 3 RCR's D Company reported 'quite a bit of excitement tonight. One of our standing patrols led by Corporal Schurman was cut [off] by a Chink patrol and had to move their position. Upon moving they became lost and moved too far into the valley. A sweeping patrol under Lieutenant Lemaire was sent out to locate them but could not find them. However, much to everyone's relief they returned at first light.'[66]

The quiet extended into June as the 25th Brigade continued to patrol actively along the division's central sector. On the nights of 2-3 and 4-5 June, the Canadians felt sufficiently experienced for RCR recce patrols to venture across the valley and reconnoitre the Chinese positions on Hill 113 above the destroyed village of Chinch'on. Both returned safely with 'nothing to report' on finding the hill unoccupied.[67] Despite these successes, however, the brigade major informed the battalions on 8 June that no patrols were to go beyond the Nabu-ri stream. Ten days later, the Patricias reported on the effects of the order, explaining that 'patrolling is quite restricted now, consisting only of small groups of outposts. Very few sightings have been made and all at long range. No contacts at all have been reported. There have been reports of small arms fire behind several enemy held features and a few lights but nothing more.'[68] Given the lack of contacts, it was all the more important for officers to keep their men on their toes. The Patricias' CO, Lieutenant-Colonel MacLachlan, for example, warned his men of the danger of complacency on 19 June, reminding them of

> the obvious dangers of standing patrols posting themselves on the same location night after night.
>
> In terrain where routes in and out of company localities are so restricted by wire and minefields, it becomes a tendency for patrols to relax in caution. By going to the 'same place' each night, routes and lay up spots become well known to the enemy as well as ourselves. Patrols should be constantly impressed that unless they keep varying their 'standing' positions, they are courting an enemy ambush.
>
> Ambush incidents on 355 and Warsaw and other features are examples of what can happen by becoming too habitual in standing patrol methods.
>
> Company commanders should look into the possibilities of alternate routes to general patrol areas.[69]

It was not until the last half of June that patrol contacts increased: the 'whole area' was reported 'alive and very active from 2300 hours on now. Enemy is heard, seen, but no prisoners have been taken yet.'[70] Throughout the month the Canadians maintained their vigorous patrol program, mounting fifty-seven reconnaissance, eight fighting, and nine ambush patrols. The majority of the fighting and ambush patrols came during the latter part of the month to counter the growing Chinese activity.[71] Despite the lack of prisoners, Allard 'was particularly pleased when, on the night of 24-5 June and again on the night of 30 June-1 July, the Chinese fired 500 mortar bombs to extricate their patrols. It convinced me that the new, aggressive patrol policy – implemented by the patrol school's graduates – was having the desired result. The enemy no longer dominated no man's land.'[72] Both actions involved 3 PPCLI. On 24 June, a 'patrol had a quick brush with the enemy. Lance

Corporal Michaud saw someone approach. He challenged and got a burp gun burst in reply. When the action terminated, two Chinamen had died and Lance Corporal Michaud was our only casualty. There were no other contacts.'[73] The second action referred to by Allard came in the early evening when 'an intercept indicated that the Chinese were sending out wire cutting parties to certain positions. They did. Sergeant Carlson with ten men ambushed one party and inflicted several casualties on them. Our own casualties were one killed in action and three wounded in action.'[74]

The improved Canadian performance was apparently noted by division headquarters for, on 27 June, Major-General West issued orders to rearrange his brigades. Operation Emperor, begun on 9 July, assigned the always reliable Commonwealth brigade to the battered Hook position while the Canadians were handed responsibility for the equally exposed defences on Hills 355 and 159. The bruised British brigade, after its battles on the Hook, was allowed to recuperate in the division's central sector. The Canadian commander took some pride in explaining that 'the purpose of the move was to share the burden [of] the defence. As revealed earlier, the central sector was regarded as the easiest.'[75] After suffering for more than a year, the move to the division's important right flank signalled, at least in Allard's eyes, that the Canadian brigade's reputation had been repaired. In the two and a half weeks that remained until an armistice was at last signed on 27 July, there was little enemy activity on the Commonwealth front and almost none opposite the Canadians on Hills 159 and 355. Even with the absence of enemy patrols and the anticipation of an imminent armistice, the brigade still covered its front with eight recce, eighteen fighting, twenty-one ambush, and seventeen daylight lay-up patrols throughout the month, in addition to the usual full slate of standing patrols immediately in advance of its positions.[76]

The quiet situation during July on Hill 355 was in sharp contrast to the one that had existed when the 28th Brigade had taken over the positions in late April. Facing an enemy that was 'leaning on our wire' after the 2nd US Division's occupation of the positions, the brigade had quickly established its usual aggressive patrol program.[77] Over the next two months, the Chinese and 28th Brigade engaged in a deadly game of cat-and-mouse in no man's land. Although the Commonwealth brigade initiated many of the ambushes, they often found themselves outnumbered by the larger Chinese patrols. The most daring patrol of the period – and its most frivolous – was made on the night of 1-2 June when a Durham Light Infantry patrol 'laid out the symbol E II R in fluorescent panels on the forward slopes of the Chinese-held Hill 217, the lower crest of the Maryang San, very close to the enemy's defensive line' to mark the coronation of Queen Elizabeth II.[78] As a result of its patrol clashes and the normal attrition produced by the enemy's shelling, May and June were costly; the 28th Brigade suffered 40 men killed, 249 wounded, and 10 missing. Thirty-two of the dead, 157 of the wounded, and 9 of the missing were from the two Australian battalions. The brigade itself estimated that it had killed 111 Chinese in return and wounded some 38 others, though 'there were doubtless many other

Chinese casualties which could not be counted in the darkness during patrol clashes or which were caused by artillery bombardments of their defences. The total brigade losses for this period, 299 men, attest to the fact that the war continued to be a hard-fought, bloody struggle to the last,'[79] at least for the Australians.

Even so, the Commonwealth Division's losses paled in comparison with the casualties that were incurred by the five ROK divisions holding the centre section of the Eighth Army's line between Kumhwa and Heartbreak Ridge. On 10 June the Chinese launched the offensive they hoped would allow them to claim a military victory prior to signing an armistice. Over the next nine days, the enemy succeeded in driving the ROK divisions back an average of 3,200 yards across a 14,000-yard front, inflicting over 7,300 casualties on the South Koreans. Chinese losses were estimated at over 6,600. By 18 June, however, the entire front returned to its usual defensive activity.[80]

On that same day, the president of the Republic of Korea, Syngman Rhee, unilaterally released some 25,000 North Korean anticommunist prisoners into the countryside. Rhee's gambit created uncertainty that an armistice would be concluded in the near future. An extended postponement in reaching an agreement, however, would disrupt the communists' apparent intention of claiming a military victory by signing an armistice immediately following some success in their summer attacks.[81] The outraged communist negotiators temporarily broke off the peace talks while their armies renewed large-scale attacks against ROK formations on 24 June. Such was the intensity and determination of the Chinese offensive that General Clark decided to rush American reinforcements from Japan to bolster the front. As the fighting raged through the first half of July, the ROK front was pierced and many units were cut off from their parent formations. In penetrating the UN line to a depth of six miles, the communists eliminated the Kumsong salient and straightened their lines in the central sector. General Taylor eventually employed nine ROK and US divisions to stem the communist offensive and regain some of the lost ground.[82]

The chief Canadian involvement in fending off the Chinese attacks on ROK units was in supplying artillery support to the 1st ROK Division on the 25th Brigade's immediate right. Although the South Korean division did not receive nearly the attention that their countrymen holding the central front did, one of their outposts was repeatedly attacked during the last two weeks of fighting. With the 81st Field Regiment firing thousands of rounds from its 25-pounder guns in support, the embattled South Koreans were able to retain the outpost until the armistice was finally signed on 27 July.[83] On the Commonwealth front itself, the only Chinese attacks were made against 2 RAR holding the Hook position on the nights of 24-5 and 25-6 July. The action was part of a larger, divisional-sized attack against the 1st US Marine Division on the left that spilled over with diversionary assaults on the Australians. Supported by the well-coordinated fire of the divisional artillery and the tanks of the 1st Royal Tank Regiment, 2 RAR was able to repel both attacks at a relatively small cost of five killed and twenty-four wounded.[84]

The Chinese themselves showed little regard for their own casualties and left the ground in front of the Hook positions littered with corpses. The 28th Brigade commander estimated that between 2,000 and 3,000 Chinese had been killed in their assaults. It seemed certain to the Commonwealth Division's intelligence staff that the Chinese were trying to make a breakthrough to the Imjin River along the divisional boundary in order to turn the Marine division's flank. 'There is no doubt on one point,' the intelligence staff reported, 'had it not been for a few stalwart infantrymen on Hill 121, the two tanks in the blocking position between Hills 111 and 121 and for the speed and flexibility and weight of 1st Commonwealth Division's artillery, the enemy would have broken through. The consequences of such a catastrophe would have been far-reaching and frightful but easy to imagine.'[85]

In a final act of war before the armistice came into effect at 2200 hours on 27 July, the Chinese fired a record 44,000 artillery rounds into the Eighth Army positions in the last four hours – but none against the Commonwealth Division. As recorded by one Canadian officer, the war ended quietly for the men holding the division's left on Hills 159 and 355:

> The Company Command Post was a sweat box. Both the company commander and the FOO were stripped to the waist. The former had wrapped a green towel about his head, turban fashion to keep the perspiration from dripping down his face. There was no celebration in progress and all at the CP were busily preparing for the 72 hour interlude between the Cease Fire and the withdrawal ...
>
> Then at 2100 hours the platoon commanders began arriving for the O[rders] Group. By 2115, the appointed time, all concerned had arrived and plans for the demilitarization of the positions and the withdrawal were outlined. By 2145 the O Group had ended and those present began pouring drinks for a toast to the Cease Fire ... and with 'cheers' or 'good health' we drank to the end of one more war.
>
> Then we went outside. Little Gibraltar [Hill 355] was topped with cloud and we saw everything in a silver mist which the moon made beautiful. It was pleasantly warm.
>
> Off to our left we could hear Canadians yelling and cheering as if they were at a rodeo. The British or Australians were shooting flares into the sky but aside from this it was appropriately peaceful. There was no great bombardment on our front during the last hours of the war.[86]

EPILOGUE

Under the terms of the armistice agreement both sides had seventy-two hours in which to pull their forces back two kilometres (1.2 miles) from the line of contact as it stood at 2200 hours on 27 July 1953. The demilitarized zone between the two Koreas ran from just below the thirty-eighth parallel near the mouth of the Imjin River on the west coast to a position some forty miles north of the parallel on the east coast. Thus separated, the two sides were restricted to replacing troops and equipment on a man-for-man and piece-for-piece basis to prevent the expansion of either army. On the contentious prisoner of war issue that had stalled the talks for most of their two-year duration, the armistice created a Committee for Repatriation of Prisoners of War to oversee the exchange of captured soldiers. Those prisoners who wished to return to their homelands were exchanged at Panmunjom. By early September 75,000 Chinese and North Koreans had been returned to the north while 12,750 UN prisoners – including the thirty-two Canadian soldiers who had been captured – were handed over to UN authorities. The Committee for Repatriation, made up of representatives from Czechoslovakia, India, Poland, Sweden, and Switzerland, took responsibility for those prisoners who did not wish to return to their former homelands and arranged for each man to be interviewed by the side to which they had originally belonged. Despite these 'explanations,' nearly 22,000 Chinese and North Korean soldiers preferred to live in the Republic of Korea or Taiwan rather than return home. Some 350 UN prisoners, including twenty-one Americans and one British marine, also opted to remain with their captors.[1]

By the fall of 1953, the 25th Brigade had settled into the monotonous routine of guarding the UN side of the newly created DMZ against the unlikely possibility of a resumption of the fighting. Within six months of the armistice, the brigade had shifted its focus from operations to training, instituting a program that was 'geared more to long-term development than active preparation for immediate hostilities.'[2] In accordance with the rotation policies laid down two years earlier, the 3rd battalions were eventually replaced in the brigade's order of battle by battalions of the Canadian Guards, the Queen's Own Rifles of Canada, and the Black Watch (Royal Highland Regiment) of Canada. Once the ROK Army had taken over the positions nearest the DMZ in the fall of 1954, the Canadian brigade had little reason to remain on the divided peninsula. Brigade headquarters was closed down on 2 December 1954 as it and most of the other units of the brigade were repatriated to Canada. The 2nd Battalion, Queen's Own Rifles and No. 3 Canadian Field Ambulance were the only units to remain behind in a revamped 'divisional' formation under 29th British Brigade headquarters. The Queen's Own finally left the theatre in April 1955 while the medical detachment, the last remaining Canadian unit, did not return home until June 1957.[3]

The fight for a peninsula many Canadian soldiers viewed as a land of filth and poverty exacted an astounding toll in human lives. The Americans estimated communist casualties at more than 1.5 million, including captured, with some 900,000 Chinese and 500,000 North Koreans killed or wounded (fifty years after the war, China and North Korea continue to regard their casualty totals as state secrets). The South Koreans, meanwhile, have estimated that their army lost some 140,000 dead and more than 700,000 wounded in defence of their homeland. Korean civilian casualties are unknown but are believed to have been well in excess of a million. The United States, which contributed 1,319,000 personnel to the UN Command during the course of the war, suffered 33,629 killed in action, 103,284 wounded, and 5,178 missing or captured, with their ground forces, army and marines, losing 31,971 of the dead. Another 20,617 US personnel died of nonbattle causes.[4] Britain, Australia, and New Zealand collectively lost a total of 954 soldiers killed and another 3,615 wounded, while the other UN contingents suffered some 1,800 killed and 7,000 wounded, almost half of them Turks.[5]

Beside these totals, the Canadian Army's casualties of 309 killed in action, 1,202 wounded, and 32 captured indicate the degree to which the 25th Brigade had been fortunate to escape the heaviest of the fighting. They were, however, incurred by a formation whose peak strength barely exceeded 8,100 all ranks, including administrative and reinforcement units in Japan. In all, only 21,940 Canadian soldiers served in the Far East during the three years of fighting. As a percentage of the total number of personnel who served in the theatre, the Canadian casualty ratio of 7.1 percent is notably less than the American one of 10.5 percent. The difference is even greater when one considers the enormous administrative 'tail' the American forces employed on the peninsula, a supply system that the Canadian Army did not attempt to duplicate. (The 25th Brigade made extensive use of both British and American facilities in drawing supplies and services.) Not only had the Canadian brigade arrived on the peninsula after the hard-fought battles of the Pusan Perimeter and the precipitous retreat from North Korea had concluded, it had also been shielded from some of the less sound operations proposed by higher American headquarters by its inclusion in the Commonwealth Division.

As in any ground war, the bulk of the Canadian brigade's casualties were in the infantry battalions: noninfantry units suffered only fifteen of the dead, a mere 7 percent of the total.[6] Although it spent only five and a half months in the front line – and the Chinese were aggressively active only during two and a half of those – the Canadian battalion to suffer the most casualties in Korea was 1 RCR with 48 men killed, 206 wounded, and 14 captured. Another of the 1st battalions, 1 PPCLI, had the second-highest totals, 32 killed, 199 wounded, and 2 missing, the bulk of which occurred while it was serving under Rockingham's command. While Stone's 2 PPCLI was involved in some of the toughest Canadian actions in Korea, having fought its way north to the thirty-eighth parallel in the spring of 1951, stood firm on the hills north of Kap'yong, and taken part in the Commonwealth Division's advance to the Jamestown Line, it suffered only the third-highest battle casualty total with 50 killed and 137 wounded. Surprisingly, the Canadian brigade had very similar casualty totals under both Rockingham's and Bogert's commands, despite the radically different approach to operations that characterized the two formations. The aggressiveness of Rockingham's battalions, which also spent less time in reserve and had to defend against the determined Chinese counterattacks of October and November 1951, resulted in battle casualties of 104 men killed, 448 wounded, and 3 captured. The passive approach of Bogert's men, on the other hand, produced the same number of dead soldiers, 104, fewer wounded, 369, but more men captured, 15.[7]

These numbers emphasize the fact that, for Canada at least, the Korean War was fought by a rather small professional army. With no vital national interests at stake and the armed forces able to sustain themselves entirely by voluntary recruitment, the Far Eastern conflict made only a limited impression on Canadian society as a whole. Once the drama of the war's first year of thrust and counterthrust had turned into stalemate – a situation highlighted by the infuriatingly protracted and seemingly illogical negotiations at Panmunjom – it was easy for the Canadian public to forget that their country was even at war. It was the Second World War that had starkly impacted people's lives, whether as one of the more than one million Canadians serving in the armed forces (amounting to one in every eleven citizens) or, for those on the home front, by concern for loved ones in the services, the effects of wartime rationing, and the mass mobilization of industry. As far as the public was concerned, at least for those who did not personally know any of the 22,000 serving (at one in every 636 Canadians, chances were they did not), Canada's involvement in the Korean War was simply the nation's contribution to an international standoff that one only read about in the newspaper. For decades after, talk of 'the war' would continue to refer solely to the 1939-45 conflict.

In contrast to its limited impact on the nation as a whole, however, the Korean War exerted an influence on Canada's regular army that rivalled, if it did not exceed, that of the Second World War. The majority of the Canadian Army's small officer corps served in Korea, including an entire generation of junior officers who had been too young for the Second World War. With service in the Far East serving as a common bond throughout much of the professional army, Korea veterans continued to hold prominent places in the Canadian Army for the remainder of the 1950s and 1960s. In addition to their influence in individual units and commands, Generals Allard and Dextraze went on to serve as chiefs of defence staff in the late 1960s and early 1970s, while Gen. Ramsay Withers, who saw action in Korea as a young signals officer fresh out of the Royal Military College, held that position during the 1980s. The commitment of a brigade-sized force of largely professional soldiers, moreover, seemed to be an example of the sort of obligation the Canadian

Army would probably have to meet in future conflicts – whether in northwest Europe or some other distant land – rather than the mass citizen army Canada had mobilized to fight the Second World War.

The Canadian Army after the Korean War is, in that respect, analogous to the United States Army in the early years of the twentieth century. Although the American public may have looked to the US Civil War as the nation's defining military event, the officers of the small regular army were influenced as much by their more recent role as 'a border constabulary for policing unruly Indians and Mexicans.'[8] The Civil War had been 'a war of the people,' whereas the Indian wars 'had been the private concern' of regular soldiers 'professionally going about their business.'[9] For Canada's regular army, the Korean experience had a similar unifying effect. It was, as Lieutenant-Colonel Wood pointed out in his conclusion to the official history, 'a situation which the generals on the frontiers have often faced before, with reinforcements far away and only one small army. Under these conditions, the soldier must endure, without flinching, the full weight of the enemy's assault, knowing that he is not going to be permitted in return the exhilaration of victory as a reward for his endurance.'[10]

And yet, as great an impact as the Korean War had on the Canadian Army, the yearly rotation of battalions meant that units entered the line with little real knowledge of the brigade's earlier combat experience. The 1st battalions took over their positions on the Jamestown Line without realizing how well the Special Force battalions had performed – an ignorance that in part reflected their undisguised disdain for the so-called soldiers of fortune. Confident in their own abilities, the Active Force officers could not, in any event, have countenanced the possibility that Rockingham's men might have had something to teach them about the conduct of operations. Unfortunately for the men in the 1st battalions, their officers lacked the Second World War command experience of the Special Force COs while their brigade commander failed to exhibit the sort of drive and personal leadership that Rockingham provided to ensure that his units maintained a sound defence.

The static Canadian front throughout the last twenty-two months of the war also tended to obscure just how poorly the regular army's 1st battalions performed. With no serious attacks being mounted against the Canadian positions aside from the occasional raid, Bogert's officers seem to have been largely unaware of the tactical difficulties their units were experiencing – even if those shortcomings were obvious to the Australian battalions fighting alongside them, or to Jean Allard once he assumed command. To this day, for instance, 1 RCR celebrates 'Kowang San Day' to commemorate the 23 October 1952 raid on Hill 355 as if it were a Canadian victory – as 1 RCR concluded at the time after they reoccupied the position in the wake of the enemy's withdrawal – with little understanding that their battalion was actually defeated by the Chinese. For its part, the official history only hinted at the problems the Canadians created for themselves, drawing no tactical distinctions between 'Rocky's Army' and Bogert's brigade. Otherwise, *Strange Battleground* fully endorsed the myth of a hastily recruited Special Force of misfits being replaced at the front by the regular army's spit-and-polish professionals.

As strange as the Korean battleground may have seemed to Canadian soldiers, it was the war's timing, rather than its topography, that made it an aberration in the country's military history. Coming only five years after the Allied victory in 1945, the army had available a large pool of combat-experienced citizens from which to recruit a brigade group for the Far East. As we have seen, all of Rockingham's senior officers had performed the same duties during the Second World War that they were asked to carry out in the Korean conflict, a level of experience that allowed the Special Force to accelerate its training program. Nowhere was this more clearly demonstrated than in the rapid progress 3 PPCLI made in its first month after formation. With a CO, company commanders, and senior NCOs who had all seen action during the Second World War, the new battalion had solid leadership to direct the training of its keen, but inexperienced, new recruits. Its senior officers understood exactly what was required of an infantry battalion in battle and were able to concentrate on the more essential skills during unit exercises rather than simply following a prescribed syllabus. The other original units of the brigade, with their initially high proportion of wartime veterans in the ranks, also proved the validity of army headquarters' original intention that the 25th Brigade's training would 'be of an "in job" refresher character.'[11] Having completed a number of unit and formation exercises, the brigade that Rockingham took to Korea was much better prepared for active operations than were the 1st and 3rd battalions that eventually replaced it at the front.

It was more than mere preparation that differentiated the performance of the 1st and 2nd battalions, however. Under Rockingham's dynamic leadership, the Canadian brigade exhibited a thorough approach to all of its operations, most notably in its appreciation for the old adage, 'Time spent in reconnaissance is never wasted.' As 2 RCR's after-action report for Operation Snatch clearly explained in October 1951, 'Detailed meticulous planning is required down to section leader level. Compilation of information [about the enemy] over a period of time is very necessary and pays dividends.' By their continual use of reconnaissance patrols roaming to the far side of no man's land, the 2nd battalions were able to build up a reasonable picture of the enemy's dispositions and routines, knowledge that was essential to planning both offensive and defensive operations. The small size of a recce patrol, moreover, allowed it to avoid enemy contact so that information could be gained with few casualties. Their vigorous patrol program also gave Rockingham's men a familiarity with the ground over which they had to operate and the confidence that they were more than a match for their Chinese opponents 'by night or by day.'[12]

The complete absence of reconnaissance patrols from the 1st battalions' task tables, on the other hand, is nothing short of astounding. The regulars' failure to reconnoitre forward of their standing patrol positions gave their ambushes little chance of intercepting the Chinese. As we have seen, their large fighting patrols were normally sent into no man's land with little knowledge of enemy strength, the type of ground they had to cover, or the existence of old wire obstacles or minefields. The nightly presence of enemy reconnaissance parties lurking just beyond the Canadian wire also meant that fighting patrols were detected almost as soon as they entered the valley, preventing any sort of surprise and allowing the Chinese to organize a counterattack. Perhaps the most serious consequence of the 1st battalions' inactivity, however, was its psychological impact on the men. As the British official historian has pointed out, 'Soldiers occupying positions from which they never make a sortie rapidly develop an acute sense of self-preservation. If the enemy in contradistinction dominates no man's land, raids freely to take prisoners or seize local points of vantage, the image of his invincibility grows.'[13] In the case of the Canadian 1st battalions, 'the "sit tight" mentality'[14] noted by Harry Pope produced a perceptible fear of the enemy's abilities and an overreliance on the divisional artillery to protect them from serious attack. Allard's emphasis on setting up a patrol school and instituting a vigorous patrol program was, in part, meant to overcome his men's lack of confidence in operating in no man's land.

The superior performance of the 2nd battalion officers over those in the three regular infantry battalions is the most interesting aspect of the Canadian Army's involvement in the Korean War. Although General Foulkes had insisted upon a limited enlistment term for the Special Force because 'the army would not wish to retain the "soldier of fortune" type of personnel on a long term basis,'[15] it was the adventurers in the 2nd battalions – despite their limited terms of service – who proved to be the true professionals when it came to the conduct of operations. Their officers combined a willingness to fight with sufficient combat experience to understand what was required to succeed in battle. Rockingham, who candidly admitted to being 'not particularly keen about soldiering when there is no fighting involved,'[16] also provided his men with the drive and forward leadership he had demonstrated during the Second World War, a style that was all too rare in the Canadian Army. Not only did his inspections of the brigade's foremost positions keep commanders on their toes and correct deficiencies before they became a serious problem, but his continual presence at the front was also seen and appreciated by his men.

The 'dugout' mindset in the 1st battalions was, in contrast, the result of the poor battlefield leadership provided by their officers and not, as some historians have argued, the product of inadequate weapons and training.[17] Given their additional Bren guns, the regulars were, if anything, slightly better equipped than the Special Force battalions, and their unwillingness to patrol as actively as either the Australians or Rockingham's men must be seen as a failing of their senior officers. If Pope's assertion about the inclination of many Active Force company and battalion commanders toward self-preservation is true, their men could hardly have been expected to show the same confidence and determination that the well-led Special

Force volunteers had demonstrated. The weak leadership in the 1st battalions cannot, however, be interpreted as representing the Canadian Army as a whole. At the very least, Allard's ability to recognize the brigade's deficiencies and take the necessary corrective action with the 3rd battalions – as well as the performance of those Active Force officers who were good enough to serve under Rockingham's watchful eye – shows that the regular army did contain a number of efficient combat officers.

Nonetheless, it is difficult to escape the conclusion that the performance of the 1st battalions reflected the tendency of a peacetime force to adopt a garrison mentality, one geared more to military appearance and routine administration than to operations. With their emphasis on spit and polish, formal mess dinners, and smartly mounted bridge guards, the officers of the army's regular battalions seem to have forgotten the purpose of their profession. When questioned by a newly promoted brigade commander in the opening months of the US Civil War, federal Brig. Gen. C.F. Smith, an officer with thirty-five years' service in the US Army, summed up his philosophy of a professional officer's duty: 'Battle is the ultimate to which the whole life's labor of an officer should be directed. He may live to the age of retirement without seeing a battle; still, he must always be getting ready for it exactly as if he knew the hour of the day it is to break upon him. And then, whether it come late or early, he must be willing to fight – he *must* fight.'[18] If nothing else, the 25th Brigade's experience in Korea demonstrates that when an officer's motivation is suspect, his unit's operations are unlikely to succeed.

NOTES

Introduction

1 Indeed that is the subtitle of the popular history by John Melady, *Korea: Canada's Forgotten War* (Toronto: McClelland and Stewart, 1983) and the title of the introduction of David Bercuson's more academic treatment, *Blood on the Hills: The Canadian Army in the Korean War* (Toronto: University of Toronto Press, 1999).

2 Historical Section, General Staff, Army Headquarters, *Canada's Army in Korea: The United Nations Operations, 1950-53, and Their Aftermath* (Ottawa: Queen's Printer, 1956).

3 Herbert Fairlie Wood, *Strange Battleground: The Operations in Korea and Their Effects on the Defence Policy of Canada* (Ottawa: Queen's Printer, 1966).

4 Melady, *Korea: Canada's Forgotten War;* Robert Heppenstall, *Find the Dragon: The Canadian Army in Korea, 1950-1953* (Edmonton: Four Winds Publishing, 1995); Ted Barris, *Deadlock in Korea: Canadians at War, 1950-1953* (Toronto: Macmillan Canada, 1999).

5 Robert S. Peacock, *Kim-chi, Asahi and Rum: A Platoon Commander Remembers, Korea 1952-53* (Toronto: Lugus Productions, 1994); John Gardam, *Korea Volunteer: An Oral History from Those Who Were There* (Burnstown, ON: General Store Publishing, 1994); J. Charles Forbes, *Fantassin: pour mon pays, la gloire et ... des prunes* (Sillery, QC: Septentrion, 1994). Forbes' memoir is, unfortunately, available only in French.

6 Denis Stairs, *The Diplomacy of Constraint: Canada, the Korean War and the United States* (Toronto: University of Toronto Press, 1974); J.L. Granatstein and David J. Bercuson, *War and Peacekeeping: From South Africa to the Gulf – Canada's Limited Wars* (Toronto: Key Porter, 1991).

7 Anthony Farrar-Hockley, *The British Part in the Korean War,* 2 vols., (London: Her Majesty's Stationery Office, 1990-5). While not an official history, Brig. C.N. Barclay's *The First Commonwealth Division: The Story of British Commonwealth Land Forces in Korea* (Aldershot, UK: Gale and Polden, 1954) was based largely on war diaries and the divisional commander's periodic reports on operations.

8 The United States Army in the Korean War includes the following four volumes: Roy E. Appleman, *South to the Naktong, North to the Yalu, June-November 1950* (Washington, DC: US Government Printing Office, 1961); Walter G. Hermes, *Truce Tent and Fighting Front* (Washington, DC: US Government Printing Office, 1966); James F. Schnabel, *Policy and Direction: The First Year* (Washington, DC: US Government Printing Office, 1972); and Billy C. Mossman, *Ebb and Flow, November 1950-July 1951* (Washington, DC: US Government Printing Office, 1990). *US Marine Operations in Korea, 1950-1953* consists of five volumes: Lynn Montross and Nicholas Canzona, vol. 1, *The Pusan Perimeter* (Washington, DC: US Government Printing Office, 1954); Lynn Montross and Nicholas Canzona, vol. 2, *The Inchon-Seoul Operation* (Washington, DC: US Government Printing Office, 1955); Lynn Montross and Nicholas Canzona, vol. 3, *The Chosin Reservoir Campaign* (Washington, DC: US Government Printing Office, 1957); Lynn Montross, Hubard Kuokka, and Norman Hicks, vol. 4, *The East-Central Front* (Washington, DC: US Government Printing Office, 1962); and Pat Meid, vol. 5, *Operations in West Korea* (Washington, DC: US Government Printing Office, 1972). Only the last of the US Army official histories, that by Mossman published nearly twenty years after the others (and which, perhaps not coincidentally, happens to cover the American collapse following the Chinese intervention), makes use of Chinese sources. It is also the best and most insightful of the American works.

9 For example, T.R. Fehrenbach, *This Kind of War: A Study in Unpreparedness* (New York: Macmillan, 1963); David Rees, *Korea: The Limited War* (London: Macmillan, 1964); Tim Carew, *Korea: The Commonwealth at War* (London: Cassell, 1967); Max Hastings, *The Korean War* (London: Michael

Joseph, 1987); Russell Spurr, *Enter the Dragon: China at War in Korea* (London: Sidgwick and Jackson, 1989); and John Toland, *In Mortal Combat: Korea, 1950-1953* (New York: William Morrow, 1991).

10 Robert O'Neill, *Australia in the Korean War, 1950-53*, vol. 2, *Combat Operations* (Canberra: Australian Government Publishing Service, 1985), 253-4.

11 Jeffrey Grey, *The Commonwealth Armies and the Korean War: An Alliance Study* (Manchester: Manchester University Press, 1988), 150-3.

12 W.H. Pope, 'Nos patrouilles en Corée, 1952-53,' *La Citadelle* 24 (Feb. 1988): 33-5; W.H. Pope, 'La Corée: La cote 159 en septembre 1952 et le sergent Bruno Bergeron, MM,' *La Citadelle* 25, 1 (1989): 30-2; W.H. Pope, 'La roulotte, les rails de chemin de fer, et le trainard,' *La Citadelle* 25, 5 (1989): 31-2.

13 Maj. W.H. Pope, 'Infantry Patrolling in Korea,' 2 June 1953, National Defence Headquarters, Directorate of History and Heritage (hereafter DHH) 410B25.013 (D89); Maj. W.H. Pope, 'Infantry Defences in Korea,' 19 September 1953, DHH 681.009 (D11).

14 Wood, *Strange Battleground*, 241.

15 Stephen Harris and William Johnston, 'The Post-War Army and the War in Korea,' in *We Stand on Guard: An Illustrated History of the Canadian Army*, ed. John Marteinson (Montreal: Ovale, 1992), 363-7.

16 Bercuson, *Blood on the Hills*, 53, 225, 199.

17 Ibid., 163-8, 189-93; Brent Byron Watson, *Far Eastern Tour: The Canadian Infantry in Korea, 1950-1953* (Montreal and Kingston: McGill-Queen's University Press, 2002), 29-46.

Prologue

1 J.M. Rockingham to C.P. Stacey, 27 October 1948, DHH 001. (D5).

2 Brereton Greenhous, ed., *Semper Paratus: The History of the Royal Hamilton Light Infantry 1862-1977* (Hamilton, ON: RHLI Historical Association, 1977), 243; J.A. Swettenham, 'Operation "Spring," 25 Jul 1944,' nd, DHH 112.3H1.003 (D43).

3 J.A. English, *The Canadian Army and the Normandy Campaign: A Study of Failure in High Command* (New York: Praeger, 1991), 238-9.

4 Greenhous, *Semper Paratus*, 220.

5 Ibid., 232.

6 J.A. Swettenham, 'Operation "Spring," 25 Jul 1944,' nd, DHH 112.3H1.003 (D43).

7 Greenhous, *Semper Paratus*, 244. See also K. Tout, *The Bloody Battle for Tilly, Normandy, 1944* (Stroud, UK: Sutton, 2000), 87-8; Fusiliers Mont-Royal, *Cents ans d'histoire d'un Régiment canadien-français: Les Fusiliers Mont-Royal, 1869-1969* (Montreal: Éditions du Jour, 1971), 203-5.

8 English, *Canadian Army and Normandy*, 244.

9 Greenhous, *Semper Paratus*, 247.

10 Ibid. See also J.A. Swettenham, 'Operation "Spring," 25 Jul 1944,' nd, DHH 112.3H1.003 (D43).

11 J.A. Swettenham, 'Operation "Spring," 25 Jul 1944,' nd, DHH 112.3H1.003 (D43).

12 C.P. Stacey, *The Victory Campaign: The Operations in Northwest Europe, 1944-1945* (Ottawa: Queen's Printer, 1960), 191.

13 Ibid., 191-2.

14 R.H. Roy, *1944: The Canadians in Normandy* (Ottawa: Macmillan Canada, 1984), 112-13. See also Tout, *Bloody Battle for Tilly*, 89.

15 J.M. Rockingham to C.P. Stacey, 27 October 1948, DHH 001. (D5).

16 English, *Canadian Army and Normandy*, 244.

17 J.M. Rockingham to C.P. Stacey, 27 October 1948, DHH 001. (D5).

Chapter 1: War and Recruitment

1 King quoted in J.W. Pickersgill and D.F. Forster, *The Mackenzie King Record*, vol. 4, *1947-1948* (Toronto: University of Toronto Press, 1970), 6.

2 C.P. Stacey, *Six Years of War: The Army in Canada, Britain and the Pacific* (Ottawa: Queen's Printer, 1955), 433, 523.

3 Herbert Fairlie Wood, *Strange Battleground: The Operations in Korea and Their Effects on the Defence Policy of Canada* (Ottawa: Queen's Printer, 1966), 17.

4 Department of National Defence (hereafter DND), *Report of the Department of National Defence for the Fiscal Year Ending March 31, 1937* (Ottawa, 1937).
5 DND, *Report of the Department of National Defence for the Fiscal Year Ending March 31, 1946* (Ottawa, 1946), 27.
6 DND, *Report of the Department of National Defence for the Fiscal Year Ending March 31, 1947* (Ottawa, 1947); DND, *Report of the Department of National Defence for the Fiscal Year Ending March 31, 1948* (Ottawa, 1948); DND, *Report of the Department of National Defence for the Fiscal Year Ending March 31, 1949* (Ottawa, 1949).
7 Claxton quoted in Wood, *Strange Battleground,* 16.
8 Escott Reid, *Radical Mandarin: The Memoirs of Escott Reid* (Toronto: University of Toronto Press, 1989), 229.
9 Ibid., 238-9. He continues, 'In 1950, the first year of the alliance, the defence expenditures of the alliance increased in real terms by only 7 percent over the preceding year. Within two years of the outbreak of the Korean War the defence expenditures of the alliance almost tripled.'
10 Wood, *Strange Battleground,* 19; DND, *Report of the Department of National Defence for the Fiscal Year Ending March 31, 1950* (Ottawa, 1950).
11 Lester Pearson, *Mike: The Memoirs of The Right Honourable Lester B. Pearson,* vol. 1, *1897-1948* (Toronto: University of Toronto Press, 1972), 284.
12 Quoted in D.J. Goodspeed, ed., *The Armed Forces of Canada, 1867-1967: A Century of Achievement* (Ottawa: Queen's Printer, 1967), 209-10.
13 Roy E. Appleman, *South to the Naktong, North to the Yalu, June-November 1950* (Washington, DC: US Government Printing Office, 1961), 1-2.
14 Robert O'Neill, *Australia in the Korean War, 1950-53,* vol. 1, *Strategy and Diplomacy* (Canberra: Australian Government Publishing Service, 1981), 6.
15 Perhaps the best study of Korean national politics during this period is the two-volume work of Bruce Cumings, *The Origins of the Korean War:* vol. 1, *Liberation and the Establishment of Separate Regimes, 1945-1947* (Princeton, NJ: Princeton University Press, 1981); and vol. 2, *The Roaring of the Cataract, 1947-1950* (Princeton, NJ: Princeton University Press, 1990).
16 A.R. Millett, 'The Forgotten Army in the Misunderstood War: The *Hanguk Gun* in the Korean War, 1946-53,' in *The Korean War, 1950-53: A 50 Year Retrospective,* ed. P. Dennis and J. Grey (Canberra: Australian Government Publishing Service, 2000), 3-4.
17 O'Neill, *Australia in the Korean War,* 1:7.
18 United Nations resolution quoted in Anthony Farrar-Hockley, *The British Part in the Korean War,* vol. 1, *A Distant Obligation* (London: Her Majesty's Stationery Office, 1990), 16.
19 Ibid., 17; O'Neill, *Australia in the Korean War,* 1:8-9.
20 Millett, 'Forgotten Army,' 21.
21 Ibid., 22.
22 O'Neill, *Australia in the Korean War, 1950-53,* vol. 2, *Combat Operations* (Canberra: Australian Government Publishing Service, 1985), 11; Appleman, *South to the Naktong,* 16-17.
23 Appleman, *South to the Naktong,* 9, 12.
24 O'Neill, *Australia in the Korean War,* 2:11-12.
25 Truman and UN resolution quoted in Wood, *Strange Battleground,* 11-12.
26 O'Neill, *Australia in the Korean War,* 2:13-14.
27 Reid, *Radical Mandarin,* 257.
28 Lester Pearson, *Mike: The Memoirs of The Right Honourable Lester B. Pearson,* vol. 2, *1948-1957* (Toronto: University of Toronto Press, 1973), 145.
29 Denis Stairs, *The Diplomacy of Constraint: Canada, the Korean War and the United States* (Toronto: University of Toronto Press, 1974), 41n.
30 Wood, *Strange Battleground,* 13-14, 14n.
31 O'Neill, *Australia in the Korean War,* 2:13.
32 Robert F. Futrell, *The United States Air Force in Korea, 1950-1953* (Washington, DC: US Government Printing Office, 1983), 113-24.
33 Ibid., 16; Wood, *Strange Battleground,* 14-15.

34 Examples are quoted in Wood, *Strange Battleground,* 22.
35 Ibid., 19.
36 'Extract from Minutes of Chiefs of Staff Committee Meeting held in the office of the Minister on 17 Jul 50,' nd, DHH 193.009 (D53).
37 Ibid.
38 Wood, *Strange Battleground,* 21.
39 'Extracts from Chiefs of Staff Committee Minutes of a special meeting – 28 Jul 50,' nd, DHH 112.3M2 (D293).
40 Lt.-Col. B.A. Reid, letter to Brereton Greenhous, 14 March 2001.
41 Pearson, *Mike,* 2:149.
42 St. Laurent quoted in Wood, *Strange Battleground,* 23.
43 Adjutant general to minister of national defence, 30 August 1950, quoted in ibid., 25.
44 Lt.-Col. S. Galloway, 'Narrative on recruiting for Canadian Army Special Force in Central Command, August 1950,' 1959, DHH 112.3H1.001 (D9).
45 Claxton quoted in Wood, *Strange Battleground,* 28.
46 Ibid., 27, 30, 32, 88.
47 Wood, *Strange Battleground,* 34-5; A Sqn, 1/2 Armoured Regiment War Diary (hereafter WD), 8 September 1950, National Archives of Canada (hereafter NAC), Record Group (hereafter RG) 24, vol. 18,264; 57 Fd Sqn WD, 22 August 1950, NAC, RG 24, vol. 18,286.
48 J.M. Rockingham biographical file, DHH.

Chapter 2: Rocky's Army

1 J.M. Rockingham, 'Recollections of Korea,' August 1975, NAC, Manuscript Group (hereafter MG) 31 G12, p. 6.
2 'Notes, Recommendations and Decisions,' 18 December 1950, 25 Bde WD, December 1950, NAC, RG 24, vol. 18,237.
3 Herbert Fairlie Wood, *Strange Battleground: The Operations in Korea and Their Effects on the Defence Policy of Canada* (Ottawa: Queen's Printer, 1966), 33-4.
4 J.A. Dextraze biographical file, DHH.
5 J.R. Stone biographical file, DHH.
6 R.A. Keane biographical file, DHH.
7 'Nominal Roll,' 26 March 1951, 2 RCR WD, NAC, RG 24, vol. 18,341; *Canadian Army Officers List,* March 1945, DHH.
8 Canadian Army Historical Section, 'Initial Supply Problems of Canadian Army Special Force,' nd, copy received from Bill McAndrew.
9 2 RCR WD, 12 and 18 August 1950, NAC, RG 24, vol. 18,340.
10 2 PPCLI WD, 25 August and 13 September 1950, NAC, RG 24, vol. 18,317.
11 2 R22eR WD, 31 August and 25 September 1950, NAC, RG 24, vol. 18,356.
12 25 Bde WD, September 1950, app. D, 'Canadian Army Training Instruction No. 6,' 14 August 1950, NAC, RG 24, vol. 18,237.
13 2 RCR WD, 20 August 1950, NAC, RG 24, vol. 18,340.
14 2 RCHA WD, 21 September 1950, app. 9, '2 Fd Regt RCHA as at 4 Oct 1950,' nd, NAC, RG 24, vol. 18,271.
15 A Sqn, 1/2 Armoured Regiment WD, 29 August and 7 September 1950, NAC, RG 24, vol. 18,264.
16 Wood, *Strange Battleground,* 32.
17 2 PPCLI WD, 20 September 1950, NAC, RG 24, vol. 18,317.
18 2 RCHA WD, 12 September 1950, NAC, RG 24, vol. 18,271. See also A Sqn, 1/2 Armoured Regiment WD, 28 September 1950, NAC, RG 24, vol. 18,264.
19 2 RCHA WD, 15 September 1950, NAC, RG 24, vol. 18,271.
20 Ibid., 19 September 1950.
21 25 Bde WD, 30 September 1950, NAC, RG 24, vol. 18,237.
22 2 R22eR WD, 1 and 10 October 1950, NAC, RG 24, vol. 18,356.
23 2 RCR WD, 15 October 1950, NAC, RG 24, vol. 18,340.

24 2 RCHA WD, 7 November 1950, NAC, RG 24, vol. 18,271.
25 Lt.-Col. F.E. White to Col. R. Rowley, 13 September 1950, DHH 112.3M2 (D293).
26 Ibid.
27 Roy E. Appleman, *South to the Naktong, North to the Yalu, June-November 1950* (Washington, DC: US Government Printing Office, 1961), 503-41.
28 Ibid., 600-4.
29 O'Neill, *Australia in the Korean War, 1950-53*, vol. 2, *Combat Operations* (Canberra: Australian Government Publishing Service, 1985), 24.
30 Ibid., 25; Appleman, *South to the Naktong,* 615, 623, 640.
31 Appleman, *South to the Naktong,* 646-51.
32 O'Neill, *Australia in the Korean War,* 2:33; Michael Sheng, 'The Psychology of the Korean War: The Role of Ideology and Perception in China's Entry into the War,' *Journal of Conflict Studies* 22, 1 (2002): 61-6.
33 Fleury quoted in Wood, *Strange Battleground,* 42.
34 25 Bde WD, 30 October 1950, NAC, RG 24, vol. 18,237.
35 2 RCR WD, 5 November 1950, NAC, RG 24, vol. 18,340.
36 25 Bde WD, 7 November 1950, NAC, RG 24, vol. 18,237.
37 2 PPCLI WD, 10 and 25 November 1950, NAC, RG 24, vol. 18,317.
38 2 RCHA WD, 21 November 1950, NAC, RG 24, vol. 18,271.
39 25 Bde WD, 24 November 1950, NAC, RG 24, vol. 18,237.
40 2 RCR WD, 20 November 1950, NAC, RG 24, vol. 18,340.
41 25 Bde WD, 22 November 1950, NAC, RG 24, vol. 18,237.
42 2 RCR WD, 21 November 1950, NAC, RG 24, vol. 18,340.
43 Ibid., 25 November 1950.
44 25 Bde WD, 26 November 1950, NAC, RG 24, vol. 18,237.
45 2 RCR WD, 2 December 1950, NAC, RG 24, vol. 18,340.
46 Historical Section, 'Absence without Leave in the CASF,' nd, DHH 112.3H1.009 (D27).
47 Walsh to GOC, Central Command, 17 January 1951, quoted ibid.
48 Historical Section, 'Absence without Leave in the CASF,' nd, DHH 112.3H1.009 (D27).
49 25 Bde WD, 5 October 1950, NAC, RG 24, vol. 18,237.
50 Rockingham quoted in Ted Barris, *Deadlock in Korea: Canadians at War, 1950-1953* (Toronto: Macmillan Canada, 1999), 51.
51 J.M. Rockingham, 'Recollections of Korea,' August 1975, NAC, MG 31 G12, pp. 8-9.
52 Wood, *Strange Battleground,* 50; O'Neill, *Australia in the Korean War,* 2:55-6.
53 Daily intelligence summary, 14 October 1950, quoted in Wood, *Strange Battleground,* 50; Michael Sheng, 'Book review of M. Hickey, *Korean War: The West Confronts Communism,*' *Journal of Military History* 65, 1 (2001): 245-6.
54 O'Neill, *Australia in the Korean War,* 2:58; Sheng, 'Review of *Korean War,*' 244.
55 Wood, *Strange Battleground,* 52.
56 2 RCR WD, 27 and 28 November 1950, NAC, RG 24, vol. 18,340.
57 25 Bde WD, 1 December 1950, NAC, RG 24, vol. 18,237.
58 2 RCHA WD, 30 November 1950, NAC, RG 24, vol. 18,271.
59 57 Fd Sqn WD, 20 November and 22 December 1950, NAC, RG 24, vol. 18,286.
60 A Sqn, 1/2 Armoured Regiment WD, 24 November 1950 and 8 January 1951, NAC, RG 24, vol. 18,264.
61 2 RCR WD, 6 December 1950, NAC, RG 24, vol. 18,340.
62 Ibid., 8, 11, and 12 December 1950.
63 25 Bde WD, 8 January 1951, NAC, RG 24, vol. 18,237.
64 2 RCR WD, 10 January 1951, NAC, RG 24, vol. 18,341.
65 Capt. G.D. Corry, 'Weekly Summary No 12, Wed 3 Jan 51-Tues 8 Jan 51,' 1 February 1951, DHH 410B25.013 (D4).
66 3 PPCLI WD, 1 and 20 December 1950 and 3 January 1951, NAC, RG 24, vol. 18,322.
67 'Report of Interview with Lt-Col G.C. Corbould,' 10 July 1951, DHH 410B25.033 (D2).

68 Wood, *Strange Battleground,* 84.
69 25 Bde WD, 11 and 12 February 1951, NAC, RG 24, vol. 18,238.
70 Ibid., 20 February 1951.
71 'Report of Interview with Lt-Col G.C. Corbould,' 10 July 1951, DHH 410B25.033 (D2).
72 2 RCR WD, 19 October 1950, NAC, RG 24, vol. 18,340.
73 25 Bde WD, 6 December 1950, NAC, RG 24, vol. 18,237.
74 'Notes, Recommendations and Decisions,' 18 December 1950, 25 Bde WD, December 1950, NAC, RG 24, vol. 18,237.
75 25 Bde WD, 27 December 1950, NAC, RG 24, vol. 18,237.
76 Macklin to Rockingham, 15 February 1951, copy in 25 Bde WD, February 1951, NAC, RG 24, vol. 18,238.
77 Rockingham minute, nd, ibid.
78 Wood, *Strange Battleground,* 32.
79 C.P. Stacey, *Six Years of War: The Army in Canada, Britain and the Pacific* (Ottawa: Queen's Printer, 1955), 109.
80 See also Macklin to Brig. Bishop, 12 March 1951, and Macklin to Rockingham, 13 March 1951, DHH 410.B25 (D1).
81 Simonds quoted in Wood, *Strange Battleground,* 86.
82 Ibid., 88.
83 25 Bde WD, 6 and 13-15 March 1951, NAC, RG 24, vol. 18,238.
84 Wood, *Strange Battleground,* 88.
85 Capt. G.D. Corry, 'Weekly Summary No 15,' 5 February 1951, DHH 410B25.013 (D4).
86 Capt. G.D. Corry, 'Weekly Summary No 16,' 10 February 1951, DHH 410B25.013 (D4).
87 25 Bde WD, 6 and 9 February 1951, NAC, RG 24, vol. 18,238.
88 Ibid., 20 February 1951.
89 A Sqn, 1/2 Armoured Regiment WD, 2 and 3 February 1951, NAC, RG 24, vol. 18,264.
90 Ibid., 21 February 1951.
91 Capt. G.D. Corry, 'Weekly Summary No 19,' 3 March 1951, DHH 410B25.013 (D4).
92 2 RCR WD, 21 February 1951, NAC, RG 24, vol. 18,341.
93 Ibid., 24 February 1951.
94 Capt. G.D. Corry, 'Weekly Summary No 19,' 3 March 1951, DHH 410B25.013 (D4); Capt. G.D. Corry, 'Weekly Summary No 21,' 17 March 1951, DHH 410B25.013 (D4).
95 Capt. G.D. Corry, 'Weekly Summary No 23,' 6 June 1951, DHH 410B25.013 (D4).
96 Capt. G.D. Corry, 'Weekly Summary No 24,' 10 June 1951, DHH 410B25.013 (D4).
97 Ibid.
98 Capt. G.D. Corry, 'Weekly Summary No 25,' 11 June 1951, DHH 410B25.013 (D4).
99 Capt. G.D. Corry, 'Weekly Summary No 26,' 11 June 1951, DHH 410B25.013 (D4).
100 3 PPCLI WD, 2 February 1951, NAC, RG 24, 18,322.
101 Ibid., 15 March 1951.
102 Wood, *Strange Battleground,* 89; 3 PPCLI WD, 21 April and 10 May 1951, NAC, RG 24, vol. 18,322.
103 Capt. G.D. Corry, 'Weekly Summary No 27,' 22 June 1951, DHH 410B25.013 (D4).

Chapter 3: Into Battle

1 2 PPCLI WD, 8 December 1950, NAC, RG 24, vol. 18,317.
2 Billy Mossman, *Ebb and Flow, November 1950-July 1951* (Washington, DC: US Government Printing Office, 1990), 147.
3 MacArthur quoted in James F. Schnabel, *Policy and Direction: The First Year* (Washington, DC: US Government Printing Office, 1972), 281-2.
4 Robert O'Neill, *Australia in the Korean War, 1950-53,* vol. 2, *Combat Operations* (Canberra: Australian Government Publishing Service, 1985), 82.
5 Mossman, *Ebb and Flow,* 126-7.
6 Schnabel, *Policy and Direction,* 283, 294-7.

7 O'Neill, *Australia in the Korean War,* 2:80, 84-5.
8 Mossman, *Ebb and Flow,* 153-5.
9 Vice chief of the general staff quoted in Wood, *Strange Battleground,* 54.
10 Deputy minister quoted ibid.
11 2 PPCLI WD, 21 December 1950, NAC, RG 24, vol. 18,317.
12 Stone report to Rockingham, 23 December 1950, DHH 145.2P7.013 (D6).
13 2 PPCLI WD, 20 December 1950, NAC, RG 24, vol. 18,317.
14 Stone report to Rockingham, 23 December 1950, DHH 145.2P7.013 (D6).
15 Ibid.
16 J.R. Stone, 'Memoir: Kapyong,' *Infantry Journal* (Autumn 1992): 13.
17 Stone report to Rockingham, 23 December 1950, DHH 145.2P7.013 (D6).
18 2 PPCLI WD, 24 December 1950, NAC, RG 24, vol. 18,317.
19 Ibid., 5 January 1951.
20 Ibid., 7 January 1951.
21 Ibid., 8 January 1951.
22 Matthew B. Ridgway, *The Korean War* (New York: Doubleday, 1967), 82-3.
23 Ridgway quoted in Schnabel, *Policy and Direction,* 308.
24 Ridgway quoted in Mossman, *Ebb and Flow,* 180. See also O'Neill, *Australia in the Korean War,* 2:92.
25 Mossman, *Ebb and Flow,* 183, 191-2.
26 Ridgway quoted ibid., 209. See also Herbert Fairlie Wood, *Strange Battleground: The Operations in Korea and Their Effects on the Defence Policy of Canada* (Ottawa: Queen's Printer, 1966), 57.
27 O'Neill, *Australia in the Korean War,* 2:97.
28 Mossman, *Ebb and Flow,* 216-27.
29 2 PPCLI WD, 5 January 1951, NAC, RG 24, vol. 18,317. A Canadian infantry battalion consisted of battalion headquarters, four rifle companies, A to D, each of three platoons numbered 1 to 12, a support company of pioneer, mortar, machine-gun, and antitank platoons, and a headquarters company of various logistics, administrative, and military police personnel.
30 Ibid., 3 January 1951.
31 Ibid., 2 January 1951.
32 Ibid., 6 January 1951.
33 Ibid., 7 January 1951.
34 Ibid., 17 January 1951.
35 Ibid., 6 January 1951.
36 Ibid., 20 January 1951.
37 Ibid., 13 January 1951.
38 Wood, *Strange Battleground,* 67.
39 2 PPCLI WD, 18 January 1951, NAC, RG 24, vol. 18,317.
40 Ibid., 9 and 14 January 1951.
41 Ibid., 15 January 1951.
42 Lilley quoted in Wood, *Strange Battleground,* 59.
43 2 PPCLI WD, 16 and 17 January 1951, NAC, RG 24, vol. 18,317.
44 Ibid., 18 January 1951.
45 Ibid., 21 January 1951.
46 Ibid., 23 January 1951.
47 Ibid., 25 January 1951.
48 Ibid., 24 and 26 January 1951.
49 Ibid., 1 and 2 February 1951.
50 Ibid., 3 February 1951.
51 Ibid., 5 February 1951. A battalion's transport was organized into echelons: F Echelon consisted of those vehicles required by the unit to fight the battle; A Echelon, those vehicles required for the hour-to-hour replenishment of F Echelon with such items as ammunition or gasoline; and B Echelon, the remaining vehicles not needed at short notice in battle, such as the quartermaster's stores trucks.

52 Ibid., 8 February 1951.
53 'Nominal Roll of 2Bn PPCLI on strength wef 24/25 April 1951,' nd, DHH 145.2P7.065 (D2).
54 Stone, 'Memoir: Kapyong,' 11-12.
55 2 PPCLI WD, 25 February 1951, NAC, RG 24, vol. 18,317; Herbert Fairlie Wood, *The Private War of Jacket Coates* (Don Mills, ON: Longmans, 1966), 12, 37.
56 Stone, 'Memoir: Kapyong,' 12.
57 2 PPCLI WD, 11 February 1951, NAC, RG 24, vol. 18,317.
58 O'Neill, *Australia in the Korean War,* 2:103-4.
59 Mossman, *Ebb and Flow,* 279.
60 O'Neill, *Australia in the Korean War,* 2:112-13.
61 Mossman, *Ebb and Flow,* 300.
62 2 PPCLI WD, 19 February 1951, NAC, RG 24, vol. 18,317.
63 O'Neill, *Australia in the Korean War,* 2:116.
64 Mossman, *Ebb and Flow,* 308.
65 2 PPCLI WD, 21 February 1951, NAC, RG 24, vol. 18,317.
66 Ibid., 23 February 1951.
67 Ibid.
68 Ibid., 24 February 1951.
69 Ibid., 25-8 February 1951; Wood, *Strange Battleground,* 64; O'Neill, *Australia in the Korean War,* 2:118-19.
70 2 PPCLI WD, 1 and 2 March 1951, NAC, RG 24, vol. 18,318.
71 Mossman, *Ebb and Flow,* 310-17.
72 D.J. Bercuson, *Blood on the Hills: The Canadian Army in the Korean War* (Toronto: University of Toronto Press, 1999), 97.
73 O'Neill, *Australia in the Korean War,* 2:119.
74 2 PPCLI WD, 7 March 1951, NAC, RG 24, vol. 18,318.
75 Ibid.; O'Neill, *Australia in the Korean War,* 2:120.
76 2 PPCLI WD, 8 March 1951, NAC, RG 24, vol. 18,318; O'Neill, *Australia in the Korean War,* 2:121.
77 Mossman, *Ebb and Flow,* 322-34.
78 Stone to CGS, 9 March 1951, DHH 112.009 (D87).
79 Ibid.
80 2 PPCLI WD, 4 January 1951, NAC, RG 24, vol. 18,317.
81 Stone to CGS, 9 March 1951, DHH 112.009 (D87).
82 Ibid.
83 Ibid.
84 2 PPCLI WD, 16, 21 and 22 March 1951, NAC, RG 24, vol. 18,318.

Chapter 4: Kap'yong

1 2 PPCLI WD, 24 and 27 March 1951, NAC, RG 24, vol. 18,318; Robert O'Neill, *Australia in the Korean War, 1950-53,* vol. 2, *Combat Operations* (Canberra: Australian Government Publishing Service, 1985), 123.
2 2 PPCLI WD, 28 March 1951, NAC, RG 24, vol. 18,318.
3 Ibid., 29 March 1951.
4 J.M. Rockingham, 'Recollections of Korea,' August 1975, NAC, MG 31 G12, p. 13. See also Herbert Fairlie Wood, *Strange Battleground: The Operations in Korea and Their Effects on the Defence Policy of Canada* (Ottawa: Queen's Printer, 1966), 70-1.
5 MacArthur quoted in Billy C. Mossman, *Ebb and Flow, November 1950-July 1951* (Washington, DC: US Government Printing Office, 1990), 319.
6 Ridgway quoted ibid., 320.
7 Truman quoted ibid., 346.
8 O'Neill, *Australia in the Korean War,* 2:122-3.
9 Mossman, *Ebb and Flow,* 367.
10 Ibid., 347-50.

11 2 PPCLI WD, 4 March 1951, NAC, RG 24, vol. 18,318.
12 2 PPCLI WD, 6 to 8 April 1951, NAC, RG 24, vol. 18,318; O'Neill, *Australia in the Korean War,* 2:125.
13 Anthony Farrar-Hockley, *The British Part in the Korean War,* vol. 2, *An Honourable Discharge* (London: Her Majesty's Stationery Office, 1995), 93-4; O'Neill, *Australia in the Korean War,* 2:127-8.
14 2 PPCLI WD, 14 April 1951, NAC, RG 24, vol. 18,318.
15 Wood, *Strange Battleground,* 71-2.
16 Capt. A.P. Mackenzie, '2 PPCLI Action Kapyong Area – 23 to 26 Apr 51,' 26 November 1954, DHH 145.2P7.013 (D5).
17 Mossman, *Ebb and Flow,* 325-6, 379-81.
18 Farrar-Hockley, *British Part in the Korean War,* 2:104-5.
19 Ibid., 106.
20 P'eng quoted ibid., 109.
21 Wood, *Strange Battleground,* 72; O'Neill, *Australia in the Korean War,* 2:132.
22 Mossman, *Ebb and Flow,* 369-77.
23 Maj. T. Younger quoted in Max Hastings, *The Korean War* (London: Michael Joseph, 1987), 251.
24 Farrar-Hockley, *British Part in the Korean War,* 2:124.
25 Brodie and Carne quoted in ibid., 125-8.
26 Mossman, *Ebb and Flow,* 421.
27 *Royal Ulster Rifles* quoted in Farrar-Hockley, *British Part in the Korean War,* 2:134.
28 Mossman, *Ebb and Flow,* 428.
29 Van Fleet quoted in Farrar-Hockley, *British Part in the Korean War,* 2:135-6.
30 Mossman, *Ebb and Flow,* 429.
31 Farrar-Hockley, *British Part in the Korean War,* 2:136.
32 Burke quoted in ibid., 141; Mossman, *Ebb and Flow,* 382-4; O'Neill, *Australia in the Korean War,* 2:134-6.
33 Mossman, *Ebb and Flow,* 282-4.
34 Ibid., 389-91.
35 Capt. A.P. Mackenzie, '2 PPCLI Action Kapyong Area – 23 to 26 Apr 51,' 26 November 1954, DHH 145.2P7.013 (D5).
36 O'Neill, *Australia in the Korean War,* 2:136-7.
37 J.R. Stone, 'Memoir: Kapyong,' *Infantry Journal* (Autumn 1992): 13-14.
38 O'Neill, *Australia in the Korean War,* 2:137-8.
39 Ibid., 140; Mossman, *Ebb and Flow,* 401-4.
40 Farrar-Hockley, *British Part in the Korean War,* 2:143-5.
41 O'Neill, *Australia in the Korean War,* 2:142.
42 Extracts from 27 Bde WD, 24 April 1951, DHH 681.018 (D1).
43 Ibid.
44 O'Neill, *Australia in the Korean War,* 2:148-57; Farrar-Hockley, *British Part in the Korean War,* 2:146-7.
45 Capt. A.P. Mackenzie, '2 PPCLI Action Kapyong Area – 23 to 26 Apr 51,' 26 November 1954, DHH 145.2P7.013 (D5).
46 2 PPCLI WD, 24 April 1951, NAC, RG 24, vol. 18,318.
47 Capt. A.P. Mackenzie, '2 PPCLI Action Kapyong Area – 23 to 26 Apr 51,' 26 November 1954, DHH 145.2P7.013 (D5).
48 Extracts from 27 Bde WD, 24 April 1951, DHH 681.018 (D1).
49 Capt. A.P. Mackenzie, '2 PPCLI Action Kapyong Area – 23 to 26 Apr 51,' 26 November 1954, DHH 145.2P7.013 (D5); Wood, *Strange Battleground,* 78.
50 Stone, 'Memoir: Kapyong,' 14.
51 Lilley quoted in Wood, *Strange Battleground,* 79.
52 Capt. J.G.W. Mills quoted in ibid., 77-8.
53 O'Neill, *Australia in the Korean War,* 2:159-60.
54 Extracts from 27 Bde WD, 25 April 1951, DHH 681.018 (D1); 'Notes on talk given by Lt-Col J.R. Stone at AHQ, 0900 hours 5 Jun 51,' nd, DHH 681.011 (D3); Capt. A.P. Mackenzie, '2 PPCLI Action Kapyong Area – 23 to 26 Apr 51,' 26 November 1954, DHH 145.2P7.013 (D5); Wood, *Strange Battleground,* 78.

55 Stone, 'Memoir: Kapyong,' 14.
56 2 PPCLI WD, 25 April 1951, NAC, RG 24, vol. 18,318.
57 Extracts from 27 Bde WD, 25 April 1951, DHH 681.018 (D1).
58 Ibid.
59 'Notes on talk given by Lt-Col J.R. Stone at AHQ, 0900 hours 5 Jun 51,' nd, DHH 681.011 (D3).
60 Mossman, *Ebb and Flow,* 407.
61 Stone, 'Memoir: Kapyong,' 14-15.
62 Ibid., 15.
63 Ibid.
64 'Notes on talk given by Lt-Col J.R. Stone at AHQ, 0900 hours 5 Jun 51,' nd, DHH 681.011 (D3).

Chapter 5: The Brigade Arrives

1 Billy C. Mossman, *Ebb and Flow, November 1950-July 1951* (Washington, DC: US Government Printing Office, 1990), 436-7.
2 Hsu Yen, *The First Trial of Strength,* ch. 2, part 5 quoted in Anthony Farrar-Hockley, *The British Part in the Korean War,* vol. 2, *An Honourable Discharge* (London: Her Majesty's Stationery Office, 1995), 151.
3 Van Fleet quoted in Mossman, *Ebb and Flow,* 435-7.
4 Ibid., 438-9; Herbert Fairlie Wood, *Strange Battleground: The Operations in Korea and Their Effects on the Defence Policy of Canada* (Ottawa: Queen's Printer, 1966), 79.
5 Mossman, *Ebb and Flow,* 439.
6 Matthew B. Ridgway, *The Korean War* (New York: Doubleday, 1967), 2.
7 2 RCR WD, 4 May 1951, NAC, RG 24, vol. 18,341.
8 J.M. Rockingham, 'Recollections of Korea,' August 1975, NAC, MG 31 G12, p. 19.
9 2 RCR WD, 5 May 1951, NAC, RG 24, vol. 18,341.
10 J.M. Rockingham, 'Recollections of Korea,' August 1975, NAC, MG 31 G12, p. 45.
11 57 Fd Sqn WD, May 1951, app. I, NAC, RG 24, vol. 18,286.
12 J.M. Rockingham, 'Recollections of Korea,' August 1975, NAC, MG 31 G12, p. 18.
13 25 Bde WD, 6 May 1951, NAC, RG 24, vol. 18,238.
14 Ibid., 11 May 1951.
15 S.L.A. Marshall, *Infantry Operations and Weapon Usage in Korea* (London: Greenhill Books, 1988),85-6.
16 Rockingham interview, 17 November 1952, DHH 410B25.013 (D22). See also Wood, *Strange Battleground,* 94.
17 C Sqn, LdSH, 'Newsletter – Mid-April to end of May,' 5 June 1951, copy in author's possession.
18 C Sqn, LdSH WD, 17-19 May 1951, NAC, RG 24, vol. 18,264; John Gardam, *Korea Volunteer: An Oral History from Those Who Were There* (Burnstown, ON: General Store Publishing, 1994), 82.
19 J.M. Rockingham, 'Recollections of Korea,' August 1975, NAC, MG 31 G12, p. 22.
20 2 RCR WD, 17 May 1951, RG 24, vol. 18,341.
21 Farrar-Hockley, *British Part in the Korean War,* 2:153.
22 Mossman, *Ebb and Flow,* 445.
23 Ibid., 453; Farrar-Hockley, *British Part in the Korean War,* 2:155-6.
24 25 Bde WD, 17 May 1951, RG 24, vol. 18,238.
25 G.W.L. Nicholson, 'Memorandum,' 17 November 1952, DHH 410B25.013 (D22).
26 Rockingham to Nicholson, 1 July 1953, DHH 410B25.009 (D5).
27 J.M. Rockingham, 'Recollections of Korea,' August 1975, NAC, MG 31 G12, p. 22.
28 Wood, *Strange Battleground,* 97-8.
29 D.J. Bercuson, *Blood on the Hills: The Canadian Army in the Korean War* (Toronto: University of Toronto Press, 1999), 117-18; Aryeh J.S. Nusbacher, 'From Koje to Kosovo: the Development of the Canadian National Command Element,' in *The Korean War, 1950-53: A 50 Year Retrospective,* ed. Peter Dennis and Jeffrey Grey (Canberra: Australian Government Publishing Service, 2000), 59-73.
30 Bercuson, *Blood on the Hills,* 118.
31 G.W.L. Nicholson, 'Memorandum,' 17 November 1952, DHH 410B25.013 (D22).

32 Ridgway, *Korean War,* 173. See also Farrar-Hockley, *British Part in the Korean War,* 2:155-6.
33 P'eng telegram, nd, quoted in Farrar-Hockley, *British Part in the Korean War,* 2:157-8.
34 Mossman, *Ebb and Flow,* 472.
35 Farrar-Hockley, *British Part in the Korean War,* 2:158-9.
36 2 RCR WD, 19-21 May 1951, NAC, RG 24, vol. 18,341.
37 Ibid., 22 May 1951.
38 25th Division operational instructions quoted in Wood, *Strange Battleground,* 99.
39 Ibid., 99-101.
40 Mossman, *Ebb and Flow,* 491.
41 Historical Officer, 25 Bde, 'The Battle of Chail-li, 2 RCR, 30 May 1951,' nd, DHH 145.2R13.013 (D2).
42 Ibid.
43 Ibid.
44 2 RCR WD, 30 May 1951, NAC, RG 24, vol. 18,341.
45 Historical Officer, 25 Bde, 'The Battle of Chail-li, 2 RCR, 30 May 1951,' nd, DHH 145.2R13.013 (D2).
46 Ibid.
47 Ibid.
48 2 RCR WD, 30 May 1951, NAC, RG 24, vol. 18,341.
49 Historical Officer, 25 Bde, 'The Battle of Chail-li, 2 RCR, 30 May 1951,' nd, DHH 145.2R13.013 (D2).
50 2 RCR WD, 30 May 1951, NAC, RG 24, vol. 18,341.
51 Ibid.; Wood, *Strange Battleground,* 104-5.
52 Keane report on operations from 25 May to 5 June 1951, nd, DHH 145.2R13.013 (D2).
53 OC, C Company to CO, 2 RCR, 7 June 1951, DHH 145.2R13.013 (D2).
54 Keane report on operations from 25 May to 5 June 1951, nd, DHH 145.2R13.013 (D2).
55 'Notes on talk given by Lt-Col Stone at AHQ, 0900 hours 5 Jun 51,' nd, DHH 681.011 (D3).
56 OC, A Company to CO, 2 RCR, 3 June 1951, DHH 145.2R13.013 (D2).
57 Keane report on operations from 25 May to 5 June 1951, nd, DHH 145.2R13.013 (D2).
58 Ibid.
59 Hutton quoted in Gardam, *Korea Volunteer,* 72.
60 Ridgway, *Korean War,* 180; Mossman, *Ebb and Flow,* 491-3.
61 Wood, *Strange Battleground,* 106.
62 2 PPCLI WD, 12 and 27 May and 1 June 1951, NAC, RG 24, vol. 18,318.
63 25 Bde WD, 2 June 1951, NAC, RG 24, vol. 18,238.
64 2 PPCLI WD, 12 June 1951, NAC, RG 24, vol. 18,318.
65 Ibid., 14 June 1951.
66 Joint chiefs of staff to commander-in-chief, Far East, 1 June 1951, quoted in Mossman, *Ebb and Flow,* 490.
67 Acheson quoted in ibid., 495.
68 Pearson and Lie quoted in Denis Stairs, *The Diplomacy of Constraint: Canada, the Korean War, and the United States* (Toronto: University of Toronto Press, 1974), 234.
69 Nieh Jung-chen quoted in Farrar-Hockley, *British Part in the Korean War,* 2:174-5; Mossman, *Ebb and Flow,* 496-7.
70 Ridgway quoted in Mossman, *Ebb and Flow,* 501.
71 2 PPCLI WD, 3 June 1951, NAC, RG 24, vol. 18,318.
72 Ibid., 7 and 9 June 1951.
73 Ibid., 10 June 1951.
74 2 R22eR WD, 14 June 1951, NAC, RG 24, vol. 18,356.
75 2 RCR WD, 14 June 1951, NAC, RG 24, vol. 18,341.
76 Wood, *Strange Battleground,* 107-8.
77 2 PPCLI WD, 19 June 1951, NAC, RG 24, vol. 18,318.
78 Ibid., 20 June 1951.
79 25 Bde WD, 5 July 1951, NAC, RG 24, vol. 18,239.
80 2 PPCLI WD, 21 June 1951, NAC, RG 24, vol. 18,318.
81 Ibid., 26 June 1951.

82 Ibid., 23 June 1951.
83 Ibid., 1 July 1951.
84 Ibid., 27 June 1951.
85 Ibid., 22 June 1951.
86 25 Bde WD, 2 July 1951, NAC, RG 24, vol. 18,239.
87 Ibid., 6 July 1951.
88 Ibid., 24 June 1951.
89 Ibid.
90 Ibid., 3 July 1951.
91 2 PPCLI WD, 2 July 1951, NAC, RG 24, vol. 18,318.
92 25 Bde WD, 3 July 1951, NAC, RG 24, vol. 18,239.
93 2 PPCLI WD, 22 May 1951, NAC, RG 24, vol. 18, 318.
94 A.R. Menzies to Secretary of State for External Affairs, 31 October 1951, DHH 681.001 (D1).
95 25 Bde WD, 3 July 1951, NAC, RG 24, vol. 18,239.
96 Ibid., 4 July 1951.
97 Ibid., 1 July 1951.
98 Ibid., 10 July 1951.
99 2 RCR WD, July 1951, NAC, RG 24, vol. 18,342.
100 25 Bde WD, 11 July 1951, NAC, RG 24, vol. 18,239.

Chapter 6: The Commonwealth Division

1 Foulkes to Gen. J. Lawton Collins, 21 August 1950, quoted in Canadian Army Historical Section, 'Initial Supply Problems of Canadian Army Special Force,' nd, copy received from Bill McAndrew.
2 Brigadier general staff plans to vice chief of the general staff, 23 February 1951, DHH 112.009 (D96).
3 2 RCR WD, 2 May 1951, NAC, RG 24, vol. 18,341.
4 Minister of National Defence to Cabinet Defence Committee, 10 April 1951, DHH 112.009 (D96).
5 Ibid.
6 Herbert Fairlie Wood, *Strange Battleground: The Operations in Korea and Their Effects on the Defence Policy of Canada* (Ottawa: Queen's Printer, 1966), 117-18.
7 Ibid., 119.
8 Anthony Farrar-Hockley, *The British Part in the Korean War*, vol. 2, *An Honourable Discharge* (London: Her Majesty's Stationery Office, 1995), 209-10.
9 J.M. Rockingham, 'Recollections of Korea,' August 1975, NAC, MG 31 G12, p. 27.
10 Ibid., 74.
11 Ibid., 45.
12 Jeffrey Grey, *The Commonwealth Armies and the Korean War: An Alliance Study* (Manchester: Manchester University Press, 1988), 151.
13 'Account of interview given by Lt-Col N.G. Wilson-Smith,' 19 June 1952, DHH 681.013 (D14).
14 Ibid.
15 Amy quoted in John Gardam, *Korea Volunteer: An Oral History from Those Who Were There* (Burnstown, ON: General Store Publishing, 1994), 93.
16 E.A.C. Amy interview, 12 June 1953, DHH 681.009 (D9).
17 Maj.-Gen. A.J.H. Cassels, '1 Commonwealth Division Periodic Report, 2 May-15 Oct. 1951,' nd, Public Record Office UK (hereafter PRO), War Office (hereafter WO), 308/27.
18 J.M. Rockingham, 'Recollections of Korea,' August 1975, NAC, MG 31 G12, pp. 29-30.
19 25 Bde WD, 16 July 1951, NAC, RG 24, vol. 18,239.
20 Ibid., 19 July 1951.
21 2 R22eR WD, 19 July 1951, NAC, RG 24, vol. 18,357.
22 25 Bde WD, 20 July 1951, NAC, RG 24, vol. 18,239.
23 'The Imjin River Incident, 18-24 July 51,' 7 October 1951, DHH 410B25.013 (D3).
24 25 Bde WD, 20 and 21 July 1951, NAC, RG 24, vol. 18,239.
25 57 Fd Sqn WD, 21 and 22 July 1951, NAC, RG 24, vol. 18,286.
26 Wood, *Strange Battleground*, 121-4.

27 'Report by Lt-Col D.S.F. Bult-Francis, AG Rep on AHQ Team, on visit to Japan and Korea, 2 Jul-4 Aug 51,' 10 August 1951, DHH 112.009 (D87).
28 R. Rowley, 'Brief notes on visit to Korean theatre,' 23 August 1951, ibid.
29 2 RCR WD, 18 August 1951, NAC, RG 24, vol. 18,342.
30 2 PPCLI WD, 18 August 1951, NAC, RG 24, vol. 18,319.
31 'Report by Lt-Col D.S.F. Bult-Francis, AG Rep on AHQ Team, on visit to Japan and Korea, 2 Jul-4 Aug 51,' 10 August 1951, DHH 112.009 (D87).
32 2 PPCLI WD, 6 August 1951, NAC, RG 24, vol. 18,319.
33 R. Rowley, 'Brief notes on visit to Korean theatre,' 23 August 1951, DHH 112.009 (D87).
34 'Report by Lt-Col D.S.F. Bult-Francis, AG Rep on AHQ Team, on visit to Japan and Korea, 2 Jul-4 Aug 51,' 10 August 1951, DHH 112.009 (D87).
35 R. Rowley, 'Brief notes on visit to Korean theatre,' 23 August 1951, DHH 112.009 (D87).
36 Ibid.
37 S.L.A. Marshall, *Infantry Operations and Weapons Usage in Korea* (London: Greenhill Books, 1988), 67-70.
38 Rockingham to quartermaster general, 10 June 1951, quoted in Canadian Army Historical Section, 'Initial Supply Problems of Canadian Army Special Force,' nd, copy received from Bill McAndrew. See also Capt. G.D. Corry to Col. C.P. Stacey, 10 July 1951, DHH 410B25.003 (D2).
39 Maj.-Gen. A.J.H. Cassels, '1 Commonwealth Division Periodic Report, 2 May-15 Oct 1951,' nd, app. C, PRO, WO 308/27.
40 Ibid.
41 Major C.H. Lithgow, 'Report on Operation "Dirk,"' nd, DHH 410B25.016 (D8).
42 Ibid.
43 Capt. L.W.G. Hayes quoted in Wood, *Strange Battleground,* 122.
44 Major C.H. Lithgow, 'Report on Operation "Dirk,"' nd, DHH 410B25.016 (D8).
45 Capt. G.D. Corry, 'Weekly Summary 44,' 30 September 1951, DHH 410B25.013 (D99); Wood, *Strange Battleground,* 123-4.
46 Maj. C.H. Lithgow, 'Report on Operation "Dirk,"' nd, DHH 410B25.016 (D8).
47 Lt.-Col. J.A. Dextraze, '2 Bn R22eR Patrol Report, Operation "Claymore,"' 29 August 1951, DHH 410B25.016 (D7).
48 Ibid.
49 Farrar-Hockley, *British Part in the Korean War,* 2:215-16.
50 Maj.-Gen. A.J.H. Cassels, '1 Commonwealth Division Periodic Report, 2 May-15 Oct. 1951,' nd, app. B, PRO, WO 308/27.
51 J.M. Rockingham, 'Recollections of Korea,' August 1975, NAC, MG 31 G12, pp. 30-1.
52 Wood, *Strange Battleground,* 126-7.
53 2 PPCLI WD, 4 September 1951, NAC, RG 24, vol. 18,319.
54 2 R22eR WD, 15 September 1951, NAC, RG 24, vol. 18,357.
55 2 RCR, 'Night Operation "Snatch,"' October 1951, DHH 410B25.013 (D7).
56 Maj.-Gen. A.J.H. Cassels, '1 Commonwealth Division Periodic Report, 2 May-15 Oct 1951,' nd, app. C, PRO, WO 308/27.
57 2 RCR, 'Night Operation "Snatch,"' October 1951, DHH 410B25.013 (D7).
58 Ibid.
59 Ibid.
60 Ibid.
61 Ibid.
62 Ibid.
63 Max Hastings, *The Korean War* (London: Michael Joseph, 1987), 276.
64 J.M. Rockingham to Dr. A.E. Grauer, 1 March 1952, DHH 410B25.019 (D18).
65 Farrar-Hockley, *British Part in the Korean War,* 2:193.
66 Van Fleet quoted in Walter G. Hermes, *Truce Tent and Fighting Front* (Washington, DC: US Government Printing Office, 1966), 81; Farrar-Hockley, *British Part in the Korean War,* 2:202.
67 Hermes, *Truce Tent,* 82-4.

68 Farrar-Hockley, *British Part in the Korean War,* 2:203-4.
69 Hermes, *Truce Tent,* 84-6.
70 Farrar-Hockley, *British Part in the Korean War,* 2:204.
71 Hermes, *Truce Tent,* 86-96.
72 Ibid., 98; Farrar-Hockley, *British Part in the Korean War,* 2:204-5, 217-18.
73 Farrar-Hockley, *British Part in the Korean War,* 2:218-19; Wood, *Strange Battleground,* 130.
74 Farrar-Hockley, *British Part in the Korean War,* 2:219.
75 Maj.-Gen. A.J.H. Cassels, '1 Commonwealth Division Periodic Report, 2 May-15 Oct 1951,' nd, app. B, PRO, WO 308/27; Robert O'Neill, *Australia in the Korean War, 1950-53,* vol. 2, *Combat Operations* (Canberra: Australian Government Publishing Service, 1985), 186.
76 Maj.-Gen. A.J.H. Cassels, '1 Commonwealth Division Periodic Report, 2 May-15 Oct 1951,' nd, app. B and C, PRO, WO 308/27; Farrar-Hockley, *British Part in the Korean War,* 2:220-21.
77 Farrar-Hockley, *British Part in the Korean War,* 2:221.
78 Ibid., 222; O'Neill, *Australia in the Korean War,* 2:186-8.
79 Farrar-Hockley, *British Part in the Korean War,* 2:223.
80 Maj.-Gen. A.J.H. Cassels, '1 Commonwealth Division Periodic Report, 2 May-15 Oct 1951,' nd, app. C, PRO, WO 308/27.
81 2 PPCLI WD, 4 October 1951, NAC, RG 24, vol. 18,319.
82 2 RCR WD, 4 October 1951, NAC, RG 24, vol. 18,342.
83 2 R22eR WD, 5 October 1951, NAC, RG 24, vol. 18,357.
84 25 Bde WD, 5 October 1951, NAC, RG 24, vol. 18,240.
85 Farrar-Hockley, *British Part in the Korean War,* 2:224.
86 Maj.-Gen. A.J.H. Cassels, '1 Commonwealth Division Periodic Report, 2 May-15 Oct 1951,' nd, app. B, PRO, WO 308/27. See also Farrar-Hockley, *British Part in the Korean War,* 2:224-8.
87 Maj.-Gen. A.J.H. Cassels, '1 Commonwealth Division Periodic Report, 2 May-15 Oct 1951,' nd, app. B, PRO, WO 308/27.
88 Farrar-Hockley, *British Part in the Korean War,* 2:224-9.
89 Ibid., 229; Wood, *Strange Battleground,* 132.
90 Hermes, *Truce Tent,* 102.
91 Ibid., 102; Farrar-Hockley, *British Part in the Korean War,* 2:230.
92 Hermes, *Truce Tent,* 102; Farrar-Hockley, *British Part in the Korean War,* 2:230.
93 Maj.-Gen. A.J.H. Cassels, '1 Commonwealth Division Periodic Report, 2 May-15 Oct 1951,' nd, app. C, PRO, WO 308/27; Hermes, *Truce Tent,* 102.
94 Cassels quoted in Farrar-Hockley, *British Part in the Korean War,* 2:230-1.
95 2 RCR, 'Night Operation "Snatch,"' October 1951, DHH 410B25.013 (D7).

Chapter 7: The First Rotation

1 Macklin to Simonds, 'Replacement Policy,' 16 July 1951, DHH 112.009 (D87).
2 Ibid.
3 3 PPCLI WD, 11 August 1951, NAC, RG 24, vol. 18,323.
4 Ibid., 6 July 1951.
5 3 PPCLI WD, July 1951, app. 3, Lt.-Col. H.F. Wood, 'Interim Report – Experimental Training Method,' 6 July 1951, NAC, RG 24, vol. 18,323.
6 3 PPCLI WD, 26 June 1951, NAC, RG 24, vol. 18,322.
7 Ibid., 6 June 1951.
8 'Summary of Decisions Resulting from a Conference between Comd 25 Cdn Inf Bde and DGAP on 22 Sep 51,' 23 September 1951, DHH 112.009 (D87); Herbert Fairlie Wood, *Strange Battleground: The Operations in Korea and Their Effects on the Defence Policy of Canada* (Ottawa: Queen's Printer, 1966), 138.
9 'Extract from Minutes of Meeting No. 122 – CGS Conference – Held Monday, 23 Jul 51,' nd, DHH 112.3M2 (D296).
10 CGS to Minister, 2 August 1951, DHH 112.3M2 (D296).
11 Army Ottawa to Army Edmonton, 16 August 1951, DHH 112.3M2 (D296).

12 G.R. Stevens, *Princess Patricia's Canadian Light Infantry*, vol. 3, *1919-1957* (Griesbach, AB: Historical Committee of the Regiment, 1957), 278.
13 1 PPCLI WD, 23 August-20 September 1951, NAC, RG 24, vol. 18,312.
14 1 PPCLI Annual Historical Report, 1 April 1951, DHH.
15 3 PPCLI WD, 20 August 1951, NAC, RG 24, vol. 18,323.
16 Ibid., 23 August 1951.
17 Ibid., 23 and 26 August 1951.
18 Ibid., 27 August 1951.
19 Ibid., 28 August 1951.
20 Ibid., 30 August 1951.
21 Ibid., 28 August 1951.
22 Ibid., 3 September 1951.
23 T. McNamara, telephone interview with author, January 1995.
24 Wood, *Strange Battleground*, 163.
25 1 PPCLI WD, 4 October 1951, NAC, RG 24, vol. 18,312.
26 Ibid., 3 October 1951.
27 McNamara, interview; Wood, *Strange Battleground*, 144.
28 3 PPCLI WD, 'Summary,' August 1951, NAC, RG 24, vol. 18,323.
29 Ibid., 5 September 1951.
30 J.R. Stone, 'Memoir: Kapyong,' *Infantry Journal* (Autumn 1992): 12.
31 Wood, *Strange Battleground*, 146.
32 1 PPCLI WD, 12 October 1951, NAC, RG 24, vol. 18,312.
33 Maj.-Gen. A.J.H. Cassels, '1 Commonwealth Division Periodic Report, 15 October 1951-15 February 1952,' nd, app. B, PRO, WO 308/27.
34 Capt. G.D. Corry, 'Weekly Summary No. 52, Wed 10 Oct 51-Tue 16 Oct 51,' 21 October 1951, DHH 410B25.013 (D99).
35 1 PPCLI WD, 19 October 1951, NAC, RG 24, vol. 18,312.
36 'Return of Casualties of 25 CIB in Korean War,' nd, DHH 410.B25.065 (D15).
37 25 Bde WD, 18 October 1951, NAC, RG 24, vol. 18,240.
38 Ibid., 21 October 1951.
39 Capt. G.D. Corry, 'Weekly Summary No. 52, Wed 10 Oct 51-Tue 16 Oct 51,' 21 October 1951; 'Weekly Summary No. 53, Wed 17 Oct 51-Tues 23 Oct 51,' 5 December 1951, DHH 410B25.013 (D99).
40 Maj.-Gen. A.J.H. Cassels, '1 Commonwealth Division Periodic Report, 15 October 1951-15 February 1952,' nd, app. A, PRO, WO 308/27.
41 25th Bde, 'Confirmatory Notes to Brigade Commander's Verbal Orders of 22 Oct 51 for Operation Pepperpot,' 22 October 1951, DHH 410B25.016 (D15).
42 25th Bde WD, 21 October 1951, NAC, RG 24, vol. 18,240.
43 Ibid., 22 October 1951.
44 1 PPCLI WD, 21 October 1951, NAC, RG 24, vol. 18,312.
45 Ibid., 22 October 1951.
46 Ibid., 23 October 1951.
47 25 Bde Ops Log, 'Operation Pepperpot,' 23 October 1951, DHH 410B25.016 (D15); Wood, *Strange Battleground*, 148-9.
48 1 PPCLI WD, 23 October 1951, NAC, RG 24, vol. 18,312.
49 Ibid.
50 25 Bde WD, 23 October 1951, NAC, RG 24, vol. 18,240.
51 Ibid.
52 'Comments by Brig. J.M. Rockingham,' 1 July 1953, DHH 410B25.009 (D5).
53 Williams quoted in Wood, *Strange Battleground*, 149.
54 25 Bde Ops Log, 'Operation Pepperpot,' 23 October 1951, DHH 410B25.016 (D15).
55 1 Comwel Div, 'Periodic Ops Report No 168,' 23 October 1951, DHH 410B25.016 (D15); Wood, *Strange Battleground*, 148-9.
56 1 PPCLI WD, 24 October 1951, NAC, RG 24, vol. 18,312.

57 Anthony Farrar-Hockley, *The British Part in the Korean War*, vol. 2, *An Honourable Discharge* (London: Her Majesty's Stationery Office, 1995), 243.
58 25 Bde WD, 27 October 1951, NAC, RG 24, vol. 18,240.
59 Ibid., 29 October 1951.
60 Ibid., 30 October 1951.
61 C Sqn LdSH WD, 23 October 1951, NAC, RG 24, vol. 18,265.
62 Ibid., 23-30 November and 16 December 1951.
63 Ron Francis quoted in John Gardam, *Korea Volunteer: An Oral History from Those Who Were There* (Burnstown, ON: General Store Publishing, 1994), 105.
64 Capt. G.D. Corry, 'Weekly Summary No. 55, Wed 31 Oct 51-Tues 6 Nov 51,' 1 February 1952, DHH 410B25.013 (D99).
65 25 Bde WD, 1 November 1951, NAC, RG 24, vol. 18,240.
66 1 PPCLI WD, 1 November 1951, NAC, RG 24, vol. 18,312.
67 Capt. G.D. Corry, 'Weekly Summary No. 55, Wed 31 Oct 51-Tues 6 Nov 51,' 1 February 1952, DHH 410B25.013 (D99).
68 Ibid.
69 2 RCR WD, 3 November 1951, NAC, RG 24, vol. 18,343.
70 1 PPCLI WD, 3 November 1951, NAC, RG 24, vol. 18,312.
71 Maj.-Gen. A.J.H. Cassels, '1 Commonwealth Division Periodic Report, 15 October 1951-15 February 1952,' nd, app. A, PRO, WO 308/27.
72 Robert O'Neill, *Australia in the Korean War, 1950-53*, vol. 2, *Combat Operations* (Canberra: Australian Government Publishing Service, 1985), 201.
73 Maj.-Gen. A.J.H. Cassels, '1 Commonwealth Division Periodic Report, 15 October 1951-15 February 1952,' nd, app. A, PRO, WO 308/27.
74 Ibid.; Farrar-Hockley, *British Part in the Korean War*, 2:246-7.
75 O'Neill, *Australia in the Korean War*, 203-4.
76 McNamara, interview; Wood, *Strange Battleground*, 144.
77 1 PPCLI WD, 30 October and 2 November 1951, NAC, RG 24, vol. 18,312.
78 Ibid., 4 November 1951.
79 Capt. G.D. Corry, 'Weekly Summary No. 55, Wed 31 Oct 51-Tues 6 Nov 51,' 1 February 1952, DHH 410B25.013 (D99); Maj.-Gen. A.J.H. Cassels, '1 Commonwealth Division Periodic Report, 15 October 1951-15 February 1952,' nd, app. A, PRO, WO 308/27; Wood, *Strange Battleground*, 150-1.
80 1 PPCLI WD, 5 November 1951, NAC, RG 24, vol. 18,312.
81 Ibid.
82 Capt. G.D. Corry, 'Weekly Summary No. 55, Wed 31 Oct 51-Tues 6 Nov 51,' 1 February 1952, DHH 410B25.013 (D99); Wood, *Strange Battleground*, 150-2.
83 25 Bde WD, 8 November 1951, NAC, RG 24, vol. 18,240.
84 1 PPCLI WD, 6 November 1951, NAC, RG 24, vol. 18,312.
85 Ibid.
86 Wood, *Strange Battleground*, 151.
87 1 PPCLI WD, 6 November 1951, NAC, RG 24, vol. 18,312.
88 Ibid.
89 Ibid.
90 McNamara, interview.
91 1 PPCLI WD, 6 November 1951, NAC, RG 24, vol. 18,312.
92 Ibid., 11 November 1951.

Chapter 8: No Withdrawal, No Panic

1 Maj.-Gen. A.J.H. Cassels, '1 Commonwealth Division Periodic Report, 15 October 1951-15 February 1952,' nd, app. A, PRO, WO 308/27.
2 Robert O'Neill, *Australia in the Korean War, 1950-53*, vol. 2, *Combat Operations* (Canberra: Australian Government Publishing Service, 1985), 204.
3 2 R22eR WD, 2 November 1951, NAC, RG 24, vol. 18,357.

4 Ibid., 4 November 1951.
5 Ibid., 5 November 1951.
6 Capt. G.D. Corry, 'Weekly Summary No. 56, Wed 7 Nov 51-Tues 13 Nov 51,' 5 December 1951, DHH 410B25.013 (D99).
7 2 R22eR WD, 13 November 1951, NAC, RG 24, vol. 18,357.
8 Maj.-Gen. A.J.H. Cassels, '1 Commonwealth Division Periodic Report, 15 October 1951-15 February 1952,' nd, PRO, WO 308/27.
9 Capt. G.D. Corry, 'Weekly Summary No. 56, Wed 7 Nov 51-Tues 13 Nov 51,' 5 December 1951, DHH 410B25.013 (D99).
10 1 PPCLI patrol report, 13-14 November 1951, DHH 410B25.019 (D19).
11 Capt. G.D. Corry, 'Weekly Summary No. 57, Wed 14 Nov 51-Tues 20 Nov 51,' 5 December 1951, DHH 410B25.013 (D99).
12 1 PPCLI patrol report, 16-17 November 1951, DHH 410B25.019 (D19).
13 Ibid.
14 Ibid.
15 Rockingham to Dr. A.E. Grauer, 1 March 1952, DHH 410B25.019 (D18).
16 Hamilton quoted in John Gardam, *Korea Volunteer: An Oral History from Those Who Were There* (Burnstown, ON: General Store Publishing, 1994), 34.
17 25 Bde WD, 9 October 1951, NAC, RG 24, vol. 18,240.
18 1 PPCLI WD, 12 November 1951, NAC, RG 24, vol. 18,312.
19 25 Bde WD, 31 July 1951, NAC, RG 24, vol. 18,239.
20 A.R. Menzies to Secretary of State for External Affairs, 31 October 1951, DHH 681.001 (D1).
21 J.M. Rockingham, 'Recollections of Korea,' August 1975, NAC, MG 31 G12, pp. 32-3.
22 A.R. Menzies to Secretary of State for External Affairs, 31 October 1951, DHH 681.001 (D1).
23 J.M. Rockingham, 'Recollections of Korea,' August 1975, NAC, MG 31 G12, pp. 32-3.
24 Maj.-Gen. A.J.H. Cassels, '1 Commonwealth Division Periodic Report, 15 October 1951-15 February 1952,' nd, app. A, PRO, WO 308/27.
25 Ibid.
26 25 Bde WD, 18 November 1951, NAC, RG 24, vol. 18,240.
27 Maj.-Gen. A.J.H. Cassels, '1 Commonwealth Division Periodic Report, 15 October 1951-15 February 1952,' nd, app. A, PRO, WO 308/27.
28 Ibid.
29 Capt. G.D. Corry, 'Weekly Summary No. 57, Wed 14 Nov 51-Tues 20 Nov 51,' 5 December 1951, DHH 410B25.013 (D99).
30 1 PPCLI WD, 20 November 1951, NAC, RG 24, vol. 18,312.
31 Maj.-Gen. A.J.H. Cassels, '1 Commonwealth Division Periodic Report, 15 October 1951-15 February 1952,' nd, PRO, WO 308/27.
32 25 Bde WD, 21 November 1951, NAC, RG 24, vol. 18,240; 1 PPCLI WD, 21 November 1951, NAC, RG 24, vol. 18,312.
33 2 R22eR WD, November 1951, app. 6, 'Commanding Officer's Conference, 1600 hrs, 19 November 1951,' NAC, RG 24, vol. 18,357.
34 Ibid.
35 25 Bde WD, 22 November 1951, NAC, RG 24, vol. 18,240.
36 Liboiron quoted in Herbert Fairlie Wood, *Strange Battleground: The Operations in Korea and Their Effects on the Defence Policy of Canada* (Ottawa: Queen's Printer, 1996), 153.
37 2 R22eR WD, 23 November 1951, NAC, RG 24, vol. 18,357.
38 'Interview with Major R. Liboiron, Lt. R. MacDuff, Lt. W. Nash, Lt. T.R. Webb, 2 R22eR,' 1 December 1951, DHH 410B25.013 (D12).
39 2nd US Battalion journal quoted in Wood, *Strange Battleground,* 154.
40 25 Bde Ops Log, 23 November 1951, DHH 410B25.013 (D39).
41 J.M. Rockingham, 'Recollections of Korea,' August 1975, NAC, MG 31 G12, p. 33. Rockingham's story is repeated in 1 PPCLI WD, 23 November 1951, NAC, RG 24, vol. 18,312.
42 2 R22eR WD, 23 November 1951, NAC, RG 24, vol. 18,357.

43 Commander, 3rd US Division to regimental commanders, 19 November 1951, quoted in Wood, *Strange Battleground,* 154.
44 Capt. G.D. Corry, 'Weekly Summary No. 58, Wed 21 Nov 51-Tues 27 Nov 51,' 5 December 1951, DHH 410B25.013 (D99).
45 25 Bde WD, 23 November 1951, NAC, RG 24, vol. 18,240.
46 Wood, *Strange Battleground,* 154-5.
47 Ibid., 155.
48 All quotations from 25 Bde Ops Log, 23-4 November 1951, DHH 410B25.013 (D39).
49 All quotations from 25 Bde Ops Log, 23-4 November 1951, DHH 410B25.013 (D39); 25 Bde WD, 24 November 1951, NAC, RG 24, vol. 18,240; Wood, *Strange Battleground,* 157.
50 1 PPCLI WD, 23 and 24 November 1951, NAC, RG 24, vol. 18,312.
51 2 R22eR WD, 24 November 1951, NAC, RG 24, vol. 18,357.
52 25 Bde Ops Log, 24 November 1951, DHH 410B25.013 (D39).
53 Ibid.
54 25 Bde WD, 24 November 1951, NAC, RG 24, vol. 18,240.
55 'Interview with Major R. Liboiron, Lt. R. MacDuff, Lt. W. Nash, Lt. T.R. Webb, 2 R22eR,' 1 December 1951, DHH 410B25.013 (D12).
56 25 Bde Ops Log, 24 November 1951, DHH 410B25.013 (D39).
57 Ibid.
58 'Interview with Major R. Liboiron, Lt. R. MacDuff, Lt. W. Nash, Lt. T.R. Webb, 2 R22eR,' 1 December 1951, DHH 410B25.013 (D12); Wood, *Strange Battleground,* 157.
59 25 Bde Ops Log, 24 November 1951, DHH 410B25.013 (D39); Wood, *Strange Battleground,* 157.
60 All quotations from 25 Bde Ops Log, 24-5 November 1951, DHH 410B25.013 (D39).
61 Ibid. See also 1 PPCLI WD, 24 November 1951, NAC, RG 24, vol. 18,312.
62 Wood, *Strange Battleground,* 158; 25 Bde Ops Log, 25 November 1951, DHH 410B25.013 (D39).
63 25 Bde Ops Log, 25 November 1951, DHH 410B25.013 (D39).
64 2 R22eR WD, 25 November 1951, NAC, RG 24, vol. 18,357.
65 'Interview with Major R. Liboiron, Lt. R. MacDuff, Lt. W. Nash, Lt. T.R. Webb, 2 R22eR,' 1 December 1951, DHH 410B25.013 (D12).
66 25 Bde WD, 26 November 1951, NAC, RG 24, vol. 18,240.
67 Wood, *Strange Battleground,* 159.
68 Maj.-Gen. A.J.H. Cassels, '1 Commonwealth Division Periodic Report, 15 October 1951-15 February 1952,' nd, app. B, PRO, WO 308/27; Wood, *Strange Battleground,* 160.
69 Dextraze quoted in Wood, *Strange Battleground,* 158.
70 Maj.-Gen. A.J.H. Cassels, '1 Commonwealth Division Periodic Report, 15 October 1951-15 February 1952,' nd, PRO, WO 308/27.
71 Wood, *Strange Battleground,* 155.
72 Maj.-Gen. A.J.H. Cassels, '1 Commonwealth Division Periodic Report, 15 October 1951-15 February 1952,' nd, PRO, WO 308/27.
73 25 Bde Ops Log, 26 November 1951, DHH 410B25.013 (D39).
74 1 PPCLI WD, 25 November 1951, NAC, RG 24, vol. 18,312.
75 25 Bde WD, 27 November 1951, NAC, RG 24, vol. 18,240.
76 Capt. G.D. Corry, 'Weekly Summary No. 58, Wed 21 Nov 51-Tues 27 Nov 51,' 5 December 1951, DHH 410B25.013 (D99).

Chapter 9: The Active Defence

1 Van Fleet quoted in Walter G. Hermes, *Truce Tent and Fighting Front* (Washington, DC: US Government Printing Office, 1966), 177.
2 Capt. G.D. Corry, 'Weekly Summary No. 59, Wed 28 Nov 51-Tues 4 Dec 51,' 5 December 1951, DHH 410B25.013 (D99).
3 Newspaper report and Ridgway quoted in Hermes, *Truce Tent,* 177-8.
4 Capt. G.D. Corry, 'Weekly Summary No. 59, Wed 28 Nov 51-Tues 4 Dec 51,' 5 December 1951, DHH 410B25.013 (D99).

5 1 PPCLI WD, 1 December 1951, NAC, RG 24, vol. 18,313.
6 2 RCR WD, 30 November 1951, NAC, RG 24, vol. 18,343.
7 Maj.-Gen. A.J.H. Cassels, '1 Commonwealth Division Periodic Report, 15 October 1951-15 February 1952,' nd, app. B, PRO, WO 308/27.
8 2 RCR WD, 1 December 1951, NAC, RG 24, vol. 18,344.
9 1 PPCLI WD, 4 December 1951, NAC, RG 24, vol. 18,313.
10 2 RCR WD, 6 and 7 December 1951, NAC, RG 24, vol. 18,344. See also Capt. G.D. Corry, 'Weekly Summary No. 59, Wed 28 Nov 51-Tues 4 Dec 51,' 5 December 1951, DHH 410B25.013 (D99); 25 Bde Ops Log, 1 and 7 December 1951, DHH 410B25.013 (D39).
11 1 PPCLI WD, 6 December 1951, NAC, RG 24, vol. 18,313.
12 25 Bde WD, 8 December 1951, NAC, RG 24, vol. 18,240.
13 Maj.-Gen. A.J.H. Cassels, '1 Commonwealth Division Periodic Report, 15 October 1951-15 February 1952,' nd, PRO, WO 308/27; 25 Bde Ops Log, 7 December 1951, DHH 410B25.013 (D39).
14 1 PPCLI WD, 7 December 1951, NAC, RG 24, vol. 18,313.
15 25 Bde Ops Log, 8 December 1951, DHH 410B25.013 (D39).
16 Ibid., 8-9 December 1951.
17 1 PPCLI WD, 10 December 1951, NAC, RG 24, vol. 18,313.
18 Ibid.; C Sqn, LdSH WD, 10 December 1951, NAC, RG 24, vol. 18,265.
19 1 PPCLI WD, 10 December 1951, NAC, RG 24, vol. 18,313.
20 Ibid.
21 Ibid.
22 Herbert Fairlie Wood, *Strange Battleground: The Operations in Korea and Their Effects on the Defence Policy of Canada* (Ottawa: Queen's Printer, 1966), 173.
23 1 PPCLI WD, 10 December 1951, NAC, RG 24, vol. 18,313; 25 Bde WD, 10 December 1951, NAC, RG 24, vol. 18,240.
24 2 RCR WD, 11 December 1951, NAC, RG 24, vol. 18,344.
25 25 Bde WD, 11 December 1951, NAC, RG 24, vol. 18,240.
26 Capt. G.D. Corry, 'Weekly Summaries Nos. 61-65,' 1, 2, and 5 February 1952, DHH 410B25.013 (D99).
27 25 Bde WD, 23 December 1951, NAC, RG 24, vol. 18,240.
28 Ibid., 19 December 1951.
29 Capt. G.D. Corry, 'Weekly Summaries Nos. 61-65,' 1, 2, and 5 February 1952, DHH 410B25.013 (D99).
30 2 RCR WD, 13 December 1951, NAC, RG 24, vol. 18,344.
31 Maj.-Gen. A.J.H. Cassels, '1 Commonwealth Division Periodic Report, 15 October 1951-15 February 1952,' nd, app. B, PRO, WO 308/27.
32 Ibid.
33 2 RCR WD, 18 December 1951, NAC, RG 24, vol. 18,344.
34 Ibid., 21 and 24 December 1951.
35 J.M. Rockingham, 'Recollections of Korea,' August 1975, NAC, MG 31 G12, p. 46.
36 1 PPCLI WD, 4 December 1951, NAC, RG 24, vol. 18,313.
37 Van Fleet quoted in Hermes, *Truce Tent,* 181.
38 Maj. R.C.W. Thomas to Maj. D.H. George, 23 December 1951, DHH 410B25.019 (D19).
39 Amy quoted in John Gardam, *Korea Volunteer: An Oral History from Those Who Were There* (Burnstown, ON: General Store Publishing, 1994), 94.
40 Maj. R.C.W. Thomas to Maj. D.H. George, 23 December 1951, DHH 410B25.019 (D19).
41 Maj. R.C.W. Thomas to Maj. D.H. George, 21 January 1952, DHH 410B25.019 (D19).
42 Maj. R.C.W. Thomas to Maj. D.H. George, 23 January 1952, DHH 410B25.019 (D19).
43 J.M. Rockingham, 'Recollections of Korea,' August 1975, NAC, MG 31 G12, pp. 43-4.
44 Lt.-Col. G.C. Corbould interview, 14 July 1951, DHH 410B25.033 (D2).
45 1 PPCLI WD, 11 January 1952, NAC, RG 24, vol. 18,313.
46 Ibid., 12 January 1952.
47 Ibid., 8 January 1952.
48 Ibid., 12 January 1952.
49 2 RCR WD, 13-18 January 1952, NAC, RG 24, vol. 18,344; 25 Bde WD, 14-18 January 1952, NAC, RG 24, vol. 18,240.

50 25 Bde WD, 14 January 1952, NAC, RG 24, vol. 18,240.
51 Ibid., 15 January 1952.
52 Wood, *Strange Battleground,* 173-4.
53 2 R22eR WD, 16 July 1951, NAC, RG 24, vol. 18,357; Wood, *Strange Battleground,* 112n.
54 1 PPCLI WD, 22 November 1951, NAC, RG 24, vol. 18,312.
55 C Sqn, LdSH WD, 19 and 20 January 1951, NAC, RG 24, vol. 18,265.
56 Capt. G.D. Corry, 'Weekly Summary No. 69, Wed 6 Feb 52-Tue 12 Feb 52,' 22 February 1952, DHH 410B25.013 (D99). See also Maj. D.H. George to 2 RCR, 1 PPCLI, 2 R22eR, 29 January 1952, DHH 410B25.019 (D19).
57 2 RCR to 25 Bde HQ, 3 February 1952, DHH 410B25.019 (D19).
58 2 RCR WD, 20 February 1952, NAC, RG 24, vol. 18,344.
59 1 PPCLI WD, 12 February and 8 March 1952, NAC, RG 24, vol. 18,313. See also 2 RCR WD, 25 February 1952, NAC, RG 24, vol. 18,344.
60 Maj. D.H. George, 'Patrol Demonstration,' 22 February 1952, DHH 410B25.019 (D19).
61 25 Bde HQ to battalions, 29 January 1952, DHH 410B25.019 (D19).
62 Capt. G.D. Corry, 'Weekly Summary No. 69, Wed 6 Feb 52-Tue 12 Feb 52,' 22 February 1952, DHH 410B25.013 (D99). See also Maj. D.H. George to 2 RCR, 1 PPCLI, 2 R22eR, 29 January 1952, DHH 410B25.019 (D19).
63 1 PPCLI WD, 11 February 1952, NAC, RG 24, vol. 18,313.
64 Ibid., 15 February 1952. See also Wood, *Strange Battleground,* 174-5.
65 Maj.-Gen. A.J.H. Cassels, '1 Commonwealth Division Periodic Report, 15 October 1951-15 February 1952,' nd, PRO, WO 308/27.
66 2 PPCLI WD, 6 June 1951, NAC, RG 24, vol. 18,318.
67 J.M. Rockingham, 'Recollections of Korea,' August 1975, NAC, MG 31 G12, p. 57.
68 25 Bde WD, 10 February 1952, NAC, RG 24, vol. 18, 241.
69 Capt. G.D. Corry, 'Weekly Summary No. 71, Wed 20 Feb 52-Tue 26 Feb 52,' 6 March 1952, DHH 410B25.013 (D99).
70 Capt. G.D. Corry, 'Weekly Summary No. 72, Wed 27 Feb 52-Tue 4 Mar 52,' 7 March 1952, DHH 410B25.013 (D99).
71 25 Bde WD, 29 February 1952, NAC, RG 24, vol. 18,241.
72 2 RCR WD, 10 March 1952, NAC, RG 24, vol. 18,345.
73 25 Bde WD, 16 March 1952, NAC, RG 24, vol. 18,241.
74 Ibid., 20 March 1952.
75 Ibid., 21 March 1952.
76 Capt. G.D. Corry, 'Weekly Summary No. 75, Wed 19 Mar 52-Tue 25 Mar 52,' 9 May 1952, DHH 410B25.013 (D99).
77 25 Bde WD, 22-25 March 1952, NAC, RG 24, vol. 18,241.
78 'Interview with Capt C Short MC OC C Coy 1 PPCLI and Sgt F Buxton commanding No 7 Platoon concerning attack on the No 7 Platoon 26 Mar 52,' 27 March 1952, DHH 145.2P7.013 (D3).
79 Ibid.
80 Ibid.
81 2 RCR WD, 26 March 1952, NAC, RG 24, vol. 18,345.
82 Maj.-Gen. A.J.H. Cassels, '1 Commonwealth Division Periodic Report 15 February-30 June 1952,' 5 July 1952, app. B, PRO, WO 308/27.
83 Wood, *Strange Battleground,* 175-6; Capt. G.D. Corry, 'Weekly Summary No. 76, Wed 26 Mar 52-Tue 1 Apr 52,' 9 May 1952, DHH 410B25.013 (D99).
84 Maj.-Gen. A.J.H. Cassels, '1 Commonwealth Division Periodic Report 15 February-30 June 1952,' 5 July 1952, app. B, PRO, WO 308/27.
85 2 RCR WD, 31 March 1952, NAC, RG 24, vol. 18,345.
86 Maj.-Gen. A.J.H. Cassels, '1 Commonwealth Division Periodic Report, 15 February-30 June 1952,' 5 July 1952, app. A and B, PRO, WO 308/27.
87 Capt. G.D. Corry, 'Weekly Summary No. 77, Wed 2 Apr 52-Tue 8 Apr 52,' nd, DHH 410B25.013 (D99).
88 25 Bde WD, 11 March 1952, NAC, RG 24, vol. 18,241.
89 Wood, *Strange Battleground,* 177.

90 1 PPCLI WD, 13 April 1952, NAC, RG 24, vol. 18,314.
91 Capt. G.D. Corry, 'Weekly Summaries Nos. 78 and 79,' nd, DHH 410B25.013 (D99).
92 Capt. G.D. Corry, 'Weekly Summary No. 80,' nd, DHH 410B25.013 (D99).

Chapter 10: The Professionals

1 P.R. Bingham interview, 14 May 1952, DHH 145.2R13.013 (D4).
2 1 RCR WD, 12 April and 21 May 1952, NAC, RG 24, vol. 18,336.
3 'Notes prepared after an interview with Major-General J.M. Rockingham at his Headquarters in Montreal,' March 1960, DHH 112.3H1.001 (D13).
4 Herbert Fairlie Wood, *Strange Battleground: The Operations in Korea and Their Effects on the Defence Policy of Canada* (Ottawa: Queen's Printer, 1966), 184.
5 Ibid., 257.
6 RCR Historical Report, June and July 1951, DHH.
7 1 RCR WD, 4 January 1952, NAC, RG 24, vol. 18,336.
8 3 RCR WD, 3, 28 and 29 January 1952, NAC, RG 24, vol. 18,253.
9 Serge Bernier, *The Royal 22e Regiment, 1914-1999* (Montreal: Art Global, 2000), 214.
10 P.R. Bingham interview, 14 May 1952, DHH 145.2R13.013 (D4).
11 Ibid.
12 1 RCR WD, 5 February 1952, NAC, RG 24, vol. 18,336.
13 Bingham quoted in Wood, *Strange Battleground,* 167.
14 RCR Historical Report, August 1951, DHH.
15 P.R. Bingham interview, 14 May 1952, DHH 145.2R13.013 (D4).
16 T. McKay quoted in John Melady, *Korea: Canada's Forgotten War* (Toronto: McClelland and Stewart, 1983), 151.
17 1 RCR WD, 18 April 1952, NAC, RG 24, vol. 18,336.
18 M.P. Bogert biographical file, DHH; G.W.L. Nicholson, *The Canadians in Italy, 1943-1945* (Ottawa: Queen's Printer, 1956), 225-7, 538-9, 690-1.
19 E.A.C. Amy, letter to author, 6 August 1999.
20 Wood, *Strange Battleground,* 177-8, app. D.
21 J.R. Cameron biographical file, DHH; T.H. Randall, *West Novas: A History of the West Nova Scotia Regiment* (np nd), 169-298.
22 L.F. Trudeau biographical file, DHH.
23 Lt.-Col. B.A. Reid to Brereton Greenhous, 14 March 2001, copy in author's possession.
24 P.R. Bingham biographical file, DHH.
25 Maj.-Gen. A.J.H. Cassels, '1 Commonwealth Division Periodic Report, 15 February-30 June 1952,' 5 July 1952, app. B, PRO, WO 308/27.
26 Ibid.
27 Ridgway quoted in Walter G. Hermes, *Truce Tent and Fighting Front* (Washington, DC: US Government Printing Office, 1966), 187.
28 Anthony Farrar-Hockley, *The British Part in the Korean War,* vol. 2, *An Honourable Discharge* (London: Her Majesty's Stationery Office, 1995), 356.
29 Maj.-Gen. A.J.H. Cassels, '1 Commonwealth Division Periodic Report, 15 February-30 June 1952,' 5 July 1952, app. B, PRO, WO 308/27.
30 1 RCR WD, 10 June 1952, NAC, RG 24, vol. 18,337.
31 Wood, *Strange Battleground,* 189.
32 2 RCR, 'Night Operation Snatch,' October 1951, DHH 410B25.013 (D7).
33 25 Bde Ops Log, 7 May 1952, NAC, RG 24, vol. 18,242.
34 25 Bde Ops Log, 5 June 1952, NAC, RG 24, vol. 18,243.
35 Capt. F.R. McGuire, 'RCR Fighting Patrol to Hill 113, 1/2 May 52,' nd, DHH 145.2R13.013 (D3).
36 Ibid.
37 Ibid.
38 Capt. F.R. McGuire, 'The Destruction of Chinch'on Village, 8/9 May 52,' DHH 145.2R13.013 (D5).
39 25 Bde Ops Log, May 1952, NAC, RG 24, vol. 18,242.

40 Cassels quoted in Wood, *Strange Battleground,* 190.
41 1 PPCLI WD, 23 May 1952, NAC, RG 24, vol. 18,314.
42 Maj. W.H. Pope, 'Infantry Patrolling in Korea,' 2 June 1953, DHH 410B25.013 (D89).
43 W.H. Pope, 'Nos patrouilles en Corée, 1952-53,' *La Citadelle* 24 (Feb. 1988): 34.
44 Ibid.
45 Ibid.
46 1 PPCLI WD, 13 June 1952, NAC, RG 24, vol. 18,314.
47 Maj. W.H. Pope, 'Infantry Defences in Korea,' 19 September 1953, DHH 681.009 (D11).
48 Pope quoted in John Gardam, *Korea Volunteer: An Oral History from Those Who Were There* (Burnstown, ON: General Store Publishing, 1994), 130-1.
49 E.A.C. Amy interview, 12 June 1953, DHH 681.009 (D9).
50 Robert S. Peacock, *Kim-chi, Asahi and Rum: A Platoon Commander Remembers, Korea 1952-53* (Toronto: Lugus Productions, 1994), 39, 21.
51 J.R. Cameron interview, 27 October 1952, DHH 410B25.013 (D25).
52 1 PPCLI WD, 29 May 1952, NAC, RG 24, vol. 18,314.
53 Peacock, *Kim-chi, Asahi and Rum,* 12.
54 1 RCR WD, 29 September 1952, NAC, RG 24, vol. 18,338.
55 Peacock, *Kim-chi, Asahi and Rum,* 40.
56 Robert O'Neill, *Australia in the Korean War, 1950-53,* vol. 2, *Combat Operations* (Canberra: Australian Government Publishing Service, 1985), 268.
57 W.H. Pope, 'La Corée: La cote 159 en septembre 1952 et le sergent Bruno Bergeron, MM,' *La Citadelle* 25, 1 (1989): 31.
58 Maj. W.H. Pope, 'Infantry Patrolling in Korea,' 2 June 1953, DHH 410B25.013 (D89).
59 W.H. Pope, 'La roulotte, les rails de chemin de fer, et le trainard,' *La Citadelle* 25, 5 (1989): 32.
60 Ibid.
61 Kenneth L. Campbell interview, 27 June 1953, DHH 410B25.013 (D57).
62 25 Bde WD, 2 June 1952, NAC, RG 24, vol. 18,243.
63 1 PPCLI WD, app. 1, 'Patrol Policy,' 3 June 1952, NAC, RG 24, vol. 18,315; Wood, *Strange Battleground,* 188.
64 1 PPCLI WD, June 1952, app. 1, 'Patrol Policy,' 3 June 1952, NAC, RG 24, vol. 18,315.
65 1 RCR WD, 7 and 8 June 1952, NAC, RG 24, vol. 18,337.
66 1 RCR WD, June 1952, app. E, 'Patrol Policy,' NAC, RG 24, vol. 18,337.
67 25 Bde WD, 13 June 1952, NAC, RG 24, vol. 18,243.
68 Ibid., 11 June 1952.
69 Ibid., 21 June 1952.
70 25 Bde Ops Log, May and June 1952, NAC, RG 24, vols. 18,242 and 18,243.
71 1 PPCLI WD, June 1952, app. 45, 'Report on Fighting Patrol, 20/21 June,' NAC, RG 24, vol. 18,315.
72 Maj.-Gen. A.J.H. Cassels, '1 Commonwealth Division Periodic Report, 15 February-30 June 1952,' 5 July 1952, app. B, PRO, WO 308/27.
73 1 PPCLI WD, 21 June 1952, app. 45, 'Report on Fighting Patrol, 20/21 June,' NAC, RG 24, vol. 18,315.
74 1 RCR WD, 13 June 1952, NAC, RG 24, vol. 18,337.
75 'Interview with Maj D.E. Holmes re "C" Coy 1 RCR raid on Point 113,' 8 July 1952, DHH 410B25.013 (D31).
76 1 RCR WD, 22 June 1952, NAC, RG 24, vol. 18,337; Wood, *Strange Battleground,* 188.
77 Capt. F.W. Webb interview, 27 August 1952, DHH 410B25.013 (D15).
78 Maj.-Gen. A.J.H. Cassels, '1 Commonwealth Division Periodic Report, 15 February-30 June 1952,' 5 July 1952, app. B, PRO, WO 308/27.
79 Capt. F.R. McGuire, 'Weekly Summary No. 88, 18-24 June 52,' 6 July 1952, DHH 410B25.013 (D99); 25 Bde Ops Log, June 1952, NAC, RG 24, vol. 18,243; Wood, *Strange Battleground,* 188-9.
80 C.N. Barclay, *The First Commonwealth Division: The Story of British Commonwealth Land Forces in Korea, 1950-1953* (Aldershot, UK: Gage and Polden, 1954), 127.
81 Maj.-Gen. M.M.A.R. West, '1 Commonwealth Division Periodic Report, 1 July-1 November 1952,' 8 November 1952, app. B, PRO, WO 308/27.

82 Farrar-Hockley, *British Part in the Korean War,* 2:356-7.
83 Barclay, *First Commonwealth Division,* 127.
84 Maj.-Gen. A.J.H. Cassels, '1 Commonwealth Division Periodic Report, 15 February-30 June 1952,' 5 July 1952, PRO, WO 308/27.
85 Ibid.
86 Hermes, *Truce Tent and Fighting Front,* 188.

Chapter 11: The Inactive Defence

1 Maj.-Gen. M.M.A.R. West, '1 Commonwealth Division Periodic Report, 1 July-1 November 1952,' 8 November 1952, PRO, WO 308/27.
2 Ibid.
3 Robert O'Neill, *Australia in the Korean War, 1950-53,* vol. 2, *Combat Operations* (Canberra: Australian Government Publishing Service, 1985), 249.
4 Maj.-Gen. M.M.A.R. West, '1 Commonwealth Division Periodic Report, 1 July-1 November 1952,' 8 November 1952, app. B, PRO, WO 308/27.
5 Ibid., app. A.
6 Ibid., app. B.
7 Ibid.
8 Ibid.
9 Ibid.
10 Maj.-Gen. A.J.H. Cassels, '1 Commonwealth Division Periodic Report, 15 February-30 June 1952,' 5 July 1952, PRO, WO 308/27.
11 1 PPCLI WD, 23 June 1952, NAC, RG 24, vol. 18,315.
12 B Sqn, LdSH WD, 21 June 1952, NAC, RG 24, vol. 18,264.
13 Ibid., 24 June 1952.
14 E.A.C. Amy interview, 12 June 1953, DHH 681.009 (D9). For the increase in Chinese firepower, see C.N. Barclay, *The First Commonwealth Division: The Story of British Commonwealth Land Forces in Korea* (Aldershot, UK: Gale and Polden, 1954), 126; O'Neill, *Australia in the Korean War,* 2:230; Russell Spurr, *Enter the Dragon: China at War in Korea* (London: Sidgwick and Jackson, 1989), 118.
15 Maj.-Gen. M.M.A.R. West, '1 Commonwealth Division Periodic Report, 1 July-1 November 1952,' 8 November 1952, PRO, WO 308/27.
16 '25 Cdn Inf Bde NCOs School,' 11 August 1952, DHH 410B25.033 (D4).
17 1 RCR WD, 19 August 1952, NAC, RG 24, vol. 18,338.
18 Maj.-Gen. M.M.A.R. West, '1 Commonwealth Division Periodic Report, 1 July-1 November 1952,' 8 November 1952, app. A and B, PRO, WO 308/27.
19 Ibid.
20 25 Bde WD, 16 August 1952, NAC, RG 24, vol. 18,243.
21 Ibid., 19 August 1952.
22 Ibid., 'Patrol Task Table,' August 1952.
23 1 PPCLI WD, 10 August 1952, NAC, RG 24, vol. 18,315.
24 1 PPCLI WD, 7 September 1952, NAC, RG 24, vol. 18,316.
25 1 PPCLI WD, 10 August 1952, NAC, RG 24, vol. 18,315.
26 Ibid., 11 August 1952.
27 Ibid., 23 August 1952.
28 Ibid., 26 August 1952.
29 Ibid., 27 August 1952.
30 25 Bde WD, 31 August 1952, NAC, RG 24, vol. 18,244.
31 1 PPCLI WD, 1 September 1952, NAC, RG 24, vol. 18,316.
32 25 Bde WD, September 1952, app. 5, Bde Ops Log, 6 September 1952, NAC, RG 24, vol. 18,244.
33 Herbert Fairlie Wood, *Strange Battleground: The Operations in Korea and Their Effects on the Defence Policy of Canada* (Ottawa: Queen's Printer, 1966), 204.
34 1 RCR WD, 8 September 1952, NAC, RG 24, vol. 18,338.
35 1 PPCLI WD, 9 September 1952, NAC, RG 24, vol. 18,316.

36 25 Bde WD, 8 September 1952, NAC, RG 24, vol. 18,244.
37 Maj. W.H. Pope, 'Infantry Patrolling in Korea,' 2 June 1953, DHH 410B25.013 (D89).
38 Robert S. Peacock, *Kim-chi, Asahi, and Rum: A Platoon Commander Remembers, Korea 1952-53* (Toronto: Lugus Productions, 1994), 17.
39 Ibid., 27, 28.
40 Ibid., 24.
41 1 PPCLI WD, 6 September 1952, NAC, RG 24, vol. 18,316.
42 25 Bde WD, September 1952, app. 5, Bde Ops Log, NAC, RG 24, vol. 18,244.
43 1 PPCLI WD, 11 September 1952, NAC, RG 24, vol. 18,316.
44 Walter G. Hermes, *Truce Tent and Fighting Front* (Washington, DC: US Government Printing Office, 1966), 299-303.
45 1 PPCLI WD, 11, 18, and 29 September 1952, NAC, RG 24, vol. 18,316.
46 Wood, *Strange Battleground,* 203.
47 25 Bde WD, September 1952, app. 5, Bde Ops Log, NAC, RG 24, vol. 18,244.
48 Maj. W.H. Pope, 'Infantry Patrolling in Korea,' 2 June 1953, DHH 410B25.013 (D89).
49 25 Bde Ops Log, 7 and 15 September 1952, DHH 410B25.019 (D22).
50 Maj. W.H. Pope, 'Infantry Patrolling in Korea,' 2 June 1953, DHH 410B25.013 (D89).
51 Ibid.
52 25 Bde Ops Log, 10 and 14 September 1952, DHH 410B25.019 (D22).
53 CRE, 1 Comwel Div, Liaison Letter No. 5, 11 December 1952, DHH 112.3E1.003 (D1).
54 23 Fd Sqn WD, 16-26 September 1952, NAC, RG 24, vol. 18,285.
55 CRE, 1 Comwel Div, Liaison Letter No. 5, 11 December 1952, DHH 112.3E1.003 (D1).
56 25 Bde Ops Log, 10 and 14 September 1952, DHH 410B25.019 (D22).
57 1 RCR WD, 16 September 1952, NAC, RG 24, vol. 18,338.
58 2 RCR WD, 20 February 1952, NAC, RG 24, vol. 18,344.
59 Ibid., 26 March 1952; 1 RCR WD, 26 August 1952, NAC, RG 24, vol. 18,338.
60 'RCR Fighting Patrol,' nd, DHH 410B25.013 (D17).
61 Ibid.
62 Wood, *Strange Battleground,* 204.
63 Loomis quoted in John Gardam, *Korea Volunteer: An Oral History from Those Who Were There* (Burnstown, ON: General Store Publishing, 1994), 145-6.
64 Barclay, *First Commonwealth Division,* 125, 205.
65 O'Neill, *Australia in the Korean War,* 2:230.
66 Ibid., 2:235.
67 25 Bde Ops Log, September 1952, DHH 410B25.019 (D22).
68 O'Neill, *Australia in the Korean War,* 2:251-2.
69 Ibid., 235.
70 HQ 28 BritCom Inf Bde, 'Notes on Patrolling in Korea,' April 1953, DHH 410B25.019 (D238).
71 Ibid.
72 Ibid.
73 O'Neill, *Australia in the Korean War,* 2:230.
74 Maj.-Gen. M.M.A.R. West, '1 Commonwealth Division Periodic Report, 1 November 1952-1 April 1953,' 1 April 1953, app. B, PRO, WO 308/27; 'Battle Casualties and Ordinary Deaths, 25 Cdn Inf Bde,' nd, DHH 410B25.065 (D15).
75 O'Neill, *Australia in the Korean War,* 2:230.
76 25 Bde WD, 1 October 1952, NAC, RG 24, vol. 18,245.
77 B Sqn, LdSH WD, 14 September, 2 and 13 October 1952, NAC, RG 24, vol. 18,264.
78 1 RCR WD, 2 and 7 October 1952, NAC, RG 24, vol. 18,338; Maj.-Gen. M.M.A.R. West, '1 Commonwealth Division Periodic Report, 1 July-1 November 1952,' 8 November 1952, app. B, PRO, WO 308/27.
79 25 Bde Ops Log, 21 September 1952, DHH 410B25.019 (D22).
80 25 Bde WD, October 1952, app. 35, 'Debriefing of B Company Patrol 12/13 Oct 52,' 13 October 1952, NAC, RG 24, vol. 18,245.

81 1 PPCLI WD, 4 October 1952, NAC, RG 24, vol. 18,316.
82 Ibid., 16 October 1952.
83 1 RCR WD, 21 October 1952, NAC, RG 24, vol. 18,338.
84 'Report by ACBO 25 Cdn Inf Bde on hostile shelling and mortaring prior to attack on B Coy 1 RCR 23 Oct 1952,' nd, DHH 410B25.013 (D27).
85 'Enemy Action against Pt 355, 22 and 23 Oct 52,' 30 October 1952, DHH 410B25.013 (D26).
86 'The Attack on "Little Gibraltar" (Pt 355), 23 Oct 52,' nd, DHH 410B25.013 (D24).
87 Maj.-Gen. M.M.A.R. West, '1 Commonwealth Division Periodic Report, 1 July-1 November 1952,' 8 November 1952, app. B, PRO, WO 308/27.
88 'Report by ACBO 25 Cdn Inf Bde on hostile shelling and mortaring prior to attack on B Coy 1 RCR 23 Oct 1952,' nd, DHH 410B25.013 (D27).
89 Maj. W.H. Pope, 'Infantry Defences in Korea,' 19 September 1953, DHH 681.009 (D11).
90 Capt. F.R. McGuire, 'Interviews with Per of RCR re Chinese Attack on "B" Coy 1 RCR, 23 October 1952,' nd, DHH 410B25.013 (D24).
91 Capt. F.R. McGuire, 'Acct of interview with Lt H.R. Gardner,' 30 October 1952, DHH 410B25.013 (D26).
92 Capt. F.R. McGuire, 'Interviews with Per of RCR re Chinese Attack on "B" Coy 1 RCR, 23 October 1952,' nd, DHH 410B25.013 (D24).
93 Wood, *Strange Battleground,* 209; 'Report by ACBO 25 Cdn Inf Bde on hostile shelling and mortaring prior to attack on B Coy 1 RCR 23 Oct 1952,' nd, DHH 410B25.013 (D27).
94 Capt. F.R. McGuire, 'Interviews with Per of RCR re Chinese Attack on "B" Coy 1 RCR, 23 October 1952,' nd, DHH 410B25.013 (D24).
95 Ibid.; Wood, *Strange Battleground,* 208-10; Capt. F.R. McGuire, 'Enemy Action against PT 355, 22 and 23 October 1952,' 30 October 1952, DHH 410B25.013 (D26).
96 Wood, *Strange Battleground,* 210.
97 Maj.-Gen. M.M.A.R. West, '1 Commonwealth Division Periodic Report, 1 July-1 November 1952,' 8 November 1952, app. B, PRO, WO 308/27.
98 1 RCR WD, 24 October 1952, NAC, RG 24, vol. 18,338.
99 Maj. W.H. Pope, 'Infantry Defences in Korea,' 19 September 1953, DHH 681.009 (D11).
100 1 PPCLI WD, 23 October 1952, NAC, RG 24, vol. 18,316.
101 25 Cdn Inf Bde, 'Ops/Int Summary,' 25 October 1952, app. A, DHH 410B25.013 (D23).
102 Maj.-Gen. M.M.A.R. West, '1 Commonwealth Division Periodic Report, 1 July-1 November 1952,' 8 November 1952, app. B, PRO, WO 308/27.
103 25 Bde WD, 31 October 1952, NAC, RG 24, vol. 18,245.

Chapter 12: On the Hook

1 Robert O'Neill, *Australia in the Korean War, 1950-53,* vol. 2, *Combat Operations* (Canberra: Australian Government Publishing Service, 1985), 253.
2 Ibid.
3 Ibid., 2:253-4.
4 Ibid., 2:265.
5 Jeffrey Grey, *The Commonwealth Armies and the Korean War: An Alliance Study* (Manchester: Manchester University Press, 1988), 150-1. O'Neill does not indicate that there were any complaints when 3 RAR relieved the Canadian 2nd battalions in January 1952. O'Neill, *Australia in the Korean War,* 2:216. Moreover, such tactically damaging behaviour would not have been tolerated by Rockingham during his frequent inspections of the battalions' foremost positions.
6 Maj.-Gen. M.M.A.R. West, '1 Commonwealth Division, Periodic Report, 1 November 1952-1 April 1953,' 1 April 1953, PRO, WO 308/27.
7 Lt.-Col. E.A.C. Amy interview, 12 June 1953, DHH 681.009 (D9). See also Grey, *Commonwealth Armies,* 151.
8 E.A.C. Amy letter to author, 6 August 1999.
9 Ibid.

10 Ibid.
11 E.A.C. Amy letter to author, 18 September 1999.
12 Walter G. Hermes, *Truce Tent and Fighting Front* (Washington, DC: US Government Printing Office, 1966), 281-2.
13 Ibid., 420.
14 Ibid., 306.
15 Ibid., 310-18.
16 Maj.-Gen. M.M.A.R. West, '1 Commonwealth Division Periodic Report, 1 July-1 November 1952,' 8 November 1952, PRO, WO 308/27.
17 1 RCR WD, 1 December 1952, NAC, RG 24, vol. 18,339.
18 Ibid., 4 December 1952.
19 Ibid., 13 November 1952.
20 3 PPCLI WD, 30 May 1952, NAC, RG 24, vol. 18,324.
21 Herbert Fairlie Wood, *Strange Battleground: The Operations in Korea and Their Effects on the Defence Policy of Canada* (Ottawa: Queen's Printer, 1966), 170.
22 3 PPCLI WD, 26 October 1952, NAC, RG 24, vol. 18,324.
23 Ibid., 27 October 1952.
24 Ibid., 4 November 1952.
25 Wood, *Strange Battleground,* 212.
26 3 PPCLI WD, 5 November 1952, NAC, RG 24, vol. 18,324.
27 Ibid., 7 November 1952.
28 Ibid., 12 and 17 November 1952.
29 J.R. Cameron interview, 27 October 1952, DHH 410B25.013 (D25).
30 Ibid.
31 'Extract from a letter dated 30 Dec. 1952 addressed to the CGS from Major-General M.M.A.R. West,' nd, H.F. Wood personnel file, NAC, National Personnel Records Centre.
32 H.F. Wood, 'Extract from narrative "How Special Can We Get?,"' October 1956, DHH 410B25.011 (D12).
33 Robert S. Peacock, *Kim-chi, Asahi and Rum: A Platoon Commander Remembers, Korea 1952-53* (Toronto: Lugus Productions, 1994), xi. Wood's novel was described by Peacock as a 'ribald collection of real and half-real incidents that occurred in Korea.'
34 Ibid., 83.
35 3 PPCLI WD, 15 November 1952, NAC, RG 24, vol. 18,324.
36 Ibid., 17 November 1952.
37 Maj.-Gen. M.M.A.R. West, '1 Commonwealth Division Periodic Report, 1 November 1952-1 April 1953,' 1 April 1953, PRO, WO 308/27; Pat Meid, *US Marine Operations in Korea, 1950-1953,* vol. 5, *Operations in West Korea* (Washington, DC: US Government Printing Office, 1972), 185-215.
38 Maj.-Gen. M.M.A.R. West, '1 Commonwealth Division Periodic Report, 1 November 1952-1 April 1953,' 1 April 1953, PRO, WO 308/27.
39 Ibid.
40 Ibid.
41 3 PPCLI WD, 19 November 1952, NAC, RG 24, vol. 18,324.
42 Ibid., 22 November 1952.
43 Wood, *Strange Battleground,* 214.
44 3 PPCLI WD, 23 November 1952, NAC, RG 24, vol. 18,324.
45 Ibid., 24 November 1952.
46 E.A.C. Amy interview, 12 June 1953, DHH 681.009 (D9).
47 Operational Research Section, Korea, 'The Field Defences of 1 Commonwealth Division up to February 1953,' March 1953, DHH 681.013 (D63); 23 Fd Sqn WD, December 1952-February 1953, NAC, RG 24, vol. 18,285; Wood, *Strange Battleground,* 214-15.
48 Maj. J.E. Leach, 'Patrol Policy – 25 Cdn Inf Bde,' 2 December 1952, 25 Bde WD, December 1952, app. 14, NAC, RG 24, vol. 18,246.

49 Ibid.
50 Maj. J.E. Leach, 'Forecast of Patrols,' 3 December 1952, 25 Bde WD, December 1952, app. 15, NAC, RG 24, vol. 18,246.
51 Wood, *Strange Battleground,* 218.
52 25 Bde WD, December 1952, app. 6A, 'Patrol Task Tables,' NAC, RG 24, vol. 18,246.
53 3 PPCLI WD, 6 December 1952, NAC, RG 24, vol. 18,324.
54 Ibid., 16 December 1952.
55 Wood, *Strange Battleground,* 219.
56 25 Bde WD, December 1952, app. 6A, 'Patrol Task Tables,' NAC, RG 24, vol. 18,246.
57 Wood, *Strange Battleground,* 218.
58 Maj. J.E. Leach, 'Patrol Policy – 25 Cdn Inf Bde,' 2 December 1952, 25 Bde WD, December 1952, app. 14, NAC, RG 24, vol. 18,246.
59 W.H. Pope, 'La Corée: La cote 159 en septembre 1952 et le sergent Bruno Bergeron, MM,' *La Citadelle* 25 (Feb. 1989): 31.
60 Ibid.
61 Peacock, *Kim-chi, Asahi, and Rum,* 80.
62 Maj.-Gen. M.M.A.R. West, 'Periodic Reports,' 1 July 1952 to 1 August 1953, PRO, WO 308/27; Terry Copp and Bill McAndrew, *Battle Exhaustion: Soldiers and Psychiatrists in the Canadian Army, 1939-1945* (Montreal: McGill-Queen's University Press, 1990), 58.
63 1 RCR WD, 2 January 1953, NAC, RG 24, vol. 18,339.
64 Ibid., 6 January 1953.
65 'Patrol Debriefing,' 7 January 1953, 1 RCR WD, January 1953, app. 8, NAC, RG 24, vol. 18,339.
66 1 RCR WD, 9 and 10 January 1953, NAC, RG 24, vol. 18,339.
67 'Debriefing of Fighting Patrol to Seattle (MR 100104) Night 12/13 Jan,' nd, 1 RCR WD, January 1953, app. 10, NAC, RG 24, vol. 18,339.
68 1 RCR WD, 21 and 25 January 1953, NAC, RG 24, vol. 18,339.
69 Ibid., 21 January 1953.
70 Maj.-Gen. M.M.A.R. West, '1 Commonwealth Division Periodic Report, 1 November 1952-1 April 1953,' 1 April 1953, app. C, PRO, WO 308/27.
71 Ibid.
72 Ibid.
73 Ibid.
74 O'Neill, *Australia in the Korean War,* 2:260.
75 Maj.-Gen. M.M.A.R. West, '1 Commonwealth Division Periodic Report, 1 November 1952-1 April 1953,' 1 April 1953, PRO, WO 308/27.
76 E.A.C. Amy interview, 12 June 1953, DHH 681.009 (D9).
77 Maj.-Gen. M.M.A.R. West, '1 Commonwealth Division Periodic Report, 1 November 1952-1 April 1953,' 1 April 1953, app. A, 'GOC Personal Memorandum No. 9 – Patrol Policy,' 23 January 1953, PRO, WO 308/27.
78 Ibid.
79 Ibid.
80 Maj.-Gen. M.M.A.R. West, '1 Commonwealth Division Periodic Report, 1 November 1952-1 April 1953,' 1 April 1953, app. B, PRO, WO 308/27.
81 Maj.-Gen. M.M.A.R. West, '1 Commonwealth Division Periodic Report, 1 November 1952-1 April 1953,' 1 April 1953, PRO, WO 308/27.
82 Hermes, *Truce Tent,* 366-8, 389-91.
83 Wood, *Strange Battleground,* 220-2.
84 Hermes, *Truce Tent,* 392-3, 396-7.
85 Maj.-Gen. M.M.A.R. West, '1 Commonwealth Division Periodic Report, 1 November 1952-1 April 1953,' 1 April 1953, PRO, WO 308/27.
86 Maj.-Gen. M.M.A.R. West, '1 Commonwealth Division Periodic Report, 1 April 1953-1 August 1953,' 1 August 1953, PRO, WO 308/27.
87 O'Neill, *Australia in the Korean War,* 2:266-8.

88 Pope quoted in Wood, *Strange Battleground,* 223.
89 W.H. Pope, 'Pour devenir maître entre les lignes,' *La Citadelle* 24, 2 (1988): 39.
90 Ibid., 40.
91 Lt.-Col. L.F. Trudeau interview, 21 April 1953, DHH 410B25.013 (D41).

Chapter 13: The Third Battalions

1 Kim Il Sung and P'eng Teh-huai to Mark Clark, 28 March 1953, quoted in Walter G. Hermes, *Truce Tent and Fighting Front* (Washington, DC: US Government Printing Office, 1966), 411-19.
2 Ibid., 422.
3 J.V. Allard with Serge Bernier, *The Memoirs of General Jean V. Allard* (Vancouver: UBC Press, 1988), passim.
4 Ibid.; G.R. Stevens, *The Royal Canadian Regiment,* vol. 2, *1933-1966* (London, ON: London Printing and Lithographing, 1967), 375; G.R. Stevens, *Princess Patricia's Canadian Light Infantry,* vol. 3, *1919-1957* (Griesbach, AB: Historical Committee of the Regiment, 1957), 409.
5 3 RCR WD, 22-3 January and 5 February 1953, NAC, RG 24, vol. 18,350.
6 Ibid., 25-6 February 1953; Herbert Fairlie Wood, *Strange Battleground: The Operations in Korea and Their Effects on the Defence Policy of Canada* (Ottawa: Queen's Printer, 1966), 223.
7 25 Bde WD, May 1953, app. 11, 'Brigadier's Personal Memorandum No. 1, Notes on Defence,' 1 May 1953, NAC, RG 24, vol. 18,250.
8 Allard, *Memoirs,* 174.
9 25 Bde WD, May 1953, app. 11, 'Brigadier's Personal Memorandum No. 1, Notes on Defence,' 1 May 1953, NAC, RG 24, vol. 18,250.
10 Lt.-Col. K.L. Campbell, 'Summary of Experiences, Korean Campaign,' 25 March 1954, DHH 145.2R13.019 (D1).
11 K.L. Campbell interview, 27 June 1953, DHH 410B25.013 (D57).
12 Brig. J.V. Allard, 'Command of 25 Cdn Inf Bde,' 13 June 1954, DHH 410B25.013 (D100).
13 J.V. Allard interview, 17 December 1963, DHH 112.3H1.001 (D7).
14 K.L. Campbell interview, 27 June 1953, DHH 410B25.013 (D57).
15 Ibid.
16 J.V. Allard interview, 17 December 1963, DHH 112.3H1.001 (D7).
17 Brig. J.V. Allard, 'Command of 25 Cdn Inf Bde,' 13 June 1954, DHH 112.3H1.001 (D7).
18 Allard, *Memoirs,* 175.
19 Pte. H.A. MacDonald interview, 5 May 1953, DHH 410B25.013 (D44).
20 K.L. Campbell interview, 27 June 1953, DHH 410B25.013 (D57).
21 Wood, *Strange Battleground,* 233-4.
22 Maj.-Gen. M.M.A.R. West, 'Periodic Report, 1 April 1953 to 1 August 1953,' 1 August 1953, annex 1 to app. B, PRO, WO 308/27.
23 J.V. Allard interview, 17 December 1963, DHH 112.3H1.001 (D7); Wood, *Strange Battleground,* 234-5.
24 Maj.-Gen. M.M.A.R. West, 'Periodic Report, 1 April 1953 to 1 August 1953,' 1 August 1953, annex 1 to app. B, PRO, WO 308/27.
25 Cpl. J.J.A. Pelletier interview, 7 and 8 August 1953, DHH 410B25.023 (D15).
26 'Interrogation Report on 2/Lt C.G. Owen,' 2 October 1953, DHH 410B25.023 (D19).
27 Wood, *Strange Battleground,* 235; K.L. Campbell interview, 27 June 1953, DHH 410B25.013 (D57); E.H. Hollyer interview, 6 May 1953, DHH 410B25.013 (D45).
28 Maj.-Gen. M.M.A.R. West, 'Periodic Report, 1 April 1953 to 1 August 1953,' 1 August 1953, annex 1 to app. B, PRO, WO 308/27.
29 Ibid., app. A.
30 E.A.C. Amy interview, 12 June 1953, DHH 681.009 (D9).
31 Wood, *Strange Battleground,* 236.
32 K.L. Campbell interview, 27 June 1953, DHH 410B25.013 (D57).
33 J.G. Poulin interview, 31 May 1953, DHH 410B25.013 (D53).
34 Maj. C.E.C. MacNeill interview, 12 May 1953, DHH 410B25.013 (D49).
35 Brig. J.V. Allard, 'Command of 25 Cdn Inf Bde,' 13 June 1954, DHH 410B25.013 (D100).

36 Ibid.
37 Ibid.
38 Ibid.
39 P.R. Bingham interview, 14 May 1952, DHH 410B25.013 (D33).
40 Wood, *Strange Battleground,* 252-3.
41 Pope quoted in John Gardam, *Korea Volunteer: An Oral History from Those Who Were There* (Burnstown, ON: General Store Publishing, 1994), 130-1.
42 J.V. Allard interview, 10 June 1953, DHH 410B25.013 (D51); J.V. Allard interview, 17 December 1963, DHH 112.3H1.001 (D7); Brig. J.V. Allard, 'Command of 25 Cdn Inf Bde,' 13 June 1954, DHH 410B25.013 (D100).
43 J.V. Allard interview, 10 June 1953, DHH 410B25.013 (D51).
44 Allard, *Memoirs,* 177.
45 Syllabus of Course No. 5, nd, DHH 410B25.019 (D238); 25 Bde WD, 22 June 1953, NAC, RG 24, vol. 18,251.
46 J.V. Allard interview, 10 June 1953, DHH 410B25.013 (D51).
47 Ibid.
48 Allard, *Memoirs,* 177.
49 Wood, *Strange Battleground,* 239; Allard interview, 10 June 1953, DHH 410B25.013 (D51).
50 Maj.-Gen. M.M.A.R. West, 'Periodic Report, 1 April 1953-1 August 1953,' 1 August 1953, app. A, PRO, WO 308/27.
51 Ibid., app. A, part 4, 'Prisoners of War.'
52 Ibid.
53 Maj.-Gen. M.M.A.R. West, 'Periodic Report, 1 April 1953-1 August 1953,' 1 August 1953, app. B, annex 2, PRO, WO 308/27.
54 Ibid., app. A.
55 Ibid.
56 Maj.-Gen. M.M.A.R. West, 'Periodic Report, 1 April 1953-1 August 1953,' 1 August 1953, PRO, WO 308/27.
57 E.A.C. Amy interview, 12 June 1953, DHH 618.009 (D9).
58 Maj.-Gen. M.M.A.R. West, 'Periodic Report, 1 April 1953-1 August 1953,' 1 August 1953, Part 5, 'Artillery,' PRO, WO 308/27.
59 Hermes, *Truce Tent,* 462.
60 Ibid., 464.
61 Ibid., 465.
62 25 Bde WD, app. 10, 'Patrol Task Tables,' May 1953, NAC, RG 24, vol. 18,250.
63 3 R22eR WD, 26 May 1953, NAC, RG 24, vol. 18,364.
64 3 PPCLI WD, 9 May 1953, NAC, RG 24, vol. 18,325.
65 3 R22eR WD, 20 May and 13 June 1953, copy of '25 Bde Int. Summary, 20 May 1953,' NAC, RG 24, vol. 18,364.
66 3 RCR WD, 31 May 1953, NAC, RG 24, vol. 18,350.
67 Ibid., 4 June 1953; 25 Bde WD, June 1953, app. 2, 'Patrol Task Tables,' NAC, RG 24, vol. 18,251.
68 3 PPCLI WD, 18 June 1953, NAC, RG 24, vol. 18,326.
69 3 PPCLI WD, June 1953, app. 16, Lt.-Col. MacLachlan, 'Standing Patrols,' 19 June 1953, NAC, RG 24, vol. 18,326.
70 3 R22eR WD, 27 June 1953, NAC, RG 24, vol. 18,364.
71 25 Bde WD, app. 2, 'Patrol Task Tables,' June 1953, NAC, RG 24, vol. 18,251.
72 Brig. J.V. Allard, 'Command of 25 Cdn Inf Bde,' 13 June 1954, DHH 410B25.013 (D100).
73 3 PPCLI WD, 24 June 1953, NAC, RG 24, vol. 18,326.
74 Ibid., 30 June 1953.
75 Maj.-Gen. M.M.A.R. West, 'Periodic Report,' 1 August 1953, PRO, WO 308/27; Brig. J.V. Allard, 'Command of 25 Cdn Inf Bde,' 13 June 1954, DHH 410B25.013 (D100).
76 25 Bde WD, July 1953, app. 4, 'Patrol Task Tables,' NAC, RG 24, vol. 18,252.

77 Robert O'Neill, *Australia in the Korean War, 1950-53*, vol. 2, *Combat Operations* (Canberra: Australian Government Publishing Service, 1985), 268.
78 Ibid., 2:271.
79 Ibid., 2:274.
80 Hermes, *Truce Tent*, 466-9.
81 Ibid., 469.
82 Ibid., 475-6.
83 Wood, *Strange Battleground*, 240.
84 Maj.-Gen. M.M.A.R. West, 'Periodic Report,' 1 August 1953, app. B, 'Special Intelligence Aspects,' PRO, WO 308/27; O'Neill, *Australia in the Korean War*, 2:282.
85 Maj.-Gen. M.M.A.R. West, 'Periodic Report,' 1 August 1953, app. B, 'Special Intelligence Aspects,' PRO, WO 308/27.
86 Unnamed officer quoted in Brig. J.V. Allard, 'Command of 25 Cdn Inf Bde,' 13 June 1954, DHH 410B25.013 (D100).

Epilogue

1 Herbert Fairlie Wood, *Strange Battleground: The Operations in Korea and Their Effects on the Defence Policy of Canada* (Ottawa: Queen's Printer, 1966), 247-9.
2 Ibid., 255.
3 Ibid., 256-7.
4 Republic of Korea, Ministry of National Defense, *The History of The United Nations Forces in the Korean War* (Seoul: Ministry of National Defense, 1976), 5:477; Walter G. Hermes, *Truce Tent and Fighting Front* (Washington: DC, US Government Printing Office, 1966), 501; Harry G. Summers, *Korean War Almanac* (New York: Facts on File, 1990), 75-7.
5 Max Hastings, *The Korean War* (London: Michael Joseph, 1987), 407.
6 Wood, *Strange Battleground*, 257.
7 'Return of Casualties of 25 CIB in Korean War,' nd, DHH 410B25.065 (D15).
8 Russell F. Weigley, *Eisenhower's Lieutenants: The Campaign of France and Germany, 1944-1945* (Bloomington: Indiana University Press, 1981), 2.
9 John Keegan, *Six Armies in Normandy: From D-Day to the Liberation of Paris, June 6th-August 25th, 1944* (New York: Viking Press, 1982), 24-5.
10 Wood, *Strange Battleground*, 260.
11 25 Bde WD, September 1950, app. D, 'Canadian Army Training Instruction No. 6,' 14 August 1950, NAC, RG 24, vol. 18,237.
12 2 RCR, 'Night Operation "Snatch,"' October 1951, DHH 410B25.013 (D7).
13 Anthony Farrar-Hockley, *The British Part in the Korean War*, vol. 2, *An Honourable Discharge* (London: Her Majesty's Stationery Office, 1995), 356.
14 Pope quoted in John Gardam, *Korea Volunteer: An Oral History from Those Who Were There* (Burnstown, ON: General Store Publishing, 1994), 130-1.
15 'Extracts from Chiefs of Staff Committee Minutes of a special meeting – 28 Jul 50,' nd, DHH 112.3M2 (D293).
16 Rockingham to Dr. A.E. Grauer, 1 March 1952, DHH 410B25.019 (D18).
17 Brent Byron Watson, *Far Eastern Tour: The Canadian Infantry in Korea, 1950-1953* (Montreal and Kingston: McGill-Queen's University Press, 2002), 27-46; David J. Bercuson, *Blood on the Hills: The Canadian Army in the Korean War* (Toronto: University of Toronto Press, 1999), 163-8, 189-93.
18 Bruce Catton, *This Hallowed Ground* (New York: Doubleday, 1955), 87-8.

BIBLIOGRAPHY

This account is based largely on the Canadian unit war diaries held at the National Archives of Canada and the files collected by the old Army Historical Section held at the Directorate of History and Heritage, National Defence Headquarters, Ottawa. Since these are already fully cited in the notes, the following is a selected list of published sources.

Allard, J.V., with Serge Bernier. *The Memoirs of General Jean V. Allard.* Vancouver: University of British Columbia Press, 1988.

Appleman, Roy E. *South to the Naktong, North to the Yalu, June-November 1950.* United States Army in the Korean War. Washington, DC: US Government Printing Office, 1961.

Barclay, C.N. *The First Commonwealth Division: The Story of British Commonwealth Land Forces in Korea.* Aldershot, UK: Gale and Polden, 1954.

Barris, Ted. *Deadlock in Korea: Canadians at War, 1950-1953.* Toronto: Macmillan Canada, 1999.

Bercuson, David J. *Blood on the Hills: The Canadian Army in the Korean War.* Toronto: University of Toronto Press, 1999.

Bernier, Serge. *The Royal 22e Regiment, 1914-1999.* Montreal: Art Global, 2000.

Carew, Tim. *Korea: The Commonwealth at War.* London: Cassell, 1967.

Catton, Bruce. *This Hallowed Ground.* New York: Doubleday and Company, 1955.

Copp, Terry, and Bill McAndrew. *Battle Exhaustion: Soldiers and Psychiatrists in the Canadian Army, 1939-1945.* Montreal: McGill-Queen's University Press, 1990.

Cumings, Bruce. *The Origins of the Korean War.* 2 vols. Princeton, NJ: Princeton University Press, 1981-90.

English, J.A. *The Canadian Army and the Normandy Campaign: A Study of Failure in High Command.* New York: Praeger, 1991.

Farrar-Hockley, Anthony. *The British Part in the Korean War.* Vol. 1, *A Distant Obligation.* London: Her Majesty's Stationery Office, 1990.

–. *The British Part in the Korean War.* Vol. 2, *An Honourable Discharge.* London: Her Majesty's Stationery Office, 1995.

Fehrenbach, T.R. *This Kind of War: A Study in Unpreparedness.* New York: Macmillan, 1963.

Forbes, J. Charles. *Fantassin: pour mon pays, la gloire et ... des prunes.* Sillery, QC: Septentrion, 1994.

Fusiliers Mont-Royal. *Cents ans d'histoire d'un Régiment canadien-français: Les Fusiliers Mont-Royal, 1869-1969.* Montreal: Éditions du Jour, 1971.

Futrell, Robert F. *The United States Air Force in Korea, 1950-1953.* Washington, DC: US Government Printing Office, 1983.

Gardam, John. *Korea Volunteer: An Oral History from Those Who Were There.* Burnstown, ON: General Store Publishing, 1994.

Goodspeed, D.J., ed. *The Armed Forces of Canada, 1867-1967: A Century of Achievement.* Ottawa: Queen's Printer, 1967.

Granatstein, J.L., and David J. Bercuson. *War and Peacekeeping: From South Africa to the Gulf – Canada's Limited Wars.* Toronto: Key Porter, 1991.

Greenhous, Brereton, ed. *Semper Paratus: The History of the Royal Hamilton Light Infantry, 1862-1977.* Hamilton: RHLI Historical Association, 1977.

Grey, Jeffrey. *The Commonwealth Armies and the Korean War: An Alliance Study.* Manchester: Manchester University Press, 1988.

Harris, Stephen, and William Johnston. 'The Post-War Army and the War in Korea.' In *We Stand on Guard: An Illustrated History of the Canadian Army,* ed. John Marteinson. Montreal: Ovale, 1992.

Hastings, Max. *The Korean War.* London: Michael Joseph, 1987.

Heppenstall, Robert. *Find the Dragon: The Canadian Army in Korea, 1950-1953.* Edmonton: Four Winds Publishing, 1995.

Hermes, Walter G. *Truce Tent and Fighting Front.* United States Army in the Korean War. Washington, DC: US Government Printing Office, 1966.

Historical Section, General Staff, Army Headquarters. *Canada's Army in Korea: The United Nations Operations, 1950-1953, and Their Aftermath.* Ottawa: Queen's Printer, 1956.

Keegan, John. *Six Armies in Normandy: From D-Day to the Liberation of Paris, June 6th-August 25th 1944.* New York: Viking Press, 1982.

Korea, Republic of. *The History of the United Nations Forces in the Korean War.* 6 vols. Seoul: Ministry of National Defense, 1972-7.

Marshall, S.L.A. *Infantry Operations and Weapon Usage in Korea.* London: Greenhill Books, 1988.

Meid, Pat. *US Marine Operations in Korea, 1950-1953.* Vol. 5, *Operations in West Korea.* Washington, DC: US Government Printing Office, 1972.

Melady, John. *Korea: Canada's Forgotten War.* Toronto: McClelland and Stewart, 1983.

Millett, A.R. 'The Forgotten Army in the Misunderstood War: The *Hanguk Gun* in the Korean War, 1946-53,' in *The Korean War, 1950-53: A 50 Year Retrospective,* ed. Peter Dennis and Jeffrey Grey. Canberra: Australian Government Publishing Service, 2000.

Montross, Lynn, and Nicholas Canzona. *US Marine Operations in Korea, 1950-1953.* Vol. 1, *The Pusan Perimeter.* Washington, DC: US Government Printing Office, 1954.

–. *US Marine Operations in Korea, 1950-1953.* Vol. 2, *The Inchon-Seoul Operation.* Washington, DC: US Government Printing Office, 1955.

–. *US Marine Operations in Korea, 1950-1953.* Vol. 3, *The Chosin Reservoir Campaign.* Washington, DC: US Government Printing Office, 1957.

Montross, Lynn, Hubard Kuokka, and Norman Hicks. *US Marine Operations in Korea, 1950-1953.* Vol. 4, *The East-Central Front.* Washington, DC: US Government Printing Office, 1962.

Mossman, Billy C. *Ebb and Flow, November 1950-July 1951.* United States Army in the Korean War. Washington, DC: US Government Printing Office, 1990.

Nicholson, G.W.L. *Official History of the Canadian Army in the Second World War.* Vol. 2, *The Canadians in Italy, 1943-1945.* Ottawa: Queen's Printer, 1957.

Nusbacher, Aryeh J.S. 'From Koje to Kosovo: the Development of the Canadian National Command Element,' in *The Korean War, 1950-53: A 50 Year Retrospective,* ed. Peter Dennis and Jeffrey Grey. Canberra: Australian Government Publishing Service, 2000.

O'Neill, Robert. *Australia in the Korean War, 1950-53.* Vol. 1, *Strategy and Diplomacy.* Canberra: Australian Government Publishing Service, 1981.

–. *Australia in the Korean War, 1950-53.* Vol. 2, *Combat Operations.* Canberra: Australian Government Publishing Service, 1985.

Peacock, Robert S. *Kim-chi, Asahi and Rum: A Platoon Commander Remembers, Korea 1952-53.* Toronto: Lugus Productions, 1994.

Pearson, Lester. *Mike: The Memoirs of The Right Honourable Lester B. Pearson.* Vol. 1, *1897-1948.* Toronto: University of Toronto Press, 1972.

–. *Mike: The Memoirs of The Right Honourable Lester B. Pearson.* Vol. 2, *1948-1957.* Toronto: University of Toronto Press, 1973.

Pickersgill, J.W., and D.F. Forster. *The Mackenzie King Record.* Vol. 4, *1947-1948.* Toronto: University of Toronto Press, 1970.

Pope, W.H. 'La Corée: La cote 159 en septembre 1952 et le sergent Bruno Bergeron, MM.' *La Citadelle* 25, 1 (1989): 30-2.

–. 'La roulotte, les rails de chemin de fer, et le trainard.' *La Citadelle* 25, 5 (1989): 31-2.

–. 'Nos patrouilles en Corée, 1952-53.' *La Citadelle* 24, 1 (1988): 33-5.

–. 'Pour devenir maître entre les lignes.' *La Citadelle* 24, 2 (1988): 37-40.

Randall, T.H. *West Novas: A History of the West Nova Scotia Regiment.* Np, nd.

Rees, David. *Korea: The Limited War.* London: Macmillan, 1964.

Reid, Escott. *Radical Mandarin: The Memoirs of Escott Reid.* Toronto: University of Toronto Press, 1989.

Ridgway, Matthew B. *The Korean War.* New York: Doubleday, 1967.

Roy, R.H. *1944: The Canadians in Normandy.* Ottawa: Macmillan Canada, 1984.

Schnabel, James F. *Policy and Direction: The First Year.* United States Army in the Korean War. Washington, DC: US Government Printing Office, 1972.

Sheng, Michael. 'The Psychology of the Korean War: The Role of Ideology and Perception in China's Entry into the War.' *Journal of Conflict Studies* 22, 1 (2002): 56-72.

–. 'Review of M. Hickey, *The Korean War: The West Confronts Communism.*' *Journal of Military History* 65, 1 (2001): 245-6.

Spurr, Russell. *Enter the Dragon: China at War in Korea.* London: Sidgwick and Jackson, 1989.

Stacey, C.P. *Official History of the Canadian Army in the Second World War.* Vol. 1, *Six Years of War: The Army in Canada, Britain and the Pacific.* Ottawa: Queen's Printer, 1955.

–. *Official History of the Canadian Army in the Second World War.* Vol. 3, *The Victory Campaign: The Operations in Northwest Europe, 1944-1945.* Ottawa: Queen's Printer, 1960.

Stairs, Denis. *The Diplomacy of Constraint: Canada, the Korean War, and the United States.* Toronto: University of Toronto Press, 1974.

Stevens, G.R. *The Princess Patricia's Canadian Light Infantry.* Vol. 3, *1919-1957.* Griesbach, AB: Historical Committee of the Regiment, 1957.

–. *The Royal Canadian Regiment.* Vol. 2, *1933-1966.* London, ON: London Printing and Lithographing, 1967.

Stone, J.R. 'Memoir: Kap'yong.' *Infantry Journal* (Autumn 1992): 11-15.

Summers, Harry G. *Korean War Almanac.* New York: Facts on File, 1990.

Toland, John. *In Mortal Combat: Korea, 1950-1953.* New York: William Morrow, 1991.

Tout, K. *The Bloody Battle for Tilly, Normandy, 1944.* Stroud, UK: Sutton, 2000.

Watson, Brent Byron. *Far Eastern Tour: The Canadian Infantry in Korea, 1950-1953.* Montreal and Kingston: McGill-Queen's University Press, 2002.

Weigley, Russell F. *Eisenhower's Lieutenants: The Campaign in France and Germany, 1944-1945.* Bloomington: Indiana University Press, 1981.

Wood, Herbert Fairlie. *The Private War of Jacket Coates.* Don Mills, ON: Longmans, 1966.

–. *Strange Battleground: The Operations in Korea and Their Effects on the Defence Policy of Canada.* Ottawa: Queen's Printer, 1966.

INDEX

Note: Military units are listed under country, e.g., "25th Canadian Infantry Brigade" is under "Canadian Army"; (m) indicates a map, (p) a photograph

Printed and bound in Canada by Friesens
Set in Minion and Bodoni by Artegraphica Design Co. Ltd.
Copy editor: Sarah Wight
Proofreader: Gail Copeland
Indexer: Patricia Buchanan
Cartographer: Eric Leinberger